Annual Review of Biophysics

Production Editor: Elizabeth Rislove Etler
Managing Editors: Linley E. Hall, Nina G. Perry
Bibliographic Quality Control: Mary A. Glass
Electronic Content Coordinators: Suzanne K. Moses, Erin H. Lee
Illustration Editor: Alan Stonebraker

Annual Review of Biophysics

Volume 44, 2015

Ken A. Dill, *Editor*

Laufer Center for Physical and Quantitative Biology,
Stony Brook University

Xiaowei Zhuang, *Associate Editor*

Harvard University

www.annualreviews.org • science@annualreviews.org • 650-493-4400

Annual Reviews
4139 El Camino Way • P.O. Box 10139 • Palo Alto, California 94303-0139

Annual Reviews
Palo Alto, California, USA

International Standard Serial Number: 1936-122X
International Standard Book Number: 978-0-8243-1844-4
Library of Congress Control Number: 2007215102

All Annual Reviews and publication titles are registered trademarks of Annual Reviews.

⊗ The paper used in this publication meets the minimum requirements of American National Standards for Information Sciences—Permanence of Paper for Printed Library Materials, ANSI Z39.48-1992.

Annual Reviews and the Editors of its publications assume no responsibility for the statements expressed by the contributors to this *Annual Review*.

TYPESET BY APTARA
PRINTED AND BOUND BY SHERIDAN BOOKS, INC., CHELSEA, MICHIGAN

Annual Review of
Biophysics
Volume 44, 2015

Contents

Index

Errata

An online log of corrections to *Annual Review of Biophysics* articles may be found at
http://www.annualreviews.org/errata/biophys

Related Articles

From the ***Annual Review of Biochemistry***, Volume 83 (2014)

Dynamics and Timekeeping in Biological Systems
Christopher M. Dobson

Bringing Dynamic Molecular Machines into Focus by Methyl-TROSY NMR
Rina Rosenzweig and Lewis E. Kay

Intrinsically Disordered Proteins and Intrinsically Disordered Protein Regions
Christopher J. Oldfield and A. Keith Dunker

Progress Toward Synthetic Cells
J. Craig Blain and Jack W. Szostak

Selection-Based Discovery of Druglike Macrocyclic Peptides
Toby Passioura, Takayuki Katoh, Yuki Goto, and Hiroaki Suga

From the ***Annual Review of Cell and Developmental Biology***, Volume 30 (2014)

Liquid-Liquid Phase Separation in Biology
Anthony A. Hyman, Christoph A. Weber, and Frank Jülicher

Cellular and Molecular Mechanisms of Synaptic Specificity
Shaul Yogev and Kang Shen

Electrochemical Control of Cell and Tissue Polarity
Fred Chang and Nicolas Minc

From the ***Annual Review of Genetics***, Volume 48 (2014)

Self-Organization of Meiotic Recombination Initiation: General Principles and Molecular Pathways
Scott Keeney, Julian Lange, and Neeman Mohibullah

Archaeal DNA Replication
Lori M. Kelman and Zvi Kelman

From the ***Annual Review of Pharmacology and Toxicology***, Volume 55 (2015)

Identifying Predictive Features in Drug Response Using Machine Learning: Opportunities and Challenges
Mathukumalli Vidyasagar

Modeling Active Mechanosensing in Cell–Matrix Interactions

Bin Chen,[1] Baohua Ji,[2,*] and Huajian Gao[3,*]

[1] Department of Engineering Mechanics, Zhejiang University, Hangzhou 310027, China; email: chenb6@zju.edu.cn

[2] Biomechanics and Biomaterials Lab, Department of Applied Mechanics, Beijing Institute of Technology, Beijing 100081, China; email: bhji@bit.edu.cn

[3] School of Engineering, Brown University, Providence, Rhode Island 02912; email: huajian_gao@brown.edu

Annu. Rev. Biophys. 2015. 44:1–32

The *Annual Review of Biophysics* is online at biophys.annualreviews.org

This article's doi: 10.1146/annurev-biophys-051013-023102

Copyright © 2015 by Annual Reviews. All rights reserved

*Corresponding authors

Keywords

receptor–ligand interaction, focal adhesion, stress fiber, cell traction, cell reorientation, multiscale modeling

Abstract

Cells actively sense the mechanical properties of the extracellular matrix, such as its rigidity, morphology, and deformation. The cell–matrix interaction influences a range of cellular processes, including cell adhesion, migration, and differentiation, among others. This article aims to review some of the recent progress that has been made in modeling mechanosensing in cell–matrix interactions at different length scales. The issues discussed include specific interactions between proteins, the structure and mechanosensitivity of focal adhesions, the cluster effects of the specific binding, the structure and behavior of stress fibers, cells' sensing of substrate stiffness, and cell reorientation on cyclically stretched substrates. The review concludes by looking toward future opportunities in the field and at the challenges to understanding active cell–matrix interactions.

Contents

INTRODUCTION

As the structural and functional unit of life, cells actively sense and respond to mechanical stimuli in their surroundings (140). The mechanical properties of the extracellular matrix (ECM), such as stiffness, surface topology, and deformation, are transduced into biochemical signals through interactions between the cell and the matrix; these interactions then regulate various cellular processes, including morphology, differentiation, motility, fate, and gene expression (19, 55, 65, 125). In general, cells adopt more rounded configurations on softer substrates, and spread into flatter, more pancake-like configurations on stiffer substrates (104). Matrix rigidity directs the differentiation of stem cells toward different lineage cell types (37), and neurons grow fastest on a matrix that has a stiffness similar to that of brain tissue (20). Cells migrate from softer to stiffer matrices, and their speed increases with the rigidity gradient (86, 155); they reorient themselves on cyclically stretched substrates in a direction nearly perpendicular to the direction of the stretch (73); and they distinguish between 2D and 3D environments in gene expression (124). The cell–matrix interaction also plays an essential part during development as cells evolve from a monolayer to a complex organism, with particular physical features associated with specific functions (83, 148).

Almost five decades ago interference reflection light microscopy was used to visualize cell–matrix adhesion in the form of discrete adhesion sites between fibroblasts and glass substrates (30). It was later recognized that these adhesion sites are located near the termini of contractile stress fibers (SFs), and physically couple the cytoskeleton to the ECM (67). At the molecular level, almost 200 different proteins, including integrin, vinculin, talin, paxillin, and tensin (17, 54), have been associated with cell–matrix adhesion (150). These proteins exist in multiple types and vary widely in structure and function (147). At the cellular level, cell–matrix interaction involves multiple subcellular structures, including focal adhesions (FAs), SFs, and microtubules, which collectively participate in cellular mechanotransduction (**Figure 1**) (127). Compared with adhesion problems in conventional engineering systems, a key feature of cell–matrix adhesion is that cells actively probe, pull, and push on the extracellular matrix.

In spite of recent developments in super-resolution fluorescence microscopy (70) and advanced bionanotechnology, understanding of the fundamental mechanisms of active mechanosensing in

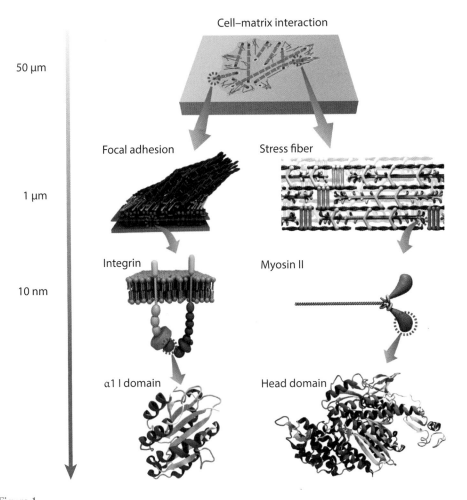

Cell–matrix interaction

50 µm

Focal adhesion

Stress fiber

1 µm

Integrin

Myosin II

10 nm

α1 I domain

Head domain

Figure 1

Schematics of stress fibers and focal adhesions—the main structures involved in cellular mechanosensing—and some critical components at multiple length scales.

cell–matrix interactions is still largely elusive. Although the total body of literature concerning cell–matrix interactions is rapidly growing, it is often focused on different scattered aspects or components of the problem, such as the structures and functions of individual proteins, FAs, and contractile SFs. The accumulative progress in the field calls for more efforts to be aimed at integrating different components of the problem into a more systematic and comprehensive understanding of active mechanosensing by cells.

The application of mechanics to the understanding of cellular phenomena is a burgeoning subject (14). This article aims to review, mainly from a mechanistic point of view, some of the recent progress made in modeling cell mechanosensing in cell–matrix interactions at multiple length scales. The issues to be discussed include specific interactions between adhesion proteins and mechanosensing at the molecular level, the structure and mechanosensitivity of FAs, the cluster effects of specific binding, the structure and behavior of SFs, cell sensing of substrate elasticity, the effect of cell shape on the distribution of traction force, the distance and depth that cells feel into a substrate, and cell reorientation on cyclically stretched substrates. The review concludes with a look at future opportunities in the field, and the challenges to understanding active mechanosensing in cell–matrix interactions.

MECHANOSENSING AT THE MOLECULAR LEVEL

Mechanosensing in cells starts at the molecular level. In many cases, mechanical forces can induce conformational changes and expose the buried peptide sequences of a protein, open ion channels, and alter the dynamics of receptor–ligand binding (71). For example, integrins are adhesion molecules that mediate cell–cell and cell–matrix interactions (88, 156), as well as transmit signals bidirectionally across the plasma membrane (149) via receptor–ligand interactions, thereby playing a central role in mechanosensing during various cellular processes (**Figure 1**). Talin is a cytoskeletal molecule that directly connects integrin to cytoskeletal filaments (15, 72, 159) via multiple vinculin binding sites (60). The initially buried vinculin-binding sites within the talin rod can be exposed by mechanical forces for binding with vinculins; this activates a cascade of signals leading to the assembly and reorganization of the cytoskeleton (33). Mechanical forces can also unfold ligands, such as fibronectin, on the surface of the ECM (133). Such force-induced activation can be pervasive during signal transduction. For example, mechanical forces enable the phosphorylation of Cas in p130Cas, which then activates downstream signaling (123). Here we focus on the molecular interactions in FAs and SFs.

Molecular Components and Interactions Within Focal Adhesions

FAs are discrete regions of a cell that provide sites for mechanical attachment to the ECM (58). The attachment of FAs to the ECM is mediated by members of the integrin family of transmembrane proteins. Integrin-mediated adhesions are multiprotein complexes that link the extracellular matrix to the actin cytoskeleton (**Figure 1**). FA plaques at the cell–matrix interface connect SFs inside the cell to the ECM via a layer of transmembrane receptors that are primarily composed of integrins and probably also syndecans (98). Besides integrin, almost 200 different proteins are involved in FAs, including talin, tensin, α-actinin, paxillin, zyxin, vinculin, and a tyrosine kinase known as FAK (or focal adhesion kinase). It has been shown that the stretching of talin may have a major role in the integrin-mediated mechanosensing of focal adhesions (70a).

As a major force-bearing adhesion-receptor protein, integrin has a central role in adhesion-mediated cellular processes (109, 149a). During cell migration, integrins bind to the matrix at the leading cell edge, aggregate in the plasma membrane as part of increasingly strengthened adhesion complexes, then unbind, and are ultimately recycled (109). Within this bind–unbind mechanical cycle, integrins exhibit conformational changes that regulate their binding affinity, which depends on the mechanical force. Recent studies have shown that integrins have three conformational states: (*a*) a bent or low-affinity state, (*b*) a straight or intermediate-affinity state, and (*c*) a separating or high-affinity state featuring separation of their α and β subunit legs (109, 149). In the high-affinity state, integrins interact strongly with ligands on the ECM to form bonds, e.g., when they aggregate to promote the growth of FAs (26).

In their mechanical cycle, integrins are supposed to be first activated by the binding of talin with the intracellular tail of the β-subunit (109, 135). Once activated, they may form bonds with ligands on the matrix, and then the contractile force of the cytoskeleton may induce further conformational change of the integrins. The contractile force can alter the interdomain headpiece hinge via separation of the heterodimer legs as the β-subunit aligns along the force vector. In this scenario, a further increase in force will strengthen the FAs by accelerating the aggregation or clustering of integrins and associated adhesion proteins. Two generic molecular interactions that depend on the applied force are critically important for the mechanosensing of FAs (79): One is the clustering of integrins and the associated adhesion proteins, and the other is the interaction between integrins and ligands on the ECM that forms the receptor–ligand bonds.

Molecular Components and Interactions Within Stress Fibers

Contractile SFs are collections of actin filaments formed by the contractile interaction of actin and myosin; they are bundled by cross-linking proteins, such as α-actinin (**Figure 1**). Large ventral SFs are anchored at both ends by FAs (69). This physical arrangement allows intracellular forces to be transmitted to the ECM, and extracellular forces to be transmitted to the cytoskeleton (87). Along the axis of SFs, regions containing the actin cross-linking protein α-actinin alternate with those containing myosin, and the polarity of the actin filaments is periodic. The nonmuscle form of the giant spring-like protein, titin or c-titin, also localizes to SFs in a periodic pattern. These observations are consistent with a sarcomeric structure similar to that of muscle fibrils, although SFs appear to be less ordered (134). A sarcomere is approximately cylindrical in shape, and an SF is built from many sarcomere units connected in series (134).

For SFs, a prominent example of mechanosensing at the molecular level is the force-controlled regulation of chemomechanical cycles of molecular motors, including nonmuscle myosin IIA, IIB, and IIC. Muscle myosin II undergoes an actin–myosin–ATP cycle, described by the Lymn–Taylor scheme, that comprises several stages (89). When myosins attach to the actin filament, molecular bonds are formed, similar to the receptor–ligand interaction. Within the power stroke of muscle myosin II, a light-chain binding region serves as a lever arm to amplify the movements of the converter domain (28). Without force constraint, the lever arm would swing all the way to complete the power stroke. However, if there is a force constraint, the swing can be arrested (52). For myosin II in skeletal muscle, it has been proposed that the swing of a lever arm is arrested at a transitional state when the motor force is approximately 6 pN (21), at which the reversible binding of P_i to the myosin head prevents ADP release (52). It has been argued that the swing being stuck at this translational state plays an important part in allowing the motor force to be self-regulated (21).

Modeling the Receptor–Ligand Interaction

The binding between a pair of receptor–ligand proteins is often mediated by weak but specific interaction via a lock-and-key mechanism. The dissociation of a specific bond is regulated by forces and often considered to be a thermally assisted escape over an energy barrier (42, 46). Because the dissociation rate of the bond depends on the applied force, there exist three categories of bond behaviors: (*a*) ideal bonds, with dissociation rates independent of the force; (*b*) slip bonds, with dissociation rates increasing as the force increases; and (*c*) catch bonds, with dissociation rates decreasing with increasing force.

For a slip bond, the dissociation rate, k_{off}, increases exponentially with the force according to Bell's law (8):

$$k_{off} = k_0 e^{f/f_0},$$
1.

where f_0 is an intrinsic force scale and k_0 is the spontaneous dissociation rate in the absence of a force; $1/k_0$ typically ranges from a fraction of a second to around 100 s (46).

Under time-dependent forces, the stiffness of a molecular bond can strongly influence its lifetime. For example, for a bond being pulled at a constant velocity V, the force increases linearly with time as $f(t) = k_{LR}Vt$, where k_{LR} is the spring constant of the bond, and the mean lifetime of the bond is (45):

$$T = \frac{1}{\mu k_0} e^{-1/\mu} E\left(\frac{1}{\mu}\right),$$ 2.

where $\mu = k_{LR} V / k_0 f_0$ and $E(x) = \int_x^\infty \frac{e^{-v}}{v} dv$.

The strength of a bond is defined as the most frequently measured force at rupture, which, following Equation 1, is predicted to have a linear dependence on the logarithm of the loading rate (45):

$$f^* = f_0 \ln\left(\frac{KV}{k_0 f_0}\right).$$ 3.

This prediction was verified by experimental measurements using a biomembrane force probe (44). The experiments showed a linear dependence of bond strength on the logarithm of the loading rate when extracting a test lipid molecule from a lipid bilayer. A similar trend was observed in the rupture of a biotin–streptavidin bond, albeit with a piecewise linear dependence due to the existence of multiple energy barriers (42) instead of a single energy barrier as assumed in Equation 1.

Equation 3 also predicts that the rupture force will diminish to zero or even negative value when the loading rate is vanishingly small. This is because Bell's model and similar models consider an irreversible rupture process and do not take into account bond rebinding (42). Therefore, such models may not be applicable at very low loading rates. To address this issue, Li & Ji (85) have recently reexamined the problem using Brownian dynamics simulations, and developed a new theoretical model by allowing bond rebinding. They treated bond rupture as the escape of a particle from a single energy well under external force (**Figure 2a**), and showed that when the loading rate is lower than a critical value, bond rebinding dominates the rupture process, resulting in a rate-independent rupture force that corresponds to a nonzero bond strength at an ultralow loading rate (**Figure 2b**). Notably, the rupture force increases with the loading stiffness, suggesting that the receptors and ligands would form stronger bonds on stiffer substrates leading to more

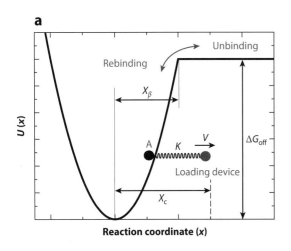
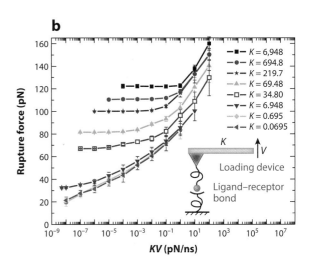

Figure 2

(*a*) Illustration of a particle, A, escaping from an energy well to mimic the rupture of the receptor–ligand bond under an external force. (*b*) Bond strength depends on the logarithm of the loading rate [obtained from Brownian dynamics simulations for different values of the spring constant *K* (pN/nm)]. Figure adapted from Reference 85 with permission.

stable cell adhesion when compared with softer substrates. This result provides further evidence for the mechanosensitivity of cell–matrix interactions at the molecular level.

In studying bond rebinding within a confined environment, Erdmann & Schwarz (40, 41) derived a relationship between the rebinding rate and the separation of a ligand–receptor pair as:

$$k_{on} = k_{on}^0 \frac{l_{bind}}{Z} \exp\left(-\frac{k_{LR}\delta^2}{2k_B T}\right), \qquad 4.$$

where k_B is Boltzmann's constant, T is the absolute temperature, k_{on}^0 is a reference association rate when the receptor–ligand pair are within a binding radius l_{bind}, and Z is the partition function for a receptor confined in a harmonic potential between zero and δ. Qian et al. (112, 113) adopted this relationship to study the effect of substrate stiffness on the lifetime and strength of a cluster of receptor–ligand bonds between elastic media.

For catch bonds, the dissociation rate counterintuitively decreases with the applied force. These bonds, first proposed by Dembo et al. (34), have been reported in binding between FimH and mannose, L-selectin and endoglycan, P-selectin and P-selectin glycoprotein ligand-1, and myosin and actin (43, 62, 93, 122, 138), as well as between $\alpha_5\beta_1$ integrin and fibronectin (80). A number of theoretical models have been proposed for catch bonds, with dissociation following a single pathway, or two pathways, or even more complex modes (137a, 158). For example, assuming that a ligand escapes the receptor binding site via a catch pathway opposed by the force and a slip pathway promoted by the force, a formula for the dissociation rate of a catch–slip bond in a two-pathway model was derived as (106):

$$k_{off} = k_c e^{x_c f/k_B T} + k_s e^{x_s f/k_B T}, \qquad 5.$$

where k_c and k_s are rate constants for unbinding through the catch and slip barriers with coordinates x_c and x_s, respectively, with x_c being negative.

MECHANOSENSING AT THE SUBCELLULAR LEVEL

Focal Adhesions

There are different forms of FAs. Nascent adhesions (focal complexes) appear as small dots 0.5–1 µm in size (10) within the lamellipodium; they have a lifetime on the order of seconds (147). They can either disassemble or mature into FAs depending on the mechanical forces (1, 25, 36, 69, 116). Mature FAs generally have an elongated shape 3–10 µm in length and several µm² in area (53, 67). The tension required to stabilize FAs is about a few nNs per µm² (6, 9). In some cases, FAs appear in the form of fibrillar adhesions (151, 152), as in fibronectin fibrillogenesis (91, 102). Other types of cell–matrix adhesion also exist, such as podosomes (118) or invadopodia (5, 59), which are mainly found in fast-moving cells, with invadopodia often existing in invading cells, such as tumor cells.

To understand the nucleation of FAs, Peng et al. (105) simulated the nucleation of integrin clusters using a kinetic Monte Carlo method, where integrin diffusion, activation, and the dynamics of receptor–ligand binding were considered. Their simulation indicated that high substrate stiffness would enhance the nucleation of FAs. Bihr et al. (13) studied the nucleation time and the critical number of receptor–ligand bonds needed for nucleation, accounting for the effect of membrane fluctuation. Shemesh et al. (131a) showed that the process of nucleation and growth of FAs is crucial to the formation of lamellipodium–lamellum interface in cell motility.

FAs can be induced to grow by mechanical force, such as by pulling the cell edge (116) or stretching the matrix adjoining the cell edge (76), and they undergo turnover when the force is relaxed. A model has been proposed to explain the mechanosensitivity of FAs (131) based on the hypothesis that stresses generated by pulling within a protein complex lower its chemical potential

(68). The model considered a 1D aggregate of identical molecules anchored on a substrate and subjected to pulling along the aggregation axis. The aggregate was assumed to exchange molecules with the surrounding medium at any point. Depending on the force level and distribution along the aggregate, a few modes of assembly were predicted, including disintegration, unlimited growth, unlimited growth after a critical length, and growth with a stable and finite steady-state length, in accordance with previous experimental observations (131). However, it was also found that when the SF assembly is selectively impaired while retaining a contractile lamella, the maturation of FAs as well as remodeling of fibronectin on the ECM is impeded, suggesting that tension is required but not sufficient for FA maturation without an SF template (101).

However, FAs can be disassembled when the force becomes too strong. To study the stability and disassembly of cell adhesion, a bond-cluster model is commonly adopted, in which the kinetics of bond breaking and reforming are considered using Bell's theory (8). Seifert (128) investigated the behaviors of a cluster of bonds subjected to linearly ramping forces. Erdmann & Schwarz (38, 39) adopted a one-step master equation approach to study the lifetime of a bond cluster. Their results suggest that an increase in the number of bonds enhances the stability of the cluster and many bonds together may have long-term and robust stability due to rebinding.

To investigate the effect of substrate stiffness on the lifetime and strength of FAs, Gao and coworkers (112, 113) developed a stochastic elasticity model of clusters of molecular bonds between two elastic media (**Figure 3**). A dimensionless parameter was identified as a controlling parameter to determine how the interfacial traction, $\sigma(x)$, is distributed within the adhesion domain between the cluster and substrate, which is written as follows:

$$\alpha = \frac{a\rho_{\mathrm{LR}}k_{\mathrm{LR}}}{E^*}, \qquad\qquad 6.$$

where a is the half-width of the adhesion cluster, and ρ_{LR} and k_{LR} are the bond density and stiffness, respectively; $E^* = 1/(\frac{1-v_c^2}{E_c} + \frac{1-v_s^2}{E_s})$ is the combined elastic modulus of cell and substrate, with v_c and v_s being the Poisson ratio and E_c and E_s the stiffness of cell and substrate, respectively. When $\alpha \to 0$, corresponding to a rigid substrate, the applied force is equally shared among all bonds within the cluster; in contrast, when $\alpha \to \infty$, corresponding to an extremely soft substrate, the distribution of bond force becomes highly nonuniform, with severe stress or force concentrated at the adhesion edges, suggesting that substrate rigidity has a strong effect on the strength and lifetime of the bond cluster.

Monte Carlo simulations have confirmed that the lifetime of a bond cluster can indeed be strongly affected by the rigidity of the substrate (**Figure 3b**) (50, 113). The lifetime of a periodic array of clusters has been calculated as a function of cluster size for different values of substrate rigidity represented by E^*, with results indicating that there exists a size window for relatively stable adhesion. The simulations also showed that the lifetime of the cluster array can be regulated by the pulling angle. For a given magnitude of the applied loading, decreasing the pulling angle tends to stabilize the adhesion (**Figure 3c**), suggesting there is a regulation mechanism that allows cells to switch between long- and short-lived adhesions by adjusting the pulling direction.

In addition to the stress-concentration effect, soft matrices also suppress rebinding in a bond cluster by increasing the local separation distance between open bonds (110). This has been demonstrated by showing that lifetime still varies with substrate rigidity when a uniform stress is directly applied to a bond cluster. It has been shown that the rebinding rate of an open bond anchored on two opposing elastic media is governed by the nondimensional parameter (50):

$$\chi = \sqrt{\frac{k_{\mathrm{LR}}}{2k_{\mathrm{B}}T}} \left(\frac{4}{E^*} + \frac{b}{k_{\mathrm{LR}}}\right) pb, \qquad\qquad 7.$$

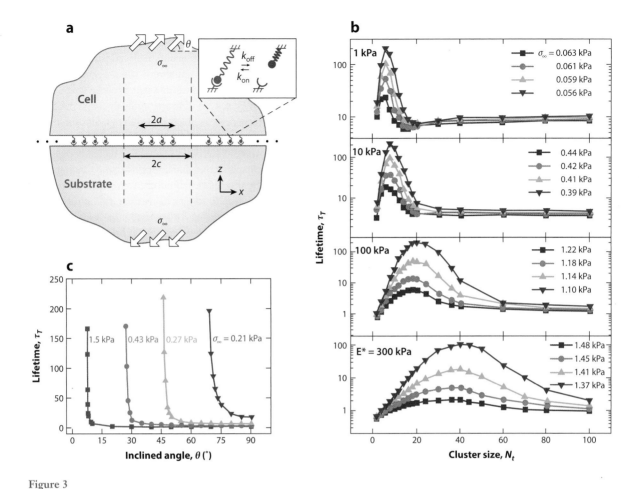

Figure 3

A mechanics model of cell adhesion illustrating the effect of adhesion size and cell–substrate elasticity on the adhesion lifetime:
(*a*) schematic illustration of a periodic array of adhesion clusters between two dissimilar elastic media under an inclined tensile stress;
(*b*) the lifetime of the periodic adhesion clusters as a function of the cluster size for different values of the reduced modulus E*; (*c*) the
lifetime of the periodic adhesion clusters as a function of the pulling angle θ at various levels of applied stress. Adapted from
Reference 113 with permission.

where p is the applied uniform stress on the cluster and b is the bond spacing, expressed in an
exponential form as $\exp(-\chi^2)$. Therefore, the larger the χ, the smaller the rebinding rate. The
mechanism by which an elastic modulus affects the rebinding rate is that on a soft substrate, the
local surface separation due to the rupture of a pair of bonds is so large that rebinding becomes
impossible, leading to a substantially shortened lifetime for the cluster. This result also suggests
that the local stiff structure of an FA plaque (an assembly of nearly 200 different proteins) may
have evolved from the necessity to maintain a stable adhesion cluster. However, the effect of
substrate elasticity on adhesion lifetime could also be mitigated by pre-tension in the SFs. It has
been demonstrated that pre-tension can shift the interfacial failure mode from crack-like failure
towards uniform bond rupture and, thus, increase the lifetime of the cluster (23); this suggests
that cell adhesion can be actively controlled by modulating the magnitude and pattern of myosin
activities within the cytoskeleton.

According to Equation 7, the strength and lifetime of the molecular bonds in FAs can also be influenced by the spacing between neighboring bonds: the larger the spacing b, the larger the parameter χ, and the smaller the rebinding rate. This is qualitatively consistent with the experimental observations that FAs are inhibited and cells do not spread when ligand spacing is greater than 73 nm, but the formation of FAs and cells spreading to a pancake-like shape occur normally when ligand spacing is smaller than 58 nm (3, 4, 129). FAs are highly dynamic structures and their mechanical responses are biphasic with respect to the magnitude of applied forces: They grow under relatively small forces, but disassemble under relatively large ones. This biphasic behavior has been studied by Kong et al. (78, 79) using a microscopic model in which two generic molecular mechanisms were introduced, i.e., integrin clustering and integrin–ligand binding, both of which depend on mechanical force. Their results showed that there are two critical forces that determine the dynamics of FAs. The force-induced growth of FAs happens at a relatively small-scale force, which is dominated by the clustering of integrin and associated adhesion molecules. In contrast, the disassembly of FAs occurs at a relatively large-scale force, which is dominated by the binding dynamics of integrin–ligand bonds.

Stress Fibers

SFs are force-generating mechanotransducers in cells. There exist three types of SFs: ventral stress fibers, transverse arcs, and dorsal stress fibers within the cell (99) (**Figure 4a**). Both ventral SFs and transverse arcs are composed of periodic distributions of myosin, α-actinin, and other cross-linking proteins on actin filaments, which make them contractile. In contrast, dorsal SFs are not contractile. SFs are also different in how they physically attach to FAs (99). Although ventral SFs are generally associated with FAs at both ends, transverse arcs are generally indirectly connected to the matrix via dorsal SFs, which attach to FAs at one end, with the other end rising toward the dorsal section of the cell (132). A ventral SF typically has a diameter of approximately 300 nm, a length of approximately 50 μm, a tension modulus of approximately 50 nN, and a pre-tensional load of a few nanoNewtons (32). An SF is built from many sarcomere units connected in series.

The intrinsic properties of SFs, such as pre-tension, viscoelastic relaxation, and motor-force homeostasis, are crucial to the mechanosensitive responses of cells to mechanical stimuli (23, 78, 114, 121, 157). It has been found that well-spread cells exert tension on their surroundings (35), which is caused mostly by the contractility of SFs. The existence of pre-tension has been demonstrated in isolated cells and their constituents, both directly (29, 82, 144) and indirectly (108, 145). For example, directly removing the tension in SFs by severing them with a laser caused the cut ends to retract (82, 87). When SFs were severed with femtosecond laser ablation, the length of the sarcomere decreased in an instantaneous elastic response, which was followed by a slower change in length due to myosin activity and viscoelasticity. Such retraction behaviors can be described by a viscoelastic cable model (82).

A mechanical model of sarcomere contraction that is consistent with experimental observation has been proposed, whereby an active element with tension generated by myosin is in series with a passive elastic element, and an impenetrable barrier prevents further sarcomere contraction (120). A model also has been developed to study the contractile behavior of SFs. The coupling between biochemistry and mechanics was taken into account with a system of reaction–diffusion equations in the model for inhomogeneous SF contraction occurring through the activation of myosin II motors along the Rho pathway. In this model, the sarcomere unit was simplified to a passive elastic spring, an active contractile module, and a viscous dashpot connected in parallel, and the whole SF was regarded as a string of such sarcomere units (11, 12), shown schematically in **Figure 4b**. A quantitative analysis showed that protein localization and force were closely correlated in SFs and

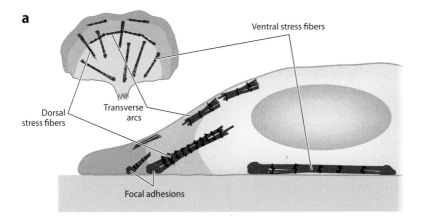

a

Ventral stress fibers

Dorsal
stress fibers

Transverse
arcs

Focal adhesions

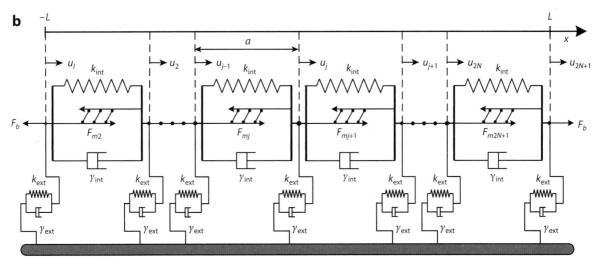

b

Figure 4

(*a*) Three types of stress fibers: dorsal stress fibers, transverse arcs, and ventral stress fibers. Panel adapted from MBInfo, National University of Singapore, available at **http://www.mechanobio.info**. (*b*) A viscoelastic mechanics model for stress fibers with inhomogeneous contraction. Panel adapted from Reference 11 with permission. Abbreviations: ext, exterior; int, interior.

suggested that a very direct force-sensing mechanism might exist along the length of an SF (27). For example, zyxin, a zinc-binding phosphoprotein that concentrates at FAs and along the actin cytoskeleton, was found to be recruited very quickly to substrate anchor points that were highly tensed upon SF release.

Owing to the structural similarity between an SF and a skeletal muscle fibril, a simple linear form of the empirical Hill's law, originally developed for muscle contraction, is often used to describe the relation between force F and contraction velocity V of an SF associated with myosin activity (12):

$$V = V_0 \left(1 - \frac{F}{F_0}\right), \qquad 8.$$

where F_0 is the isometric force and V_0 a reference contraction velocity. A behavior of interest is motor-force homeostasis. Using the structural unit of a sarcomere, a molecular model for

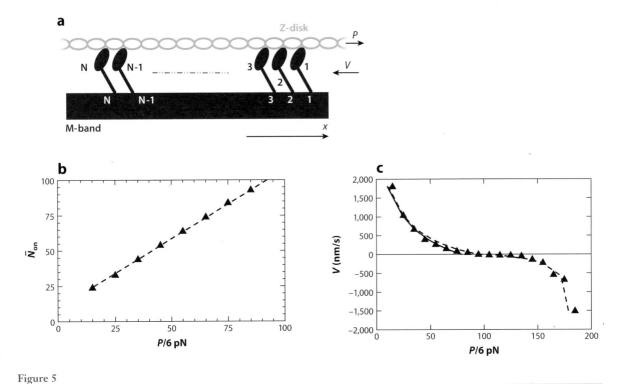

Figure 5

(*a*) Molecular model of a sarcomere during skeletal muscle contraction. The Z-disc is a structure existing between the dark lines (Z-lines) in electron micrographs of muscle fiber, and the M-band is a structure in the middle of a sarcomere. (*b*) The number of working motors increases linearly in proportion to the filament load, with force per motor at approximately 6 pN. (*c*) Simulated Hill's law for the contractile velocity of the actin thin filament versus the applied loads, with simulation results (*triangles*), fitted curve for the contractile part according to the equation $(P + 150)(V + 920) = $ Constant (*solid line*), and fitted curve with equation $P = 570[1 - 1.2V/(V + 650)]$ for the contractile part and $P = 630[1 + (15/\pi) \arctan(-12V/1800)]$ for the lengthening part (*dashed line*) (22). The units for P and V are pN and nm/s, respectively. Figure adapted from Reference 22 with permission.

SF contraction (**Figure 5***a*) was implemented within a coupled stochastic–elastic framework at two timescales (22). At the lower timescale, the system was considered elastic, and forces and displacements were solved using the finite element method; the results were then used to determine the reaction rates of motor binding and unbinding. The system's configuration was subsequently updated with a Monte Carlo method at the upper timescale. The simulation results indicated that the number of motors in the work state increases almost linearly with the filament load (**Figure 5***b*) and the motor force was regulated at approximately 6 pN, which is in agreement with other experimental data. The analysis indicated that the precise regulation of motor force in such an apparently chaotic system was due to both the stochastic feature and the force–stretch behavior of a single motor. The model has been further validated by recovering Hill's law between applied force and contractile velocity (**Figure 5***c*).

To investigate whether and how pre-tension in the cytoskeleton influences cell adhesion, Chen & Gao (23) developed a stochastic elasticity model of an SF attached to a rigid substrate via FAs. By comparing variations in adhesion lifetime and observing the sequences of bond breaking with and without pre-tension in the SF under the same applied force, they demonstrated that the effect of pre-tension is to shift the interfacial failure mode from crack-like propagation toward uniform bond failure within the contact region, thereby greatly increasing the lifetime of the adhesion.

This study suggests a feasible mechanism by which cell adhesion could be actively controlled via cytoskeletal contractility.

It has been postulated that the pre-strain in SFs is homeostatic and may be closely related to the overall pre-strain of the cell (66). It has been shown that SFs can shorten by approximately 15% within 1 s of being mechanically dislodged from a rigid substrate (82). Deguchi et al. (32) found pre-strain to be approximately 20%. Lu et al. (87) found that the pre-strain of SFs in endothelial cells increased from 10% to 26% when they were treated with 2 nM of calyculin A, a serine/threonine phosphatase inhibitor that elevates myosin light-chain phosphorylation; pre-strain decreased to 5% when they were treated with 10 μM blebbistatin, a selective inhibitor of actin–myosin interactions that has a high affinity for myosin II. These results indicate that SFs under isometric contraction exhibit a target tensional strain that is dependent on the degree of actin–myosin interaction.

MECHANOSENSING AT THE CELLULAR LEVEL

Experimental Observations

Cells actively probe their external environment and respond to various cues related to mechanical properties, such as stiffness, geometry, and dimensionality. In particular, substrate stiffness is recognized as playing a key part in the mechanosensing of cells. The stiffness of the human body varies from approximately 1 kPa in brain tissue to more than 1 MPa in bone. The stiffness of a particular tissue may also change with time, for example, due to aging or upon invasion by cancer cells (56, 103). There are many experimental reports concerning the effect of substrate stiffness on the behaviors of cells. Cells are more rounded on softer substrates, but spread out more like a pancake on stiffer substrates (57, 104, 137). Fibroblasts pull less on a softer matrix than on a stiffer matrix (86). In some studies, cells preferred to spread along the stiffest direction on a matrix patterned with anisotropic micropillars (57, 121). Most spectacularly, depending on the stiffness of the matrix, mesenchymal stem cells differentiate toward different cell types (37). Clearly, the stiffness of the ECM regulates many cellular behaviors, including morphology, adhesion, migration, and differentiation.

With newly developed experimental techniques, quantitative measurements of the mechanosensitivity of cells have been accumulating. For example, experiments have indicated that substrate stiffness has significant effects on both the traction forces at the cell–substrate interface and the area of a cell that is spread on the substrate surface. On a substrate patterned with arrays of microposts, Fu and coworkers (49, 146) observed that the cell-traction force, cell-spreading area, and total area of FAs all increased with the stiffness of the microposts, and the total traction force is linearly proportional to the cell-spreading area. Tan et al. (136) reported that the average force on the microposts increased as the cell-spreading area increased. Ladoux and coworkers (57, 121) found that the average force, as well as the strongest force, on a micropost both exhibit a biphasic dependence on the stiffness of the post; i.e., they increase linearly with the stiffness of the post when the post is relatively soft, but then level off to a plateau value on sufficiently stiff posts (**Figure 6a**). On a continuous substrate, it has been reported that cell traction is proportional to the cell-spreading area (115); this area exhibits a similar biphasic dependence on the substrate stiffness (130). Such biphasic dependence of cell traction on substrate stiffness has not been satisfactorily explained. This lack of understanding has resulted in an ongoing debate about whether cells on an elastic substrate sense force or deformation (48, 121, 136).

In addition to its magnitude, the distribution of cell traction has also received considerable attention. Rape et al. (114) conducted a systematic study of the dependence of cell traction on

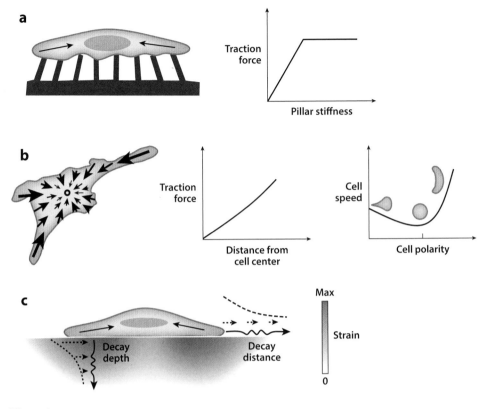

Figure 6

Representative mechanosensing events of cells on elastic substrates. (*a*) The cell exerts traction forces and deflects an array of elastomeric microposts on the substrate. Cell traction exhibits a biphasic dependence on the stiffness of the microposts. (*b*) The traction–distance law in cellular mechanosensing: the larger the distance from the cell center, the higher the cell traction. The commonly observed polarized cell shape is expected to play a crucial part in distributing the traction force and controlling cell-migration behaviors. (*c*) The cell-induced deformation field in the substrate decays with the depth or distance away from the cell. Figure adapted from Reference 66 with permission.

cell geometry and spreading area, and observed that cell traction and the size of FAs are both proportional to the distance from the cell center (**Figure 6*b***). Gardel et al. (51) and Dembo & Wang (35) showed that cell traction decreases in migrating keratocytes and fibroblasts as the distance from the cell edge increases. Similar relationships between traction and distance have been observed in cell colonies (96) and cells cultured in 3D matrices (84). A general observation is that the cell-traction force increases as distance from the cell center increases: the larger the distance, the higher the traction force. Surprisingly, until recently there has been relatively little discussion of the mechanisms underlying the observed relationship between force and distance (66), which may have important implications for the role of cell shape in regulating the distribution of traction and cell-migration behaviors (**Figure 6*b***).

In addition to the mechanical properties of the ECM, cells also actively respond to various external stimuli. For example, cells can sense deformation or force from the substrate (**Figure 6*c***). Some cells, such as vascular endothelial cells, are subject to cyclic loads under physiological conditions. It has been observed that upon cyclic stretch, initially randomly oriented cells on substrates rotate and reorient themselves almost perpendicularly to the loading direction (73, 100, 143).

The studies discussed above suggest that a few basic questions are critically important for understanding mechanosensitivity at the cellular scale.

- How does substrate stiffness influence the magnitude and distribution of cell traction?
- Why is cell traction distributed in a distance-dependent manner? What implications does this have for cell-migration behaviors? Can cell migration be controlled by regulating the distribution of cell traction?
- How far and how deeply can cells feel into a substrate?
- How do cells respond to the substrate's cyclic stretching?

Modeling the Cell–Matrix Interaction

Clarifying cell-traction force. He et al. (66) developed a contracting-disk model of cells interacting with an elastic substrate via adhesion molecules at the cell–substrate interface (**Figure 7**). To enable the model to be as simple as possible without losing the essential physics of the problem, they treated an adherent cell as a pre-strained elastic disk with the following constitutive equation:

$$\sigma_{ij} = \frac{E_c}{1+\nu_c}\left(\varepsilon_{ij} + \frac{\nu_c}{1-\nu_c}\varepsilon_{kk}\delta_{ij}\right) + \frac{E_c}{1-\nu_c}\varepsilon_0\delta_{ij}, \qquad 9.$$

where E_c is Young's modulus; ν_c is Poisson's ratio of the cell; and $i, j = 1, 2$ are coordinates in the plane of the disk. The second term on the right-hand side of the above equation accounts for cytoskeletal contractility.

The cell traction $\tau_c(r)$ at the interface is related to the elongation $\Delta_r(r)$ of molecular bonds as:

$$\tau_c(r) = \rho k_b \Delta_r(r), \qquad 10.$$

where ρk_b is the areal stiffness of the interfacial bonds, and ρ and k_b denote bond density and bond stiffness, respectively; $\Delta_r(r) = u_s(r) - u_c(r)$; and $u_c(r)$ and $u_s(r)$ are the displacements of the cell and substrate at the interface, respectively (**Figure 7**).

For a semi-infinite substrate, He et al. (66) derived a perturbation solution for the traction force between cell and substrate, as well as deformation in the cell and substrate. It was shown that the solution is governed by two dimensionless parameters: $a = \frac{2\rho k_b R}{\pi E_s^*}$ and $b = \frac{\rho k_b R^2}{E_c^* b_c}$, where R is the cell size, b_c is the cell thickness, E_c^* and E_s^* represent $\frac{E_c}{1-\nu_c^2}$ and $\frac{E_s}{1-\nu_s^2}$, respectively, where E_s and ν_s denote Young's modulus and Poisson's ratio of the substrate, respectively. Here the mechanical properties of the substrate should be interpreted as the effective properties of the substrate coupled with an adhesive protein layer to which the cell is attached (139a).

The zeroth-order solution of the traction, corresponding to cells adhering to a rigid substrate, is:

$$\bar{\tau}_{c(0)}(\bar{r}) = -\frac{b_c b}{R}C_{1(0)}\text{BesselI}(1, \sqrt{b}\bar{r}). \qquad 11.$$

For a substrate of finite thickness, an approximate solution of cell traction was derived as:

$$\bar{\tau}_c = -\frac{b_c}{R}[C_1 A^2 C\text{BesselI}(1, A\bar{r}) + C_2 B^2 D\text{BesselI}(1, B\bar{r})], \qquad 12.$$

where A, B, C, C_1 and C_2 are constants whose detailed expressions can be found in (66). Note that in He et al.'s study (66) the traction is assumed to be along the horizontal direction, and the vertical force between the cell and the substrate is neglected. This assumption is reasonable for a relatively stiff substrate. For a very soft substrate (much softer than a cell), the measurements from Legant et al. (83a) have shown that the vertical component of cell traction can be as large as 30–50% of the horizontal component. Nevertheless, the theory of He et al. captured the essence

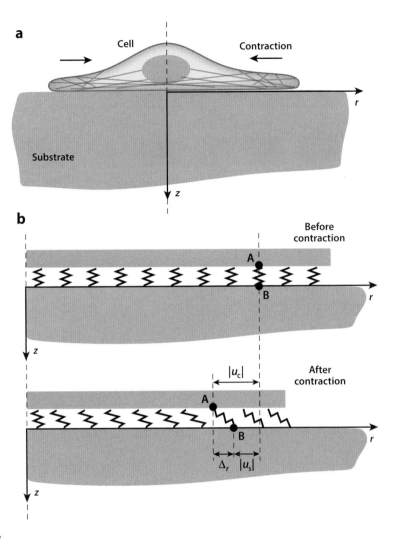

Figure 7

The contracting-disk model of cell–matrix interaction. (*a*) Schematic of a cell adhering to and pulling on an elastic substrate, owing to the intrinsic contractility of the cell. (*b*) The cell is modeled as an elastic contracting disk that is anchored to the substrate via molecular bonds (treated as elastic springs) at the cell–substrate interface. r and z are radial and vertical coordinates, respectively, u_c and u_s are displacements of the cell and substrate, respectively, and $\Delta_r = u_s - u_c$. A and B are the points on the surface of the cell and substrate, respectively, connected by a molecular bond. Figure adapted from Reference 66 with permission.

of the mechanics of cell–matrix interactions, and their predictions show broad agreement with experiments (66). For instance, it was predicted that horizontal traction alone could induce vertical displacement on the substrate, which is consistent with experimental measurements (83a, 94a).

Effect of substrate stiffness: Do cells sense force or deformation of their substrates?
Substrate stiffness has a significant effect on cell displacement and traction. For example, cell displacement varies linearly with distance on a soft substrate, but it varies exponentially on a stiff substrate. Cell traction also varies linearly with distance near the center on a soft substrate,

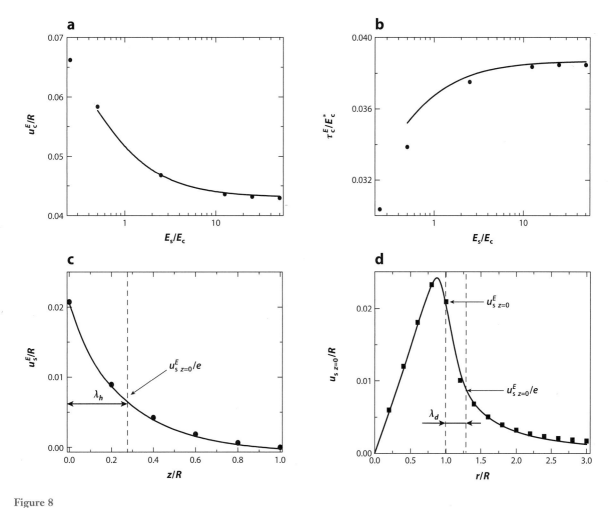

Figure 8

Cell-induced elasticity and deformation occurring during interaction with a substrate. (*a*) Cell displacement is inversely proportional to substrate stiffness when the stiffness is low, but it decreases to a plateau value when the stiffness is high. (*b*) Cell traction also exhibits a biphasic dependence on substrate stiffness. (*c*) Variations of radial displacement at the cell edge, with depth z into the substrate, $\lambda_{\rm h}$ being the characteristic depth of decay. (*d*) Variation in radial displacement on the substrate surface with distance from the cell center, $\lambda_{\rm d}$ being the characteristic lateral distance of decay from the cell edge. Figure adapted from Reference 66 with permission.

but it rises dramatically at the cell's periphery. Particularly, the results from the contracting-disk model indicate that peripheral cell displacement is inversely proportional to substrate stiffness for $E_{\rm s}/E_{\rm c} < 5$, and that it asymptotically settles to a plateau for $E_{\rm s}/E_{\rm c} > 5$ (**Figure 8a**). In comparison, cell traction first increases and then levels off to a constant value with increasing substrate stiffness (**Figure 8b**). These results suggest that cells cannot sense changes in substrate stiffness once it rises above a critical value (66). Similar conclusions had been reached earlier based on a simple two-spring model (126). In that model, the interfacial bonds and substrate are modeled as two elastic springs connected in series, with an overall effective stiffness of $k_{\rm eff} = k_{\rm b}k_{\rm s}/(k_{\rm b} + k_{\rm s})$, $k_{\rm s}$ being the effective spring constant of the substrate, and $k_{\rm b}$ the effective spring constant of the interfacial bonds. If $k_{\rm s} \gg k_{\rm b}$, then $k_{\rm eff} \rightarrow k_{\rm b}$; i.e., the stiffness of the interfacial bond dominates the overall stiffness of the system. In this situation, the cell can hardly sense any changes in substrate stiffness. A similar idea was adopted by Marcq and colleagues (92) in a 1D model.

These results shed light on a long pursued and debated and frequently asked question—that is, whether cells sense force or deformation in their microenvironment. Saez et al. (121) have shown that the traction forces of epithelial cells are linearly proportional to the rigidity of the substrate, suggesting that cellular forces are regulated by the deformation of the matrix in trying to maintain a homeostatic strain. However, measurements by Freyman et al. (48, 123a) have shown that cell traction is limited by the force rather than the displacement of the medium. This puzzle suggests that there is not a simple monotonic relationship between cell traction and substrate stiffness. The contracting-disk model of He et al. (66) provided a feasible explanation for this apparent paradox in that cells appear to maintain constant strain on soft substrates and constant traction on stiff substrates.

How far can cells feel? This is a central question in cell mechanosensing that can be understood by studying the cell-induced deformation and stress fields of the substrate. He et al. (66) showed that both displacement and stress fields in the substrate decay exponentially according to their depth and distance from the adhering cell, with a characteristic decay length on the same order as that of the cell radius (**Figure 8c,d**). That is, cell-induced displacement and stress fields in the substrate essentially vanish beyond a critical depth or distance that is comparable to the cell's size, which is consistent with experimental observations (95). This behavior is related to the question of how far cells feel into their microenvironment (130). The decay length is thus defined as the mechanosensing length of the cell. It also has been shown that the mechanosensing length is not sensitive to substrate stiffness for a wide range of stiffnesses.

The concept of mechanosensing length provides useful insights into the mechanisms that bone cells use to sense mechanical signals associated with bone remodeling: Osteoblasts and osteoclasts are normally at the surface of the bone, but osteocytes are embedded in the bone matrix. In this scenario, it is important to know how far the cells can sense mechanical stimuli (141, 142). In the literature on bone remodeling (119), the mechanosensing length is often chosen to be 100 μm, which is consistent with the predictions made by He et al. (66).

Mechanosensing length, as described above, also has important implications for the experimental measurement of cell-traction forces associated with the surface deformation of a substrate with finite thickness. The contracting-disk model suggests that a substrate with a depth that is greater than the cell's radius can be considered to be a semi-infinite substrate (90). Essentially, the substrate chosen should be thicker than the mechanosensing length if the traction force is to be determined based on the Boussinesq–Cerruti solution.

What is the role of the cell-shape-dependent distribution of traction in cell migration? This question is important for understanding how cells produce and regulate the driving force for cell migration. Migrating cells normally have a polarized shape (81, 153). For instance, migrating fibroblasts display a large front (lamellipodia) and a long tail. In this specific shape, the area of the cell's front is much larger than the tail, and the cell's center is located closer to the front (35). Correspondingly, polarized keratocytes have a crescent-like shape consisting of a large front and two flank-like rears (18), and the cell's center is also closer to the front. According to the traction–distance relationship predicted from the contracting-disk model, the larger the distance from the cell center, the greater the cell's traction (66). Therefore, traction should be greater at the cell's tail than at the front.

This law of the distribution of traction that is dependent on cell shape is consistent with experimentally measured traction distributions in fibroblasts and keratocytes (18, 35, 47), and it is central to cell migration. At the cell front, relatively low traction is used to promote the formation of FAs (79), while greater traction at the cell rear induces the disassembly of FAs (78, 79), causing detachment of the cell rear, which produces a driving force for cell migration (155). These results also suggest that cell shape could be employed to control cell motility because different cell shapes induce different distributions of cell traction. For instance, it has been found that the higher a cell's polarity, the higher the driving force produced for cell migration (66, 153, 154, 156), which demonstrates the pivotal role cell shape has in cell migration by regulating the distribution of traction in the cell.

Cell Reorientation Upon Cyclic Stretch

Systematic experiments have shown that upon cyclic stretch, initially randomly oriented cells often reorient themselves perpendicularly to the loading direction (**Figure 9a**) (73, 100, 143).

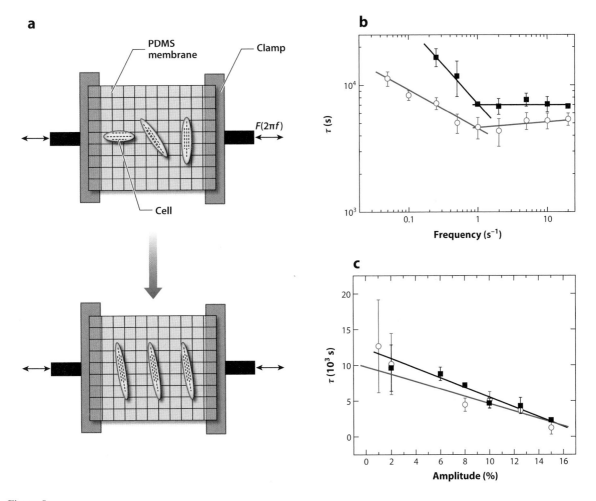

Figure 9

Cell reorientation on an elastic substrate subject to cyclic stretching force, denoted by F, with stretching frequency f. (*a*) Schematic illustration. (*b*) The characteristic time τ for cell reorientation decreases with cyclic frequency until it saturates beyond 1 Hz for two different cell types under subconfluent conditions. (*c*) The characteristic time τ for cell reorientation decreases linearly with strain amplitude at a cyclic frequency of 1 Hz. Figure adapted from Reference 73 with permission. Abbreviation: PDMS, polydimethylsiloxane.

The duration of the reorientation process strongly depends on both the cycling frequency and amplitude. For cells at subconfluent densities, there exists a lower threshold frequency below which the reorientation process ceases to occur. As the cycling frequency increases, the characteristic time of reorientation decreases monotonically until it saturates at a minimum value beyond 1 Hz (73) (**Figure 9b**). The characteristic time of reorientation also decreases monotonically with the cycling amplitude (**Figure 9c**).

A phenomenological model of a force dipole has suggested that the nearly perpendicular reorientation of SFs is caused by a cell's inherent tendency to establish an optimal internal stress (31). However, the same model also predicted that cells should align in parallel with the stretch direction at the limit of very low frequencies, which appears to be inconsistent with experimental observations (73). When considering the effect of cyclic loads on SFs (75, 78), it has been shown that SFs behave elastically at high stretch frequencies, but can adjust their reference lengths at low frequencies to maintain tensional homeostasis (16, 97). Thus, cell reorientation can be viewed as a consequence of the disassembly of SFs under high cyclic frequencies together with a gradual accumulation of SFs in orientations that avoid rapid length changes (75, 157).

Since FAs are one of the key players in cellular reorientation under cyclic stretch (61), an elastosarcomere-adhesion (ELSA) model (schematically shown in **Figure 10a**) has been developed to integrate the dynamic behaviors of an SF adhering on a substrate via two FAs (24). This model has also incorporated the experimental observations that $\alpha_5\beta_1$ integrin, which is a catch bond (80), plays a dominant role in determining the mechanical strength of FAs (117). Interestingly, the effect of force on the stability of catch bonds is similar to the mechanosensitivity of FAs; i.e., a small force promotes stability and growth, but a large force induces instability. The ELSA model postulates that FAs are catch-bond clusters, and the force in each catch bond is initially close to the optimal value corresponding to the longest lifetime at which FAs are expected to be most stable. SFs were assumed to actively resist stretching, according to the linear Hill's law. However, the

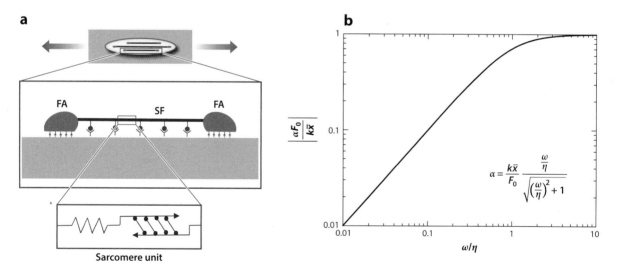

Figure 10

An elastosarcomere-adhesion (ELSA) model of cellular response on a cyclically stretched substrate. (*a*) Schematic illustration of the model. (*b*) The predicted amplitude of steady-state force oscillation in a homogeneously activated stress fiber (SF) as a function of the stretching frequency, *f*. Note that $\omega = 2\pi f$, k is the spring constant of a sarcomere unit, F_0 is the isometric load, $\bar{x}$ is the stretching amplitude, and η is the characteristic frequency of an SF. Figure adapted from Reference 24 with permission. Abbreviation: FA, focal adhesion.

shortening or lengthening of an SF can be nonuniform along its length (107, 134). In the ELSA model, two activation modes of SF contraction were assumed. In the localized activation mode, only one or a few sarcomere units in an SF are activated at any given time, but in the homogeneous activation mode, all or a large majority of sarcomere units are simultaneously activated (24). As schematically shown in **Figure 10a**, it has been suggested that there are multiple localized anchor points along an SF (64), and these are expected to have intrinsic relaxation timescales that are much shorter than those of mature FAs. At low stretch frequencies, the interaction forces between the SF and the substrate via the localized anchor points may be fully relaxed due to bond rupturing and rebinding. However, at high frequencies, there may not be sufficient time for these bonds to relax, and the whole SF would then be stretched directly by the substrate via these anchoring points, which would lead to homogeneous activation of all or a majority of the sarcomere units (24).

The ELSA model also predicted that the force within the SF oscillates around the isometric load upon cyclic stretch, with the amplitude increasing with that of the cyclic strain and also with the stretch frequency until it saturates beyond a critical frequency (**Figure 10b**). The saturation frequency was predicted to be controlled by two intrinsic clocks in the SF (24). The upper intrinsic clock corresponds to the characteristic frequency associated with the homogeneous activation mode of an SF:

$$f_h = \frac{kV_0}{2\pi F_0},$$ 13a.

where $k \sim 1$ pN/nm is the spring constant of the SF; the lower intrinsic clock corresponds to the characteristic frequency associated with the homogeneous activation mode of an SF:

$$f_l = \frac{kV_0}{2N\pi F_0},$$ 13b.

where N is the total number of sarcomere units in an SF along its length. It was estimated that $f_l \sim 0.002$–0.02 Hz, and $f_h \sim 0.12$–1.2 Hz (24). The observed threshold frequencies for cell reorientation are 0.01 Hz for rat fibroblasts and 0.1 Hz for human fibroblasts (73), which are close to f_l, suggesting that the localized activation mode of SFs may govern reorientation behavior in the low-frequency regime. In contrast, f_h is close to the experimentally reported saturation frequency, around 1 Hz, and beyond which the characteristic time of cell reorientation no longer changes (73). This is consistent with the assumption that the homogeneous activation mode of SFs governs reorientation behavior in the high-frequency regime (24).

The ELSA model also predicted that FAs essentially maintain their sizes upon cyclic stretch due to the much longer characteristic timescale associated with FA growth or shrinkage (24), which is consistent with the observation that massive FA rearrangements under cyclic stretch are accomplished by sliding instead of de novo formation of FAs during the initial process (61). As the force in the catch bonds oscillates periodically about the optimal load, the bond lifetime was predicted to decrease with cycling frequency until it reached approximately 1 Hz, beyond which it saturates to a constant (24). The bond lifetime also has been shown to decrease monotonically with cycling amplitude. These results are qualitatively consistent with the reported behaviors of the characteristic time it takes for cell reorientation (73). The ELSA model also predicted that SFs would favor an orientation nearly perpendicular to the stretch direction, where the minimum stretch amplitude exists. With less stable FAs postulated to slide or relocate to more stable configurations, the rotation velocity was estimated using a simple transition-state model (24).

Experiments have shown that stretching affects the reorientation of stress fibers more significantly than does relaxation (139). To understand this effect, it had been assumed that in the vicinity of the isometric force the shortening speed of an SF is higher than its lengthening speed (24), similar to the behavior of skeletal muscle (22). The effect of cyclic stretch with triangular waveforms was then investigated, and this showed that applying a high lengthening rate leads to much larger forces within SFs than applying a fast shortening rate (24). This implies that, at the same strain rate, lengthening should be more effective in destabilizing catch bonds, and this explains the observed asymmetric effect that SFs are more responsive to lengthening than to shortening (139). The ELSA model cautioned that there could be alternative physical interpretations for the catch-bond-like behaviors of FAs.

Zhong et al. (157) also predicted the biphasically frequency-dependent cell reorientation by modeling the disassembly of original SFs along the stretching direction as well as the formation of new SFs perpendicular to the loading direction. More recently, Qian et al. (111) developed another promising model of cyclic stretch-induced reorientation of spindle-shaped cells from the point of view of competitive coupling between the assembly and disassembly of SFs, the growth and disruption of FAs, the stiffening of the substrate during stretch, and rotation of the whole cell. The hypothesis that cells tend to orient in the direction where the formation of SFs is energetically most favorable suggests that the final alignment of cells reflects the competition between the elevated force within SFs that accelerates their disassembly and the disruption of cell–substrate adhesion, and an effectively increased substrate rigidity that promotes more stable FAs. The model integrates observations about the dependence of stable adhesions on substrate rigidity and the dependence of cell realignment on stretching frequency and amplitude, and also provides a simple explanation of the regulation of the protein Rho in the formation of stretch-induced SFs in cells.

FUTURE CHALLENGES

Understanding the mechanics of active mechanosensing by cells is a multiscale problem that is full of challenges and opportunities. A cell is a complex, multiscale living system with a myriad of functions and processes occurring from the molecular to the subcellular and cellular levels. At the level of FAs and SFs, there exist all kinds of interactions among numerous proteins in the mechanosensing of cells. The nanoscale architecture of FAs has been identified using interferometric photoactivated localization microscopy (74). This revealed that integrins and actin are vertically separated by a 40 nm FA core region, consisting of multiple protein-specific layers, including an integrin-signaling layer, an intermediate-force transduction layer, and an uppermost actin-regulatory layer. There are also complex interactions at the subcellular level, including those among sarcomere-like units of SFs and their connected cell–matrix adhesive structures. Cell adhesion, cell migration, and other adhesion-related behaviors all require coordination among multiple cell–matrix adhesion sites. There also exists crosstalk between cell–ECM and cell–cell contacts (94). Collective cell migration requires coordination among FAs in different cells. In addition, the actin–myosin contractility in striated fibers close to the basal membrane induces substrate strain that gives rise to an elastic interaction between neighboring striated fibers, which in turn favors interfiber registry and predicts the dependence of interfiber registry on externally controllable elastic properties in the substrate. Modeling such a complex system is challenging. It will be desirable to identify a minimal modeling system for each length scale.

The timescale and its interplay with the length scale are also important issues in the mechanosensing of cells. Clearly, events involved in the active mechanosensing of cells often occur at multiple timescales. Ion channel protein is activated as quickly as 0.1 s (77); the association or dissociation of a molecular complex can happen within seconds; the assembly of mature FAs takes approximately 3 minutes; and gene regulation in stem-cell differentiation can take up to a few days. Correspondingly, the size of a single protein at a specific state with a particular structure is approximately 10 nm; the size of an FA is approximately 1 μm; and the length of an SF or the size of a cell is approximately 50 μm. Consequently, the events that take place in cell–matrix adhesion at any of those timescales or length scales may be critical, especially when their effects are highly magnified through multiple rounds of mechanosensing at multiple sites. Thus, it is important to first identify all these events at different timescales and length scales, and then provide an integrated hierarchical modeling system to quantitatively evaluate the contributions of these events in the active cell–matrix adhesion.

In moving toward an integrated approach, there is a compelling need to integrate different subcellular components with sufficient structural details at the molecular level to elucidate specific functions and behaviors at the higher structural levels of cells (65) with the aim of establishing a comprehensive theoretical framework to understand and guide mounting experimental observations. One example would be to study the underlying mechanisms that control the magnitude of pre-strain in living systems at different length scales: For instance, pre-strain in stress fibers is 0.1–0.2, and at the cellular level is approximately 0.1, according to experimental findings (32, 87). There even exist homeostatic eigenstrains at the scale of tissue such as bone, tendon, or blood vessel (2, 7, 63). However, the underlying mechanisms—which seem to involve many length scales, from molecular to subcellular to cellular—that determine the value of the eigenstrains in cells and tissues remain to be fully clarified. Another example is the biphasic dependence of cell sensing on substrate stiffness at both the cellular and molecular levels. It will be interesting to find the connections among stiffness sensing at different length scales.

CONCLUSIONS

In this article we have reviewed some recent modeling studies of active mechanosensing in cell–matrix interactions at different length scales. It is clear that cells can sense mechanical cues at different length scales through different responding mechanisms. The mechanosensing structures involved include receptor–ligand bonds at the molecular level, FA complex and associated SFs at the subcellular level, and the overall structure and alignment of the cytoskeleton, as well as contractile deformation and associated cell traction at the cellular level.

The mechanical cues, including rigidity, morphology, and deformation of the matrix, as well as internal and external forces, play critical parts in regulating the mechanosensing of cells. The influence of the mechanical cues will either propagate from the molecular scale to the cellular scale via force transduction, or propagate down to the molecular scale. For instance, on one hand, micropatterns and the stiffness of the ECM will influence the distribution of traction force at the cellular scale, which then locally (at the subcellular level) influences the stability of FAs, such as the formation at cell front and de-adhesion at cell rear. At the molecular level, the traction force can influence the binding and unbinding dynamics of receptor–ligand bonds in FAs. On the other hand, substrate stiffness not only influences the deformation and traction of cells at the cellular scale, but also directly influences the stability of FAs (bond clusters), as well as the binding and unbinding of bonds at the molecular level.

It has been observed that there exist intrinsic biphasic features in the mechanosensing behaviors of cells. These biphasic behaviors can happen at different length scales. Cells do not have simple monotonic responses to an external stimulus. For example, at the cellular level, the magnitude of cell traction depends biphasically on matrix stiffness. At the subcellular level, the stability of FAs depends biphasically on the magnitude of the traction force. At the molecular level, the bond-rupture force depends biphasically on the loading stiffness and loading rate.

There are intrinsic and internal relationships among the different mechanisms of mechanosensing behaviors. For example, in the mechanisms of cells regulating cell–matrix adhesion, the cellular-level traction–distance relationship combined with the subcellular-level biphasic dependence of the stability of FAs on the traction force forms the basis of cells regulating their migration behaviors. This mechanism allows cells to form adhesion (FA complexes) at the cell front and to detach at the cell rear.

We have also discussed some interesting size effects in cellular mechanosensing. For example, the size of a molecular cluster has a crucial role in the adhesion strength of FAs; cell size influences the magnitude of cell traction (the larger the cell size or the larger the distance from the cell center, the stronger the traction); and mechanosensing length depends on cell size. The timescale also matters. For example, the loading frequency has important roles in cell reorientation: At a sufficiently low loading frequency, cells barely change their orientation, but at a higher loading frequency, cells reorient themselves to align perpendicularly to the loading direction. Bond rupture also depends on the loading rate: When the loading rate is high, the rupture strength decreases with the loading rate, but when the loading rate decreases to a critical loading rate, the rupture force will level off to a saturation value that is independent of the loading rate.

SUMMARY POINTS

1. Mechanosensing events take place at the single-molecule level with the aid of mechanical forces induced by myosin motors in stress fibers.

2. The interaction among proteins is mediated by weak but specific binding. Three types of bonds have been reported: ideal bonds, slip bonds, and catch bonds. The loading rate, loading magnitude, and elasticity have a strong effect on the binding kinetics among proteins.

3. Focal adhesions are mechanosensitive and also heterogeneous in many aspects.

4. A cluster of bonds has a much longer lifetime than a single bond due to cooperative binding within a confined environment; however, this is influenced by the elasticity of the substrate, bond spacing, and pre-tension within the cytoskeleton.

5. A coupled stochastic–elastic framework can be adapted to build a molecular model to study the mechanical behavior of stress fibers.

6. Cell traction generally increases as distance from the cell center increases. This law of traction–distance distribution suggests that cell shape (polarization) has an important role in regulating the speed and direction of cell migration.

7. Cell traction exhibits a biphasic dependence on substrate stiffness: It increases as the stiffness of a soft substrate increases (corresponding to a constant deformation or strain), and then levels off to a constant value on a stiff substrate.

8. Cells rotate upon cyclic stretch. Both the cycling frequency and the amplitude regulate the duration of the cell-reorientation process.

FUTURE ISSUES

1. What is the complete list of mechanosensing events at the molecular level?

2. How does the loading rate of focal adhesions that is due to sarcomere contraction depend on matrix rigidity?

3. How is a stress fiber assembled?

4. What are the potential roles of catch bonds in the dynamics of focal adhesion and in the regulation of cell migration?

5. How does matrix rigidity regulate gene expression?

6. Which level of rigidity does a cell sense on a highly heterogeneous matrix?

7. Is there any physical connection between stress fibers and the matrix beyond the two ends?

8. How does a stress fiber shorten or lengthen upon cyclic stretch?

9. How does a focal adhesion remodel under cyclic stretch?

10. How does a cell distinguish between 2D and 3D environments?

DISCLOSURE STATEMENT

The authors are not aware of any affiliations, memberships, funding, or financial holdings that might be perceived as affecting the objectivity of this review.

ACKNOWLEDGMENTS

This work was supported by the National Natural Science Foundation of China (grant nos. 11372279, 11321202, 11372042, and 11221202) and Fundamental Research Funds for the Central Universities (no. 2013QNA4045). The work of H.G. has been supported by the US National Science Foundation (grant no. CMMI-1028530) and the Center for Mechanics and Materials at Tsinghua University.

LITERATURE CITED

1. Alexandrova AY, Arnold K, Schaub S, Vasiliev JM, Meister J-J, et al. 2008. Comparative dynamics of retrograde actin flow and focal adhesions: Formation of nascent adhesions triggers transition from fast to slow flow. *PLOS ONE* 3:e3234

2. Arampatzis A, Karamanidis K, Albracht K. 2007. Adaptational responses of the human Achilles tendon by modulation of the applied cyclic strain magnitude. *J. Exp. Biol.* 210:2743–53

3. Arnold M, Cavalcanti-Adam EA, Glass R, Blummel J, Eck W, et al. 2004. Activation of integrin function by nanopatterned adhesive interfaces. *ChemPhysChem* 5:383–88

4. Arnold M, Hirschfeld-Warneken VC, Lohmuller T, Heil P, Blummel J, et al. 2008. Induction of cell polarization and migration by a gradient of nanoscale variations in adhesive ligand spacing. *Nano Lett.* 8:2063–69

5. Ayala I, Baldassarre M, Caldieri G, Buccione R. 2006. Invadopodia: a guided tour. *Eur. J. Cell Biol.* 85:159–64

6. Balaban NQ, Schwarz US, Riveline D, Goichberg P, Tzur G, et al. 2001. Force and focal adhesion assembly: a close relationship studied using elastic micropatterned substrates. *Nat. Cell Biol.* 3:466–72

7. Bayraktar HH, Keaveny TM. 2004. Mechanisms of uniformity of yield strains for trabecular bone. *J. Biomech.* 37:1671–78

8. Bell GI. 1978. Models for the specific adhesion of cells to cells. *Science* 200:618–27

9. Bershadsky AD, Balaban NQ, Geiger B. 2003. Adhesion-dependent cell mechanosensitivity. *Annu. Rev. Cell Dev. Biol.* 19:677–95

10. Bershadsky AD, Tint IS, Neyfakh AA, Vasiliev JM. 1985. Focal contacts of normal and RSV-transformed quail cells. Hypothesis of the transformation-induced deficient maturation of focal contacts. *Exp. Cell Res.* 158:433–44

11. Besser A, Colombelli J, Stelzer EHK, Schwarz US. 2011. Viscoelastic response of contractile filament bundles. *Phys. Rev. E* 83:051902

12. Besser A, Schwarz US. 2007. Coupling biochemistry and mechanics in cell adhesion: a model for inhomogeneous stress fiber contraction. *New J. Phys.* 9:425

13. Bihr T, Seifert U, Smith A-S. 2012. Nucleation of ligand-receptor domains in membrane adhesion. *Phys. Rev. Lett.* 109:258101

14. Boal D. 2002. *Mechanics of the Cell.* Cambridge, UK: Cambridge Univ. Press

15. Brown NH, Gregory SL, Rickoll WL, Fessler LI, Prout M, et al. 2002. Talin is essential for integrin function in *Drosophila*. *Dev. Cell* 3:569–79

16. Brown RA, Prajapati R, McGrouther DA, Yannas IV, Eastwood M. 1998. Tensional homeostasis in dermal fibroblasts: mechanical responses to mechanical loading in three-dimensional substrates. *J. Cell. Physiol.* 175:323–32

17. Burridge K, Chrzanowska-Wodnicka M. 1996. Focal adhesions, contractility, and signaling. *Annu. Rev. Cell Dev. Biol.* 12:463–519

18. Burton K, Park JH, Taylor DL. 1999. Keratocytes generate traction forces in two phases. *Mol. Biol. Cell* 10:3745–69

19. Byron A, Morgan MR, Humphries MJ. 2010. Adhesion signalling complexes. *Curr. Biol.* 20:R1063–67

20. Chan CE, Odde DJ. 2008. Traction dynamics of filopodia on compliant substrates. *Science* 322:1687–91

21. Chen B. 2013. Self-regulation of motor force through chemomechanical coupling in skeletal muscle contraction. *J. Appl. Mech.* 80:051013

22. Chen B, Gao H. 2011. Motor force homeostasis in skeletal muscle contraction. *Biophys. J.* 101:396–403

23. Chen B, Gao HJ. 2010. Mechanical principle of enhancing cell-substrate adhesion via pre-tension in the cytoskeleton. *Biophys. J.* 98:2154–62

24. Chen B, Kemkemer R, Deibler M, Spatz J, Gao H. 2012. Cyclic stretch induces cell reorientation on substrates by destabilizing catch bonds in focal adhesions. *PLOS ONE* 7:e48346

25. Choi CK, Vicente-Manzanares M, Zareno J, Whitmore LA, Mogilner A, Horwitz AR. 2008. Actin and α-actinin orchestrate the assembly and maturation of nascent adhesions in a myosin II motor-independent manner. *Nat. Cell Biol.* 10:1039–50

26. Clark K, Pankov R, Travis MA, Askari JA, Mould AP, et al. 2005. A specific $\alpha_5\beta_1$-integrin conformation promotes directional integrin translocation and fibronectin matrix formation. *J. Cell Sci.* 118:291–300

27. Colombelli J, Besser A, Kress H, Reynaud EG, Girard P, et al. 2009. Mechanosensing in actin stress fibers revealed by a close correlation between force and protein localization. *J. Cell Sci.* 122:1665–79

28. Cooke R. 1986. The mechanism of muscle contraction. *CRC Crit. Rev. Biochem.* 21:53–118

29. Costa KD, Hucker WJ, Yin FCP. 2002. Buckling of actin stress fibers: a new wrinkle in the cytoskeletal tapestry. *Cell Motil. Cytoskelet.* 52:266–74

30. Curtis AS. 1964. The mechanism of adhesion of cells to glass. A study by interference reflection microscopy. *J. Cell Biol.* 20:199–215

31. De R, Zemel A, Safran SA. 2007. Dynamics of cell orientation. *Nat. Phys.* 3:655–59

32. Deguchi S, Ohashi T, Sato M. 2006. Tensile properties of single stress fibers isolated from cultured vascular smooth muscle cells. *J. Biomech.* 39:2603–10

33. del Rio A, Perez-Jimenez R, Liu R, Roca-Cusachs P, Fernandez JM, Sheetz MP. 2009. Stretching single talin rod molecules activates vinculin binding. *Science* 323:638–41

34. Dembo M, Torney DC, Saxman K, Hammer D. 1988. The reaction-limited kinetics of membrane-to-surface adhesion and detachment. *Proc. R. Soc. Lond. B* 234:55–83

35. Dembo M, Wang Y-L. 1999. Stresses at the cell-to-substrate interface during locomotion of fibroblasts. *Biophys. J.* 76:2307–16

36. Endlich N, Otey CA, Kriz W, Endlich K. 2007. Movement of stress fibers away from focal adhesions identifies focal adhesions as sites of stress fiber assembly in stationary cells. *Cell Motil. Cytoskelet.* 64:966–76

37. Engler AJ, Sen S, Sweeney HL, Discher DE. 2006. Matrix elasticity directs stem cell lineage specification. *Cell* 126:677–89

38. Erdmann T, Schwarz US. 2004. Stability of adhesion clusters under constant force. *Phys. Rev. Lett.* 92:108102

39. Erdmann T, Schwarz US. 2004. Stochastic dynamics of adhesion clusters under shared constant force and with rebinding. *J. Chem. Phys.* 121:8997–9017

40. Erdmann T, Schwarz US. 2006. Bistability of cell-matrix adhesions resulting from non-linear receptor-ligand dynamics. *Biophys. J.* 91:L60–62

41. Erdmann T, Schwarz US. 2007. Impact of receptor-ligand distance on adhesion cluster stability. *Eur. Phys. J. E* 22:123–37

42. Evans E. 2001. Probing the relation between force—lifetime—and chemistry in single molecular bonds. *Annu. Rev. Biophys. Biomol. Struct.* 30:105–28

43. Evans E, Leung A, Heinrich V, Zhu C. 2004. Mechanical switching and coupling between two dissociation pathways in a P-selectin adhesion bond. *PNAS* 101:11281–86

44. Evans E, Ludwig F. 2000. Dynamic strengths of molecular anchoring and material cohesion in fluid biomembranes. *J. Phys. Condens. Matter* 12:A315

45. Evans E, Ritchie K. 1997. Dynamic strength of molecular adhesion bonds. *Biophys. J.* 72:1541–55

46. Evans EA, Calderwood DA. 2007. Forces and bond dynamics in cell adhesion. *Science* 316:1148–53

47. Fournier MF, Sauser R, Ambrosi D, Meister J-J, Verkhovsky AB. 2010. Force transmission in migrating cells. *J. Cell Biol.* 188:287–97

48. Freyman TM, Yannas IV, Yokoo R, Gibson LJ. 2002. Fibroblast contractile force is independent of the stiffness which resists the contraction. *Exp. Cell Res.* 272:153–62

49. Fu J, Wang Y-K, Yang MT, Desai RA, Yu X, et al. 2010. Mechanical regulation of cell function with geometrically modulated elastomeric substrates. *Nat. Methods* 7:733–36

50. Gao H, Qian J, Chen B. 2011. Probing mechanical principles of focal contacts in cell-matrix adhesion with a coupled stochastic-elastic modelling framework. *J. R. Soc. Interface* 8:1217–32

51. Gardel ML, Sabass B, Ji L, Danuser G, Schwarz US, Waterman CM. 2008. Traction stress in focal adhesions correlates biphasically with actin retrograde flow speed. *J. Cell Biol.* 183:999–1005

52. Geeves MA, Holmes KC. 1999. Structural mechanism of muscle contraction. *Annu. Rev. Biochem.* 68:687–728

53. Geiger B, Bershadsky A. 2001. Assembly and mechanosensory function of focal contacts. *Curr. Opin. Cell Biol.* 13:584–92

54. Geiger B, Bershadsky A, Pankov R, Yamada KM. 2001. Transmembrane extracellular matrix-cytoskeleton crosstalk. *Nat. Rev. Mol. Cell Biol.* 2:793–805

55. Geiger B, Spatz JP, Bershadsky AD. 2009. Environmental sensing through focal adhesions. *Nat. Rev. Microbiol.* 10:21–33

56. Georges PC, Janmey PA. 2005. Cell type-specific response to growth on soft materials. *J. Appl. Physiol.* 98:1547–53

57. Ghibaudo M, Saez A, Trichet L, Xayaphoummine A, Browaeys J, et al. 2008. Traction forces and rigidity sensing regulate cell functions. *Soft Matter* 4:1836–43

58. Gilmore AP, Burridge K. 1996. Molecular mechanisms for focal adhesion assembly through regulation of protein–protein interactions. *Structure* 4:647–51

59. Gimona M, Buccione R. 2006. Adhesions that mediate invasion. *Int. J. Biochem. Cell Biol.* 38:1875–92

60. Gingras AR, Ziegler WH, Frank R, Barsukov IL, Roberts GCK, et al. 2005. Mapping and consensus sequence identification for multiple vinculin binding sites within the talin rod. *J. Biol. Chem.* 280:37217–24

61. Goldyn AM, Rioja BA, Spatz JP, Ballestrem C, Kemkemer R. 2009. Force-induced cell polarisation is linked to RhoA-driven microtubule-independent focal-adhesion sliding. *J. Cell Sci.* 122:3644–51

62. Guo B, Guilford WH. 2006. Mechanics of actomyosin bonds in different nucleotide states are tuned to muscle contraction. *PNAS* 103:9844–49

63. Guo X, Lu X, Kassab GS. 2005. Transmural strain distribution in the blood vessel wall. *Am. J. Physiol. Heart Circ. Physiol.* 288:H881–86

64. Guthardt Torres P, Bischofs IB, Schwarz US. 2012. Contractile network models for adherent cells. *Phys. Rev. E* 85:011913

65. Hanein D, Horwitz AR. 2012. The structure of cell-matrix adhesions: the new frontier. *Curr. Opin. Cell Biol.* 24:134–40

66. He S, Su Y, Ji B, Gao H. 2014. Some basic questions on mechanosensing in cell–substrate interaction. *J. Mech. Phys. Solids* 70:116–35

67. Heath JP, Dunn GA. 1978. Cell to substratum contacts of chick fibroblasts and their relation to the microfilament system. A correlated interference-reflexion and high-voltage electron-microscope study. *J. Cell Sci.* 29:197–212

68. Hill TL. 1987. *Linear Aggregation Theory in Cell Biology.* New York: Springer-Verlag

69. Hotulainen P, Lappalainen P. 2006. Stress fibers are generated by two distinct actin assembly mechanisms in motile cells. *J. Cell Biol.* 173:383–94

70. Huang B, Babcock H, Zhuang X. 2010. Breaking the diffraction barrier: super-resolution imaging of cells. *Cell* 143:1047–58

70a. Hytönen VP, Vogel V. 2008. How force might activate talin's vinculin binding sites: SMD reveals a structural mechanism. *PLOS Comput. Biol.* 4:e24

71. Ji B, Bao G. 2011. Cell and molecular biomechanics: perspectives and challenges. *Acta Mech. Solida Sin.* 24:27–51

72. Jiang G, Giannone G, Critchley DR, Fukumoto E, Sheetz MP. 2003. Two-piconewton slip bond between fibronectin and the cytoskeleton depends on talin. *Nature* 424:334–37

73. Jungbauer S, Gao H, Spatz JP, Kemkemer R. 2008. Two characteristic regimes in frequency-dependent dynamic reorientation of fibroblasts on cyclically stretched substrates. *Biophys. J.* 95:3470–78

74. Kanchanawong P, Shtengel G, Pasapera AM, Ramko EB, Davidson MW, et al. 2010. Nanoscale architecture of integrin-based cell adhesions. *Nature* 468:580–84

75. Kaunas R, Hsu H-J, Deguchi S. 2011. Sarcomeric model of stretch-induced stress fiber reorganization. *Cell Health Cytoskelet.* 3:13–22

76. Kaverina I, Krylyshkina O, Beningo K, Anderson K, Wang Y-L, Small JV. 2002. Tensile stress stimulates microtubule outgrowth in living cells. *J. Cell Sci.* 115:2283–91

77. Kobayashi T, Sokabe M. 2010. Sensing substrate rigidity by mechanosensitive ion channels with stress fibers and focal adhesions. *Curr. Opin. Cell Biol.* 22:669–76

78. Kong D, Ji B, Dai L. 2008. Stability of adhesion clusters and cell reorientation under lateral cyclic tension. *Biophys. J.* 95:4034–44

79. Kong D, Ji B, Dai L. 2010. Stabilizing to disruptive transition of focal adhesion response to mechanical forces. *J. Biomech.* 43:2524–29

80. Kong F, García AJ, Mould AP, Humphries MJ, Zhu C. 2009. Demonstration of catch bonds between an integrin and its ligand. *J. Cell Biol.* 185:1275–84

81. Kozlov MM, Mogilner A. 2007. Model of polarization and bistability of cell fragments. *Biophys. J.* 93:3811–19

82. Kumar S, Maxwell IZ, Heisterkamp A, Polte TR, Lele TP, et al. 2006. Viscoelastic retraction of single living stress fibers and its impact on cell shape, cytoskeletal organization, and extracellular matrix mechanics. *Biophys. J.* 90:3762–73

83. Lecuit T, Lenne P-F. 2007. Cell surface mechanics and the control of cell shape, tissue patterns and morphogenesis. *Nat. Rev. Microbiol.* 8:633–44

83a. Legant WR, Choi CK, Miller JS, Shao L, Gao L, et al. 2013. Multidimensional traction force microscopy reveals out-of-plane rotational moments about focal adhesions. *PNAS* 110:881–86

84. Legant WR, Miller JS, Blakely BL, Cohen DM, Genin GM, Chen CS. 2010. Measurement of mechanical tractions exerted by cells in three-dimensional matrices. *Nat. Methods* 7:969–71

85. Li D, Ji B. 2014. Predicted rupture force of a single molecular bond becomes rate independent at ultralow loading rates. *Phys. Rev. Lett.* 112:078302

86. Lo C-M, Wang H-B, Dembo M, Wang Y-l. 2000. Cell movement is guided by the rigidity of the substrate. *Biophys. J.* 79:144–52

87. Lu L, Feng Y, Hucker WJ, Oswald SJ, Longmore GD, Yin FCP. 2008. Actin stress fiber pre-extension in human aortic endothelial cells. *Cell Motil. Cytoskelet.* 65:281–94

88. Luo B-H, Carman CV, Springer TA. 2007. Structural basis of integrin regulation and signaling. *Annu. Rev. Immunol.* 25:619–47

89. Lymn RW, Taylor EW. 1971. Mechanism of adenosine triphosphate hydrolysis by actomyosin. *Biochemistry* 10:4617–24

90. Maloney J, Walton E, Bruce C, Van Vliet K. 2008. Influence of finite thickness and stiffness on cellular adhesion-induced deformation of compliant substrata. *Phys. Rev. E* 78:041923

91. Mao Y, Schwarzbauer JE. 2005. Fibronectin fibrillogenesis, a cell-mediated matrix assembly process. *Matrix Biol.* 24:389–99

92. Marcq P, Yoshinaga N, Prost J. 2011. Rigidity sensing explained by active matter theory. *Biophys. J.* 101:L33–35

93. Marshall BT, Long M, Piper JW, Yago T, McEver RP, Zhu C. 2003. Direct observation of catch bonds involving cell-adhesion molecules. *Nature* 423:190–93

94. Maruthamuthu V, Sabass B, Schwarz US, Gardel ML. 2011. Cell-ECM traction force modulates endogenous tension at cell–cell contacts. *PNAS* 108:4708–13

94a. Maskarinec SA, Franck C, Tirrell DA, Ravichandran G. 2009. Quantifying cellular traction forces in three dimensions. *PNAS* 106:22108–13

95. Merkel R, Kirchgessner N, Cesa CM, Hoffmann B. 2007. Cell force microscopy on elastic layers of finite thickness. *Biophys. J.* 93:3314–23

96. Mertz A, Banerjee S, Che Y, German G, Xu Y, et al. 2012. Scaling of traction forces with the size of cohesive cell colonies. *Phys. Rev. Lett.* 108:198101

97. Mizutani T, Haga H, Kawabata K. 2004. Cellular stiffness response to external deformation: tensional homeostasis in a single fibroblast. *Cell Motil. Cytoskelet.* 59:242–48

98. Morgan MR, Humphries MJ, Bass MD. 2007. Synergistic control of cell adhesion by integrins and syndecans. *Nat. Rev. Microbiol.* 8:957–69

99. Naumanen P, Lappalainen P, Hotulainen P. 2008. Mechanisms of actin stress fibre assembly. *J. Microsc.* 231:446–54

100. Neidlinger-Wilke C, Wilke HJ, Claes L. 1994. Cyclic stretching of human osteoblasts affects proliferation and metabolism: a new experimental method and its application. *J. Orthop. Res.* 12:70–78

101. Oakes PW, Beckham Y, Stricker J, Gardel ML. 2012. Tension is required but not sufficient for focal adhesion maturation without a stress fiber template. *J. Cell Biol.* 196:363–74

102. Pankov R, Cukierman E, Katz BZ, Matsumoto K, Lin DC, et al. 2000. Integrin dynamics and matrix assembly: tensin-dependent translocation of $\alpha_5\beta_1$ integrins promotes early fibronectin fibrillogenesis. *J. Cell Biol.* 148:1075–90

103. Paszek MJ, Zahir N, Johnson KR, Lakins JN, Rozenberg GI, et al. 2005. Tensional homeostasis and the malignant phenotype. *Cancer Cell* 8:241–54

104. Pelham RJ, Wang YL. 1997. Cell locomotion and focal adhesions are regulated by substrate flexibility. *PNAS* 94:13661–65

105. Peng X, Huang J, Xiong C, Fang J. 2012. Cell adhesion nucleation regulated by substrate stiffness: a Monte Carlo study. *J. Biomech.* 45:116–22

106. Pereverzev YV, Prezhdo OV, Forero M, Sokurenko EV, Thomas WE. 2005. The two-pathway model for the catch-slip transition in biological adhesion. *Biophys. J.* 89:1446–54

107. Peterson LJ, Rajfur Z, Maddox AS, Freel CD, Chen Y, et al. 2004. Simultaneous stretching and contraction of stress fibers in vivo. *Mol. Biol. Cell* 15:3497–508

108. Pourati J, Maniotis A, Spiegel D, Schaffer JL, Butler JP, et al. 1998. Is cytoskeletal tension a major determinant of cell deformability in adherent endothelial cells? *Am. J. Physiol. Cell Physiol.* 274:C1283–89

109. Puklin-Faucher E, Sheetz MP. 2009. The mechanical integrin cycle. *J. Cell Sci.* 122:179–86

110. Qian J, Gao H. 2010. Soft matrices suppress cooperative behaviors among receptor-ligand bonds in cell adhesion. *PLOS ONE* 5:e12342

111. Qian J, Liu H, Lin Y, Chen W, Gao H. 2013. A mechanochemical model of cell reorientation on substrates under cyclic stretch. *PLOS ONE* 8:e65864

112. Qian J, Wang J, Gao H. 2008. Lifetime and strength of adhesive molecular bond clusters between elastic media. *Langmuir* 24:1262–70

113. Qian J, Wang JZ, Lin Y, Gao HJ. 2009. Lifetime and strength of periodic bond clusters between elastic media under inclined loading. *Biophys. J.* 97:2438–45

114. Rape AD, Guo W-h, Wang Y-l. 2011. The regulation of traction force in relation to cell shape and focal adhesions. *Biomaterials* 32:2043–51

115. Reinhart-King CA, Dembo M, Hammer DA. 2005. The dynamics and mechanics of endothelial cell spreading. *Biophys. J.* 89:676–89

116. Riveline D, Zamir E, Balaban NQ, Schwarz US, Ishizaki T, et al. 2001. Focal contacts as mechanosensors: externally applied local mechanical force induces growth of focal contacts by an mDia1-dependent and ROCK-independent mechanism. *J. Cell Biol.* 153:1175–86

117. Roca-Cusachs P, Gauthier NC, del Rio A, Sheetz MP. 2009. Clustering of $\alpha_5 \beta_1$ integrins determines adhesion strength whereas $\alpha_v \beta_3$ and talin enable mechanotransduction. *PNAS* 106:16245–50

118. Rottiers P, Saltel F, Daubon T, Chaigne-Delalande B, Tridon V, et al. 2009. TGFβ-induced endothelial podosomes mediate basement membrane collagen degradation in arterial vessels. *J. Cell Sci.* 122:4311–18

119. Ruimerman R, Hilbers P, van Rietbergen B, Huiskes R. 2005. A theoretical framework for strain-related trabecular bone maintenance and adaptation. *J. Biomech.* 38:931–41

120. Russell RJ, Xia S-L, Dickinson RB, Lele TP. 2009. Sarcomere mechanics in capillary endothelial cells. *Biophys. J.* 97:1578–85

121. Saez A, Buguin A, Silberzan P, Ladoux B. 2005. Is the mechanical activity of epithelial cells controlled by deformations or forces? *Biophys. J.* 89:L52–54

122. Sarangapani KK, Yago T, Klopocki AG, Lawrence MB, Fieger CB, et al. 2004. Low force decelerates L-selectin dissociation from P-selectin glycoprotein ligand-1 and endoglycan. *J. Biol. Chem.* 279:2291–98

123. Sawada Y, Tamada M, Dubin-Thaler BJ, Cherniavskaya O, Sakai R, et al. 2006. Force sensing by mechanical extension of the Src family kinase substrate p130Cas. *Cell* 127:1015–26

123a. Schoen I, Pruitt BL, Vogel V. 2013. The yin-yang of rigidity sensing: how forces and mechanical properties regulate the cellular response to materials. *Annu. Rev. Mater. Res.* 43:589–618

124. Schwartz MA, Chen CS. 2013. Cell biology. Deconstructing dimensionality. *Science* 339:402–4

125. Schwartz MA, Ginsberg MH. 2002. Networks and crosstalk: integrin signalling spreads. *Nat. Cell Biol.* 4:E65–68

126. Schwarz US, Erdmann T, Bischofs IB. 2006. Focal adhesions as mechanosensors: the two-spring model. *BioSystems* 83:225–32

127. Schwarz US, Gardel ML. 2012. United we stand: integrating the actin cytoskeleton and cell-matrix adhesions in cellular mechanotransduction. *J. Cell Sci.* 125:3051–60

128. Seifert U. 2000. Rupture of multiple parallel molecular bonds under dynamic loading. *Phys. Rev. Lett.* 84:2750

129. Selhuber-Unkel C, Erdmann T, López-García M, Kessler H, Schwarz US, Spatz JP. 2010. Cell adhesion strength is controlled by intermolecular spacing of adhesion receptors. *Biophys. J.* 98:543–51

130. Sen S, Engler AJ, Discher DE. 2009. Matrix strains induced by cells: computing how far cells can feel. *Cell. Mol. Bioeng.* 2:39–48

131. Shemesh T, Geiger B, Bershadsky AD, Kozlov MM. 2005. Focal adhesions as mechanosensors: a physical mechanism. *PNAS* 102:12383–88

131a. Shemesh T, Verkhovsky AB, Svitkina TM, Bershadsky AD, Kozlov MM. 2009. Role of focal adhesions and mechanical stresses in the formation and progression of the lamellum interface. *Biophys. J.* 97:1254–64

132. Small JV, Rottner K, Kaverina I. 1999. Functional design in the actin cytoskeleton. *Curr. Opin. Cell Biol.* 11:54–60

133. Smith ML, Gourdon D, Little WC, Kubow KE, Eguiluz RA, et al. 2007. Force-induced unfolding of fibronectin in the extracellular matrix of living cells. *PLOS Biol.* 5:e268

134. Stachowiak MR, O'Shaughnessy B. 2008. Kinetics of stress fibers. *New J. Phys.* 10:025002

135. Tadokoro S, Shattil SJ, Eto K, Tai V, Liddington RC, et al. 2003. Talin binding to integrin β tails: a final common step in integrin activation. *Science* 302:103–6

136. Tan JL, Tien J, Pirone DM, Gray DS, Bhadriraju K, Chen CS. 2003. Cells lying on a bed of microneedles: an approach to isolate mechanical force. *PNAS* 100:1484

137. Tee S-Y, Fu J, Chen CS, Janmey PA. 2011. Cell shape and substrate rigidity both regulate cell stiffness. *Biophys. J.* 100:L25–27

137a. Thomas W, Forero M, Yakovenko O, Nilsson L, Vicini P, et al. 2006. Catch-bond model derived from allostery explains force-activated bacterial adhesion. *Biophys. J.* 90:753–64

138. Thomas WE, Trintchina E, Forero M, Vogel V, Sokurenko EV. 2002. Bacterial adhesion to target cells enhanced by shear force. *Cell* 109:913–23

139. Tondon A, Hsu H-J, Kaunas R. 2012. Dependence of cyclic stretch-induced stress fiber reorientation on stretch waveform. *J. Biomech.* 45:728–35

139a. Trappmann B, Gautrot JE, Connelly JT, Strange DGT, Li Y, et al. 2012. Extracellular-matrix tethering regulates stem-cell fate. *Nat. Mater.* 11:642–49

140. Vogel V, Sheetz M. 2006. Local force and geometry sensing regulate cell functions. *Nat. Rev. Mol. Cell Biol.* 7:265–75

141. Wang H, Ji B, Liu XS, Guo XE, Huang Y, Hwang K-C. 2012. Analysis of microstructural and mechanical alterations of trabecular bone in a simulated three-dimensional remodeling process. *J. Biomech.* 45:2417–25

142. Wang H, Ji B, Liu XS, van Oers RFM, Guo XE, et al. 2014. Osteocyte-viability-based simulations of trabecular bone loss and recovery in disuse and reloading. *Biomech. Model. Mechanobiol.* 13:153–66

143. Wang JH, Goldschmidt-Clermont P, Wille J, Yin FC. 2001. Specificity of endothelial cell reorientation in response to cyclic mechanical stretching. *J. Biomech.* 34:1563–72

144. Wang N, Naruse K, Stamenovic D, Fredberg JJ, Mijailovich SM, et al. 2001. Mechanical behavior in living cells consistent with the tensegrity model. *PNAS* 98:7765–70

145. Wang N, Tolić-Nørrelykke IM, Chen J, Mijailovich SM, Butler JP, et al. 2002. Cell prestress. I. Stiffness and prestress are closely associated in adherent contractile cells. *Am. J. Physiol. Cell Physiol.* 282:C606–16

146. Weng S, Fu J. 2011. Synergistic regulation of cell function by matrix rigidity and adhesive pattern. *Biomaterials* 32:9584–93

147. Wolfenson H, Henis YI, Geiger B, Bershadsky AD. 2009. The heel and toe of the cell's foot: a multi-faceted approach for understanding the structure and dynamics of focal adhesions. *Cell Motil. Cytoskelet.* 66:1017–29

148. Wozniak MA, Chen CS. 2009. Mechanotransduction in development: a growing role for contractility. *Nat. Rev. Microbiol.* 10:34–43

149. Xiao T, Takagi J, Coller BS, Wang J-H, Springer TA. 2004. Structural basis for allostery in integrins and binding to fibrinogen-mimetic therapeutics. *Nature* 432:59–67

149a. Yu C-H, Law JBK, Suryana M, Low HY, Sheetz MP. 2011. Early integrin binding to Arg-Gly-Asp peptide activates actin polymerization and contractile movement that stimulates outward translocation. *PNAS* 108:20585–90

150. Zaidel-Bar R, Itzkovitz S, Ma'ayan A, Iyengar R, Geiger B. 2007. Functional atlas of the integrin adhesome. *Nat. Cell Biol.* 9:858–67

151. Zamir E, Katz BZ, Aota S, Yamada KM, Geiger B, Kam Z. 1999. Molecular diversity of cell-matrix adhesions. *J. Cell Sci.* 112:1655–69

152. Zamir E, Katz M, Posen Y, Erez N, Yamada KM, et al. 2000. Dynamics and segregation of cell-matrix adhesions in cultured fibroblasts. *Nat. Cell Biol.* 2:191–96

153. Zhong Y, He S, Dong C, Ji B, Hu G. 2014. Cell polarization energy and its implications for cell migration. *C. R. Mec.* 342:334–46

154. Zhong Y, He S, Ji B. 2012. Mechanics in mechanosensitivity of cell adhesion and its roles in cell migration. *Int. J. Comput. Mater. Sci. Eng.* 1:1250032

155. Zhong Y, Ji B. 2013. Impact of cell shape on cell migration behavior on elastic substrate. *Biofabrication* 5:015011

156. Zhong Y, Ji B. 2014. How do cells produce and regulate the driving force in the process of migration? *Eur. Phys. J. Special Top.* 223:1373–90

157. Zhong Y, Kong D, Dai L, Ji B. 2011. Frequency-dependent focal adhesion instability and cell reorientation under cyclic substrate stretching. *Cell. Mol. Bioeng.* 4:442–56

158. Zhu C, Lou J, McEver RP. 2005. Catch bonds: physical models, structural bases, biological function and rheological relevance. *Biorheology* 42:443–62

159. Ziegler WH, Gingras AR, Critchley DR, Emsley J. 2008. Integrin connections to the cytoskeleton through talin and vinculin. *Biochem. Soc. Trans.* 36:235–39

Biostructural Science Inspired by Next-Generation X-Ray Sources

Sol M. Gruner[1,2,3] and Eaton E. Lattman[4,5,6]

[1]Department of Physics, [2]Cornell High Energy Synchrotron Source (CHESS), [3]Kavli Institute at Cornell for Nanoscale Science, Cornell University, Ithaca, New York 14853; email: smg26@cornell.edu

[4]Hauptman-Woodward Medical Research Institute, Buffalo, New York 14203

[5]Department of Structural Biology, School of Medicine and Biomedical Sciences, SUNY Buffalo, Buffalo, New York 14203

[6]BioXFEL Center, Buffalo, New York 14203

Annu. Rev. Biophys. 2015. 44:33–51

First published online as a Review in Advance on February 26, 2015

The *Annual Review of Biophysics* is online at biophys.annualreviews.org

This article's doi: 10.1146/annurev-biophys-060414-033813

Keywords

microcrystallography, nanocrystallography, biomolecular solution scattering, synchrotron radiation sources, X-ray free-electron laser, energy recovery linac, bright storage ring sources

Abstract

Next-generation synchrotron radiation sources, such as X-ray free-electron lasers, energy recovery linacs, and ultra-low-emittance storage rings, are catalyzing novel methods of biomolecular microcrystallography and solution scattering. These methods are described and future trends are predicted. Importantly, there is a growing realization that serial microcrystallography and certain cutting-edge solution scattering experiments can be performed at existing storage ring sources by utilizing new technology. In this sense, next-generation sources are serving two distinct functions, namely, provision of new capabilities that require the newer sources and inspiration of new methods that can be performed at existing sources.

Contents

INTRODUCTION

Synchrotron radiation (SR) methods have vastly expanded the ability to determine the molecular structure and properties of biological materials. This accomplishment is a direct consequence of the steady improvements in storage-ring-based SR facilities that have enabled diffraction experiments not feasible with conventional X-ray machines. Recently, next-generation synchrotron X-ray sources with greatly enhanced capabilities, e.g., X-ray free-electron lasers (XFELs) (64), energy recovery linacs (ERLs) (14), and ultra-low-emittance storage rings (UESRs) (13), have moved from concept to feasible implementation.

XFELs, the first of the next-generation sources (NGS) to come online, have already catalyzed novel experimental approaches in biostructural science, which have been excellently reviewed elsewhere (11, 30, 100). Our intent with this review is somewhat different from that of prior reviews and is based on two observations. First, routine availability of NGS is still the better part of a decade away; therefore, most experiments over the coming decade will continue to be performed at existing storage ring sources. Second, novel experimental approaches inspired by NGS experiments are being developed at existing storage ring sources.

To make these observations concrete, consider a proof-of-principle serial microcrystallography experiment (17) demonstrated at the Linac Coherent Light Source (LCLS) at SLAC (now SLAC National Accelerator Laboratory), the world's first hard XFEL. What, specifically, is novel about this experiment? Novelty is not confined to the XFEL source: The X-ray beamline, the sample delivery system, the X-ray detector, the data collection protocol, and the way in which the data were handled and analyzed are quite different from what is found at conventional crystallographic beamlines. This begs a question: If one were to likewise reconsider all parts of the crystallographic experiment in terms of in-principle physical limits, could one perform significantly more advanced serial microcrystallography at storage ring sources? The answer, as we shall show, is almost certainly yes.

This review is, therefore, forward-looking and focused on experiments that are likely to evolve over the next decade at existing storage ring sources, as well as at NGS. We identify specific future methods that are suggested by recent advances in order to provide a roadmap for future research. In some cases this involves the development of technology initiated at storage rings that will come to fruition at NGS. In other cases fruition will arrive at existing storage ring sources, such that the primary role of NGS will be inspiration and motivation.

SERIAL MICROCRYSTALLOGRAPHY

Serial microcrystallography (SMX) refers to techniques that obtain atomic structure from multiple microcrystals. The use of multiple crystals to obtain structure dates back to the very beginnings of protein crystallography, but the ability do this with microcrystals is very much at the cutting edge of biostructural research. The scientific motivation is the assumption that many important protein systems that are difficult to obtain as large single crystals may be more readily available as many small, high-diffraction-quality crystals (34, 46, 68, 79, 102). For the purposes of this review, microcrystallography refers to crystals that are less than a few microns across; the distinguishing feature is that the crystals are too small to allow complete data sets to be obtained from a single crystal before radiation damage becomes limiting. Therefore, our use of the term microcrystallography includes nanocrystallography.

Successful demonstration of SMX experiments has driven much of the excitement at XFELs (11, 20, 48, 49, 60, 104). Significantly, examination of a seminal SMX XFEL experiment (17) reveals that almost every aspect of the experiment differs from routine crystallography at storage rings, leading to an important question: What are the limits in principle of what can be done at other bright sources, including present and future storage rings and ERLs, if one reconsiders the entire crystallography experiment? For example, will SMX be routinely performed at non-XFEL sources? This answer is important because the availability of XFEL beamlines will be limited for at least the better part of the next decade.

What Is Required for a Complete Data Set?

Proof-of-principle XFEL experiments involved crystals that were typically a few microns in size, so consider the number of crystals that is needed to obtain a complete data set if each crystal has a volume of, say, $(2 \ \mu m)^3$. Further, assume a unit cell size on the order of 100 Å across. Sliz et al. (94) based their examination of this issue on the experience at the time, i.e., using cryocooled crystals, phosphor-coupled CCD (charge-coupled device) detectors, and typical state-of-the art macromolecular beamlines at storage rings in 2003. They concluded that complete data sets at 3.5 Å resolution required crystals roughly $(20 \ \mu m)^3$. Because radiation damage for cryocooled crystals scales linearly with dose (42), i.e., with energy absorbed per unit mass, data collection is ultimately limited by the total number of protein molecules involved. A crystal of $(20 \ \mu m)^3$ has the same number of proteins as 10^3 cryocooled crystals, each with a volume of $(2 \ \mu m)^3$. For the sake of reference, call this a worst-case scenario because the Sliz et al. (94) scenario was based on extrapolations from experience and was not an optimization based on first principles. One fully expects that elimination of background scatter from beamline optics or reduction of detector noise would reduce the required number of crystals.

Holton & Frankel (43) started from first principles and assumed nearly ideal photon background and photon detection. They found that a complete data set with a signal-to-noise ratio of 2 at 2 Å resolution would be attainable from a cryocooled perfect lysozyme crystal sphere 1.2 μm in diameter. They noted that this diameter is further reduced by roughly a factor of 2 to 3 if photoelectron escape effects (67, 84) are taken into account; the resultant estimate is a reduction in volume by a factor of approximately 10. Lysozyme has roughly one-tenth the unit cell volume considered in the previous paragraph (10^6 Å^3), but the resolution considered is higher (2 Å versus 3.5 Å). It is reasonable, therefore, to say that in a best-case scenario (further discussed below) one cryocooled crystal 2 μm across should yield a complete data set at ~2 Å resolution for a unit cell approximately 100 Å across. Thus, the best- and worst-case scenarios as described above bracket the number of 2-μm crystals required for complete 2 Å data sets to be from 1 to 10^3 cryocooled crystals. This finding is supported by recent results at PETRA III (34).

How many ~10-keV incident X-rays will cause severe radiation damage to the 2-μm crystal? Although this number is dependent on the desired resolution and varies from one type of protein to another, a rule of thumb is that a 20-MGy dose limits the diffraction resolution to 2 Å (42, 45). A layer of protein or water 2 μm thick absorbs approximately 10^{-3} of the incident X-rays. Assume a beamline capable of delivering 10^{12} X-rays into the $(2\text{-μm})^2$ cross-sectional area of the crystal. Some beamlines already exceed this (72), and brighter sources under development will increase this by orders of magnitude (14). This corresponds to 10^9 absorbed X-rays in the $(2 \text{ μm})^3$ volume, which is a dose rate of 200 MGy/s. The crystal will last ~0.1 s, which is the best-case-scenario time for a complete data set. For the worst case, assume the crystals are delivered serially into the beam one after the other; then the time to get a complete data set from 1,000 crystals is 100 s.

The above estimates are for cryocooled crystals. How about noncryocooled crystals? In round numbers, cryoprotection increases the number of absorbed X-rays to a given level of radiation damage by a factor of 100 if delivered quickly (66), so the best- and worst-case scenarios given above scale to 10^2 and 10^5 noncryocooled crystals, respectively, with corresponding total exposure times of 10 s and 10^4 s. These numbers of crystals sound big, but the total volume of protein involved is actually modest: A single conventional crystal 200 μm on a side has the same volume as 10^6 of the 2-μm crystals.

Even if the worst case takes ten times longer, the data collection times are still on the order of a day for a complete data set. And with forthcoming synchrotron sources with orders of magnitude more brightness, the time estimates fall by corresponding orders of magnitude. The important conclusion is that serial microcrystallography is feasible in principle at many types of existing synchrotron sources, and even more so with forthcoming brighter sources. Very recent first (and, therefore, not ideally optimized) results at PETRA III support this conclusion (98).

Obviously, the above estimates do not take into account many practical problems of implementation, such as crystal manipulation, heating, or orientation. But these problems are ones of engineering, not fundamental diffraction physics. With enough clever engineering effort, most practical problems can be resolved. This is precisely the philosophy that was and is being successfully taken in the case of microcrystallography at the XFELs, hence the title of this review.

Experimental Considerations for Serial Microcrystallography

In the following sections we examine the literature on approaches to practical implementations and extrapolate areas in need of attention.

Beam brightness. Practical SMX is dependent upon the ability to focus sufficient and suitable X-ray flux onto a microcrystal to determine a structure in a reasonable amount of time. In this regard, what beam characteristics are important?

X-ray beams are characterized by their spectral brightness (X-rays/s/mm²/mrad²/0.1% bandwidth). The units indicate that X-ray beams, being electromagnetic radiation, are subject to the brightness theorem, a formulation of Liouville's theorem (12, 54). In practice, this means that the spectral brightness is at best constant along the beam path and that one may trade beam width for divergence, as long as the product of the two is kept constant. Both spectral brightness and transverse coherence are inversely proportional to the transverse electron emittances, defined as proportional to the product of the generating electron beam width and divergence transverse to the direction of electron beam propagation. This is the primary motivation behind the quest for ever-brighter synchrotron sources: the smaller the electron beam emittances, the brighter the potential X-ray beams, which translates in turn to potential to put more X-rays into a low-divergence microbeam. Note the word "potential." Although a given electron emittance sets an upper bound on the X-ray beam spectral brightness and coherence, there are always ways to lose X-rays and lower the brightness (14, 33).

Just as with visible light, the diffraction limit set by the wavelength, λ, of the radiation determines the ultimate smallest width, Δx, and angular divergence, $\Delta \theta$, as $\Delta x \Delta \theta \geq \lambda / 4\pi \approx 8\text{pm}$ for 10-keV X-rays. The emittance of PETRA III, among the world's brightest rings as of 2014, is ~ 1 nm, about 100 times the diffraction limit. UESRs, and especially ERLs on the drawing boards, would approach the diffraction limit. Today's best storage rings and X-ray optics deliver sufficiently monochromatic beams with $\sim 10^{12}$ X-rays/s/μm^2. Beams of far higher specific intensity are possible with lower-emittance X-ray sources. For example, if suitable X-ray optics can be devised, an ERL design advocated by Cornell University would be able to deliver $\sim 10^{11}$–10^{12} X-rays/s/nm^2 (14).

Radiation damage. The ability to extract structural information from protein crystals is ultimately limited by radiation damage, a broad term encompassing a multitude of destructive processes resulting from ionizing radiation (32, 80, 101). These processes include bond scission, chemical alteration, and charge movement, leading to displacement of atoms and consequent loss of inherent structure. In the noncryocooled case, chemically destructive entities, such as free radicals, readily diffuse and multiply damage. This takes significant time. As a result, the damage continues to increase even after the X-ray beam is turned off; i.e., radiation damage is time dependent and accumulates faster than linearly with the X-ray dose. (There are hints that at sufficiently high dose rates at storage ring sources, one might be able to begin to outrun radiation damage—this is a current area of research. This is not to be confused with dosing in femtoseconds at XFELs, where damage can be outrun.) If the crystal is cryocooled prior to irradiation to prevent diffusion, damage will be localized to primary sites of electron ejection and Compton scattering. In this case, the damage increases linearly with the X-ray dose (absorbed X-ray energy per unit mass of specimen). The damage is locked in at cryotemperatures by the inability of atoms to move about. If the crystal is warmed to allow diffusion, degraded diffraction from the irradiated regions quickly becomes evident.

Another consequence of the absorption of X-ray energy is the production of heat. At low rates of X-ray fluence the heat may be effectively conducted out of the crystal to surrounding cold gas in a cryostream. As the specific X-ray intensity rises, however, a point is reached where energy is deposited faster than it can be conducted away and the local temperature rises. This ultimately sets the limit of microbeam intensity for crystallography at storage ring sources.

XFELs can produce microbeams of $>10^{12}$ X-rays in a pulse only femtoseconds long. The pulse is scattered from a microcrystal before the tens of femtoseconds required for atomic nuclei to move appreciably. The result is that the diffracted X-rays have exited the sample before the sample is vaporized into plasma. This diffract-before-destroy regime gives XFELs the ability to largely outrun radiation damage. The number of diffracted X-rays, however, is ultimately limited by the number of electrons in the sample; after all, X-rays scatter primarily off the electrons. Typically 1 in 10 X-rays that interact with the sample is diffracted; the remainder photoeject electrons. At sufficiently high XFEL fluences, so many photoelectrons are ejected at the leading edge of the X-ray pulse that few electrons remain to scatter the remaining X-rays in the pulse. In other words, the diffraction becomes self-limiting (10, 39, 40, 112). Diffraction occurs only for the part of reciprocal space that intersects the Ewald sphere; thus, to gather a complete data set one must sample many orientations of crystals relative to the beam. The consequence is that, even with

XFELs, many microcrystals at different orientations need to be diffracted to obtain a complete data set. The primary potential advantage of XFELs is therefore the ability to obtain complete data sets with fewer unfrozen crystals than at storage rings or ERLs. Whether this translates in practice to a more feasible experiment depends on myriad details of experimental execution and facility access (see below).

X-ray background reduction and efficient detectors. X-ray background reduction is absolutely essential for microcrystallography. Holton & Frankel's (43) calculation that a complete data set can be obtained with a 1-μm crystal assumes recording of diffraction spots with a signal-to-noise (SNR) ratio of 2. In the absence of X-ray background and with an ideal detector, a SNR of 2 is achieved with $N = 4$ X-rays; i.e., SNR $= 4/\sqrt{4} = 2$. Few crystallographers would consider a measurement of four X-rays to be a viable diffraction spot, but this is simply because past experience typically involved detectors that had significant noise or sample situations with unnecessary X-ray background.

Modern electronic pixel array detectors, of both the photon-counting and photon-integrating variety, measure X-ray signals to an accuracy limited by the shot noise inherent in the signal being measured, i.e., the square root of the number of incident X-rays in the measurement area. In this regard, it is often said that modern pixel array detectors are noiseless. This phrase has no technical meaning, as no detector has infinitely precise ability to accurately measure X-ray signals. Limitations, which can be made small, arise from, e.g., variations in window absorption, partial transparency of the detector sensors to X-rays, and calibration imperfections. Another misconception is that photon-counting detectors make more accurate measurements than photon-integrating detectors do, especially for very-low-dose measurements. In fact, the accuracy with which a detector makes a measurement is dependent in all cases on the specific details of the detector and the measurement being made. For example, most photon-counting detectors installed on crystallographic beamlines to date lose X-rays because of charge division between neighboring pixels (35, 36). Newer technologies just now being developed promise to eliminate this flaw (8). Integrating detectors avoid this false-negative counting and perform in experiments even at remarkably low doses of a few X-rays per frame (6, 75), but these too are available only as custom devices. Even so, demonstrated technologies, for both photon-counting and photon-integrating pixel array detectors, prove that detectors need not be a limiting factor in SMX experiments.

Reducing background X-ray scatter to near-ideal levels is also possible but to date has not been implemented at practically any crystallographic beamlines. To set the scale, a suitable goal would be to reduce background scatter to levels inherent to the sample itself (see **Figure 1**). Most protein crystals are half water, the bulk of which is not crystallographically bound and therefore contributes to the diffuse background scatter. For a crystal 2 μm on a side, the irreducible scatter is therefore equivalent to 1 μm thickness of water. Water has roughly 10^3 times the density of air or nitrogen; hence, background scatter equivalent to 1 μm water is obtained by an air or nitrogen main beam path length of 1 mm. If gas is required for cooling, helium, with roughly one-twentieth the scattering cross-section of air, is a better choice. SMX experiments at the LCLS occur in a vacuum, with background determined largely by the water or lipidic medium used to convey microcrystals into the XFEL beam (17, 60, 81, 102). This is necessary in part because X-ray windows would not survive passage of the XFEL beam.

X-ray windows and sample supports, when present, contribute X-ray background. Plastic windows usually have a scattering cross-section comparable to that of water, so two windows even 0.5 μm thick produce scatter equivalent to that of the internal crystal water. Likewise, crystals held, for example, in a 10-μm-thick film of vitreous water contribute many times the background scatter of the inherent crystal water.

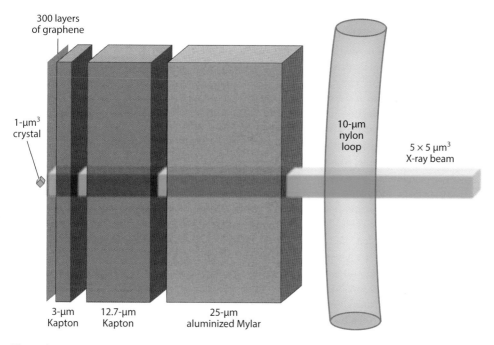

Figure 1

All stray matter in the 5×5 μm X-ray beam shown contributes to unwanted X-ray background. To appreciate relative magnitudes, consider a 1-μm³ protein crystal, shown at the left. It consists of about 50% water, which is the source of a minimum level of background scatter. All other materials that might be in the beam, some of which are shown to scale, contribute roughly in proportion to their volume in the beam. The desirability of eliminating all these sources of background is obvious. The graphene multilayer at the left represents 300 layers of graphene at the scale shown, because a few layers would be too thin a line to be seen in the drawing. The few layers of graphene that would actually be needed would contribute insignificantly to the X-ray background.

Ideally windows and sample supports should utilize materials that are no more than a few atoms thick for negligible background scatter. This is possible with graphene: A single layer of graphene, one carbon atom thick, is sufficiently strong to be used as a helium- and vacuum-tight window over multimicron-wide areas (19). Microcrystals encapsulated in liquid bubbles trapped between graphene sheets have been imaged in the high-vacuum environment of the electron microscope (109, 110). Wierman et al. (106) demonstrated the use of graphene sheets as a crystal support capable of spanning the better part of a millimeter. Free-standing, high-quality graphene is certain to become commercially available. Alternative window materials, such as silicon nitride windows hundreds of nanometers thick, are commercially available. Their thickness makes them less desirable than graphene but still sufficiently thin to serve for many SMX experiments.

Crystal preparation and delivery into the X-ray beam. SMX is justified by the assertion that large numbers of microcrystals of important systems are more readily obtainable than larger single crystals. Although the strength of the asserted case will become clearer as the community gathers experience, there is evidence that microcrystals are more easily obtained. Smaller crystals appear more readily in crystallization screens (79) of aqueously soluble proteins. Crystals produced by lipidic phase methods (49) are in most cases very small. Crystals grown in vivo in cells are necessarily small (34, 81). Thus, even if the assertion is not universally true, it is likely to be true enough in certain important cases to warrant continued development of SMX.

A related question is whether the diffraction quality of microcrystals is generally better than that of larger crystals. Protein crystals usually have larger mosaicity than perfect crystals do, presumably because they consist of smaller mosaic blocks of more perfect crystals (68, 95). This suggests that as the size of the crystal approaches the size of the mosaic block, the mosaic spread should decrease. A reduction in disordered protein at the boundaries of mosaic blocks may also improve diffraction quality. Although there are few systematic studies on these issues, evidence for the improved quality of microcrystals is slowly accumulating as more microcrystal systems are studied. For example, Weierstall et al. (102) reported that they solved the structure of a G protein–coupled receptor complex with microcrystals using SMX at the LCLS. However, they were unsuccessful in solving the structure at a storage ring source with larger crystals because of poorer-quality diffraction from the larger crystals. Systematic investigations of the diffraction quality and, just as important, the heterogeneity in quality as a function of crystal size are needed. Typically, crystal mosaicity increases when crystals are cryocooled. It is not known how this effect scales with crystal size. It is possible that microcrystals are less disrupted by the cryocooling process. Systematic studies of questions such as these have been difficult to perform because microcrystals have been difficult to study. NGS are enabling in this regard. The studies should be done.

SMX depends on the availability of a sufficient quantity of suitable crystals and ways to serially feed these crystals into the beam. The literature to date on SMX at the LCLS is dominated by batch crystal preparation procedures (3, 17, 24, 48, 49, 53, 60, 81) and stochastic insertion of crystals into the beam with either an aqueous liquid jet (16, 96, 103) or a lipidic phase gel injector (102). The liquid injector is an ingenious device whereby a fluid jet studded with microcrystals is focused to micron sizes by a coaxial carrier gas sheath. Because the liquid stream moves at high speeds (meters per second), it consumes much protein. By contrast, the lipidic phase gel injector uses less protein because it slowly extrudes a few-microns-wide toothpaste-like column of highly viscous lipidic gel studded with membrane proteins within a coaxial gas sheath. Although the injector was designed to work with the lipidic gel phase in which membrane protein crystals are grown, it takes no stretch of imagination to consider using it with an appropriate polymer gel carrier for nonmembrane proteins.

The advantage of these methods is conceptual, if not actual, simplicity. But there is work to be done: Researchers must devise batch crystal preparation and delivery procedures to provide crystals of a homogenous size. Stochastic injection methods require decisions about the concentration of crystals to put into the carrier medium: If the concentration is too low, many laser pulses may encounter no crystals; at too high a concentration, more than one crystal at a time may be in the beam. Stochastic injection of crystals of heterogeneous sizes argues for a beam size that is larger than the average crystal size to maximize the probability of having a complete crystal in the beam. In this case, even if the crystal is centered in the beam, many X-rays bypass the crystal entirely, hitting only, perhaps, the carrier fluid and thereby contributing to unwanted background scatter. All these factors result in experiments that take both more time and more protein than ideally required. The consequence to date is that each SMX structure solved at the LCLS has required huge numbers of crystals. But these are early days for SMX at XFELs, and more efficient methods will certainly be devised.

It is instructive to compare two seminal SMX experiments, one done at the LCLS XFEL and one done at the PETRA III storage ring. Both experiments solved the structure of the glycosylated precursor complex of *Trypanosoma brucei* cathepsin B grown in vivo in bacteria. The LCLS structure solved at 2.1 Å used liquid jet injection involving many unfrozen crystals, of which $\sim 3 \times 10^5$ were diffracted (81). The PETRA III experiments used essentially the same source of crystals—papers describing the two experiments have several authors in common—but in this case the crystals were spread across a ~20-μm-thick film of liquid spanning a 0.7-mm-diameter cryoloop, which was subsequently cryocooled. The loop was then raster-scanned using a microbeam and a conventional diffractometer at the microfocus P14 beamline at PETRA III. The loop yielded diffraction data from approximately 80 crystals that were used to solve the structure to 3.0 Å. The authors noted that background from the cryocooled liquid film was a limitation, but the background could have been be reduced if crystal supports derived from electron microscopy (68) or graphene (106) were used.

Obviously, one could consider doing a similar frozen cryoloop experiment at an XFEL that would be very conservative of protein. Cryocooled crystals, however, are biologically inactive. Alternatively, one might consider a spread of microcrystals at near room temperature, each within a tiny surrounding fluid volume, encapsulated between sheets of graphene. This is hardly fanciful— it has already been done with nanoparticles in electron microscope studies (109, 110).

Another very recent seminal SMX experiment at PETRA III used a flow of room-temperature lysozyme crystals down a glass capillary (98). A 9-μm-diameter beam was used with 2×10^{12} 9,800-eV X-rays/s. The flow rate of crystals in the capillary resulted in exposures of 1 to 3 ms. Forty thousand diffraction patterns were acquired and refined at 2.1 Å resolution. Although the crystals were relatively large (~135 μm^3), this promising experiment supports our conclusion that SMX will become feasible at storage rings.

Ideally, all crystals would be produced at the beamline; all would be of a very similar size and fed one at a time into a microbeam with a cross-sectional diameter footprint that matched the projected area of the crystal. Scientists are currently developing microfluidic chips that screen proteins for crystallization conditions, make the crystals, and then shuttle them on-chip for serial in situ X-ray diffraction (41, 73, 91, 92). By controlling the feedback using small-growth volumes in the crystallization cells, scientists can create microdroplets with crystals of uniform size, with one crystal per microdrop (41). One can envision a system in which a microfluidic chip is used to create microcrystals of a uniform size that are then shuttled to an in situ diffraction chamber equipped with graphene or other ultrathin X-ray windows. Excess surrounding droplet fluid is then withdrawn, the crystal is diffracted while the entire chip undergoes small-angle oscillations, and then the crystal is flushed away. There is no reason why this cannot occur many times per second in an automated process. This would minimize handling of very delicate crystals.

Data handling and diffraction signal strength. One frontier experiment that motivated XFELs is the possibility of determining the structure of noncrystalline particles (11, 86, 96, 100). In this type of experiment many images are accumulated from individual particles encountering the X-ray pulse, one at a time. The challenge is to devise ways to sum the many images, given that each particle encounters the beam in a random, unknown orientation. Because the number of scattered X-rays is limited by the number of electrons in the particle, each diffraction image is severely Poisson noise limited, i.e., contains so few X-rays that no single image contains enough information to determine the orientation of the particle when it encountered the X-ray pulse. Such images are called sparse. Remarkably, so-called expand–maximize–compress (EMC) algorithms resolve this problem, given enough protein scattering events (27, 63). Practical demonstrations have proven that structures with even very sparse images can be recovered (6, 62, 74). Alternative methods to the EMC approach are also being developed (44), though it is not yet clear how well these approaches work with extremely sparse data.

As recently shown, EMC algorithms can be applied to sparse crystallographic data (5, 7). Further experiments needed to prove that EMC algorithms can be applied to SMX will likely soon be forthcoming. The key conclusion would be that it is not necessary for each microcrystal to diffract enough X-rays to determine the orientation of the crystal. Given enough randomly oriented crystals, one can still determine the reciprocal space Bragg pattern, even though the orientation of each individual crystal is unknown. This conclusion has a remarkable corollary: The ability to do SMX is not limited by the strength of the X-ray source. In principle, SMX is possible with a conventional laboratory source, though the data collection times may be impractically long. Data collection times will certainly be feasible at storage ring sources.

SMX can generate copious quantities of data and is pushing X-ray crystallography into previously uncharted areas of truly massive data sets. Procedures that have been used to turn SMX into real structures are evolving quickly (9, 18, 25, 31, 85, 96, 104, 105).

The Future of SMX

Given the considerations above, it is useful to speculate about the future of SMX as this serves to stimulate research. We confine attention to static SMX; the special case of very fast time-resolved SMX (70, 87) is beyond the scope of this review.

Compelling considerations that will shape the future of SMX include (*a*) the availability of SMX beamlines and better detectors, (*b*) a reduction in X-ray background, (*c*) a desire to reduce the amount of protein needed to obtain a complete data set, and (*d*) the size of the crystals. What kind of X-ray source will enable SMX? SMX is already being performed at XFELs and at bright storage rings (see below). The feasibility of SMX will certainly be enhanced as XFELs become more stable, perhaps with seeded operation; as ERLs and UESRs are built; and as technical innovations downstream of the source come online. The arguments given above therefore suggest that the capabilities of SMX will grow at all the different types of very bright sources. The simple availability of beamlines and the wealth of crystals in the micron-sized range will catalyze a rapid increase in storage-ring-based capabilities. Much depends on the size of the crystals. As crystal sizes shrink below 1 μm, XFEL sources will look increasingly attractive, at least initially. Further, one can envision high-throughput XFEL capabilities. But as crystal sizes shrink and technical advances allow researchers to manipulate crystals in high-vacuum environments, electron microscope diffraction will also become increasingly attractive (1, 58, 68, 69, 88, 90), given that electrons have $\sim 10^4$ times the scattering cross-section of X-rays and that difficulties resulting from multiple scattering decrease with sample thickness.

Storage ring beamlines can readily be adapted to deal with cryocooled crystals ranging from 1 to 20 μm (34). This size range is also readily within reach of room-temperature experiments (98). In cases in which sample protein is limited, in situ diffraction in microfluidic chips will become especially useful (41, 73).

Especially as crystals sizes shrink, background reduction will compel SMX beamlines to utilize vacuum environments from source to detector except for perhaps the immediate environment around the crystals. In the case of cryocooled crystals spread on, e.g., graphene or thin polymer films, the crystals themselves can be introduced into the vacuum environment. Because XFEL pulses are shorter in duration than heat transfer times, it would simply be necessary to maintain enough distance between crystals so that the sample destruction induced by a XFEL pulse is sufficiently isolated from the remaining crystals. Continuous cryocooling may be required for storage ring experiments in which exposure times are longer than phonon timescales. One can envision, for example, crystals on a planar graphene support that is raster-scanned through a microbeam in an enclosed space on the order of a millimeter across through which there is a flow of cold helium gas. This enclosed space is in the vacuum environment of the beamline, and X-rays are admitted into and out of the enclosed space via small windows made of graphene or other low-background scattering material.

The toothpaste extrusion–injection system (102) is an elegant room-temperature solution that uses relatively little protein. It is likely to be adapted for both XFEL and storage ring systems, and for both membrane and fully aqueous proteins. Noncryocooled crystals can suffer only very brief exposure to vacuum. A gas sheath was utilized in XFEL experiments; however, in a storage ring beamline it is easy to visualize use within a narrow enclosed space as described in the previous paragraph. Likewise, microfluidic chip delivery systems with integral vacuum windows are likely to be developed for storage ring SMX (41, 73). These systems may be more difficult to use at XFELs because the windows would likely be destroyed by the XFEL pulse.

In summary, these are exciting times for developments in SMX. XFELs have catalyzed innovative thinking, both for XFEL and non-XFEL SMX. One thing is certain: Future crystallography options will be far more diverse than they have been in the past.

NONCRYSTALLINE SPECIMENS

The possibility of using XFELs to image single particles (e.g., proteins or viruses) in vacuum has been well reviewed elsewhere (11, 61, 62, 71, 86). It is not discussed here other than to note that the process is challenging and faces intense competition from single-particle imaging by electron microscopy (38). Rather, we discuss structural measurements of molecules in solution that are enabled by NGS.

Time-Resolving Fast Structural Changes

Very-short-duration NGS X-ray pulses enable the study of very rapid structural changes. An elegant example is an experiment at the LCLS (4) that examined fast changes upon light absorption in the photosynthetic reaction center (PRC). The PRC faces unique problems of energy management because the energy of a single green light photon is approximately equal to the activation energy for unfolding the molecule. Photons absorbed by the light-harvesting antennae in the PRC are rapidly funneled to the reaction center through dedicated, specialized channels. Excess energy deposited in the protein is hypothesized to emanate as displacement waves before damage can be done by a process called protein quakes (2, 111).

Multiphoton absorption was used to trigger the PRC (22) and wide-angle X-ray scattering (WAXS) was monitored for progress of the structural change. Red light laser pulses 500 fs in duration were focused onto a microjet of PRC solution prior to the arrival of X-ray pulses. The delay time between the laser and XFEL pulses was calibrated to ≤5 ps, and WAXS patterns were collected over a series of 41 time delays up to 100 ps. Curves showing the difference in scattering between activated and dark (unactivated) molecules were generated at each time point. The light-induced perturbation appeared within a few picoseconds and subsequently decayed over ~10 ps. Importantly, the perturbation preceded the propagation of heat through the protein.

The results relied on knowledge of the equilibrium molecular structure of the complex (23), as well as molecular dynamics simulations and modeling. A combination of molecular dynamics simulations of heat deposition and flow in a molecule and spectral decomposition of the time-resolved difference scattering curves provided the basis for an understanding of energy propagation in the system. Because the light pulse was tuned to the frequency of the photosystem antennae, cofactors were heated to few thousand Kelvins, which decayed with a halftime of ~7 ps via heat flow to the remainder of the PRC. Signatures of protein structural changes appeared with clarity in oscillations of a component (termed C2) of the spectral decomposition of the data. This study illustrates both the rapid evolution of the technology and experimental prowess of the field and an application to a biologically important problem.

Another example of a study of a light-activated system measured changes in the size and shape of photoactive yellow protein (PyP) following photoactivation (21). This work was a sequel to an earlier study in which PyP was studied by time-resolved Laue crystallography (89). The Laue study illustrated a PyP photocycle involving four intermediate states. The solution scattering study was undertaken in part to dispel questions about the effects of lattice constraints on the observed structural changes in the protein.

The experimental protocol contained a number of innovative elements. The PyP solution was pumped with a circularly polarized laser flash. Because the flash is absorbed primarily by the p-coumaric acid chromophore, the protein molecules being excited are selected to align the chromophore transition dipole with the electric field of the illumination. This alignment gave rise to mildly anisotropic scattering, providing additional information in the pattern. Isolated $\sim$100-ps X-ray pulses at the BioCARS 14-ID-B beamline at the US Department of Energy's Advanced Photon Source probed the PyP solution. High-resolution data ($q_{max} = 2.5$ Å^{-1}) were observed. The pulse length was longer than the lifetime of the excited state, such that there were multiple opportunities to excite each molecule. The story of how the authors handled the weak signal from the experiment is a lesson in care and thoughtfulness.

In this study, a rapid 0.3% compaction of the protein was modeled along the direction of the electronic transition moment of the p-coumaric acid, accompanied by expansion along perpendicular directions, producing a change in overall volume of approximately -0.25%. The 150-ps time resolution of the experiment was too slow to track the compaction, suggesting avenues for future work on XFELs. The solution scattering results were largely supportive of the original model derived from the Laue crystal work. These two studies illustrate requirements for future studies: a worthy photo-activatable system; X-ray pulses capable of producing WAXS in time intervals shorter than the time constants of the process being monitored; structural knowledge of the unactivated (dark) system; and an ability to use scattering to model the changes arising from the activation.

Structure from Molecules in Solution

Traditional solution scattering involves X-ray illumination of a volume of the solution and collection of the resulting X-ray scatter. Because the sample contains many randomly oriented molecules, the measured diffraction pattern is cylindrically symmetric (i.e., azimuthally averaged) about the incident beam axis. The resulting curve of scattered intensity versus angle from the incident beam is relatively smooth. Even so, the resulting low-resolution curve, obtained from small-angle X-ray scattering (SAXS), can yield important information about the size, shape, and volume of the molecule (15, 37, 57, 76, 78). Work by Svergun & Koch (99) and Shneerson & Saldin (93) has resulted in a suite of computer programs that facilitate SAXS analysis.

The extraction of much information from a simple curve challenges intuition. However, Hura et al. (47) calculated SAXS curves for many proteins and showed that molecules of different folds do indeed have distinguishable curves. Also, because proteins are compact objects (i.e., have a finite support), the range of possible curves is severely limited.

Still, SAXS reconstructions without additional constraints can vary considerably. Fast, intense NGS pulses offer additional constraints: SAXS data can be obtained on timescales that are fast relative to the rotational motion of the particles. This sort of experiment has come to be called fluctuational solution scattering (FSS). Kam and colleagues (50–52) pointed out the possibilities of FSS long ago, but the requisite X-ray sources did not exist. Now XFELs are motivating intense interest in FSS (26, 28, 29, 56, 59, 77, 82, 83). The reader is referred to a masterful tutorial by Kirian (55) for insights into how FSS works.

FSS data methodology is in its formative stages. Liu et al. (59) applied angular correlation methods to simulated data from two globular proteins, the icosahedral *Satellite tobacco necrosis virus* (STNV) protein and the torus-shaped protein peroxiredoxin. Reconstructions were carried out at low resolution using an elaborated version of the Kam method, in which expanded Zernike polynomials and symmetrized basis functions played a key role. The spatial correlation coefficients between the reconstructed models and the original Protein Data Bank model were >75%. Intermediate results of the reconstruction yielded computed curves equivalent to those obtained in traditional SAXS experiments; reconstructions based solely on these models were flawed compared with reconstructions that received the full FSS treatment. Liu et al. (59) also examined an experimental system of ellipsoidal iron oxide nanoparticles and produced promising reconstructions.

An important feasibility experiment performed at the LCLS examined dumbbell-shaped particles formed from two polystyrene spheres of equal size that were dispersed in micron-sized aerosol droplets (97). Cylindrical symmetry of the specimen was used to recover the three-dimensional angular correlation function. Obtaining the corresponding calculations for an object with no symmetry would be a much more formidable task. Nevertheless, this paper appears to represent the first three-dimensional reconstruction of an object using FSS 2D data. As such, it serves as a pathway to more realistic specimens.

Another important proof-of-principle experiment for FSS involved ab initio structure determination of gold rods from soft X-ray diffraction patterns of arrays of such rods confined to a plane (82). The rods were approximately 90×25 nm and were imaged lying on a 30-nm-thick silicon nitride membrane. The authors formed the angular multiparticle correlation functions for each of the observed diffraction patterns and summed these to derive the single-particle correlation function from which the low-resolution structure of the rods was determined.

The Kam formalism is not limited to low-resolution reconstructions, as shown by another recent proof-of-principle experiment on silver nanocrystals (65). Because the SSRL (Stanford Synchrotron Radiation Lightsource) storage ring used as a source has relatively long pulses, the silver nanocrystal suspension was frozen to preclude particle rotation. Three angular correlation functions were computed: within the ring containing the 111 reflections; within the ring containing the 200 reflections; and between the rings, obtaining the 111 and the 200 reflections. The resultant correlation signals at effectively atomic resolution were in agreement with theory. Conventional powder analysis techniques applied to the same specimens would have produced only two signals, those from the 111 ring and the 200 ring. Coherent X-ray imaging, including the angular correlation peaks, provided five signals. One can foresee many important applications of this technique as methodology improves. This study opens the door to high-resolution studies in more complex systems, such as proteins.

In conclusion, to illustrate future potential, we consider a specific biological system, RNA folding, that might benefit from the capacity of NGS to map out large new regions of this experimental space. The world of noncoding RNAs is filled with large structures essential for protein synthesis, splicing, and many other cellular processes (107, 108). The folding and assembly of these systems is of intense interest. RNA folding differs in many ways from protein folding. The unfolded state is generally characterized by persistent secondary structure, that is, the existence of RNA helices, hairpins, and related secondary structures. Formation of tertiary structure normally requires increasing concentrations of divalent cations, particularly magnesium, as well as the presence of companion proteins in many cases. Folding is also characterized by the existence of stable intermediates that exist at Mg^{2+} concentrations below that necessary for complete folding. In addition, complex kinetics leads to the formation of off-pathway structures. Finally, the range of time constants involved is very broad.

Imagine the experimental problem of mapping the folding of a complicated RNA or ribonucleoprotein complex. We want to know the time constants for the formation and dissipation of kinetic intermediates, as well as their structures. We would like to know the structures and concentrations of intermediates at local minima in the folding process. Much more detailed questions will arise for each individual system.

Although solution SAXS has already made significant contributions to our understanding of RNA folding (76), NGS time-resolved WAXS and SAXS provide new opportunities. One great benefit of RNA as a system for study is that partial structures of many of the intermediates will be known. The ability to recover the intensity transform from SAXS, or to bin structural information in the case of alternative confirmations, depends critically on relatively modest amounts of additional information. For example, Elser (28) has shown that recovery of intensity transform from solution scattering experiments on particles having no symmetry and fully random orientations is undetermined. When the orientation of one axis in the particle is fixed in space, the problem becomes tractable. Thus, the variety of known structures in the RNA system becomes an enormous advantage. In addition, the high phosphate content provides stronger scattering, improving signal-to-noise ratios. What would be needed are X-ray pulses short enough to freeze the rotations of the particles and outrun overt radiation damage. NGS will provide such pulses.

CONCLUSION

NGS are contributing to biostructural science both by providing new capabilities and by inspiring new approaches at existing storage ring sources. The resultant excitement is palpable. The ultimate benefits to biology are certain to be immense.

SUMMARY POINTS

1. SMX refers to crystallographic methods used to determine the structure of macromolecules from a series of small crystals (a few microns across or smaller) that are individually too small to yield complete data sets prior to irreversible radiation damage.

2. SMX will be most useful for systems in which only small crystals are readily obtained. Examples of particular interest include membrane proteins and macromolecular complexes.

3. As the technology advances, it is increasingly clear that SMX will be feasible both at next-generation X-ray sources (X-ray free-electron lasers, energy recovery linac sources, and ultra-low-emittance storage rings) and existing high-spectral-brightness storage ring sources.

4. Intense X-ray free-electron laser pulses enable powerful new methods, such as WAXS from noncrystalline specimens and solutions, for femtosecond studies.

FUTURE ISSUES

1. A great deal of developmental work remains to be done before SMX becomes routine at any synchrotron source. Currently (as of December 2014), SMX for unfrozen crystals micron-sized or smaller has been successfully demonstrated only at X-ray free-electron lasers.

2. Single-particle imaging at XFELs awaits significant progress in source intensity, noise reduction, detector technology, and other experimental aspects.

3. Femtosecond time-resolved X-ray studies of biological specimens are still at the very early stages. One may anticipate rapid progress at X-ray free-electron laser sources as user time becomes increasingly available.

DISCLOSURE STATEMENT

The authors are not aware of any affiliations, memberships, funding, or financial holdings that might be perceived as affecting the objectivity of this review.

ACKNOWLEDGMENTS

S.M.G. is grateful for support from CHESS (supported by NSF and NIH-NIGMS via DMR-1332208), MacCHESS (NIH GM-103485), and DOE (DE-FG02-10ER46693). E.E.L. is grateful for support from the NSF (DBI-1231306).

LITERATURE CITED

1. Amunts A, Brown A, Bai XC, Llácer JL, Hussain T, et al. 2014. Structure of the yeast mitochondrial large ribosomal subunit. *Science* 343:1485–89

2. Ansari A, Berendzen J, Bowne SF, Frauenfelder H, Iben IET, et al. 1985. Protein states and proteinquakes. *PNAS* 82:5000–4

3. Aquila A, Hunter MS, Doak RB, Kirian RA, Fromme P, et al. 2012. Time-resolved protein nanocrystallography using an X-ray free-electron laser. *Opt. Express* 20:2706–16

4. Arnlund D, Johansson LC, Wickstrand C, Barty A, Williams GJ, et al. 2014. Visualizing a protein quake with time-resolved X-ray scattering at a free-electron laser. *Nat. Methods* 11:923–26

5. Ayyer K. 2014. *Reconstructing images from sparse data*. PhD Thesis, Cornell Univ. Press

6. Ayyer K, Philipp HT, Tate MW, Elser V, Gruner SM. 2014. Real-space X-ray tomographic reconstruction of randomly oriented objects with sparse data frames. *Opt. Express* 22:2403–13

7. Ayyer K, Philipp HT, Tate MW, Wierman JL, Elser V, Gruner SM. 2014. Determination of crystallographic intensities from sparse data. *IUCrJ* 2:29–34

8. Ballabriga R, Alozy J, Campbell M, Fiederle M, Fröjdh E, et al. 2013. The Medipix3RX: a high resolution, zero dead-time pixel detector readout chip allowing spectroscopic imaging. *J. Instrum.* 8:2

9. Barends TRM, Foucar L, Botha S, Doak RB, Shoeman RL, et al. 2014. De novo protein crystal structure determination from X-ray free-electron laser data. *Nature* 505:244–47

10. Barty A, Caleman C, Aquila A, Timneanu N, Lomb L, et al. 2012. Self-terminating diffraction gates femtosecond X-ray nanocrystallography measurements. *Nat. Photonics* 6:35–40

11. Barty A, Küpper J, Chapman HN. 2013. Molecular imaging using X-ray free-electron lasers. *Annu. Rev. Phys. Chem.* 64:415–35

12. Bass M, ed. 2001. *Handbook of Optics. Volume III: Classical Optics, Vision Optics, X-Ray Optics*. New York: McGraw-Hill

13. Bei M, Borland M, Cai Y, Elleaume P, Gerig R, et al. 2010. The potential of an ultimate storage ring for future light sources. *Nuclear Instrum. Methods Phys. Res. A* 622:518–35

14. Bilderback DH, Brock JD, Dale DS, Finkelstein KD, Pfeifer MA, Gruner SM. 2010. Energy recovery linac (ERL) coherent hard X-ray sources. *New J. Phys.* 12:035011

15. Blanchet CE, Svergun DI. 2013. Small-angle X-ray scattering on biological macromolecules and nanocomposites in solution. *Annu. Rev. Phys. Chem.* 64:37–54

16. Bogan MJ. 2013. X-ray free electron lasers motivate bioanalytical characterization of protein nanocrystals: serial femtosecond crystallography. *Anal. Chem.* 85:3464–71

17. Boutet S, Lomb L, Williams GJ, Barends TRM, Aquila A, et al. 2012. High-resolution protein structure determination by serial femtosecond crystallography. *Science* 337:362–64

18. Brehm W, Diederichs K. 2014. Breaking the indexing ambiguity in serial crystallography. *Acta Crystallogr. D* 70:101–9

19. Bunch JS, Verbridge SS, Alden JS, van der Zande AM, Parpia JM, et al. 2008. Impermeable atomic membranes from graphene sheets. *Nano Lett.* 8:2458–62

20. Chapman HN, Fromme P, Barty A, White TA, Kirian RA, et al. 2011. Femtosecond X-ray protein nanocrystallography. *Nature* 470:73–77

21. Cho HS, Schotte F, Dashdorj N, Kyndt J, Anfinrud PA. 2013. Probing anisotropic structure changes in proteins with picosecond time-resolved small-angle X-ray scattering. *J. Phys. Chem. B* 117:15825–32

22. Cogdell RJ, Gall A, Köhler J. 2006. The architecture and function of the light-harvesting apparatus of purple bacteria: from single molecules to in vivo membranes. *Q. Rev. Biophys.* 39:227–324

23. Deisenhofer J, Epp O, Sinning I, Michel H. 1995. Crystallographic refinement at 2.3 Å resolution and refined model of the photosynthetic reaction centre from *Rhodopseudomonas viridis*. *J. Mol. Biol.* 246:429–57

24. Demirci H, Sierra RG, Laksmono H, Shoeman RL, Botha S, et al. 2013. Serial femtosecond X-ray diffraction of 30S ribosomal subunit microcrystals in liquid suspension at ambient temperature using an X-ray free-electron laser. *Acta Crystallogr. F* 69:1066–69

25. Donatelli JJ, Sethian JA. 2014. Algorithmic framework for X-ray nanocrystallographic reconstruction in the presence of the indexing ambiguity. *PNAS* 111:593–98

26. Elser V. 2003. Phase retrieval by iterated projections. *J. Opt. Soc. Am. A* 20:40–55

27. Elser V. 2009. Noise limits on reconstructing diffraction signals from random tomographs. *IEEE Trans. Inf. Theory* 55:4715–22

28. Elser V. 2011. Strategies for processing diffraction data from randomly oriented particles. *Ultramicroscopy* 111:788–92

29. Elser V. 2011. Three-dimensional structure from intensity correlations. *New J. Phys.* 13:123014

30. Falcone R, Jacobsen C, Kirz J, Marchesini S, Shapiro D, Spence J. 2011. New directions in X-ray microscopy. *Contemp. Phys.* 52:293–318

31. Foucar L, Barty A, Coppola N, Hartmann R, Holl P, et al. 2012. CASS—CFEL-ASG software suite. *Comput. Phys. Commun.* 183:2207–13

32. Garman EF, Nave C. 2009. Radiation damage in protein crystals examined under various conditions by different methods. *J. Synchrotron Radiat.* 16:129–32

33. Gasbarro A, Bazarov I. 2014. Reduced forms of the Wigner distribution function for the numerical analysis of rotationally symmetric synchrotron radiation. *J. Synchrotron Radiat.* 21:289–99

34. Gati C, Bourenkov G, Klinge M, Rehders D, Stellato F, et al. 2014. Serial crystallography on in vivo grown microcrystals using synchrotron radiation. *IUCrJ* 1:87–94

35. Gimenez EN, Ballabriga R, Campbell M, Horswell I, Dolbnya I, et al. 2011. Characterization of Medipix3 with synchrotron radiation. *IEEE Trans. Nuclear Sci.* 58:323–32

36. Gimenez EN, Ballabriga R, Campbell M, Horswell I, Llopart X, et al. 2011. Study of charge-sharing in MEDIPIX3 using a micro-focused synchrotron beam. *J. Instrum.* 6:C01031

37. Glatter O, Kratky O. 1982. *Small Angle X-Ray Scattering*. New York: Academic

38. Greber BJ, Boehringer D, Leitner A, Bieri P, Voigts-Hoffmann F, et al. 2014. Architecture of the large subunit of the mammalian mitochondrial ribosome. *Nature* 505:515–19

39. Hau-Riege SP. 2012. Photoelectron dynamics in X-ray free-electron-laser diffractive imaging of biological samples. *Phys. Rev. Lett.* 108:238101

40. Hau-Riege SP. 2013. Nonequilibrium electron dynamics in materials driven by high-intensity X-ray pulses. *Phys. Rev. E* 87:053102

41. Heymann M, Opthalage A, Wierman JL, Akella S, Szebenyi DME, et al. 2014. Room-temperature serial crystallography using a kinetically optimized microfluidic device for protein crystallization and on-chip X-ray diffraction. *IUCrJ* 1:349–60

42. Holton JM. 2009. A beginner's guide to radiation damage. *J. Synchrotron Radiat.* 16:133–42

43. Holton JM, Frankel KA. 2010. The minimum crystal size needed for a complete diffraction data set. *Acta Crystallogr. D* 66:393–408

44. Hosseinizadeh A, Schwander P, Dashti A, Fung R, D'Souza RM, Ourmazd A. 2014. High-resolution structure of viruses from random diffraction snapshots. *Philos. Trans. R. Soc. B* 369:20130326

45. Howells MR, Beetz T, Chapman HN, Cui C, Holton JM, et al. 2009. An assessment of the resolution limitation due to radiation-damage in X-ray diffraction microscopy. *J. Electron Spectrosc. Relat. Phenom.* 170:4–12

46. Hunter MS, Fromme P. 2011. Toward structure determination using membrane-protein nanocrystals and microcrystals. *Methods* 55:387–404

47. Hura GL, Menon AL, Hammel M, Rambo RP, Poole FL 2nd, et al. 2009. Robust, high-throughput solution structural analyses by small angle X-ray scattering (SAXS). *Nat. Methods* 6:606–12

48. Johansson LC, Arnlund D, Katona G, White TA, Barty A, et al. 2013. Structure of a photosynthetic reaction centre determined by serial femtosecond crystallography. *Nat. Commun.* 4:2911

49. Johansson LC, Arnlund D, White TA, Katona G, DePonte DP, et al. 2012. Lipidic phase membrane protein serial femtosecond crystallography. *Nat. Methods* 9:263–65

50. Kam Z. 1977. Determination of macromolecular structure in solution by spatial correlation of scattering fluctuations. *Macromolecules* 10:927–34

51. Kam Z, Gafni I. 1985. Three-dimensional reconstruction of the shape of human wart virus using spatial correlations. *Ultramicroscopy* 17:251–62

52. Kam Z, Koch MHJ, Bordas J. 1981. Fluctuation X-ray-scattering from biological particles in frozen solution by using synchrotron radiation. *PNAS* 78:3559–62

53. Kang HJ, Lee C, Drew D. 2013. Breaking the barriers in membrane protein crystallography. *Int. J. Biochem. Cell Biol.* 45:636–44

54. Kim KJ. 1986. Brightness, coherence and propagation characteristics of synchrotron radiation. *Nuclear Instrum. Methods Phys. Res. A* 246:71–76

55. Kirian RA. 2012. Structure determination through correlated fluctuations in X-ray scattering. *J. Phys. B* 45:223001

56. Kirian RA, Schmidt KE, Wang X, Doak RB, Spence JC. 2011. Signal, noise, and resolution in correlated fluctuations from snapshot small-angle X-ray scattering. *Phys. Rev. E* 84:011921

57. Koch MHJ, Vachette P, Svergun DI. 2003. Small-angle scattering: a view on the properties, structures and structural changes of biological macromolecules in solution. *Q. Rev. Biophys.* 36:147–227

58. Kuhlbrandt W. 2014. The resolution revolution. *Science* 343:1443–44

59. Liu HG, Poon BK, Saldin DK, Spence JCH, Zwart PH. 2013. Three-dimensional single-particle imaging using angular correlations from X-ray laser data. *Acta Crystallogr. A* 69:365–73

60. Liu W, Wacker D, Gati C, Han GW, James D, et al. 2013. Serial femtosecond crystallography of G protein-coupled receptors. *Science* 342:1521–24

61. Loh ND. 2014. A minimal view of single-particle imaging with X-ray lasers. *Philos. Trans. R. Soc. B* 369:20130328

62. Loh ND, Bogan MJ, Elser V, Barty A, Boutet S, et al. 2010. Cryptotomography: reconstructing 3D Fourier intensities from randomly oriented single-shot diffraction patterns. *Phys. Rev. Lett.* 104:225501

63. Loh NTD, Elser V. 2009. Reconstruction algorithm for single-particle diffraction imaging experiments. *Phys. Rev. E* 80:026705

64. McNeil BWJ, Thompson NR. 2010. X-ray free-electron lasers. *Nat. Photonics* 4:814–21

65. Mendez D, Lane TJ, Sung J, Sellberg J, Levard C, et al. 2014. Observation of correlated X-ray scattering at atomic resolution. *Philos. Trans. R. Soc. B* 369:20130315

66. Nave C, Garman EF. 2005. Towards an understanding of radiation damage in cryocooled macromolecular crystals. *J. Synchrotron Radiat.* 12:257–60

67. Nave C, Hill MA. 2005. Will reduced radiation damage occur with very small crystals? *J. Synchrotron Radiat.* 12:299–303

68. Nederlof I, Li YW, van Heel M, Abrahams JP. 2013. Imaging protein three-dimensional nanocrystals with cryo-EM. *Acta Crystallogr. D* 69:852–59

69. Nederlof I, van Genderen E, Li YW, Abrahams JP. 2013. A Medipix quantum area detector allows rotation electron diffraction data collection from submicrometre three-dimensional protein crystals. *Acta Crystallogr. D* 69:1223–30

70. Neutze R, Moffat K. 2012. Time-resolved structural studies at synchrotrons and X-ray free electron lasers: opportunities and challenges. *Curr. Opin. Struct. Biol.* 22:651–59

71. Neutze R, Wouts R, van der Spoel D, Weckert E, Hajdu J. 2000. Potential for biomolecular imaging with femtosecond X-ray pulses. *Nature* 406:752–57

72. Ohashi H, Yamazaki H, Yumoto H, Koyama T, Senba Y, et al. 2013. Stable delivery of nano-beams for advanced nano-scale analyses. *J. Phys.* 425:052018

73. Perry SL, Guha S, Pawate AS, Bhaskarla A, Agarwal V, et al. 2013. A microfluidic approach for protein structure determination at room temperature via on-chip anomalous diffraction. *Lab Chip* 13:3183–87

74. Philipp HT, Ayyer K, Tate MW, Elser V, Gruner SM. 2012. Solving structure with sparse, randomly-oriented X-ray data. *Opt. Express* 20:13129–37

75. Philipp HT, Ayyer K, Tate MW, Elser V, Gruner SM. 2013. Recovering structure from many low-information 2-D images of randomly selected samples. *J. Phys.* 425:192016

76. Pollack L. 2011. SAXS studies of ion–nucleic acid interactions. *Annu. Rev. Biophys.* 40:225–42

77. Poon HC, Saldin DK. 2011. Beyond the crystallization paradigm: structure determination from diffraction patterns from ensembles of randomly oriented particles. *Ultramicroscopy* 111:798–806

78. Putnam CD, Hammel M, Hura GL, Tainer JA. 2007. X-ray solution scattering (SAXS) combined with crystallography and computation: defining accurate macromolecular structures, conformations and assemblies in solution. *Q. Rev. Biophys.* 40:191–285

79. Quevillon-Cheruel S, Dominique L, Leulliot N, Graille M, Poupon A, et al. 2004. The Paris-Sud yeast structural genomics pilot-project: from structure to function. *Biochimie* 86:617–23

80. Ravelli RBG, Garman EF. 2006. Radiation damage in macromolecular cryocrystallography. *Curr. Opin. Struct. Biol.* 16:624–29

81. Redecke L, Nass K, DePonte DP, White TA, Rehders D, et al. 2013. Natively inhibited *Trypanosoma brucei* cathepsin B structure determined by using an X-ray laser. *Science* 339:227–30

82. Saldin DK, Poon HC, Bogan MJ, Marchesini S, Shapiro DA, et al. 2011. New light on disordered ensembles: ab initio structure determination of one particle from scattering fluctuations of many copies. *Phys. Rev. Lett.* 106:115501

83. Saldin DK, Poon HC, Schwander P, Uddin M, Schmidt M. 2011. Reconstructing an icosahedral virus from single-particle diffraction experiments. *Opt. Express* 19:17318–35

84. Sanishvili R, Yoder DW, Pothineni SB, Rosenbaum G, Xu SL, et al. 2011. Radiation damage in protein crystals is reduced with a micron-sized X-ray beam. *PNAS* 108:6127–32

85. Sauter NK, Hattne J, Grosse-Kunstleve RW, Echols N. 2013. New Python-based methods for data processing. *Acta Crystallogr. D* 69:1274–82

86. Schlichting I, Miao J. 2012. Emerging opportunities in structural biology with X-ray free-electron lasers. *Curr. Opin. Struct. Biol.* 22:613–26

87. Schmidt M. 2013. Mix and inject: reaction initiation by diffusion for time-resolved macromolecular crystallography. *Adv. Condens. Matter Phys.* **http://dx.doi.org/10.1155/2013/167276**

88. Schmidt-Krey I, Cheng Y, eds. 2013. *Electron Crystallography of Soluble and Membrane Proteins.* Heidelberg, Ger.: Springer

89. Schotte F, Cho HS, Kaila VRI, Kamikubo H, Dashdorj N, et al. 2012. Watching a signaling protein function in real time via 100-ps time-resolved Laue crystallography. *PNAS* 109:19256–61

90. Shi D, Nannenga BL, Iadanza MG, Gonen T. 2013. Three-dimensional electron crystallography of protein microcrystals. *Elife* 2:e0 1345:1–17

91. Shim JU, Cristobal G, Link DR, Thorsen T, Fraden S. 2007. Using microfluidics to decouple nucleation and growth of protein crystals. *Crystal Growth Design* 7:2192–94

92. Shim JU, Cristobal G, Link DR, Thorsen T, Jia YW, et al. 2007. Control and measurement of the phase behavior of aqueous solutions using microfluidics. *J. Am. Chem. Soc.* 129:8825–35

93. Shneerson VL, Saldin DK. 2009. Molecular shapes from small-angle X-ray scattering: extension of the theory to higher scattering angles. *Acta Crystallogr. A* 65:128–34

94. Sliz P, Harrison SC, Rosenbaum G. 2003. How does radiation damage in protein crystals depend on X-ray dose? *Structure* 11:13–19

95. Snell EH, Helliwell JR. 2005. Macromolecular crystallization in microgravity. *Rep. Prog. Phys.* 68:799–853

96. Spence JCH, Weierstall U, Chapman HN. 2012. X-ray lasers for structural and dynamic biology. *Rep. Prog. Phys.* 75:102601

97. Starodub D, Aquila A, Bajt S, Barthelmess M, Barty A, et al. 2012. Single-particle structure determination by correlations of snapshot X-ray diffraction patterns. *Nat. Commun.* 3:1276

98. Stellato F, Oberthür D, Liang M, Bean R, Gati C, et al. 2014. Room-temperature macromolecular serial crystallography using synchrotron radiation. *IUCrJ* 1:204–12

99. Svergun DI, Koch MHJ. 2002. Advances in structure analysis using small-angle scattering in solution. *Curr. Opin. Struct. Biol.* 12:654–60

100. Thibault P, Elser V. 2010. X-ray diffraction microscopy. *Annu. Rev. Condens. Matter Phys.* 1:237–55

101. Warkentin M, Badeau R, Hopkins J, Thorne RE. 2011. Dark progression reveals slow timescales for radiation damage between T = 180 and 240 K. *Acta Crystallogr. D* 67:792–803

102. Weierstall U, James D, Wang C, White TA, Wang D, et al. 2014. Lipidic cubic phase injector facilitates membrane protein serial femtosecond crystallography. *Nat. Commun.* 5:3309

103. Weierstall U, Spence JCH, Doak RB. 2012. Injector for scattering measurements on fully solvated biospecies. *Rev. Sci. Instrum.* 83:035108

104. White TA, Barty A, Stellato F, Holton JM, Kirian RA, et al. 2013. Crystallographic data processing for free-electron laser sources. *Acta Crystallogr. D* 69:1231–40

105. White TA, Kirian RA, Martin AV, Aquila A, Nass K, et al. 2012. CrystFEL: a software suite for snapshot serial crystallography. *J. Appl. Crystallogr.* 45:335–41

106. Wierman JL, Alden JS, Kim CU, McEuen PL, Gruner SM. 2013. Graphene as a protein crystal mounting material to reduce background scatter. *J. Appl. Crystallogr.* 46:1501–7

107. Woodson SA. 2010. Compact intermediates in RNA folding. *Annu. Rev. Biophys.* 39:61–77

108. Woodson SA. 2011. RNA folding pathways and the self-assembly of ribosomes. *Acc. Chem. Res.* 44:1312–19

109. Yuk JM, Kim K, Aleman B, Regan W, Ryu JH, et al. 2011. Graphene veils and sandwiches. *Nano Lett.* 11:3290–94

110. Yuk JM, Park J, Ercius P, Kim K, Hellebusch DJ, et al. 2012. High-resolution EM of colloidal nanocrystal growth using graphene liquid cells. *Science* 336:61–64

111. Zang C, Stevens JA, Link JJ, Guo LJ, Wang LJ, Zhong DP. 2009. Ultrafast proteinquake dynamics in cytochrome *c*. *J. Am. Chem. Soc.* 131:2846–52

112. Ziaja B, Chapman HN, Faustlin R, Hau-Riege S, Jurek Z, et al. 2012. Limitations of coherent diffractive imaging of single objects due to their damage by intense X-ray radiation. *New J. Phys.* 14:114015

Contemporary NMR Studies of Protein Electrostatics

Mathias A.S. Hass[1] and Frans A.A. Mulder[2]

[1]Institute of Chemistry, Gorlaeus Laboratories, Leiden University, 2300 RA Leiden, The Netherlands

[2]Department of Chemistry and Interdisciplinary Nanoscience Center (iNANO), Aarhus University, DK-8000 Aarhus C, Denmark; email: fmulder@chem.au.dk

Annu. Rev. Biophys. 2015. 44:53–75

First published online as a Review in Advance on February 26, 2015

The *Annual Review of Biophysics* is online at biophys.annualreviews.org

This article's doi:
10.1146/annurev-biophys-083012-130351

Keywords

nuclear magnetic resonance (NMR) spectroscopy, chemical shift titration, protonation, pK_a, protein electrostatics

Abstract

Electrostatics play an important role in many aspects of protein chemistry. However, the accurate determination of side chain proton affinity in proteins by experiment and theory remains challenging. In recent years the field of nuclear magnetic resonance spectroscopy has advanced the way that protonation states are measured, allowing researchers to examine electrostatic interactions at an unprecedented level of detail and accuracy. Experiments are now in place that follow pH-dependent ^{13}C and ^{15}N chemical shifts as spatially close as possible to the sites of protonation, allowing all titratable amino acid side chains to be probed sequence specifically. The strong and telling response of carefully selected reporter nuclei allows individual titration events to be monitored. At the same time, improved frameworks allow researchers to model multiple coupled protonation equilibria and to identify the underlying pH-dependent contributions to the chemical shifts.

Contents

INTRODUCTION

Protonation is a ubiquitous process in biology. Electrostatic interactions, ligand recognition, protein folding, enzyme catalysis, membrane potentials, and the energetics of cells depend on ionization and proton transfer. Protonation is the most common ionization process in protein molecules. In order to understand how protonation influences biology, it is important to know the thermodynamics and kinetics of protonation of individual groups in the specific proteins involved in these processes (1, 13, 18, 47, 52, 67, 73). Furthermore, the experimental study of protonation is an important tool used to understand the electrostatics in proteins and serves as a benchmark for computational models (2, 41, 73).

Experimental studies of the thermodynamics of protonation equilibria involve the determination of pK_a values; the kinetics concerns the study of proton transfer rates. The most basic way to measure pK_a values is by potentiometric proton binding curves, which report the net proton uptake of a molecule. However, for proteins with numerous different protonatable groups, potentiometric curves report only the macroscopic behavior of the protein, without giving much insight into atomic details. A more complete picture of how protonation controls biological function requires microscopic information at the level of individual titrating groups in a protein.

The NMR frequency is highly sensitive to changes in the nuclear environment, which makes the NMR chemical shift an ideal probe for protonation events. This property is utilized in pH chemical shift titration measurements, which constitute the most important NMR tool used for studying protonation equilibria. A pH chemical shift titration curve represents the pH dependence of the observed chemical shift of a given nucleus. The curve contains information about the thermodynamics of one or more protonation events in proximity to the nucleus, and about the chemical shift perturbations caused by these events (65).

The exquisite sensitivity of the NMR chemical shift causes it to be susceptible to long-range effects from more distant protonation sites; therefore, nuclei may probe more than one titrating site. The most idiosyncratic and site-specific probes are the nuclei directly in the protonating group, which usually are dominated by short-range effects (74). The development of NMR experiments tailored for the observation of these nuclei has recently been invigorated and is discussed in the first part of this review.

In the second part, we consider how the measured NMR chemical shift data reflect the extent of proton binding. Because proteins contain multiple titrating residues, NMR titration curves more often than not reflect multiple titration events. An additional layer of complexity is added by the energetic coupling between protonation sites. This effect, also known as cooperativity, provides not only valuable information but also additional challenges in the interpretation of the data. In general, determining microscopic parameters, including so-called intrinsic pK_a values and interaction energies, from chemical shift titrations alone leads to ambiguous results (59); it is necessary to combine chemical shift titration data with additional information. It is becoming increasingly clear that access to ^{13}C and ^{15}N chemical shift titrations, coupled with computational models in the analysis, can provide accurate answers (38, 41, 60). Here electrostatic models (26) are of special importance, but chemical shift prediction methods may also provide the information required to extract reliable microscopic parameters. Site-directed mutagenesis of titrating residues offers further ways to resolve ambiguities in the interpretation of chemical shift titration data (38).

Unfortunately, space restrictions do not permit us to cover the subject of protonation kinetics, which can have pronounced effects on chemical shifts and line shape over the titration course (24, 48, 49, 63). Fortunately, in most applications proton exchange is sufficiently rapid and does not need to be considered in titration data analysis.

NMR EXPERIMENTS FOR MEASURING pK_a CONSTANTS

Indirect Detection of Heteronuclear Side Chain Chemical Shifts

Titratable residues in proteins are ionized at either oxygen, sulfur, or nitrogen atoms. When protonated, the hydrogen atoms bound to O, S, and N are labile; i.e., they rapidly (within seconds or less) exchange with the solvent. Therefore, in NMR, protonation events do not generally lead to the observation of new signals, as the labile protons are broadened beyond detection because of rapid exchange with the solvent water. As a consequence, the integral of the signal arising from the bound proton cannot be used to determine the position of the protonation equilibrium. In practice, the position of the equilibrium is therefore often determined by proxy: Another nearby nucleus senses the change in protonation state of the titrated group through the influence this event has on the chemical shift of the reporter nucleus. In much of the literature, proxy protons have been used as the probes for the equilibrium because of (a) the exquisite sensitivity of ^{1}H NMR and (b) the ~100% natural abundance of the spin-1/2 ^{1}H isotope. This approach sidesteps isotope labeling but does not provide much resolution, even in 2D spectra. Moreover, there is a more fundamental caveat: Because the sensor protons are typically several bonds and/or Ångströms removed from the titration site, they experience irregular pH-dependent chemical shift changes that cannot be unambiguously linked to a single titration event. As a consequence, the deconvolution of multiple titration events must be resolved by multiparametric curve fitting, and the assignment of sites may be ambiguous (16). Because heteronuclear chemical shifts can typically be measured much more closely to the site of protonation, and because these nearby nuclei usually demonstrate larger responses (in parts per million, ppm) due to the ionization of a particular side chain than to nearby electric fields, they are much better suited to the study of side chain protonation states and pK_a constants than protons are (74). A summary of suitable sensor nuclei is provided in **Table 1**, including the typically observed pH-dependent chemical shift changes observed in proteins.

This review describes NMR experiments devised to obtain access to the heteronuclear chemical shifts that respond sensitively and, in many cases, exclusively to the (de)protonation equilibrium. We emphasize published methods that describe comprehensive analyses of side chain protonation states. This typically involves experiments designed to specifically detect the correlations for individual amino acid types in uniformly ^{13}C- and ^{15}N-enriched protein samples. Such samples are commonly produced to obtain resonance assignments and perform structure calculations,

Table 1 Typical heteronuclear pH-shifts and pK_a constants[a]

Amino acid	pK_a[c]	Nucleus	δ_1	δ_0	$\Delta\delta$	Reference(s)
Asp	4.0	CG	176	180	−4	61
		CB	38	41	−3	54
Glu	4.4	CD	179	183	−4	61
		CG	32	36	−4	54
His	6.8	**NE2/ND1**	177	250	−73	50
		ND1/NE2	177	168	9	50
		CG	131	135	−4	55
		CE1	136	139	−3	55
Tyr	9.6	CZ	157	167	−10	42
		CG	131	124	7	42
Lys	10.4	**NZ**	33	26	7	4
		CD	29	33	−4	55
Arg[b]	13.5	**NH1/2**	68	78	−10	–
		CZ	157	160	−3	–
		NE	83	88	−5	–
Cys	8.3	CB	25	28	−3	11
N terminus	8.0	**N**	38	25	13	4, 78
C terminus	3.6	C	180	183	−3	35

[a]Definitions: δ_1 is the chemical shift for the protonated form, δ_0 is the chemical shift for deprotonated form, and $\Delta\delta = \delta_1 - \delta_0$ is the pH-shift observed upon proton binding. Values are quoted in parts per million (ppm), and only side chain nuclei for which $|\Delta\delta| > 1$ ppm are included. Atoms in boldface refer to atoms that directly bind the proton. All values are relative to DSS (4,4-dimethyl-4-silapentane-1-sulfonic acid) as internal reference, and we use IUPAC conventions for indirect referencing. We added 1.0 ppm to the ^{13}C values of Richarz & Wüthrich (55).

[b]These shifts were measured by direct observation of ^{13}C and ^{15}N for 0.1 M L-arginine hydrochloride salt in 90%/10% v/v H_2O/D_2O. A value of 12.5 is typically quoted, although a value of 13.5 is inferred from these measurements.

[c]These are consensus values based on findings in the protein and peptide NMR titration literature. For reference, values recently determined by Platzer et al. (53) for peptides containing a single titratable group, in the presence of 50 mM NaCl, are Asp (3.86), Glu (4.34), His (6.45), Tyr (9.76), Lys (10.34), Arg (13.9), Cys (8.49), N terminus (8.23), and C terminus (3.55).

and they are routinely and cost-effectively produced by overexpression in host systems such as *Escherichia coli*. Moreover, a single protein sample can be used to determine the individual side chain protonation states and pK_a constants for all amino acids at once, thereby reducing cost and labor and avoiding differences in protein, buffer, or salt concentration between multiple samples. This approach supersedes a number of traditional pH titration studies in which specific isotope labels were strategically introduced at a small subset of residues.

We adopt the common usage of short acronyms that identify the flow of magnetization in the NMR experiment and indicate which of the nuclei are correlated in the spectra. For example, the H2(C)CO experiment transfers magnetization from the two methylene protons adjacent to carbonyl/carboxyl groups via the intervening ^{13}C nucleus. This nucleus is noted in parentheses, indicating that its chemical shift is not registered. Most experiments that we discuss employ proton magnetization for excitation and detection, as this generally provides higher sensitivity. The magnetization is channeled to the heteronuclear spins in an out-and-back fashion, and the ^{13}C and ^{15}N shifts are thus observed through indirect detection. Owing to page restrictions, we refer the interested reader to the original literature for details of the pulse sequences.

Glutamate and Aspartate

The most accurate method for measuring the side chain pK_a constants of aspartate and glutamate likely involves the detection of the carboxylate ^{13}C chemical shifts, and this is typically performed using the H2(C)CO experiment (43). The experiment correlates the nonexchangeable protons at the methylene carbon next to the site of protonation in a 2D correlation spectrum (Hβ to Cγ for Asp, and Hγ to Cδ for Glu). An example of a variant of protein GB1 (PGB1-QDD) (34), is shown in **Figure 1a**. The experiment affords high resolution because of significant site-to-site variation in the carboxylate ^{13}C chemical shifts of the individual Asp and Glu residues, which also occur in separate regions of the spectrum. Although not indicated in **Figure 1a** for clarity, each peak in the spectrum due to Asp or Glu is assigned sequence specifically to its unique place in the primary structure, thereby providing access to individual pH titration data as the chemical shifts change with pH. Typically, a 2D spectrum is recorded over a large pH interval upon small (~0.2) changes in sample pH. The position of the $^{13}C'$ shift for each Asp and Glu is then plotted versus pH, as shown in **Figure 2a,b**. Owing to the dominating effect of side chain protonation on the $^{13}C'$ shifts, pK_a constants can be readily identified from the inflection points of the curves. Alternatively, they can be gauged from the derivative plot, where each maximum marks the location of the associated inflection point. The interpretation of the different shapes of the curves are discussed below.

Alternatively, the $^{13}C\gamma$ shift of Glu and the $^{13}C\beta$ shift of Asp can be probed, as they too display significant variation with ionization (see **Table 1**). The most convenient correlation experiment in such cases is the 3D C(CO)NH experiment, which was originally designed to assign side chain aliphatic carbon chemical shifts. As the pK_a constants of carboxylic acidic groups are generally below 7, backbone amides remain observable throughout the titration of Asp and Glu residues, even for exposed and disordered segments. However, 3D spectroscopic titration experiments are time-consuming, which has affected the quality of titration curves obtained by this approach (12, 54).

Cysteine

Because of the lower occurrence of cysteine residues in proteins, there have been comparatively fewer studies of the pK_a constants of these side chains. However, several important classes of proteins employ active site cysteine residues, and knowledge of their pK_a constants is therefore

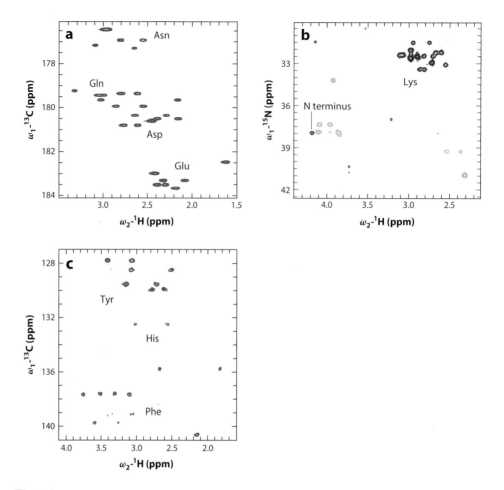

Figure 1

Typical examples of (*a*) H2(C)CO, (*b*) H2(C)N, and (*c*) CG(CB)HB spectra recorded for small proteins. (*a*) Asp/Glu and C-terminal carboxylic acid $^{13}C'$ chemical shifts are obtained from a H2(C)CO spectrum. (*b*) Lys and N-terminal primary amine ^{15}N chemical shifts are obtained from a H2(C)N spectrum. (*c*) Tyr side chain $^{13}C\gamma$ shifts are collected from a CG(CB)HB spectrum. Because uniformly $^{13}C/^{15}N$-enriched proteins are used, $^{15}N\varepsilon$ signals due to Arg are also detected in panel *b*, and $^{13}C\gamma$ signals due to His are also observed in panel *c*. Reprinted with permission from Reference 4: I. André, S. Linse, and F.A.A. Mulder *J. Am. Chem. Soc.* 129, 15805–13. Copyright (2007) The American Chemical Society; and Reference 44: N.A. Oktaviani, T.J. Pool, H. Kamikubo, J. Slager, R.M. Scheek, M. Kataoka M, and F.A.A. Mulder *Biophys. J.* 102, 579–86. Copyright (2012) The authors.

of particular relevance. For example, thioredoxin has received much attention and a combination of NMR titrations and site-directed mutagenesis has provided insight into the microscopic pK_a values of the active site residues, including Cys32 (11). In their study, Chivers et al. (11) obtained cysteine pK_a constants by ^{13}C detection NMR spectroscopy, coupled with specific incorporation of [$^{13}C\beta$]-Cys into the growth medium. Following work on Cys $^{13}C\beta$ chemical shifts, Jensen et al. (29) detected nonexchangeable protons in uniformly ^{13}C-labeled proteins, and peptide studies indicate that backbone $^{13}C\alpha$ and ^{15}N chemical shifts can be just as telling (53).

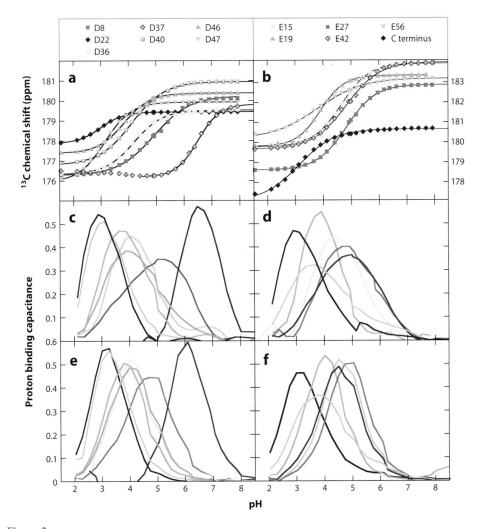

Figure 2

Titration curves of (*a*) the seven Asp residues and (*b*) the five Glu residues and the C terminus in PGB1-QDD at low salt concentrations. (*c–f*) Capacitance curves for all carboxyl groups and the C terminus in PGB1-QDD. (*c,d*) Asp/Glu at a low salt concentration, respectively. (*e,f*) Asp/Glu at a salt concentration of 0.5 M. Reprinted with permission from Reference 35: S. Lindman, S. Linse, F.A.A. Mulder, and I. André, *Biochemistry* 45, 13993–4002. Copyright (2006) The American Chemical Society.

Histidine

The imidazole ring of histidine has three commonly observed protonation states: the fully protonated, positively charged form and two neutral tautomers with similar energies, called the ε-tautomer and δ-tautomer. Often all three protonation states are significantly populated and coexist in fast exchange. Even though there are two different neutral forms, the titration curve of histidine follows the Henderson-Hasselbalch curve (HH-curve), unless affected by other titrating groups. As for any other conformational exchange process, tautomerization cannot explain deviations from the HH-curve (31). Which tautomer dominates depends on the local environment of the imidazole group.

Henderson-
Hasselbalch curve
(HH-curve):
observed in the case of
a single protonation
event; reflects the
fractions of the species
in the protonation
equilibrium as a
function of proton
concentration
(expressed by pH)

Constant-time
^1H–^{13}C HSQC: a 2D
^1H–^{13}C correlation
experiment for
uniformly
^{13}C-enriched proteins,
without splitting due
to ^{13}C-^{13}C J-couplings

pH-shift: the change
in chemical shift (in
ppm) upon
protonation

For nonlabeled proteins in 100% D_2O, the δ and ε ^1H signals are often well resolved, even in 1D spectra (36, 51). For ^{15}N-labeled proteins, histidine pK_a values are conveniently measured with ^1H–^{15}N multiple-bond correlation experiments (50), providing information on tautomeric and protonation states at the same time. Because of the overwhelming pH-dependent chemical shift changes (**Table 1**), problems can arise from line broadening caused by the (de)protonation and tautomerization equilibria (21). High buffer concentrations may improve the quality of the spectrum in such a case, by increasing proton transfer rates (20, 21, 23). In uniformly ^{15}N,^{13}C-labeled proteins, the two proton-bound ^{13}C nuclei can be observed in a constant-time ^1H–^{13}C HSQC experiment, in which $^{13}C\varepsilon^1$ is a suitable reporter nucleus of the protonation state (**Table 1**) and $^{13}C\varepsilon^2$ can be used to assign the tautomer state (62).

The imidazole chemical shifts are good indicators of the protonation state. The shifts associated with protonation and tautomerization have been characterized in detail in liquid (50, 71), solid-state (33), and NMR and quantum chemical computations (71, 72). Therefore, it is possible to determine, to a good approximation, the protonation and tautomer states of histidine residues from the ^{15}N and ^{13}C ring chemical shifts.

Lysine

Relative lysine pK_a values can be obtained by the combined use of reductive alkylation with ^{13}C-enriched reagents, although these modifications introduce nonnative substituents and require spectral assignment via mutagenesis (28). Alternatively, the Lys side chain $^{13}C\delta$ chemical shift shows a -4 ppm pH-shift upon proton binding (**Table 1**), which dominates over pH-dependent conformational effects. Lys side chain titrations were monitored by specific incorporation using [5-^{13}C]-lysine to avoid overlap with signals from other amino acid side chains (17).

In uniformly labeled proteins, lysine side chain $^{13}C\delta$ carbon chemical shifts are in principle well resolved in C(CO)NH spectra, but their use is precluded by the rapid exchange of backbone amide protons at the elevated pH needed to titrate the Lys side chains. An alternative approach was therefore sought by André et al. (4), who followed the amine $^{15}N\zeta$ chemical shifts via an H2(C)N experiment. Because the change upon protonation is $\sim$7 ppm the $^{15}N\zeta$ chemical shift is an excellent sensor of the Lys protonation state. H2(C)N spectra are sufficiently well resolved for small proteins, as shown for Calbindin D_{9k} in **Figure 1b**, and pulse schemes for the assignment of the correlations have been published (4).

Tyrosine

The effect of ionization of the phenolic group on the ^{13}C chemical shifts of tyrosine was investigated by Norton & Bradbury (42), and these values are listed in **Table 1**. As might be expected, the largest pH-shift, -10.4 ppm, was observed for $^{13}C\zeta$ at the hydroxyl group. However, the second-largest effect, a change of 6.2 ppm, was observed for the $^{13}C\gamma$ chemical shift. ^{13}C signals of tyrosine residues have been observed by direct ^{13}C detection, by utilizing specific labeling with 4-^{13}C-Tyr (30): The $^{13}C\zeta$ resonances fall into a region of approximately 155–160 ppm when the side chains are protonated. The assignment of the signals required eliminating each tyrosine in turn by mutagenesis, followed by recording the NMR spectrum of each sample.

As an alternative, the coherence transfer scheme HE(CE)CZ allows the $^{13}C\zeta$ shifts to be read out in a 2D spectrum on uniformly ^{13}C-enriched proteins. This approach was successfully applied to *Bacillus circulans* xylanase (6) and to *E. coli* peptidyl-prolyl *cis-trans* isomerase b in the context of stereo-array isotope labeling (66). However, this approach failed for the photoactive yellow protein (PYP) from *Halorhodospira halophila*, likely because of exchange broadening by tyrosine ring flips on the intermediate NMR timescale (approximately milliseconds). Oktaviani et al. (44)

therefore resorted to a semiconstant time implementation of the CG(CB)HB experiment and followed the $^{13}C\gamma$ shifts of all tyrosine residues in the protein (**Figure 1c**). Their experiment is unaffected by 180° tyrosine ring flips about the χ^2 dihedral angle, as none of the nuclei involved in magnetization transfer undergo a change in chemical shift in the process. The correlation with $^{13}C\beta$ chemical shifts can be particularly advantageous, as tyrosine $^1H\beta$ chemical shifts are often available from spectra that correlate the side chain aliphatic resonances with backbone amide frequencies, thereby bypassing the need to assign the aromatic spin system altogether.

Arginine

Detecting heteronuclear shifts in the guanidinium headgroup in order to determine arginine pK_a constants is difficult or nearly impossible for the following reasons. First, because of the exchange with solvent, proton signals for solvent-exposed groups are increasingly broadened at pH above 7. Second, rotation around the $N\varepsilon$-$C\zeta$ partial double bond is slow (milliseconds), which leads to intermediate exchange and severe line broadening for $^1H\eta$ and $^{15}N\eta$ signals, such that guanidino headgroup signals are often unobservable, even at lower pH (25, 39, 77). Rather, André et al. (4) demonstrated that HD(NE)CZ spectra could be obtained for Arg, offering a route to the ^{13}C nucleus closest to the site of protonation, but the experiment suffers from poor sensitivity. However, measurements on L-arginine (**Table 1**) reveal that the more sensitive H2(C)N experiment (which is used for Lys) may be equally well suited for Arg, as the pH-shift for $^{15}N\varepsilon$ is at least as large as that for $^{13}C\zeta$. Alternatively, both $^{15}N\varepsilon$ and $^{13}C\zeta$ could be monitored simultaneously by making use of 2D $^{15}N\varepsilon$–$^{13}C\zeta$ correlation spectroscopy with ^{13}C detection (75).

N and C Termini

The H2(C)CO experiment is also perfectly suited for determining carboxy-terminal pK_a values. The resonance frequency of the carboxylate ^{13}C is generally observed at approximately 180–181 ppm at neutral pH and shows a pH-shift of approximately −3 ppm, similar to that observed for side chain carboxylates (**Table 1**), such that these $^{13}C'$ resonances are accessible from a single experiment.

The N-terminal amino group is generally unobservable owing to rapid exchange of the amine protons with solvent water. In this case the ^{15}N chemical shift can be observed indirectly in a 2D H2(C)N spectrum, where the carrier frequencies are appropriately placed (4): The α-amino ^{15}N chemical shift typically appears at approximately 38 ppm at acidic pH and shifts by approximately −13 ppm upon deprotonation (**Table 1**).

ANALYSIS OF CHEMICAL SHIFT TITRATION CURVES

NMR Titration of a Single Protonation Site

The simplest case of protonation is the protonation of a single site within a molecule, where a site refers to a specific basic group B that can absorb one proton and become its conjugate acid, AH^+. The acid-base equilibrium between these two protonation states,

$$AH^+ \rightleftarrows B + H^+,$$ 1.

is commonly associated with the acid dissociation constant,

$$K_a = \frac{[B][H^+]}{[AH^+]} = \frac{p_0}{p_1}[H^+],$$ 2.

where p_0 and p_1 are the populations of the deprotonated form, B, and protonated form, AH^+, respectively. The pH is defined by $-\log_{10}([H^+])$ and the pK_a value by $-\log_{10}(K_a)$.

The NMR chemical shift of a nucleus close to a protonation site depends on the protonation state of that site. Because the exchange between protonation states in most cases is fast on the NMR chemical shift timescale, the observed chemical shift at equilibrium, δ_{obs}, is a population-weighted average of the deprotonated and protonated states,

$$\delta_{obs} = p_0\delta_0 + p_1\delta_1. \qquad 3.$$

Here δ_1 and δ_0 are the chemical shifts of the protonated state and the deprotonated state, respectively. The observed chemical shift as a function of pH is given by

$$\delta_{obs} = \delta_0 + \frac{\Delta\delta}{1 + 10^{[pH-pK_a]}}, \qquad 4.$$

where $\Delta\delta = \delta_1 - \delta_0$ is herein called the pH-shift and represents the chemical shift change upon proton binding. The equation is analogous to the Henderson-Hasselbalch (HH) equation.

Multiple Noninteracting Protonation Sites

Proteins have many protonation sites; therefore, protein resonances are likely to be affected by several protonation events, resulting in more complex titration curves. For noninteracting protonation sites the contributions from each titration are additive. Thus, for N protonation sites that influence the chemical shift of a nucleus, the chemical shift as a function of pH is given by (59).

$$\delta_{obs} = \delta_0 + \sum_{i=1}^{N} \frac{\Delta\delta_i}{1 + 10^{[pH-pK_{ai}]}}. \qquad 5.$$

Here δ_0 is the chemical shift of the fully deprotonated state with respect to all N titrations. The pH-shifts, $\Delta\delta_i$, can be positive or negative and therefore Equation 5 can produce nonmonotonous chemical shift titration curves (**Figure 3**). A statistical F-test can be used to determine the number of sites, N, that is appropriate (15, 61). As a rule of thumb, it is possible to experimentally determine N pK_a values from a single titration curve as reliable only if (*a*) they differ by more than one pK_a unit, (*b*) data are acquired over a pH range of at least $2N$, and (*c*) all the pK_a values lie within this range. In situations where these criteria are not met (**Figure 3d**), one of the pK_a values must be known in order to determine the others.

Two Interacting Protonation Sites

Equation 5 is almost always sufficient for the empirical analysis of chemical shift titration data (45). However, just because a given model is able to reproduce experimental data does not imply that the parameters obtained have an obvious physical interpretation (37, 38, 45). Important aspects of interpreting the physical reality behind chemical shift titration curves are illustrated by considering the case of two interacting protonation sites (**Figure 4**). In the following sections we consider this case in detail from several different viewpoints: general microscopic and macroscopic viewpoints and furthermore two commonly used special cases of the microscopic model. Their comparison leads us to the decoupled site representation—a relatively recently formulated view on pH titrations that attempts to clarify the connection between the microscopic reality of protonation equilibria and the macroscopic observables.

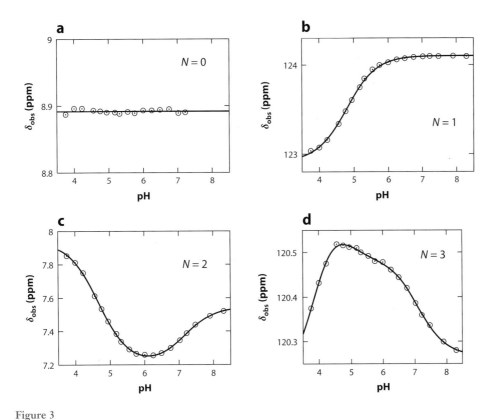

Figure 3

Examples of experimental backbone amide chemical shift titration curves, fitted with Equation 5 (see text). Data are shown for (*a*) ^{1}HN of K106, (*b*) ^{15}N of C78, (*c*) ^{1}HN of H40, and (*d*) ^{15}N of K59 for pseudoazurin from *Alcaligenes faecalis* (19, 23). Adapted with permission from Reference 23: M.A.S. Hass, M. Vlasie, M. Ubbink, J.J. Led *Biochemistry* 48, 50–58. Copyright (2009) The American Chemical Society.

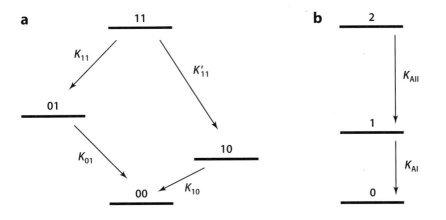

Figure 4

Schematic energy diagram of (*a*) the microscopic model for two interacting protonation sites and (*b*) the corresponding macroscopic model. K_{10}, K_{01}, K_{11}, and K'_{11} are the microscopic acid dissociation constants. K_{AI} and K_{AII} are the macroscopic dissociation constants.

The General Microscopic Model for Two Interacting Sites

If two protonation sites are sufficiently close to each other, they interact and give rise to cooperative protonation. Cooperativity between protonation reactions is usually negative because of the electric repulsion between two like charges; however, positive cooperativity can occur when structural changes are involved (58).

For two interacting sites there are four microstates, 00, 10, 01, and 11, where 0(1), in the first and second positions, refer to the nonprotonated(protonated) state of the first and second sites, respectively (**Figure 4a**). The equilibrium state of the system can be defined by a set of four independent equations (59). For example,

$$K_{10} = \frac{p_{00}}{p_{10}}[H^+], \quad K_{01} = \frac{p_{00}}{p_{01}}[H^+], \quad K_{11} = \frac{p_{01}}{p_{11}}[H^+], \quad p_{00} + p_{10} + p_{01} + p_{11} = 1. \quad 6.$$

From these equations the populations (or probabilities) of each microstate can be obtained:

$$p_{10} = p_{00}10^{[pK_{10}-pH]}, \quad p_{01} = p_{00}10^{[pK_{01}-pH]}, \quad p_{11} = p_{00}10^{[pK_{01}+pK_{11}-2pH]}, \quad p_{00} = \frac{1}{Z}, \quad 7.$$

where Z is the partition function (also known as the binding polynomial) for two protonation sites, given by

$$Z = 1 + 10^{[pK_{10}-pH]} + 10^{[pK_{01}-pH]} + 10^{[pK_{01}+pK_{11}-2pH]}. \quad 8.$$

The fourth acid dissociation constant in **Figure 4a** is given by the other three: $K'_{11} = K_{11}K_{01}/K_{10}$. The interaction energy between the two sites is given by

$$w = -RT \ \ln(10)(pK_{11} - pK_{10}), \quad 9.$$

where T is the temperature and R is the gas constant. In the absence of conformational changes this energy is the electrostatic interaction energy.

Each nucleus has a chemical shift in each microstate. Assuming fast exchange on the NMR timescale, the observed chemical shift is the population-weighted average:

$$\delta_{obs} = p_{00}\delta_{00} + p_{10}\delta_{10} + p_{01}\delta_{01} + p_{11}\delta_{11}. \quad 10.$$

Equation 10 is the general equation for two interacting sites and contains seven physically independent parameters: three microscopic pK_a values and four chemical shifts. It is often convenient to represent the three microscopic pK_a values by two intrinsic pK_a values (pK_{10} and pK_{01}) and one interaction energy, w (Equation 9), where the intrinsic value refers to the pK_a value of a site when all other sites are uncharged.

The General Macroscopic Model for Two Sites

It is equally valid to describe interacting sites from a macroscopic viewpoint (14, 38, 69). In this view, individual microstates are of no concern. The macroscopic protonation states are defined by the number of protons absorbed by the system. The microscopic and macroscopic models differ by their viewpoint and are mathematically equivalent for any number of interacting sites; no approximations are made. Thus, for two sites there are three macroscopic protonation states (compared to four microstates), corresponding to zero, one, and two protons absorbed by the system (**Figure 4b**). Here the single protonated state represents the sum of the two microstates 01 and 10 in **Figure 4a**. For two sites, there are two macroscopic pK_a values termed pK_{AI} and pK_{AII}. At equilibrium the system is defined by

$$K_{AI} = \frac{p_0}{p_1}[H^+], \quad K_{AII} = \frac{p_1}{p_2}[H^+], \quad p_0 + p_1 + p_2 = 1. \quad 11.$$

The populations of the three macrostates are then given by

$$p_1 = p_0 10^{[\text{p}K_{\text{AI}} - \text{pH}]}, \quad p_2 = p_0 10^{[\text{p}K_{\text{AI}} + \text{p}K_{\text{AII}} - 2\text{pH}]}, \quad p_0 = \frac{1}{Z}, \qquad 12.$$

where the partition function is

$$Z = 1 + 10^{[\text{p}K_{\text{AI}} - \text{pH}]} + 10^{[\text{p}K_{\text{AI}} + \text{p}K_{\text{AII}} - 2\text{pH}]}. \qquad 13.$$

If all protonation states are in fast exchange, the observed chemical shift is

$$\delta_{\text{obs}} = p_0 \delta_0 + p_1 \delta_1 + p_2 \delta_2. \qquad 14.$$

The macroscopic parameters are related to the microscopic parameters by

$$K_{\text{AI}} = \left(\frac{1}{K_{01}} + \frac{1}{K_{10}} \right)^{-1}, \quad K_{\text{AII}} = K_{11} + K_{11}', \quad \delta_1 = \frac{K_{\text{AI}}}{K_{01}} \delta_{01} + \frac{K_{\text{AI}}}{K_{10}} \delta_{10}. \qquad 15.$$

$$\delta_0 = \delta_{00} \quad \delta_2 = \delta_{11}$$

The macroscopic model contains only five independent parameters, two $\text{p}K_a$ values and three chemical shifts, whereas the microscopic model has seven physically independent parameters. As a consequence, only five of its seven parameters can be obtained when fitting the microscopic model to a chemical shift titration curve (59, 69).

Simplifications of the Microscopic Model for Two Sites

The comparison between the general microscopic and macroscopic models shows that five parameters are sufficient to describe any two-site titration, even though the microscopic model contains seven physically independent parameters (59). Thus, two parameters are undetermined. On the other hand, the physical interpretation of three of the five macroscopic parameters (δ_1, $\text{p}K_{\text{AI}}$, and $\text{p}K_{\text{AII}}$) is not obvious. To illustrate the relationship between experimental observables and microscopic parameters, we return to the microscopic model and simplify it so that it, like the macroscopic model, contains only five independent parameters that can be uniquely determined from a titration curve. This simplification requires two assumptions.

First, assume that the pH-shifts are additive, so that $\delta_{00} - \delta_{01} = \delta_{10} - \delta_{11}$. If structural changes upon protonation either are absent or have no impact on the chemical shift, this assumption is justified. Equation 10 can then be simplified to

$$\delta_{\text{obs}} = p_{00}\delta_{00} + p_{10}(\delta_{00} + \Delta\delta_1) + p_{01}(\delta_{00} + \Delta\delta_2) + p_{11}(\delta_{00} + \Delta\delta_1 + \Delta\delta_2), \qquad 16.$$

where $\Delta\delta_1 = \delta_{10} - \delta_{00}$ and $\Delta\delta_2 = \delta_{11} - \delta_{10}$ are the pH-shifts upon protonation of the first and second sites, respectively. This simplification is not valid when two sites X and Y interact, and the protein unfolds when Y protonates, for example. The pH-shift of a given nucleus on protonation of X is likely to be different in the folded and unfolded states of the protein, and thus the pH-shift of X depends on the protonation state of Y.

A second assumption that reduces the number of independent parameters to five may be made in the following two ways, giving rise to two different models:

Model 1: $\Delta\delta_2 = 0$,

Model 2: $w = 0$.

Model 1 includes cooperativity but assumes that only one of the two protonation events affects the chemical shift. In Model 2 the two sites are noncooperative and Equation 16 reduces to Equation 5 with $N = 2$.

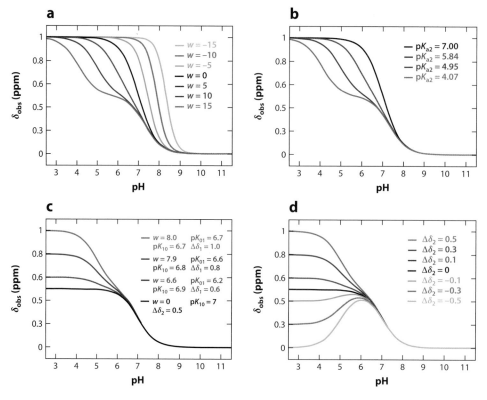

Figure 5

Simulated chemical shift titration curves for (*a,c*) two interacting sites according to Model 1 using Equation 16 with Equation 7, and for (*b,d*) two noninteracting sites according to Model 2 using Equation 5. For all curves in panel *a* $pK_{01} = 7$, $pK_{10} = 7$, $\Delta\delta_1 = 1.0$, $\Delta\delta_2 = 0$, $\delta_{00} = 0$; in panel *b* $pK_{a1} = 7$, $\Delta\delta_1 = 0.5$, $\Delta\delta_2 = 0.5$, $\delta_0 = 0$; in panel *c* $\Delta\delta_2 = 0$, $\delta_{00} = 0$; and in panel *d* $pK_{a1} = 7$, $pK_{a2} = 5$, $\Delta\delta_1 = 0.5$, $\delta_0 = 0$. Note that the titration curves of the same color in panels *a* and *b* are exactly the same, likewise for panels *b* and *d*. Interaction energies are in kJ/mol and chemical shifts are in ppm. The values shown in panels *b* and *c* are rounded off. The black curves are Henderson-Hasselbalch curves.

Model 1 and Model 2 describe different physical realities. In Model 1 the two sites interact, but the chemical shift is affected only by one of the sites. In other words, the titration curve is site specific. In Model 2 the sites are not interacting while the chemical shift responds to both sites; thus, the titration curve is not site specific. Surprisingly, maybe, they are mathematically identical, at least as long as cooperativity is nonpositive and the titration curves they describe are monotonous (see below and **Figure 5**). Model 1 and Model 2 provide two physically different microscopic interpretations of the macroscopic model.

The Decoupled Site Representation

The fact that Model 1 and Model 2 are interchangeable has been generalized to any number of sites (37, 45, 69). The titration of *N* interacting sites can always be described by *N* noninteracting quasi-sites. Usually, although not always (37), this means that the titration curve can be represented as a weighted sum of *N* HH-curves (as in Equation 5) if all interactions energies are nonnegative (45). This representation is called the decoupled site representation (DSR) (31, 37, 45, 46).

For cooperative protonation the quasi-sites in the DSR do not represent the titration of individual groups; rather they represent a phase in the collective protonation of all interacting residues. This representation is in some respects similar to the macroscopic model, although not identical (38). The pK_a values of the quasi-sites refer to the inflection points of the individual HH-curves, but they are often similar to the macroscopic pK_a values. For two interacting sites the quasi-pK_a values will differ at most by $\pm \log_{10}(2)$ from the macroscopic value.

The DSR is based on the factorization of the partition function, Z, where the quasi-pK_a values are obtained from the roots of Z. The factorization can always be done because the partition function is a polynomial of the order N, where N is the number of interacting sites. For two interacting sites, the pK_a values of the two quasi-sites are given by

$$pK_{a1} = -\log_{10}(-\lambda_+), \quad pK_{a2} = -\log_{10}(-\lambda_-), \qquad 17.$$

where λ_+ and λ_- are the roots of Z (Equation 8).

In the case $\Delta\delta_2 = 0$, Equation 16 reduces to

$$\delta_{obs} = \delta_{00} + (p_{10} + p_{11})\Delta\delta_1. \qquad 18.$$

If Equation 7 is inserted into Equation 18 using the factorized form of the partition function, it can be found that

$$\delta_{obs} = \delta_{00} + \frac{a\,\Delta\delta_1}{(1 + 10^{[pH-pK_{a1}]})} + \frac{(1-a)\Delta\delta_1}{(1 + 10^{[pH-pK_{a2}]})}, \qquad 19.$$

where the prefactor a is given by

$$a = \frac{K'_{11} - K_{a1}}{K_{a2} - K_{a1}} = \frac{K_{11} - K_{a2}}{K_{a1} - K_{a2}}. \qquad 20.$$

Because a is a constant independent of pH, it follows that Equation 19 (i.e., Model 1) has the same form as Equation 5 with $N = 2$ (i.e., Model 2). Thus, as long as Z has real roots, the cooperative model (Model 1) is indistinguishable from the noncooperative one (Model 2).

The DSR parameters of two interacting sites, K_{a1}, K_{a2}, and a can be converted to a unique set of microscopic dissociation constants if, as assumed in Model 1, $\Delta\delta_2 = 0$ (69):

$$K_{11} = a K_{a1} + (1-a)K_{a2}, \quad K_{01} = \frac{K_{a1}K_{a2}}{a K_{a1} + (1-a)K_{a2}}, \quad K_{10} = \frac{K_{a1}K_{a2}}{a K_{a2} + (1-a)K_{a1}}. \qquad 21.$$

However, not all sets of DSR parameters in Model 1 are physically meaningful. For any given set of quasi-pK_a values, there exists a nonpositive value of $a = a_{min}$ and a value $a = a_{max} = 1 - a_{min}$, where the DSR parameters represent sites with infinite negative interaction energies (37). For $a < a_{min}$ or $a > a_{max}$, Equation 21 gives rise to nonphysical negative dissociation constants equivalent to imaginary microscopic pK_a values. Such cases represent chemical shift titration curves that are nonmonotonous, where $\Delta\delta_2 \neq 0$ and the signs of $\Delta\delta_2$ and $\Delta\delta_1$ are opposite (e.g., **Figure 3c**). The incorporation of one additional parameter, however, also leaves the model underdetermined, and it is no longer possible to convert the DSR parameters to a unique set of microscopic parameters.

More than Two Interacting Protonation Sites

More than two interacting sites can give rise to complicated and potentially counterintuitive titration curves. Overall, the methods used for two sites can be extended to describe any number of sites. A recent formal treatment of any number of interacting protonation sites is given by Ullmann and colleagues (7, 37, 45, 69). Here we point out three features that are not present when considering only two interacting sites. (a) Nonmonotonous titration curves can occur also when the chemical shift senses only one site. (*b*) The interaction energies between two sites can be pH dependent if structural changes occur. (*c*) The number of parameters in the microscopic model increases dramatically with the number of sites.

Three or more interacting sites can result in proton binding curves that are nonmonotonous. This means that lowering pH causes deprotonation of one of the three sites over a certain range of pH values. A classic example of a nonmonotonous proton binding curve is the titration of the central amino group in diethylenetriamine pentaacetate (DTPA) (45, 64). It is tempting to think that three or more titrating groups close to each other in a protein will show similar behavior for certain geometric arrangements of the protonation sites.

It is common to assume that the pairwise interactions between protonation sites are independent of other sites. However, for more than two interacting sites, the interaction energies between two sites may themselves depend on the protonation state of other sites. Such dependencies may occur when structural changes are involved. Similar arguments that were used for chemical shifts to obtain Equation 16 apply here: If structural changes can be ignored, the additive property of electric fields implies that the pairwise interaction energies are independent of the protonation state of other sites. The assumption will greatly reduce the number of independent parameters for larger numbers of interacting sites. There will be cases for which the assumption is not valid. For example, if two sites X and Y interact and the protein unfolds upon the protonation of a third site Z, one would expect that the interaction energy between X and Y depends on the protonation state of Z.

The number of physically independent variables in the general microscopic model increases with the power of the number of sites, N, whereas the reduced models assuming pH independence of interaction energies and chemical shift changes only increase with the square of N, and the noncooperative models and macroscopic models increase linearly. The number of parameters contained in the macroscopic model defines the maximum number of parameters that can be determined from a titration curve, which leaves a large number of underdetermined parameters in any microscopic model.

The Hill Model

An approximation of cooperative protonation is the Hill model:

$$\delta_{obs} = \delta_0 + \frac{\Delta\delta}{1 + 10^{n[pH - pK_a]}},$$ 22.

where n is the Hill coefficient. If $n < 1$, it suggests that cooperativity is negative; $n = 1$ suggests no cooperativity; and $n > 1$ suggests positive cooperativity. The number of interacting sites is not specified. The Hill model qualitatively describes the broadening or narrowing of the pH range where a site protonates, resulting from negative and positive cooperativity, respectively, but does not reproduce multiphasic titrations. Equation 22 assumes that the chemical shift is affected by only one protonation site. The Hill model contains only four independent parameters and is therefore a useful approximation. In this context, the Hill coefficient is the physical interpretation of the linear pH dependence of the pK_a value (34).

Proton Binding Capacitance

When visualizing titration data, it can be helpful to plot not only the chemical shift titration curve but also its derivative, as shown in **Figure 2c,d**. If only one site exclusively affects the chemical shift, the normalized titration curve is identical to the proton occupancy of this site, χ, which in this case becomes $(\delta_{obs} - \delta_0)/\Delta\delta$. The derivative of χ with respect to pH is called the proton binding capacitance (PBC) (34). For a simple HH-titration (Equation 4) the PBC is given by

$$\frac{d\chi}{d\mathrm{pH}} = \ln(10)\frac{10^{[\mathrm{pH}-\mathrm{p}K_a]}}{(1 + 10^{[\mathrm{pH}-\mathrm{p}K_a]})^2}.$$

23.

Here the PBC has a maximum at $\mathrm{pH} = \mathrm{p}K_a$, where its value is $\ln(10)/4 = 0.58$. Experimental values significantly larger than this indicate positive cooperativity, whereas smaller values indicate negative cooperativity. In the framework of the Hill model, the maximum value of the PBC is proportional to the Hill coefficient (34). PBC curves have the advantage that they very clearly display changes in the electrostatics of the system. As **Figure 2e,f** show, the addition of salt screens electrostatic interactions on the PGB1-QDD protein surface, leading to (*a*) shifts in the curve maxima toward model $\mathrm{p}K_a$ values and (*b*) sharper and more symmetric curves, marking the reduction in multiple, negatively cooperative interactions.

DETERMINING MICROSCOPIC PARAMETERS

When analyzing NMR titration data, one generally needs to make assumptions about the chemical shifts and the interaction energies. The question remains, Is it possible to obtain genuine microscopic parameters experimentally?

Global Fitting of Titration Curves

NMR titration curves can be obtained for all NMR-observable nuclei in a protein, producing vast data sets. Although titration curves obtained from different nuclei do provide independent information (60), global fitting does not resolve the intrinsic problems of determining microscopic parameters (59, 69). If experimental errors are ignored, the maximum information for N interacting sites is obtained from N titration curves. Any additional curves will be linear combinations of those curves and will not provide independent information (69). In a global fit of an N-site model to N titration curves, the parameters in the reduced microscopic model are underdetermined, even for $N = 2$ (59). Furthermore, for a large number of sites N becomes similar to the number of individual measuring points in an experimental titration curve (typically 5–20). In this case the global DSR model will also be underdetermined, because each titration curve is associated with a unique set of $N + 1$ chemical shifts in the DSR (Equation 5).

Computational Models

A truly general approach to analyzing protein chemical shift titration curves would be to assume that all titrating groups in a protein interact, thereby invoking models with very large numbers of parameters. Fortuitously, many interaction energies would be moderated because the sites are far from each other. In addition, pH-shifts become insignificant for nuclei far from the protonation site. Restricting the interaction energies and pH-shifts to be nonzero only for cases that meet certain criteria, for example, the sites are within a certain distance from each other, could greatly reduce the number of parameters. Then, at least in principle, it would be feasible to determine microscopic values; however, because many protein $\mathrm{p}K_a$ values are often similar to each other, the successfulness of this approach is questionable. Additional assumptions about the chemical shift, e.g., for nuclei with highly predictable pH-shifts, are likely to be essential. For example, a virtually complete reference set of pH-dependent chemical shifts was recently reported for all nuclei in short random-coil peptides (53). A possible solution to the problem is to use global optimization algorithms that include an electrostatic model and some kind of method that predicts chemical shifts. The most ambitious approach along these lines published thus far is by Nielsen and colleagues (32, 60).

For example, ten pairwise interaction energies for five sites may be obtained from electrostatic calculations based on the protein structure by utilizing Poisson-Boltzmann continuum electrostatics (5, 26, 56, 57) or Monte Carlo simulations (70). This would at least in principle allow the remaining 11 microscopic parameters to be determined. In favorable cases some of the pH-shifts may be predicted with reasonable accuracy, further reducing parameters. Protein dynamics may be incorporated into the calculation by averaging the interaction energies over different side chain conformations or a molecular dynamics trajectory (41, 70).

Software packages for analyzing and simulating titration curves are available. The pKaTool, developed by Nielsen and colleagues (40, 60), is an interactive graphical tool used to analyze experimental titration data. The database Titration_DB (15) contains a large number of experimental protein chemical shift titration curves. Generalized Monte Carlo Titration (GMCT) (70) by Ullmann and colleagues is a simulation program that models receptor binding and can incorporate continuum electrostatics and conformational changes. In addition, pK_a prediction methods are continuously being refined (2, 3, 41), although this topic is beyond the scope of this review.

Systematic Mutations of Protonation Sites

Another possible approach is to employ mutations that systematically deplete protonation sites (13). For example, imagine five interacting aspartate residues. Hypothetically, one could mutate four of them into nontitratable analogs (e.g., asparagine) and then by mutagenesis reintroduce the aspartates one by one. It would be necessary to determine only three parameters from each of the first two mutants. Four and five new parameters could be determined from the third and fourth mutants, respectively, and six parameters from the wild-type protein. In this way one could in principle determine all 21 parameters in the reduced microscopic model, although this approach requires that the mutations do not significantly perturb the structure of the protein.

Case in point, recent studies by McIntosh et al. (38) dissect the electrostatic interactions in *B. circulans* xylanase by NMR-monitored titrations and mutagenesis. The interested reader will find many of the concepts introduced in this review exemplified in their study.

ORIGINS OF pH-DEPENDENT CHEMICAL SHIFTS

Understanding the effect of protonation on the chemical shifts is essential for interpreting chemical shift titration curves. As discussed above, knowledge about the pH-shift can allow one to distinguish between otherwise indistinguishable cooperative and noncooperative models. Furthermore, the pH-shift can provide valuable information about structural changes (32) and electrostatics (22) in a protein.

Nonetheless, it remains challenging to disentangle the large variety of effects that contribute to the NMR chemical shifts of proteins (27, 76). Qualitatively, the pH-shift may be regarded as the sum of a through-bond contribution, hydrogen bond contributions, contributions from structural changes, and through-space electrostatic contributions.

Through-bond shifts are most important for nuclei very close to the protonation site, such as carboxylate ^{13}C in aspartate, glutamate, or C termini; the imidazole ring signals of histidine; $^{13}C^{\beta}$ of cysteines; the side chain ^{15}N signals of lysines and arginines; and the aromatic ^{13}C nuclei of tyrosines. The pH-shifts for these nuclei are dominated by through-bond contributions that depend little on local structure. Therefore, the shifts of these residues tend to be similar and they are often reasonably well approximated (**Table 1**), although special structural features may cause these shifts to deviate significantly from standard values. For example, (*a*) metal coordination or exceptionally strong hydrogen bonds are expected to cause large perturbations in nuclear shielding; (*b*) protonation often leads to disruption and/or formation of new hydrogen bonds, so nuclei in the hydrogen donor and acceptor groups directly interacting with the protonation site can be strongly affected (10, 68); (*c*) changes in the electrostatic potential and hydrogen-bonding network can trigger additional changes in the geometric structure of the protein, and, depending on the protein, these changes may range from local side chain conformational changes to large-scale global structural changes that can affect nuclei far from the protonation site; (*d*) the change in electric field due to protonation can affect the chemical shifts of nuclei over considerable distances directly through space (9). The magnitude of this long-range dipole–dipole electric field effect has long been underestimated, although recent studies show that it can be a sizeable contribution to the pH-shifts of backbone amide nuclei (8, 22, 32).

CONCLUSIONS

Recent advances in NMR spectroscopy have made it possible to measure to an unprecedented level of detail the pH-dependent protonation states of individual acidic and basic groups in proteins. The development of a suite of dedicated pulse sequences provides access to microscopic protonation equilibria for the titratable amino acids, which allows researchers to quantitatively determine electrostatic interactions in proteins. The exquisite data quality that can now be routinely obtained greatly facilitates and improves the modeling of the underlying energetics, which ultimately is needed to explain pH-dependent protein stability and function.

SUMMARY POINTS

1. NMR chemical shifts are highly sensitive reporters of changes in electrostatics of the nuclear environment, and these effects are convoluted.

2. The accurate determination of protonation states and pK_a constants crucially depends on access to ^{13}C and ^{15}N reporter nuclei at side chain positions.

3. NMR pulse schemes are available to follow pH titrations for all acidic and basic side chains in uniformly isotopic-enriched proteins.

4. The high level of detail in chemical shift titration curves allows scientists to test and differentiate sophisticated electrostatic models.

5. A true appreciation of protein electrostatics requires the integration of accurate experimental and computational techniques.

FUTURE ISSUES

1. Further investigation and consideration of electric field effects on chemical shifts are needed.

2. Extension of NMR methods to measure ^{13}C and ^{15}N reporter nuclei at side chain positions of larger proteins, such as enzymes, is desirable.

3. The expanding body of accurate experimental NMR titration data and the development of computational methods will be mutually beneficial.

4. Intrinsically disordered proteins will serve as exciting testing grounds for experiments and for modeling electrostatic interactions.

5. Protonation kinetics are often neglected in pH titration studies, but they have pronounced effects on chemical shifts. This area needs invigoration.

DISCLOSURE STATEMENT

The authors are not aware of any affiliations, memberships, funding, or financial holdings that might be perceived as affecting the objectivity of this review.

ACKNOWLEDGMENTS

We thank Dr. Matthias Ullmann and Dr. Lawrence McIntosh for helpful comments. F.A.A.M. thanks his collaborators at Lund University, Sweden, for sparking an interest in this area of research, and his former colleagues and students at the University of Groningen, The Netherlands, for the careful measurement and thorough analysis of numerous NMR titration curves. The authors thank the Netherlands Organization for Scientific Research (NWO) for funding their research.

LITERATURE CITED

1. Alberty RA. 2000. Effect of pH on protein–ligand equilibria. *J. Phys. Chem. B* 104:9929–34
2. Alexov E, Mehler EL, Baker N, Baptista AM, Huang Y, et al. 2011. Progress in the prediction of pK_a values in proteins. *Proteins* 79:3260–75
3. Anandakrishnan R, Aguilar B, Onufriev AV. 2012. *H*++ 3.0: automating pK prediction and the preparation of biomolecular structures for atomistic molecular modeling and simulations. *Nucleic Acids Res.* 40:W537–41

4. Performs an H2(C)N experiment to study lysine, arginine, and N terminus pK_a constants.

4. André I, Linse S, Mulder FAA. 2007. Residue-specific pK_a determination of lysine and arginine side chains by indirect ^{15}N and ^{13}C spectroscopy: application to *apo* calmodulin. *J. Am. Chem. Soc.* 129:15805–13
5. Antosiewicz J, McCammon JW, Gilson MK. 1994. Prediction of pH-dependent properties of proteins. *J. Mol. Biol.* 238:415–36
6. Baturin SJ, Okon M, McIntosch LP. 2011. Structure, dynamics, and ionization equilibria of the tyrosine residues in *Bacillus circulans* xylanase. *J. Biomol. NMR* 51:379–94
7. Bombarda E, Ullmann GM. 2010. pH-dependent pK_a values in proteins—a theoretical analysis of protonation energies with practical consequences for enzymatic reactions. *J. Phys. Chem. B* 114:1994–2003

8. Makes quantum mechanical calculations of the polarizability due to nuclear shielding.

8. Boyd J, Domene C, Redfield C, Ferraro MB, Lazzeretti P. 2003. Calculation of dipole-shielding polarizability ($\sigma^I_{\alpha\beta\gamma}$): the influence of uniform electric field effects on the shielding of backbone nuclei in proteins. *J. Am. Chem. Soc.* 125:9556–57
9. Buckingham AD. 1960. Chemical shifts in the nuclear magnetic resonance spectra of molecules containing polar groups. *Can. J. Chem.* 38:300–7
10. Castaneda CA, Fitch CA, Majumdar A, Khangulov V, Schlessman JL, et al. 2009. Molecular determinants of the pK_a values of Asp and Glu residues in staphylococcal nuclease. *Proteins* 77:570–88
11. Chivers PT, Prehoda KE, Volkman BF, Kim BM, Markley JL, Raines RT. 1997. Microscopic pK_a values of *Escherichia coli* thioredoxin. *Biochemistry* 36:14985–91
12. Croke RL, Patil SM, Quevreaux J, Kendall DA, Alexandrescu AT. 2011. NMR determination of pK_a values in α-synuclein. *Protein Sci.* 20:256–69

13. Di Cera E. 1998. Site-specific thermodynamics: understanding cooperativity in molecular recognition. *Chem. Rev.* 98:1563–91

14. Edsall JT, Martin RB, Hollingworth BR. 1958. Ionization of individual groups in dibasic acids, with application to the amino and hydroxyl groups of tyrosine. *PNAS* 44:505–18

15. Farrell D, Miranda ES, Webb H, Georgi N, Crowley PB, et al. 2010. TitrationDB: storage and analysis of NMR-monitored protein pH titration curves. *Proteins* 78:843–57

16. Forman-Kay JD, Clore GM, Gronenborn AM. 1992. Relationship between electrostatics and redox function in human thioredoxin: characterization of pH titration shifts using two-dimensional homo- and heteronuclear NMR. *Biochemistry* 31:3442–52

17. Gao G, Prasad R, Lodwig SN, Unkefer CJ, Beard WA, et al. 2006 Determination of lysine pK values using [5-^{13}C]lysine: application to the lyase domain of DNA Pol β. *J. Am. Chem. Soc.* 128:8104–5

18. Harris TK, Turner GJ. 2002 Structural basis of perturbed pK_a values of catalytic groups in enzyme active sites. *IUBMB Life* 53:85–98

19. Hass MAS. 2007. *Motions in proteins on the microsecond time-scale characterized by NMR: applications to histidine dynamics in blue copper proteins*. PhD Thesis, Univ. Copenhagen

20. Hass MAS, Christensen HEM, Zhang JD, Led JJ. 2007. Kinetics and mechanism of the acid transition of the active site in plastocyanin. *Biochemistry* 46:14619–28

21. Hass MAS, Hansen DF, Christensen HEM, Led JJ, Kay LE. 2008. Characterization of conformational exchange of a histidine side chain: protonation, rotamerization, and tautomerization of His61 in plastocyanin from *Anabaena variabilis*. *J. Am. Chem. Soc.* 130:8460–70

22. Hass MAS, Jensen MR, Led JJ. 2008. Probing electric fields in proteins in solution by NMR spectroscopy. *Proteins* 72:333–43

23. Hass MAS, Vlasie M, Ubbink M, Led JJ. 2009. Conformational exchange in pseudoazurin: different kinds of microsecond to millisecond dynamics characterized by their pH and buffer dependence using ^{15}N NMR relaxation. *Biochemistry* 48:50–58

24. Hass MAS, Yilmaz A, Christensen HEM, Led JJ. 2009. Histidine side-chain dynamics and protonation monitored by ^{13}C CPMG NMR relaxation dispersion. *J. Biomol. NMR* 44:225–33

25. Henry GD, Sykes BD. 1995. Determination of the rotational dynamics and pH dependence of the hydrogen exchange rates of the arginine guanidino group using NMR spectroscopy. *J. Biomol. NMR* 6:59–66

26. Honig B, Nicholls A. 1995. Classical electrostatics in biology and chemistry. *Science* 268:1144–49

27. Hunter CA, Packer MJ, Zonta C. 2005. From structure to chemical shift and vice-versa. *Prog. Nucl. Magn. Reson. Spectrosc.* 47:27–39

28. Huque ME, Vogel HJ. 1993. Carbon-13 NMR studies of the lysine side chains of calmodulin and its proteolytic fragments. *J. Protein Chem.* 12:695–707

29. Jensen KS, Pedersen JT, Winther JR, Teilum K. 2014. The pK_a value and accessibility of cysteine residues are key determinants for protein substrate discrimination by glutaredoxin. *Biochemistry* 53:2533–40

30. Kato-Toma Y, Iwashita T, Masuda K, Oyama Y, Ishiguro M. 2003. pK_a measurements from nuclear magnetic resonance of tyrosine-150 in class C beta-lactamase. *Biochem. J.* 371:175–81

31. Klingen AR, Bombarda E, Ullmann GM. 2006. Theoretical investigation of the behavior of titratable groups in proteins. *Photochem. Photobiol. Sci.* 5:588–96

32. Kukić P, Farrell D, Søndergaard CR, Bjarnadottir U, Bradley J, et al. 2009. Improving the analysis of NMR spectra tracking pH-induced conformational changes: removing artifacts of the electric field on the NMR chemical shift. *Proteins* 78:971–84

33. Li SH, Hong M. 2011. Protonation, tautomerization, and rotameric structure of histidine: a comprehensive study by magic-angle-spinning solid-state NMR. *J. Am. Chem. Soc.* 133:1534–44

34. Lindman S, Linse S, Mulder FAA, André I. 2006. Electrostatic contributions to residue-specific protonation equilibria and proton binding capacitance for a small protein. *Biochemistry* 45:13993–4002

35. Lindman S, Linse S, Mulder FAA, André I. 2007. pK_a values for side-chain carboxyl groups of a PGB1 variant explain salt and pH-dependent stability. *Biophys. J.* 92:257–66

36. Markley JL. 1975. Observation of histidine residues in proteins by means of nuclear magnetic resonance spectroscopy. *Acc. Chem. Res.* 8:70–80

37. Martini JWR, Ullmann GM. 2013. A mathematical view on the decoupled sites representation. *J. Math. Biol.* 66:477–503

21. Examines tautomers, rotamers, charge states, and proton exchange of histidine.

22. Identifies electric field effects on chemical shifts.

32. Combines electrostatic models and chemical shift prediction to identify structural changes.

34. Discusses proton binding capacitance and provides an explanation for the Hill parameter in pH titrations.

38. Investigates in great detail the electrostatic interaction between two active site residues.

38. **McIntosh LP, Naito D, Baturin SJ, Okon M, Joshi MD, Nielsen JE. 2011. Dissecting electrostatic interpretations in** *Bacillus circulans* **xylanase through NMR-monitored pH titrations.** *J. Biomol. NMR* 51:5–19

39. Mulder FA, Spronk CA, Slijper M, Kaptein R, Boelens R. 1996. Improved HSQC experiments for the observation of exchange broadened signals. *J. Biomol. NMR* 8:223–28

40. Nielsen JE. 2007. Analysing the pH-dependent properties of proteins using pK_a calculations. *J. Mol. Graph. Model.* 25:691–99

41. Forms the pK_a cooperative, a forum on protein electrostatics for experimentalists and theoreticians.

41. **Nielsen JE, Gunner MR, García-Moreno B. 2011. The pK_a Cooperative: a collaborative effort to advance structure-based calculations of pK_a values and electrostatic effects in proteins.** *Proteins* 79:3249–59

42. Norton RS, Bradbury JH. 1974. Carbon-13 nuclear magnetic resonance study of tyrosine titrations. *J. Chem. Soc. Chem. Comm.* 919:870–71

43. Applies the H2(C)CO experiment to study carboxylate pK_a constants.

43. **Oda Y, Yamazaki T, Nagayama K, Kanaya S, Kuroda Y, Nakamura H. 1994. Individual ionization constants of all the carboxyl groups in ribonuclease HI from** *Escherichia coli* **determined by NMR.** *Biochemistry* 33:5275–84

44. Oktaviani NA, Pool TJ, Kamikubo H, Slager J, Scheek RM, et al. 2012. Comprehensive determination of protein tyrosine pK_a values for photoactive yellow protein using indirect ^{13}C NMR spectroscopy. *Biophys. J.* 102:579–86

45. Onufriev A, Case DA, Ullmann GM. 2001. A novel view of pH titration in biomolecules. *Biochemistry* 40:3413–19

46. Describes the decoupled site representation.

46. **Onufriev A, Ullmann GM. 2004. Decomposing complex cooperative ligand binding into simple components: connections between microscopic and macroscopic models.** *J. Phys. Chem.* 108:11157–69

47. Pace CN, Grimsley GR, Scholtz JM. 2009. Protein ionizable groups: pK values and their contribution to protein stability and solubility. *J. Biol. Chem.* 284:13285–89

48. Palmer AG 3rd, Kroenke CD, Loria JP. 2001. Nuclear magnetic resonance methods for quantifying microsecond-to-millisecond motions in biological macromolecules. *Methods Enzymol.* 339:204–38

49. Paquin R, Ferrage F, Mulder FAA, Akke M, Bodenhausen G. 2008. Multiple-timescale dynamics of side-chain carboxyl and carbonyl groups in proteins by ^{13}C nuclear spin relaxation. *J. Am. Chem. Soc.* 130:15805–7

50. Pelton JG, Torchia DA, Meadow ND, Roseman S. 1993. Tautomeric states of the active-site histidines of phosphorylated and unphosphorylated III^{Glc}, a signal-transducing protein from *Escherichia coli*, using two-dimensional heteronuclear NMR techniques. *Protein Sci.* 2:543–58

51. Pérez-Cañadillas JM, Campos-Olivas R, Lacadena J, Martínez del Pozo A, Gavilanes JG, et al. 1998. Characterization of pK_a values and titration shifts in the cytotoxic ribonuclease α-sarcin by NMR. Relationship between electrostatic interactions, structure, and catalytic function. *Biochemistry* 37:15865–76

52. Perutz MF. 1978. Electrostatic effects in proteins. *Science* 201(4362):1187–91

53. Platzer G, Okon M, McIntosh LP. 2014. pH-dependent random coil ^{1}H, ^{13}C, and ^{15}N chemical shifts of the ionizable amino acids: a guide for protein pK_a measurements. *J. Biomol. NMR* 60:109–29

54. Pujato M, Navarro A, Versace R, Mancusso R, Ghose R, Tasayco ML. 2006. The pH-dependence of amide chemical shift of Asp/Glu reflects its pK_a in intrinsically disordered proteins with only local interactions. *Biochim. Biophys. Acta* 1764:1227–33

55. Richarz R, Wüthrich K. 1978. Carbon-13 NMR chemical-shifts of common amino-acid residues measured in aqueous-solutions of linear tetrapeptides H-Gly-Gly-X-L-Ala-OH. *Biopolymers* 17:2133–41

56. Rocchia W, Alexov E, Honig B. 2001. Extending the applicability of the nonlinear Poisson-Boltzmann equation: multiple dielectric constants and multivalent ions. *J. Phys. Chem. B* 105:6507–14

57. Rocchia W, Sridharan S, Nicholls A, Alexov E, Chiabrera A, Honig B. 2002. Rapid grid-based construction of the molecular surface for both molecules and geometric objects: applications to the finite difference Poisson-Boltzmann method. *J. Comp. Chem.* 23:128–37

58. Rostovtseva TK, Liu T, Colombini M, Parsegian VA, Bezrukov SM. 2000. Positive cooperativity without domains or subunits in a monomeric membrane channel. *PNAS* 97:7819–22

59. Shrager RI, Cohen JS, Heller SR, Sachs DH, Schechter AN. 1972. Mathematical models for interacting groups in nuclear magnetic resonance titration curves. *Biochemistry* 11:541–47

60. Søndergaard CR, McIntosh LP, Pollastri G, Nielsen JE. 2008. Determination of electrostatic interaction energies and protonation state populations in enzyme active sites. *J. Mol. Biol.* 376:269–87

61. Spitzner N, Löhr F, Pfeiffer S, Koumanov A, Karshikoff A, Rüterjans H. 2001. Ionization properties of titratable groups in ribonuclease T1. *Eur. Biophys. J.* 30:186–97

62. Sudmeier JL, Bradshaw EM, Haddad KE, Day RM, Thalhauser CJ, et al. 2003. Identification of histidine tautomers in proteins by 2D ^{1}H/^{13}C$^{\delta 2}$ one-bond correlated NMR. *J. Am. Chem. Soc.* 125:8430–31

63. Sudmeier JL, Evelhoch JL, Jonsson NB-H. 1980. Dependence of NMR lineshape analysis upon chemical rates and mechanisms: implications for enzyme histidine titrations. *J. Mag. Reson.* 40:377–90

64. Sudmeier JL, Reilley CN. 1964. Nuclear magnetic resonance studies of protonation of polyamine and aminocarboxylate compounds in aqueous solution. *Anal. Chem.* 36:1698–706

65. Szakács Z, Kraszni M, Noszál B. 2004. Determination of microscopic acid-base parameters from NMR-pH titrations. *Anal. Bioanal. Chem.* 378:1428–48

66. Takeda M, Jee J, Ono AM, Terauchi T, Kainosho M. 2009. Hydrogen exchange rate of tyrosine hydroxyl groups in proteins as studied by the deuterium isotope effect on Cζ chemical shifts. *J. Am. Chem. Soc.* 131:18556–62

67. Tollinger M, Crowhurst KA, Kay LE, Forman-Kay JD. 2003. Site-specific contributions to the pH dependence of protein stability. *PNAS* 100:4545–50

68. Tomlinson JH, Green VL, Baker PJ, Williamson MP. 2010. Structural origins of pH-dependent chemical shifts in the B1 domain of protein G. *Proteins* 14:3000–16

69. Ullmann GM. 2003. Relation between protonation constants and titration curves in polyprotic acids: a critical view. *J. Phys. Chem. B* 107:1263–71

70. Ullmann RT, Ullmann GM. 2012. GMCT: a Monte Carlo simulation package for macromolecular receptors. *J. Comp. Chem.* 33:887–900

71. Vila JA. 2012. Limiting values of the ^{15}N chemical shift of the imidazole ring of histidine at high pH. *J. Phys. Chem.* 116:6665–69

72. Vila JA, Arnautova YA, Vorobjev Y, Scheraga HA. 2011. Assessing the fractions of tautomeric forms of the imidazole ring of histidine in proteins as a function of pH. *PNAS* 108:5602–7

73. Warshel A, Aqvist J. 1991. Electrostatic energy and macromolecular function. *Annu. Rev. Biophys. Biophys. Chem.* 20:267–98

74. Webb H, Tynan-Connolly BM, Gregory ML, Farrell D, O'Meara F, et al. 2011. Remeasuring HEWL pK_a values by NMR spectroscopy: methods, analysis, accuracy, and implications for theoretical pK_a calculations. *Proteins* 79:685–702

75. Werbeck ND, Kirkpatrick J, Hansen DF. 2013. Probing arginine side-chains and their dynamics with carbon-detected NMR spectroscopy: application to the 42 kDa human histone deacetylase 8 at high pH. *Angew. Chem. Int. Ed. Engl.* 52:3145–47

76. Wishart DS, Case DA. 2001. Use of chemical shift in molecular structure determination. *Methods Enzymol.* 338:3–34

77. Yamazaki T, Pascal SM, Singer AU, Forman-Kay JD, Kay LE. 1995. NMR pulse sequences for the sequence-specific assignment of arginine guanidino ^{15}N and ^{1}H chemical shifts in proteins. *J. Am. Chem. Soc.* 117:3556–64

78. Zhu L, Kemple MD, Yuan P, Prendergast FG. 1995. N-terminus and lysine side chain pK_a values of melittin in aqueous solutions and micellar dispersions measured by ^{15}N NMR. *Biochemistry* 34:13196–202

Anatomy of Nanoscale Propulsion

Vinita Yadav,[1] Wentao Duan,[1] Peter J. Butler,[2,*]
and Ayusman Sen[1,*]

[1]Department of Chemistry and [2]Department of Biomedical Engineering, The Pennsylvania
State University, University Park, Pennsylvania 16802; email: pbutler@psu.edu, asen@psu.edu

Annu. Rev. Biophys. 2015. 44:77–100

The *Annual Review of Biophysics* is online at
biophys.annualreviews.org

This article's doi:
10.1146/annurev-biophys-060414-034216

*Corresponding authors

Keywords

nanomotors, micromotors, micropumps, enzyme motors, enzyme pumps,
electrophoresis, diffusiophoresis, chemotaxis

Abstract

Nature supports multifaceted forms of life. Despite the variety and complexity of these forms, motility remains the epicenter of life. The applicable
laws of physics change upon going from macroscales to microscales and
nanoscales, which are characterized by low Reynolds number (Re). We
discuss motion at low Re in natural and synthetic systems, along with various
propulsion mechanisms, including electrophoresis, electrolyte diffusiophoresis, and nonelectrolyte diffusiophoresis. We also describe the newly
uncovered phenomena of motility in non-ATP-driven self-powered enzymes
and the directional movement of these enzymes in response to substrate gradients. These enzymes can also be immobilized to function as fluid pumps in
response to the presence of their substrates. Finally, we review emergent collective behavior arising from interacting motile species, and we discuss the
possible biomedical applications of the synthetic nanobots and microbots.

Contents

INTRODUCTION

Motility is a critical feature of life. The abilities to sense one's environment, to advance toward food and away from toxins, and to communicate are as vital to the survival of a bacterium as they are to that of a blue whale. However, as one goes from macro to micro and ultimately to nano scale, the applicable laws of physics change, necessitating the use of different mechanisms to achieve motility. As size decreases, the ratio of surface area to volume increases, implying that volume-dependent forces (such as inertia), which dominate at longer length scales, become less relevant as objects are scaled down. Instead, surface-dependent forces must be utilized to induce motion (107, 130). This review focuses on motion at the nanoscale and microscale and on the physics that governs this motion.

Reynolds Number

The Reynolds number (Re) refers to a dimensionless quantity defined as the ratio of inertial to viscous forces, and this number helps to predict transport properties at different scales:

$$Re = \rho V l / \eta, \hspace{4cm} 1.$$

where ρ is the density of the fluid, V is the mean velocity relative to the fluid, l is the characteristic linear dimension or the traveled length in the fluid, and η is the dynamic viscosity of the fluid. A low Re implies that viscosity is the dominant force, and a high Re implies that inertia dominates. Bacteria and other unicellular organisms are the best examples of low Re swimmers; for these swimmers, $Re = 10^{-4}$, whereas for an average-sized human being in water, $Re = 10^4$. According to the scallop theorem, only nonreciprocal motion can lead to net propulsion in the low-Re regime (68). Nonreciprocal motion requires that time-reversal symmetry be broken, for example, by the introduction of the asymmetry in the swimmer design. Although a low Re represents the first challenge to nanoscale and microscale motion, this challenge is not the only one.

Brownian Passive Diffusion Versus Directed Motion

At low Re, microscale objects are subject to the rapid thermal bumping by solvent molecules, and are driven into motion when collisions are uneven. This effect creates what is known as Brownian diffusion where the objects diffuse and wander around in a solution. Thermal bumping also causes an object to rotate and randomly change orientation, known as Brownian rotation. In contrast, directed motion requires an input of energy.

The translational particle diffusion coefficient, D_t, can be calculated as follows:

$$D_t = k_B T/6\pi \eta a, \qquad\qquad 2.$$

whereas the rotational particle diffusion coefficient, D_r, is governed by the following equation:

$$D_r = k_B T/(8\pi \eta a^3). \qquad\qquad 3.$$

In both equations above, k_B is the Boltzmann constant, T is the absolute temperature, η is the viscosity of fluid through which the particle moves, and a is the radius of such a particle.

To examine the nature of particle motion, the mean-squared displacement (MSD) over different time intervals (τ) is calculated by analyzing the trajectories of particles. For several idealized types of motions, the MSD has been shown to increase as a function of τ raised to some power α (Equation 4) (81).

$$\text{MSD} = K\tau^\alpha \qquad\qquad 4.$$

K is a constant with a value that depends on the diffusion coefficient of the particle. For particles undergoing a purely diffusive, two-dimensional random Brownian walk, K is equal to four times the diffusion coefficient of the particles, and the MSD increases linearly with τ (i.e., $\alpha = 1$) (96). Because typical Brownian diffusion is by far the most commonly observed, systems in which α does not equal 1 are often deemed as having anomalous diffusive behavior. Values of α that are greater than 1 correspond to superdiffusive systems, and those that are less than 1 correspond to subdiffusive systems (21, 24, 79). Consider the example of the Brownian motion of an inert colloid suspended in a solvent: during a given time interval τ, the MSD of the particle does indeed go as τ, except when the time interval is very small, for example, the interval between collisions. At these very small timescales, the particle may appear to be undergoing what is defined as ballistic motion as it traverses its mean free path between solvent collisions (96). For particles that migrate along a linear trajectory with a constant ballistic velocity, $\alpha = 2$. In contrast, however, labeled messenger RNA molecules in a living *Escherichia coli* cell undergo subdiffusion with α values of approximately 0.7 (79).

INSPIRATIONS FROM NATURE

A motor is a machine that consumes some form of energy and converts it into mechanical work. Motion is an inextricable part of life, and nature has employed several different chemically powered motors to sustain life. Some examples of molecular motors include myosins, dyneins, and kinesins, all of which are known as cytoplasmic motors. These molecules utilize ATP as their energy source and achieve directionality by moving on tracks (e.g., microtubules). ATP hydrolysis causes a conformational change that is further amplified and translated into mobility. In this respect, synthetic motors and pumps are similar to their biological counterparts. Both biological and synthetic motors expend energy: Biological motors utilize ATP hydrolysis and convert it into mechanical motion, and synthetic motors use chemical, electrical, or magnetic energy to do the same. The working mechanisms of these two kinds of motors often resemble each other: Specifically, proton gradients cause transport across membranes in living systems and are responsible for the propulsion of bimetallic nanorods and fluid pumping in bimetallic pumps (see the subsection titled "Self-electrophoresis") (64). Although synthetic motors do exhibit directionality, another interesting goal involves motion along a predefined track, replicating kinesin translocation along a microtubule. A recent study reveals that almost all enzymes, not just the ones functioning as cytoplasmic motors, are capable of exhibiting motion. Further, these enzymes exhibit a rudimentary form of chemotaxis in the presence of their substrate gradient (see the subsection titled "Enzyme Motors and Pumps").

The following subsections discuss two classical biological molecular machines: the dynein motor that powers the motion of cilia and flagella (57, 100), and the classical sodium–potassium pump (17). Their synthetic analogs have also been constructed and are discussed in the sections titled "Synthetic Adaptations" and "Artificial Motors and Pumps for Biomedical Applications."

Cilia and Flagella

For individual cilia and flagella, the Re falls between 10^{-4} and 10^{-6}. For Re values in this range, the inertial force takes into account the mass and propulsion velocity of the organism, and the viscous forces are derived from the liquid environment of the organism.

Cilia and eukaryotic flagella enable organisms to exhibit motility. Both are driven by dynein motors and utilize ATP as a primary energy source, helping the organism move to new sources of food and, in turn, giving motile species a marked advantage over their nonmotile counterparts. The oscillations produced by cilia and eukaryotic flagella translate into an average forward motion (37). In prokaryotes, motility is exhibited by flagella that are anchored on the inner cell membrane and that undergo rotary motion powered by motors at their bases (7). The motor for each flagellum derives its power from a proton or sodium ion flux across the bacterial cell membrane.

Although some organisms propel themselves using single flagella, others can enjoy enhanced locomotion by phase adjusting the oscillatory beat patterns of individual flagella in their flagellar bundles (14, 45). Similar favorable interactions are also observed in groups of individual organisms moving in close proximity to each other. The subsection titled "Emergent Collective Behavior" discusses these phenomena and their laboratory counterparts in greater detail.

Cilia are tiny hair-like structures that are essentially short flagella that occur in large arrays, and neighboring cilia cause fluid flow by synchronous movement stemming from an in-phase relationship between their beats (9). The synchronized beating of neighboring cilia produces metachronal waves that in turn accomplish complex tasks including fluid motion and sensing. As an example, fluid motion induced by the cilia lining the gills of nonmotile marine animals is vital for water ingestion and filter feeding (116). These tiny antennas can be triggered by external mechanical or chemical stimuli. Stimulation of the cilia in turn initiates complex cascading chemical reactions that help transmit signals within the cells (29, 110). Cilia are also involved in sensing; for example, fish use hair-like sensors to detect fluid disturbances made by approaching predators (28). The importance of ciliary systems also extends to other areas: For example, cilia lining the brain ventricles have a significant effect on transmural transport (113). Similarly, a single California mussel, *Mytilus californianus*, can remove impurities suspended in water using its cilia-lined gills at an average filtration rate of 2.6 L/h (27).

Axonemes form the core structures of the eukaryotic cilia and flagella. Dynein motors are important building blocks of axonemes and provide the power for ciliary and flagellar motility. Dyneins form the basic framework of the nine cylindrically arranged microtubule (MT) doublets in each axoneme. The oscillatory beats produced by flagella and cilia result from an ATP-driven mechanochemical cycle, in which the dynein motor on one MT doublet interacts with the

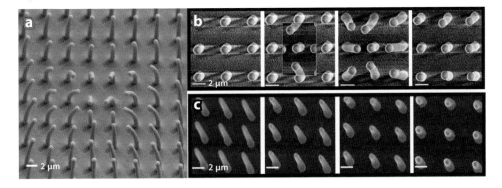

Figure 1

Scanning electron microscope image of synthetic ciliated surface. (*a*) The surface was fabricated using soft lithography and actuated using an electron-beam. (*b* and *c*) Actuated epoxy nanoposts are observed to reversibly bend and tilt within seconds of electron-beam focusing. Figure adapted from Reference 95 with permission from John Wiley and Sons.

binding sites on the adjoining doublet, resulting in sliding motion that is subsequently converted to bending (57, 100).

Because of the myriad of potential applications, current research efforts are focused on replicating the efficient natural motor systems (66, 95, 111, 112, 124, 125, 143) (**Figure 1**). Actuated synthetic cilia can be employed to alter the fluid environment locally and to regulate transport at surfaces. As observed in nature, controlling the shape, size, and oscillation frequency of the structural material enables a broad range of microfluidic applications. Lab-on-a-chip devices integrate several laboratory functions into a single small-scale chip, and these devices require regulated fluid transport that can be achieved by ciliated surfaces. Studies have also demonstrated that surfaces embedded with cilia-like nanostructures show self-cleaning and self-repair properties (95, 112, 135).

Although mimicking the independent actuation of individual biocilia presents a formidable challenge, one study has demonstrated coordinated movement using magnetic actuation (133). In addition, Dogic and coworkers (104) have replicated a ciliary beating pattern using a bottom-up approach. They used biotin labeled kinesin motors bound into clusters through streptavidin-stabilized microtubules. Polyethylene glycol was added to induce attractive interactions between the MTs. This design enables the kinesin clusters to simultaneously bind and walk along the neighboring MTs.

The in vitro artificial design described above enabled the study of both isolated active microtubule bundles and synchronous emergent behavior arising from interacting beating bundles, for example, metachronal waves observed in cilia. Importantly, however, it also provides a design for active materials for fluid transport. Finally, Aizenberg and colleagues developed surfaces bearing arrays of nanostructures put in motion by environment-responsive gels that can be designed to confer a wide range of adaptive motion-generating, self-cleaning and other behaviors (95, 112, 135).

The Sodium–Potassium Pump

The transport of ions and molecules into and out of cells is critical to the functioning of cellular machinery. Both transport against concentration gradients and movement of hydrophilic molecules across lipid bilayers pose challenges that are overcome by active transport. The movement of sodium and potassium against concentration gradients is effected by the Na^+/K^+ ATPase, a membrane-bound ion pump. The energy for this action is derived from ATP hydrolysis, which the enzyme uses to generate electrochemical gradients for Na^+ and K^+ across the plasma membranes of cells (23, 114, 115). Such electrochemical gradients play a critical role in the cellular uptake of ions and nutrients and in the regulation of intracellular pH and cell volume. This ion transport is made possible by conformational changes in the Na^+/K^+ ATPase; the two conformational states of the ATPase selectively bind three Na^+ ions and two K^+ ions. Hence, for every hydrolyzed ATP molecule, three Na^+ ions are exported, and two K^+ ions are imported. Some functional aspects of these naturally occurring pumps have been duplicated in the laboratory (137), and the subsection titled "Diffusiophoretic Motors" discusses them in greater detail.

SYNTHETIC ADAPTATIONS

Researchers have designed several synthetic, self-powered micron-sized and nano-sized machines inspired by biological counterparts. To overcome the dominance of viscous forces and randomization from Brownian motion in low-Re regimes, asymmetric swimming and a constant net force are necessary to induce motion of either the machines themselves or the ambient fluid. In the following subsection, we discuss new advances in the design of synthetic motors and pumps and the recent discovery of enzymes as new molecular machines and pumps.

Synthetic Motors and Pumps

Motors and pumps are the two major synthetic machines of interest, and both generate mechanical forces and cause directional transport by converting energy either from chemical fuels (34, 39, 41, 48, 61, 87, 91, 92, 118, 121, 136, 140, 141) or from external sources including magnetic (20, 33, 36, 123), electric (11, 13), light (1, 47, 70, 86), acoustic (2, 54, 132), and thermal fields (6, 52, 97). Unlike motors that propel themselves, pumps do not move themselves; rather, they induce the movement of nearby fluids and inert tracer particles. The motors require a gradient along the surface (e.g., in chemical concentration, temperature, surface tension, or pressure) to induce motion. They are mostly designed as rods or spheres that have asymmetric compositions (e.g., Janus particles, which have an active material on one side and an inert material on the other) (39), activity (different chemical reaction rates at the two ends) (93), or shape (e.g., motors that are concave on one end and convex on the other) (129). Early micropump designs were based on the generation of local electric fields (47, 51, 62, 77, 90, 92). Recent designs include polymeric or enzymatic micropumps, which pump fluids by generating chemical concentration gradients (108, 109, 139, 142).

Propulsion Mechanisms

The generation of the propulsive force, asymmetry, and, ultimately, motion can arise from a variety of mechanisms. These mechanisms may be based on either chemical concentration gradients, as in self-electrophoresis and self-diffusiophoresis, or the gradients of external fields.

Self-electrophoresis. Electrophoresis is a phenomenon in which charged species are transported through a liquid medium (usually an aqueous solution) under an electric field. In an electric field (E), charged particles migrate with velocity ($\mathbf{U}$) governed by the Smoluchowski equation for particles with thin double layers (3, 117):

$$\mathbf{U} = \frac{\zeta_{\mathrm{p}}\varepsilon}{\mu}E. \qquad 5.$$

Here, ζ_{p} is the zeta potential of the particle surface, which is related to the surface charge, and ε and μ are the permittivity and dynamic viscosity of the medium, respectively. Unlike conventional electrophoresis, which requires an external electric field, redox reactions occurring at different parts of a particle surface can result in an ion concentration gradient, and hence local electric field, leading to the motion of the object itself. This process is called self-electrophoresis, and it has been exploited in various synthetic micromachine and nanomachine systems over the past decade.

The first such system was discovered by the Sen and Mallouk groups at The Pennsylvania State University (93). In this system, Au–Pt nanorods (2–3 μm long and ∼400 nm in diameter) were observed to move autonomously in dilute hydrogen peroxide (H_2O_2), with the Pt ends leading at a speed of approximately 10 μm/s. The Ozin group (26) independently made similar observations with Au–Ni nanorods of similar dimensions.

In self-electrophoresis, the charged microparticle moves in a self-generated electric field as a result of an asymmetric distribution of ions. For example, **Figure 2a** shows that in the case of Au–Pt bimetallic nanomotors, oxidation of H_2O_2 occurs at the anode (Pt end), and reduction of H_2O_2 (and that of O_2) occurs at the cathode (Au end), leading to a proton concentration gradient oriented from the Pt end to the Au end. This asymmetric distribution results in an electric field that has the opposite direction as the proton concentration gradient. The negatively charged nanorod therefore moves toward the Pt end, an effect similar to traditional electrophoresis.

The discovery of bimetallic motors has inspired the design of other synthetic machines, including motors that are based on different shapes (38, 134), fuels (71, 75), and power sources (72). **Figure 2b** shows that redox chemical reactions that are responsible for self-electrophoresis and motor propulsion can also be triggered by electric fields by means of bipolar chemistry. In one such system, Zn micromotors are propelled under an electric potential: Zn metal is oxidized and dissolved at one end, and Zn ions are reduced, and metal deposited, at the other end.

Micropumps that are based on self-electrophoresis have also been designed. A motor moves through fluid, so by inverse, immobilizing it will induce fluid flow in the vicinity of the motor. The first examples of micropumps (51, 53, 60, 62, 63) were developed using the same principle as those used in the development of bimetallic Au–Pt motors (described above). When fuel is added to the system, electrochemical reactions take place at the surface of the two metals: The cathode reduces fuel and consumes protons, and the anode oxidizes fuel and produces protons (see **Figure 2c**). The redox reaction creates a proton gradient in solution over the metals, and thus it also creates an electric field. This field acts both phoretically on charged tracer particles and osmotically on the electric double-layer on the charged metal surface, leading to fluid motion. Only the electrophoretic effect matters in determining the direction of motion for tracer particles suspended in solution, whereas the combination or competition of the electrophoretic and electroosmotic effects decides the direction of movement for particles near the metal surface. Changing the fuel can lead to changes in pumping direction, as demonstrated in **Figure 2d**.

Self-diffusiophoresis. Similar to self-electrophoresis, self-diffusiophoresis is a mechanism that originates from chemical concentration gradients that are produced by surface chemical reactions. Self-diffusiophoresis can be classified into two categories, electrolyte and nonelectrolyte self-diffusiophoresis, depending on whether the chemical species contributing to the gradient are charged or uncharged, respectively.

Electrolyte self-diffusiophoresis. Electrolyte self-diffusiophoresis is more commonly exploited in the synthetic motor and pump systems. This mechanism works when a gradient of electrolytes ∇c is formed across a charged surface with zeta potential ζ_p. For diffusiophoresis near a wall with zeta potential ζ_w, two effects contribute to the movement of a particle: an electrophoretic effect and a chemophoretic effect. In such cases, the speed U of the diffusiophoretic movement can be approximated by Equation 6 (3):

$$U = \underbrace{\frac{\nabla c}{c_0}\left[\left(\frac{D^+ - D^-}{D^+ + D^-}\right)\left(\frac{k_B T}{e}\right)\frac{\varepsilon(\zeta_p - \zeta_w)}{\eta}\right]}_{\text{Electrophoretic Term}} + \underbrace{\frac{\nabla c}{c_0}\left[\left(\frac{2\varepsilon k_B^2 T^2}{\eta e^2}\right)\left\{\ln\left(1 - \gamma_w^2\right) - \ln\left(1 - \gamma_p^2\right)\right\}\right]}_{\text{Chemophoretic Term}}, \quad 6.$$

where D^+ and D^- are the diffusion coefficients of the cation and anion, respectively, c_0 is the bulk concentration of ions, e is the charge of an electron, k_B is the Boltzmann constant, T is the

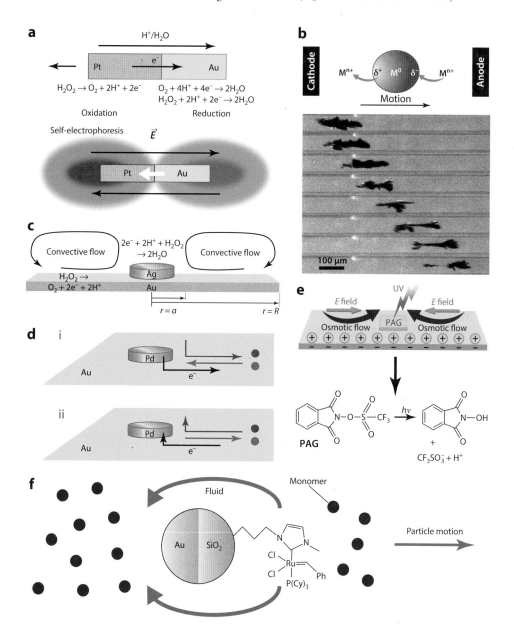

Figure 2

Micromotors and pumps with different propulsion mechanisms. (*a*) Propulsion of bimetallic Au–Pt nanorods in H_2O_2 solution powered by self-electrophoresis. Panel adapted from Reference 93, with permission from the American Chemical Society. (*b*) Propulsion of Zn microparticles in 0.1 M zinc sulfate solution mediated by bipolar chemistry under an external electric field. Panel adapted from Reference 72, with permission from the American Chemical Society. (*c*) Immobilization of bimetallic motors on a surface induces fluid flows in its vicinity. Panel adapted from Reference 62, with permission from the American Chemical Society. (*d*) Direction of movement of negative SiO_2 colloids (*blue*), positive amidine-functionalized colloids (*red*), and electrons (*black*) over an Au surface relative to a Pd feature in a solution containing different fuels: (*i*) hydrazine (N_2H_4) or (*ii*) dimethyl hydrazine ($N_2Me_2H_2$). Panel adapted from Reference 51, with permission from the American Chemical Society. (*e*) Exposure to ultraviolet (UV) light leads to formation of ions from the photoacid generator (PAG). The faster diffusivity of protons leads to inward electric fields that act both phoretically on the colloids and osmotically on the ions near the charged substrate surface. The combination of the two causes inward motion of positive, amine-functionalized polystyrene (NH_2-PS) particles, which gather around the photoacid. Panel adapted from Reference 139, with permission from the American Chemical Society. (*f*) Propulsion of a Janus particle under nonelectrolyte self-diffusiophoresis owing to ring-opening metathesis polymerization of norbornene (monomer) by the immobilized Ru catalyst. Panel adapted from Reference 91, with permission from John Wiley & Sons.

absolute temperature, ε is the dielectric permittivity of the solution, η is the viscosity, and $\gamma_w = \tanh(e\zeta_w/4k_BT)$, $\gamma_p = \tanh(e\zeta_p/4k_BT)$. If the cation and the anion exhibit different diffusivities, a net electric field emerges, resulting in the electrophoretic term in Equation 6. The electric field acts both diffusiophoretically on the nearby charged particles and osmophoretically on the fluid near the double layer of the wall. The interplay between phoretic and osmotic components depends on the difference between the zeta potentials of the particles (ζ_p) and the wall (ζ_w), and this interplay can lead to schooling and exclusion behaviors that are discussed later in the subsection titled "Self-assembly and collective patterns." In addition, because ionic strength influences the thickness of the electric double layer, the electrolyte concentration gradient causes a gradient in the thickness of the electric double layer. Higher "pressure" where the double layer is thinner drives fluid flow from an area of relatively high electrolyte concentration to one of lower concentration. This behavior is described by the chemophoretic term in Equation 6. In most cases, the chemophoretic effect is negligible, and diffusiophoretic transport is governed by the electrophoretic effect, unless the diffusivities of the cations and the anions are very similar.

Because of their high diffusivities and significant contribution to electrophoretic effect, self-diffusiophoretic systems often involve chemical reactions that generate gradients of H^+ or OH^-. The first example of such a system is the UV light–powered silver chloride (AgCl) micromotor reported by Ibele et al. (49). Under UV light, AgCl is reduced to Ag metal, and produces protons and chloride ions. Because protons have a significantly higher diffusivity ($D_{H^+} = 9.311 \times 10^{-5}$ cm^{2}s^{-1}, $D_{Cl^-} = 1.385 \times 10^{-5}$ cm^{2}s^{-1} at 298 K), an electric field is generated. This field points toward the AgCl particles and results in both electrophoresis of these particles and electroosmosis along the wall. Irregular shapes and/or different reactivities of the AgCl particles break the spherical symmetry around them, driving them into motion by means of the unbalanced electric field and diffusiophoretic flow. More recent electrolyte self-diffusiophoretic systems employ other reactions, such as dissociation of acids (98), but these newer systems follow essentially the same protocol. Such a protocol can also be extended to design micropumps that drive fluid motion via photogeneration of ions (139) (**Figure 2e**) or dissolution of salts (138).

Nonelectrolyte self-diffusiophoresis. As shown in Equation 6, high electrolyte concentrations suppress electrolyte-driven diffusiophoretic transport, and, as a result, synthetic machines powered by this mechanism cannot operate in media with high ionic strengths. Thus, although the propulsive forces generated by nonelectrolyte diffusiophoresis (based on neutral solute gradients) are generally weaker than those generated by its electrolyte analog, this mechanism remains effective in powering motion at high ionic strength. Pavlick et al. (91) described one such system: The catalysis of norbornene polymerization by a Grubbs catalyst attached to the SiO_2 end of a SiO_2–Au Janus particle resulted in the enhanced diffusivity of Janus spheres. The propulsive force in the system is believed to arise from the asymmetric distribution of monomer molecules on the two sides of the sphere, as monomers are consumed on the catalyst end (SiO_2 end) (see **Figure 2f**). Consumption of the monomer by the Grubbs catalyst attached on the particle surface creates a monomer gradient that leads to a pressure gradient. This gradient in turn powers the motion of the particles (16, 40). The inverse of this polymerization-powered motor system, in which one side of the particle creates more solute molecules than the other, has also been explored (32, 48, 58, 142).

Self-electrophoresis versus electrolyte self-diffusiophoresis. Self-electrophoresis and electrolyte self-diffusiophoresis are two of the most commonly exploited mechanisms for the design of synthetic micromachines and nanomachines. Both mechanisms are based on surface chemical reactions and on the generation of chemical gradients and local electric fields. The differences between the two mechanisms and the associated systems can be summarized as follows. Electric fields generated by self-electrophoretic motors are more localized and do not extend as far as those generated by electrolyte self-diffusiophoretic systems. As a result, interactions between the self-electrophoretic motors are short range, leading to only the assembly of doublets or triplets, whereas electrolyte self-diffusiophoretic interactions can lead to the formation of collective patterns such as schools. In addition, interactions between self-electrophoretic motors are anisotropic and are highly influenced by the relative positions and/or orientations of the motors. Electrolyte self-diffusiophoretic motors, in contrast, can emit and receive chemical signals in an isotropic manner. Lastly, formation of electric fields requires self-electrophoretic systems to be conductive (67), which is not necessary for their electrolyte self-diffusiophoretic counterparts.

Other mechanisms. Bubble propulsion is another mechanism that can power motion at high ionic strengths. In this mechanism, oxygen or hydrogen microbubbles are generated via H_2O_2 decomposition or reduction of water. When bubbles detach from the motors, the associated recoil force pushes the motors in the opposite direction (35, 39, 83, 119).

Many other important propulsion mechanisms exist in addition to those discussed in the preceding subsections. These include mechanisms based on self-generated gradients, such as self-acoustophoresis and self-thermophoresis, as well as mechanisms that follow the gradients generated by external fields including, for example, electric and magnetic fields. We present specific examples of and elaborate further on these mechanisms in the subsection titled "Enzyme Motors and Pumps" and the section "Artificial Motors and Pumps for Biomedical Applications." A few review articles touch upon these topics and are recommended for interested readers (25, 42, 78, 84).

Emergent Collective Behavior

Communication and cooperation between individual agents are commonly observed in natural systems, and the subsequent self-organization of these agents can lead to the emergence of biological phenomena such as locust swarms, flocking birds, and ant colonies. The transition from individual to collective behavior arises from the interactions of units in response to the changes in their local environment. These emergent systems are inspirations for the design of micromachines or nanomachines that can communicate and cooperate with each other to achieve potential applications in the fields of drug delivery, particle assembly, and chemical sensing (4, 18, 31, 44, 55, 56, 74, 85, 89, 103, 122, 127).

Chemotaxis. Micromotors and nanomotors that are powered by chemical gradients can move preferentially in a direction defined by an externally applied chemical gradient, a phenomenon known as chemotaxis. Chemotaxis has long been observed in biological systems (8), and it has also been observed recently in synthetic systems and in enzymes in vitro (5, 46, 91, 106), although the mechanism in the latter systems is not as well-understood. When Pt–Au nanorods are placed in a gradient of H_2O_2, they gradually diffuse to the source of the chemical, using a combination of active and stochastic diffusion (see **Figure 3a**) (46). A similar behavior was also discovered in the polymerization motor system discussed in subsection titled "Nonelectrolyte self-diffusiophoresis" (91), as well as in bubble-propelled catalytic microengines (5). Hong et al. (46) have proposed that catalytic motors preferentially diffuse up fuel concentration gradients to regions with higher diffusivities, and a similar mechanism has recently been described by Saha et al. (101).

Self-assembly and collective patterns. Similar to many natural systems, synthetic micromotors and nanomotors respond to externally generated chemical gradients and interact to form assemblies or collective patterns. For example, self-propelling bimetallic nanomotors that are moving in the same directions can attract each other to form doublets or even triplets (131). In addition, many collective micromotor systems have been designed based on the electrolyte self-diffusiophoresis mechanism. For example, AgCl micromotors can interact with each other when the particle concentration is increased (105) and can cluster to form so-called schools that resemble the behavior of flocking birds and schooling fishes (49). A predator–prey behavior is observed when negatively charged passive SiO_2 particles are added to this system, as the SiO_2 particles also respond to ion gradients generated by the active AgCl particles (**Figure 3b**). Micromotor systems that show interactions over long distances can be designed by incorporating other chemical reactions. For example, researchers have observed spatiotemporal oscillation patterns among AgCl and SiO_2 particles under UV light in H_2O_2 solution (50). In addition, coupling different reactions may result in transitions between two collective behavior patterns: Duan et al. (22) reported that silver orthophosphate microparticles (Ag_3PO_4) in aqueous media show transitions between "exclusion" and "schooling" behaviors, which are triggered either by shifts in the chemical equilibrium (via addition or removal of ammonia) or in response to UV light (**Figure 3c**). Because each different combination of two inputs (ammonia and UV) results in one of two outputs (schooling and exclusion), one can design a NOR logic gate, opening up a new avenue for computations using synthetic nanomachines and micromachines.

Enzyme Motors and Pumps

Recent studies have shown that most active enzymes can harvest energy from substrate turnover to generate mechanical force. This force powers the movement of the enzymes themselves and that of nearby particles, as well as the pumping of the surrounding fluid.

Enzyme motors. It has been demonstrated that similar to other chemically driven motors, enzymes are able to power their own motion by turnover of their respective substrates (10, 106). This ability is manifested in the form of substrate-dependent enhancement in diffusivity, as measured at the single-molecule level using fluorescence correlation spectroscopy (FCS). The observed diffusion enhancement disappears upon the addition of an inhibitor. The precise mechanism for turnover-induced enhanced diffusivity remains to be established, although several mechanistic possibilities have been suggested. In one proposal, enzymes in solution propel themselves during substrate turnover by undergoing a sequence of nonreciprocal conformational changes during the substrate-binding and product-release steps (102). Alternatively, Colberg & Kapral (15) have suggested that molecular-scale catalysts can propel themselves via the production of products that can interact with the catalyst via Lennard-Jones interaction potentials. Spatially asymmetric

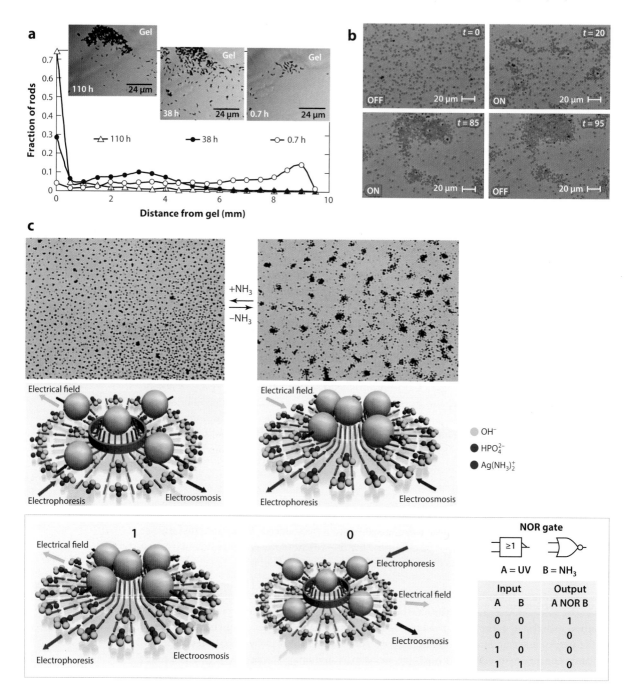

Figure 3

Collective behavior demonstrated by synthetic nanomotors and micromotors. (*a*) Chemotaxis of Au–Pt bimetallic nanomotors toward the source of H_2O_2 fuel (gel in the upper part of each image), depicted as an increase in the number of rods over time. Panel adapted from Reference 46, with permission from the American Physical Society. (*b*) Formation of predator–prey schools of active AgCl micromotors (*black dots*, prey) and inert SiO_2 tracer particles (*gray dots*, predators) under ultraviolet (UV) light. Panel adapted from Reference 49, with permission from John Wiley & Sons. (*c*) Reversible transition between two collective behaviors: Ag_3PO_4 micromotors disperse and cluster reversibly with the addition and removal of ammonia. The transition from dispersion to clustering can be halted by UV irradiation, and the two different responses of the micromotors under these two orthogonal inputs enable the design of a NOR logic gate. Panel adapted from Reference 22, with permission from the American Chemical Society.

catalysis can lead to an inhomogeneous distribution of products. This distribution creates a concentration gradient that can cause propulsion, depending on the features of the products and the solvent (self-diffusiophoresis). Finally, heat generation via reaction exothermicity can also lead to enhanced diffusion. In several instances, however, the bulk rise in solution temperature due to enzymatic catalysis has been estimated and found to be in the micro-Kelvin range; too small to account for the observed enhanced diffusion (106, 109). Nevertheless, a local, instantaneous, reaction-induced rise in temperature cannot be ruled out.

By using Langevin/Brownian dynamics simulations, it was determined that forces of 12 and 9 pN per turnover were sufficient to cause enhanced diffusion of urease and catalase, respectively. These forces are comparable to those produced by myosin, kinesin, and dynein motors (approximately 11 pN) (120) and by other molecular-scale systems (73, 77), and they are within the range needed to activate integrins (128), which are biological adhesion molecules responsible for mechanosensation by cells. Thus, force production by enzyme catalysis is a potentially novel and mechanobiology-relevant event.

In the presence of a gradient in substrate concentration, the enzyme molecules migrate toward regions with higher substrate concentrations—a form of molecular chemotaxis (106). It has been hypothesized (106, 109) that the chemotactic behavior of the enzyme molecules arises from the enhanced diffusion mechanism because the substrate concentration changes continuously as the enzyme diffuses along the gradient. Thus, at every point in space, the diffusion rate increases on moving up the gradient and decreases on moving down the gradient. A higher diffusion coefficient leads to greater spreading of the enzyme molecules in areas with high substrate concentrations, so the center of gravity of the enzyme ensemble moves toward higher substrate concentrations. As with any nonequilibrium system, continuous energy input is required for directional movement; in this case, energy input is needed to maintain the substrate gradient. The proposed mechanism is stochastic in nature and differs from biological chemotaxis, which requires temporal memory of the concentration gradient. The experimental findings on chemotaxis are supported by a finite-element simulation of the convection–diffusion equation in which the relationship between the enzyme diffusion coefficient and the substrate concentration was determined by FCS and was input into the simulation as a substrate concentration–dependent diffusion coefficient (106).

The observed chemotactic behavior of single enzymes suggests that when an enzyme acts on the products of a second enzymatic reaction nearby, the acting enzyme molecules might exhibit collective movement up the substrate gradient toward this second enzyme. This is an example of collective behavior at the molecular level. For example, catalase was observed to migrate toward glucose oxidase in the presence of glucose because H_2O_2 is a product in glucose oxidation (106).

The chemotactic migration of active enzymes toward areas of higher substrate concentration was utilized to separate enzymes from one another in a microfluidic device (19, 106). If one places a mixture of two enzymes in one channel and places the substrate for only one of them in the other channel, the catalytically active biomolecules can be isolated from the corresponding inactive (or less active) ones. The procedure allows enzyme molecules of similar sizes and isoelectric points to be separated, and such separation is unprecedented in the literature. In principle, chemotactic separation can also be used to separate other active catalysts from their less-active or inactive counterparts in the presence of their respective substrates, so this technique should find wide applicability.

Enzyme pumps. Surface-anchored enzymes transfer their chemically generated force to the surrounding fluid; in effect, immobilized enzyme systems can be used as micropumps in the presence of enzyme-specific substrates (108). Thus, enzymes transduce chemical energy from substrate turnover into fluid motion. This discovery enables the design of nonmechanical self-powered enzyme-based devices that act as both sensor and pump, precisely controlling the flow rate and turning on and off in response to specific analytes. Most enzyme pumps that have been studied so far (glucose oxidase, catalase, lipase, DNA polymerase) catalyze exothermic reactions and therefore pump fluid and tracer particles inward along the bottom surface of a microchannel using thermal gradients (**Figure 4**). Urease (which hydrolyzes urea to bicarbonate and ammonium ions) increases the solution density, however, and thus pumps fluid outward. These experiments establish two important concepts: (*a*) Essentially all surface-anchored enzymes act as pumps during substrate turnover, and (*b*) these pumps are selective for the substrate or promoter of the particular enzyme.

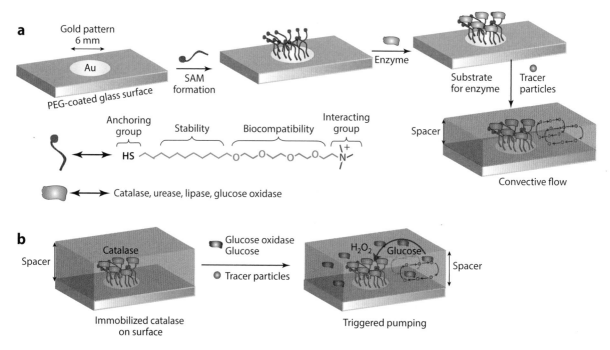

Figure 4

Schematic depiction of the fabrication and functioning of enzymatic micropumps. (*a*) Au patterned on a polyethylene glycol (PEG)-coated glass surface is functionalized with a quaternary ammonium thiol, which electrostatically binds to the negatively charged groups on the enzyme. Triggered fluid pumping is initiated by introducing the enzyme-specific substrate. (*b*) Cascading fluid pumping is observed when the enzyme catalase is actuated by production of its substrate in situ by the enzyme glucose oxidase and its substrate glucose, enabling microfluidic regulation and logic. Abbreviations: HS, thiol; SAM, self-assembled monolayer.

Like the diffusivity of freely swimming enzymes, the pumping velocity of the enzyme pumps increases with increasing substrate concentration and reaction rate. Similar pumping can also occur in gel particles in which the enzymes are immobilized. For example, bound glucose oxidase pumps insulin out of gel particles when glucose is added to the surrounding solution (108).

ARTIFICIAL MOTORS AND PUMPS FOR BIOMEDICAL APPLICATIONS

Inspired by biological counterparts discussed in the section titled "Inspirations from Nature," several artificial motors have been designed for potential biomedical applications, both in vivo and in vitro. These motors can be classified into four groups on the basis of how they are powered: diffusiophoretic motors, bubble-propelled motors, magnetically driven motors, or acoustically powered motors.

Diffusiophoretic Motors

Autonomous pumps based on ion gradients have been described previously and are of particular interest for orthopedic applications because of the high mineral content of bone. Yadav et al. (137) have reported a micropump-based strategy that utilizes the substrate itself as both the trigger and the fuel. Because this technique does not require an external power supply, it appears to be ideal for targeted drug delivery. Bone is composed of the mineral hydroxyapatite, which undergoes hydrolysis at physiological pH, as described by Equation 7.

$$Ca_{10}(PO_4)_6(OH)_2 + 12H_2O \rightarrow 10Ca^{2+} + 6H_2PO_4^- + 14OH^- \qquad 7.$$

A crack in a bone releases ions into the surrounding solution, and the large difference in diffusion coefficients between the cation (Ca^{2+}) and the faster anion (OH^-) [$D(Ca^{2+}) = 0.789 \times 10^{-5}$ cm^2/s, $D(OH^-) = 5.273 \times 10^{-5}$ cm^2/s, and $D(H_2PO_4^-) = 0.959 \times 10^{-5}$ cm^2/s] induces a local electric field pointed away from the crack in the bone surface (i.e., the ion source). Negatively charged moieties introduced into the system respond to this electric field by undergoing diffusiophoretic transport toward the damage site. Thus, the damaged matrix itself provides both the fuel and the trigger for detection and repair. **Figure 5a** shows how negatively charged quantum dots were used to demonstrate the detection process. In addition, the delivery of a bone growth factor incorporated into a polymeric particle was achieved. This technique provides a mechanism for actively targeting the damage site, in contrast to the traditional mechanism of transporting drugs via passive diffusion.

Bubble-Propelled Motors

Identification, separation, and isolation of target analytes, such as specific proteins, nucleic acids, or other biomarkers, are extremely important in biomedical research. Bubble-propelled motors can sense, capture, and transport biological analytes ranging from molecules to cells via surface modification and functionalization (119). In several publications, Wang and coworkers demonstrated that receptor-modified tubular microengines can selectively isolate a wide range of target bioanalytes, including bacteria (12), DNA molecules (136), and cancer cells (4). For example, catalytic microengines that have an outer surface functionalized with the Concanavalin A (ConA) lectin receptor can recognize and selectively bind to carbohydrate constituents of bacterial surfaces (12). As proof of this concept, these researchers demonstrated that E. coli can be isolated from untreated seawater and drinking water samples (**Figure 5b**). With the help of external magnetic

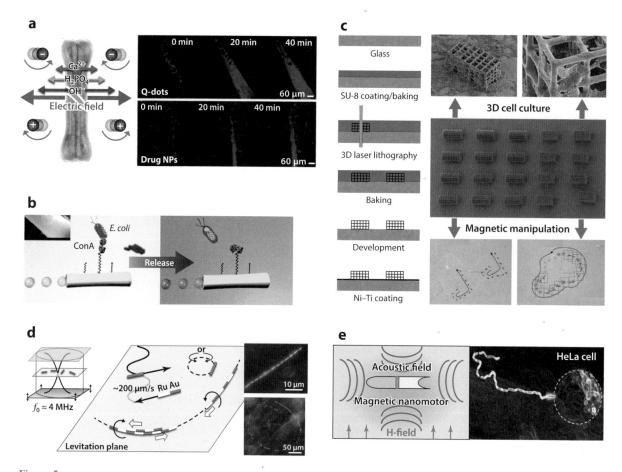

Figure 5

Artificial motors and pumps for biomedical applications. (*a*) Ions that leach from the bone crack induce self-diffusiophoretic flows that lead to the enrichment of negatively charged fluorescent quantum dots (Q-dots) and drug nanoparticles (NPs) at the crack site. Panel adapted from Reference 137, with permission from John Wiley & Sons. (*b*) Isolation of bacteria from seawater or drinking water samples using Concanavalin A (ConA) functionalized catalytic motors. Panel adapted from Reference 12, with permission from the American Chemical Society. (*c*) Fabrication and magnetic manipulation of cage-like micromotors for transportation of cells. Panel adapted from Reference 59, with permission from John Wiley & Sons. (*d*) Propagation and assembly of bimetallic rods under acoustic fields. Panel adapted from Reference 129, with permission from the American Chemical Society. (*e*) Navigation of an acoustically powered motor toward a HeLa cell under magnetic field guidance. Panel adapted from Reference 132, with permission from John Wiley and Sons. Abbreviations: *E. coli, Escherichia coli*.

fields, tubular catalytic microengines can function as concentrating systems (99) and can achieve directional transport and delivery of cells (103).

Bubble-propelled motors can be used to achieve controlled drug release by coating their surfaces with polymeric layers. For example, Mou et al. (82) demonstrated that Mg–Pt Janus motors coated with a thermoresponsive poly(N-isopropylacrylamide) (PNIPAM) hydrogel layer released drug molecules in response to a temperature change. Despite these potential applications, in vivo applications of bubble-propelled motors are hindered by electrolyte- and blood plasma–induced attenuation of their motility, as Pumera and colleagues reported (126, 144).

Magnetically Driven Motors

A problem for bubble-propelled motors is their general lack of directionality, owing to Brownian randomization at longer timescales. One way to overcome this problem is to introduce magnetic components into the motors. Although such motors are still powered by chemical fuels, they are also subject to guidance by external magnetic fields.

Another method is to simply replace the power source with external magnetic fields. Motors powered by external magnetic fields, when actuated, can be employed both in vitro and in vivo (94). Nelson and colleagues (30, 59, 81) reported several examples of cell transportation and drug delivery by artificial flagella using this technique. Cell transportation was accomplished by fabricating cage-like micromotors and allowing cells to grow inside them (see **Figure 5c**). These motors were subsequently activated and propelled using an external rotating magnetic field (59). Drug delivery was accomplished using motor surfaces that were modified with drug-loaded chitosan or with liposomes (30, 81); these motors then migrated toward targets and released drugs.

Nelson and colleagues also reported wireless manipulation of micromotors inside eye cavity via the OctoMag electromagnetic control system (65, 76). The OctoMag can control motors in three dimensions, and it has a workspace of ~20 × 20 × 20 mm that covers the posterior segment of a human eye. Micromotors are injected into eyes using a 23G needle syringe, and, once inside, they are powered and manipulated with magnetic fields.

Acoustically Powered Motors

Low-power acoustic waves are safe and used extensively for in vivo imaging; thus, these waves are useful for powering motors. In an acoustic field, suspended microparticles experience acoustic radiation forces, which are strongest when standing waves are formed under acoustic excitation.

A recent work by Wang et al. (130) described a MHz-frequency ultrasound-powered autonomous micromotor system. In their system, bimetallic microrods are suspended in water and levitated to a plane at the midpoint of the cell by a vertical standing wave (**Figure 5d**). In the plane, the rods exhibit axial propulsion at speeds as high as 200 μm/s (~100 body lengths per second). These bimetallic rods also form patterns in the nodal plane. Motion of the motors is significantly affected by their composition, as only metallic rods show fast axial motion; polymeric rods do not.

The exact propulsion mechanism is not completely understood, but self-acoustophoresis has been suggested as a possibility. Acoustic motors, under the guidance of magnetic fields, can be steered to capture and transport various bioanalytes, such as cells (**Figure 5e**) (2). Wang and colleagues (132) also reported the motion of acoustic motors inside living HeLa cells. This report is the first example of artificial motors inside living cells. The motors attach strongly to the external surfaces of the cells, and they are readily internalized after incubation for periods of at least 24 h. These motors are actuated at 4 MHz, and they exhibit axial propulsion and spinning while the cells remain viable. Such systems can provide a new tool for probing the response of living cells to internal mechanical excitation and for related biomedical applications.

CONCLUSION

Challenges to the large-scale use of synthetic motors in biological systems include developing effective fabrication and optimal actuation mechanisms, precise control over motion, and biocompatibility. Synthetic motors, which are discussed in this review, can be divided roughly into two groups: motors that are powered externally by, for example, electric, magnetic, or acoustic fields, and motors that are powered by self-generated gradients, for example, those powered by self-electrophoresis and self-diffusiophoresis. In the former group, the external field is applied from a macroscopic source, and all of the motors are subject to similar forces and migrate along the projected field lines. Such external control is a desired functionality for directed navigation. In comparison, motors that are powered by self-generated gradients are autonomous, in that each motor makes its own decision on the basis of its local environment. This ability to respond to an environment and to move autonomously grants versatility, and it is the foundation of collective behaviors such as swarming and schooling, which indicate intermotor communication. In addition it is beneficial to have motors that can independently carry out operations such as sensing and reporting, where different populations of interacting motors perform different tasks. Because the two kinds of motors have their own advantages, combining both propulsion methods in one single motor system would be desirable. Such a system would include motors that are orthogonally powered by external fields and self-generated gradients: The former can guide the directed migration to desired sites, and the latter enable communication and cooperation between motors.

Despite the reported progress in the design of synthetic motors, they cannot carry out complex tasks in the same manner as their biological counterparts. More integrated functionalities (69) and better division of labor are two key elements future designs of synthetic motors should consider. The ultimate goal in the emerging area of synthetic motors and pumps is to create functional building blocks that have the following attributes: (*a*) mobility resulting from biomimetic energy harvested from the local environment, (*b*) rapid and reversible assembly capabilities provided by emergent self-assembly, (*c*) the intelligence and communication capabilities seen in interacting microorganisms, and (*d*) the ability to perform specific tasks in response to signals from each other and from the environment.

The observation that enzymes such as urease, catalase, lipase, DNA polymerase, and others undergo powered movement and pump fluids while catalyzing substrate turnover amends the paradigm that ATP-powered biomotors are a special class of enzymes. This observation clearly suggests that (*a*) single-enzyme molecules generate sufficient mechanical force via substrate turnover to cause their own movement and that of the surrounding particles and fluid, and (*b*) the movement becomes directional when a gradient in substrate concentration is imposed. Indeed, other than the presence of so-called tracks that provide directionality, there may not be a significant difference between traditional motor proteins and free-swimming enzymes. In addition, it will be interesting to examine the role played by membrane-bound enzymes in cell membrane fluctuations. The results described open up a new area of mechanobiology: intrinsic force generation by non-ATP-dependent enzymes and their role in the biochemical regulation of cell function. These enzymes, as well as nontraditional ATP-dependent enzymes, can provide sufficient force for the stochastic motion of the cytoplasm and for the convective transport of fluid in cells (43). Further, they may be responsible for the observed glass-to-fluid transition that occurs in active bacterial cells (88).

SUMMARY POINTS

1. Nature displays efficient forms of biological motors and pumps that serve as inspirations for the design of both self-powered synthetic nanomotors and micromotors and pumps.

2. As the size of an object scales down, surface forces such as viscosity dominate over volume forces such as inertia. This shift in force dominance is characteristic of the low-Re regime.

3. Synthetic motors and pumps are powered by various propulsion mechanisms, such as electrophoresis, electrolyte and nonelectrolyte diffusiophoresis, and acoustophoresis.

4. Similar to many natural systems, the synthetic micromotors and nanomotors respond to chemical gradients generated by each other to form assemblies or collective patterns.

5. Non-ATP-powered enzymes generate sufficient mechanical force via substrate turnover to cause their own movement and that of the surrounding particles and fluid. The movement becomes directional through the imposition of a substrate gradient.

6. Surface-anchored enzymes transfer their chemically generated force to the surrounding fluid, in effect functioning as micropumps in the presence of their respective substrates.

7. Self-powered nanomotors and micromotors have many potential applications including the capture, transport, and concentration of bioanalytes, as well as the targeted delivery of drugs and antidotes in response to the presence of specific biomarkers.

DISCLOSURE STATEMENT

The authors are not aware of any affiliations, memberships, funding, or financial holdings that might be perceived as affecting the objectivity of this review.

ACKNOWLEDGMENTS

We gratefully acknowledge financial support from The Pennsylvania State University Materials Research Science and Engineering Center under National Science Foundation grant DMR-1420620 and supported in part by the Defense Threat Reduction Agency (HDTRA1-13-1-0039).

LITERATURE CITED

1. Abid J-P, Frigoli M, Pansu R, Szeftel J, Zyss J, et al. 2011. Light-driven directed motion of azobenzene-coated polymer nanoparticles in an aqueous medium. *Langmuir* 27:7967–71

2. Ahmed S, Wang W, Mair LO, Fraleigh RD, Li S, et al. 2013. Steering acoustically propelled nanowire motors toward cells in a biologically compatible environment using magnetic fields. *Langmuir* 29:16113–18

3. Anderson JL. 1989. Colloid transport by interfacial forces. *Annu. Rev. Fluid Mech.* 21:61–99

4. Balasubramanian S, Kagan D, Jack Hu C-M, Campuzano S, Lobo-Castañon MJ, et al. 2011. Micromachine-enabled capture and isolation of cancer cells in complex media. *Angew. Chem. Int. Ed.* 50:4161–64

5. Baraban L, Harazim SM, Sanchez S, Schmidt OG. 2013. Chemotactic behavior of catalytic motors in microfluidic channels. *Angew. Chem. Int. Ed.* 52:5552–56

6. Baraban L, Streubel R, Makarov D, Han L, Karnaushenko D, et al. 2012. Fuel-free locomotion of Janus motors: magnetically induced thermophoresis. *ACS Nano* 7:1360–67

7. Baykov AA, Malinen AM, Luoto HH, Lahti R. 2013. Pyrophosphate-fueled Na^+ and H^+ transport in prokaryotes. *Microbiol. Mol. Biol. Rev.* 77:267–76

8. Berg HC, Brown DA. 1972. Chemotaxis in *Escherichia coli* analysed by three-dimensional tracking. *Nature* 239:500–4

9. Brennen C, Winet H. 1977. Fluid mechanics of propulsion by cilia and flagella. *Annu. Rev. Fluid Mech.* 9:339–98

10. Butler PJ, Dey KK, Sen A. 2015. Impulsive enzymes: a new force in mechanobiology. *Cell. Molec. Bioeng.* 8:106–18

11. Calvo-Marzal P, Sattayasamitsathit S, Balasubramanian S, Windmiller JR, Dao C, Wang J. 2010. Propulsion of nanowire diodes. *Chem. Commun.* 46:1623–24

12. Campuzano S, Orozco J, Kagan D, Guix M, Gao W, et al. 2011. Bacterial isolation by lectin-modified microengines. *Nano Lett.* 12:396–401

13. Chang ST, Paunov VN, Petsev DN, Velev OD. 2007. Remotely powered self-propelling particles and micropumps based on miniature diodes. *Nat. Mater.* 6:235–40

14. Cleveland LR, Cleveland BT. 1966. The locomotory waves of *Koruga*, *Deltotrichonympha* and *Mixotricha*. *Arch. Protistenk* 109:39–63

15. Colberg PH, Kapral R. 2014. Angström-scale chemically powered motors. *Europhys. Lett.* 106:30004

16. Córdova-Figueroa UM, Brady JF. 2008. Osmotic propulsion: the osmotic motor. *Phys. Rev. Lett.* 100:158303

17. Dean RB. 1941. Theories of electrolyte equilibrium in muscle. *Biol. Symp.* 3:331–48

18. Detrain C, Deneubourg J-L. 2006. Self-organized structures in a superorganism: Do ants "behave" like molecules? *Phys. Life Rev.* 3:162–87

19. Dey KK, Das S, Poyton MF, Sengupta S, Butler PJ, et al. 2014. Chemotactic separation of enzymes. *ACS Nano* 8:11941–49

20. Dreyfus R, Baudry J, Roper ML, Fermigier M, Stone HA, Bibette J. 2005. Microscopic artificial swimmers. *Nature* 437:862–65

21. Duan W, Ibele M, Liu R, Sen A. 2012. Motion analysis of light-powered autonomous silver chloride nanomotors. *Eur. Phys. J. E* 35:77–84

22. Duan W, Liu R, Sen A. 2013. Transition between collective behaviors of micromotors in response to different stimuli. *J. Am. Chem. Soc.* 135:1280–83

23. Dubyak GR. 2004. Ion homeostasis, channels, and transporters: an update on cellular mechanisms. *Adv. Physiol. Educ.* 28:143–54

24. Dunderdale G, Ebbens S, Fairclough P, Howse J. 2012. Importance of particle tracking and calculating the mean-squared displacement in distinguishing nanopropulsion from other processes. *Langmuir* 28:10997–1006

25. Fischer P, Ghosh A. 2011. Magnetically actuated propulsion at low Reynolds numbers: towards nanoscale control. *Nanoscale* 3:557–63

26. Fournier-Bidoz S, Arsenault AC, Manners I, Ozin GA. 2005. Synthetic self-propelled nanorotors. *Chem. Commun.* 41:441–43

27. Fox DL, Coe WR. 1943. Biology of the California sea-mussel (*Mytilus californianus*). II. Nutrition, metabolism, growth and calcium deposition. *J. Exp. Zool.* 93:205–49

28. Fraser PJ, Shelmerdine RL. 2002. Dogfish hair cells sense hydrostatic pressure. *Nature* 415:495–96

29. Fratzl P, Barth FG. 2009. Biomaterial systems for mechanosensing and actuation. *Nature* 462:442–48

30. Fusco S, Chatzipirpiridis G, Sivaraman KM, Ergeneman O, Nelson BJ, Pané S. 2013. Chitosan electrodeposition for microrobotic drug delivery. *Adv. Healthcare Mater.* 2:1037–44

31. Gangwal S, Pawar A, Kretzschmar I, Velev OD. 2010. Programmed assembly of metallodielectric patchy particles in external AC electric fields. *Soft Matter* 6:1413–18

32. Gao W, Pei A, Dong R, Wang J. 2014. Catalytic iridium-based Janus micromotors powered by ultralow levels of chemical fuels. *J. Am. Chem. Soc.* 136:2276–79

33. Gao W, Sattayasamitsathit S, Manesh KM, Weihs D, Wang J. 2010. Magnetically powered flexible metal nanowire motors. *J. Am. Chem. Soc.* 132:14403–5

34. Gao W, Sattayasamitsathit S, Orozco J, Wang J. 2011. Highly efficient catalytic microengines: template electrosynthesis of polyaniline/platinum microtubes. *J. Am. Chem. Soc.* 133:11862–64

35. Garcia-Gradilla V, Orozco J, Sattayasamitsathit S, Soto F, Kuralay F, et al. 2013. Functionalized ultrasound-propelled magnetically guided nanomotors: toward practical biomedical applications. *ACS Nano* 7:9232–40

36. Ghosh A, Fischer P. 2009. Controlled propulsion of artificial magnetic nanostructured propellers. *Nano Lett.* 9:2243–45

37. Gibbons IR. 1981. Cilia and flagella of eukaryotes. *J. Cell Biol.* 91:107–24

38. Gibbs JG, Fragnito NA, Zhao Y. 2010. Asymmetric Pt/Au coated catalytic micromotors fabricated by dynamic shadowing growth. *Appl. Phys. Lett.* 97:253107

39. Gibbs JG, Zhao Y-P. 2009. Autonomously motile catalytic nanomotors by bubble propulsion. *Appl. Phys. Lett.* 94:163104

40. Golestanian R. 2009. Anomalous diffusion of symmetric and asymmetric active colloids. *Phys. Rev. Lett.* 102:188305

41. Golestanian R, Liverpool TB, Ajdari A. 2005. Propulsion of a molecular machine by asymmetric distribution of reaction products. *Phys. Rev. Lett.* 94:220801

42. Guix M, Mayorga-Martinez CC, Merkoçi A. 2014. Nano/micromotors in (bio)chemical science applications. *Chem. Rev.* 114:6285–322

43. Guo M, Ehrlicher AJ, Jensen MH, Renz M, Moore JR, et al. 2014. Probing the stochastic, motor-driven properties of the cytoplasm using force spectrum microscopy. *Cell* 158:822–32

44. Gupta S, Alargova RG, Kilpatrick PK, Velev OD. 2009. On-chip dielectrophoretic coassembly of live cells and particles into responsive biomaterials. *Langmuir* 26:3441–52

45. Hand WG, Haupt W. 1971. Flagellar activity of the colony members of *Volvox aureus* Ehrbg. during light stimulation. *J. Protozool.* 18:361–64

46. Hong Y, Blackman NMK, Kopp ND, Sen A, Velegol D. 2007. Chemotaxis of nonbiological colloidal rods. *Phys. Rev. Lett.* 99:178103

47. Hong Y, Diaz M, Córdova-Figueroa UM, Sen A. 2010. Light-driven titanium-dioxide-based reversible microfireworks and micromotor/micropump systems. *Adv. Funct. Mater.* 20:1568–76

48. Howse JR, Jones RAL, Ryan AJ, Gough T, Vafabakhsh R, Golestanian R. 2007. Self-motile colloidal particles: from directed propulsion to random walk. *Phys. Rev. Lett.* 99:048102

49. Ibele M, Mallouk TE, Sen A. 2009. Schooling behavior of light-powered autonomous micromotors in water. *Angew. Chem. Int. Ed.* 48:3308–12

50. Ibele ME, Lammert PE, Crespi VH, Sen A. 2010. Emergent, collective oscillations of self-mobile particles and patterned surfaces under redox conditions. *ACS Nano* 4:4845–51

51. Ibele ME, Wang Y, Kline TR, Mallouk TE, Sen A. 2007. Hydrazine fuels for bimetallic catalytic microfluidic pumping. *J. Am. Chem. Soc.* 129:7762–63

52. Jiang HR, Yoshinaga N, Sano M. 2010. Active motion of a Janus particle by self-thermophoresis in a defocused laser beam. *Phys. Rev. Lett.* 105:268302

53. Jun I-K, Hess H. 2010. A biomimetic, self-pumping membrane. *Adv. Mater.* 22:4823–25

54. Kagan D, Benchimol MJ, Claussen JC, Chuluun-Erdene E, Esener S, Wang J. 2012. Acoustic droplet vaporization and propulsion of perfluorocarbon-loaded microbullets for targeted tissue penetration and deformation. *Angew. Chem. Int. Ed.* 51:7519–22

55. Kagan D, Campuzano S, Balasubramanian S, Kuralay F, Flechsig G-U, Wang J. 2011. Functionalized micromachines for selective and rapid isolation of nucleic acid targets from complex samples. *Nano Lett.* 11:2083–87

56. Kagan D, Laocharoensuk R, Zimmerman M, Clawson C, Balasubramanian S, et al. 2010. Rapid delivery of drug carriers propelled and navigated by catalytic nanoshuttles. *Small* 6:2741–47

57. Kardon JR, Vale RD. 2009. Regulators of the cytoplasmic dynein motor. *Nat. Rev. Mol. Cell Biol.* 10:854–65

58. Ke H, Ye S, Carroll RL, Showalter K. 2010. Motion analysis of self-propelled Pt–Silica particles in hydrogen peroxide solutions. *J. Phys. Chem. A* 114:5462–67

59. Kim S, Qiu F, Kim S, Ghanbari A, Moon C, et al. 2013. Fabrication and characterization of magnetic microrobots for three-dimensional cell culture and targeted transportation. *Adv. Mater.* 25:5863–68

60. Kline TR, Iwata J, Lammert PE, Mallouk TE, Sen A, Velegol D. 2006. Catalytically driven colloidal patterning and transport. *J. Phys. Chem. B* 110:24513–21

61. Kline TR, Paxton WF, Mallouk TE, Sen A. 2005. Catalytic nanomotors: remote-controlled autonomous movement of striped metallic nanorods. *Angew. Chem.* 117:754–56

62. Kline TR, Paxton WF, Wang Y, Velegol D, Mallouk TE, Sen A. 2005. Catalytic micropumps: microscopic convective fluid flow and pattern formation. *J. Am. Chem. Soc.* 127:17150–51

63. Kline TR, Sen A. 2006. Reversible pattern formation through photolysis. *Langmuir* 22:7124–27

64. Kocherginsky N. 2009. Acidic lipids, H^+-ATPases, and mechanism of oxidative phosphorylation. Physico-chemical ideas 30 years after P. Mitchell's Nobel Prize award. *Prog. Biophys. Mol. Biol.* 99:20–41

65. Kummer MP, Abbott JJ, Kratochvil BE, Borer R, Sengul A, Nelson BJ. 2010. OctoMag: an electromagnetic system for 5-DOF wireless micromanipulation. *IEEE Trans. Robot.* 26:1006–17

66. Kwak MK, Jeong H-E, Kim T-I, Yoon H, Suh KY. 2010. Bio-inspired slanted polymer nanohairs for anisotropic wetting and directional dry adhesion. *Soft Matter* 6:1849–57

67. Laocharoensuk R, Burdick J, Wang J. 2008. Carbon-nanotube-induced acceleration of catalytic nanomotors. *ACS Nano* 2:1069–75

68. Lauga E. 2011. Enhanced diffusion by reciprocal swimming. *Phys. Rev. Lett.* 106:178101

69. Liu M, Liu L, Gao W, Su M, Ge Y, et al. 2014. A micromotor based on polymer single crystals and nanoparticles: toward functional versatility. *Nanoscale* 6:8601–5

70. Liu M, Zentgraf T, Liu Y, Bartal G, Zhang X. 2010. Light-driven nanoscale plasmonic motors. *Nat. Nanotechnol.* 5:570–73

71. Liu R, Sen A. 2011. Autonomous nanomotor based on copper–platinum segmented nanobattery. *J. Am. Chem. Soc.* 133:20064–67

72. Loget G, Kuhn A. 2010. Propulsion of microobjects by dynamic bipolar self-regeneration. *J. Am. Chem. Soc.* 132:15918–19

73. Mahadevan L, Matsudaira P. 2000. Motility powered by supramolecular springs and ratchets. *Science* 288:95–100

74. Manesh KM, Balasubramanian S, Wang J. 2010. Nanomotor-based 'writing' of surface microstructures. *Chem. Commun.* 46:5704–6

75. Mano N, Heller A. 2005. Bioelectrochemical propulsion. *J. Am. Chem. Soc.* 127:11574–75

76. Marino H, Bergeles C, Nelson BJ. 2014. Robust electromagnetic control of microrobots under force and localization uncertainties. *IEEE Trans. Automat. Sci. Eng.* 11:310–16

77. Mehta AD, Rief M, Spudich JA, Smith DA, Simmons RM. 1999. Single-molecule biomechanics with optical methods. *Science* 283:1689–95

78. Mei Y, Solovev AA, Sanchez S, Schmidt OG. 2011. Rolled-up nanotech on polymers: from basic perception to self-propelled catalytic microengines. *Chem. Soc. Rev.* 40:2109–19

79. Metzler R, Jeon J-H, Cherstvy AG, Barkai E. 2014. Anomalous diffusion models and their properties: non-stationarity, non-ergodicity, and ageing at the centenary of single particle tracking. *Phys. Chem. Chem. Phys.* 16:24128–64

80. Metzler R, Klafter J. 2000. The random walk's guide to anomalous diffusion: a fractional dynamics approach. *Phys. Rep.* 339:1–77

81. Mhanna R, Qiu F, Zhang L, Ding Y, Sugihara K, et al. 2014. Artificial bacterial flagella for remote-controlled targeted single-cell drug delivery. *Small* 10:1953–57

82. Mou F, Chen C, Zhong Q, Yin Y, Ma H-R, Guan J. 2014. Autonomous motion and temperature-controlled drug delivery of Mg/Pt-poly(N-isopropylacrylamide) Janus micromotors driven by simulated body fluid and blood plasma. *ACS Appl. Mater. Interfaces* 6:9897–903

83. Orozco J, Campuzano S, Kagan D, Zhou M, Gao W, Wang J. 2011. Dynamic isolation and unloading of target proteins by aptamer-modified microtransporters. *Anal. Chem.* 83:7962–69

84. Pak OS, Gao W, Wang J, Lauga E. 2011. High-speed propulsion of flexible nanowire motors: theory and experiments. *Soft Matter* 7:8169–81

85. Palacci J, Sacanna S, Steinberg AP, Pine DJ, Chaikin PM. 2013. Living crystals of light-activated colloidal surfers. *Science* 339:936–40

86. Palacci J, Sacanna S, Vatchinsky A, Chaikin PM, Pine DJ. 2013. Photoactivated colloidal dockers for cargo transportation. *J. Am. Chem. Soc.* 135:15978–81

87. Pantarotto D, Browne WR, Feringa BL. 2008. Autonomous propulsion of carbon nanotubes powered by a multienzyme ensemble. *Chem. Commun.* 2008:1533–35

88. Parry BR, Surovtsev IV, Cabeen MT, O'Hern CS, Dufresne ER, Jacobs-Wagner C. 2014. The bacterial cytoplasm has glass-like properties and is fluidized by metabolic activity. *Cell* 156:183–94

89. Patra D, Sengupta S, Duan W, Zhang H, Pavlick R, Sen A. 2013. Intelligent, self-powered, drug delivery systems. *Nanoscale* 5:1273–83

90. Patra D, Zhang H, Sengupta S, Sen A. 2013. Dual stimuli-responsive, rechargeable micropumps via "host–guest" interactions. *ACS Nano* 7:7674–79

91. Pavlick RA, Sengupta S, McFadden T, Zhang H, Sen A. 2011. A polymerization-powered motor. *Angew. Chem. Int. Ed.* 50:9374–77

92. Paxton WF, Baker PT, Kline TR, Wang Y, Mallouk TE, Sen A. 2006. Catalytically induced electrokinetics for motors and micropumps. *J. Am. Chem. Soc.* 128:14881–88

93. Paxton WF, Kistler KC, Olmeda CC, Sen A, St Angelo SK, et al. 2004. Catalytic nanomotors: autonomous movement of striped nanorods. *J. Am. Chem. Soc.* 126:13424–31

94. Peyer KE, Zhang L, Nelson BJ. 2013. Bio-inspired magnetic swimming microrobots for biomedical applications. *Nanoscale* 5:1259–72

95. Pokroy B, Epstein AK, Persson-Gulda MCM, Aizenberg J. 2009. Fabrication of bioinspired actuated nanostructures with arbitrary geometry and stiffness. *Adv. Mater.* 21:463–69

96. Pusey PN. 2011. Brownian motion goes ballistic. *Science* 332:802–03

97. Qian B, Montiel D, Bregulla A, Cichos F, Yang H. 2013. Harnessing thermal fluctuations for purposeful activities: the manipulation of single micro-swimmers by adaptive photon nudging. *Chem. Sci.* 4:1420–29

98. Reinmüller A, Oğuz EC, Messina R, Löwen H, Schöpe HJ, Palberg T. 2012. Colloidal crystallization in the quasi-two-dimensional induced by electrolyte gradients. *J. Chem. Phys.* 136:164505–10

99. Restrepo-Peréz L, Soler L, Martínez-Cisneros C, Sánchez S, Schmidt OG. 2014. Biofunctionalized self-propelled micromotors as an alternative on-chip concentrating system. *Lab Chip* 14:2914–17

100. Roberts AJ, Kon T, Knight PJ, Sutoh K, Burgess SA. 2013. Functions and mechanics of dynein motor proteins. *Nat. Rev. Molec. Cell Biol.* 14:713–26

101. Saha S, Golestanian R, Ramaswamy S. 2014. Clusters, asters, and collective oscillations in chemotactic colloids. *Phys. Rev. E* 89:062316

102. Sakaue T, Kapral R, Mikhailov AS. 2010. Nanoscale swimmers: hydrodynamic interactions and propulsion of molecular machines. *Eur. Phys. J. B* 75:381–87

103. Sanchez S, Solovev AA, Schulze S, Schmidt OG. 2011. Controlled manipulation of multiple cells using catalytic microbots. *Chem. Commun.* 47:698–700

104. Sanchez T, Welch D, Nicastro D, Dogic Z. 2011. Cilia-like beating of active microtubule bundles. *Science* 333:456–59

105. Sen A, Ibele M, Hong Y, Velegol D. 2009. Chemo and phototactic nano/microbots. *Faraday Discuss.* 143:15–27

106. Sengupta S, Dey KK, Muddana HS, Tabouillot T, Ibele ME, et al. 2013. Enzyme molecules as nanomotors. *J. Am. Chem. Soc.* 135:1406–14

107. Sengupta S, Ibele ME, Sen A. 2012. Fantastic voyage: designing self-powered nanorobots. *Angew. Chem. Int. Ed.* 51:8434–45

108. Sengupta S, Patra D, Rivera IO, Agrawal A, Dey KK, et al. 2014. Self-powered enzyme micropumps. *Nat. Chem.* 6:415–22

109. Sengupta S, Spiering MM, Dey KK, Duan W, Patra D, et al. 2014. DNA polymerase as a molecular motor and pump. *ACS Nano* 8:2410–18

110. Shah AS, Ben-Shahar Y, Moninger TO, Kline JN, Welsh MJ. 2009. Motile cilia of human airway epithelia are chemosensor. *Science* 325:1131–34

111. Shields AR, Fiser BL, Evans BA, Falvo MR, Washburn S, Superfine R. 2010. Biomimetic cilia arrays generate simultaneous pumping and mixing regimes. *PNAS* 107:15670–75

112. Sidorenko A, Krupenkin T, Taylor A, Fratzl P, Aizenberg J. 2007. Reversible switching of hydrogel-actuated nanostructures into complex micropatterns. *Science* 315:487–90

113. Sigrist-Nelson K. 1975. Dipeptide transport in isolated intestinal brush border membrane. *Biochim. Biophys. Acta* 394:220–26

114. Skou JC. 1957. The influence of some cations on an adenosine triphosphatase from peripheral nerves. *Biochim. Biophys. Acta* 23:394–401

115. Skou JC. 1965. Enzymatic basis for active transport of Na^+ and K^+ across cell membrane. *Physiol. Rev.* 45:596–617

116. Sleigh MA, Aiello E. 1972. The movement of water by cilia. *Acta Protozool.* 11:265–77

117. Solomentsev Y, Anderson JL. 1994. Electrophoresis of slender particles. *J. Fluid Mech.* 279:197–215

118. Solovev AA, Mei Y, Bermúdez Ureña E, Huang G, Schmidt OG. 2009. Catalytic microtubular jet engines self-propelled by accumulated gas bubbles. *Small* 5:1688–92

119. Solovev AA, Sanchez S, Pumera M, Mei YF, Schmidt OG. 2010. Magnetic control of tubular catalytic microbots for the transport, assembly, and delivery of micro-objects. *Adv. Funct. Mater.* 20:2430–35

120. Spudich J, Rice SE, Rock RS, Purcell TJ, Warrick HM. 2011. Optical traps to study properties of molecular motors. *Cold Spring Harb. Protoc.* 11:1305–18

121. Stock C, Heureux N, Browne WR, Feringa BL. 2008. Autonomous movement of silica and glass micro-objects based on a catalytic molecular propulsion system. *Chem. Eur. J.* 14:3146–53

122. Sundararajan S, Sengupta S, Ibele ME, Sen A. 2010. Drop-off of colloidal cargo transported by catalytic Pt–Au nanomotors via photochemical stimuli. *Small* 6:1479–82

123. Tottori S, Zhang L, Qiu F, Krawczyk KK, Franco-Obregón A, Nelson BJ. 2012. Magnetic helical micromachines: fabrication, controlled swimming, and cargo transport. *Adv. Mater.* 24:811–16

124. van Oosten CL, Bastiaansen CWM, Broer DJ. 2009. Printed artificial cilia from liquid-crystal network actuators modularly driven by light. *Nat. Mater.* 8:677–82

125. Vilfan M, Potočnik A, Kavčič B, Osterman N, Poberaj I, et al. 2010. Self-assembled artificial cilia. *PNAS* 107:1844–47

126. Wang H, Zhao G, Pumera M. 2013. Blood electrolytes exhibit a strong influence on the mobility of artificial catalytic microengines. *Phys. Chem. Chem. Phys.* 15:17277–80

127. Wang J, Gao W. 2012. Nano/microscale motors: biomedical opportunities and challenges. *ACS Nano* 6:5745–51

128. Wang N, Butler JP, Ingber DE. 1993. Mechanotransduction across the cell surface and through the cytoskeleton. *Science* 260:1124–27

129. Wang W, Castro LA, Hoyos M, Mallouk TE. 2012. Autonomous motion of metallic microrods propelled by ultrasound. *ACS Nano* 6:6122–32

130. Wang W, Duan W, Ahmed S, Mallouk TE, Sen A. 2013. Small power: autonomous nano- and micro-motors propelled by self-generated gradients. *Nano Today* 8:531–54

131. Wang W, Duan W, Sen A, Mallouk TE. 2013. Catalytically powered dynamic assembly of rod-shaped nanomotors and passive tracer particles. *PNAS* 110:17744–49

132. Wang W, Li S, Mair L, Ahmed S, Huang TJ, Mallouk TE. 2014. Acoustic propulsion of nanorod motors inside living cells. *Angew. Chem.* 126:3265–68

133. Wang Y, Gao Y, Wyss H, Anderson P, den Toonder J. 2013. Out of the cleanroom, self-assembled magnetic artificial cilia. *Lab Chip* 13:3360–66

134. Wheat PM, Marine NA, Moran JL, Posner JD. 2010. Rapid fabrication of bimetallic spherical motors. *Langmuir* 26:13052–55

135. Wong T-S, Kang SH, Tang SKY, Smythe EJ, Hatton BD, et al. 2011. Bioinspired self-repairing slippery surfaces with pressure-stable omniphobicity. *Nature* 477:443–47

136. Wu J, Balasubramanian S, Kagan D, Manesh KM, Campuzano S, Wang J. 2010. Motion-based DNA detection using catalytic nanomotors. *Nat. Commun.* 1:36

137. Yadav V, Freedman JD, Grinstaff M, Sen A. 2013. Bone-crack detection, targeting and repair using ion gradients. *Angew. Chem. Int. Ed.* 52:10997–1001

138. Yadav V, Pavlick RA, Meckler SM, Sen A. 2014. Triggered detection and deposition: toward the repair of microcracks. *Chem. Mater.* 26:4647–52

139. Yadav V, Zhang H, Pavlick R, Sen A. 2012. Triggered "on/off" micropumps and colloidal photodiode. *J. Am. Chem. Soc.* 134:15688–91

140. Zhang H, Duan W, Liu L, Sen A. 2013. Depolymerization-powered autonomous motors using biocom-patible fuel. *J. Am. Chem. Soc.* 135:15734–37

141. Zhang H, Duan W, Lu M, Zhao X, Shklyaev S, et al. 2014. Self-powered glucose-responsive micropumps. *ACS Nano* 8:8537–42

142. Zhang H, Yeung K, Robbins JS, Pavlick RA, Wu M, et al. 2012. Self-powered microscale pumps based on analyte-initiated depolymerization reactions. *Angew. Chem. Int. Ed.* 51:2400–4

143. Zhang L, Peyer KE, Nelson BJ. 2010. Artificial bacterial flagella for micromanipulation. *Lab Chip* 10:2203–15

144. Zhao G, Wang H, Khezri B, Webster RD, Pumera M. 2013. Influence of real-world environments on the motion of catalytic bubble-propelled micromotors. *Lab Chip* 13:2937–41

Mechanisms of Autophagy

Nobuo N. Noda[1,2] and Fuyuhiko Inagaki[2,3]

[1]Institute of Microbial Chemistry (BIKAKEN), Tokyo 141-0021, Japan; email: nn@bikaken.or.jp

[2]CREST, Japan Science and Technology Agency, 7, Gobancho, Chiyoda-ku, Tokyo 102-0076, Japan

[3]Faculty of Advanced Life Science, Hokkaido University, Sapporo 001-0021, Japan; email: finagaki@pharm.hokudai.ac.jp

Annu. Rev. Biophys. 2015. 44:101–22

First published online as a Review in Advance on February 26, 2015

The *Annual Review of Biophysics* is online at biophys.annualreviews.org

This article's doi: 10.1146/annurev-biophys-060414-034248

Keywords

Atg1 complex, Atg8-PE, Atg12-Atg5-Atg16 complex, pre-autophagsomal structure, autophagosome formation, structural biology

Abstract

The formation of the autophagosome, a landmark event in autophagy, is accomplished by the concerted actions of Atg proteins. The initial step of starvation-induced autophagy in yeast is the assembly of the Atg1 complex, which, with the help of other Atg groups, recruits Atg conjugation systems and initiates the formation of the autophagosome. In this review, we describe from a structural-biological point of view the structure, interaction, and molecular roles of Atg proteins, especially those in the Atg1 complex and in the Atg conjugation systems.

Contents

INTRODUCTION

Autophagosome:
a double-membrane
organelle that emerges
and sequesters
cytoplasmic
components during
autophagy

Atg:
autophagy-related
proteins

PI3K:
phosphatidylinositol
3-kinase

**Pre-autophagosomal
structure (PAS):** a
perivacuolar structure
observed in yeast to
which most Atg
proteins localize and
generate
autophagosomes

Autophagy is an intracellular degradation system conserved among eukaryotes (74). The landmark event in autophagy is the generation of a double-membrane structure called the autophagosome. When autophagy is induced by starvation, a membrane sac called an isolation membrane appears and expands into an autophagosome. During this process, a portion of the cytoplasm including proteins and organelles is confined to the lumen of the autophagosome, and upon fusion between an autophagosome and a lysosome (or a vacuole in the case of yeast and plants), the inside contents are degraded by lysosomal hydrolases.

Using budding yeast, *Saccharomyces cerevisiae*, researchers have identified many autophagy-related (Atg) proteins that function in autophagy (51, 117, 118). Among these, 18 Atg proteins in six distinct groups help form the autophagosome: the Atg1 complex, the transmembrane protein Atg9, an autophagy-specific phosphatidylinositol 3-kinase (PI3K) complex, the Atg2-Atg18 complex, and the Atg8 and Atg12 conjugation systems (74, 79) (**Figure 1**). These six functional groups are localized to the pre-autophagosomal structure (or phagophore assembly site, PAS) and cooperate to generate autophagosomes (111, 113, 114). A systematic and quantitative analysis using fluorescence microscopy established a hierarchy map of these six groups involved in PAS assembly (113) (**Figure 1**). The most upstream and downstream groups in the map are the Atg1 complex and the Atg8 and Atg12 conjugation systems, respectively, and they are linked to each other through the other three Atg groups (74, 114). Most of these core Atg proteins and their interactions have been conserved evolutionarily, suggesting that the basic mechanism of autophagosome formation is also evolutionarily conserved.

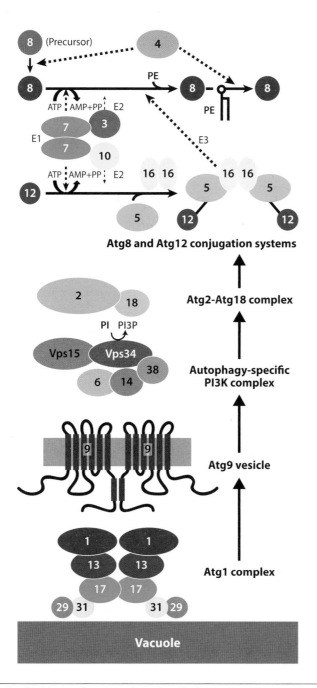

Figure 1

The six Atg groups involved in autophagosome formation. Six Atg groups target a perivacuolar site in a hierarchical manner. Abbreviations: PE, phosphatidylethanolamine; PI3K, phosphatidylinositol 3-kinase; PI3P, phosphatidylinositol 3-phosphate.

KD: kinase domain

IDR: intrinsically disordered region

Many recent reviews on the physiology and cell biology of autophagy (59, 60, 70, 74, 98), as well as on the structural biology of autophagy (33, 52, 84), have been published. In this review, we focus on the core Atg proteins, especially those forming the Atg1 complex and the two Atg conjugation systems, and update from a structural-biological point of view the current understanding of their structure and molecular role in autophagosome formation.

Atg1 COMPLEX: THE INITIATOR OF AUTOPHAGOSOME FORMATION

Formation of the PAS is critical for initiating the formation of the autophagosome (111). Upon starvation, the first step in creating the PAS is the assembly of the Atg1 complex (113). Atg1 is a serine-threonine kinase and its kinase activity is essential for the formation of the autophagosome (43). In *S. cerevisiae*, Atg1 forms a complex with four other Atg proteins, Atg13, Atg17, Atg29, and Atg31, upon starvation (7, 46). The Atg1-Atg13-Atg17-Atg29-Atg31 complex (referred to as the Atg1 complex hereafter) recruits Atg9 and the autophagy-specific PI3K complex, which in turn recruit the Atg2-Atg18 complex and the Atg conjugation systems, and thus complete PAS assembly (113) (**Figure 1**). Formation of the Atg1 complex enhances the kinase activity of Atg1, which is also important for the progress of autophagy (43). The elevated kinase activity itself is not required for recruiting downstream Atg proteins to the PAS, but it is required for cycling the Atg proteins between the PAS and other membrane compartments (97).

Architecture of Atg1

Atg1 can be structurally divided into three regions: an N-terminal kinase domain (KD); a C-terminal globular domain; and an intrinsically disordered region (IDR), which connects the first two (**Figure 2a**). The structure of the Atg1 KD, which has not been determined experimentally, is predicted to belong to a protein kinase superfamily fold owing to the high sequence similarity. Thr226 and Ser230 (residue types and numbers in this review refer to *S. cerevisiae* Atg when not otherwise specified) in the activation loop of the Atg1 KD are autophosphorylation sites and their phosphorylation is critical for both kinase activity and autophagy (48, 128). Yeh et al. (127) proposed a model in which Atg13 induces dimerization of Atg1, which promotes autophosphorylation of Thr226 and thus activates the kinase activity of Atg1. Additional structural studies of the Atg1 KD are needed to validate these models.

X-ray crystallography has determined the structure of the C-terminal domain (CTD) as a complex with the Atg1-binding region of Atg13 (13) (**Figure 2a**). The CTD of Atg1 consists of

→

Figure 2

Structure and phosphoregulation of the Atg1 complex. (*a*) Architecture of Atg1 and its interaction with Atg13. The Atg1^{tMIT}-Atg13^{MIM} complex model was generated using PDB ID 4P1N. All structural models in this article were prepared using the program PyMOL. The IDRs are indicated by curved lines. The inset denotes the region shown in panel *d*. (*b*) Structure of Atg13^{HORMA} and how it compares with Mad2. Structural models for the HORMA domains of Atg13 and Mad2 (closed and open conformations) were generated using PDB IDs 4J2G and 1GO4, respectively. (*c*) Architecture of the Atg17-Atg29-Atg31 complex. The structure of the Atg13^{17BR}-Atg17-Atg29-Atg31 complex (PDB ID 4P1W) was used to generate models. The inset denotes the region shown in panel *e*. (*d*) Close-up view of the interaction between Atg1^{MIT2} and Atg13$^{MIM(N)}$. (*e*) Close-up view of the interaction between Atg13^{17BR} and Atg17; broken lines indicate possible hydrogen bonds. Abbreviations: AIM, Atg8-family-interacting motif; C, carboxy termini; HORMA, Hop1p, Rev7p, and Mad2; IDR, intrinsically disordered region; MIM, MIT-interacting motif; MIT, microtubule-interacting and transport domain; N, amino termini; P, phosphorylation.

six α-helices, which fold into two three-helix bundles, and these two bundles interact to form one globular fold. Each bundle resembles a microtubule-interacting and transport (MIT) domain—hence the names MIT1 and MIT2. The MIT domains are often observed in proteins involved in membrane traffic such as the multivesicular body pathway, and they function as a binding module that connects proteins (34). Tandem MIT domains (tMIT) of Atg1 are responsible for binding Atg13, and their mode for recognizing Atg13 is similar to how other MIT domains recognize

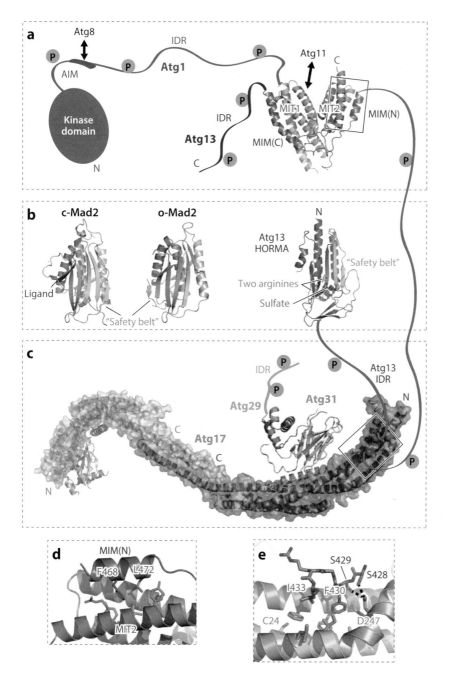

Cytoplasm-to-
vacuole targeting
(Cvt) pathway:
a yeast-specific system
that constitutively
delivers some vacuolar
enzymes to the vacuole
using mechanisms
similar to autophagy

MIT: microtubule-
interacting and
transport domain

AIM: Atg8-family-
interacting
motif

their targets (described below). In addition to binding Atg13, the CTD of Atg1 was suggested to bind Atg11 (65), the scaffold protein essential for selective autophagy, such as the Cvt (cytoplasm-to-vacuole targeting) pathway, and membranes, especially those with high curvature (96). The Atg11-binding site, which is distinct from the Atg13-binding site (the first and the third α-helices of MIT2, as described below), was assigned to be the second α-helix of MIT2 (65) and thus Atg11 might not compete with Atg13 for Atg1 binding. The structure of Atg1 tMIT does not possess a surface suitable for sensing membrane curvature; thus, further studies are needed to determine its membrane-related functions.

The IDR of Atg1, which consists of ~300 residues, connects the KD and the tMIT. It remains to be elucidated whether the Atg1 IDR connects them as a random coil and whether the relative positioning of the two globular domains is completely variable or fixed to some extent. The Atg1 IDR contains an abundance of serines and threonines, many of which are phosphorylated by various kinases (5, 16, 24, 48, 104). The roles of phosphorylation at these sites are largely unknown; however, Budovskaya et al. (5) have shown that Ser508 and Ser515 in the Atg1 IDR are phosphorylated by the cAMP-dependent protein kinase and that these phosphorylations regulate the localization of Atg1 to the PAS but not its kinase activity. Structural information on Atg1, including its IDR, is urgently required to establish the biological significance of each phosphorylation site in the IDR. The Atg1 IDR possesses an Atg8-family-interacting motif (AIM) (85) and directly interacts with Atg8 (55, 78). This interaction is dispensable for targeting Atg1 to PAS but essential for tethering Atg1 to the isolation membrane. Although the Atg1-Atg8 interaction is important for efficient autophagy, the role of Atg1 in relation to isolation membranes remains to be established.

Architecture of Atg13

Atg13 can be structurally divided into two regions: an N-terminal globular domain and a C-terminal IDR. X-ray crystallography has determined the structure of the NTD of Atg13 (37) (**Figure 2b**). The core of the NTD consists of a five-stranded antiparallel β-sheet and four α-helices on the same side of the sheet. A smaller three-stranded antiparallel β-sheet is located at the C-terminal side of the core. The topology of the core structure is essentially identical to that of the Hop1p, Rev7p, and Mad2 (HORMA) domains (2), which is why the NTD of Atg13 was named HORMA. Structural studies of the Mad2 HORMA domain showed that Mad2 possesses an open conformation (o-Mad2) and a closed conformation (c-Mad2), and that ligand binding shifts the equilibrium to c-Mad2 (63) (**Figure 2b**). The Atg13 HORMA domain is topologically similar to c-Mad2, and it remains to be elucidated whether the Atg13 HORMA domain also has two conformations. In the crystal structure of the Atg13 HORMA domain, a sulfate ion was bound in proximity to the basic side chains of two arginines that are located at the core β-sheet and at the loop region, called the safety-belt (37). In the case of Mad2, the safety-belt undergoes a large conformational change upon ligand binding and locks the ligand by functioning as a fastened safety-belt (63). Because sulfate ions are often observed in the phosphate-binding pocket of a protein, scientists speculated that phosphorylated serine and threonine residues in Atg13 or an Atg13-binding protein could bind to the two arginines in a manner similar to that of the sulfate ion, and that this interaction could switch the conformation of the Atg13 HORMA domain from open to closed as in the case of Mad2. However, the conservation of the two arginines is restricted to species closely related to *S. cerevisiae*; they are not conserved in mammalian Atg13 (37). The Atg13 HORMA domain is necessary for targeting the autophagy-specific PI3K complex, but not the Atg1 complex, to the PAS (37). However, direct interaction between the Atg13 HORMA domain and the PI3K complex has not been observed. In the case of mammals, the Atg13 HORMA domain binds Atg101; however, Atg101 is not conserved in budding yeast (29, 67). To establish the specific function of the Atg13 HORMA domain in autophagy, its binding partner(s) must be identified.

The Atg13 IDR has been predicted to be quite long (~470 amino acids) and contains abundant serines and threonines, many of which are phosphorylated by various kinases (4, 13, 24, 32, 44, 61, 104–106). The Atg13 IDR is responsible for binding both Atg1 and Atg17 (8, 43); thus phosphorylation at the Atg13 IDR regulates autophagy by changing the affinity of Atg13 to Atg1 and Atg17 (described below). The Atg1-binding region was assigned to the ~60-residue region (residues 460–521), whereas only a 13-residue region (residues 424–436) is sufficient for binding Atg17 (13). Circular dichroism spectroscopy confirmed that the Atg1-binding region is intrinsically disordered when in free form, whereas two α-helices were induced upon Atg1 binding (13) (described below). The Atg17-binding region is too short to contain a globular fold. Because the Atg13 IDR is phosphoregulated by nutrient conditions, Jao et al. (37) speculated that a phosphorylated IDR could bind to the two arginines in the HORMA domain of the same protein by which Atg13 is fixed to a closed conformation and that starvation-induced dephosphorylation of IDR releases the closed conformation, enabling the HORMA domain to bind downstream factors. However, no interaction between the IDR and the HORMA domain of Atg13 has been observed. A structural analysis of full-length Atg13 is needed to substantiate these speculations.

Architecture of the Atg17-Atg29-Atg31 Complex

Atg17, Atg29, and Atg31 form a 2:2:2 stable complex in vitro (41). Further, they constitutively form a complex with each other irrespective of nutrient conditions in vivo (41). In total, they may be considered as one structural unit. The crystal structure of full-length Atg17 with full-length Atg31 and Atg29 lacking its C-terminal IDR has been determined (96) (**Figure 2c**). The Atg17 protomer consists of four α-helices, which fold into a crescent-like structure, and Atg17 dimerizes via its C-terminal region, which results in its unique S-shaped architecture. Single-particle electron microscopy has also shown that Atg17 is S-shaped when in complex with Atg29 and Atg31, but that in free form Atg17 has a more elongated conformation that is rodlike rather than crescent-like (9, 65).

Atg31 has a β-sandwich fold consisting of eight β-strands, one of which is derived from the N-terminal region of Atg29, and thus Atg31 appears to not retain its folded structure in the absence of Atg29 (96) (**Figure 2c**). In addition to the β-sandwich fold, Atg31 has one α-helix at the C terminus, which binds tightly to Atg17 by forming an intermolecular four-helix bundle with the three α-helices of Atg17 (96). In contrast, the β-sandwich moiety of Atg31 showed little interaction with Atg17. Atg29 consists of the N-terminal β-strand, which forms the Atg31 β-sandwich fold; three α-helices; and the C-terminal IDR (96). Both Atg29 and Atg31 bind to the middle of the concave surface of the crescent-like fold of Atg17 mainly via the C-terminal helix of Atg31. Atg29 does not directly interact with Atg17 in the crystal structure, although there remains a possibility that the Atg29 IDR directly interacts with Atg17.

The Atg29 IDR contains many serine and threonine residues that are phosphorylated upon starvation (65). Although deletion of the Atg29 IDR did not impair autophagic activity, unphosphorylatable mutations at the Atg29 IDR severely impaired autophagy (65). These observations suggest that the Atg29 IDR inhibits autophagy and that phosphorylation of the IDR impairs its inhibiting activity and promotes autophagy. The molecular mechanism of the inhibitory activity of the Atg29 IDR remains to be established. Atg11 interacts directly with the phosphorylated IDR of Atg29, which promotes the recruitment of the Atg17-Atg29-Atg31 complex to the PAS in cells lacking Atg1 and Atg13 (65). However, Atg11 is not required for the assembly of the

Atg1 complex under starvation or for starvation-induced autophagy (43, 46, 49). To better understand this process, the significance of the Atg11-Atg29 interaction in autophagy requires further investigation.

MIM:
MIT-interacting motif

17BR: Atg17-binding
region

TORC1: target of
rapamycin (TOR)
complex 1

Structural Basis of the Atg1-Atg13 Interaction

In general, proteins that interact with MIT domains utilize an MIT-interacting motif (MIM) (34). There are several types of MIMs, most of which have a helical conformation and form an intermolecular helix bundle by binding to the groove formed between two α-helices of the MIT (34). The Atg1-binding region of Atg13 also binds to Atg1^{tMIT} with a helical conformation: The N-terminal helix binds to the groove formed between the first and third helices of Atg1^{MIT2}, whereas the C-terminal helix binds to the groove formed between the second and third helices of Atg1^{MIT1} (13); the N- and C-terminal helices of Atg13 are called MIM(N) and MIM(C) (**Figure 2a**). The buried surface between Atg13$^{MIM(C)}$ and Atg1^{MIT1} is larger than that between Atg13$^{MIM(N)}$ and Atg1^{MIT2}; nevertheless, in vitro studies have shown that the affinity between Atg1 and Atg13 is endowed primarily by the Atg1^{MIT2}-Atg13$^{MIM(N)}$ interaction and that the Atg1^{MIT1}-Atg13$^{MIM(C)}$ interaction secondarily reinforces it (13). Consistently, Phe468 and Leu472 in Atg13$^{MIM(N)}$, which are deeply bound to the hydrophobic groove of Atg1^{MIT2} (**Figure 2d**), are essential for the interaction with Atg1 (13, 55).

Structural Basis of the Atg13-Atg17 Interaction

The minimum Atg17-binding region (17BR) of Atg13 is composed of 13 amino acids. Crystallographic study of Atg13^{17BR} in complexes with the Atg17-Atg29-Atg31 complex showed that only six residues in 17BR had a defined electron density, and thus modeling was performed on these six residues (13) (**Figure 2e**). Atg13^{17BR} is bound to the hydrophobic groove of the N-terminal region of Atg17 using the two hydrophobic side chains Phe430 and Ile433. Further, Ser428 and Ser429 of Atg13 form hydrogen bonds with Asp247 of Atg17. Alanine substitution at these hydrophobic residues and serines in Atg13 severely impairs the interaction between Atg13^{17BR} and Atg17 (13). Further, the D247A mutation in Atg17 severely impaired both the interaction of full-length Atg13 with Atg17 and the autophagy progression in vivo (13). This finding suggests that the Atg13^{17BR}-Atg17 interaction observed in the crystal structure is essential for the Atg13-Atg17 interaction and for autophagy.

The Atg13 IDR is very long (as many as ~470 residues), and regions in the IDR other than 17BR might also be involved in the interaction with Atg17. An in vitro study showed that mutations at 17BR did not completely impair the interaction between full-length Atg13 and Atg17 (Y. Fujioka & N.N. Noda, unpublished observations). A previous study reported that a single point mutation at Cys24 with arginine in Atg17 impaired the interaction with Atg13 (39). The Cys24 is located at the N-terminal region of Atg17 but is not involved in the formation of the binding site for Atg13^{17BR} (**Figure 2e**). Because the side chain of Cys24 is buried and surrounded by hydrophobic residues, its arginine substitution may have remotely disturbed the conformation of the Atg13^{17BR}-binding site. Further characterization of the Atg13 IDR other than in 17BR and MIM may provide more information on the functions of Atg13.

Dephosphorylation of Atg13 Leads to the Formation of the Atg1 Complex

Autophagy is strongly induced by starvation and is believed to be regulated by the nutrient sensor TORC1 [target of rapamycin (Tor) complex 1] (87). Under nutrient-rich conditions, TORC1 is active and directly phosphorylates Atg13. Starvation inhibits TORC1 activity, leading to imme-diate dephosphorylation of Atg13 possibly by an unidentified phosphatase(s) (43). The following events that initiate autophagy are currently unconfirmed. One possible model is that dephos-phorylated Atg13 increases the affinity of Atg13 to both Atg1 and Atg17, which then leads to the formation of the Atg1 complex and to PAS assembly (13, 43). Eight serines in the Atg13 IDR were identified as TORC1-phosphorylating sites responsible for regulating autophagy, and importantly, overexpression of Atg13 with alanine substitution at all eight serines induced au-tophagy even under growth conditions (44). These data strongly suggest that dephosphorylation at the Atg13 IDR is sufficient to induce autophagy. Further, three serines in the Atg13 IDR were identified as phosphorylation sites by cAMP-dependent protein kinase, and their alanine sub-stitution promoted PAS targeting of Atg13, possibly by interacting with Atg17 (106). However, owing to a lack of structural information, these studies did not establish the molecular mecha-nisms of phosphorylation-mediated regulation of the Atg1 complex assembly. Via structure-based analysis we recently identified specific serines in the Atg13 IDR that are directly involved in the Atg13-Atg17 interaction (13).

Both Atg13$^{MIM(C)}$ and Atg13^{17BR}, which are responsible for binding Atg1 and Atg17, respec-tively, contain serines that are phosphorylated under nutrient-rich conditions and dephosphory-lated upon treatment with rapamycin. Aspartate mutation at five serines in Atg13$^{MIM(C)}$ that mimic phosphorylation moderately weakened the Atg1-Atg13 interaction, whereas aspartate mutation at Ser429 in Atg13^{17BR} severely impaired the Atg13-Atg17 interaction both in vitro and in vivo (13). Consistent with this finding, autophagy was partially and severely impaired when these serines were mutated to aspartate in Atg13$^{MIM(C)}$ and Atg13^{17BR}, respectively (13). Ser429 of Atg13 forms an important hydrogen bond with Asp247 of Atg17, as described above (**Figure 2e**). Phosphory-lation at Ser429 would not only destroy the hydrogen bond but also cause electrostatic repulsion between the introduced phosphate group and Asp247, which could account for the complete in-hibition of the Atg13-Atg17 interaction by an S429D mutation. Phosphorylation at Ser428 would also inhibit the interaction in a similar mechanism. In contrast, the Atg1-Atg13 interaction, which is mediated mainly by Atg13$^{MIM(N)}$, is regulated by multiple phosphorylations at Atg13$^{MIM(C)}$. Be-cause Atg13$^{MIM(C)}$ enhances the Atg1-Atg13$^{MIM(N)}$ interaction, phosphorylation at Atg13$^{MIM(C)}$ is not sufficient to completely destroy the Atg1-Atg13 interaction. This mild regulation of the Atg1-Atg13 interaction may be needed to retain a small population of the Atg1-Atg13 complex required for the Cvt pathway under nutrient-rich conditions. This is in contrast to the Atg13-Atg17 inter-action, which is not required for the Cvt pathway; thus, its complete inhibition would be possible. Recently, Kraft et al. (55) reported that Atg13 constitutively forms a complex with Atg1 and that the phosphorylated state of Atg13 does not affect formation of the complex. Although the exact reason for the various different observations remains to be elucidated, one possible explanation is that the formation of the Atg1-Atg13 complex is not fully regulated by the nutrient conditions, which makes it technically difficult to detect starvation-dependent increases in the Atg1-Atg13 complex. The data reported so far may indicate that the starvation-dependent interaction of Atg13 with Atg17, rather than the interaction of Atg13 with Atg1, is more important for fully regulating autophagy.

The Mammalian ULK1 Complex

In higher eukaryotes such as mammals, ULK1 and ULK2 are the orthologs of yeast Atg1 (69). ULK1 and ULK2, along with several other proteins including mammalian Atg13 (6, 15, 27, 38); RB1-inducible coiled-coil protein 1 (RB1CC1), also known as FIP200 (15, 20, 27, 38); and Atg101 (29, 67), contribute to the initial step of autophagosome formation in complexes. RB1CC1 has been suggested to be a functional homolog of yeast Atg17 on the basis of observations that it directly interacts with Atg13, and is predicted to possess coiled coils similar to those in Atg17, although little sequence homology is observed between RB1CC1 and Atg17 (20). The C-terminal region of RB1CC1 shows sequence homology to that of Atg11, suggesting that RB1CC1 may be a hybrid homolog of yeast Atg11 and Atg17. The mammalian ULK1/2 complex lacks Atg29 and Atg31 counterparts but possesses Atg101, which is not conserved in budding yeast. Fission yeast conserves an Atg101 homolog, Mug66, but lacks Atg29 and Atg31 (29, 109). The Atg29-Atg31 pair and Atg101 appear to be mutually exclusive throughout evolution; thus, it could be speculated that they play equivalent roles. However, although the Atg29-Atg31 pair directly interacts with Atg17 but not with Atg13, the binding partner of Atg101 is Atg13 and not the Atg17 counterpart, RB1CC1. Further, the structure of Atg101 was predicted to be similar to that of the HORMA domains (23), which is quite different from the structure of the Atg29-Atg31 pair (96) (**Figure 2**). Another important difference from the yeast Atg1 complex is that the ULK1/2 complex exists constitutively and its formation is not regulated by nutrient conditions (69). However, mammalian Atg13 is also phosphorylated by mTORC1, suggesting a general regulatory mechanism of starvation-induced autophagy that is at least partly shared between mammals and yeast.

Downstream Factors of the Atg1 Complex

Atg9, present in single-membrane vesicles with a diameter of 30–60 nm called the Atg9 vesicles, travels between the PAS and other membrane compartments (126). Although there are no structural studies of Atg9, Atg9 is predicted to have six transmembrane helices followed by a coiled coil and to be present as a homodimer via the dimerization of the coiled coil (21). Targeting Atg9 to the PAS requires the Atg1 complex but not the kinase activity of Atg1 (97, 113). Atg9 is a direct target of Atg1 and phosphorylated Atg9 is responsible for efficiently recruiting Atg8 and Atg18 to the PAS (93). However, how Atg9 targets the PAS and recruits downstream factors to the PAS and how Atg1-mediated phosphorylation regulates Atg9 function await further study, especially a structural analysis of Atg9.

The autophagy-specific PI3K complex, consisting of Vps34, Vps15, Atg6/Vps30, Atg14, and Atg38, targets the PAS via the Atg1 complex (1, 47). Vps34 is the catalytic subunit of the PI3K complex; Vps15, Atg6/Vps30, and Atg14 regulate the activity and the localization of Vps34; and Atg38 may be important for the integrity of the PI3K complex (1). The PI3K complex targets the PAS depending on both Atg9 and the Atg1 complex (113). Thus far we know the Atg14 complex, the BARA domain of Atg6, and the HORMA domain of Atg13 are required for the PI3K complex to target the PAS (37, 82, 89). However, a direct interaction(s) that connects the PI3K complex to Atg9 or to the Atg1 complex has not been reported. Further investigations are required to elucidate how the PI3K complex targets the PAS.

Atg CONJUGATION SYSTEMS: THE WORKERS THAT EXPAND ISOLATION MEMBRANES

In autophagy, there are two ubiquitin-like conjugation systems: the Atg8 and Atg12 systems (90) (**Figure 1**). The Atg12 system contains five Atg proteins: Atg5, Atg7, Atg10, Atg12, and Atg16 (72, 73, 103). Atg12 is activated by Atg7, an E1-like enzyme (73), and is then transferred to Atg10, an E2-like enzyme (103). Finally, the C-terminal glycine of Atg12 is conjugated to the side chain of Lys149 of Atg5 (73). The unique feature of the Atg12 system is that E3 enzymes are not required for this conjugation reaction. There is no deconjugation enzyme, and the Atg12-Atg5 conjugate is formed constitutively in vivo. The Atg12-Atg5 conjugate further forms a complex with a dimeric protein, Atg16 (Atg16L in the case of mammals and plants), with which Atg5 interacts noncovalently (12, 71, 72).

The Atg8 system contains four Atg proteins: Atg3, Atg4, Atg7, and Atg8 (35) (**Figure 1**). Nascent Atg8 is processed by Atg4, a cysteine protease, to expose a glycine residue at its C terminus (50). The processed Atg8 is then activated by Atg7, the same E1-like enzyme as in the Atg12 system, and transferred to Atg3, an E2-like enzyme (35). Finally, the C-terminal glycine of Atg8 is conjugated to the amine moiety of phosphatidylethanolamine (PE) (35). The final step in conjugation requires the E3-like Atg12-Atg5-Atg16 complex, the product of the Atg12 system (18). Atg4 also works as a deconjugation enzyme that cleaves Atg8-PE so that Atg8 may be reused. The unique feature of the Atg8 system is that Atg8 is conjugated to a lipid, not to a protein.

PE: phos-phatidylethanolamine

Atg8: A Ubiquitin-Like Protein

X-ray crystallography and NMR have shown that Atg8 and its homologs in mammals, *Bombyx mori*, *Plasmodium falciparum*, and *Trypanosoma brucei* share a similar structure composed of a ubiquitin-core fold and two α-helices at its N-terminal side (17, 30, 54, 58, 83, 94, 107) (**Figure 3a**). The two α-helices endow Atg8 with two unique properties. First, Atg8-PE-containing liposomes are tethered together via the self-association property of Atg8-PE in vitro, for which the two α-helices are essential (77, 120). Second, there is a deep hydrophobic pocket, called the W-site, between the two α-helices and the ubiquitin core. The W-site, together with another hydrophobic pocket in the ubiquitin core, called the L-site, plays an important role in selective autophagy. The Cvt pathway is a well-characterized example of selective autophagy in which vacuolar enzymes such as aminopeptidase I (Ape1) and α-mannosidase (Ams1) are selectively packaged in an autophagosome-like structure called a Cvt vesicle and delivered into the vacuole under nutrient-rich conditions (64). The adaptor protein Atg19 links the vacuolar enzymes to the Cvt vesicle by interacting with both the vacuolar enzymes and Atg8 (102), the latter of which is mediated by an AIM (83, 85). The Atg19 AIM has a WEEL sequence and uses the side chains of Trp and Leu in the sequence to bind to the above-mentioned W- and L-sites on Atg8 (83) (**Figure 3a**). In addition, the backbone of the AIM forms a parallel β-sheet with Atg8 β2, which is similar to the interaction between the SUMO and SUMO-interacting motif (22). Mammalian Atg8 homologs such as LC3 also recognize a WXXL-like sequence in a manner similar to that of Atg8; thus, such a sequence in mammals is called the LC3-interacting region (LIR) (36, 83, 92). The AIM/LIR is conserved in other adaptor proteins such as Atg32, Atg34, Atg36, and Cue5 in yeast and p62, Nix, and Tollip in mammals, and the interaction between the AIM/LIR and Atg8-family proteins is also conserved (53, 62, 75, 88, 92, 112). Further, AIM/LIR is observed in core Atg proteins such as Atg1, Atg3, Atg12, and mammalian Atg4B and Atg13, and appears to tether these factors to autophagic membranes via the interaction with Atg8-PE (45, 55, 78, 100, 110, 124).

Atg4: Processing and Deconjugation

Atg4 mediates both processing of nascent Atg8 and deconjugation of Atg8-PE conjugates (40, 50). Structural studies of the human Atg4 ortholog, HsAtg4B, in free form and in complex with LC3 have been published (57, 100, 108) (**Figure 3b**). HsAtg4B has a papain fold with a catalytic triad consisting of Cys74, Asp278, and His280. A notable feature is that the catalytic site of HsAtg4B is buried, covered by the regulatory loop, Trp142, and the N-terminal tail (108) (**Figure 3b**, free HsAtg4B), making it inaccessible in the free form. The crystal structure of HsAtg4B in complex with LC3 showed that HsAtg4B binds two LC3 proteins; one LC3 binds

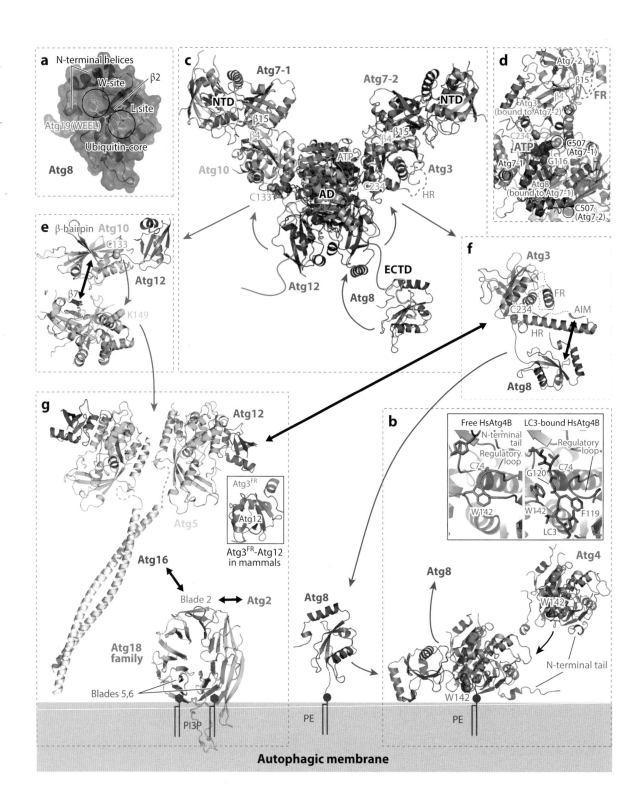

a

N-terminal helices

W-site

β2

L-site

Atg19(WEEL)

Ubiquitin-core

Atg8

c

Atg7-1

Atg7-2

NTD

NTD

β15

β15

β4

β4

Atg10

ATP

Atg3

AD

C234

C133

HR

Atg12

ECTD

Atg8

d

Atg7-2

β15

FR

β4

Atg3
(bound to Atg7-2)

C234

C507
(Atg7-1)

ATP

G116

Atg7-1

Atg8
(bound to Atg7-1)

C507
(Atg7-2)

e

β-hairpin Atg10

C133

Atg12

β7

K149

f

Atg3

FR

C234

AIM

HR

Atg8

g

Atg12

Atg5

Atg3^FR

Atg12

Atg3^FR-Atg12
in mammals

Atg16

Blade 2

Atg2

Atg18
family

Blades 5,6

PI3P

b

Free HsAtg4B

LC3-bound HsAtg4B

N-terminal tail

Regulatory
loop

Regulatory
loop

C74

C74

G120

W142

W142

F119

LC3

Atg8

Atg8

Atg4

W142

PE

N-terminal tail

W142

PE

Autophagic membrane

to the LIR in the N-terminal tail, which opens the exit of the catalytic site, and the other LC3 binds to the papain fold and extends the C-terminal tail into the cleft to expose the scissile bond to the catalytic cysteine, Cys74 (100). A remarkable feature is the large conformational change around the regulatory loop and Trp142: The insertion of the C-terminal tail, especially Phe119, of LC3 dislocates the root of the regulatory loop and thereby disrupts the interaction between Trp142 and the regulatory loop (**Figure 3b**, LC3-bound HsAtg4B). This disruption allows the C-terminal tail of the LC3 precursor to enter the catalytic site. Trp142 of HsAtg4B and Phe119 of LC3 are conserved, suggesting that these interaction modes are also evolutionarily conserved. The C-terminal LC3 peptide alone does not induce the conformational change, and both the ubiquitin core and the C-terminal tail are essential for LC3 to be processed by HsAtg4B.

AD: adenylation domain

ECTD: extreme C-terminal domain

Atg7: An Activating (E1-Like) Enzyme

The E1-like enzyme Atg7 first adenylates two ubiquitin-like proteins (Ubls), Atg8 and Atg12, consuming ATP, then forms a thioester intermediate with both, and finally transfers them to each cognate E2 enzyme, Atg3 and Atg10. X-ray crystallography of Atg7 has established the unique architecture of Atg7 (26, 86, 116) (**Figure 3c**). Atg7 is composed of the NTD, the CTD, and a short linker that connects them. The CTD is subdivided into the adenylation domain (AD) and the extreme C-terminal domain (ECTD). The AD forms a homodimer whose architecture is similar to the heterodimeric architecture of the active and nonactive ADs in canonical E1 enzymes (26, 86, 101, 116). However, in addition to the AD, the structure of Atg7 is totally distinct from that of the canonical E1 enzymes in ubiquitin-related systems; Atg7 has neither a ubiquitin-fold domain nor a catalytic cysteine domain, which is conserved among canonical E1 enzymes. The NTD and ECTD of Atg7 have never been observed in other E1 enzymes, and these structural features suggest that Atg7 works by a mechanism different from that used by canonical E1 enzymes.

The crystal structure of the Atg7 CTD in complex with Atg8 and MgATP showed that Atg8 and MgATP are loaded on both CTDs within a dimer (26, 86), confirming that both activation domains are active. In contrast, in the case of canonical E1 enzymes, one of the activation domains is inactive. The catalytic cysteine in Atg7 is located on a crossover loop, which covers the Atg8-binding surface in the free form but shows a local conformation change and exposes the surface upon binding Atg8 (26, 86). Using hydrophobic residues (Ala75, Phe77, Phe79, Leu84, and Thr87), the ubiquitin core of Atg8 binds to the central β-sheet of the AD. The C-terminal tail of Atg8 extends under the

---

Figure 3

Structure and mechanism of the Atg conjugation systems. (*a*) Structure of Atg8 in complex with the WEEL sequence of Atg19 (PDB ID 2ZPN). (*b*) Structure of human Atg4B alone and in complex with LC3 (PDB ID 2CY7, 2ZZP). (*c*) Modeled structure of the Atg7-Atg3-Atg8-Atg10-Atg12 complex. The model was generated by superimposing the structures of the Atg7-Atg3 and Atg7-Atg10 complexes (PDB ID 4GSL, 4GSK) and plant Atg12b (PDB ID 1WZ3) on the structure of the Atg7-Atg8-MgATP complex (PDB ID 3VH4). The loop region containing Cys133 of Atg10 was derived from the Atg10 structure (PDB ID 4EBR). The model of Atg8 in complex with the loop of Atg7^{ECTD} was generated using the NMR structure of the Atg8-Atg7^{C30} complex (PDB ID 2LI5). One Atg7 protomer in complex with Atg8 and Atg10 is labeled Atg7-1 (*gray*); the other Atg7 protomer in complex with Atg3 and Atg12 is labeled Atg7-2 (*green*). (*d*) Close-up view of the catalytic site in panel *c*. Atg8 Gly116 and the side chains of Atg3 Cys234 and Atg7 Cys507 as well as ATP are shown with space-filling models. (*e*) Structure of Atg5 (PDB ID 2DYO) and Atg10 (PDB ID 2LPU). The side chains of Atg10 Cys133 and Atg5 Lys149 are shown with a space-filling model. (*f*) Structure of Atg3 (PDB ID 2DYT). The side chain of Atg3 Cys234 is shown with a space-filling model. (*g*) Structure of the Atg12-Atg5-Atg16 complex (PDB ID 3W1S, 3A7P) and the Atg18-family protein Hsv2 (PDB ID 3VU4). The interaction between Atg12 and Atg3^{FR} (PDB ID 4NAW) is shown in the inset. Red and blue arrows indicate the flow of Atg8 and Atg12, respectively. The black double-headed arrow indicates possible interactions. Abbreviations: AD, adenylation domain; AIM, Atg8-family-interacting motif; ECTD, extreme C-terminal domain; FR, flexible region; HR, handle region; NTD, N-terminal domain; PE, phosphatidylethanolamine; PI3P: phosphatidylinositol 3-phosphate.

crossover loop and the C-terminal Gly116 of Atg8 is located around the bound MgATP and the catalytic cysteine, Cys507 (**Figure 3***d*). This structure supports the idea that the adenylation of Atg8 Gly116 and its subsequent thioester formation with Atg7 Cys507 proceed with only a local conformational change in Atg7. This process is different for canonical E1 enzymes, in which a drastic domain rearrangement occurs during activation reactions (101). Although the C-terminal residues of the Atg7 ECTD were not visible in the crystal structure, they play an essential role in binding and activating Atg8 by Atg7. The NMR structure of Atg8 in complex with the C-terminal 30-residue peptide of Atg7 (Atg7 C30) showed that Atg7 C30 binds to the W- and L-sites in Atg8 with extensive hydrophobic and hydrophilic interactions, which are important for the activation reaction (86).

A two-step recognition model was proposed on the basis of these observations: Atg8 is first captured by the C-terminal tail of Atg7 and then recruited to the AD as in the crystal structure and from here the activation reaction proceeds (**Figure 3***c*). Recognition and activation of another Ubl, Atg12, by Atg7 seem similar to that of Atg8 by Atg7 (see **Figure 3***c* for a model of the Atg7-Atg12 complex), although a structural study has not been performed. Atg12 does not possess the W-site because the N-terminal helices are absent, suggesting that many of the interactions that Atg7 C30 forms with Atg8 may be impossible with Atg12. This implies that compared with Atg12, Atg8 may be more efficiently captured and activated by Atg7, which would be advantageous as autophagy requires a large amount of Atg8-PE but only a small amount of Atg12-Atg5 (28, 121).

Atg3 and Atg10: Conjugating (E2-Like) Enzymes

Atg8 or Atg12 bound to Atg7 via a thioester bond is transferred to the E2-like enzymes Atg3 or Atg10 to form the Atg8~Atg3 or the Atg12~Atg10 thioester intermediate, respectively (35). Atg3 and Atg10 share an E2-core fold that is somewhat different from that in canonical E2 enzymes: It lacks the C-terminal two α-helices. In addition, Atg10 possesses a characteristic β-hairpin that extends over the core β-sheet (25, 122, 125) (**Figure 3***e*). Atg10 directly recognizes Atg5 at β7 using the β-hairpin and catalyzes the Atg12-Atg5 conjugation without an E3 enzyme (125). In addition to the E2-core fold, Atg3 has two unique insertions, a handle region (HR) and a flexible region (FR), giving Atg3 a hammer-like shape consisting of a head (E2 core) and a handle (HR) (122) (**Figure 3***f*). Many of the residues forming the components of the protruding α-helix in the handle region are disordered in the crystal structure of the Atg3-Atg7 complex (42) (**Figure 3***c*), suggesting that the unique structure of the handle region is possibly due to crystal contacts. Atg3^{FR} (residues 84–162) has a highly acidic character and most of its residues are intrinsically disordered. The handle region contains an AIM that binds to Atg8 (124), whereas the flexible region has a small α-helical region that binds to the Atg7 NTD (116, 122) (**Figure 3***d*). The N-terminal region of Atg3, which is disordered in the crystal structure but is essential for autophagy, has been suggested to form an amphipathic helix and to bind membranes with high curvature (19, 80). However, the proper targeting of Atg3 to autophagic membranes requires the E3-like Atg12-Atg5-Atg16 complex in vivo (14).

The Structural Basis of the Transfer of Atg8 and Atg12 from Atg7 to E2 Enzymes

Data from recent crystallographic studies of the Atg7-Atg3 and Atg7-Atg10 complexes explain the mechanism by which Atg7 transfers Atg8 and Atg12 to E2 enzymes (42, 123). The Atg7-Atg3 and Atg7-Atg10 interactions are similar to each other yet distinct from canonical E1-E2 interactions

(31). Both Atg3 and Atg10 are wedged between the NTD and CTD of Atg7 and interact with β15 of the Atg7 NTD using the same loop region that follows β4 (**Figure 3c**). The loop region of Atg10 forms an intermolecular β-sheet with Atg7 β15, whereas in the case of Atg3 no such β-sheet is formed and the interactions are mediated mainly by side chains. In addition, the short helix in Atg3^{FR} is bound to the hydrophobic shoulder groove in the Atg7 NTD (**Figure 3d**). The catalytic cysteine of both Atg3 and Atg10 is positioned distal to the catalytic Cys507 of the Atg7 protomer to which Atg3 and Atg10 are bound, but much nearer to the Cys507 of the other Atg7 protomer within a dimer (**Figure 3d**). This suggests that both Atg8 and Atg12 are transferred from the Cys507 of one Atg7 protomer to the catalytic cysteine of the cognate E2 bound to the other Atg7 protomer within a dimer. This *trans* reaction model, which was confirmed by biochemical studies using heterodimerized Atg7 mutants (86, 116), is unique to Atg7 among E1 enzymes and explains why the homodimer architecture is essential for Atg7's functions. Atg7 transfers Atg8 to Atg3 and Atg12 to Atg10 in vivo; however, in vitro studies showed that Atg7 can transfer Atg8 to Atg10 and Atg12 to Atg3, and importantly that the transfer of Atg12 to Atg3 was more efficient than the transfer of Atg12 to Atg10 (123). Further studies are required to determine the mechanisms that govern the specific formation of Atg8~Atg3 and Atg12~Atg10 thioester intermediates in vivo.

The Atg12-Atg5-Atg16 Complex: An E3-Like Enzyme

The Atg12-Atg5 conjugate forms a complex with Atg16 and functions as an E3-like enzyme in the Atg8 conjugation system (11, 14, 18, 72). In vitro studies have shown that the Atg12-Atg5 conjugate facilitates the transfer reaction of Atg8 from Atg3 to PE through a reorganization of the catalytic center of the E2-like enzyme Atg3 (99). Atg16 has no E3-like activity in vitro and its role in vivo is considered to target the Atg12-Atg5 conjugate to the autophagic membranes (14).

Crystallographic studies unveiled the unique architecture of the Atg12-Atg5-Atg16 complex, which is distinct from that of other E3 enzymes (12, 66, 81, 91, 115) (**Figure 3g**). Atg12 and Atg5 contain one and two ubiquitin folds, respectively, giving the Atg12-Atg5 conjugate a three-ubiquitin-fold architecture. Atg16 is composed of the Atg5-binding domain and the dimeric coiled-coil domain. As a result the Atg12-Atg5-Atg16 complex forms a 2:2:2 complex and thus contains six ubiquitin folds. However, the biological significance of this unique architecture remains to be established. In higher eukaryotes, Atg3^{FR} contains a motif that specifically binds Atg12 (68) (**Figure 3g**); thus, for Atg3, binding to Atg12 and Atg7 is mutually exclusive (95), whereas yeast Atg3 does not have such an Atg12-binding motif and the affinity between Atg3 and Atg12 is much lower than that between their human counterparts (K. Matoba & N.N. Noda, unpublished observations). The currently accepted model of the Atg8-PE conjugation mediated by the Atg12-Atg5-Atg16 complex is as follows: The Atg12-Atg5-Atg16 complex targets the autophagic membrane via the Atg5-Atg16 complex moiety and then recruits a Atg3~Atg8 thioester intermediate via the interaction between Atg3 and Atg12. These interactions play at least two roles in the reaction: One role is to activate the catalytic site of Atg3 (99) and the other is to locate the Atg3~Atg8 thioester near the PE. Structural studies on the full-length E2-E3 complex are needed to uncover the molecular mechanisms of this unique conjugation reaction.

PAS-Targeting Mechanism of Atg Conjugation Systems

The original hierarchy map showed that the Atg conjugation systems depend on the PI3K complex but not the Atg2-Atg18 complex to target the PAS (113). However, studies using fission yeast have shown that Atg8 depends on Atg18a to target the PAS and that Atg18a interacts with Atg5,

PI3P:
phosphatidylinositol
3-phosphate

which leads to a proposed model in which Atg18a recruits Atg8 to the PAS through the Atg12-Atg5-Atg16 complex (109). Further, studies of mammalian autophagy have shown that an Atg18 homolog, WIPI2b, interacts directly with the mammalian Atg16 ortholog, Atg16L1, and that this interaction is essential for autophagy (10). Furthermore, Atg18-family proteins target to the PAS by binding to PI3P (phosphatidylinositol 3-phosphate), which is produced by PI3K (74). These data indicate that Atg18-family proteins that localize to the PAS by binding to PI3P directly recruit the Atg12-Atg5-Atg16 complex, which then recruits Atg8 to the PAS.

Crystallographic studies have shown in detail the architecture of Atg18 on an Atg18 paralog, Hsv2 (3, 56, 119) (**Figure 3g**). Hsv2 has a seven-bladed β-propeller fold and possesses two binding pockets for PI3P at blades 5 and 6. Both WIPI2b and Atg18 utilize blade 2 to interact with Atg16L1 and Atg2, respectively (10, 119). Therefore, Atg2 and Atg16 may compete to bind to Atg18 if both proteins can bind to the same Atg18 paralog. Alternatively, each Atg18 paralog might have a specific binding partner: one specific to Atg2 and another specific to Atg16. In *S. cerevisiae*, there are three Atg18 paralogs: Atg18, Atg21, and Hsv2. Although only Atg18 is essential for autophagy, Atg18 and Atg21 cooperate to recruit Atg8 to the PAS (76). Detailed functional and structural studies are needed to establish the molecular role of each paralog in autophagy.

CONCLUDING REMARKS

Structural biological studies on core Atg proteins, especially those forming the Atg1 complex and the Atg conjugation systems, have developed rapidly. However, the structures of the protein Atg9, the Atg2-Atg18 complex, and the PI3K complex have yet to be fully unveiled. Furthermore, most of the interactions connecting the six functional groups are poorly understood. A determination of the structures of all core Atg proteins and the critical interactions among them would serve as a powerful compass to guide researchers toward a better understanding of the molecular mechanisms in autophagy.

SUMMARY POINTS

1. Atg1 and Atg13 have elongated KD-IDR-MIT and HORMA-IDR architectures, respectively, whereas Atg17 has a unique S-shaped architecture.

2. The Atg13 IDR binds directly to Atg1 MIT using MIM and to Atg17 using a short sequence.

3. Upon starvation, the interaction of Atg13 with both Atg1 and Atg17 is enhanced by dephosphorylation at specific serines in Atg13, leading to the formation of the Atg1 complex.

4. Atg4 has a papain-like fold with unique insertions that enable specific recognition and delipidation of Atg8.

5. Atg7 (E1), Atg3 (E2), and Atg10 (E2) in Atg conjugation systems possess both canonical and noncanonical structural features and mediate the activation reaction of Atg8 and Atg12 with a unique *trans* mechanism.

6. The Atg12-Atg5-Atg16 complex (E3), which is not structurally similar to other E3 enzymes, mediates both activation and membrane-targeting of Atg3 for Atg8 lipidation.

FUTURE ISSUES

1. How does the Atg1 complex form a higher-order assembly at the PAS?

2. How do Atg13 and Atg17 activate the Atg1 kinase?

3. How does the Atg1 complex recruit downstream factors such as Atg9 to the PAS?

4. How does Atg7 properly transfer Atg8 and Atg12 to each cognate E2 enzyme in vivo?

5. How does the Atg12-Atg5-Atg16 complex activate Atg3 and target it to the PAS?

6. How is Atg4-mediated delipidation of Atg8 spatiotemporally regulated?

DISCLOSURE STATEMENT

The authors are not aware of any affiliations, memberships, funding, or financial holdings that might be perceived as affecting the objectivity of this review.

ACKNOWLEDGMENTS

This work was supported in part by the Japan Society for the Promotion of Sciences KAKENHI Grant Number 25111004 (to NNN) and 22121008 (to FI) from the Ministry of Education, Culture, Sports, Science and Technology of Japan.

LITERATURE CITED

1. Araki Y, Ku WC, Akioka M, May AI, Hayashi Y, et al. 2013. Atg38 is required for autophagy-specific phosphatidylinositol 3-kinase complex integrity. *J. Cell Biol.* 203:299–313

2. Aravind L, Koonin EV. 1998. The HORMA domain: a common structural denominator in mitotic checkpoints, chromosome synapsis and DNA repair. *Trends Biochem. Sci.* 23:284–86

3. Baskaran S, Ragusa MJ, Boura E, Hurley JH. 2012. Two-site recognition of phosphatidylinositol 3-phosphate by PROPPINs in autophagy. *Mol. Cell* 47:339–48

4. Bodenmiller B, Wanka S, Kraft C, Urban J, Campbell D, et al. 2010. Phosphoproteomic analysis reveals interconnected system-wide responses to perturbations of kinases and phosphatases in yeast. *Sci. Signal.* 3:rs4

5. Budovskaya YV, Stephan JS, Deminoff SJ, Herman PK. 2005. An evolutionary proteomics approach identifies substrates of the cAMP-dependent protein kinase. *PNAS* 102:13933–38

6. Chan EY, Longatti A, McKnight NC, Tooze SA. 2009. Kinase-inactivated ULK proteins inhibit autophagy via their conserved C-terminal domains using an Atg13-independent mechanism. *Mol. Cell. Biol.* 29:157–71

7. Cheong H, Nair U, Geng J, Klionsky DJ. 2008. The Atg1 kinase complex is involved in the regulation of protein recruitment to initiate sequestering vesicle formation for nonspecific autophagy in *Saccharomyces cerevisiae*. *Mol. Biol. Cell* 19:668–81

8. Cheong H, Yorimitsu T, Reggiori F, Legakis JE, Wang CW, Klionsky DJ. 2005. Atg17 regulates the magnitude of the autophagic response. *Mol. Biol. Cell* 16:3438–53

9. Chew LH, Setiaputra D, Klionsky DJ, Yip CK. 2013. Structural characterization of the *Saccharomyces cerevisiae* autophagy regulatory complex Atg17-Atg31-Atg29. *Autophagy* 9:1467–74

10. Dooley HC, Razi M, Polson HEJ, Girardin SE, Wilson MI, Tooze SA. 2014. WIPI2 links LC3 conjugation with PI3P, autophagosome formation, and pathogen clearance by recruiting Atg12–5-16L1. *Mol. Cell* 55:238–52

11. Fujioka Y, Noda NN, Fujii K, Yoshimoto K, Ohsumi Y, Inagaki F. 2008. In vitro reconstitution of plant Atg8 and Atg12 conjugation systems essential for autophagy. *J. Biol. Chem.* 283:1921–28

12. Fujioka Y, Noda NN, Nakatogawa H, Ohsumi Y, Inagaki F. 2010. Dimeric coiled-coil structure of *Saccharomyces cerevisiae* Atg16 and its functional significance in autophagy. *J. Biol. Chem.* 285:1508–15

13. Fujioka Y, Suzuki SW, Yamamoto H, Kondo-Kakuta C, Kimura Y, et al. 2014. Structural basis of starvation-induced assembly of the autophagy initiation complex. *Nat. Struct. Mol. Biol.* 21:513–21

14. Fujita N, Itoh T, Omori H, Fukuda M, Noda T, Yoshimori T. 2008. The Atg16L complex specifies the site of LC3 lipidation for membrane biogenesis in autophagy. *Mol. Biol. Cell* 19:2092–100

15. Ganley IG, Lam DH, Wang J, Ding X, Chen S, Jiang X. 2009. ULK1·ATG13·FIP200 complex mediates mTOR signaling and is essential for autophagy. *J. Biol. Chem.* 284:12297–305

16. Gnad F, de Godoy LMF, Cox J, Neuhauser N, Ren S, et al. 2009. High-accuracy identification and bioinformatic analysis of in vivo protein phosphorylation sites in yeast. *Proteomics* 9:4642–52

17. Hain AU, Weltzer RR, Hammond H, Jayabalasingham B, Dinglasan RR, et al. 2012. Structural characterization and inhibition of the *Plasmodium* Atg8-Atg3 interaction. *J. Struct. Biol.* 180:551–62

18. Hanada T, Noda NN, Satomi Y, Ichimura Y, Fujioka Y, et al. 2007. The Atg12-Atg5 conjugate has a novel E3-like activity for protein lipidation in autophagy. *J. Biol. Chem.* 282:37298–302

19. Hanada T, Satomi Y, Takao T, Ohsumi Y. 2009. The amino-terminal region of Atg3 is essential for association with phosphatidylethanolamine in Atg8 lipidation. *FEBS Lett.* 583:1078–83

20. Hara T, Takamura A, Kishi C, Iemura S, Natsume T, et al. 2008. FIP200, a ULK-interacting protein, is required for autophagosome formation in mammalian cells. *J. Cell Biol.* 181:497–510

21. He C, Baba M, Cao Y, Klionsky DJ. 2008. Self-interaction is critical for Atg9 transport and function at the phagophore assembly site during autophagy. *Mol. Biol. Cell* 19:5506–16

22. Hecker C-M, Rabiller M, Haglund K, Bayer P, Dikic I. 2006. Specification of SUMO1- and SUMO2-interacting motifs. *J. Biol. Chem.* 281:16117–27

23. Hegedűs K, Nagy P, Gáspári Z, Juhász G. 2014. The putative HORMA domain protein Atg101 dimerizes and is required for starvation-induced and selective autophagy in *Drosophila*. *BioMed Res. Int.* 2014:470482

24. Helbig AO, Rosati S, Pijnappel PW, van Breukelen B, Timmers MH, et al. 2010. Perturbation of the yeast *N*-acetyltransferase NatB induces elevation of protein phosphorylation levels. *BMC Genomics* 11:685

25. Hong SB, Kim BW, Kim JH, Song HK. 2012. Structure of the autophagic E2 enzyme Atg10. *Acta Crystallogr. D* 68:1409–17

26. Hong SB, Kim BW, Lee KE, Kim SW, Jeon H, et al. 2011. Insights into noncanonical E1 enzyme activation from the structure of autophagic E1 Atg7 with Atg8. *Nat. Struct. Mol. Biol.* 18:1323–30

27. Hosokawa N, Hara T, Kaizuka T, Kishi C, Takamura A, et al. 2009. Nutrient-dependent mTORC1 association with the ULK1-Atg13-FIP200 complex required for autophagy. *Mol. Biol. Cell* 20:1981–91

28. Hosokawa N, Hara Y, Mizushima N. 2006. Generation of cell lines with tetracycline-regulated autophagy and a role for autophagy in controlling cell size. *FEBS Lett.* 580:2623–29

29. Hosokawa N, Sasaki T, Iemura S, Natsume T, Hara T, Mizushima N. 2009. Atg101, a novel mammalian autophagy protein interacting with Atg13. *Autophagy* 5:973–79

30. Hu C, Zhang X, Teng YB, Hu HX, Li WF. 2010. Structure of autophagy-related protein Atg8 from the silkworm *Bombyx mori*. *Acta Crystallogr. F* 66:787–90

31. Huang DT, Paydar A, Zhuang M, Waddell MB, Holton JM, Schulman BA. 2005. Structural basis for recruitment of Ubc12 by an E2 binding domain in NEDD8's E1. *Mol. Cell* 17:341–50

32. Huber A, Bodenmiller B, Uotila A, Stahl M, Wanka S, et al. 2009. Characterization of the rapamycin-sensitive phosphoproteome reveals that Sch9 is a central coordinator of protein synthesis. *Genes Dev.* 23:1929–43

33. Hurley JH, Schulman BA. 2014. Atomistic autophagy: the structures of cellular self-digestion. *Cell* 157:300–11

34. Hurley JH, Yang D. 2008. MIT domainia. *Dev. Cell* 14:6–8

35. Ichimura Y, Kirisako T, Takao T, Satomi Y, Shimonishi Y, et al. 2000. A ubiquitin-like system mediates protein lipidation. *Nature* 408:488–92

36. Ichimura Y, Kumanomidou T, Sou YS, Mizushima T, Ezaki J, et al. 2008. Structural basis for sorting mechanism of p62 in selective autophagy. *J. Biol. Chem.* 283:22847–57

37. Jao CC, Ragusa MJ, Stanley RE, Hurley JH. 2013. A HORMA domain in Atg13 mediates PI 3-kinase recruitment in autophagy. *PNAS* 110:5486–91

38. Jung CH, Jun CB, Ro S-H, Kim Y-M, Otto NM, et al. 2009. ULK-Atg13-FIP200 complexes mediate mTOR signaling to the autophagy machinery. *Mol. Biol. Cell* 20:1992–2003

39. Kabeya Y, Kamada Y, Baba M, Takikawa H, Sasaki M, Ohsumi Y. 2005. Atg17 functions in cooperation with Atg1 and Atg13 in yeast autophagy. *Mol. Biol. Cell* 16:2544–53

40. Kabeya Y, Mizushima N, Yamamoto A, Oshitani-Okamoto S, Ohsumi Y, Yoshimori T. 2004. LC3, GABARAP and GATE16 localize to autophagosomal membrane depending on form-II formation. *J. Cell Sci.* 117:2805–12

41. Kabeya Y, Noda NN, Fujioka Y, Suzuki K, Inagaki F, Ohsumi Y. 2009. Characterization of the Atg17-Atg29-Atg31 complex specifically required for starvation-induced autophagy in *Saccharomyces cerevisiae*. *Biochem. Biophys. Res. Commun.* 389:612–15

42. Kaiser SE, Mao K, Taherbhoy AM, Yu S, Olszewski JL, et al. 2012. Noncanonical E2 recruitment by the autophagy E1 revealed by Atg7-Atg3 and Atg7-Atg10 structures. *Nat. Struct. Mol. Biol.* 19:1242–49

43. Kamada Y, Funakoshi T, Shintani T, Nagano K, Ohsumi M, Ohsumi Y. 2000. Tor-mediated induction of autophagy via an Apg1 protein kinase complex. *J. Cell Biol.* 150:1507–13

44. Kamada Y, Yoshino K, Kondo C, Kawamata T, Oshiro N, et al. 2010. Tor directly controls the Atg1 kinase complex to regulate autophagy. *Mol. Cell. Biol.* 30:1049–58

45. Kaufmann A, Beier V, Franquelim HG, Wollert T. 2014. Molecular mechanism of autophagic membrane-scaffold assembly and disassembly. *Cell* 156:469–81

46. Kawamata T, Kamada Y, Kabeya Y, Sekito T, Ohsumi Y. 2008. Organization of the pre-autophagosomal structure responsible for autophagosome formation. *Mol. Biol. Cell* 19:2039–50

47. Kihara A, Noda T, Ishihara N, Ohsumi Y. 2001. Two distinct Vps34 phosphatidylinositol 3-kinase complexes function in autophagy and carboxypeptidase Y sorting in *Saccharomyces cerevisiae*. *J. Cell Biol.* 152:519–30

48. Kijanska M, Dohnal I, Reiter W, Kaspar S, Stoffel I, et al. 2010. Activation of Atg1 kinase in autophagy by regulated phosphorylation. *Autophagy* 6:1168–78

49. Kim J, Kamada Y, Stromhaug PE, Guan J, Hefner-Gravink A, et al. 2001. Cvt9/Gsa9 functions in sequestering selective cytosolic cargo destined for the vacuole. *J. Cell Biol.* 153:381–96

50. Kirisako T, Ichimura Y, Okada H, Kabeya Y, Mizushima N, et al. 2000. The reversible modification regulates the membrane-binding state of Apg8/Aut7 essential for autophagy and the cytoplasm to vacuole targeting pathway. *J. Cell Biol.* 151:263–76

51. Klionsky DJ, Cregg JM, Dunn WA Jr, Emr SD, Sakai Y, et al. 2003. A unified nomenclature for yeast autophagy-related genes. *Dev. Cell* 5:539–45

52. Klionsky DJ, Schulman BA. 2014. Dynamic regulation of macroautophagy by distinctive ubiquitin-like proteins. *Nat. Struct. Mol. Biol.* 21:336–45

53. Kondo-Okamoto N, Noda NN, Suzuki SW, Nakatogawa H, Takahashi I, et al. 2012. Autophagy-related protein 32 acts as autophagic degron and directly initiates mitophagy. *J. Biol. Chem.* 287:10631–38

54. Koopmann R, Muhammad K, Perbandt M, Betzel C, Duszenko M. 2009. *Trypanosoma brucei* ATG8: structural insights into autophagic-like mechanisms in protozoa. *Autophagy* 5:1085–91

55. Kraft C, Kijanska M, Kalie E, Siergiejuk E, Lee SS, et al. 2012. Binding of the Atg1/ULK1 kinase to the ubiquitin-like protein Atg8 regulates autophagy. *EMBO J.* 31:3691–703

56. Krick R, Busse RA, Scacioc A, Stephan M, Janshoff A, et al. 2012. Structural and functional character-ization of the two phosphoinositide binding sites of PROPPINs, a β-propeller protein family. *PNAS* 109:E2042–49

57. Kumanomidou T, Mizushima T, Komatsu M, Suzuki A, Tanida I, et al. 2006. The crystal structure of human Atg4b, a processing and de-conjugating enzyme for autophagosome-forming modifiers. *J. Mol. Biol.* 355:612–18

58. Kumeta H, Watanabe M, Nakatogawa H, Yamaguchi M, Ogura K, et al. 2010. The NMR structure of the autophagy-related protein Atg8. *J. Biomol. NMR* 47:237–41

59. Lamb CA, Yoshimori T, Tooze SA. 2013. The autophagosome: origins unknown, biogenesis complex. *Nat. Rev. Mol. Cell Biol.* 14:759–74

60. Levine B, Mizushima N, Virgin HW. 2011. Autophagy in immunity and inflammation. *Nature* 469:323–35

61. Li X, Gerber SA, Rudner AD, Beausoleil SA, Haas W, et al. 2007. Large-scale phosphorylation analysis of α-factor-arrested *Saccharomyces cerevisiae*. *J. Proteome Res.* 6:1190–97

62. Lu K, Psakhye I, Jentsch S. 2014. Autophagic clearance of polyQ proteins mediated by ubiquitin-Atg8 adaptors of the conserved CUET protein family. *Cell* 158:549–63

63. Luo X, Yu H. 2008. Protein metamorphosis: the two-state behavior of Mad2. *Structure* 16:1616–25

64. Lynch-Day MA, Klionsky DJ. 2010. The Cvt pathway as a model for selective autophagy. *FEBS Lett.* 584:1359–66

65. Mao K, Chew LH, Inoue-Aono Y, Cheong H, Nair U, et al. 2013. Atg29 phosphorylation regulates coordination of the Atg17-Atg31-Atg29 complex with the Atg11 scaffold during autophagy initiation. *PNAS* 110:E2875–84

66. Matsushita M, Suzuki NN, Obara K, Fujioka Y, Ohsumi Y, Inagaki F. 2007. Structure of Atg5· Atg16, a complex essential for autophagy. *J. Biol. Chem.* 282:6763–72

67. Mercer CA, Kaliappan A, Dennis PB. 2009. A novel, human Atg13 binding protein, Atg101, interacts with ULK1 and is essential for macroautophagy. *Autophagy* 5:649–62

68. Metlagel Z, Otomo C, Takaesu G, Otomo T. 2013. Structural basis of ATG3 recognition by the autophagic ubiquitin-like protein ATG12. *PNAS* 110:18844–49

69. Mizushima N. 2010. The role of the Atg1/ULK1 complex in autophagy regulation. *Curr. Opin. Cell Biol.* 22:132–39

70. Mizushima N, Komatsu M. 2011. Autophagy: renovation of cells and tissues. *Cell* 147:728–41

71. Mizushima N, Kuma A, Kobayashi Y, Yamamoto A, Matsubae M, et al. 2003. Mouse Apg16L, a novel WD-repeat protein, targets to the autophagic isolation membrane with the Apg12-Apg5 conjugate. *J. Cell Sci.* 116:1679–88

72. Mizushima N, Noda T, Ohsumi Y. 1999. Apg16p is required for the function of the Apg12p-Apg5p conjugate in the yeast autophagy pathway. *EMBO J.* 18:3888–96

73. Mizushima N, Noda T, Yoshimori T, Tanaka Y, Ishii T, et al. 1998. A protein conjugation system essential for autophagy. *Nature* 395:395–98

74. Mizushima N, Yoshimori T, Ohsumi Y. 2011. The role of Atg proteins in autophagosome formation. *Annu. Rev. Cell Dev. Biol.* 27:107–32

75. Motley AM, Nuttall JM, Hettema EH. 2012. Pex3-anchored Atg36 tags peroxisomes for degradation in *Saccharomyces cerevisiae*. *EMBO J.* 31:2852–68

76. Nair U, Cao Y, Xie Z, Klionsky DJ. 2010. Roles of the lipid-binding motifs of Atg18 and Atg21 in the cytoplasm to vacuole targeting pathway and autophagy. *J. Biol. Chem.* 285:11476–88

77. Nakatogawa H, Ichimura Y, Ohsumi Y. 2007. Atg8, a ubiquitin-like protein required for autophagosome formation, mediates membrane tethering and hemifusion. *Cell* 130:165–78

78. Nakatogawa H, Ohbayashi S, Sakoh-Nakatogawa M, Kakuta S, Suzuki SW, et al. 2012. The autophagy-related protein kinase Atg1 interacts with the ubiquitin-like protein Atg8 via the Atg8 family interacting motif to facilitate autophagosome formation. *J. Biol. Chem.* 287:28503–7

79. Nakatogawa H, Suzuki K, Kamada Y, Ohsumi Y. 2009. Dynamics and diversity in autophagy mechanisms: lessons from yeast. *Nat. Rev. Mol. Cell Biol.* 10:458–67

80. Nath S, Dancourt J, Shteyn V, Puente G, Fong WM, et al. 2014. Lipidation of the LC3/GABARAP family of autophagy proteins relies on a membrane-curvature-sensing domain in Atg3. *Nat. Cell Biol.* 16:415–24

81. Noda NN, Fujioka Y, Hanada T, Ohsumi Y, Inagaki F. 2013. Structure of the Atg12-Atg5 conjugate reveals a platform for stimulating Atg8-PE conjugation. *EMBO Rep.* 14:206–11

82. Noda NN, Kobayashi T, Adachi W, Fujioka Y, Ohsumi Y, Inagaki F. 2012. Structure of the novel C-terminal domain of vacuolar protein sorting 30/autophagy-related protein 6 and its specific role in autophagy. *J. Biol. Chem.* 287:16256–66

83. Noda NN, Kumeta H, Nakatogawa H, Satoo K, Adachi W, et al. 2008. Structural basis of target recognition by Atg8/LC3 during selective autophagy. *Genes Cells* 13:1211–18

84. Noda NN, Ohsumi Y, Inagaki F. 2009. ATG systems from the protein structural point of view. *Chem. Rev.* 109:1587–98

85. Noda NN, Ohsumi Y, Inagaki F. 2010. Atg8-family interacting motif crucial for selective autophagy. *FEBS Lett.* 584:1379–85

86. Noda NN, Satoo K, Fujioka Y, Kumeta H, Ogura K, et al. 2011. Structural basis of Atg8 activation by a homodimeric E1, Atg7. *Mol. Cell* 44:462–75

87. Noda T, Ohsumi Y. 1998. Tor, a phosphatidylinositol kinase homologue, controls autophagy in yeast. *J. Biol. Chem.* 273:3963–66

88. Novak I, Kirkin V, McEwan DG, Zhang J, Wild P, et al. 2010. Nix is a selective autophagy receptor for mitochondrial clearance. *EMBO Rep.* 11:45–51

89. Obara K, Sekito T, Ohsumi Y. 2006. Assortment of phosphatidylinositol 3-kinase complexes–Atg14p directs association of complex I to the pre-autophagosomal structure in *Saccharomyces cerevisiae*. *Mol. Biol. Cell* 17:1527–39

90. Ohsumi Y. 2001. Molecular dissection of autophagy: two ubiquitin-like systems. *Nat. Rev.* 2:211–16

91. Otomo C, Metlagel Z, Takaesu G, Otomo T. 2013. Structure of the human ATG12~ATG5 conjugate required for LC3 lipidation in autophagy. *Nat. Struct. Mol. Biol.* 20:59–66

92. Pankiv S, Clausen TH, Lamark T, Brech A, Bruun J-A, et al. 2007. p62/SQSTM1 binds directly to Atg8/LC3 to facilitate degradation of ubiquitinated protein aggregates by autophagy. *J. Biol. Chem.* 282:24131–45

93. Papinski D, Schuschnig M, Reiter W, Wilhelm L, Barnes CA, et al. 2014. Early steps in autophagy depend on direct phosphorylation of Atg9 by the Atg1 kinase. *Mol. Cell* 53:471–83

94. Paz Y, Elazar Z, Fass D. 2000. Structure of GATE-16, membrane transport modulator and mammalian ortholog of autophagocytosis factor Aut7p. *J. Biol. Chem.* 275:25445–50

95. Qiu Y, Hofmann K, Coats JE, Schulman BA, Kaiser SE. 2013. Binding to E1 and E3 is mutually exclusive for the human autophagy E2 Atg3. *Protein Sci.* 22:1691–97

96. Ragusa MJ, Stanley RE, Hurley JH. 2012. Architecture of the Atg17 complex as a scaffold for autophagosome biogenesis. *Cell* 151:1501–12

97. Reggiori F, Tucker KA, Stromhaug PE, Klionsky DJ. 2004. The Atg1-Atg13 complex regulates Atg9 and Atg23 retrieval transport from the pre-autophagosomal structure. *Dev. Cell* 6:79–90

98. Rubinsztein DC, Shpilka T, Elazar Z. 2012. Mechanisms of autophagosome biogenesis. *Curr. Biol.* 22:R29–34

99. Sakoh-Nakatogawa M, Matoba K, Asai E, Kirisako H, Ishii J, et al. 2013. Atg12-Atg5 conjugate enhances E2 activity of Atg3 by rearranging its catalytic site. *Nat. Struct. Mol. Biol.* 20:433–39

100. Satoo K, Noda NN, Kumeta H, Fujioka Y, Mizushima N, et al. 2009. The structure of Atg4B-LC3 complex reveals the mechanism of LC3 processing and delipidation during autophagy. *EMBO J.* 28:1341–50

101. Schulman BA, Harper JW. 2009. Ubiquitin-like protein activation by E1 enzymes: the apex for downstream signaling pathways. *Nat. Rev. Mol. Cell Biol.* 10:319–31

102. Scott SV, Guan J, Hutchins MU, Kim J, Klionsky DJ. 2001. Cvt19 is a receptor for the cytoplasm-to-vacuole targeting pathway. *Mol. Cell* 7:1131–41

103. Shintani T, Mizushima N, Ogawa Y, Matsuura A, Noda T, Ohsumi Y. 1999. Apg10p, a novel protein-conjugating enzyme essential for autophagy in yeast. *EMBO J.* 18:5234–41

104. Soufi B, Kelstrup CD, Stoehr G, Fröhlich F, Walther TC, Olsen JV. 2009. Global analysis of the yeast osmotic stress response by quantitative proteomics. *Mol. Biosyst.* 5:1337–46

105. Soulard A, Cremonesi A, Moes S, Schütz F, Jenö P, Hall MN. 2010. The rapamycin-sensitive phosphoproteome reveals that TOR controls protein kinase A toward some but not all substrates. *Mol. Biol. Cell* 21:3475–86

106. Stephan JS, Yeh YY, Ramachandran V, Deminoff SJ, Herman PK. 2009. The Tor and PKA signaling pathways independently target the Atg1/Atg13 protein kinase complex to control autophagy. *PNAS* 106:17049–54

107. Sugawara K, Suzuki NN, Fujioka Y, Mizushima N, Ohsumi Y, Inagaki F. 2004. The crystal structure of microtubule-associated protein light chain 3, a mammalian homologue of *Saccharomyces cerevisiae* Atg8. *Genes Cells* 9:611–18

108. Sugawara K, Suzuki NN, Fujioka Y, Mizushima N, Ohsumi Y, Inagaki F. 2005. Structural basis for the specificity and catalysis of human Atg4B responsible for mammalian autophagy. *J. Biol. Chem.* 280:40058–65

109. Sun LL, Li M, Suo F, Liu XM, Shen EZ, et al. 2013. Global analysis of fission yeast mating genes reveals new autophagy factors. *PLOS Genet.* 9:e1003715

110. Suzuki H, Tabata K, Morita E, Kawasaki M, Kato R, et al. 2014. Structural basis of the autophagy-related LC3/Atg13 LIR complex: recognition and interaction mechanism. *Structure* 22:47–58

111. Suzuki K, Kirisako T, Kamada Y, Mizushima N, Noda T, Ohsumi Y. 2001. The pre-autophagosomal structure organized by concerted functions of APG genes is essential for autophagosome formation. *EMBO J.* 20:5971–81

112. Suzuki K, Kondo C, Morimoto M, Ohsumi Y. 2010. Selective transport of α-mannosidase by autophagic pathways: identification of a novel receptor, Atg34p. *J. Biol. Chem.* 285:30019–25

113. Suzuki K, Kubota Y, Sekito T, Ohsumi Y. 2007. Hierarchy of Atg proteins in pre-autophagosomal structure organization. *Genes Cells* 12:209–18

114. Suzuki K, Ohsumi Y. 2010. Current knowledge of the pre-autophagosomal structure (PAS). *FEBS Lett.* 584:1280–86

115. Suzuki NN, Yoshimoto K, Fujioka Y, Ohsumi Y, Inagaki F. 2005. The crystal structure of plant ATG12 and its biological implication in autophagy. *Autophagy* 1:119–26

116. Taherbhoy AM, Tait SW, Kaiser SE, Williams AH, Deng A, et al. 2011. Atg8 transfer from Atg7 to Atg3: a distinctive E1-E2 architecture and mechanism in the autophagy pathway. *Mol. Cell* 44:451–61

117. Thumm M, Egner R, Koch B, Schlumpberger M, Straub M, et al. 1994. Isolation of autophagocytosis mutants of *Saccharomyces cerevisiae*. *FEBS Lett.* 349:275–80

118. Tsukada M, Ohsumi Y. 1993. Isolation and characterization of autophagy-defective mutants of *Saccharomyces cerevisiae*. *FEBS Lett.* 333:169–74

119. Watanabe Y, Kobayashi T, Yamamoto H, Hoshida H, Akada R, et al. 2012. Structure-based analyses reveal distinct binding sites for Atg2 and phosphoinositides in Atg18. *J. Biol. Chem.* 287:31681–90

120. Weidberg H, Shpilka T, Shvets E, Abada A, Shimron F, Elazar Z. 2011. LC3 and GATE-16 N termini mediate membrane fusion processes required for autophagosome biogenesis. *Dev. Cell* 20:444–54

121. Xie Z, Nair U, Klionsky DJ. 2008. Atg8 controls phagophore expansion during autophagosome formation. *Mol. Biol. Cell* 19:3290–98

122. Yamada Y, Suzuki NN, Hanada T, Ichimura Y, Kumeta H, et al. 2007. The crystal structure of Atg3, an autophagy-related ubiquitin carrier protein (E2) enzyme that mediates Atg8 lipidation. *J. Biol. Chem.* 282:8036–43

123. Yamaguchi M, Matoba K, Sawada R, Fujioka Y, Nakatogawa H, et al. 2012. Noncanonical recognition and UBL loading of distinct E2s by autophagy-essential Atg7. *Nat. Struct. Mol. Biol.* 19:1250–56

124. Yamaguchi M, Noda NN, Nakatogawa H, Kumeta H, Ohsumi Y, Inagaki F. 2010. Autophagy-related protein 8 (Atg8) family interacting motif in Atg3 mediates the Atg3-Atg8 interaction and is crucial for the cytoplasm-to-vacuole targeting pathway. *J. Biol. Chem.* 285:29599–607

125. Yamaguchi M, Noda NN, Yamamoto H, Shima T, Kumeta H, et al. 2012. Structural insights into Atg10-mediated formation of the autophagy-essential Atg12-Atg5 conjugate. *Structure* 20:1244–54

126. Yamamoto H, Kakuta S, Watanabe TM, Kitamura A, Sekito T, et al. 2012. Atg9 vesicles are an important membrane source during early steps of autophagosome formation. *J. Cell Biol.* 198:219–33

127. Yeh YY, Shah KH, Herman PK. 2011. An Atg13 protein-mediated self-association of the Atg1 protein kinase is important for the induction of autophagy. *J. Biol. Chem.* 286:28931–39

128. Yeh YY, Wrasman K, Herman PK. 2010. Autophosphorylation within the Atg1 activation loop is required for both kinase activity and the induction of autophagy in *Saccharomyces cerevisiae*. *Genetics* 185:871–82

Single-Cell Physiology

Sattar Taheri-Araghi,[1] Steven D. Brown,[1]
John T. Sauls,[1] Dustin B. McIntosh,[1]
and Suckjoon Jun[1,2]

[1]Department of Physics, [2]Section of Molecular Biology, Division of Biological Science,
University of California, San Diego, La Jolla, California 92093; email: suckjoon.jun@gmail.com

Annu. Rev. Biophys. 2015. 44:123–42

First published online as a Review in Advance on
February 26, 2015

The *Annual Review of Biophysics* is online at
biophys.annualreviews.org

This article's doi:
10.1146/annurev-biophys-060414-034236

Keywords

cell cycle, growth, microbiology, microfluidics, systems biology,
quantitative biology

Abstract

Single-cell techniques have a long history of unveiling fundamental
paradigms in biology. Recent improvements in the throughput, resolution,
and availability of microfluidics, computational power, and genetically encoded fluorescence have led to a modern renaissance in microbial physiology.
This resurgence in research activity has offered new perspectives on physiological processes such as growth, cell cycle, and cell size of model organisms
such as *Escherichia coli*. We expect these single-cell techniques, coupled with
the molecular revolution of biology's recent half-century, to continue illuminating unforeseen processes and patterns in microorganisms, the bedrock of
biological science. In this article we review major open questions in single-
cell physiology, provide a brief introduction to the techniques for scientists of diverse backgrounds, and highlight some pervasive issues and their
solutions.

Contents

INTRODUCTION

The late François Jacob (89) is said to have remarked, "The dream of every cell is to become two cells." There are several basic steps for cellular reproduction: growth of the cell, replication and segregation of the genetic materials, and cell division. The physiological study of microorganisms aims to understand the fundamental controls underlying these processes. In particular, a single-cell approach can reveal causal relationships that are inaccessible to population-level experiments, and provide key insights into the underlying control mechanisms. Researchers were interested in single-cell measurements of microorganisms nearly a century ago (15). However, it is only in the last decade that the field has come of age with the rapid development of video microscopy and lab-on-a-chip technologies, along with computers that are powerful enough to analyze large amounts of data.

A telling example is the study of cell size. In the classic literature, cell size was measured by optical density of a growing culture and colony counts, assuming that light absorbance per cell was proportional to the cell size (79). Data from batch culture, however, do not disclose cell-to-cell variations and may not reveal important correlations. See, for instance, the relationship between the size of newborn *Escherichia coli* cells and their respective generation time between birth and division (**Figure 1***a*). They are negatively correlated; i.e., cells born smaller than the population average take longer to divide than cells born larger than the population average. This finding is a strong indication for a mechanism of cell size control, which would not have been possible to measure in batch culture.

Control of gene expression is another important example for which single-cell approaches have been immensely valuable. The study of gene expression mechanisms dates back to the 1950s,

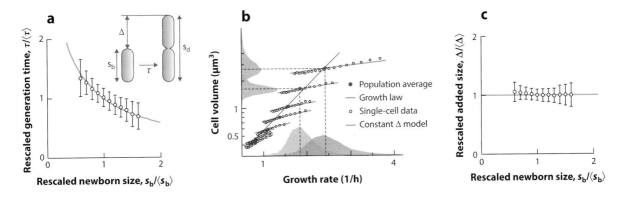

Figure 1

Single-cell experiments of *Escherichia coli* reveal the size control mechanism by parameters that are not accessible in a population average experiment. (*a*) Generation time, τ, is negatively correlated with newborn size, s_b, ruling out the timer model. (*b*) Single-cell data show a systematic deviation from the growth law. The population average data (*red lines* and *red symbols*) confirm the classic work of Schaechter et al. (79), but single-cell data (*black symbols*) systematically deviate from the growth law. This deviation is related to how cells control their size in a steady-state growth condition. (*c*) Cells add a constant size, Δ, from birth to division, independent of their size at birth, s_b. Figure based on data from Wang et al. (98).

such as the analysis of the *lac* operon induction levels by Novick & Weiner (75). This experiment revealed that the smooth, correlated increase in protein expression observed in batch culture experiments was not due to the equal and gradual induction of all cells. Instead, discrete subpopulations of cells transition from fully repressed to fully induced states. Novick & Weiner's observation inspired modern systems biology studies on bistability of gene expression at the single-cell level (77). Noise in gene expression has also benefited from single-cell methods (34, 76). The revelation of new behaviors and mechanisms through single-cell experiments is integral to biology.

We anticipate two audiences will read this review article. The first audience consists of researchers trained in quantitative fields of science and engineering who want to enter biology and tackle long-standing problems in cell physiology. We introduce key scientific questions in single-cell physiology that can benefit from the tools and ways of thinking from the physical sciences and engineering. The second audience consists of biologists who want to use single-cell technologies for their research. Similarly, we introduce key technical approaches that can complement existing molecular assays. Like any technology, single-cell methods produce good data only when used appropriately. Unfortunately, virtually all current techniques suffer from varying degrees of artifacts and physiological compromises. It can take years of painstaking control experiments to discover and (hopefully) correct these problems. For both audiences, we discuss some of the most common problems and how to troubleshoot them.

Although this is a review article, space constraints mean that we must focus and impose our own view of this important branch of basic science through the selection of material. As such, we use examples from bacterial cell physiology that share the same natural core with eukaryotes. We also apologize to our colleagues whose work should have been cited otherwise. We provide a partial solution by introducing excellent review articles for the important materials we are unable to discuss.

FUNDAMENTAL QUESTIONS IN SINGLE-CELL PHYSIOLOGY

Growing cells have been the subject of endless fascination since their first observation by Antony van Leeuwenhoek (30). Many individuals have recorded with great care and accuracy the basic properties of cells. In the 1940s, Jacques Monod (71) studied cells utilizing multiple carbon sources in a growth medium. His study on cells transitioning from metabolizing glucose to lactose, known as the diauxic shift, was one of the major stepping stones for the later study with Jacob and Lwoff on the mechanism of gene expression—the *lac* operon (49).

For those trained at the interface between biological and physical sciences, reading the literature from the early-twentieth century until the beginning of the 1970s is a refreshing experience. See, for example, the work by Schaechter et al. (79) on bacterial growth in the late 1950s. They established the basic principle in bacterial physiology known as the growth law on the basis of meticulous measurements of cell mass, RNA, and DNA content with respect to nutrient-imposed growth rate. The growth law states that the average cell size increases exponentially with respect to nutrient-imposed growth rate. Remarkably, this exponential relationship is independent of the chemical details of the growth media. Similar and equally important quantitative approaches to bacterial physiology and the bacterial cell cycle continued in the 1960s. Koch & Schaechter (59), among many others, based their study of cell size distributions on the elongation model of individual cells. Cooper & Helmstetter (28) established the phenomenological kinematic rule of the bacterial cell cycle, which explained the timing of chromosome replication and cell division under a wide range of nutrient-imposed growth rates.

Although most classic studies relied on population-level measurements, their interests were deeply rooted in single-cell behavior. However, the lack of single-cell data has hindered our ability to answer many fundamental questions because population averages can conceal important causal insights and because throughput suffers when resolution is increased (see **Figure 1**). Some of these questions include, How do cells coordinate growth and cell cycle? How do cells control their size and shape? How do cells know when to replicate their chromosome and when to divide? How do cells die? We follow with how single-cell methods are needed to address these questions.

Growth and Cell Size

Cell size control is a long-standing, multifaceted problem in biology. First, many single-celled microorganisms, including yeast (52) and bacteria (79), change their average size with respect to growth conditions. The growth law shows that the average cell size increases exponentially as the nutrient-imposed growth rate increases. Second, even in a steady-state growth condition, cell size, among other cell cycle parameters, exhibits significant variability. Using single-cell measurements, we now know that the size of *E. coli* varies about 15% at division (92, 98). Although this finding implies cell size is subject to stochastic fluctuation, the size distribution of a population remains unchanged over generations, indicating that cells respond to fluctuations to maintain size homeostasis.

Two classes of models, sizer and timer, account for size control and homeostasis in microorganisms. Sizer presumes cells trigger division at a specific size, whereas timer assumes cell division occurs after a set elapsed time. Thus, sizer predicts that the division size is independent of the birth size, whereas timer indicates that generation time is constant irrespective of the birth size. Testing these predictions requires single-cell data, in which the growth of a large population of individual cells can be tracked to find correlations between growth parameters. Data collected from 10^5 individual cells (presented in **Figure 1a**) preclude the timer model since the generation time is negatively correlated with newborn size. Similar analysis (92) of single-cell data showed that size at division is correlated with size at birth, precluding sizer.

Our analysis of the growth law at a single-cell level led to a surprising discovery: The growth law breaks down at a single-cell level (92) (**Figure 1b**). That is, the population average data confirm the original growth law, but single-cell data systematically deviate from it. These deviations are related to how individual cells control their size in the presence of fluctuations in a steady-state growth condition: Cells add a constant size from birth to division, independent of their size at birth. This fundamental and simple size homeostasis mechanism operates in both *E. coli* and *Bacillus subtilis* (see **Figure 1c** for *E. coli*). Following this "adder" principle, cell size deviations are restored after several generations by geometric regression to the mean (23, 53, 92, 97).

New developments in molecular physiology have created opportunities to potentially perturb cell size control mechanisms. Levin and colleagues (46, 101) have reported a metabolic sensor in *B. subtilis* that links nutrient availability with division machinery, specifically the FtsZ constriction ring. This metabolic sensor is thought to regulate an inhibitor of constriction ring assembly to control cell size in a nutrient-dependent manner. How the metabolic sensor integrates with other molecular mechanisms and ultimately leads to a quantitative relationship between the average cell size and the nutrient-imposed growth rate is still unknown. Kinetic information is needed if we are to understand these processes. By revisiting classic nutrient shift-up experiments (26, 79) to measure the response in size and the cell cycle of individual cells during the transition from one steady-state growth condition to another, researchers may discriminate among these hypotheses.

"Adder" principle: a model for cell size homeostasis based on added size from birth to division

Cell Cycle

The cell cycle is composed of a set of processes that must be faithfully performed in order to create two viable daughter cells. Undergraduate biology textbooks focus on the cell cycle of eukaryotes, in which the chromosome is duplicated once and partitioned among the two daughter cells and checkpoints arrest the cycle if the process goes awry (3, 69). Unlike eukaryotes, most prokaryotes are capable of multifork replication, i.e., of maintaining multiple overlapping rounds of DNA synthesis (28), as shown in **Figure 2**. Significant questions remain pertaining to how these cells

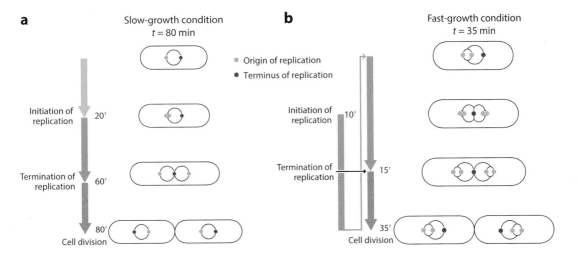

Figure 2

Cell cycle of *Escherichia coli* cells. (*a*) In slow-growth conditions (generation time larger than C and D periods combined), the cell cycle has three distinct steps: the time between birth and initiation of chromosome replication (B period, *green arrow*; length depends on generation time), the time of chromosome replication (C period, *blue arrow*; 40 min), and the gap between termination of chromosome replication and division (D period, *orange arrow*; 20 min). (*b*) In fast-growth conditions, multiple cell cycles must overlap because the period C + D is constant and longer than the generation time. The illustration shows chromosome replication spanning two generations. Under all growth conditions, one round of the replication cycle must be coupled to one round of the division cycle.

can coordinate growth, size, DNA replication, and division to create two functioning daughter cells without incident.

In a series of studies in the 1960s, Helmstetter, Cooper, and colleagues (26, 28, 44, 45) developed experimental methods to measure the duration of chromosome replication, known as C period (analogous to S phase in eukaryotes), in the model organism *E. coli*. For a wide range of growth conditions at 37°C, C period is constant, approximately 40 min for their strain of *E. coli* B/r. In addition, a constant amount of time known as D period (20 min; analogous to G2 phase in eukaryotes) passes between replication termination and cell division. Thus, C and D periods combined last for approximately 60 min, although *E. coli* can divide as frequently as every 20 min. This seeming conflict, namely that DNA replication can take longer than the generation time, led Cooper & Helmstetter to conclude that cell cycles in *E. coli* must overlap. Their influential model predicted that *E. coli* initiates DNA replication C + D minutes prior to each cell division.

An obvious question is, What is the relationship between cell cycle timing and cell size? In an important theoretical study, Donachie (32) showed that the Helmstetter-Cooper model together with the growth law by Schaechter et al. implies that replication initiates when cell mass per replication origin reaches a critical value, independent of the growth condition. The notion of critical mass, however, remains controversial (14, 27).

Single-cell data can provide fundamental insights into cell cycle control mechanisms not available from population-level data. For example, the negative correlations between the generation time and the newborn size (**Figure 1**) clearly show the presence of a size control mechanism. Similarly, the following questions can be answered only by single-cell experiments, which were not possible when the Helmstetter-Cooper model was developed in the 1960s: How variable are C and D periods under constant growth conditions? Will replication always initiate when the cell reaches a critical mass as Donachie predicted? More generally, how is the cell cycle maintained when cells deviate from the average growth rate or size of the population or when cells experience stochastic variation at the initiation of replication? Subsequent analyses of various *E. coli* strains revealed deviations in the duration and arrangement of different growth periods (73). In consideration of these differences even within one species, how general are the aforementioned models to diverse strains and organisms that perform multifork replication? Rigorous single-cell measurements of replication timing will shed light on the above questions and may reveal whether fundamental processes underlie cell cycle control across diverse microbes.

Metabolism

Intimately connected with growth, metabolism represents the entire complex chemical network underlying living organisms. Despite ongoing work to characterize and model these networks, metabolism in vivo remains woefully unquantified. This is partially due to the difficulty of simultaneously measuring the kinetics, abundances, and fluctuations of the many players in these complex systems. Can we quantitatively understand metabolism without measuring seemingly endless parameters? This dilemma captures one of the central problems of systems biology: how to bridge bottom-up and top-down methods in order to uncover guiding principles.

Single-cell data can provide fundamental insights into the general properties of metabolism. Recently, Kiviet et al. (57) continuously and simultaneously monitored instantaneous growth rate and metabolic production (e.g., *lac* expression) in single cells. This exposed fluctuations at timescales far below that of the generation time and allowed them to measure how growth and gene expression influence each other. By computing cross correlations between measured growth rate and the level of gene expression, they showed that noise propagates bidirectionally. Because correlations in fluctuations were also observed in the Krebs cycle at metabolic nodes distant from the *lac* operon, these observations are likely a general feature of noise propagation in metabolism. It also gives us hope that single-cell studies can provide general and critical insights into even the most complex systems.

Cell Shape

Cell shape may be considered a topic in cell biology or mathematical biology rather than physiology. Early attempts to quantify shape focused on the physical constraints on the forms unicellular organisms can take (58). More recently, the role of bacterial cell walls and cytoskeletal components has become an important avenue of investigation to understand cell shape control. We believe the subject can greatly benefit from a physiological approach that focuses on responses of cell shape to changing growth conditions. Woldringh et al. (104) addressed how *E. coli* cell shape changes during the transition from one steady-state growth condition to another, i.e., from slow growth in minimal glycerol to fast growth in synthetic rich media. Their critical observation was that cell morphology changes anisotropically; although both cell length and cell width increased immediately after nutrient shift-up, many cells continued to possess a tapered old pole (**Figure 3a**). This

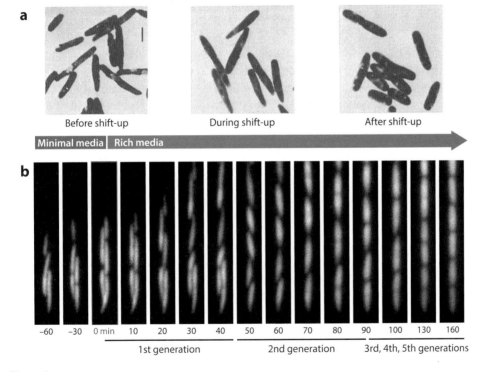

Before shift-up   During shift-up   After shift-up

Minimal media | Rich media

-60   -30   0 min   10   20   30   40   50   60   70   80   90   100   130   160

1st generation   2nd generation   3rd, 4th, 5th generations

Figure 3

Shape changes of *Escherichia coli* cells during the transition from slow-growth to fast-growth conditions. (*a*) Anisotropic change of cell morphology observed by Woldringh et al. (104) leading to the conclusion that the old pole is metabolically inert in terms of the turnover rate of constituent materials relative to the sides of the cell wall. (*b*) A nutrient shift-up experiment in a microfluidic device consistent with and extending the anisotropic interpretation. The tapered pole was indeed the result of the old pole dimensions changing slower than the size of the adjacent side walls. The tapered old pole eventually regained normal shape and dimensions, indicating the cell pole is not completely inert. Panel *a* is reprinted from Reference 104, with permission from Elsevier.

observation suggests that the old pole is metabolically inert relative to the sides of the cell wall in terms of the turnover rate of constituent materials. We performed a nutrient shift-up experiment and continuously monitored cell shape changes at the single-cell level (**Figure 3b**; S. Jun & P. Wang, unpublished results). The tapered pole was indeed the result of the slow change of the old pole dimensions compared with the faster increase in size of the side walls, consistent with the previous anisotropic observations. However, the tapered old pole eventually achieved normal shape and dimensions, indicating that the cell pole is not completely inert—an observation not possible without modern microfluidic techniques.

This type of single-cell growth experiment can be combined with modern imaging techniques that can directly visualize cell wall synthesis (31, 37, 96). Furthermore, we can now easily manipulate the shape of individual cells using controllable forces (4, 99) or geometrical constraints of microfabricated devices (67, 93). How does a cell maintain the correct shape in the face of a fluctuating physical environment? A lesson from these recent single-cell studies is that growth and physiology are important for understanding cell shape maintenance.

Mother machine: a microfluidic device with many narrow parallel growth channels that has one closed end and one open end exposed to fresh media

SOS: a group of bacterial functions that act to repair and recover from DNA damage

Senescence and Death

Whether the two daughter cells resulting from cell division are physiologically and genetically identical and whether they are indistinguishable from the mother cell remain important open questions. These questions have often been addressed in the context of senescence, which has required single-cell approaches beginning with the first experiments. The classic study by Mortimer & Johnston (72) discovered that morphologically asymmetric dividing budding yeast accumulate bud scars on the mother cell and that she dies after several dozen divisions. Experimental reports indicate that even for bacteria the two daughter cells are different in both morphologically asymmetric and symmetric organisms (1, 90). Specifically, these authors found that the growth rate of the daughter cells continuously decreases with respect to the replicative age of the cells. Follow-up studies by several groups (65, 103) reported correlations between protein aggregation (formation of inclusion bodies) and decrease of growth rate, although whether protein aggregation actually reduces growth rate has not been shown.

A new class of experiments using microfluidic devices has painted a different picture (70). Our group (98) used a simple microfluidic habitat (the mother machine) to observe the long-term growth patterns of many single *E. coli* cells. Cells grew and replicated while the growth medium was continuously replenished in the device. *E. coli* mother cells trapped in narrow, dead-end growth channels grew without any decrease in growth rates for several hundred generations in steady-state conditions. Instead, the frequency of filamentation (and by inference, SOS induction) had a dramatic effect on the rate of death. To determine the heritable material driving an increased rate of cell death or filamentation, a combination of single-cell cultivation and monitoring by single-cell DNA sequencing will ultimately resolve questions about the nature of bacterial senescence. We feel that this is a field where microfluidics and single-cell technology are already mature and ready for more serious genetics and physiological approaches.

Evolution

Single-cell approaches can unexpectedly impact the study of evolution and the genetic origin of physiology (54). An early implementation of single-cell sequencing that targeted discrete loci observed the genetic progression of mouse tumor cell lineages and linked specific mutations to the appearance of tumor phenotypes (36). Because mutations and selection happen at the individual level, efforts to quantify the rate of evolution are somewhat futile without single-cell resolution.

This is particularly intriguing considered in the context of directed evolution in microfluidic devices (106). Single-cell evolution experiments could decouple selection scheme design from growth rate, which is impossible in traditional adaptive laboratory evolution. A method to rapidly sequester individual cells could possibly be combined with a single-cell-level phenotypic assay (e.g., quantitative mass spectrometry), eliminating the need to couple the analyte of interest with continued rapid growth and division. A chosen cell could subsequently seed a new round of growth and selection, and sequencing could trace the effects of evolution on physiology.

SINGLE-CELL EXPERIMENTS WITH MICROFLUIDICS: LESSONS LEARNED AND SHARED

We have outlined fundamental questions in cell physiology that can benefit from quantitative single-cell approaches. Unfortunately, implementation of these approaches is not an easy feat. Observation of growth in individual cells has been recorded since at least 1932 (15) but micrographs alone portray limited information. Two elegant technologies developed in the mid-twentieth century, the baby machine and the Coulter counter, were an enormous leap forward (22, 28, 42, 44). Today we are fortunate to be armed with even more precise and robust technology for direct tracking and manipulation of individual cells.

Microfluidics paired with microscopy has become chief among these tools, enabling many studies that were not possible with bulk culture. Its adoption has been accelerated by advances in the miniaturization of electronics and parallel liquid sample handling methods for chemical analysis (80, 102). Low-cost and accessible soft-lithography techniques pioneered and matured by the Whitesides laboratory (105) were major contributions to the field. Rapid development of a complex microfluidic manipulation system by the Quake laboratory (95) has thrust microfluidics to the forefront of biology. A salient example of a previously inaccessible study is Balaban et al. (10), which characterized the bacterial persistence phenotype as a nongenetic switch between growth and nongrowth. Monitoring growth of single cells, the authors were able to directly observe individual persistent cells that survive antibiotic treatment without developing genetic resistance to the antibiotic. Other efforts to characterize cellular growth took advantage of the mother machine (98). Studies of both rod-shaped bacteria such as *B. subtilis* (74) and single-cell eukaryotes such as fission yeast (74, 87) utilized the high-throughput and long-term experimental capabilities of this device. In addition to answering existing questions, the use of microfluidic devices has enabled researchers to observe dynamic systems that were otherwise relegated to theory. For instance, it is now possible to directly observe competition and rapid evolution within a population of single cells (55).

With awareness of the limitations imposed by microfluidic techniques, it is possible to conceive, design, and successfully execute exciting experiments. Our philosophical compass for making decisions herein is guided by three central tenets: (*a*) Results must be reproducible; (*b*) quantitative distributions, as opposed to means or cherry-picked images, must be presented; and (*c*) averages calculated from the distributions must agree with population-level control experiments.

In the following sections we review useful technologies, pitfalls we faced in the past, and lessons we have learned along the way. In our experience, the application of these practices with great care dramatically improves the reliability and reproducibility of experimental data.

Design Strategy

The growth environment of microfluidic-based single-cell experiments is different from that of batch culture or continuous culture devices, e.g., chemostats and turbidostats. One consideration is that the volume of the liquid environment surrounding the cells is reduced such that a single cell can

Baby machine: a device based on membrane elution to produce synchronized populations of cells

Turbidostat: a continuous bulk culture device that maintains a constant concentration of cells by exchanging old media for new media at a variable rate

PDMS:
polydimethylsiloxane

LB: lysogeny broth

Prototroph: an
organism capable of
synthesizing all its
metabolites from
inorganic material,
requiring no organic
nutrients

be in constant contact with several sides of the vessel's walls. Thus, cells growing in microchannels can be influenced by the physical presence of channel walls, a phenomenon absent in liquid culture experiments. These forces along with fluid dynamics may drive unexpected behavior that may be anticipated at the device design stage (88).

Most of the current single-cell microfluidic devices are based on polydimethylsiloxane (PDMS) annealed to a coverslip, allowing microscopy from one side of the glass. PDMS-based devices are robust, reproducible, and economic. However, PDMS is relatively stiff, which can introduce mechanical stress to cells under specific circumstances. Cluzel and colleagues (70) designed a microfluidic device based on printing micron-scale channels on a block of agarose gel. The soft, transparent, and porous nature of agarose gel makes it favorable for cell trapping; the physical pressure on cells is minimal while the gel allows delivery of nutrients. Another advantage of agarose gel over PDMS is its optical properties. With an index of refraction almost similar to that of water, agarose gel improves the quality of transmission light microscopy. Unfortunately, agarose itself is less stable than PDMS over time; agarose-based microfluidic devices are thus less suitable for long-term experiments.

The isolation of individual cells is often a prerequisite for single-cell studies. Although some laboratory strains have lost the ability to form biofilms, their occurrence can clog a microfluidic device and render the experiment useless. Clever and elaborate device designs have been critical in resolving these challenges. Quake and colleagues (11) created a lab-on-a-chip bioreactor that uses microfluidic plumbing networks to allow long-term growth of small populations of *E. coli* while actively preventing biofilm formation. Even organisms that do not form biofilms can spontaneously adhere to surfaces. We have empirically found that media flow rates on the order of 10 mm/s inside the mother machine will successfully evacuate cells (98).

Microfluidic habitats currently have long development cycles. Complex designs that alleviate biological problems require longer development cycles before the question of interest is actually addressed. Direct 3D printing and two-photon fabrication are two technologies with the potential to dramatically reduce the time from design to implementation to a single day. In addition, they remove the need for clean room photolithography. Current 3D printing technology allows feature scales as small as tens of microns, whereas the feature size attainable by two-photon systems is limited by optical resolution to 200–300 nm. These two technologies can in principle be combined to design 3D devices that cannot be realized by traditional photolithography techniques. For interested readers, we recommend recent reviews (48, 56, 87).

Growth Media and Culturability

Not all organisms and cells grow in a microfluidic device. Microorganisms grown under seemingly identical nutrient conditions sometimes show different growth rates depending on the cultivation methods, e.g., liquid culture, surfaces, or microfluidic devices. For example, in rich media such as lysogeny broth (LB), prototrophic *B. subtilis* strains grow well in both a microfluidic device and batch culture and show the same average growth rate. However, in defined minimal media (e.g., S7$_{50}$), the same strains grow much more slowly, if at all, in a microfluidic device compared with the batch culture of the same medium.

The barrier to growth might be traced to the one of the advantages of microfluidics itself. The precise control over media composition—including oxygenation (2)—possible in microfluidics can also be the source of artifacts and challenges. Molecules secreted by cells to improve their environment are immediately washed away, whereas in batch culture they persist and are available to the population. To troubleshoot this type of growth problem in a microfluidic device, we suggest trying conditioned, filtered medium prepared from batch culture in exponential or stationary phase. If the cells grow in a conditioned medium in a microfluidic device, it is likely that small molecules secreted by cells in batch culture are important for growth. Such molecules are constantly removed in a typical microfluidic device and cells are likely to experience nutrient conditions akin to infinite dilution.

FACS: fluorescence-activated cell sorting

Once the cause of the problem is identified, the next step is to add the essential molecules that are present in batch culture but not in the defined media. This step can be painstaking and requires a priori knowledge of the physiological demands of the specific strain or organism. In the case of *B. subtilis* grown in $S7_{50}$, the addition of sodium citrate and ferric chloride to $S7_{50}$ medium immediately revived growth. Indeed, the secretion of siderophores to increase the availability of metal salts, particularly iron, is essential for growth (62, 78). Other secreted agents such as autoinducer-2 (29), indole (63), and outer membrane vesicles (68) can build to levels in batch and turbidostat cultures that can alter transcription or physiology. The effect of these environment-conditioning agents on data obtained from various culture conditions is largely unexplored, and microfluidic growth devices are a powerful tool for investigators in this field.

Physical Manipulation of Single Cells

The physical capture of single cells is a prerequisite for some advanced analytics but it poses significant challenges. For example, aside from the unbiased amplification of DNA, the physical isolation of cells is a major hurdle in single-cell sequencing. Unfortunately, best practices in single-cell capture may not be intuitively obvious and are not refined enough to be immediately successful for new investigators. Microfluidic solutions are preferable to alternative methods such as flow sorting, micropipetting, or laser dissection. Although FACS (fluorescence-activated cell sorter) is high throughput and unbiased, large amounts of cells are needed, precluding studies of individual microorganisms that have ceased growth. Micropipetting and laser microdissection are low-throughput manual methods subject to operator bias. On the other hand, microfluidic techniques can be high throughput, provide visual confirmation of capture, and can be automated to diminish operator bias (66). The small reagent volumes required also reduce costs and suppress the frequency of contamination.

Actuated microfluidics and optical traps (also known as laser tweezers) offer rapidly maturing solutions that are often employed hand-in-hand. Actuated microfluidics is a highly controllable fluid flow system that utilizes micron-scale valves and pressure gradients that can sequester cells without undue stress. Researchers are developing increasingly sophisticated devices that can capture single cells in nanoliter volumes and deliver picoliter volume reagents to reaction chambers in a defined manner (64). Droplet microfluidics is another emerging technique that allows for the manipulation of individually isolated nanoliter volumes of liquid that can contain cells or reagents (41). Optical traps were applied to biological studies the year after their unveiling (7, 8). They can isolate specific single cells, in contrast to actuated microfluidics, in which liquid and molecules surrounding cells are cotransported. Complete optical trap systems can be purchased, but advanced do-it-yourself systems can be constructed for significantly less (J. Xu, personal communication). Intrigued readers might start with the book chapter on setting up an optical trap for cell isolation by Block (20) and a recent review by Landry et al. (61).

Imaging and Phototoxicity

Fluorescence imaging is powerful and often essential in single-cell studies, but it can also severely compromise the physiological state of individual cells. Phototoxicity is arguably the most serious and yet poorly understood problem associated with fluorescence microscopy for single-cell experiments. Upon excitation with a fluorescent light source, live cells will grow more slowly or stop growing altogether. The primary mechanism of phototoxicity seems to be the production of radical oxygen species. Radical oxygen species are highly reactive and can bind to and damage any number of important cellular constituents. In many cases this can be attributed directly to the fluorescent protein itself (39) but also to naturally occurring metabolites (e.g., NAD$^+$, flavins) that might otherwise confound the use of the green spectrum for detailed quantitative studies (16, 25).

Intense illumination is associated with growth defects in a number of organisms and is no less important in studies of bacteria, although the few quantitative analyses of the effect that have been performed are often relegated to supplementary information (91). To better understand the adverse effect of fluorescence illumination on bacterial physiology and, in particular, bacterial growth, we examined the effect of fluorescent illumination on the doubling rate of *E. coli* (D. McIntosh, unpublished results). Using a strain of *E. coli* that constitutively expresses a GFP fusion of a single-stranded binding protein, we took phase-contrast and fluorescence images 20 times per cell division in slow-growth media using a GFP filter set (see **Figure 4**). The growth

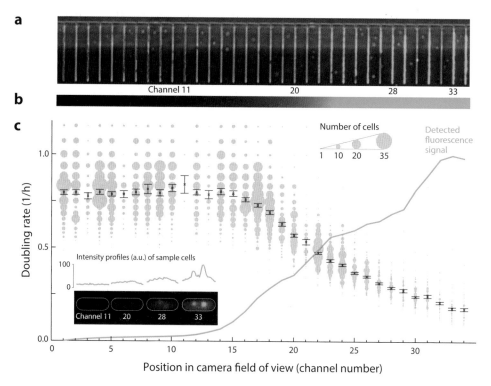

Figure 4

Strong effect of fluorescence imaging on growth. (*a*) A phase contrast/GFP overlay of a single field of view of *Escherichia coli* cells expressing Ssb-GFP (a GFP fusion of a single-stranded binding protein) grown in steady-state conditions. Cells imaged approximately 20 times per cell cycle for approximately 3 days with a fluorescence excitation illumination gradient across the field of view (cells on the left-hand side experience minimal illumination, whereas the exposure is maximum on the right-hand side). (*b*) A slice from an image taken with the same optical alignment of an FITC (fluorescein isothiocyanate) solution showing the intensity gradient. (*c*) Co-plot of FITC fluorescence intensity (a.u.) and growth rate (1/h) versus position in the field of view. As fluorescence intensity increases, the growth rate decreases. The insets show the intensity profile of the fluorescence image along a line passing through cells from different channels, as they experience different excitation light intensity.

rate of the cells is attenuated with increasing illumination intensity. Clearly, fluorescence imaging has a dramatic effect on the physiology of the cells.

Phototoxicity is correlated primarily with the illumination power delivered to the cell. Assuming that the illumination, exposure, camera triggering, and shutter opening have been optimized to the lowest possible levels that still permit accurate quantification, it will be necessary to upgrade to the most sensitive detectors available. Other methods to consider include (a) illuminating with longer wavelength light for two-photon excitation to reduce the unwanted excitation of metabolites, reducing the burden of associated reactive oxygen species (84, 107); (b) limiting the excitation area to only a small region of interest within the specimen, sparing the remainder of the specimen from unnecessary damage (47); and (c) avoiding chromophore overexcitation and thus phototoxicity (51) by using a pulsed laser with an interpulse time exceeding the lifetime of the triplet excited state (33).

Although most single-cell techniques rely on light microscopy, alternatives to visual observation that provide high-resolution insights do exist. Manalis and colleagues (85) designed a novel microchannel resonator to measure the ultralow volume of particles passing through a suspended resonator. Together with the Kirschner laboratory (38), they studied growth of single cells by measuring the buoyant mass of cells at femtogram resolution. Their experimental data based on *B. subtilis*, *E. coli*, *S. cerevisiae*, and mouse lymphoblasts were consistent with exponential growth of cells during the cell cycle.

Choice of Fluorescent Proteins

Fluorescence microscopy can provide valuable information about protein interactions and localizations and metabolic activities of cells. With the advent of modern genetics, fluorescent proteins became more and more popular for tracking gene expression and protein interactions (81). The efficiency of the method and the possibility of live-cell visualization outpaced immunofluorescence techniques, the previous gold standard. A review article by Tsien and colleagues (82) still provides a nice guideline for choosing fluorescent proteins.

The drawback of fusion fluorescent proteins is that fusion can affect the function of the tagged protein. Sometimes the artifact leads to an obvious phenotypic problem, such as slow growth rate or unusual morphology (82). But the dangerous artifacts are those that are not obvious. In a remarkable report, Landgraf et al. (60) performed extensive and extremely careful studies on a previously reported ClpX protein localization pattern. They used two methods to validate the localization: (a) tracking the downstream processes in the daughter cells in both wild-type and tagged cells and (b) using alternative fluorescent proteins. They confirmed the observed foci were an artifact of fluorescent protein dimerization. An important lesson from this study is that scientists must construct and test different reporter proteins for any serious experiments employing fluorescent fusion proteins. In addition, results based on fluorescent fusion proteins should be validated by independent means.

Temperature Control

Temperature affects the growth rate of the cells as well as the brightness of most fluorescent proteins. Most laboratories use a heated microscope stage or a thermal incubator made of plexiglass coupled to a feedback-controlled heated air blower. These methods work to an extent, but we recommend careful measurements of the temperature for important physiological experiments. Sometimes the timescale for cyclic heating and cooling of the incubator can be similar to the timescale of the physiological parameters of interest. This makes it difficult, when interpreting the data, to decouple otherwise orthogonal external (e.g., environmental fluctuations) and internal

BSA: bovine serum
albumin

TTL:
transistor-transistor
logic

(e.g., physiological variability) factors that can influence the physiological state of the cells. A carefully designed and regulated environmental chamber in which a microscope, a microscope table, and other small equipment can be stationed at a constant temperature is an excellent solution to solve all problems related to temperature fluctuations. In contrast to the quest for uniformity, Groisman et al. (40) designed a microfluidic chemostat that provided unique temperature and pressure control for growing microorganisms in micron-sized traps.

Passivity of the Cellular Environment

The problems of passivation of microfluidic devices, motility of cells, and the infusion rate of growth media are often related in a typical single-cell experiment. If the internal surfaces of the microfluidic device are not properly passivated, cells can stick to the walls and affect the growth of other cells. For PDMS-based microfluidic devices, we find preloading with 50 mg/ml BSA (bovine serum albumin) for several minutes and 0.5 mg/ml BSA in the supplied growth medium is sufficient for passivation. Another method is to add mild neutral detergents such as Tween, which prevents cells from sticking to the glass surface (94). If the strain is motile, the cells may swim against incoming nutrient flow and can eventually clog the inlet and the tubing of the microfluidic device. We have found that keeping flow rates high (>10 mm/s), as well as simply knocking out motility genes, can abrogate this problem (see Strain Selection, below).

Communication Among the Electronics

Consider typical time-lapse imaging of multiple fields of view, or fast fluorescent particle tracking in vivo using a microscope equipped with a motorized stage, a mechanical shutter, fluorescence filter cubes or filter wheels, and a white fluorescence illumination source such as a mercury or xenon lamp. The microscope software sends an instruction from the computer to the microscope to (a) move the stage to the preregistered position, (b) find the focal plane, (c) open the mechanical shutter, (d) acquire an image, (e) send the image back to the computer, and (f) close the mechanical shutter. For multicolor imaging, additional steps cause further delay while the filter cube or filter wheel changes the illumination color and takes additional images. Each of these steps involves communication between equipment and waiting time, which all add up and can cause a significant discrepancy between the actual exposure time and the nominal exposure time (from tens to hundreds of milliseconds). Such a discrepancy can affect both the reliability of the acquired data and the physiology of the cells because of phototoxicity. To prevent these problems, we recommend fast communication methods such as TTL (transistor-transistor logic) and replacing mechanical components with electronic components where possible. For example, use LEDs or lasers with multiband filter cubes instead of mechanical shutters and use mercury lamps with single-band filter wheels.

Primary Image Analysis

Although bioinformatics is popularly considered the domain of next-generation sequencing, we propose that it includes the analysis of data produced by any high-throughput experimental technique and in particular the processing of time-lapse video data. In our view, this is one of the most difficult challenges of high-throughput single-cell experiments. Despite the ubiquity of publicly available image analysis software such as microbeTracker (83), Cell Profiler (24), and the mother machine–specific MMJ (6), we have not found a one-size-fits-all solution for high-throughput image analysis of the images generated from microfluidics-based single-cell experiments. The wide range of experimental conditions, the requirements dictated by the types of hypotheses under consideration, and the vagaries of superficially simple issues such as the perceived sharpness of focus all contribute to complex and evolving requirements for data analysis. Developing dedicated image analysis software can take several years of effort in addition to constant customization and maintenance for different experimental configurations. The science as a whole will benefit from community-level efforts to improve the available algorithms. We are optimistic that, like sequencing, image analysis will increasingly become the realm of engineering rather than art.

Strain Selection

Since its landmark sequencing, *E. coli* MG1655 (19) has become one of the most widely used *E. coli* strains. The related strains W3110 (43) and BW25113 have also been used extensively; BW25113 is the basis for the enormously useful Keio knockout collection (9). Unfortunately, there are increasingly well-known problems with the anabolic pathways of these and other strains derived from W1485, particularly pyrimidine biosynthesis (50), amino acid biosynthesis (5), and carbon metabolism (21). This picture is further complicated by MG1655's lack of lambda prophage and the emerging importance of phage elements in mediating the host's resistance to external stresses (13, 100). If MG1655 is nonetheless required, it is imperative to ensure that the correct substrain of MG1655 is selected (12, 35).

Our prototrophic strain of choice is the K12 derivative NCM3722 by the late Sydney Kustu. NCM3722 has been corrected for several defects found in MG1655 (86). To further improve this strain's broad suitability for physiology studies, we recently derived an F− NCM3722 strain (SJ358), which is available from our laboratory and from the *E. coli* Genetic Stock Center.

When physical constraints do not fix the position of cells, natural motility systems can interfere with long-term monitoring. Genetically engineered defects in the flagellar system of *E. coli* can render cells nonmotile but will have unequal consequences on the physiology of the cell (17, 18). This is in addition to potential differences in the natural biological factors (e.g., insertion sequences) that contribute to motility (12). We have employed $\Delta motA$ and $\Delta fliC$ strains in the past but either of these may not be desirable depending on the nature of the assay under consideration.

CONCLUSIONS

Addressing fundamental questions in cellular physiology requires single-cell techniques that can capture the growth and cell cycle events of individual unicellular organisms. Given the extent of the intrinsic fluctuations in biological systems, population-level measurements mask important causal relationships underlying the biological phenomena. In this article we reviewed some of the questions from different aspects of bacterial physiology, including cell cycle, cell size, shape, metabolism, and cell death. Although recent advances in single-cell technologies have allowed us to answer some of the long-standing problems, many fundamental problems remain to be understood.

Among various single-cell techniques, microfluidics combined with high-resolution time-lapse imaging is popular and powerful. They not only allow for the investigation of individual cells, but also enable high-throughput observation such that researchers can draw quantitative conclusions about a cell's physiology. However, as all technology is blind to its implementation, it is up to the prudent investigator to responsibly apply experimental techniques in order to minimize confounding artifacts. The hurdle here is not of desire but of painstaking trial and error. We hope the lessons we have shared in this article save the reader aggravation and encourage discovery in this exciting field.

SUMMARY POINTS

1. Despite decades of study, many basic aspects of microbial physiology remain poorly understood. Single-cell data can greatly improve our understanding of these aspects.

2. Single-cell approaches help us unravel cell-to-cell variations and correlations that are otherwise averaged out in population-level measurements.

3. Microfluidic devices coupled with high-resolution microscopy imaging are a powerful means available to physiologists.

4. When collecting data and interpreting results from single-cell experiments, researchers must follow the three tenets: (*a*) Results must be reproducible; (*b*) quantitative distributions, as opposed to means or cherry-picked images, must be presented; and (*c*) averages calculated from the distributions must agree with population-level control experiments.

FUTURE ISSUES

1. Progression of the cell cycle involves a set of processes that lead to cell division. Precise description of how these processes are coordinated is an open question that relies on future single-cell data.

2. The growth law, one of the first quantitative rules in bacterial physiology, states that cell size is exponentially related to growth rate. How individual cells recognize growth rate and their size remains to be understood.

3. Recent single-cell studies revealed that bacteria, including *E. coli* and *B. subtilis*, maintain size homeostasis by the "adder" principle. That is, cells add a constant size to each cell cycle. Yet, we need to find out how this principle results from growth and cell cycle coordination, especially in the context of evolution.

4. Current imaging techniques can disrupt the physiology of living cells. Phototoxicity is a major challenge that needs to be solved.

DISCLOSURE STATEMENT

The authors are not aware of any affiliations, memberships, funding, or financial holdings that might be perceived as affecting the objectivity of this review.

ACKNOWLEDGMENTS

This work was supported by the Paul G. Allen Foundation, the Pew Charitable Trusts, and the National Science Foundation CAREER Award (to S.J.).

LITERATURE CITED

1. Ackermann M, Stearns SC, Jenal U. 2003. Senescence in a bacterium with asymmetric division. *Science* 300:1920

2. Adler M, Erickstad M, Gutierrez E, Groisman A. 2012. Studies of bacterial aerotaxis in a microfluidic device. *Lab Chip* 12:4835–47

3. Alberts B, Johnson A, Lewis J, Raff M, Roberts K, Walter P. 2003. *Molecular Biology of the Cell*. New York: Garland Science

4. Amir A, Babaeipour F, McIntosh DB, Nelson DR, Jun S. 2014. Bending forces plastically deform growing bacterial cell walls. *PNAS* 111:5778–83

5. Andersen DC, Swartz J, Ryll T, Lin N, Snedecor B. 2001. Metabolic oscillations in an *E. coli* fermentation. *Biotechnol. Bioeng.* 75:212–18

6. Arnoldini M, Vizcarra IA, Peña-Miller R, Stocker N, Diard M, et al. 2014. Bistable expression of virulence genes in *Salmonella* leads to the formation of an antibiotic-tolerant subpopulation. *PLOS Biol.* 12:e1001928

7. Ashkin A, Dziedzic J, Bjorkholm JE, Chu S. 1986. Observation of a single-beam gradient-force optical trap for dielectric particles in air. *Opt. Lett.* 22:816–18

8. Ashkin A, Dziedzic J, Yamane T. 1987. Optical trapping and manipulation of single cells using infrared laser beams. *Nature* 330:769–71

9. Baba T, Ara T, Hasegawa M, Takai Y, Okumura Y, et al. 2006. Construction of *Escherichia coli* K-12 in-frame, single-gene knockout mutants: the Keio collection. *Mol. Syst. Biol.* 2:2006.0008

10. Balaban NQ, Merrin J, Chait R, Kowalik L, Leibler S. 2004. Bacterial persistence as a phenotypic switch. *Science* 305:1622–25

11. Balagadde F, You L, Hansen C, Arnold F, Quake S. 2005. Long-term monitoring of bacteria undergoing programmed population control in a microchemostat. *Science* 309:137–40

12. Barker CS, Prüss BM, Matsumura P. 2004. Increased motility of *Escherichia coli* by insertion sequence element integration into the regulatory region of the *flhD* operon (MG1655). *J. Bacteriol.* 186:7529–37

13. Barondess J, Beckwith J. 1995. *bor* gene of phage λ, involved in serum resistance, encodes a widely conserved outer membrane lipoprotein. *J. Bacteriol.* 177:1247–53

14. Bates D, Kleckner N. 2005. Chromosome and replisome dynamics in *E. coli*: Loss of sister cohesion triggers global chromosome movement and mediates chromosome segregation. *Cell* 121:899–911

15. Bayne-Jones S, Adolph EF. 1932. Growth in size of micro-organisms measured from motion pictures: II. *Bacillus megatherium*. *J. Cell. Comp. Physiol.* 1:388–407

16. Benson RC, Meyer RA, Zaruba ME, McKhann GM. 1979. Cellular autofluorescence—Is it due to flavins? *J. Histochem. Cytochem.* 27:44–48

17. Berg HC. 2003. The rotary motor of bacterial flagella. *Annu. Rev. Biochem.* 72:9–54

18. Blair DF, Berg HC. 1990. The MotA protein of *E. coli* is a proton-conducting component of the flagellar motor. *Cell* 60:439–49

19. Blattner FR, Plunkett GI, Bloch CA, Perna NT, Burland V, et al. 1997. The complete genome sequence of *Escherichia coli* K-12. *Science* 277:1453–62

20. Block SM. 1998. Construction of optical tweezers. In *Cells: A Laboratory Manual*, Vol. 3, ed. D Spector, R Goldman, L Leinwand, pp. 81.1–81.14. Cold Spring Harbor, NY: Cold Spring Harbor Press

21. Brinkkötter A, Klöss H, Alpert CA, Lengeler JW. 2000. Pathways for the utilization of *N*-acetyl-galactosamine and galactosamine in *Escherichia coli*. *Mol. Microbiol.* 37:125–35

22. Campbell A. 1957. Synchronization of cell division. *Bacteriol. Rev.* 21:263–72

23. Campos M, Surovtsev IV, Kato S, Paintdakhi A, Beltran B, et al. 2014. A constant size extension drives bacterial cell size homeostasis. *Cell* 159:1433–466

24. Carpenter AE, Jones TR, Lamprecht MR, Clarke C, Kang IH, et al. 2006. CellProfiler: image analysis software for identifying and quantifying cell phenotypes. *Genome Biol.* 7:R100

25. Chance B, Cohen P, Jobsis F, Schoener B. 1962. Intracellular oxidation-reduction states in vivo. *Science* 137:499–508

26. **Cooper S. 1969. Cell division and DNA replication following a shift to a richer medium. *J. Mol. Biol.* 43:1–11**

27. Cooper S. 2006. Regulation of DNA synthesis in bacteria: analysis of the Bates/Kleckner licensing/initiation-mass model for cell cycle control. *Mol. Microbiol.* 62:303–7

28. **Cooper S, Helmstetter CE. 1968. Chromosome replication and the division cycle of *Escherichia coli* B/r. *J. Mol. Biol.* 31(3):519–40**

29. DeLisa M, Valdes J, Bentley W. 2001. Mapping stress-induced changes in autoinducer AI-2 production in chemostat-cultivated *Escherichia coli* K-12. *J. Bacteriol.* 183:2918–28

26. Shows that chromosome replication initiates once accumulation of hypothetical initiator(s) reaches a threshold; rate of accumulation depends on growth rate.

28. Demonstrates that periods of chromosome replication and the gap between termination of replication and cell division are constant, independent of growth rate.

30. Dobell C. 1923. *Antony Van Leeuwenhoek and His "Little Animals"*. New York: Harcourt, Brace

31. Domínguez-Escobar J, Chastanet A, Crevenna AH, Fromion V, Wedlich-Söldner R, Carballido-López R. 2011. Processive movement of MreB-associated cell wall biosynthetic complexes in bacteria. *Science* 333:225–28

32. Donachie W. 1968. Relationship between cell size and time of initiation of DNA replication. *Nature* 219:1077–79

33. Donnert G, Eggeling C, Hell SW. 2009. Triplet-relaxation microscopy with bunched pulsed excitation. *Photochem. Photobiol. Sci.* 8:481–85

34. Elowitz M, Levine A, Siggia E, Swain P. 2002. Stochastic gene expression in a single cell. *Science* 297:1183–86

35. Freddolino PL, Amini S, Tavazoie S. 2012. Newly identified genetic variations in common *Escherichia coli* MG1655 stock cultures. *J. Bacteriol.* 194:303–6

36. Frumkin D, Wasserstrom A, Itzkovitz S, Stern T, Harmelin A, et al. 2008. Cell lineage analysis of a mouse tumor. *Cancer Res.* 68:5924–31

37. Garner EC, Bernard R, Wang W, Zhuang X, Rudner DZ, Mitchison T. 2011. Coupled, circumferential motions of the cell wall synthesis machinery and MreB filaments in *B. subtilis*. *Science* 333:222–25

38. Godin M, Delgado FF, Son S, Grover WH, Bryan AK, et al. 2010. Using buoyant mass to measure the growth of single cells. *Nat. Methods* 7:387–90

39. Greenbaum L, Rothmann C, Lavie R, Malik Z. 2000. Green fluorescent protein photobleaching: a model for protein damage by endogenous and exogenous singlet oxygen. *Biol. Chem.* 381:1251–58

40. Groisman A, Lobo C, Cho H. 2005. A microfluidic chemostat for experiments with bacterial and yeast cells. *Nat. Methods* 2:685–89

41. Guo MT, Rotem A, Heyman JA, Weitz DA. 2012. Droplet microfluidics for high-throughput biological assays. *Lab Chip* 12:2146–55

42. Harvey R, Marr A, Painter P. 1967. Kinetics of growth of individual cells of *Escherichia coli* and *Azotobacter agilis*. *J. Bacteriol.* 93:605–17

43. Hayashi K, Morooka N, Yamamoto Y, Fujita K, Isono K, et al. 2006. Highly accurate genome sequences of *Escherichia coli* K-12 strains MG1655 and W3110. *Mol. Syst. Biol.* 2:2006.0007

44. Helmstetter C. 1967. Rates of DNA synthesis during the division cycle of *Escherichia coli* B/r. *J. Mol. Biol.* 24:417–27

45. Helmstetter CE, Cummings DJ. 1963. Bacterial synchronization by selection of cells at division. *PNAS* 50:767–74

46. Hill NS, Buske PJ, Shi Y, Levin PA. 2013. A moonlighting enzyme links *Escherichia coli* cell size with central metabolism. *PLOS Genet.* 9:e1003663

47. Hoebe RA, Van Oven CH, Gadella TWJ, Dhonukshe PB, Van Noorden CJF, Manders EMM. 2007. Controlled light-exposure microscopy reduces photobleaching and phototoxicity in fluorescence live-cell imaging. *Nat. Biotechnol.* 25:249–53

48. Hribar KC, Soman P, Warner J, Chung P, Chen S. 2014. Light-assisted direct-write of 3D functional biomaterials. *Lab Chip* 14:268–75

49. Jacob F, Monod J. 1961. Genetic regulatory mechanisms in the synthesis of proteins. *J. Mol. Biol.* 3(3):318–56

50. Jensen KF. 1993. The *Escherichia coli* K-12 "wild types" W3110 and MG1655 have an *rph* frameshift mutation that leads to pyrimidine starvation due to low *pyrE* expression levels. *J. Bacteriol.* 175:3401–7

51. Johnson ID. 2006. Practical considerations in the selection and application of fluorescent probes. In *Handbook of Biological Confocal Microscopy*, ed. JB Pawley, pp. 353–67. New York: Springer

52. Johnston GC, Ehrhardt CW, Lorincz A, Carter BLA. 1979. Regulation of cell size in the yeast *Saccharomyces cerevisiae*. *J. Bacteriol.* 137:1–5

53. Jun S, Taheri-Araghi S. 2014. Cell-size maintenance: universal strategy revealed. *Trends Microbiol.* 23:4–6

54. Kalisky T, Quake SR. 2011. Single-cell genomics. *Nat. Methods* 8:311–14

55. Keymer JE, Galajda P, Muldoon C, Park S, Austin RH. 2006. Bacterial metapopulations in nanofabricated landscapes. *PNAS* 103:17290–95

56. Kitson PJ, Rosnes MH, Sans V, Dragone V, Cronin L. 2012. Configurable 3D-printed millifluidic and microfluidic 'lab on a chip' reactionware devices. *Lab Chip* 12:3267–71

57. Kiviet DJ, Nghe P, Walker N, Boulineau S, Sunderlikova V, Tans SJ. 2014. Stochasticity of metabolism and growth at the single-cell level. *Nature* 514:376–79

58. Koch AL. 2001. *Bacterial Growth and Form.* New York: Springer

59. Koch AL, Schaechter M. 1962. A model for statistics of the cell division process. *J. Gen. Microbiol.* 29:435–54

60. **Landgraf D, Okumus B, Chien P, Baker TA, Paulsson J. 2012. Segregation of molecules at cell division reveals native protein localization. *Nat. Methods* 9:480–82**

61. Landry ZC, Giovanonni SJ, Quake SR, Blainey PC. 2013. Optofluidic cell selection from complex microbial communities for single-genome analysis. *Methods Enzymol.* 531:61–69

62. Lankford C, Byers B. 1973. Bacterial assimilation of iron. *Crit. Rev. Microbiol.* 2:273–331

63. Lee JH, Lee J. 2010. Indole as an intercellular signal in microbial communities. *FEMS Microbiol. Rev.* 34:426–44

64. Leung K, Zahn H, Leaver T, Konwar KM, Hanson NW, et al. 2012. A programmable droplet-based microfluidic device applied to multiparameter analysis of single microbes and microbial communities. *PNAS* 109:7665–70

65. Lindner AB, Madden R, Demarez A, Stewart EJ, Taddei F. 2008. Asymmetric segregation of protein aggregates is associated with cellular aging and rejuvenation. *PNAS* 105:3076–81

66. Macaulay IC, Voet T. 2014. Single cell genomics: advances and future perspectives. *PLOS Genet.* 10:e1004126

67. Männik J, Driessen R, Galajda P, Keymer JE, Dekker C. 2009. Bacterial growth and motility in sub-micron constrictions. *PNAS* 106:14861–66

68. Mashburn-Warren LM, Whiteley M. 2006. Special delivery: vesicle trafficking in prokaryotes. *Mol. Microbiol.* 61:839–46

69. Mitchison JM. 1971. *The Biology of the Cell Cycle.* Cambridge, UK: Cambridge Univ. Press

70. Moffitt JR, Lee JB, Cluzel P. 2012. The single-cell chemostat: an agarose-based, microfluidic device for high-throughput, single-cell studies of bacteria and bacterial communities. *Lab Chip* 12:1487–94

71. Monod J. 1949. The growth of bacterial cultures. *Annu. Rev. Microbiol.* 3:371–94

72. Mortimer R, Johnston J. 1959. Life span of individual yeast cells. *Nature* 183:1751–52

73. Nanninga N, Woldringh C. 1985. *Molecular Cytology of Escherichia coli: Cell Growth, Genome Duplication, and Cell Division.* London: Academic

74. Norman TM, Lord ND, Paulsson J, Losick R. 2013. Memory and modularity in cell-fate decision making. *Nature* 503:481–86

75. Novick A, Weiner M. 1957. Enzyme induction as an all-or-none phenomenon. *PNAS* 43:553–66

76. **Ozbudak EM, Thattai M, Kurtser I, Grossman AD, van Oudenaarden A. 2002. Regulation of noise in the expression of a single gene. *Nat. Genet.* 31:69–73**

77. Ozbudak EM, Thattai M, Lim HN, Shraiman BI, Van Oudenaarden A. 2004. Multistability in the lactose utilization network of *Escherichia coli*. *Nature* 427:737–40

78. Rolfe MD, Rice CJ, Lucchini S, Pin C, Thompson A, et al. 2012. Lag phase is a distinct growth phase. *J. Bacteriol.* 194:686–701

79. **Schaechter M, Maaløe O, Kjeldgaard NO. 1958. Dependency on medium and temperature of cell size and chemical composition during balanced growth of *Salmonella typhimurium*. *J. Gen. Microbiol.* 19:592–606**

80. Schaller RR. 1997. Moore's law: past, present, and future. *IEEE Spectrosc.* 6:52–59

81. Shaner NC, Patterson GH, Davidson MW. 2007. Advances in fluorescent protein technology. *J. Cell Sci.* 120:4247–60

82. Shaner NC, Steinbach PA, Tsien RY. 2005. A guide to choosing fluorescent proteins. *Nat. Methods* 2:905–9

83. Sliusarenko O, Heinritz J, Emonet T, Jacobs-Wagner C. 2011. High-throughput, subpixel precision analysis of bacterial morphogenesis and intracellular spatio-temporal dynamics. *Mol. Microbiol.* 80:612–27

84. So P, Dong C. 2000. Two-photon excitation fluorescence microscopy. *Annu. Rev. Biomed. Eng.* 2:399–429

85. Son S, Grover W, Burg T, Manalis S. 2008. Suspended microchannel resonators for ultralow volume universal detection. *Anal. Chem.* 80:4757–60

60. Explicitly demonstrates potential confounding effects of fluorescent fusion proteins in physiologic investigations.

76. Shows that protein copy number noise is a function of translation (stochastic ribosomal activity) as opposed to transcription (gene expression).

79. Introduces growth law stating that cell size is exponentially related to growth rate.

86. Soupene E, van Heeswijk WC, Plumbridge J, Stewart V, Bertenthal D, et al. 2003. Physiological studies of *Escherichia coli* strain MG1655: growth defects and apparent cross-regulation of gene expression. *Am. Soc. Microbiol.* 185:5611–26

87. Spivey EC, Xhemalce B, Shear JB, Finkelstein IJ. 2014. 3D-printed microfluidic microdissector for high-throughput studies of cellular aging. *Anal. Chem.* 86:7406–12

88. Squires T, Quake SR. 2005. Microfluidics: fluid physics at the nanoliter scale. *Rev. Modern Phys.* 77:977–1026

89. Starka J. 1974. Avant-propos (foreword). *Ann. Microbiol.* 125B:133–34

90. Stewart EJ, Madden R, Paul G, Taddei F. 2005. Aging and death in an organism that reproduces by morphologically symmetric division. *PLOS Biol.* 3:e45

91. Strack RL, Hein B, Bhattacharyya D, Hell SW, Keenan RJ, Glick BS. 2009. A rapidly maturing far-red derivative of DsRed-Express2 for whole-cell labeling. *Biochemistry* 48:8279–81

92. Taheri-Araghi S, Bradde S, Sauls JT, Hill NS, Levin PA, et al. 2015. Cell size control in bacteria. *Curr. Biol.* http://dx.doi.org/10.1016/j.cub.2014.12.009

93. Takeuchi S, DiLuzio WR, Weibel DB, Whitesides GM. 2005. Controlling the shape of filamentous cells of *Escherichia coli*. *Nano Lett.* 5:1819–23

94. Turner L, Zhang R, Darnton NC, Berg HC. 2010. Visualization of flagella during bacterial swarming. *J. Bacteriol.* 192:3259–67

95. Unger MA, Chou H-P, Thorsen T, Scherer A, Quake SR. 2000. Monolithic microfabricated valves and pumps by multilayer soft lithography. *Science* 288:113–16

96. Van Teeffelen S, Wang S, Furchtgott L, Huang KC, Wingreen NS, et al. 2011. The bacterial actin MreB rotates, and rotation depends on cell-wall assembly. *PNAS* 108:15822–27

97. Voorn WJ, Koppes LJ, Grover N. 1993. Mathematics of cell division in *Escherichia coli*. *Curr. Top. Mol. Genet.* 187–94

98. Wang P, Robert L, Pelletier J, Dang WL, Taddei F, et al. 2010. Robust growth of *Escherichia coli*. *Curr. Biol.* 20:1099–103

99. Wang S, Arellano-Santoyo H, Combs PA, Shaevitz JW. 2010. Actin-like cytoskeleton filaments contribute to cell mechanics in bacteria. *PNAS* 107:9182–85

100. Wang X, Kim Y, Ma Q, Hong SH, Pokusaeva K, et al. 2010. Cryptic prophages help bacteria cope with adverse environments. *Nat. Commun.* 1:147

101. Weart RB, Lee AH, Chien AC, Haeusser DP, Hill NS, Levin PA. 2007. A metabolic sensor governing cell size in bacteria. *Cell* 130:335–47

102. Whitesides GM. 2006. The origins and the future of microfluidics. *Nature* 442:368–73

103. Winkler J, Seybert A, König L, Pruggnaller S, Haselmann U, et al. 2010. Quantitative and spatio-temporal features of protein aggregation in *Escherichia coli* and consequences on protein quality control and cellular ageing. *EMBO J.* 29:910–23

104. Woldringh C, Grover N, Rosenberger R, Zaritsky A. 1980. Dimensional rearrangement of rod-shaped bacteria following nutritional shift-up. II. Experiments with *Escherichia coli* B/r. *J. Theor. Biol.* 86:441–54

105. Xia Y, Whitesides GM. 1998. Soft lithography. *Annu. Rev. Mater. Sci.* 28:153–84

106. Zhang Q, Lambert G, Liao D, Kim H, Robin K, et al. 2011. Acceleration of emergence of bacterial antibiotic resistance in connected microenvironments. *Science* 333:1764–67

107. Zipfel WR, Williams RM, Webb WW. 2003. Nonlinear magic: multiphoton microscopy in the biosciences. *Nat. Biotechnol.* 21:1369–77

92. Demonstrates that bacteria maintain size homeostasis by adding a constant size in each cell cycle.

98. Overturned widespread belief that cell age and growth rate were inversely correlated by using microfluidic growth chambers instead of agarose pads.

Roles for Synonymous Codon Usage in Protein Biogenesis

Julie L. Chaney[1] and Patricia L. Clark[1,2]

[1]Department of Chemistry and Biochemistry, [2]Department of Chemical and Biomolecular Engineering, University of Notre Dame, Notre Dame, Indiana 46556; email: jchaney@nd.edu, pclark1@nd.edu

Annu. Rev. Biophys. 2015. 44:143–66

First published online as a Review in Advance on February 26, 2015

The *Annual Review of Biophysics* is online at biophys.annualreviews.org

This article's doi:
10.1146/annurev-biophys-060414-034333

Keywords

translation, ribosome, cotranslational folding, protein aggregation, protein degradation

Abstract

Owing to the degeneracy of the genetic code, a protein sequence can be encoded by many different synonymous mRNA coding sequences. Synonymous codon usage was once thought to be functionally neutral, but evidence now indicates it is shaped by evolutionary selection and affects other aspects of protein biogenesis beyond specifying the amino acid sequence of the protein. Synonymous rare codons, once thought to have only negative impacts on the speed and accuracy of translation, are now known to play an important role in diverse functions, including regulation of cotranslational folding, covalent modifications, secretion, and expression level. Mutations altering synonymous codon usage are linked to human diseases. However, much remains unknown about the molecular mechanisms connecting synonymous codon usage to efficient protein biogenesis and proper cell physiology. Here we review recent literature on the functional effects of codon usage, including bioinformatics approaches aimed at identifying general roles for synonymous codon usage.

Contents

INTRODUCTION

The genetic code is degenerate: 61 trinucleotide codons are used to encode the 20 standard amino acids. Whereas both methionine and tryptophan are encoded by only one codon, each of the other 18 amino acids is encoded by two to six synonymous codons (**Figure 1**). Because synonymous codons do not alter the encoded amino acid sequence, they were historically considered equivalent and interchangeable. Accordingly, DNA mutations that alter synonymous codon usage are referred to as "silent" mutations and are often assumed to be neutral in models of mutation and selection (29, 62, 72, 78, 117). Indeed, commonly used models of molecular evolution are based on the assumption that synonymous codon changes are merely genomic background noise (62, 72). However, a growing body of evidence has revealed that synonymous codon choice is nonrandom and can affect multiple aspects of protein biogenesis in diverse organisms, including humans. Here we review the current status of our understanding of synonymous codon usage and its impacts on diverse aspects of protein biogenesis, including transcription, translation, cotranslational folding, secretion, and posttranslational modifications. We also provide an overview of algorithms used to identify and quantify patterns in synonymous codon usage, as well as our current understanding of the effects of these patterns on protein biogenesis.

Codon Bias

Usage frequencies of synonymous codons within the same genome often differ, in some cases by more than an order of magnitude (56, 57). Although almost all organisms use the same genetic code (**Figure 1a**), the specific synonymous codons that are rare versus common vary between organisms and correlate with genome %GC bias (19, 40). For many sets of synonymous codons, the base composition at the first and second codon positions is fixed and varies only at the third

	NTN		NCN		N		NGN	
TNN	TTT	Phe	TCT	Ser	TAT	Tyr	TGT	Cys
	TTC		TCC		TAC		TGC	
	TTA	Leu	TCA		TAA	STOP	TGA	STOP
	TTG		TCG		TAG		TGG	Trp
CNN	CTT	Leu	CCT	Pro	CAT	His	CGT	Arg
	CTC		CCC		CAC		CGC	
	CTA		CCA		CAA	Gln	CGA	
	CTG		CCG		CAG		CGG	
ANN	ATT	Ile	ACT	Thr	AAT	Asn	AGT	Ser
	ATC		ACC		AAC		AGC	
	ATA		ACA		AAA	Lys	AGA	Arg
	ATG	Met	ACG		AAG		AGG	
GNN	GTT	Val	GCT	Ala	GAT	Asp	GGT	Gly
	GTC		GCC		GAC		GGC	
	GTA		GCA		GAA	Glu	GGA	
	GTG		GCG		GAG		GGG	

b
```
Met-Leu-Asp-Gly-Pro
ATG TTA GAT GGT CCT
    TTG GAC GGC CCC
    CTT     GGA CCA
    CTC     GGG CCG
    CTA
    CTG
```

Figure 1

(*a*) The standard genetic code. (*b*) A hypothetical peptide sequence and its possible coding sequences. Most amino acids are encoded by a set of synonymous codons that differ only at the wobble position. There are five exceptions: Leucine, serine, and arginine are each encoded by six codons and therefore also include different nucleotides at the first (all three) and second (serine only) codon positions. Methionine and tryptophan are each encoded by only one codon.

(wobble) position (**Figure 1*b***). For example, proline is encoded by CCN, where N can be any nucleotide. Thus, for protein coding sequences, the average %GC content can be adjusted by altering the %GC content at the third codon position (%GC3). In genomes with a high average %GC, common synonymous codons typically end in G or C, whereas in low average %GC genomes, common codons are more likely to end in A or T (91). Historically, it was thought that average %GC was driven primarily by an organism's growth temperature (90), although it now appears that other effects can also be important drivers (87, 101, 102, 134).

Direct Effects of Synonymous Codon Usage

Compared with more common synonymous codons, rare codons generally correlate with lower levels of cognate tRNA or weaker interactions at the wobble position with the same tRNA (27, 39, 59, 63, 64, 116). For these reasons, rare codons are generally thought to be translated more slowly than common codons, and experimental evidence supports this hypothesis (80, 98, 114, 115). Indeed, although average translation rates are ~20 amino acids (aa)/s in prokaryotes and ~5 aa/s in

%GC3: percentage of guanine (G) and cytosine (C) nucleotides at the third nucleotide position in codons

eukaryotes, local translation rates can vary by more than an order of magnitude (20, 114). However, codon rarity is not the only determinant of translation rate, and a detailed understanding of all factors that affect translation rate has been limited by the technical challenges of measuring absolute translation rates of individual codons in vivo. Translation rates measured from in vitro translation systems are typically much slower and less variable than rates measured in vivo (18, 103, 123). Ribosome profiling is a new method that measures relative ribosome occupancy of mRNA sites on a transcriptome-wide level (65, 81), and in one case it has been possible to convert these occupancies to absolute translation rates (66). Most ribosomal profiling studies have not identified a broad connection between codon usage and ribosome occupancy except in a few specific cases caused by the depletion of charged tRNA or the presence of Shine-Dalgarno (SD) motifs (81). However, most ribosome profiling studies have focused on the most extreme translational pauses across an entire proteome. In contrast, a new analysis of yeast ribosome profiling data, designed to quantify comparatively subtle differences in translation rate associated with synonymous codon usage, discovered that rare codons are on average translated more slowly than synonymous common codons (50).

Two systems were recently developed to measure the relative effects of individual or small segments of synonymous codons on translation rates in vivo. The first is a fluorescent biosensor called YKB. YKB consists of three fluorescent half-domains connected by flexible linkers (104) (**Figure 2b**). The N-terminal Y half-domain and the C-terminal B half-domain compete with each other to interact with the central K half-domain, and the outcome of this competition determines whether a yellow or cyan fluorescent protein is formed. Translational pauses in a switch region at the 5′ end of the B half-domain allow additional time for a Y-K interaction to form cotranslationally, thus increasing the proportion of Y-K (yellow) fluorescence observed. Introducing synonymous rare codons into the switch region slowed translation rates, resulting in increased yellow fluorescence and decreased cyan fluorescence. This yellow/cyan fluorescence ratio changed predictably with the rareness of the synonymous codons used, and showed directly for the first time that synonymous codons, presumably because of their effects on translation rate, can alter not just a protein folding pathway but also the final, folded structure of the encoded protein (104).

While the YKB biosensor represents an engineered approach to measuring codon-specific effects on translation rate, a second translation rate sensor system is based on the naturally occurring His operon (20). Fast translation of the His leader peptide results in transcriptional termination, reducing expression of the downstream genes, whereas slow translation enhances expression. Replacing the downstream genes with β-galactosidase enabled researchers to relatively compare the translation rates for codons inserted into the leader peptide coding sequence and demonstrate that translation rate varies considerably for different codons, including synonymous codons decoded by the same tRNA (see also the sidebar, What Determines the Translation Rate of a Codon?). Codon context (the identity of the 5′ and 3′ flanking codons) also affected translation rates (20).

Although beyond the scope of this review, the amino acid sequence of the nascent chain can also perturb the local translation rate. Positively charged amino acids can reduce the translation rate because of their interaction with negative charges in the ribosome exit tunnel (16, 82). Rates of peptide bond formation vary among amino acids (137) and are especially slow for proline, leading to translational pauses at polyproline motifs (31, 132, 139). Specific peptide motifs, including the well-characterized *Escherichia coli* SecM (secretion monitor) stalling sequence (23, 41, 67, 139), can also stall translation. Nascent peptide effects add an extra layer of complexity to the interpretation of translation rate changes, as codon usage effects may be hidden among these and other translation rate regulatory mechanisms.

Translational accuracy is slightly lower for rare codons than for common codons (69, 75, 110), although as for translation rates, experimental data for the translational accuracy of specific codons

Shine-Dalgarno (SD) motif: an mRNA nucleotide motif (consensus AGGAGG) in bacteria that interacts with the 16S rRNA and may introduce translational pauses

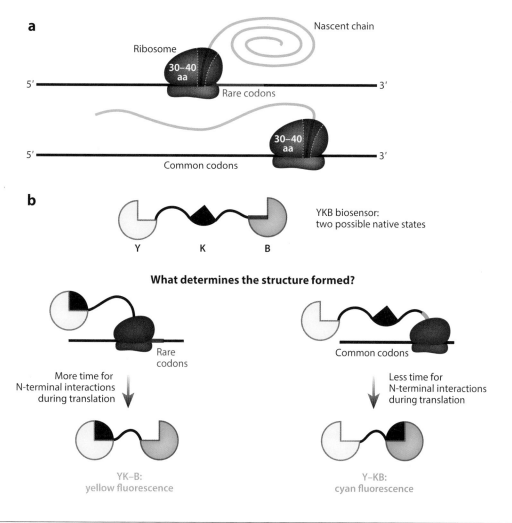

a

Nascent chain

Ribosome

30–40 aa

5' ——————— 3'

Rare codons

30–40 aa

5' ——————— 3'

Common codons

b

YKB biosensor:
two possible native states

Y   K   B

What determines the structure formed?

Rare codons

More time for
N-terminal interactions
during translation

YK–B:
yellow fluorescence

Common codons

Less time for
N-terminal interactions
during translation

Y–KB:
cyan fluorescence

Figure 2

(*a*) Rare codons are hypothesized to introduce translational pauses that modulate cotranslational protein folding. A translational pause could allow additional time for the nascent chain to form a 3D structure. The most C-terminal 30–40 amino acids of the nascent protein are constrained in the ribosomal exit tunnel and unable to form a 3D structure. Hence a rare codon cluster that promotes the folding of a protein structural unit is expected to be offset 30–40 codons from the region encoding that structural unit. (*b*) The YKB biosensor is a split fluorescence system designed to detect changes in translation rates due to synonymous codon usage (104). YKB consists of three fluorescent half-domains: The N-terminal Y half-domain and the C-terminal B half-domain compete to interact with the central K half-domain, and the resulting native structure determines the color of fluorescence observed. YK/KB fluorescence ratios show a stronger correlation with relative codon usage than do tRNA levels, a tRNA wobble metric, %GC, or mRNA stability (24, 104).

is limited. Certain codons may also be rare in specific genomes because they form deleterious nucleotide motifs and are thus subject to negative selection. For example, CG dinucleotide pairs have an increased mutational susceptibility in methylated eukaryotic genomes (99). As a result, in the human genome NCG is rarely used to encode amino acids encoded by NCN codons (149).

Synonymous codon usage within coding sequences can also alter the stability of mRNA structure, affecting cell physiology. An analysis of mutations in a bacterial long-term evolution experiment indicated that mutations that alter mRNA stability were selected against (21).

WHAT DETERMINES THE TRANSLATION RATE OF A CODON?

Codon usage frequencies generally correlate with levels of the cognate tRNAs. However, due to wobble pairing rules, some tRNAs recognize multiple synonymous codons, and the strength of the wobble pairing interaction can also influence the translation rate. If the translation rate is determined by the tRNA level alone, codons decoded by the same tRNA should be translated at the same rate.

For example, *Escherichia coli* has only one Glu tRNA, which decodes both Glu codons, GAA and GAG (see **Supplemental Figure 1**; follow the **Supplemental Material link** from the Annual Reviews home page at **http://www.annualreviews.org**). Sørensen & Pedersen (115) compared the translation rates of the GAA and GAG codons. The rarer GAG codon was translated three times more slowly than the common codon GAA, indicating that tRNA levels are not the sole determinant of translation rates. In addition to wobble pairing, other effects, including codon context, can modulate translation rates (see main text).

Stable mRNA structures can cause translational pauses (129), so mRNA structure provides an additional mechanism to regulate translation speed and, by extension, the temporal coordination of cotranslational folding and/or interactions of the nascent chain with other cellular components (see Cotranslational Protein Folding and Cotranslational Interactions with Other Cellular Components, below). For example, in the polytopic membrane protein CFTR, a synonymous mutation (Ile507 ATC→ATT) exacerbates the protein folding defect caused by the ΔF508 mutation linked to cystic fibrosis. This synonymous mutation is hypothesized to alter mRNA structure by introducing large single-stranded loops that lead to slower translation (7, 79).

Selection for mRNA structure is an example of synonymous codon selection that can affect protein biogenesis, and hence cell physiology and fitness, for reasons not directly related to the decoding of those codons at the ribosome. Functionally significant RNA motifs are another example. For example, synonymous single nucleotide polymorphisms (SNPs) may either weaken or strengthen splice sites (105, 120). Likewise, ribosomal profiling experiments have shown that bacterial ribosomes accumulate at internal SD motifs (consensus sequence AGGAGGT), which bind to the complementary anti-SD motif found within small subunit rRNA (81). SD motifs may occur in any reading frame and are underrepresented within coding sequences, suggesting that they are generally under negative selection. The selection against SD motifs appears to influence synonymous codon usage in *E. coli*: Glycine-glycine pairs are unlikely to be encoded by GGA-GGT and GGA is the rarest glycine codon in *E. coli*. In support of this interpretation, translation of internal SD motifs by ribosomes that lack an anti-SD motif did not increase ribosome occupancy at these motifs (81).

Single nucleotide polymorphism (SNP): a single nucleotide variant common in a population, sometimes associated with a disease

Selective Pressures on Codon Usage: Why Are Rare Codons Used at All?

Rare codons were historically viewed as mildly deleterious because of their lower rates of translation speed and accuracy. Scientists assumed that evolution favored common codons in general, but because the negative selective pressure was not strong enough to completely eliminate rare codons, some continued to be incorporated as a result of mutational drift (14, 108, 113). However, synonymous rare codons are not distributed randomly across coding sequences; instead, they tend to appear in clusters within the protein coding sequences of most species (24, 25, 96). This discovery led to the hypothesis that rare codons are under positive selection in certain locations because of some functional role (25). In support of the selection hypothesis, Pechmann & Frydman

(97) discovered that rare codons from homologous coding sequences of 10 closely related yeast species tend to occur in similar locations. Analogous to the conservation of functionally important amino acid residues, their observation suggested that synonymous rare codons could be functionally important within these protein families. However, other selection forces could also cause the appearance of rare codon clustering. For example, if selection favors common codons, but this selection is strong in some parts of coding sequences and weak or absent in others, mutational drift will result in a higher concentration of rare codons in the regions of weak selection. If these regions of weak codon selection occur in equivalent regions of homologous coding sequences, this can create the appearance of conservation.

Because of their lower translational accuracy, rare codons are hypothesized to be under stronger negative selection in coding sequence regions encoding functionally important amino acids (35, 151). Highly expressed sequences tend to be encoded by more common codons (8, 51, 52, 63), and this finding has led to the hypothesis that common codons are under stronger positive selection in highly expressed genes because of their faster translation rate, leading to more efficient protein production (55, 109). Thus, rare codons would be expected to cluster in more lowly expressed genes with weaker selection for translational efficiency. However, in many organisms numerous highly expressed genes, such as those encoding ribosomal proteins, contain rare codon clusters (24). The ambiguity of these results underscores the importance of examining experimental data for the functional importance of codon usage.

EFFECTS OF SYNONYMOUS CODON USAGE ON PROTEIN BIOGENESIS

Cotranslational Protein Folding

Protein synthesis occurs at the peptidyltransferase active site of the ribosome, which is located within the core of its roughly spherical, ~25-nm-diameter structure. As the ribosome decodes the mRNA sequence, the newly synthesized nascent chain initially passes through a narrow, ~10-nm-long exit tunnel (6, 143) (**Figure 2a**). This tunnel constrains the conformations of the most recently synthesized 30–40 aa of the nascent protein chain, as it is too narrow to permit the nascent chain to adopt significant tertiary structure (although it is wide enough to permit, and even stabilize, an α-helical conformation) (138). After a nascent chain is 30–40 aa long, its N-terminus emerges at the surface of the ribosome, and these conformational restrictions are significantly reduced.

The vectorial appearance of the nascent chain during its synthesis means that in vivo the N-terminus of a polypeptide chain has an opportunity to begin folding before its C-terminus appears. To what extent this folding vector can alter folding mechanisms or the final folded structure of an encoded protein remains controversial. To date, researchers have studied protein folding primarily in vitro, by diluting full-length protein chains from a chemical denaturant, using small, simple model proteins that fold robustly, meaning they can assume their native structure from a wide variety of unfolded conformations (22). Results from this approach have led to the current dominant thermodynamic paradigm, developed by Anfinsen (1), that the amino acid sequence of a protein provides all the information necessary to specify its native, 3D structure. Under this paradigm, the structure that a protein adopts should be unaffected by the starting conformation, and synonymous variations within the mRNA coding sequence that alter local translation rate should not affect the folded structure of the protein.

However, the model proteins commonly used to study folding do not wholly capture the complexities of protein structural and folding properties across the proteome (12), nor do in vitro folding experiments accurately mimic in vivo folding conditions. For example, the native structure of a protein need not represent a unique thermodynamic energy minimum: For some proteins, the native structure represents a kinetically trapped state (95, 140), which can lead to the population of more than one native structure (5, 15, 83, 112, 130). Compared with current folding models, larger proteins with more complex structural properties might be more dependent on cotranslational folding to avoid protein misfolding and aggregation. Indeed, multidomain proteins can undergo misfolding owing to interactions between adjacent structural domains, and the amino acid sequences of these proteins have evolved to avoid such interactions (11). Vectorial folding during translation could enable an N-terminal domain to fold before the appearance of a potentially interfering C-terminal domain, and modulating the translation rate via synonymous codon substitutions could provide still more time for the N-terminus to fold. In this fashion, synonymous codon usage would add an additional layer of information to the coding sequence by encoding the translation rate as well as the amino acid sequence (73, 93, 100, 104) (**Figure 2**).

Supporting this hypothesis, several studies have shown that synonymous rare codon substitutions inhibit the function of specific proteins, presumably by disfavoring the formation of the functional native structure. Two broad types of synonymous substitution folding effects have been observed: (*a*) those that alter the structure and/or function of the encoded protein, and (*b*) those that produce even more dramatic effects, altering the partitioning between proper folding and aggregation and thereby reducing the yield of correctly folded proteins.

A classic example of the first type is chloramphenicol acetyltransferase (CAT). The wild-type CAT coding sequence contains two large rare codon clusters. Replacing one of these clusters with more common synonymous codons resulted in faster translation but reduced CAT specific activity by ~20%, suggesting that some portion of CAT translated with more common codons, although soluble, adopts a structure distinct from the functional native structure (74). Sun et al. (119) identified in a library of galactose oxidase mutants with altered substrate specificity similar synonymous mutations that reduce enzymatic activity. A more recent study showed that synonymous codon substitutions can also impact organism physiology. Zhou et al. (150) examined the effects of codon usage in FRQ, a fungal circadian clock regulator protein encoded largely by rare codons. Replacing the rare codons with more common synonymous codons impaired FRQ function and the circadian properties of the fungus. FRQ protein translated from the common codon sequence showed different protease susceptibility than FRQ translated from the wild-type coding sequence, suggesting that the functional effects were caused by a difference in FRQ protein structure.

Alternatively, slowly translated, rare synonymous codons can reduce protein misfolding and aggregation (Type *b* from above). Cortazzo et al. (26) examined the in vivo folding of synonymous variants of a fatty-acid-binding protein. Replacing five rare codons with common synonymous substitutions lowered the yield of soluble proteins and induced a cellular stress response, suggesting misfolding occurred (26). Increasing cellular tRNA levels is expected to raise the translation rate of codons with low levels of cognate tRNA, reducing translational pauses. Increasing tRNA levels in *E. coli* produced an overall decrease in soluble protein and increase in insoluble aggregates, suggesting translational pauses are important for the folding of many proteins (43).

Although these examples provide a compelling case for the impact of synonymous codon usage for proper cotranslational folding of some proteins, the extent to which synonymous codon usage affects cotranslational folding in general remains unknown. There is a pressing need to study codon usage in a systematic way in order to develop a predictive model for its effects on cotranslational protein folding, and to determine to what extent these effects are due to slow decoding versus alterations to mRNA structure or other effects. The development of such a predictive model is further challenged because the factors that affect translation rate likely differ between organisms. For example, the prokaryotic ribosome has helicase activity (122, 127), and therefore prokaryotes are expected to be less susceptible to stalling induced by mRNA structures than eukaryotes are.

Cotranslational Interactions with Other Cellular Components

During translation, nascent chains may form cotranslational interactions with other cellular components and undergo covalent modifications (68, 76). Perhaps the most well-studied example is cotranslational interactions between N-terminal nascent chain signal sequences and the signal recognition particle, which initially arrests translation elongation to ensure subsequent cotranslational translocation of the nascent polypeptide chain once it arrives at the ER translocon (133, 135, 136). Because the 5′ ends of coding sequences of secreted proteins are more enriched in rare codons than those of cytosolic proteins, it has been hypothesized that they might contribute to increased membrane targeting and secretion efficiency (25). Rare-codon-induced translational pauses are hypothesized to allow extra time for other cotranslational interactions as well (24). For example, a rare-codon-induced reduction of translation rate in actin increases the likelihood of cotranslational arginylation (145), a covalent modification that regulates actin activity and prevents aggregation of actin filaments (70). In addition, many multimeric protein complexes can form cotranslationally (37). Although less well explored, codon usage and other mechanisms that control local translation rates might help regulate other well-characterized steps in nascent chain biogenesis including interactions with molecular chaperones (94) and enzymes that catalyze N-glycosylation (85).

Functional Regulation of Expression Level

In addition to affecting translation rates and cotranslational processes, codon usage can significantly alter protein expression levels. Indeed, because of the known negative effects of rare codons on expression yield, it is common practice when expressing a human gene in *E. coli* or another expression host to replace the arginine codons AGA and AGG, which are common in *Homo sapiens* but very rare in *E. coli*, with more common versions to maximize expression level (see Heterologous Protein Expression, below). In support of this approach, the coding sequences of many highly expressed genes are enriched in common codons. This observation is often interpreted as support for the hypothesis that selection favors common codons, allowing most rare codons to accumulate in lowly expressed sequences, which are thought to be under weaker selection (109).

However, recent results have challenged this longstanding view by demonstrating functional significance of expression level regulation by rare codons in certain sequences. Xu et al. (142) tested the effects of codon usage in cyanobacterium (*Synechococcus elongatus*) circadian clock proteins KaiB and KaiC, whose wild-type coding sequences contain many rare codons. Replacing these rare codons with common synonymous codons increased protein expression level, and this increase in expression disrupted the circadian growth rhythms of the organism (142). This result suggested that synonymous codons may be under selection to regulate protein expression level and are not merely a by-product of mutational drift in lowly expressed genes. Likewise, Subramaniam et al. (118) discovered that bacterial biofilm formation is inhibited by SinR, and the SinR coding sequence contains a number of serine codons susceptible to pausing under serine-starving conditions (81, 118). As a result, the production of SinR decreases when nutrients are limited, initiating biofilm formation. In support of the ideas that highly expressed transcripts are not the only coding sequences subject to synonymous codon selection and that synonymous codon-related regulation such as this might be widespread, tRNA levels differ with cell cycle stage and growth conditions, as do the expression levels of genes with different codon usage (10, 124). Likewise, cell cycle–regulated genes show atypical codon usage (46).

Viral Codon Usage

Viruses provide another example of how genes adapt to expression conditions. Viral genes rely on host translational machinery for expression and, as a consequence, have evolved diverse mechanisms to exploit host codon usage biases. Viral coding sequences, particularly those with high expression, typically have codon usage biases similar to those of their host organisms (4). However, certain viral genes are enriched in codons that are rare in their hosts' genomes, and this rare codon usage is hypothesized to provide a mechanism to reduce viral protein expression and minimize host immune system responses (89, 128). Some viruses also encode their own tRNA (often a tRNA that is rare in the host) to allow more efficient, selective translation of viral transcripts (34).

Codon Usage in Horizontally Transferred Genes

In contrast to the examples of functionally significant rare codon usage provided above, some genes have unusual codon usage because they were horizontally transferred between different species or strains. Horizontal transfer often involves plasmids, and horizontally transferred genes in bacteria are often related to virulence or antibiotic resistance, but this process can also occur in eukaryotes and transferred genes can be incorporated into the genome (61, 121). Genes that have recently undergone horizontal transfer often have unusual GC content and codon usage compared with their host genome, and researchers have used this unusual codon usage to develop algorithms to identify putative horizontally transferred genes (49). However, not all horizontally transferred genes have unusual codon usage, and not all genes with unusual codon usage have been horizontally transferred (46). When evaluating a gene with unusual codon usage, researchers should consider the possibility of horizontal transfer before assuming that the unusual codon bias resulted from selection.

Heterologous Protein Expression

Analogous to naturally occurring horizontal gene transfer, genes are also frequently transferred between species in the laboratory. Because synonymous codon usage can be functionally significant, and the distribution of rare and common codons within the same coding sequence can be drastically different, differences in codon usage frequencies between organisms can have consequences for heterologous protein expression (**Figure 3**). This finding has led to a number of algorithms that adjust the codon usage of a sequence for expression in a particular organism (47, 58, 60). Because of the traditional focus on rare codons as deleterious, these algorithms typically seek to optimize a coding sequence by increasing the number of amino acids encoded by common codons (38). The emphasis on common codons is due partly to the association between codon commonness and high expression and to the desire to produce large amounts of protein from heterologous expression. However, this approach ignores potential contributions of rare codons to cotranslational folding or other processes, such as interactions with molecular chaperones. Hence, if the goal is to produce the highest possible yield of soluble, natively folded proteins, then designing a coding sequence for uniformly fast translation may not be the most effective approach. An alternative strategy, called codon harmonization, involves replicating the coding sequence's original distribution of rare and common codons in the context of the heterologous expression system (2). Harmonization was used to design mRNA sequences for *E. coli* expression of proteins

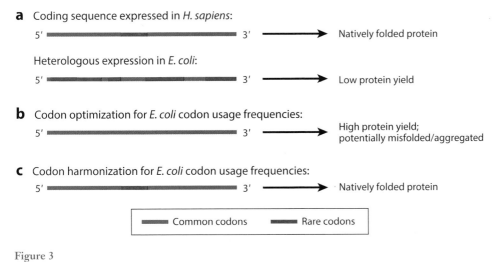

a Coding sequence expressed in *H. sapiens*:

5′ ■■■■■■■■■■■■■■■ 3′ ⟶ Natively folded protein

Heterologous expression in *E. coli*:

5′ ■■■■■■■■■■■■■■■ 3′ ⟶ Low protein yield

b Codon optimization for *E. coli* codon usage frequencies:

5′ ■■■■■■■■■■■■■■■ 3′ ⟶ High protein yield; potentially misfolded/aggregated

c Codon harmonization for *E. coli* codon usage frequencies:

5′ ■■■■■■■■■■■■■■■ 3′ ⟶ Natively folded protein

■■ Common codons   ■■ Rare codons

Figure 3

Hypothetical example of heterologous expression of a human coding sequence in *Escherichia coli*. (*a*) Because many codons that are common in *Homo sapiens* are rare in *E. coli*, a human coding sequence often contains more rare codons when expressed in *E. coli*. This can lower protein expression levels. (*b*) To solve this problem, coding sequences are frequently optimized for the codon usage of the heterologous expression host by selecting only synonymous codons that are common in the host. This approach often results in increased expression levels, but much of the resulting protein product may be misfolded. (*c*) Codon harmonization is based on the hypothesis that the original pattern of rare and common codon usage, under native expression conditions, promotes proper folding. Instead of choosing all common synonymous codons, codons that are rare in *H. sapiens* are replaced by codons that are rare in *E. coli*, and codons that are common in *H. sapiens* are replaced by codons that are common in *E. coli*.

from the eukaryotic pathogen *Plasmodium falciparum*. *E. coli* and *P. falciparum* have very different genome %GC bias and codon usage levels, and codon harmonization improved expression level and soluble protein yield relative to conventional codon optimization (2, 3). More generally, translating eukaryotic coding sequences in *E. coli* strains that translate more slowly, at a rate more similar to eukaryotic translation rates, increased folding yield for some eukaryotic proteins (111).

Rare Codons at Coding Sequence Termini

Rare codons are enriched at the 5′ termini of many coding sequences in many species (25, 131, 144); however, the functional significance of this enrichment is still a matter of debate (**Figure 4**). Ribosome profiling has identified higher ribosome occupancies at the 5′ termini of coding sequences, although it is not clear whether this was caused by slower translation or premature termination (65). A 5′ rare codon cluster is not expected to regulate cotranslational folding, because at the time of its translation the nascent chain has not yet exited the ribosome (**Figure 2a**). According to one hypothesis, because rare codons reduce translation rate, they create a ramp at the 5′ end of the coding sequence, which optimizes ribosome spacing on the mRNA and prevents ribosome traffic jams (88, 131). In contrast, the 5′ enrichment of rare codons is proposed to be a by-product of selection for GC content. High %GC generally leads to more stable mRNA structures, and stable 5′ structures may interfere with translation initiation. Less stable 5′ mRNA structures are correlated with higher protein expression levels (77, 107, 148).

Evidence from recent large-scale screening studies suggests that the enrichment of rare codons at the 5′ termini does result primarily from selection for low %GC codons, at least in bacteria

a Ramp hypothesis: ribosome spacing

b Secretion hypothesis: paused translation for targeting

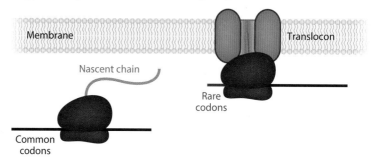

c mRNA structure hypothesis: translation initiation

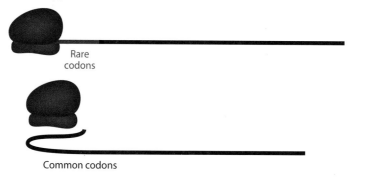

Figure 4

Proposed functions of 5′ rare codons. (*a*) The ramp hypothesis (131) suggests that 5′ rare codons introduce a region of slow translation that keeps ribosomes more widely spaced on the mRNA, as ribosomes will move more quickly after leaving the ramp. (*b*) The secretion hypothesis (25, 144) suggests that 5′ rare codons cause a translational pause to allow time for targeting before the nascent chain is translated. (*c*) The mRNA structure hypothesis (9, 54) suggests that 5′ codon usage is under selection for reduced mRNA structure so that translation may be initiated more efficiently.

(9, 44, 54). These studies indicated that low %GC codons are enriched at the 5′ termini. In organisms with high %GC content, most low %GC codons are rare, so selection for low %GC codons results in a corresponding coincidental enrichment of rare codons.

The rare codons at the 5′ termini in the transcripts of secreted proteins are hypothesized to slow translation and allow additional time for the ribosome to be targeted to the membrane (144). Consistent with this hypothesis, in bacteria secreted proteins are more likely to contain synonymous rare codons near the 5′ end of their coding sequences (25), suggesting these rare codons might play a role in efficient translocation in addition to their role in enhancing translation initiation. A recent study of several eukaryotic species also showed a 5′ enrichment of rare codons in coding sequences of secreted proteins but not cytosolic proteins (84), supporting the hypothesis that a lowered translation rate could promote secretion.

In addition to the enrichment of rare codons at the 5′ termini, some species show an enrichment of rare codons at the 3′ termini of coding sequences (25). Compared with 5′-end rare codons, 3′-end rare codons have received far less attention in the literature, but they have been hypothesized to tether a synthesized protein to the ribosome to allow additional time for cotranslational folding before translation termination and release of the nascent chain (25).

Codon Usage and Human Health

Emerging connections between synonymous codon usage and human health further underscore the importance of understanding the mechanisms by which synonymous codon substitutions alter protein biogenesis. Although many disease-associated SNPs are nonsynonymous, some synonymous SNPs have been identified as disease associated (105). One example is the CFTR synonymous mutation Ile507 ATC→ATT, which alters mRNA stability and exacerbates the effects of the cystic fibrosis mutation ΔF508 (see Direct Effects of Synonymous Codon Usage, above). In *MDR1*, a gene encoding a transmembrane efflux pump involved in multidrug resistance, three disease-associated SNPs (two synonymous and one nonsynonymous) correlate with patient responses to chemotherapy (48, 71). *MDR1* expressed in a human cell line with these SNPs produced an efflux pump with an altered structure (assessed by protease susceptibility and antibody binding) and altered drug-pumping activity compared with wild-type *MDR1*. In addition to altering cotranslational folding, pathogenic synonymous SNPs can alter splicing motifs, leading to alternative splicing (28, 36, 42, 53, 86). Supek et al. (120) discovered that synonymous mutations are often driver mutations in human cancers, and speculated that some of these synonymous SNPs could affect protein folding, as they are enriched near the beginning of α-helical regions in oncogenes. This study also found that cancer-driving synonymous substitutions are both rare to common and common to rare, underscoring that increasing both codon rarity and commonness can be deleterious in specific circumstances.

MEASURING AND TRACKING SYNONYMOUS CODON USAGE

Quantifying Codon Usage and Predicting Translation Rates

Although the growing body of experimental results described above has demonstrated that synonymous codon selection can play a functional role in specific coding sequences, such results have not yet led to a general understanding of the roles for synonymous codon usage in protein biogenesis. Alongside functional studies, bioinformatics studies of codon usage patterns have provided a valuable strategy for developing and testing broad, general hypotheses about synonymous codon usage.

To study the functional importance of synonymous codon usage, it is first necessary to develop an algorithm to classify or quantify codon usage. A number of these algorithms have been developed, some of which merely quantify codon usage while others attempt to use codon usage frequencies and other information to predict translation rates (24, 33, 97, 109, 116, 147) (**Figure 5**). Whereas some algorithms quantify codon usage across an entire gene (returning a

Calculating synonymous codon usage

There are multiple algorithms to calculate synonymous codon usage. Some examples include the following:

Leu-Leu-Cys	Protein sequence
CTG-CTA-TGC	Codons

a Absolute rareness

Uses codon usage frequencies from the genome. This method does not control for the influence of the amino acid sequence (in this example, Cys is a rare amino acid).

CTG	CTA	TGC
51.1	3.9	6.4

b Codon optimality: Codon Adaptation Index (CAI)

This method compares the codon usage of a sequence to the codon usage of a set of highly expressed genes (in this case, *E. coli* ribosomal proteins). Highly expressed genes are hypothesized to use more translationally optimal codons.

CTG	CTA	TGC	
379	1	17	Codon frequency
379	379	17	Most common codon frequency

The frequency of each codon in the codon usage set is divided by the frequency of the most common codon in that synonymous set. The CAI for the full sequence is the geometric mean:

$$[(379/379) \times (1/379) \times (17/17)]/3 = 0.00088$$

c Relative codon usage: %MinMax

Relative measures of codon usage control for amino acid frequencies: The usage frequency of a codon is compared to others in its synonymous set. The %MinMax algorithm was designed to highlight clusters of rare codons. Usage frequencies of the codons in a coding sequence are compared with the maximum, minimum, and average possible for a given amino acid sequence.

CTG	CTA	TGC	
51.1	3.9	6.4	Genome-wide usage frequencies
51.1	51.1	6.4	Max. for synonymous set
3.9	3.9	5.2	Min. for synonymous set
17.3	17.3	5.8	Avg. for synonymous set

%MinMax scores are typically calculated for a sequence window:

$$\%\text{MinMax} = 100x(\text{Actual} - \text{Avg.})/(\text{Max} - \text{Avg.}) =$$

$$100x\frac{((51.1 + 3.9 + 6.4) - (17.3 + 17.3 + 5.8))}{((51.1 + 51.1 + 6.4) - (17.3 + 17.3 + 5.8))} = 30.7$$

Figure 5

Metrics commonly used to calculate and compare the codon usage of mRNA sequences. Examples of calculations using (*a*) absolute rareness, (*b*) Codon Adaptation Index (CAI) (109), and (*c*) %MinMax (24). For absolute rareness and %MinMax calculations, using data from the Codon Usage Database (92), the codon usage frequencies are shown in units of frequency per 1,000 codons in genome open reading frames.

single codon usage value per coding sequence), position-specific codon usage algorithms that analyze individual codons or short sliding windows along the coding sequence are more useful for identifying local perturbations of codon usage that might affect cotranslational folding and other aspects of protein biogenesis.

While some algorithms focus on codon usage, others classify codons according to levels of cognate tRNA. Unlike codon usage frequencies, which are available for all fully sequenced genomes, absolute tRNA concentrations are available for only a few species. Although tRNA levels in general correlate with tRNA gene copy number, and in many cases gene copy numbers have been used as a proxy for tRNA concentration, cellular levels of tRNA and charged tRNA vary with cell cycle and growth conditions (32, 81) and between different cell types in multicellular organisms (30), limiting these approximations. Some algorithms incorporate additional factors predicted to affect the connection between codon usage and translation rate, for example, by including an additional term representing the strength of wobble pairing between a given codon and anticodon (116). There is some experimental evidence that codon usage metrics in addition to codon rarity do correlate with translation rates, although the difficulty of measuring the absolute translation rate of individual codons or local sequence regions has hindered comparisons between these metrics and actual translation rates. For example, Spencer et al. (116) used pulse-chase analysis to compare the translation rates of synonymous luciferase variants with predicted fast or slow translation based on a wobble velocity metric. Experimental results were globally consistent with predictions, but the experimental methods were not sufficiently sensitive to test predictions of translation rate in local sequence regions. Zhang et al. (146) identified partially translated products, showing that clusters of slow-translating codons (as predicted by their tRNA level algorithm) caused translational pauses. Similar results were observed for the %MinMax algorithm, a measure of relative codon rareness (24) (**Figure 6**). Translation-rate-dependent cotranslational folding of the YKB biosensor (**Figure 2**; described in Direct Effects of Synonymous Codon Usage, above) was more

%MinMax: an algorithm based on relative codon usage used to quantify the codon usage within a gene

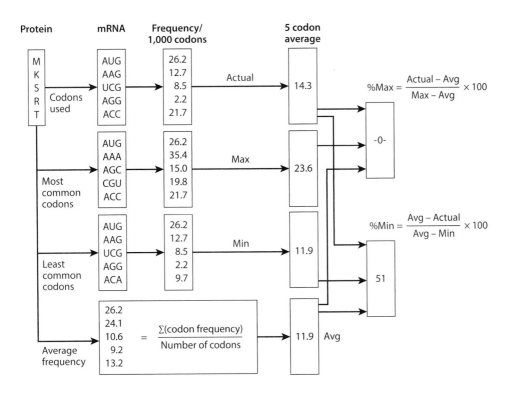

Figure 6

Flowchart for %MinMax analysis. The minimum, maximum, and average usage frequencies are calculated for each set of synonymous codons. The usage frequency of the actual codon used is compared with these values. Common codons result in positive %MinMax scores and rare codons result in negative %MinMax scores. In this simple example results are averaged over a window of 5 codons; in practice, a sliding window of 17 codons is typically used. Figure reproduced from Reference 24 with permission.

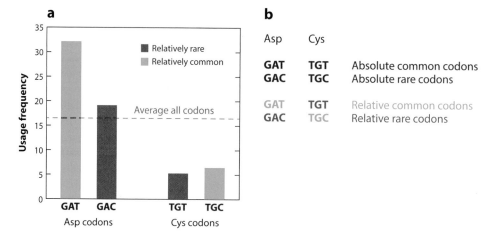

Figure 7

Absolute versus relative codon rareness. (*a*) Absolute codon usage frequencies of aspartate and cysteine codons in the *Escherichia coli* genome (frequency is defined as codons per 1,000 genome codons). The gray dashed line indicates the average usage frequency of all 61 sense codons. Both aspartate codons have high absolute usage frequencies, and both cysteine codons have low absolute usage frequencies, because aspartate is a common amino acid and cysteine is a rare one. (*b*) If codons are classified according to absolute rareness, all cysteine codons are considered rare and all aspartate codons are considered common. However, measures of relative rareness control for amino acid frequencies and classify a codon as rare or common on the basis of how it compares to other codons encoding the same amino acid.

accurately predicted by an algorithm that considers only codon usage frequency than by several other algorithms, including those based on tRNA concentration and wobble velocity (104).

Even among algorithms that evaluate only codon usage frequency, comparisons can be based on either absolute or relative codon usage frequencies. Because amino acid usage frequencies differ widely, these results are not equivalent (**Figure 7**). A codon is rare in absolute terms if its usage frequency is lower than the average of all codons that encode amino acids, but it is rare in relative terms if its usage frequency is lower than the usage frequency of other codons encoding the same amino acid. Relative rareness is often more useful for studies of codon usage because it allows for correction based on amino acid conservation. For example, cysteine is a rare amino acid, so even the most common cysteine codon may be rare in absolute terms, but its presence in a codon sequence indicates selection for cysteine, not for a rare codon. Some algorithms, including the widely used Codon Adaptation Index (CAI) (**Figure 5**), are based on codon usage frequencies in highly expressed genes rather than whole genomes, assuming that highly expressed genes are under stronger selection and contain more optimal codons (109).

As data for translation rates of specific codons become available, methods of quantifying codon usage can be refined. Until this becomes possible, bioinformatics analyses are limited to identifying coding sequence regions with statistically unusual codon usage. A crucial aspect for every bioinformatics study to consider is the development of an appropriate null model to control for the effects of amino acid sequence and other irrelevant variables on codon selection. A common choice is random reverse translations, in which control mRNA sequences are constructed by randomly selecting synonymous codons for a given protein sequence (24). Synonymous codons may be chosen according to probabilities determined from the species codon usage or by randomly shuffling the synonymous codons in a single protein.

Codon Adaptation Index (CAI): an algorithm used to quantify the codon usage of an entire gene; based on comparisons to codon usage in highly expressed genes

Identifying Patterns in Synonymous Codon Usage

Many bioinformatics studies have sought to identify correlations between the locations of rare codon clusters and structural units in the encoded protein, on the basis of the hypothesis that rare codon clusters promote cotranslational folding of these units. However, the scientific community has not reached a clear consensus on the location and functional significance of rare codon clusters, primarily because different studies have yielded dramatically different results. This inconsistency is not surprising, given the differences in the algorithms and data sets used. In particular, studies that focus on proteins of known structure tend to rely on small data sets, which can introduce bias.

One attractive hypothesis is that rare codons might separate the cotranslational folding of individual domains in a multidomain protein. Several studies have tested whether rare codons are enriched at domain boundaries or, given the shielding by the ribosome exit tunnel of the nascent chain C-terminus, 30 to 40 codons downstream relative to domain boundaries (**Figure 2**). However, whereas Thanaraj & Argos (126) determined that rare codons were enriched at domain boundaries in a set of 37 multidomain *E. coli* proteins with solved structures, Saunders & Deane (106) observed the opposite trend and concluded that rare codons were underenriched at domain boundaries in human, yeast, and *E. coli* sequences. The sample size used by Saunders & Deane was larger than that used by Thanaraj & Argos, but still represented only a small fraction of the entire proteome: Their largest sample, from *E. coli*, consisted of only 121 proteins.

Different secondary structure types, which have different topologies and fold at different rates, are hypothesized to exhibit distinct codon usage patterns. An analysis of 54 *E. coli* proteins of known structure indicated α-helices are associated with common codon usage, whereas β-sheets and coil regions are associated with rare codon usage, which was hypothesized to be related to the slower folding rate of β-sheets (125). Similarly, Saunders & Deane (106) found that certain codons have different usage frequencies at regions of transition between secondary structure types. But in contrast to the study above, they found "fast" codons at the transition into irregular, random coil structures and "slow" codons at transitions into α-helices or β-sheets. Xie & Ding (141) examined associations between codon usage and secondary structure in 54 *E. coli* proteins and 107 mammalian (mostly human) proteins of known structure. They determined that two codons in *E. coli* and 17 codons in mammals had statistically significant different usage in different secondary structure types, but the authors did not draw any conclusions about preferences for rare and common codons in different secondary structure types. In a broader analysis, Brunak & Engelbrecht (13) analyzed 719 proteins of known structure and found no correlations between synonymous codon usage and secondary structure regions, leaving unclear the connections between codon selection and secondary structure of the encoded protein.

Others have hypothesized that the distribution of rare codons is influenced more by selection for translational accuracy than by selection for translation rate. According to this view, common codons are expected to be favored in regions where amino acid sequence is critical, whereas rare codons are clustered in regions (for example, unstructured linkers) where mistranslation is less harmful (151). However, the synonymous mutations studied by Cortazzo et al. (26) were located in a turn between two α-helices, so rare codons located between structural units (rather than in them) may still be functional.

Recent studies have sought to determine whether rare codons are conserved in homologous coding sequences during evolution, as this would imply a functional role for rare codons. Pechmann & Frydman (97) examined several yeast species and concluded that rare codons tend to align in homologs. Chartier et al. (17) reported that gene families within the Pfam database contain many conserved rare codon clusters. However, the Chartier et al. study relied on measures of absolute codon rareness and failed to control for amino acid content, so their analysis may have detected conservation of rare amino acids rather than conservation of rare synonymous codons.

CONCLUSIONS

A growing body of experimental evidence has demonstrated that synonymous codon usage is under evolutionary selection and has functional significance for the biogenesis of some proteins. However, although experimental evidence for the functional significance of rare codons is accumulating, we still lack a general, predictive understanding of the mechanisms by which synonymous codon selection impacts protein biogenesis. An understanding of these mechanisms will enhance synthetic gene design and heterologous protein expression and further our understanding of the mechanisms underlying human diseases. Although it is not yet possible to accurately predict which synonymous mutations have functional impact, bioinformatics analyses based on wider, more representative data sets and more extensive statistical analyses, coupled with additional broadscale experimental testing, will be invaluable for clarifying the currently exciting but murky picture of the effects of codon usage on protein biogenesis.

SUMMARY POINTS

1. Synonymous codon usage can be functionally significant and impacts multiple steps of protein biogenesis.

2. Evidence suggests that synonymous codon usage is under evolutionary selection.

3. Synonymous codon changes can affect human health.

4. Although extensive evidence shows that synonymous codon usage affects biogenesis-specific proteins, we still lack a general, predictive understanding of these effects.

FUTURE ISSUES

1. Will broader bioinformatics studies reveal correlations between codon usage and protein structure?

2. Can we accurately predict which synonymous codon changes will most likely negatively impact protein biogenesis and lead to disease?

3. Will an improved understanding of synonymous codon usage lead to rules for codon selection that can be applied to improve folding yields for rational protein design?

DISCLOSURE STATEMENT

The authors are not aware of any affiliations, memberships, funding, or financial holdings that might be perceived as affecting the objectivity of this review.

ACKNOWLEDGMENTS

This work was supported by National Institutes of Health grants R01 GM074807 and U54 GM105816.

LITERATURE CITED

1. Anfinsen CB. 1973. Principles that govern the folding of protein chains. *Science* 181:223–30
2. Angov E, Hillier CJ, Kincaid RL, Lyon JA. 2008. Heterologous protein expression is enhanced by harmonizing the codon usage frequencies of the target gene with those of the expression host. *PLOS ONE* 3:e2189
3. Angov E, Legler PM, Mease RM. 2011. Adjustment of codon usage frequencies by codon harmonization improves protein expression and folding. *Methods Mol. Biol.* 705:1–13
4. Bahir I, Fromer M, Prat Y, Linial M. 2009. Viral adaptation to host: a proteome-based analysis of codon usage and amino acid preferences. *Mol. Syst. Biol.* 5:311
5. Baker D, Agard DA. 1994. Influenza hemagglutinin: kinetic control of protein function. *Structure* 2:907–10
6. Ban N, Nissen P, Hansen J, Moore PB, Steitz TA. 2000. The complete atomic structure of the large ribosomal subunit at 2.4 Å resolution. *Science* 289:905–20
7. Bartoszewski RA, Jablonsky M, Bartoszewska S, Stevenson L, Dai Q, et al. 2010. A synonymous single nucleotide polymorphism in ΔF508 *CFTR* alters the secondary structure of the mRNA and the expression of the mutant protein. *J. Biol. Chem.* 285:28741–48
8. Bennetzen JL, Hall BD. 1982. Codon selection in yeast. *J. Biol. Chem.* 257:3026–31
9. Bentele K, Saffert P, Rauscher R, Ignatova Z, Blüthgen N. 2013. Efficient translation initiation dictates codon usage at gene start. *Mol. Syst. Biol.* 9:675
10. Berg OG, Kurland CG. 1997. Growth rate-optimised tRNA abundance and codon usage. *J. Mol. Biol.* 270:544–50
11. Borgia MB, Borgia A, Best RB, Steward A, Nettels D, et al. 2011. Single-molecule fluorescence reveals sequence-specific misfolding in multidomain proteins. *Nature* 474:662–65
12. Braselmann E, Chaney JL, Clark PL. 2013. Folding the proteome. *Trends Biochem. Sci.* 38:337–44
13. Brunak S, Engelbrecht J. 1996. Protein structure and the sequential structure of mRNA: alpha-helix and beta-sheet signals at the nucleotide level. *Proteins* 25:237–52
14. Bulmer M. 1991. The selection-mutation-drift theory of synonymous codon usage. *Genetics* 129:897–907
15. Burmann BM, Knauer SH, Sevostyanova A, Schweimer K, Mooney RA, et al. 2012. An α-helix to β-barrel domain switch transforms the transcription factor RfaH into a translation factor. *Cell* 150:291–303
16. Charneski CA, Hurst LD. 2013. Positively charged residues are the major determinants of ribosomal velocity. *PLOS Biol.* 11:e1001508
17. Chartier M, Gaudreault F, Najmanovich R. 2012. Large-scale analysis of conserved rare codon clusters suggests an involvement in co-translational molecular recognition events. *Bioinformatics* 28:1438–45
18. Chen C, Stevens B, Kaur J, Cabral D, Liu H, et al. 2011. Single-molecule fluorescence measurements of ribosomal translocation dynamics. *Mol. Cell* 42:367–77
19. Chen SL, Lee W, Hottes AK, Shapiro L, McAdams HH. 2004. Codon usage between genomes is constrained by genome-wide mutational processes. *PNAS* 101:3480–85
20. Chevance FF, Le Guyon S, Hughes KT. 2014. The effects of codon context on in vivo translation speed. *PLOS Genet.* 10:e1004392
21. Chursov A, Frishman D, Shneider A. 2013. Conservation of mRNA secondary structures may filter out mutations in *Escherichia coli* evolution. *Nucleic Acids Res.* 41:7854–60
22. Clark PL. 2004. Protein folding in the cell: reshaping the folding funnel. *Trends Biochem. Sci.* 29:527–34
23. Clark PL, Ugrinov KG. 2009. Measuring cotranslational folding of nascent polypeptide chains on ribosomes. *Methods Enzymol.* 466:567–90
24. Clarke TF, Clark PL. 2008. Rare codons cluster. *PLOS ONE* 3:e3412
25. Clarke TF, Clark PL. 2010. Increased incidence of rare codon clusters at 5′ and 3′ gene termini: implications for function. *BMC Genomics* 11:118
26. Cortazzo P, Cervenansky C, Marin M, Reiss C, Ehrlich R, Deana A. 2002. Silent mutations affect in vivo protein folding in *Escherichia coli*. *Biochem. Biophys. Res. Commun.* 293:537–41
27. Curran JF. 1995. Decoding with the A-I wobble pair is inefficient. *Nucleic Acids Res.* 23:683–88
28. Daidone V, Gallinaro L, Grazia Cattini M, Pontara E, Bertomoro A, et al. 2011. An apparently silent nucleotide substitution (c.7056C>T) in the von Willebrand factor gene is responsible for type 1 von Willebrand disease. *Haematologica* 96:881–87

29. Dees ND, Zhang Q, Kandoth C, Wendl MC, Schierding W, et al. 2012. MuSiC: identifying mutational significance in cancer genomes. *Genome Res.* 22:1589–98

30. Dittmar KA, Goodenbour JM, Pan T. 2006. Tissue-specific differences in human transfer RNA expression. *PLOS Genet.* 2:e221

31. Doerfel LK, Wohlgemuth I, Kothe C, Peske F, Urlaub H, Rodnina MV. 2013. EF-P is essential for rapid synthesis of proteins containing consecutive proline residues. *Science* 339:85–88

32. Dong H, Nilsson L, Kurland CG. 1996. Co-variation of tRNA abundance and codon usage in *Escherichia coli* at different growth rates. *J. Mol. Biol.* 260:649–63

33. dos Reis M, Savva R, Wernisch L. 2004. Solving the riddle of codon usage preferences: a test for translational selection. *Nucleic Acids Res.* 32:5036–44

34. Dreher TW. 2010. Viral tRNAs and tRNA-like structures. *Wiley Interdiscip. Rev. RNA* 1:402–14

35. Drummond DA, Wilke CO. 2008. Mistranslation-induced protein misfolding as a dominant constraint on coding-sequence evolution. *Cell* 134:341–52

36. Du YZ, Dickerson C, Aylsworth AS, Schwartz CE. 1998. A silent mutation, C924T (G308G), in the L1CAM gene results in X linked hydrocephalus (HSAS). *J. Med. Genet.* 35:456–62

37. Duncan CD, Mata J. 2011. Widespread cotranslational formation of protein complexes. *PLOS Genet.* 7:e1002398

38. Elena C, Ravasi P, Castelli ME, Peirú S, Menzella HG. 2014. Expression of codon optimized genes in microbial systems: current industrial applications and perspectives. *Front. Microbiol.* 5:21

39. Elf J, Nilsson D, Tenson T, Ehrenberg M. 2003. Selective charging of tRNA isoacceptors explains patterns of codon usage. *Science* 300:1718–22

40. Ermolaeva MD. 2001. Synonymous codon usage in bacteria. *Curr. Issues Mol. Biol.* 3:91–97

41. Evans MS, Ugrinov KG, Frese M-A, Clark PL. 2005. Homogeneous stalled ribosome nascent chain complexes produced in vivo or in vitro. *Nat. Methods* 2:757–62

42. Faa' V, Coiana A, Incani F, Costantino L, Cao A, Rosatelli MC. 2010. A synonymous mutation in the *CFTR* gene causes aberrant splicing in an Italian patient affected by a mild form of cystic fibrosis. *J. Mol. Diagn.* 12:380–83

43. Fedyunin I, Lehnhardt L, Böhmer N, Kaufmann P, Zhang G, Ignatova Z. 2012. tRNA concentration fine tunes protein solubility. *FEBS Lett.* 586:3336–40

44. Firnberg E, Labonte JW, Gray JJ, Ostermeier M. 2014. A comprehensive, high-resolution map of a gene's fitness landscape. *Mol. Biol. Evol.* 31:1581–92

45. Frenkel-Morgenstern M, Danon T, Christian T, Igarashi T, Cohen L, et al. 2012. Genes adopt non-optimal codon usage to generate cell cycle-dependent oscillations in protein levels. *Mol. Syst. Biol.* 8:572

46. Friedman R, Ely B. 2012. Codon usage methods for horizontal gene transfer detection generate an abundance of false positive and false negative results. *Curr. Microbiol.* 65:639–42

47. Fuglsang A. 2003. Codon optimizer: a freeware tool for codon optimization. *Protein Expr. Purif.* 31:247–49

48. Fung KL, Pan J, Ohnuma S, Lund PE, Pixley JN, et al. 2014. *MDR1* synonymous polymorphisms alter transporter specificity and protein stability in a stable epithelial monolayer. *Cancer Res.* 74:598–608

49. Garcia-Vallve S, Guzman E, Montero MA, Romeu A. 2003. HGT-DB: a database of putative horizontally transferred genes in prokaryotic complete genomes. *Nucleic Acids Res.* 31:187–89

50. Gardin J, Yeasmin R, Yurovsky A, Cai Y, Skiena S, Futcher B. 2014. Measurement of average decoding rates of the 61 sense codons in vivo. *Elife* 3:e03735

51. Ghaemmaghami S, Huh WK, Bower K, Howson RW, Belle A, et al. 2003. Global analysis of protein expression in yeast. *Nature* 425:737–41

52. Goetz RM, Fuglsang A. 2005. Correlation of codon bias measures with mRNA levels: analysis of transcriptome data from *Escherichia coli*. *Biochem. Biophys. Res. Commun.* 327:4–7

53. Gonzalez-Paredes FJ, Ramos-Trujillo E, Claverie-Martin F. 2014. Defective pre-mRNA splicing in *PKD1* due to presumed missense and synonymous mutations causing autosomal dominant polycystic disease. *Gene* 546:243–49

54. Goodman DB, Church GM, Kosuri S. 2013. Causes and effects of N-terminal codon bias in bacterial genes. *Science* 342:475–79

55. Gouy M, Gautier C. 1982. Codon usage in bacteria: correlation with gene expressivity. *Nucleic Acids Res.* 10:7055–74

56. Grantham R, Gautier C, Gouy M. 1980. Codon frequencies in 119 individual genes confirm consistent choices of degenerate bases according to genome type. *Nucleic Acids Res.* 8:1893–912

57. Grantham R, Gautier C, Gouy M, Mercier R, Pave A. 1980. Codon catalog usage and the genome hypothesis. *Nucleic Acids Res.* 8:r49–r62

58. Grote A, Hiller K, Scheer M, Münch R, Nörtemann B, et al. 2005. JCat: a novel tool to adapt codon usage of a target gene to its potential expression host. *Nucleic Acids Res.* 33:W526–31

59. Guo FB, Ye YN, Zhao HL, Lin D, Wei W. 2012. Universal pattern and diverse strengths of successive synonymous codon bias in three domains of life, particularly among prokaryotic genomes. *DNA Res.* 19:477–85

60. Gustafsson C, Govindarajan S, Minshull J. 2004. Codon bias and heterologous protein expression. *Trends Biotechnol.* 22:346–53

61. Gyles C, Boerlin P. 2014. Horizontally transferred genetic elements and their role in pathogenesis of bacterial disease. *Vet. Pathol.* 51:328–40

62. Hurst LD. 2002. The *Ka/Ks* ratio: diagnosing the form of sequence evolution. *Trends Genet.* 18:486

63. Ikemura T. 1985. Codon usage and transfer-RNA content in unicellular and multicellular organisms. *Mol. Biol. Evol.* 2:13–34

64. Ikemura T, Ozeki H. 1983. Codon usage and transfer RNA contents: organism-specific codon-choice patterns in reference to the isoacceptor contents. *Cold Spring Harb. Symp. Quant. Biol.* 47(Pt. 2):1087–97

65. Ingolia NT, Ghaemmaghami S, Newman JR, Weissman JS. 2009. Genome-wide analysis in vivo of translation with nucleotide resolution using ribosome profiling. *Science* 324:218–23

66. Ingolia NT, Lareau LF, Weissman JS. 2011. Ribosome profiling of mouse embryonic stem cells reveals the complexity and dynamics of mammalian proteomes. *Cell* 147:789–802

67. Ito K, Chiba S, Pogliano K. 2010. Divergent stalling sequences sense and control cellular physiology. *Biochem. Biophys. Res. Commun.* 393:1–5

68. Jha S, Komar AA. 2011. Birth, life and death of nascent polypeptide chains. *Biotechnol. J.* 6:623–40

69. Kane JF. 1995. Effects of rare codon clusters on high-level expression of heterologous proteins in *Escherichia coli. Curr. Opin. Biotechnol.* 6:494–500

70. Karakozova M, Kozak M, Wong CC, Bailey AO, Yates JR 3rd, et al. 2006. Arginylation of β-actin regulates actin cytoskeleton and cell motility. *Science* 313:192–96

71. Kimchi-Sarfaty C, Oh JM, Kim IW, Sauna ZE, Calcagno AM, et al. 2007. A "silent" polymorphism in the *MDR1* gene changes substrate specificity. *Science* 315:525–28

72. Kimura M. 1980. A simple method for estimating evolutionary rates of base substitutions through comparative studies of nucleotide sequences. *J. Mol. Evol.* 16:111–20

73. Komar AA. 2009. A pause for thought along the co-translational folding pathway. *Trends Biochem. Sci.* 34:16–24

74. Komar AA, Lesnik T, Reiss C. 1999. Synonymous codon substitutions affect ribosome traffic and protein folding during in vitro translation. *FEBS Lett.* 462:387–91

75. Kramer EB, Farabaugh PJ. 2007. The frequency of translational misreading errors in *E. coli* is largely determined by tRNA competition. *RNA* 13:87–96

76. Kramer G, Boehringer D, Ban N, Bukau B. 2009. The ribosome as a platform for co-translational processing, folding and targeting of newly synthesized proteins. *Nat. Struct. Mol. Biol.* 16:589–97

77. Kudla G, Murray AW, Tollervey D, Plotkin JB. 2009. Coding-sequence determinants of gene expression in *Escherichia coli. Science* 324:255–58

78. Lawrence MS, Stojanov P, Polak P, Kryukov GV, Cibulskis K, et al. 2013. Mutational heterogeneity in cancer and the search for new cancer-associated genes. *Nature* 499:214–18

79. Lazrak A, Fu LW, Bali V, Bartoszewski R, Rab A, et al. 2013. The silent codon change I507-ATC → ATT contributes to the severity of the ΔF508 CFTR channel dysfunction. *FASEB J.* 27:4630–45

80. Letzring DP, Dean KM, Grayhack EJ. 2010. Control of translation efficiency in yeast by codon-anticodon interactions. *RNA* 16:2516–28

81. Li GW, Oh E, Weissman JS. 2012. The anti-Shine-Dalgarno sequence drives translational pausing and codon choice in bacteria. *Nature* 484:538–41

82. Lu JL, Deutsch C. 2008. Electrostatics in the ribosomal tunnel modulate chain elongation rates. *J. Mol. Biol.* 384:73–86

83. Luo XL, Tang ZY, Xia GH, Wassmann K, Matsumoto T, et al. 2004. The Mad2 spindle checkpoint protein has two distinct natively folded states. *Nat. Struct. Mol. Biol.* 11:338–45

84. Mahlab S, Linial M. 2014. Speed controls in translating secretory proteins in eukaryotes–an evolutionary perspective. *PLOS Comput. Biol.* 10:e1003294

85. Malaby HLH, Kobertz WR. 2013. Molecular determinants of co- and post-translational N-glycosylation of type I transmembrane peptides. *Biochem. J.* 453:427–34

86. Meijer J, Nakajima Y, Zhang C, Meinsma R, Ito T, Van Kuilenburg AB. 2013. Identification of a novel synonymous mutation in the human β-ureidopropionase gene *UPB1* affecting pre-mRNA splicing. *Nucleosides Nucleotides Nucleic Acids* 32:639–45

87. Meunier J, Duret L. 2004. Recombination drives the evolution of GC-content in the human genome. *Mol. Biol. Evol.* 21:984–90

88. Mitarai N, Sneppen K, Pedersen S. 2008. Ribosome collisions and translation efficiency: optimization by codon usage and mRNA destabilization. *J. Mol. Biol.* 382:236–45

89. Mueller S, Papamichail D, Coleman JR, Skiena S, Wimmer E. 2006. Reduction of the rate of poliovirus protein synthesis through large-scale codon deoptimization causes attenuation of viral virulence by lowering specific infectivity. *J. Virol.* 80:9687–96

90. Musto H, Naya H, Zavala A, Romero H, Alvarez-Valín F, Bernardi G. 2004. Correlations between genomic GC levels and optimal growth temperatures in prokaryotes. *FEBS Lett.* 573:73–77

91. Muto A, Osawa S. 1987. The guanine and cytosine content of genomic DNA and bacterial evolution. *PNAS* 84:166–69

92. Nakamura Y, Gojobori T, Ikemura T. 2000. Codon usage tabulated from international DNA sequence databases: status for the year 2000. *Nucleic Acids Res.* 28:292

93. Novoa EM, Ribas de Pouplana L. 2012. Speeding with control: codon usage, tRNAs, and ribosomes. *Trends Genet.* 28:574–81

94. Oh E, Becker AH, Sandikci A, Huber D, Chaba R, et al. 2011. Selective ribosome profiling reveals the cotranslational chaperone action of trigger factor in vivo. *Cell* 147:1295–308

95. Park C, Zhou S, Gilmore J, Marqusee S. 2007. Energetics-based protein profiling on a proteomic scale: identification of proteins resistant to proteolysis. *J. Mol. Biol.* 368:1426–37

96. Parmley JL, Huynen MA. 2009. Clustering of codons with rare cognate tRNAs in human genes suggests an extra level of expression regulation. *PLOS Genet.* 5:e1000548

97. Pechmann S, Frydman J. 2013. Evolutionary conservation of codon optimality reveals hidden signatures of cotranslational folding. *Nat. Struct. Mol. Biol.* 20:237–43

98. Pedersen S. 1984. *Escherichia coli* ribosomes translate in vivo with variable rate. *EMBO J.* 3:2895–98

99. Pfeifer GP. 2006. Mutagenesis at methylated CpG sequences. *Curr. Top. Microbiol. Immunol.* 301:259–81

100. Purvis IJ, Bettany AJ, Santiago TC, Coggins JR, Duncan K, et al. 1987. The efficiency of folding of some proteins is increased by controlled rates of translation in vivo. A hypothesis. *J. Mol. Biol.* 193:413–17

101. Raghavan R, Kelkar YD, Ochman H. 2012. A selective force favoring increased G+C content in bacterial genes. *PNAS* 109:14504–7

102. Rocha EPC, Danchin A. 2002. Base composition bias might result from competition for metabolic resources. *Trends Genet.* 18:291–94

103. Rosenblum G, Chen C, Kaur J, Cui X, Zhang H, et al. 2013. Quantifying elongation rhythm during full-length protein synthesis. *J. Am. Chem. Soc.* 135:11322–29

104. Sander IM, Chaney JL, Clark PL. 2014. Expanding Anfinsen's principle: contributions of synonymous codon selection to rational protein design. *J. Am. Chem. Soc.* 136:858–61

105. Sauna ZE, Kimchi-Sarfaty C. 2011. Understanding the contribution of synonymous mutations to human disease. *Nat. Rev. Genet.* 12:683–91

106. Saunders R, Deane CM. 2010. Synonymous codon usage influences the local protein structure observed. *Nucleic Acids Res.* 38:6719–28

107. Schauder B, McCarthy JEG. 1989. The role of bases upstream of the Shine-Dalgarno region and in the coding sequence in the control of gene expression in *Escherichia coli*: translation and stability of messenger RNAs in vivo. *Gene* 78:59–72

108. Sharp PM, Li WH. 1986. Codon usage in regulatory genes in *Escherichia coli* does not reflect selection for 'rare' codons. *Nucleic Acids Res.* 14:7737–49

109. Sharp PM, Li WH. 1987. The codon adaptation index—a measure of directional synonymous codon usage bias, and its potential applications. *Nucleic Acids Res.* 15:1281–95

110. Shpaer EG. 1986. Constraints on codon context in *Escherichia coli* genes. Their possible role in modulating the efficiency of translation. *J. Mol. Biol.* 188:555–64

111. Siller E, DeZwaan DC, Anderson JF, Freeman BC, Barral JM. 2010. Slowing bacterial translation speed enhances eukaryotic protein folding efficiency. *J. Mol. Biol.* 396:1310–18

112. Sinclair JF, Ziegler MM, Baldwin TO. 1994. Kinetic partitioning during protein-folding yields multiple native states. *Nat. Struct. Biol.* 1:320–26

113. Smith NGC, Eyre-Walker A. 2001. Why are translationally sub-optimal synonymous codons used in *Escherichia coli*? *J. Mol. Evol.* 53:225–36

114. Sørensen MA, Kurland CG, Pedersen S. 1989. Codon usage determines translation rate in *Escherichia coli*. *J. Mol. Biol.* 207:365–77

115. Sørensen MA, Pedersen S. 1991. Absolute in vivo translation rates of individual codons in *Escherichia coli*. The two glutamic acid codons GAA and GAG are translated with a threefold difference in rate. *J. Mol. Biol.* 222:265–80

116. Spencer PS, Siller E, Anderson JF, Barral JM. 2012. Silent substitutions predictably alter translation elongation rates and protein folding efficiencies. *J. Mol. Biol.* 422:328–35

117. Strauss BS. 1998. Hypermutability and silent mutations in human carcinogenesis. *Semin. Cancer Biol.* 8:431–38

118. Subramaniam AR, DeLoughery A, Bradshaw N, Chen Y, O'Shea E, et al. 2013. A serine sensor for multicellularity in a bacterium. *Elife* 2:e01501

119. Sun L, Petrounia IP, Yagasaki M, Bandara G, Arnold FH. 2001. Expression and stabilization of galactose oxidase in *Escherichia coli* by directed evolution. *Protein Eng.* 14:699–704

120. Supek F, Miñana B, Valcárcel J, Gabaldón T, Lehner B. 2014. Synonymous mutations frequently act as driver mutations in human cancers. *Cell* 156:1324–35

121. Syvanen M. 2012. Evolutionary implications of horizontal gene transfer. *Annu. Rev. Genet.* 46:341–58

122. Takyar S, Hickerson RP, Noller HF. 2005. mRNA helicase activity of the ribosome. *Cell* 120:49–58

123. Talkad V, Schneider E, Kennell D. 1976. Evidence for variable rates of ribosome movement in *Escherichia coli*. *J. Mol. Biol.* 104:299–303

124. Taylor RC, Webb Robertson B-J, Markillie LM, Serres MH, Linggi BE, et al. 2013. Changes in translational efficiency is a dominant regulatory mechanism in the environmental response of bacteria. *Integr. Biol.* 5:1393–406

125. Thanaraj TA, Argos P. 1996. Protein secondary structural types are differentially coded on messenger RNA. *Protein Sci.* 5:1973–83

126. Thanaraj TA, Argos P. 1996. Ribosome-mediated translational pause and protein domain organization. *Protein Sci.* 5:1594–612

127. Thomas JO, Kolb A, Szer W. 1978. Structure of single-stranded nucleic acids in the presence of ribosomal protein S1. *J. Mol. Biol.* 123:163–76

128. Tindle RW. 2002. Immune evasion in human papillomavirus-associated cervical cancer. *Nat. Rev. Cancer* 2:59–65

129. Tu C, Tzeng TH, Bruenn JA. 1992. Ribosomal movement impeded at a pseudoknot required for frameshifting. *PNAS* 89:8636–40

130. Tuinstra RL, Peterson FC, Kutlesa S, Elgin ES, Kron MA, Volkman BF. 2008. Interconversion between two unrelated protein folds in the lymphotactin native state. *PNAS* 105:5057–62

131. Tuller T, Carmi A, Vestsigian K, Navon S, Dorfan Y, et al. 2010. An evolutionarily conserved mechanism for controlling the efficiency of protein translation. *Cell* 141:344–54

132. Ude S, Lassak J, Starosta AL, Kraxenberger T, Wilson DN, Jung K. 2013. Translation elongation factor EF-P alleviates ribosome stalling at polyproline stretches. *Science* 339:82–85

133. Walter P, Blobel G. 1981. Translocation of proteins across the endoplasmic reticulum III. Signal recognition protein (SRP) causes signal sequence-dependent and site-specific arrest of chain elongation that is released by microsomal membranes. *J. Cell Biol.* 91:557–61

134. Wang HC, Susko E, Roger AJ. 2006. On the correlation between genomic G+C content and optimal growth temperature in prokaryotes: data quality and confounding factors. *Biochem. Biophys. Res. Commun.* 342:681–84

135. Wickner W, Schekman R. 2005. Protein translocation across biological membranes. *Science* 310:1452–56

136. Wiedmann M, Huth A, Rapoport TA. 1986. A signal sequence is required for the functions of the signal recognition particle. *Biochem. Biophys. Res. Commun.* 134:790–96

137. Wohlgemuth I, Brenne S, Beringer M, Rodnina MV. 2008. Modulation of the rate of peptidyl transfer on the ribosome by the nature of substrates. *J. Biol. Chem.* 283:32229–35

138. Woolhead CA, McCormick PJ, Johnson AE. 2004. Nascent membrane and secretory proteins differ in FRET-detected folding far inside the ribosome and in their exposure to ribosomal proteins. *Cell* 116:725–36

139. Woolstenhulme CJ, Parajuli S, Healey DW, Valverde DP, Petersen EN, et al. 2013. Nascent peptides that block protein synthesis in bacteria. *PNAS* 110:E878–87

140. Xia K, Manning M, Hesham H, Lin Q, Bystroff C, Colón W. 2007. Identifying the subproteome of kinetically stable proteins via diagonal 2D SDS/PAGE. *PNAS* 104:17329–34

141. Xie T, Ding D. 1998. The relationship between synonymous codon usage and protein structure. *FEBS Lett.* 434:93–96

142. Xu Y, Ma PJ, Shah P, Rokas A, Liu Y, Johnson CH. 2013. Non-optimal codon usage is a mechanism to achieve circadian clock conditionality. *Nature* 495:116–20

143. Yusupov MM, Yusupova GZ, Baucom A, Lieberman K, Earnest TN, et al. 2001. Crystal structure of the ribosome at 5.5 Å resolution. *Science* 292:883–96

144. Zalucki YM, Beacham IR, Jennings MP. 2009. Biased codon usage in signal peptides: a role in protein export. *Trends Microbiol.* 17:146–50

145. Zhang FL, Saha S, Shabalina SA, Kashina A. 2010. Differential arginylation of actin isoforms is regulated by coding sequence-dependent degradation. *Science* 329:1534–37

146. Zhang G, Hubalewska M, Ignatova Z. 2009. Transient ribosomal attenuation coordinates protein synthesis and co-translational folding. *Nat. Struct. Mol. Biol.* 16:274–80

147. Zhang G, Ignatova Z. 2009. Generic algorithm to predict the speed of translational elongation: implications for protein biogenesis. *PLOS ONE* 4:e5036

148. Zhang W, Xiao W, Wei H, Zhang J, Tian Z. 2006. mRNA secondary structure at start AUG codon is a key limiting factor for human protein expression in *Escherichia coli*. *Biochem. Biophys. Res. Commun.* 349:69–78

149. Zhao Z, Jiang C. 2010. Features of recent codon evolution: a comparative polymorphism-fixation study. *J. Biomed. Biotechnol.* 2010:202918

150. Zhou M, Guo JH, Cha J, Chae M, Chen S, et al. 2013. Non-optimal codon usage affects expression, structure and function of clock protein FRQ. *Nature* 495:111–15

151. Zhou T, Weems M, Wilke CO. 2009. Translationally optimal codons associate with structurally sensitive sites in proteins. *Mol. Biol. Evol.* 26:1571–80

RELATED RESOURCES

%MinMax calculator: **http://www.codons.org/**
CAIcal Server: **http://genomes.urv.cat/CAIcal/**
Codon Usage Database: **http://www.kazusa.or.jp/codon/**

Biophysics of
Channelrhodopsin

Franziska Schneider,*,# Christiane Grimm, and Peter Hegemann

Experimental Biophysics, Institute of Biology, Humboldt-Universität zu Berlin, 10115 Berlin, Germany; email: f.schneider@imperial.ac.uk, grimmchr@hu-berlin.de, hegemann@hu-berlin.de

Annu. Rev. Biophys. 2015. 44:167–86

The *Annual Review of Biophysics* is online at biophys.annualreviews.org

This article's doi: 10.1146/annurev-biophys-060414-034014

*Corresponding author

#Current address: Cardiac Biophysics and Systems Biology Group, National Heart and Lung Institute, Imperial College London, UB9 6JH, United Kingdom

Keywords

ion selectivity, photocycle, voltage dependence, color-tuning, channelrhodopsin-activation model

Abstract

Channelrhodopsins (ChRs) are directly light-gated ion channels that function as sensory photoreceptors in flagellated green algae, allowing these algae to identify optimal light conditions for growth. In neuroscience, ChRs constitute the most versatile tools for the light-induced activation of selected cells or cell types with unprecedented precision in time and space. In recent years, many ChR variants have been discovered or engineered, and countless electrical and spectroscopic studies of these ChRs have been carried out, both in host cells and on purified recombinant proteins. With significant support from a high-resolution 3D structure and from molecular dynamics calculations, scientists are now able to develop models that conclusively explain ChR activation and ion conductance on the basis of chromophore isomerization, structural changes, proton transfer reactions, and water rearrangement on timescales ranging from femtoseconds to minutes.

Contents

INTRODUCTION

Channelrhodopsins in Their Native Environment

Channelrhodopsins (ChRs) are light-gated cation channels that serve as sensory photoreceptors in motile green algae (47, 48, 68, 72). In these algae, ChRs are located at the surface of a specialized cellular compartment called the eyespot. This organelle consists of (*a*) an optical device comprising two or more layers of pigmented granules that function as quarter-wave stack antennae and provide directional sensitivity and (*b*) a specialized overlying plasma membrane that contains the ChRs and other proteins of the sensory machinery (15, 22). Upon photon absorption, ChRs mediate fast, proton- and cation-driven inward currents, resulting in plasma membrane depolarization (47, 48). At low light intensities, the electrical signal is most probably amplified by secondary voltage-gated channels, such as voltage-gated Ca^{2+} channels, whereas at high light intensities, the photocurrent is mainly mediated by ChRs directly (30). The local increase in cytosolic Ca^{2+} concentration is transmitted to the flagella base (basal bodies) by an unknown signaling cascade. The direction-modulated signal allows the alga to adjust the plane, frequency, and three-dimensional pattern of its flagellar beating, thereby enabling the alga to exhibit phototactic and photophobic responses (22, 24).

Channelrhodopsins in Optogenetics

Photocurrents:
electric currents
conducted by ChRs
upon light activation

After the initial characterization of ChRs as directly light-gated ion channels in 2002 and 2003 (47, 48), the unique combination of both photosensor and channel within a single, relatively small protein has drawn attention from not only algae researchers but also a larger scientific community of cell biologists and neuroscientists. Since their initial functional expression in human embryonic kidney (HEK) cells (48), ChRs have been successfully expressed in a large variety of vertebrate cells to depolarize the plasma membrane following light application. In neurons, ChR-mediated cation currents were shown to be sufficient for eliciting action potentials in a spatiotemporally defined manner (10, 27). This finding was another milestone in the rapidly developing field of optogenetics. Thus far, ChRs have been applied to induce synaptic plasticity (84), unravel neuronal connectivity (54), and manipulate behavior in ChR-expressing animals including worms, flies, chickens, zebrafish, and rodents (1, 11, 37, 46, 65). Potential clinical applications of ChRs include restoration of vision (9), repair of hearing impairment (66), and treatment of neural disorders such as Parkinson's disease (19).

Channelrhodopsin Variants

The first identified ChRs were two isoforms from *Chlamydomonas reinhardtii* (ChR1 and ChR2) (47, 48, 68, 72) and the two corresponding ChRs from the colonial alga *Volvox carteri* (VChR1 and VChR2) (14, 32, 82). Owing to its superior expression in host cells, ChR2 is currently not only the best-studied ChR but also the most commonly used optogenetic tool for membrane depolarization. Subsequently, a number of ChR genes were discovered in related chlorophycean algae, including *Mesostigma viride* (MChR), *Chlamydomonas augustae* (CaChR1), *Chlamydomonas yellowstonensis*, *Dunaliella salina* (DChR), *Pleodorina starii*, *Pyramimonas gelidicola*, and *Platymonas subcordiformis* (PsChR) (17, 18, 25, 83). Very recently, 61 additional ChR homologs were identified from a large genomic screen and were tested for photocurrent properties in selected cell systems (33). The two ChRs originating from *Stigeoclonium helveticum* (ShChR) and *Chlamydomonas noctigama* (CnChR1)—referred to as Chronos and Chrimson, respectively—exhibit highly distinct characteristics (see the sections titled "Color Tuning in Channelrhodopsins" and "Voltage Dependence" for details), rendering them potent candidates for optogenetic applications (33). Today, sequence comparison in combination with structural modeling facilitates our understanding of the structural and functional dynamics of the different ChRs and enables the design of new ChRs adapted to specific research questions.

CHANNELRHODOPSIN STRUCTURE

ChRs consist of an N-terminal membrane-spanning domain followed by a C-terminal intracellular domain that has been proposed to be relevant for ChR targeting and protein–protein interactions in the alga (43). The N-terminal module comprises seven transmembrane helices (H1–H7) and a retinal chromophore, and is sufficient for light-gated channel activity (47, 48). As is already apparent in the low-resolution (6 Å) structure from electron microscopy, ChR2 forms dimers in which H3 and H4 are located at the dimer interface (44). High-resolution X-ray crystallography on a ChR1/ChR2 chimera (C1C2) unveiled protomer linkage via three disulfide bridges at the N-terminal extracellular end (31). This linkage, however, has little or no relevance for ion channel functionality (62).

Retinal-Binding Pocket and Active Site Complex

As in all microbial rhodopsins, the retinal chromophore is bound to a conserved lysine residue in H7, the corresponding residue to K257[1] in ChR2, via a protonated retinal Schiff base (RSBH$^+$)

---

[1]Unless otherwise indicated, we use the ChR2 numbering of amino acids throughout this article.

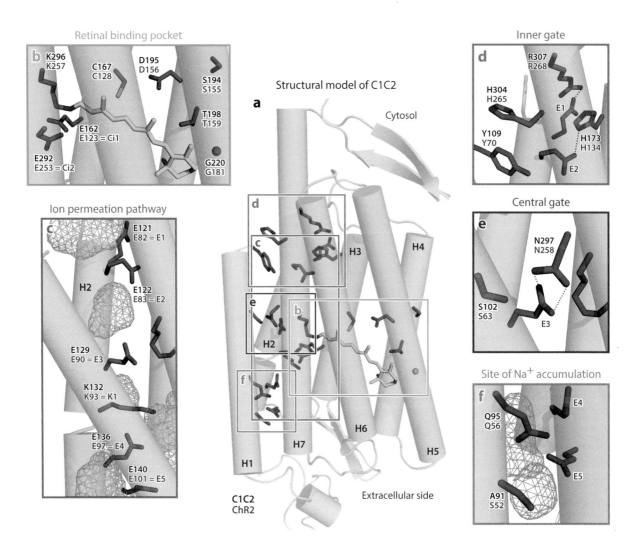

Figure 1

Important structural elements of channelrhodopsins (ChRs). The structural model depicts the C1C2 chimera and is based on its crystal structure solved by Kato et al. (31) (PDB ID: 3UG9). The model reflects dark-adapted C1C2, and thus a closed channel conformation. Helices H1–H5 originate from ChR1, and H6 and H7 originate from ChR2. The retinal is shown in lime green. (*a*) Overall protein structure with framed regions of interest; (*b*) retinal binding pocket; (*c*) ion permeation pathway; (*d*) inner gate; (*e*) central gate; (*f*) site of Na$^+$ accumulation. The gray wireframes in panels *c* and *f* depict cavities within the protein in which water molecules and cations may reside.

linkage (**Figure 1a,b**). The charge of the RSBH$^+$ is stabilized by a counterion complex comprising two glutamate residues, E123 and E253 [termed counterion-1 (Ci1) and counterion-2 (Ci2) in the remainder of this article] (**Figure 1b**). In the C1C2 structure, distances between the RSB nitrogen and the Ci1 and Ci2 (in this case E162 and D292) carboxyl groups are almost equal (3.4 and 3.0 Å, respectively) (31). Moreover, theoretical calculations of pK$_a$ values propose that, in the dark, Ci1 is protonated and Ci2 is deprotonated, suggesting that Ci2 functions as a proton acceptor in C1C2 (31). The nearest water molecule is more distal (4.4 Å) than the respective glutamate carboxyl groups are, proposing a direct proton transfer from the RSBH$^+$ to Ci2 (31), in clear contrast to the case of bacteriorhodopsin (BR), in which Ci1 and Ci2 are connected to the RSB nitrogen via water 402 (42). Accordingly, mutation of Ci2 to alanine almost completely abolishes photocurrents, whereas mutation of Ci1 to threonine, alanine, or glutamine in ChR2 results in functional ChRs that are widely used for fast action potential firing in neurons, owing to their accelerated photocycling. These ChR mutants are commonly referred to as channelrhodopsin-ET-accelerated (ChETA) mutants (7, 21). Recent spectroscopic findings and molecular dynamics (MD) simulations suggest that ChR2 E90 undergoes a side flip in the ChETA mutants, thereby at least partially replacing the Ci1 charge (36).

Another pair of residues that are highly relevant for gating and consecutive photocycle kinetics comprises C128 and D156 of ChR2; these residues are referred to as the DC pair or DC gate (**Figure 1b**). Individual mutation of either of these residues causes up to a ten thousand–fold deceleration in channel opening and closing [step-function rhodopsins (SFRs)] (3, 8), which in turn results in current saturation at much lower light intensities during prolonged illumination and thereby imparts increased operational light sensitivity to host cells (8). Mutations in both residues completely arrest the photocycle in the conducting state: Channel closing has not been observed for the double mutant (81). The corresponding residues in BR, T90 and D115, interact with the retinal chromophore and control H3–H4 dynamics during the photocycle (29, 42). Although evidence for different arrangements of the two residues in ChRs exists, the role of the DC gate in the coupling of retinal isomeric changes to channel gating remains to be elucidated (78).

ChR2 T159 constitutes another important amino acid of the retinal binding pocket, that is in direct contact with D156 (**Figure 1b**). Replacement of this amino acid (T159) with cysteine causes improved retinal binding and a threefold to tenfold increased stationary photocurrent, depending on the host system (7, 57, 74). In the presence of C159, step-function mutants show only moderately decelerated photocycle kinetics. Accordingly, DC pair mutations do not generate slow step-function rhodopsins in VChR1 and MChR, as both feature a cysteine at the corresponding position (VChR1 C154 and MChR C178, respectively) (57). T159 operates in conjunction with D156 and S155 to form an OH-cluster (hydrogen-bonding network) along H4 that is crucial for protein dynamics following light excitation of the chromophore (**Figure 1b**).

Ion Permeation Pathway

The high-resolution structure of the C1C2 chimera reveals a hydrophilic pore between H1, H2, H3, and H7 that was already previously assumed to serve as the cation permeation pathway in ChRs (31). Polar and charged residues of H2 that appear with a roughly seven–amino acid periodicity and face toward H3 and H7 are key elements of the pore (77). In ChR2, these polar residues include E82 (E1), E83 (E2), E90 (E3), K93 (K1), E97 (E4), and E101 (E5) (**Figure 1c**). Individual substitutions of E1, E2, E4, or E5 to alanine or glutamine reduce photocurrents by twofold to sixfold, whereas multiple substitutions result in more dramatic current reduction (71, 77). Consistent with the mutant data, MD simulations detect two preferential sites for Na^+ accumulation; the first site is located between E4, E5, S52, and Q56 (**Figure 1f**), and the second one is near the hydrophilic cluster composed of E1, E2, H134, H265, and R268 on the cytosolic side (**Figure 1d**). Moreover, E1 and E3 are highly conserved among ChRs and constitute key determinants for cation selectivity (see the section titled "Putative Selectivity Filter").

In MD simulations, the hydrophilic pore attracts water from the extracellular bulk phase; this so-called access channel with a diameter of 8 Å is framed by side chains of polar residues including the essential R120 and the polar E4 and E5 (55, 78). Near the RSBH$^+$, the water distribution is discontinuous, and the channel is blocked by S63, E3, and N258, which are interconnected by several hydrogen bonds (referred to as the central gate, see **Figure 1e**) (31, 78). A second

---

Channelrhodopsin-ET-accelerated (ChETA): ChR variants that have mutated Ci1 and that exhibit fast, voltage-insensitive photocycle kinetics

Photocycle: cyclic series of photointermediates that appear after photoexcitation of the protein-bound chromophore

DC pair: homologous residues to ChR2 C128 and D156 that are critical determinants of the kinetics of channel opening and closing

Step-function rhodopsins (SFRs): slow-cycling ChR mutants for which both on- and off-switching are triggered by light of different wavelengths

Retinal binding pocket: a cavity within the protein in which the retinal is fixed by interaction with selected amino acids and by covalent linkage to K257

Access channel: cavity within the C1C2 structure framed by polar residues; in MD simulations water molecules penetrate from the extracellular bulk phase

restriction site (referred to as the inner gate, see **Figure 1d**) is given by Y70 in combination with the hydrophilic cluster of E1 and E2 and their hydrogen-bonding partners H134 and R268, which are located on H3 and H7, respectively. The hydrogen-bonding network of both gates keeps the channel internally closed, preventing water influx from both the cytoplasmic and extracellular bulk phases. Channel opening and the resulting cation conductance thus require conformational rearrangements at the two gates (gating).

CHANNELRHODOPSIN PHOTOACTIVATION

Photocycle Models and Retinal Isomerizations

In microbial rhodopsins, photon absorption triggers retinal isomerization and initiates a sequence of thermal conformational changes that finally reestablish the original dark state (this cyclic process is known as the photocycle; see **Figure 2a** for ChR2). The electronically excited state of the chromophore is vibrationally inactivated within 150 fs after ChR2 photoexcitation (75). Following conical intersection and conversion to the electronic ground state (which occur on a 400-fs timescale), vibrational inactivation continues in conjunction with further retinal restructuring, and the early K-like intermediate is reached after 2.7 ps (64, 75). This early K-product seems either to be identical to or to smoothly fade to (without color shift) the early P500 intermediate previously identified by flash photolysis experiments (15). Major rearrangements of the protein backbone already occur during the formation of the P500 intermediate (40, 48, 60, 75) and correspond to more red-shifted photointermediates in VChR1 (P600) and CaChR (K-like, ~P580) (15, 32, 67). The RSB is then deprotonated, yielding the blue-shifted P390 state in ChR2 (4, 15, 32, 60, 67). The primary proton acceptor is Ci1 or Ci2, depending on the ChR variant and the external conditions that determine the steric configuration and protonation states of the respective residues (31, 36, 40, 78). The P390 state is in equilibrium with the P520 state, exhibiting a reprotonated RSB (4, 15, 60). Residue D156 was proposed to function as the proton donor (40), but this assumption is challenged by the fact that (a) D156 is not conserved in all ChRs, and (b) the kinetics of the D156 deprotonation does not parallel RSB reprotonation (36). Whereas there is general consensus about P520 being a conductive state, P390 is formed prior to the opening of the channel but equilibrates with P520, and the involvement of P390 in ion conduction is still under debate (4, 40, 69). It is conceivable that the retinal conformation is changed again during P390 formation, triggering the rearrangement of the inner gate and final channel gating. Thus, one could define an early P390 state and a late P390′ state for ChR; these would be analogous to the M and M′ states of BR (26). The late P390′ state in equilibrium with P520 could be the first ion conducting state that appears during the ChR photocycle. In ChRs with red-shifted dark states such as VChR1, C1V1, or ReaChR (see the section titled "Color-Tuning in Channelrhodopsins"), the absorption spectra of the dark state and the conducting state (corresponding to P520) almost completely overlap. Photoactivation of these ChRs causes apparent chromophore bleaching without an absorption shift during time-resolved spectroscopy due to lower extinction coefficients of the *cis*-chromophores (32, 38, 67, 81). In ChR2, channel closure is accompanied by the transition from the conducting P520 state to the nonconducting P480 and P480′ states that biphasically revert to the dark state (4, 59). Major conformational reorientations occur during dark state recovery on a timescale of several seconds, even in wild-type ChR2 (60).

Retinal extraction and Raman measurements indicate a mixture of retinal isoforms, even for dark-adapted (DA_{app}) ChR2 or C128T; the latter exhibits 22–40% 13-*cis* retinal and 60%–78% all-*trans* retinal (58, 59, 70). During continuous illumination, the ratio of 13-*cis* retinal to all-*trans* retinal increases, and minor amounts of 11-*cis* and 9-*cis* isoforms appear. Accordingly, it has

---

Central gate: hydrogen-bonded ChR residues that block the cation-permeation pathway from the extracellular side; channel opening requires reorientation of these residues

Inner gate: hydrophilic amino acid cluster that blocks the cation-permeation pathway from the intracellular side; reorientation of this cluster might be final step in ChR gating

Infrared (IR) difference spectroscopy: measurement of changes in IR light absorption between photocycle intermediates and dark states that represent dipole changes of molecule vibrations

a Photocycle model of ChR2

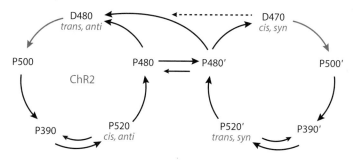

b Spectral variety of ChR activation

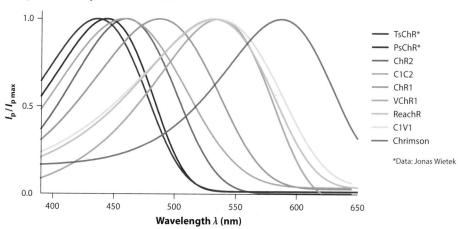

Figure 2

Channelrhodopsin (ChR) photoactivation. (*a*) Complex photocycle model for ChR2 implying photoactivation of two different dark states (D480 and D470) with distinct retinal configurations (4, 59, 60). Transition between the two cycles occurs in the presence of late P480 photointermediates. Light activation is indicated by blue arrows. (*b*) Palette of color-tuned ChRs. Normalized action spectra of selected ChRs were recorded in human embryonic kidney (HEK) 293 cells. The reader is referred to **Table 1** for the respective action maxima of each ChR and for relevant references. Abbreviations: C1C2/ReachR/C1V1, chimeric ChRs; ChR1/ChR2, *Chlamydomonas reinhardtii* ChRs; Chrimson, *Chlamydomonas noctigama* ChR; PsChR, *Platymonias subcordiformus* ChR; TsChR, *Tetraselmis striata* ChR; VChR1, *Volvox carteri* ChR.

been concluded that multiple retinal isomerizations occur in parallel in ChRs. Both all-*trans*,15-*anti* retinal and 13-*cis*,15-*syn* retinal stabilize a salt bridge between the RSB and the counterion complex, thereby favoring closed channel conformations, but both 13-*cis*,15-*anti* retinal and all-*trans*,15-*syn* retinal may evoke formation of the conducting states (53, 59, 70). The corresponding photocycles imply the photoconversion of all-*trans*,15-*anti* retinal to 13-*cis*,15-*anti* retinal, as well as that of 13-*cis*,15-*syn* retinal to all-*trans*,15-*syn* retinal, whereas the transition between the two cycles was proposed to occur during population of late photocycle intermediate states (P480); however, this hypothesis has never been experimentally verified (**Figure 2a**) (59). The two retinal conformations of the open channel states might be linked to the two conductive states with different ion selectivities, as observed in electrical measurements (see **Figure 3c,d** and the section titled "Electrophysiological Reaction Schemes") (6, 63).

a Current–voltage relationship of ChR2

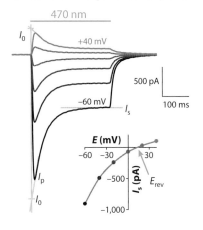

b Peak recovery kinetics of ChR2

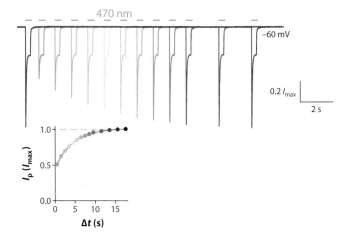

c Electrophysiological reaction schemes

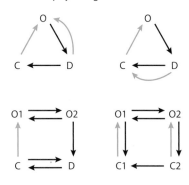

d Different reversal potentials of I_0 and I_s

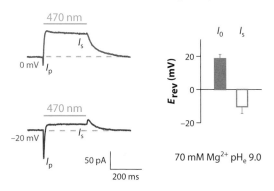

70 mM Mg^{2+} pH$_e$ 9.0

Figure 3

Electrophysiological properties of channelrhodopsins (ChRs). (*a,b,d*) Photocurrents of ChR2 measured under voltage-clamp conditions in human embryonic kidney (HEK) 293 cells. (*a*) ChR2 photocurrents at different holding potentials during continuous, high-intensity illumination. Currents exhibit peak levels (I_p) that inactivate to stationary levels of reduced amplitude (I_s). The initial current (I_0) is obtained by linear extrapolation to time zero of illumination. The corresponding current–voltage relationship of I_s is given as an inset. The blue arrow indicates the reversal potential (E_{rev}). (*b*) Recovery of ChR2 I_p depends on the time interval between two consecutive illuminations. I_s is unaffected by the dark interval. (*c*) Reaction schemes to explain the electrophysiological properties of ChRs. The upper schemes depict three-state models; C indicates a closed state, O indicates an open state, and D indicates a desensitized state (15, 48, 50). The lower schemes depicts four-state models consisting of two closed states (D and C; C1 and C2) and two open states (O1 and O2) (4, 23, 51). The bottom right scheme is consistent with the photocycle model depicted in **Figure 2*a***. Light-induced transitions are highlighted by light blue arrows. (*d*) ChR2 photocurrents measured at conditions close to the respective reversal potentials (E_{rev}) [internal solution: *N*-methyl-D-glucamine (NMG), pH 9.0]. Peak currents (I_p) are inwardly directed, whereas stationary photocurrents (I_s) are outwardly directed. Accordingly, E_{rev} of I_p/I_0 is positively shifted compared with the reversal potential of the corresponding I_s.

Color Tuning in Channelrhodopsins

The naturally occurring ChRs studied thus far exhibit action spectrum maxima between 436 nm (ChR from *Tetraselmis striata*) and 590 nm (Chrimson from *Chlamydomonas noctigama*) (33). The palette of color-tuned ChRs is supplemented by chimeric ChRs that combine helices from different ChRs, as summarized in **Figure 2*b*** and **Table 1**.

Table 1 Overview of color-tuned channelrhodopsin (ChR) variants

ChR variant	Origin	Maxima of action spectrum at pH 7.2[a]	Reference(s)
TsChR	*Tetraselmis striata*	436 nm	(33)
PsChR	*Platymonas subcordiformus*	444 nm	(17)
ChR2	*Chlamydomonas reinhardtii*	460 nm	(48)
VChR2	*Volvox carteri*	465 nm	(32)
ChR1	*Chlamydomonas reinhardtii*	487 nm	(47)
C1C2 = ChEF	*Chlamydomonas reinhardtii*	458 nm	(39, 73, 76)
VChR1	*Volvox carteri*	536 nm	(57, 82)
ReachR	*Chlamydomonas reinhardtii/Volvox carteri*	531 nm	(38)
MChR	*Mesostigma viride*	531 nm	(18)
C1V1	*Chlamydomonas reinhardtii/Volvox carteri*	536 nm	(57, 81)
Chrimson	*Chlamydomonas noctigama*	587 nm	(33)

[a]Action spectra were recorded in human embryonic kidney (HEK) 293 cells, and maxima were determined by fitting to a five-parameter Weibull function.

In general, retinal absorption depends on the conformation of the retinal (e.g., nonplanarity), electrical interactions of the RSBH$^+$ with the counterion complex, and other electrostatic interactions that either stabilize or destabilize the ground state or excited states (2, 41). Characterization of different ChR chimera showed that H7 is a major determinant for the wavelength sensitivity of ChR activation (57, 76) because the exact localization of the RSB lysine (K257 of ChR2) defines both the direct intrahelical interactions with Ci2 and interhelical interactions of the RSBH$^+$ with Ci1. Moreover, H7 may determine the number and position of water molecules along the channel pore, thereby indirectly influencing counterion arrangement. Most obvious attempts to color-shift ChR absorption included exchanging the counterion residues to vary the distance and interaction strength between the counterions and the RSBH$^+$. In ChR2 and PsChR, exchanges of Ci1 by glutamine (E123Q and E106Q) lead to bathochromically shifted absorption by 23 and 30 nm, whereas replacements of Ci2 by asparagine (D253N and D236N) induced smaller bathochromic shifts (16 and 14 nm, respectively) (17). In contrast, mutation of Ci1 in C1V1 (E162T) lead to a hypsochromic shift most likely caused by water invasion into the active site complex in the mutant (57, 81). Apart from counterion residues, the polarity of amino acids directly interacting with the retinal polyene chain, and with the β-ionone ring in particular, influences retinal geometry and electrostatics. A prominent example is that of the residue at position 181 in ChR2 (**Figure 1*b***). While all blue-light absorbing ChRs (and MChR) possess a nonpolar glycine residue, the red-shifted ChRs VChR1 (and its derivatives) and Chrimson have a polar serine residue at the corresponding position. Accordingly, C1C2 G220S is red shifted by 13 nm (F. Schneider, unpublished data), and C1V1 S220G shows a 12-nm blue shift (57). Although the retinal-binding pocket is the most important contributor to color tuning in ChRs, long-range interactions within the protein can also modulate the absorption spectrum, most likely by indirectly influencing the geometry of the counterion complex (the active site). A glutamate residue found in ChR1 (E87), PsChR1, VChR1, DChR1, and related ChRs causes bathochromic shifts upon acidification of the extracellular solution, whereas a comparable spectral shift is not present in ChR2 (17, 73). Mutation of this residue to an uncharged glutamine stabilizes the red-shifted form in ChR1-like ChRs. Because C1C2 E87 is more than 20 Å away from the RSB nitrogen, this effect can only be explained by secondary conformational changes in the protein.

CHANNELRHODOPSIN PHOTOCURRENT PROPERTIES

ChR photocurrents have been intensively characterized by electrical recordings from ChR-expressing *Xenopus* oocytes and HEK cells, mainly under voltage-clamp conditions. At negative voltages (-60 mV), cells expressing ChR exhibit inward-directed photocurrents carried by protons and cations (**Figure 3a**). Excitation of ChR1 and ChR2 with bright light pulses evokes photocurrent rise with time constants of approximately 200 µs, and the maximum of the early peak currents I_p is reached within 1–2 ms (4, 73). I_p decreases to a stationary current I_s in a process referred to as inactivation. This transition is caused by channel desensitization through equilibration of two open states (see the section titled "Electrophysiological Reaction Schemes" below) and by the accumulation of late nonconducting photocycle intermediates (P480 and P480') (6, 48). After light application, currents decline biexponentially to baseline, emphasizing the presence of at least two conducting states that contribute to I_s (23, 51). In ChR2, channel closure shows effective time constants of 10 to 20 ms. Repetitive ChR activation starts from partially dark-adapted ChRs, resulting in reduced peak currents, and the initial peak amplitude is only regained after a dark period of several seconds (23, 48) (**Figure 3b**). All kinetic parameters strongly depend on experimental conditions such as voltage, pH, and the quality of the actinic light (23, 48).

Electrophysiological Reaction Schemes

Analogous to photocycle models based on spectroscopic findings, electrophysiological reaction schemes were developed to quantitatively describe photocurrent properties. The challenge was to develop consistent models that account for (*a*) the fast closure of the channel after either a single flash or a longer light pulse, (*b*) the slow recovery of the transient peak current in the range of seconds, and (*c*) the existence of two conducting states with different selectivities (see below). Three-state models comprising a closed state (C), an open state (O), and a desensitized state (D) were employed to explain channel inactivation and the recovery kinetics of the peak current (**Figure 3c**, upper row) (15, 48, 50). These models imply a second light-dependent step in the reaction scheme, such that light either induces photoactivation of the D state with reduced efficiency or accelerates the reverse reaction from D to C (15, 50). However, all three-state models failed to reproduce both the biexponential off-kinetics of the channel current and alterations of selectivity between early and late photocurrents. Moreover, a simple four-state model implying two consecutive open states, O1 and O2 (**Figure 3c**, bottom left), could not explain both fast channel closure and slow recovery kinetics of the peak current. Only by employing a four-state model with two closed and two open states (C1, C2, O1, and O2), could the channel kinetics and dark recovery of I_p be properly modeled (**Figure 3c**, bottom right) (23, 51). Dark-adapted ChR molecules reside in the C1 state, which is photoconverted to O1 upon light excitation. During prolonged illumination, O1 and O2 equilibrate within milliseconds and eventually convert to their respective closed states, C1 and C2, whereas the C2-to-C1 back conversion needs two to ten seconds of darkness[2] (51). The C1-to-O1 photoactivation exhibits high quantum efficiency, and O1 shows high conductivity but is rather short-lived (51). Inversely, the C2-to-O2 conversion is proposed to be less effective, and O2 is less conductive but is long lived (51). Furthermore, one study of the ChR2 C128T mutant showed that the different dark-adapted states and their respective open states are populated depending on the color and duration of the preceding illumination (59). Thus, the conductivity of ChRs is adapted according to the color, duration, and intensity of the applied light (23, 51).

---

[2]In reality, full dark adaptation is more complex, as seen from the photocycle in **Figure 2a**.

Ion Selectivity

Although all ChRs primarily conduct protons, they also conduct monovalent cations, and to some extent divalent cations, especially under physiological conditions of low proton concentration. The following relative conductivities have been determined for ChR1, ChR2, VChR1, and VChR2: $p(H^+) \gg p(Li^+) > p(Na^+) > p(K^+) > p(Rb^+) > p(Cs^+) \approx p(Ca^{2+}) > p(Mg^{2+})$ (6, 15, 39, 48, 63, 73, 82). Given the reversal potentials of ChR2, the relative proton conductance has been estimated to be 10^5–10^6 times higher than the Na^+ conductivity, whereas the Ca^{2+} conductance was calculated to be ~12% of the Na^+ conductance (39, 48). In a solution containing different cations (e.g., a standard extracellular solution containing H^+, Na^+, Ca^{2+}, and Mg^{2+}), all cations present compete for binding and transport in a voltage- and pH-dependent fashion. Thus, for example, Na^+ currents are larger at pH 9.0 than they are in the presence of competing H^+ at pH 7.0 (20, 63).

Studies have shown that when recording photocurrents close to the reversal potential, the early photocurrent I_0 and the stationary current I_s can exhibit different directionalities of cation flow (e.g., inward-directed I_0 and outward-directed I_s) (**Figure 4d**). These differences in directionality most impressively demonstrate the different reversal voltages and distinct cation selectivities of I_0 and I_s (6, 63).

An enzyme kinetics model was used to quantitatively describe ChR-mediated cation transport via two open states (20, 63). The initial current, I_0, reflects conductance via only the first open state, O1, whereas the stationary photocurrent, I_s, is fed by the conductances of both open states, O1 and O2 (63). The model further implies competition between four different cationic substrates for binding to an empty binding site of the protein (63). After loading, the binding site switches from an external exposure to an internal exposure, thereby transporting cations to the other side of the membrane. Subsequently, the cation is released and the empty binding site can reorient. After independent determination of the binding affinities for H^+ and for all relevant cations, photocurrents can be dissected to understand the contributions of competing cations at a given experimental condition. The peculiar difficulty is that the competition between ions significantly depends on the applied voltage; therefore, the relative conductances cannot be determined from reversal voltages as formalized by the Goldmann–Hodgkin–Katz equation. For ChR2 at a high Na^+ concentration, pH_e 7.2, and -60 mV, the initial current, I_0, is driven mainly by protons, with a minor contribution from Na^+ (33%), whereas the stationary current, I_s, shows higher relative Na^+ currents (48%) (63). Other ChR variants, such as C1V1 and $CatCh^+$ (ChR2 L132C-T159C), show generally higher Na^+ currents than ChR2 (63). In most ChRs, considerable Ca^{2+} currents are only observed at high, nonphysiological Ca^{2+} concentrations above 10 mM (63). In contrast, Mg^{2+} is bound more tightly, resulting in small Mg^{2+} currents even at concentrations as low as a few millimolar. Only in $CatCh^+$ are Mg^{2+} currents larger; these currents contribute to 15% of I_s under standard conditions (63).

Putative Selectivity Filter

Highly selective channels, such as K^+ channels or Na^+ channels, contain so-called selectivity filters that determine the kind of transported ions. These selectivity filters represent the narrowest part of the ion-conducting pathway and adopt conserved symmetric structures that specifically bind only one ion species, for example, by mimicking the hydration shell of the respective ion (12). Although ChRs naturally occur as dimeric proteins, the ion-conducting pathway is located between H1, H2, H3, and H7 of each monomer (for details, see the section titled "Ion Permeation Pathway"), so no symmetric selectivity filter is found (31). Moreover, ChRs are relatively unselective for different

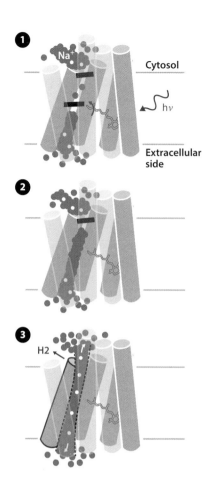

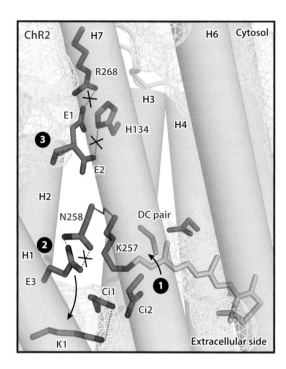

Figure 4

Helix 2 (H2)-tilt (HT) model for ChR2 activation. The numbered panels on the left depict the three steps required for ChR2 pore formation: ❶ photon absorption and retinal isomerization; ❷ disruption of the E3–N258 hydrogen bond and deprotonation and downflip of E3; and ❸ outward movement of H2, disconnection of hydrogen bonds at the inner gate, and continuous pore formation. Blue spheres depict water molecules, white spheres depict Na⁺ ions, and dark blue bars reflect closed gates or barriers in the protein. The inset on the right highlights important residues involved in pore formation. The DC pair is composed of C128 and D156 at the active site; however, its role in channel activation remains to be investigated. The ChR2 structure was gained by homology modeling using the C1C2 crystal structure as a template (31). The gray wireframe depicts cavities in which water molecules and cations may reside in dark-adapted ChR2. Hydrogen bonds depicted in this panel are drawn according to Reference 36.

cations with various atomic radii (e.g., Li⁺ versus Cs⁺), arguing against a defined binding site for a specific cation. Most likely, ChRs mediate cation flux via a water-filled pore without complete dehydration of the transported ions.

Several key elements have been identified to regulate cation selectivity in ChRs. Most importantly, ChR2 S63, E90, and N258 of the central gate (**Figure 1e**) are critical determinants. The introduction of a second negative charge into the central gate region, as, for example, in ChR2 S63D or N258D, favors the transport of divalent cations (31, 55). Mutations of ChR2 E90 result in different ion selectivities depending on the character of the introduced residue. In contrast to ChR2 E90Q and E90A, which show strongly reduced proton selectivity with only minor shifts in reversal potentials between pH 4.0 and pH 9.0, ChR2 E90H exhibits no detectable Na^+ conductivity but shows pH-dependent proton currents (13, 20, 61). The ion selectivity of ChR2 E90K has long been a mystery. At acidic pH, the mutant shows strongly enhanced inward currents; however, outward currents are also stimulated, and the reversal voltage does not change between pH 4.0 and pH 9.0 (13, 61). In fact, the introduction of a lysine or arginine residue with a net charge of $+1$ into the central gate inverts the ChR2 ion selectivity to select monovalent anions with high Cl^- conductance when this ion is available as a substrate (ChloC) (79). However, a Cl^--conducting channel has also been achieved by sequentially modeling the conducting pore, which has a negatively charged surface, into one that has a more positive surface (iC1C2) (5). Both of the Cl^--conducting ChRs, ChloC and iC1C2, exhibit only minor H^+ conductance and negligible cation conductance.

Electrophysiological characterization: time-resolved measurement of membrane current or voltage in ChR-expressing cells

The counterion residues Ci1 and Ci2 indirectly affect ion selectivity, as they are located close to the central gate but oriented toward the RSB. ChR2 E123A conducts mainly protons, consistent with increased H^+/Na^+ ratios in homologous C1C2 E162A and D292A (20, 31). Interestingly, DChR naturally contains an alanine at the Ci1 position (A178) and is itself proton selective (83). ChR2 K93 (K1) was proposed to be directly hydrogen-bonded to Ci1 from the extracellular site (**Figure 4**, right) and to form a hydrogen bond with Ci2 via an interjacent water molecule (28). Substitution of K1 with alanine in C1C2 increases the ratio of H^+/Na^+ conductance (31), possibly by favoring protonation of the counterion residues or by reorienting central gate residues such as E3.

MD simulations for ChR2 visualize two preferential Na^+ occupancies (see the section titled "Ion Permeation Pathway") (78). One occupancy site is located extracellular to the central gate, implying the involvement of S52, Q56, and E4 (**Figure 1f**). But, this assignment is questionable because S52 is not conserved, and only replacement of Q56 results in enhanced selectivity for H^+ and K^+ (31), whereas E4 exchange to alanine does not alter cation selectivity (71). A second Na^+ binding site is formed by E1, E2, H134, H265, and R268, residues that are close to or part of the inner gate (78). Of these residues, only H134 is crucial for selectivity (20). H134R, H134S, and H134N mutants show photocurrents carried by Na^+ that are strongly inhibited by both intracellular and extracellular H^+. This inhibition is explained by inefficient proton release on the cytosolic side. The nearby residue ChR2 L132 faces away from the inner gate, but its replacement in ChR2 L132C, also referred to as CatCh, indirectly influences cation binding, resulting in a 1.6-fold increase in Ca^{2+} selectivity, enlarged Mg^{2+} conductance, and high stationary currents (34, 57, 63).

Voltage Dependence

The electrophysiological characterization of ChRs is usually performed under voltage-clamp conditions; however, ChR activation in green algae or neurons rapidly depolarizes the membrane. This depolarization changes the properties of the channel because ChRs are highly voltage sensitive and exhibit inward rectification, voltage-dependent cation selectivity, and voltage-modulated photocycle kinetics (80).

ChRs display asymmetric current–voltage relations in which inward currents are stronger than outward currents (inward rectification) (**Figure 3a**). In inward-rectifying K^+ channels, cytosolic Mg^{2+} causes inward rectification by blocking channel activity in a voltage-dependent manner. In contrast, variations in the internal Mg^{2+} concentration in ChRs do not affect current sizes, reversal potentials, or the shapes of current–voltage relationships, so Mg^{2+} can be excluded as a potential source of inward rectification (20). On the basis of our previous kinetic analysis, we suggested that ChR rectification is caused by fast, voltage-dependent cation binding in cases in which protons and cations compete for one predominant external binding site (20). Accordingly, rectification is small in ChR mutants that preferentially conduct either H^+, Na^+, or Cl^-, such as the H^+-selective E90H mutant or the Cl^--selective ChloC (20, 79). Interestingly, inward rectification is reduced upon mutating selected inner gate residues (ChR2 Y70, E1, and E2) (J. Wietek, unpublished results). Thus, charged and polar inner gate residues might be part of the inherent voltage sensor of ChR that reorients in a manner dependent on the applied membrane voltage.

The current transport model implies voltage-sensitive rate constants, and the apparent voltage is determined using an elastic voltage-divider (20). In fact, ChR cation selectivity and thus the ratio of the conducted ions depend on the membrane voltage (63). At negative voltages (e.g., −60 mV), the stationary currents of selected ChRs (ChR2, C1V1, CatCh$^+$) are mediated primarily by Na^+ transport, whereas the initial current, I_0, is driven mainly by protons (63). In contrast, when considering reversal potentials, stationary currents show higher proton selectivity than do their respective initial currents (6, 63). Together, these findings demonstrate that ChR cation selectivity differs between conditions that are close to thermodynamic equilibrium and conditions in which high electrochemical gradients produce strong unidirectional driving forces. The voltage-sensitive cation selectivity of early and late photocurrents may also explain the voltage-dependent degree of photocurrent inactivation.

Whereas voltage-dependent steps in the ChR photocycle are difficult to analyze by spectroscopic means, the voltage dependence of channel opening, closing, and recovery kinetics has been determined in electrophysiological measurements. Channel opening occurs within ~200 μs as described for ChR1, ChR2, and a Volvox ChR chimera, and it shows little to no voltage dependence (4, 7, 15, 73). In contrast, ChR2 and ChR2 mutants (ChR2 H134R, ChR2 T159C) exhibit channel closing rates that are accelerated twofold to threefold at negative membrane voltages (−100 mV) compared with positive voltages (+50 or +80 mV) (4, 7). Similarly, in ChR2 and C1V1, the kinetics of peak recovery were shown to be threefold to fourfold faster at negative voltages than at positive voltages (48, 57). Mutation of ChR2 Ci1 to threonine results in fast, voltage-independent channel closing and in remarkably fast recovery kinetics (7, 21). Therefore, the counterion residue and its interaction partners, including ChR2 E3 and K1, which are involved in voltage-dependent protonation reactions, reorganization of the hydrogen network, or conformational changes, modulate channel closure and recovery of the dark-adapted state. Chronos, a ChR from *Stigeoclonium helveticum*, displays very fast photocycle kinetics (33). Most interestingly, Chronos exhibits inverse off-kinetics voltage-dependence: It displays faster channel closing at positive voltages (33). In the Chronos primary sequence, the residues corresponding to ChR2 Ci1 and T159 are replaced by methionine (M140) and asparagine (N176), respectively. To fully understand voltage sensing in ChRs, however, further structural information on photointermediates, and on the conducting states specifically, is urgently needed.

THE HELIX 2 (H2)-TILT MODEL FOR CHANNELRHODOPSIN ACTIVATION

Structural information, detailed electrical measurements, and time-resolved Fourier transform infrared (FTIR) and electron paramagnetic resonance (EPR) measurements, in combination with MD calculations, resulted in the following model for ChR activation (**Figure 4**). All-*trans* to 13-*cis* isomerization induces the movement of N258, which is next to the retinal-binding residue K257 (36). This movement is in agreement with early backbone conformational changes observed after a femtosecond flash on a picosecond timescale (49). The next early event is the disruption of one of the two hydrogen bonds between N258 and E90 (E3); this disruption causes a special rearrangement of H2 and H7 and induces an outward flip, as well as deprotonation of E3 itself

(36). The tilt of H2 in the MD simulations agrees with the light-induced movement of spin-labeled cysteines on H2 and H7, as measured by EPR of selected spin-labeled cysteines (35, 62). The outward orientation of E3 opens up a small pore, and water molecules invade from the extracellular site into the vestibule between the inner gate and the outer gate, resulting in the formation of the preopen state (36). Subsequently, only small conformational changes and proton-transfer reactions at the inner gate appear to be important for the transition from the preopen state to the fully open state (59). These conformational changes might involve separation of the salt bridges E1/R268 and E2/H134 (**Figure 1d** and **Figure 4**). As both glutamic acids are deprotonated before and after separation, however, reorientation at the inner gate is expected to be almost infrared silent, and has not been seen in time-resolved FTIR measurements thus far. Notably, a very recent electron microscopy study confirmed light-induced rearrangements of H2, H6, and H7 and suggested that H2 and H7 become more flexible after illumination (47). This observation is consistent with disruption of the interconnecting hydrogen bonds of both the central gate and the inner gate (E3/N258, E1/R268 and E2/H134).

To fully understand ChR gating, we need to accommodate the DC pair C128/D156. Modifications in these residues dramatically slow down the photocycle from milliseconds to minutes (3, 8, 81). The connection between H3 and H4 is important, as shown for the homologs T90/D115 in BR (16); however, the detailed functionality of the DC pair for ChR activation is not yet clear.

APPLICATIONS OF CHANNELRHODOPSINS

ChRs are most commonly used to depolarize the plasma membranes of excitable cells, thereby either directly activating cellular activity such as action potential firing or reducing the threshold for such events (10, 27). In fact, different ChR variants should be considered for the activation of different target cell types; for example, a fast ChR with voltage-independent off-kinetics, such as a ChETA mutant, would be most suited to eliciting action potentials in fast-spiking interneurons (7, 21). In contrast, a ChR exhibiting moderate photocycling kinetics and moderate current inactivation, as seen in ChR2 H134R, might be the preferred option to optogenetically mimic the action potential of a cardiomyocyte (80). Moreover, bistable SFRs are the best choice for the prolonged induction of subthreshold depolarization without continuous illumination (3, 8).

ChRs might also be used to alter cation distributions along both plasma membranes and intracellular membranes. Although ChRs in general are not highly selective for a single cation species, the ionic photocurrent composition differs between different ChRs and should be taken into account when choosing an appropriate ChR variant (63). For example, the Catch$^+$ mutant is probably the best-suited variant for triggering Ca^{2+} influx into the cytosol from intracellular stores because its Ca^{2+} conductance is high at high Ca^{2+} concentrations (57, 63). Two recently developed ChRs, ChloC and iC1C2, represent anion-selective ChRs that can be used to clamp the voltage to the reversal potential for Cl^-, thereby suppressing action potential firing (5, 79).

Color-tuned ChRs enable independent activation of distinct cellular populations and allow ChRs to be used in combination with fluorescent sensor proteins. Furthermore, the improved ensemble of orange- and red-light activated ChRs, including ReachR and Chrimson, allows for ChR activation in intact tissues and organs, owing to reduced absorption and scattering of red light in living tissue (33, 38). Alternatively, ChRs that exhibit an elevated two-photon absorption cross-section, such as C1V1, can be employed for two-photon activation with near-infrared light (56).

ChR properties to consider include unitary conductance, retinal binding affinity, and protein stability. Moreover, properties that strongly depend on the target cells, such as expression level and membrane targeting, are of serious and equal importance, and these should be individually tested for each ChR variant and cell type, respectively. Finally, to help users choose a ChR variant

Table 2 Overview of channelrhodopsin (ChR) variants relevant for optogenetic applications

ChR variant	Use(s) and special properties	Reference(s)
ChR2 H134R	Widely used ChR, increased Na^+ conductivity, improved retinal binding in *Caenorhabditis elegans*	(30, 39)
CatCh (ChR2 L132C)	Enhanced Mg^{2+} and Ca^{2+} selectivity, large photocurrents, low inactivation	(34, 57)
ChR2 T159C	Large photocurrents, improved retinal binding affinity	(7, 74)
CatCh$^+$ (ChR2 L132C-T159C)	Enhanced Mg^{2+} and Ca^{2+} selectivity, large photocurrents, low inactivation, provides high light sensitivity to host cells, more stable expression than CatCh	(52, 57, 63)
ChETA (ChR2 E123T-T159C)	Fast photocycle at the expense of reduced transported charge per absorbed photon, reduced voltage dependency of channel closing kinetics	(7, 21)
Chronos	Very fast photocycle, large photocurrents, inverse voltage dependency of off kinetics, provides high light sensitivity to host cells	(33)
Step-function rhodopsins (ChR2 C128A/S/T; ChR2 D156A/C/N)	Very slow photocycle kinetics and extended open-state lifetimes, provides very high light sensitivity to cells, UV light– and green light–induced channel closure (bistable rhodopsins)	(3, 8)
ChIEF	Fast photocycle, low inactivation	(39)
C1V1 (E122T-E162T)	Green light–induced activation, high two-photon cross-section	(57, 81)
ReachR	Green light–induced activation, high expression level, and large photocurrents in mammalian cells	(38)
PsChR	Violet light–induced activation, high unitary conductance and high Na^+ conductivity, low inactivation, fast recovery kinetics	(17)
Cs-Chrimson	Orange light–induced activation, improved membrane targeting by use of the CsChR (ChR87) N-terminus	(33)
Slow ChloC (ChR2 E90R-D156N T159C)	Cl^- selectivity, slow photocycle, improved photocurrents and shifted reversal potential, used for voltage clamping to the Cl^- reversal potential	(79)
iC1C2	Cl^- selectivity, used for voltage clamping to the Cl^- reversal potential	(5)

with appropriate biophysical properties, **Table 2** summarizes the most useful and most commonly applied ChR variants for optogenetic applications.

FUTURE ISSUES

1. 3D structures of different states as they occur during the cyclic reaction pathway (photocycle) and structures of the open state(s) are most urgently needed.

2. Visualization of proton dynamics including structural changes and proton transfer reactions using nuclear magnetic resonance (NMR).

3. Extension of the activation model by stepwise inclusion of structural changes, water dynamics, and proton-transfer steps.

4. Further improvement of the chloride-conducting channels and the possible generation of Na^+ and K^+-selective ChRs.

DISCLOSURE STATEMENT

The authors are not aware of any affiliations, memberships, funding, or financial holdings that might be perceived as affecting the objectivity of this review.

ACKNOWLEDGMENTS

We thank Johannes Vierock for stimulating discussions during the preparation of the manuscript, and we thank Jonas Wietek for providing action spectra of selected ChR variants. The work was supported by the Louis-Jeantet Foundation and the German Research Foundation, DFG (SFB1078 B2).

LITERATURE CITED

1. Arenkiel BR, Peca J, Davison IG, Feliciano C, Deisseroth K, et al. 2007. In vivo light-induced activation of neural circuitry in transgenic mice expressing channelrhodopsin-2. *Neuron* 54(2):205–18
2. Babitzki G, Denschlag R, Tavan P. 2009. Polarization effects stabilize bacteriorhodopsin's chromophore binding pocket: a molecular dynamics study. *J. Phys. Chem. B* 113(30):10483–95
3. Bamann C, Gueta R, Kleinlogel S, Nagel G, Bamberg E. 2010. Structural guidance of the photocycle of channelrhodopsin-2 by an interhelical hydrogen bond. *Biochemistry* 49(2):267–78
4. Bamann C, Kirsch T, Nagel G, Bamberg E. 2008. Spectral characteristics of the photocycle of channelrhodopsin-2 and its implication for channel function. *J. Mol. Biol.* 375(3):686–94
5. Berndt A, Lee SY, Ramakrishnan C, Deisseroth K. 2014. Structure-guided transformation of channel-rhodopsin into a light-activated chloride channel. *Science* 344:420–24
6. Berndt A, Prigge M, Gradmann D, Hegemann P. 2010. Two open states with progressive proton selectivities in the branched channelrhodopsin-2 photocycle. *Biophys. J.* 98(5):753–61
7. Berndt A, Schoenenberger P, Mattis J, Tye KM, Deisseroth K, et al. 2011. High-efficiency channel-rhodopsins for fast neuronal stimulation at low light levels. *PNAS* 108(18):7595–600
8. Berndt A, Yizhar O, Gunaydin LA, Hegemann P, Deisseroth K. 2009. Bi-stable neural state switches. *Nat. Neurosci.* 12(2):229–34
9. Bi A, Cui J, Ma Y-P, Olshevskaya E, Pu M, et al. 2006. Ectopic expression of a microbial-type rhodopsin restores visual responses in mice with photoreceptor degeneration. *Neuron* 50(1):23–33
10. Boyden ES, Zhang F, Bamberg E, Nagel G, Deisseroth K. 2005. Millisecond-timescale, genetically targeted optical control of neural activity. *Nat. Neurosci.* 8(9):1263–68
11. Douglass AD, Kraves S, Deisseroth K, Schier AF, Engert F. 2008. Escape behavior elicited by single, channelrhodopsin-2-evoked spikes in zebrafish somatosensory neurons. *Curr. Biol.* 18(15):1133–37
12. Doyle DA. 1998. The structure of the potassium channel: molecular basis of K+ conduction and selectivity. *Science* 280(5360):69–77
13. Eisenhauer K, Kuhne J, Ritter E, Berndt A, Wolf S, et al. 2012. In channelrhodopsin-2 glu-90 is crucial for ion selectivity and is deprotonated during the photocycle. *J. Biol. Chem.* 287(9):6904–11
14. Ernst OP, Sánchez Murcia PA, Daldrop P, Tsunoda SP, Kateriya S, Hegemann P. 2008. Photoactivation of channelrhodopsin. *J. Biol. Chem.* 283(3):1637–43
15. Foster KW, Smyth RD. 1980. Light antennas in phototactic algae. *Microbiol. Rev.* 44(4):572–630
16. Garczarek F, Gerwert K. 2006. Polarized FTIR spectroscopy in conjunction with in situ H/D exchange reveals the orientation of protein internal carboxylic acids. *J. Am. Chem. Soc.* 128(1):28–29
17. Govorunova EG, Sineshchekov OA, Li H, Janz R, Spudich JL. 2013. Characterization of a highly efficient blue-shifted channelrhodopsin from the marine alga *Platymonas subcordiformis. J. Biol. Chem.* 288:29911–22
18. Govorunova EG, Spudich EN, Lane CE, Sineshchekov OA, Spudich JL. 2011. New channelrhodopsin with a red-shifted spectrum and rapid kinetics from *Mesostigma viride. mBio* 2(3):e00115–11
19. Gradinaru V, Mogri M, Thompson KR, Henderson JM, Deisseroth K. 2009. Optical deconstruction of Parkinsonian neural circuitry. *Science* 324(5925):354–59
20. Gradmann D, Berndt A, Schneider F, Hegemann P. 2011. Rectification of the channelrhodopsin early conductance. *Biophys. J.* 101(5):1057–68
21. Gunaydin LA, Yizhar O, Berndt A, Sohal VS, Deisseroth K, Hegemann P. 2010. Ultrafast optogenetic control. *Nat. Neurosci.* 13(3):387–92
22. Hegemann P. 2008. Algal sensory photoreceptors. *Annu. Rev. Plant Biol.* 59:167–89
23. Hegemann P, Ehlenbeck S, Gradmann D. 2005. Multiple photocycles of channelrhodopsin. *Biophys. J.* 89(6):3911–18

24. Holland EM, Braun FJ, Nonnengässer C, Harz H, Hegemann P. 1996. The nature of rhodopsin-triggered photocurrents in *Chlamydomonas*. I. Kinetics and influence of divalent ions. *Biophys. J.* 70(2):924–31

25. Hou S-Y, Govorunova EG, Ntefidou M, Lane CE, Spudich EN, et al. 2011. Diversity of *Chlamydomonas* channelrhodopsins. *Photochem. Photobiol.* 88(1):119–28

26. Hu JG, Sun BQ, Bizounok M, Hatcher ME, Lansing JC, et al. 1998. Early and late M intermediates in the bacteriorhodopsin photocycle: a solid-state NMR study. *Biochemistry* 37(22):8088–96

27. Ishizuka T, Kakuda M, Araki R, Yawo H. 2006. Kinetic evaluation of photosensitivity in genetically engineered neurons expressing green algae light-gated channels. *Neurosci. Res.* 54(2):85–94

28. Ito S, Kato HE, Taniguchi R, Iwata T, Nureki O, Kandori H. 2014. Water-containing hydrogen-bonding network in the active center of channelrhodopsin. *J. Am. Chem. Soc.* 136:3475–82

29. Joh NH, Min A, Faham S, Whitelegge JP, Yang D, et al. 2008. Modest stabilization by most hydrogen-bonded side-chain interactions in membrane proteins. *Nature* 453(7199):1266–70

30. Kateriya S. 2004. "Vision" in single-celled algae. *News Physiol. Sci.* 19(3):133–37

31. Kato HE, Zhang F, Yizhar O, Ramakrishnan C, Nishizawa T, et al. 2012. Crystal structure of the channelrhodopsin light-gated cation channel. *Nature* 482(7385):369–74

32. Kianianmomeni A, Stehfest K, Nematollahi G, Hegemann P, Hallmann A. 2009. Channelrhodopsins of *Volvox carteri* are photochromic proteins that are specifically expressed in somatic cells under control of light, temperature, and the sex inducer. *Plant Physiol.* 151(1):347–66

33. Klapoetke NC, Murata Y, Kim SS, Pulver SR, Birdsey-Benson A, et al. 2014. Independent optical excitation of distinct neural populations. *Nat. Methods* 11:338–46

34. Kleinlogel S, Feldbauer K, Dempski RE, Fotis H, Wood PG, et al. 2011. Ultra light-sensitive and fast neuronal activation with the Ca^{2+}-permeable channelrhodopsin CatCh. *Nat. Neurosci.* 14(4):513–18

35. Krause N, Engelhard C, Heberle J, Schlesinger R, Bittl R. 2013. Structural differences between the closed and open states of channelrhodopsin-2 as observed by EPR spectroscopy. *FEBS Lett.* 587(20):3309–13

36. Kuhne J, Eisenhauer K, Ritter E, Hegemann P, Gerwert K, Bartl F. 2014. Early formation of the ion-conducting pore in channelrhodopsin-2. *Angew. Chemie Int. Ed.* 54:4953–57

37. Li X, Gutierrez DV, Hanson MG, Han J, Mark MD, et al. 2005. Fast noninvasive activation and inhibition of neural and network activity by vertebrate rhodopsin and green algae channelrhodopsin. *PNAS* 102(49):17816–21

38. Lin JY, Knutsen PM, Muller A, Kleinfeld D, Tsien RY. 2013. ReaChR: a red-shifted variant of channelrhodopsin enables deep transcranial optogenetic excitation. *Nat. Neurosci.* 16:1499–508

39. Lin JY, Lin MZ, Steinbach P, Tsien RY. 2009. Characterization of engineered channelrhodopsin variants with improved properties and kinetics. *Biophys. J.* 96(5):1803–14

40. Lórenz-Fonfría VA, Resler T, Krause N, Nack M, Gossing M, et al. 2013. Transient protonation changes in channelrhodopsin-2 and their relevance to channel gating. *PNAS* 110(14):E1273–81

41. Luecke H, Schobert B, Lanyi JK, Spudich EN, Spudich JL. 2001. Crystal structure of sensory rhodopsin II at 2.4 angstroms: insights into color tuning and transducer interaction. *Science* 293(5534):1499–503

42. Luecke H, Schobert B, Richter HT, Cartailler JP, Lanyi JK. 1999. Structure of bacteriorhodopsin at 1.55 Å resolution. *J. Mol. Biol.* 291(4):899–911

43. Mittelmeier TM, Boyd JS, Lamb MR, Dieckmann CL. 2011. Asymmetric properties of the *Chlamydomonas reinhardtii* cytoskeleton direct rhodopsin photoreceptor localization. *J. Cell Biol.* 193(4):741–53

44. Müller M, Bamann C, Bamberg E, Kühlbrandt W. 2011. Projection structure of channelrhodopsin-2 at 6 Å resolution by electron crystallography. *J. Mol. Biol.* 414(1):86–95

45. Müller M, Bamann C, Bamberg E, Kühlbrandt W. 2014. Light-induced helix movements in channelrhodopsin-2. *J. Mol. Biol.* 427(2):341–49

46. Nagel G, Brauner M, Liewald JF, Adeishvili N, Bamberg E, Gottschalk A. 2005. Light activation of channelrhodopsin-2 in excitable cells of *Caenorhabditis elegans* triggers rapid behavioral responses. *Curr. Biol.* 15(24):2279–84

47. Nagel G, Ollig D, Fuhrmann M, Kateriya S, Musti AM, et al. 2002. Channelrhodopsin-1: a light-gated proton channel in green algae. *Science* 296(5577):2395–98

48. Nagel G, Szellas T, Huhn W, Kateriya S, Adeishvili N, et al. 2003. Channelrhodopsin-2, a directly light-gated cation-selective membrane channel. *PNAS* 100(24):13940–45

49. Neumann-Verhoefen M-K, Neumann K, Bamann C, Radu I, Heberle J, et al. 2013. Ultrafast infrared spectroscopy on channelrhodopsin-2 reveals efficient energy transfer from the retinal chromophore to the protein. *J. Am. Chem. Soc.* 135(18):6968–76

50. Nikolic K, Degenaar P, Toumazou C. 2006. Modeling and engineering aspects of channelrhodopsin2 system for neural photostimulation. *Proc. Int. Conf. IEEE Eng. Med. Biol. Soc., 28th, New York*, pp. 1626–29. Piscataway, NJ: IEEE

51. Nikolic K, Grossman N, Grubb MS, Burrone J, Toumazou C, Degenaar P. 2009. Photocycles of channelrhodopsin-2. *Photochem. Photobiol.* 85(1):400–11

52. Pan Z-H, Ganjawala TH, Lu Q, Ivanova E, Zhang Z. 2014. ChR2 mutants at L132 and T159 with improved operational light sensitivity for vision restoration. *PLOS ONE* 9(6):e98924

53. Patzelt H, Simon B, terLaak A, Kessler B, Kühne R, et al. 2002. The structures of the active center in dark-adapted bacteriorhodopsin by solution-state NMR spectroscopy. *PNAS* 99(15):9765–70

54. Petreanu L, Huber D, Sobczyk A, Svoboda K. 2007. Channelrhodopsin-2-assisted circuit mapping of long-range callosal projections. *Nat. Neurosci.* 10(5):663–68

55. Plazzo AP, De Franceschi N, Da Broi F, Zonta F, Sanasi MF, et al. 2012. Bioinformatic and mutational analysis of channelrhodopsin-2 protein cation-conducting pathway. *J. Biol. Chem.* 287(7):4818–25

56. Prakash R, Yizhar O, Grewe B, Ramakrishnan C, Wang N, et al. 2012. Two-photon optogenetic toolbox for fast inhibition, excitation and bistable modulation. *Nat. Methods* 9:1171–79

57. Prigge M, Schneider F, Tsunoda SP, Shilyansky C, Wietek J, et al. 2012. Color-tuned channelrhodopsins for multiwavelength optogenetics. *J. Biol. Chem.* 287:31804–12

58. Radu I, Bamann C, Nack M, Nagel G, Bamberg E, Heberle J. 2009. Conformational changes of channelrhodopsin-2. *J. Am. Chem. Soc.* 131(21):7313–19

59. Ritter E, Piwowarski P, Hegemann P, Bartl FJ. 2013. Light-dark adaptation of channelrhodopsin C128T mutant. *J. Biol. Chem.* 288(15):10451–58

60. Ritter E, Stehfest K, Berndt A, Hegemann P, Bartl FJ. 2008. Monitoring light-induced structural changes of Channelrhodopsin-2 by UV-visible and Fourier transform infrared spectroscopy. *J. Biol. Chem.* 283(50):35033–41

61. Ruffert K, Himmel B, Lall D, Bamann C, Bamberg E, et al. 2011. Glutamate residue 90 in the predicted transmembrane domain 2 is crucial for cation flux through channelrhodopsin 2. *Biochem. Biophys. Res. Commun.* 410(4):737–43

62. Sattig T, Rickert C, Bamberg E, Steinhoff H-J, Bamann C. 2013. Light-induced movement of the transmembrane helix b in channelrhodopsin-2. *Angew. Chem. Int. Ed. Engl.* 52(37):9705–8

63. Schneider F, Gradmann D, Hegemann P. 2013. Ion selectivity and competition in channelrhodopsins. *Biophys. J.* 105(1):91–100

64. Scholz F, Bamberg E, Bamann C, Wachtveitl J. 2012. Tuning the primary reaction of channelrhodopsin-2 by imidazole, pH, and site-specific mutations. *Biophys. J.* 102(11):2649–57

65. Schroll C, Riemensperger T, Bucher D, Ehmer J, Völler T, et al. 2006. Light-induced activation of distinct modulatory neurons triggers appetitive or aversive learning in *Drosophila* larvae. *Curr. Biol.* 16(17):1741–47

66. Shimano T, Fyk-Kolodziej B, Mirza N, Asako M, Tomoda K, et al. 2013. Assessment of the AAV-mediated expression of channelrhodopsin-2 and halorhodopsin in brainstem neurons mediating auditory signaling. *Brain Res.* 1511:138–52

67. Sineshchekov OA, Govorunova EG, Wang J, Li H, Spudich JL. 2013. Intramolecular proton transfer in channelrhodopsins. *Biophys. J.* 104(4):807–17

68. Sineshchekov OA, Jung K-H, Spudich JL. 2002. Two rhodopsins mediate phototaxis to low- and high-intensity light in *Chlamydomonas reinhardtii. PNAS* 99(13):8689–94

69. Stehfest K, Hegemann P. 2010. Evolution of the channelrhodopsin photocycle model. *ChemPhysChem* 11(6):1120–26

70. Stehfest K, Ritter E, Berndt A, Bartl F, Hegemann P. 2010. The branched photocycle of the slow-cycling channelrhodopsin-2 mutant C128T. *J. Mol. Biol.* 398(5):690–702

71. Sugiyama Y, Wang H, Hikima T, Sato M, Kuroda J, et al. 2009. Photocurrent attenuation by a single polar-to-nonpolar point mutation of channelrhodopsin-2. *Photochem. Photobiol. Sci.* 8(3):328–36

72. Suzuki T, Yamasaki K, Fujita S, Oda K, Iseki M, et al. 2003. Archaeal-type rhodopsins in *Chlamydomonas*: model structure and intracellular localization. *Biochem. Biophys. Res. Commun.* 301(3):711–17

73. Tsunoda SP, Hegemann P. 2009. Glu 87 of channelrhodopsin-1 causes pH-dependent color tuning and fast photocurrent inactivation. *Photochem. Photobiol.* 85(2):564–69

74. Ullrich S, Gueta R, Nagel G. 2012. Degradation of channelopsin-2 in the absence of retinal and degradation resistance in certain mutants. *Biol. Chem.* 394:271–80

75. Verhoefen M-K, Bamann C, Blöcher R, Förster U, Bamberg E, Wachtveitl J. 2010. The photocycle of channelrhodopsin-2: ultrafast reaction dynamics and subsequent reaction steps. *ChemPhysChem* 11(14):3113–22

76. Wang H, Sugiyama Y, Hikima T, Sugano E, Tomita H, et al. 2009. Molecular determinants differentiating photocurrent properties of two channelrhodopsins from *Chlamydomonas*. *J. Biol. Chem.* 284(9):5685–96

77. Watanabe HC, Welke K, Schneider F, Tsunoda S, Zhang F, et al. 2012. Structural model of channelrhodopsin. *J. Biol. Chem.* 287(10):7456–66

78. Watanabe HC, Welke K, Sindhikara DJ, Hegemann P, Elstner M. 2013. Towards an understanding of channelrhodopsin function: simulations lead to novel insights of the channel mechanism. *J. Mol. Biol.* 425:1795–814

79. Wietek J, Wiegert JS, Adeishvili N, Schneider F, Watanabe H, et al. 2014. Conversion of channelrhodopsin into a light-gated chloride channel. *Science* 344:409–12

80. Williams JC, Xu J, Lu Z, Klimas A, Chen X, et al. 2013. Computational optogenetics: empirically-derived voltage- and light-sensitive channelrhodopsin-2 model. *PLOS Comput. Biol.* 9:e1003220

81. Yizhar O, Fenno LE, Prigge M, Schneider F, Davidson TJ, et al. 2011. Neocortical excitation/inhibition balance in information processing and social dysfunction. *Nature* 477(7363):171–78

82. Zhang F, Prigge M, Beyrière F, Tsunoda SP, Mattis J, et al. 2008. Red-shifted optogenetic excitation: a tool for fast neural control derived from *Volvox carteri*. *Nat. Neurosci.* 11(6):631–33

83. Zhang F, Vierock J, Yizhar O, Fenno LE, Tsunoda S, et al. 2011. The microbial opsin family of optogenetic tools. *Cell* 147(7):1446–57

84. Zhang Y-P, Oertner TG. 2007. Optical induction of synaptic plasticity using a light-sensitive channel. *Nat. Methods* 4(2):139–41

Structure and Mechanism of RNA Mimics of Green Fluorescent Protein

Mingxu You and Samie R. Jaffrey

Department of Pharmacology, Weill Medical College, Cornell University, New York, New York 10065; email: miy2003@med.cornell.edu, srj2003@med.cornell.edu

Annu. Rev. Biophys. 2015. 44:187–206

The *Annual Review of Biophysics* is online at biophys.annualreviews.org

This article's doi:
10.1146/annurev-biophys-060414-033954

Keywords

RNA, aptamers, fluorescence, microscopy, imaging

Abstract

RNAs have highly complex and dynamic cellular localization patterns. Technologies for imaging RNA in living cells are important for uncovering their function and regulatory pathways. One approach for imaging RNA involves genetically encoding fluorescent RNAs using RNA mimics of green fluorescent protein (GFP). These mimics are RNA aptamers that bind fluorophores resembling those naturally found in GFP and activate their fluorescence. These RNA–fluorophore complexes, including Spinach, Spinach2, and Broccoli, can be used to tag RNAs and to image their localization in living cells. In this article, we describe the generation and optimization of these aptamers, along with strategies for expanding the spectral properties of their associated RNA–fluorophore complexes. We also discuss the structural basis for the fluorescence and photophysical properties of Spinach, and we describe future prospects for designing enhanced RNA–fluorophore complexes with enhanced photostability and increased sensitivity.

Contents

INTRODUCTION

RNA imaging is important for determining the function and regulation of noncoding and coding RNAs. Approximately 1–2% of the genome encodes mRNA, whereas the vast majority of it encodes noncoding RNAs (ncRNAs), including microRNAs, PIWI-associated RNAs (piRNAs), circular RNAs, long intergenic ncRNAs, and small nucleolar RNAs (snoRNAs) (2, 16, 26).

Most of these ncRNAs are mysterious, and their sequences often provide little information about their potential function. This contrasts with mRNAs where sequence analysis is important for predicting the encoded protein. For ncRNAs, however, the sequence usually does not provide information that predicts function. Therefore, one of the first experiments that can provide insight into the function of an ncRNA is to determine its subcellular localization. For example, nuclear ncRNAs may have a role in regulating gene transcription, whereas cytoplasmic ncRNAs likely affect processes in this compartment. The dynamics of ncRNA localization can also provide insights into its function. Translocation of an ncRNA to a specific subcellular site or structure, such as Cajal bodies in the nucleus or P-bodies in the cytoplasm, can provide insights into possible functions or regulatory pathways for the ncRNA under study.

In addition to knowledge gained from imaging ncRNAs, information on the regulation of mRNA can be gained by studying mRNA localization in cells. mRNA is subjected to a wide range of posttranscriptional processing events, including splicing, RNA editing, exonucleolytic and endonucleolytic degradation, nonsense-mediated decay, adenosine methylation, pseudouridylation, and deadenylation (11, 42, 47). mRNAs transit through different parts of the cell as they are processed by these different pathways (1, 35, 56). Because mRNA regulatory mechanisms appear to occur in spatially defined regions or structures in cells, imaging approaches can provide insights into the pathways that regulate transcription, modification, and degradation of specific mRNAs in cells.

Altered RNA localization can also cause disease (6). For instance, fragile X syndrome, the most common genetic form of mental retardation, is associated with the loss of an RNA-trafficking protein (5). Thus, imaging approaches that reveal RNA trafficking or localization could provide insights into the underlying mechanisms of this and similar diseases.

RNA IMAGING APPROACHES

Imaging RNA with Labeled Probes

One can obtain real-time localization of RNA in living cells using chemical labeling approaches such as RNA synthesis with fluorescent nucleotides. These labeled RNAs are then microinjected into cells (60), and their fate is determined using fluorescence microscopy. However, this approach is limited by low throughput and by the difficulty of preparing these RNAs and microinjecting them into cells.

Molecular beacons are also used to image RNAs in living cells. Molecular beacons are oligonucleotides that typically contain both a fluorophore and a quencher (61). The beacon folds into a stem-loop structure that is nonfluorescent owing to the proximity of the fluorophore and quencher at either end of the oligonucleotide, that is, at the base of the stem. When an mRNA that has complementarity to the loop of the beacon hybridizes to the beacon, the stem is disrupted, separating the quencher and fluorophore and leading to fluorescence. Each mRNA requires a custom-designed beacon, however, and transfected beacons can exhibit nonspecific nuclear sequestration (43, 61). These issues can prevent adoption by many scientific laboratories.

Genetically Encoded Reporters of RNA Localization

Because of the difficulties associated with the chemical labeling approaches described above, numerous groups have developed genetically encoded reporters of RNA localization (8, 30, 62). Genetic encodability bypasses the complexities of synthesis and the toxicities associated with microinjection, and genetically encoded tools can be expressed directly in cells after a DNA sequence is introduced. Genetic encoding also enables reporters to be expressed in a cell type–specific or tissue-specific manner. Thus, genetic encoding markedly simplifies imaging.

The most commonly used genetically encoded RNA imaging technique is the green fluorescent protein (GFP)–MS2 system (8). This technique uses two components: MS2, a phage protein, which is fused to GFP, and MS2 binding RNA sequences that are inserted into the 3′ untranslated regions (UTRs) of mRNAs of interest. GFP–MS2 and MS2 element–containing RNAs are expressed in cells, and GFP–MS2 binds to the MS2 element–tagged RNA. Fluorescence in these cells derives from RNA–GFP complexes. Because unbound GFP–MS2 molecules diffuse throughout the cytosol, however, there can be fluorescence background that results from unbound GFP–MS2. To reduce this problem, the GFP–MS2 fusion protein is engineered to contain a nuclear localization signal (NLS) that causes excess GFP–MS2 to move into the nucleus (8). Variations of this protocol that use different RNA binding elements and fluorescent proteins have also been reported (30).

GFP–MS2 can potentially affect the localization of the mRNA to which it is bound (60) because it contains an NLS trafficking element. Indeed, because most heterologously expressed RNAs are designed to bind 24–48 GFP–MS2 sequences, each RNA is subjected to the effects of 24–48

NLS-targeting elements (60). In addition, because the GFP–MS2 accumulates in the nucleus, an intense nuclear fluorescence can arise and complicate the analysis of nuclear-localized RNAs. Although these issues can be addressed by careful control of GFP–MS2 expression, the system for controlling such expression can be complex to implement.

Other related approaches have been described. One involves the expression of GFP as two halves, each of which is fused to half of an RNA binding protein, eIF4A (eukaryotic initiation factor 4A) (62). RNAs that contain the eIF4A binding site nucleate the binding of the eIF4A halves, juxtaposing the two GFP halves and enabling the formation of a stable GFP complex. As the GFP complex requires ~30 min to mature into a fluorescent form (41), this method might not enable visualization of newly synthesized RNAs. Moreover, once the fluorescent complex has formed, it can spontaneously dissociate or accumulate in the cytoplasm after RNA degradation, possibly leading to high background cytoplasmic fluorescence. Thus, although this approach has high potential for use in imaging RNA in living cells, some of the potential challenges associated with it could limit its application. The approaches described above are useful for RNA imaging in live cells [as are others that were not described here owing to space limitations (60)], but they are complicated by the need to introduce different components into cells at highly specific stoichiometries.

IMAGING RNA USING MIMICS OF GREEN FLUORESCENT PROTEIN

Conditionally Fluorescent Small-Molecule Dyes for RNA Imaging

A simpler approach is to express an RNA tagged with a sequence that confers the fluorescence needed for imaging. This approach is analogous to GFP tagging of proteins. Short RNA sequences that fold into specific shapes that bind other molecules are termed aptamers. RNA aptamers can be generated readily using the SELEX (selective enrichment of ligands by exponential enrichment) technique, which we describe in more detail below. RNA aptamers have been developed that bind fluorescent dyes such as fluorescein (32, 52), but these aptamers have not been widely adopted for use in live-cell experiments because both the bound and unbound dyes are fluorescent.

Our strategy was to identify fluorophores that would be switched on (exhibit fluorescence) only when bound to a highly specific aptamer (46). Although many molecules exhibit fluorescence that can be induced by binding to various intracellular molecules (for example, ethidium bromide and Hoechst dyes become fluorescent upon binding nucleic acids), our strategy sought to identify fluorophores that are both switchable and bioorthogonal, meaning that the fluorescence is not switched on by normal cellular biomolecules. Selecting for this quality ensures that the unbound fluorophore is nonfluorescent and does not contribute to background fluorescence.

We sought to identify fluorophores that would not exhibit fluorescence upon interaction with normal cellular constituents but that would potentially be activated by specific RNA aptamers. We considered small-molecule dyes with structural features that could make them prone to exhibiting increased fluorescence upon rigidification, such as stilbenes (38), triphenylmethane dyes (e.g., pararosaniline and malachite green) (15), and cyanine dyes. Unfortunately, however, these dyes exhibit fluorescence activation when applied to cells, which is consistent with the known induction of fluorescence in malachite green and stilbenes by contact with lipids and membranes (23, 38). In addition, some molecules exhibit cytotoxicity at low micromolar concentrations. For example, malachite green generates cytotoxic radicals upon irradiation (7), leading to destruction of the RNA aptamers that bind it (21). Such destruction is problematic because malachite green is fluorescent when bound to cognate aptamers (3). Thus, the undesirable features of this dye have prevented the use of these otherwise potentially useful aptamers for RNA imaging.

Aptamer: short DNA or RNA sequences that fold into specific shapes that bind other molecules

Selective enrichment of ligands by exponential enrichment (SELEX): a technique to isolate DNA or RNA that specifically binds to a target ligand

Bioorthogonal: a molecule or reaction that neither affects nor is affected by cellular biochemical processes or molecules

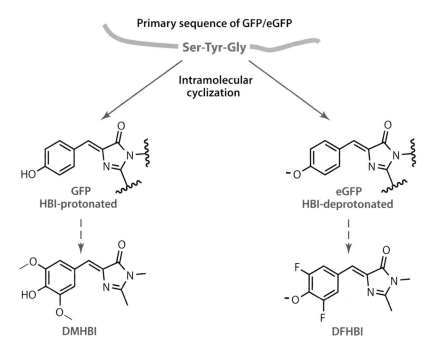

Primary sequence of GFP/eGFP

Ser-Tyr-Gly

Intramolecular
cyclization

GFP
HBI-protonated

eGFP
HBI-deprotonated

DMHBI

DFHBI

Figure 1

Structures of the green fluorescent protein (GFP) fluorophore and of fluorophores that are switched on by
RNA aptamers. The fluorophores in GFP and in its close variant, enhanced GFP (eGFP), are derived from a
Ser–Tyr–Gly tripeptide within the protein. The folded protein catalyzes an intramolecular cyclization that
converts the tripeptide into the HBI fluorophore. In eGFP, unlike in GFP, the fluorophore is predominantly
in the deprotonated, or phenolate, form; this form accounts for the higher extinction coefficient and
brightness of eGFP. RNA mimics of GFP bind to fluorophores resembling HBI. The original RNA
aptamers were designed to bind DMHBI, which resembles HBI in GFP in that the fluorophore is
predominantly protonated (*left*). The DFHBI fluorophore was designed to overcome this problem and was
designed as a biomimetic of the fluorophore in eGFP (*right*). Owing to the addition of fluorines, the DFHBI
fluorophore is deprotonated at neutral pH. Thus, RNA aptamers that bind DFHBI, such as Spinach,
Spinach2, and Broccoli, are highly bright, in part because of the higher extinction coefficient of DFHBI.
Abbreviations: DFHBI, (Z)-4-(3,5-difluoro-4-hydroxybenzylidene)-1,2-dimethyl-1H-imidazol-5(4H)-one;
DMHBI, (Z)-4-(3,5-dimethoxy-4-hydroxybenzylidene)-1,2-dimethyl-1H-imidazol-5(4H)-one; HBI,
4-hydroxy-benzylidene-imidazolinone.

We therefore considered the fluorophore that is formed within GFP, as this protein also exhibits
conditional fluorescence. After GFP is synthesized, it undergoes an autocatalytic intramolecular
cyclization reaction that involves an internal Ser–Tyr–Gly tripeptide (14). The cyclized product
is subsequently oxidized to the final 4-hydroxy-benzylidene-imidazolinone (HBI) fluorophore
(**Figure 1**). The oxidation results in delocalization of the π-electron system.

Surprisingly, when this fluorophore is chemically synthesized, it is nonfluorescent (44). Similarly, denatured GFP is nonfluorescent, and the fluorescence returns upon protein renaturation
(9). The basis for the conditional fluorescence of GFP is due to the chemical structure of the
fluorophore. After photoexcitation, a molecule can dissipate the energy of the excited state
either through a radiative (i.e., fluorescence) pathway or through a nonradiative pathway, which
usually involves vibrational or other intramolecular movements. In folded GFP, the excited-state
fluorophore dissipates its energy by radiative decay (fluorescence) (**Figure 2**) (40). GFP unfolding
allows the fluorophore to dissipate its energy by various bond rotations, however, and these

**Conditional
fluorescence:** the
emitted radiation that
occurs only when
some conditions or
requirements are met

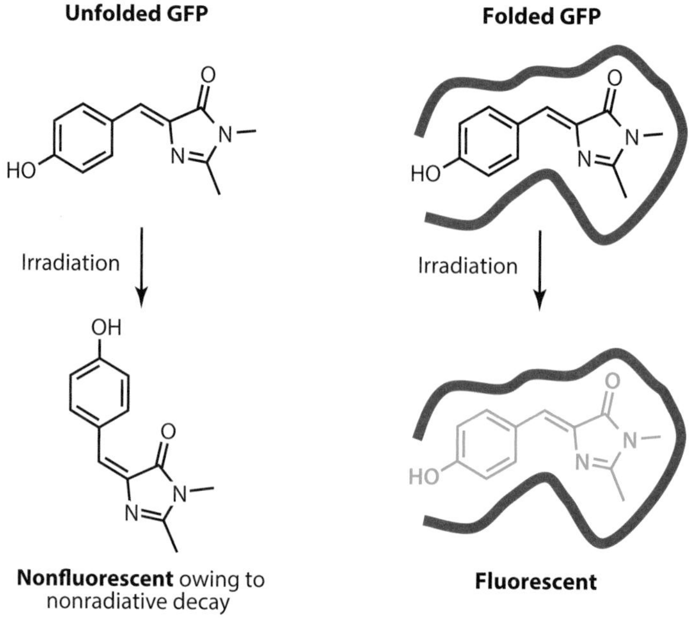

Unfolded GFP　　　　　　　**Folded GFP**

Irradiation　　　　　　　　Irradiation

Nonfluorescent owing to nonradiative decay　　　　**Fluorescent**

Figure 2

Fluorescence of green fluorescent protein (GFP) depends on the presence of protein contacts surrounding the fluorophore. GFP exhibits conditional fluorescence that depends on the folded state of the protein. When the protein is unfolded (*left*), the fluorophore portion of the protein undergoes an isomerization in response to irradiation. The folded state of the protein (*right*) inhibits this nonradiative decay pathway for dissipation of the energy of the excited state of the fluorophore. Instead, the major pathway available for the fluorophore to dissipate the energy of its excited state is fluorescence. RNA aptamers such as Spinach and Broccoli mimic the protein-suppressing effect of GFP for DFHBI [(Z)-4-(3,5-difluoro-4-hydroxybenzylidene)-1,2-dimethyl-1H-imidazol-5(4H)-one] and related GFP-like fluorophores.

rotations likely involve a twisting motion about the ethylenic bridge referred to as a "hula twist" that results in a *cis–trans* isomerization (4). The folded GFP protein prevents these motions, thereby making the radiative decay pathway the major means of dissipating the energy of the excited state fluorophore (**Figure 2**) (4, 40). Indeed, GFP variants that permit conformational freedom of the fluorophore have normal fluorophore maturation but reduced fluorescence (37).

One key experiment (44) tested the idea that fluorophore rigidification is essential for fluorescence using artificial restriction of bond movement by immobilizing the fluorophore in ethanol glass (ethanol at 77K). This treatment transformed the fluorophore into an intensely fluorescent species, in contrast to the fluorophore in ethanol solution at 25°C, which is nonfluorescent (44). Thus, the GFP contains a conditionally fluorescent fluorophore for which fluorescence arises because of immobilization induced by the GFP protein.

Identification of RNAs that Switch On the Fluorescence of Green Fluorescent Protein–Based Fluorophores

We asked whether an RNA aptamer could immobilize the GFP fluorophore in a fluorescent conformation similar to what is seen in GFP. We synthesized a variety of GFP-like fluorophores, including novel ones with potentially useful spectral properties. The synthesis of the GFP fluorophore, HBI [(Z)-4-(4-hydroxybenzylidene)-1,2-dimethyl-1H-imidazol-5(4H)-one], was described by several groups (36, 44). The main protocol for HBI synthesis is based on the work of Kojima et al. (36), and it involves an aldol condensation of *N*-acetylglycine and substituted benzaldehydes, resulting in the lactone intermediate shown in **Figure 2**. This lactone is then aminolyzed and recyclized to form the final HBI-like molecule. We made several derivatives of HBI using various substituted benzaldehydes as starting materials, and we used various acylated forms of glycine to make further derivatives. These substituents might serve as so-called handles that could help the RNA to bind the fluorophore and thereby facilitate rigidification. In addition, creation of multiple derivatives allows preparation of multiple RNA–fluorophore complexes, each of which has a different fluorescent color due to the presence of a different RNA-bound fluorophore.

HBI-like fluorophores were synthesized in two forms: (*a*) a form for use in cell-based experiments and (*b*) a form with an aminohexyl linker for immobilization on beads; this linker is required to obtain RNA aptamers in SELEX experiments. We used SELEX, a procedure that generates RNA aptamers that bind diverse types of small molecules and proteins (18), to generate RNA aptamers that bind HBI-like fluorophores. In this procedure, 10^{14}–10^{15} different RNAs of random sequence are synthesized and incubated with agarose beads that contain the target molecule of interest, which was a GFP-like fluorophore in this case. After extensive washing, RNAs that remain bound to the target molecule are eluted using buffer that contains the fluorophore. The eluted RNAs are then amplified by reverse transcription-polymerase chain reaction (RT-PCR) and transcribed to RNA. The binding and RT-PCR steps are repeated several times to select for the aptamers with the highest affinities. Because the RNA library has a high combinatorial diversity and RNAs have the ability to fold into diverse tertiary structures, this procedure often yields 10–100 different RNA aptamers for any given ligand (20). SELEX rarely fails to yield an aptamer that binds to a ligand target (20).

We tested whether RNA aptamers could induce fluorescence in GFP-based fluorophores. We initially focused on DMHBI [(Z)-4-(3,5-dimethoxy-4-hydroxybenzylidene)-1,2-dimethyl-1H-imidazol-5(4H)-one] (**Figure 1**) because this fluorophore exhibits an intense yellow-green fluorescence when immobilized in ethanol glass. DMHBI was coupled to agarose beads, and SELEX was performed to recover RNA aptamers. Of several hundred different DMHBI binding RNA aptamers tested, only a few were capable of inducing DMHBI fluorescence (46). However, these experiments did demonstrate that RNA aptamers can switch on the fluorescence of HBI-like fluorophores. To further test this concept, we generated RNA aptamers against a series of other HBI-like fluorophores and again identified aptamers capable of activating various structural derivatives of HBI (46). Taken together, these data show that RNA aptamers can switch on the fluorescence of HBI-like fluorophores and form RNA–fluorophore complexes that mimic GFP.

An RNA–Fluorophore Complex that Mimics Enhanced Green Fluorescent Protein?

The excitation and emission spectra of the first RNA–fluorophore complexes resembled those of GFP, not enhanced GFP (eGFP) (46). The difference between these proteins is due to the protonation state of the HBI fluorophore. In GFP, the fluorophore is predominantly in its protonated, or phenol, form, whereas in eGFP, the fluorophore is predominantly in its deprotonated, or phenolate, form (**Figure 1**) (59). Each form has its own absorbance peak; the phenol form has an absorbance maximum at ~390 nm, and the phenolate has an absorbance maximum at ~475 nm. Importantly, the phenolate form of the fluorophore has a significantly higher extinction coefficient than the phenol form does, and, as the degree of fluorescence depends on the extinction coefficient and the quantum yield, eGFP exhibits higher fluorescence than GFP (59).

Extinction coefficient: a measurement of how efficiently a sample absorbs light at a given wavelength

Quantum yield: the number of photons emitted per photon absorbed by a given fluorophore

Spinach   DFHBI   Spinach
                                                  + DFHBI

Figure 3

Fluorescence of the Spinach–DFHBI complex. The Spinach RNA aptamer robustly activates the fluorescence of DFHBI. Each tube contains the indicated solution, and all tubes were irradiated at 365 nm. Only the tube containing both Spinach and DFHBI exhibits fluorescence following irradiation. Abbreviation: DFHBI, (Z)-4-(3,5-difluoro-4-hydroxybenzylidene)-1,2-dimethyl-1H-imidazol-5(4H)-one.

Because the absorbance spectra of RNA–DMHBI complexes indicated that the fluorophore was in the phenol form, these RNA–fluorophore complexes were similar to the original GFP rather than to eGFP (46). We therefore used a biomimetic strategy to create an RNA mimic of eGFP. To do this, we synthesized a new fluorophore that contains a phenolate, resembling the form of the fluorophore normally found in eGFP. To ensure that the new fluorophore, DFHBI [(Z)-4-(3,5-difluoro-4-hydroxybenzylidene)-1,2-dimethyl-1H-imidazol-5(4H)-one], remained in the phenolate form, it was synthesized to contain fluorine atoms (**Figure 1**). The fluorine atoms lower the pK_a of the phenolic proton to 5.5, compared with 8.1 for HBI (46). This ensures that the fluorophore will present the phenolate state at physiological pH, including at the pH used for generating aptamers via SELEX.

We used SELEX to identify RNA aptamers that bind and switch on the fluorescence of DFHBI (**Figure 3**). The most efficient aptamer binds DFHBI with a K_d of ~500 nM and exhibits high fluorescence: Its quantum yield is 0.72, and its total molar brightness is equal to half that of eGFP. Control RNAs, such as cellular RNA, tRNA, or scrambled RNA sequences, exhibit no fluorescence upon incubation with DFHBI. Because this RNA–fluorophore complex is very similar to GFP, we named it after the vegetable spinach, in analogy to the fruits that have been used in naming fluorescent proteins (46).

OPTIMIZING RNA–FLUOROPHORE COMPLEXES

Directed Evolution to Generate Cell-Compatible RNA–Fluorophore Complexes

One of the major challenges in working with RNA aptamers is that they often fail to function as expected in living cells. Once expressed in cells, aptamers are susceptible to RNA degradation and often fail to fold (39). Misfolding can result from competing folding pathways, thermal instability, or dependence on high magnesium ion concentrations that are not normally found in cells (49, 67). In addition, adjacent sequences in a target RNA into which an aptamer is inserted can interfere with folding (39, 57).

Analysis of Spinach showed that it exhibits poor folding in vitro and in cells (57). As a result, the overall fluorescence in Spinach-expressing cells was reduced. To address this, Spinach was systematically mutagenized to identify mutations that resulted in improved folding in vitro (57). Thus, an enhanced version of Spinach, designated Spinach2, exhibits improved cellular fluorescence due to improved folding (57).

Because it is difficult to identify mutations that improve folding, using selection protocols that produce aptamers that are already highly efficient at folding in cells is desirable. Thus, we modified the standard SELEX protocol to use bead-bound fluorophores for the initial rounds of aptamer selection and to use fluorescence screening to select for aptamers that exhibit fluorescence in cells (19). The fluorescence screening is performed by expressing the aptamers in *Escherichia coli*, followed by fluorescence-activated cell sorting (FACS). As these aptamers already exhibit fluorescence in cells, this selection process isolates those aptamers that show a combination of high fluorescence, high folding in cells, and compatibility with cellular ion concentrations.

After identification, aptamers can be further optimized for cellular performance by a process called directed evolution. In this approach, parent aptamer sequences are used to guide the synthesis of random libraries designed to resemble the parent aptamer. This process is similar to one previously described for ribozyme and aptamer mutant libraries (22, 29). Briefly, a DNA library is synthesized in which each encoded aptamer resembles the parent aptamer. At each position, every nucleotide has a controlled probability of being converted into one of the other three nucleotides, and this probability is mathematically calculated such that the resulting DNA library encodes all aptamers that differ from the parent aptamer by all possible 1-, 2-, 3-, 4-, 5-, 6-, 7-, or 8-nucleotide (nt) changes (19). The library is then subjected to one or two rounds of SELEX to remove aptamers that are incapable of binding the fluorophore, and the remaining aptamers are expressed in *E. coli* and processed using FACS to identify the best mutants. This procedure provides a simple method to test every possible aptamer mutant that has a similar overall sequence to that of the parent aptamer.

We used this approach to develop Broccoli, a 49-nt aptamer that exhibits bright green fluorescence upon binding DFHBI or DFHBI-1T [(Z)-4-(3,5-difluoro-4-hydroxybenzylidene)-2-methyl-1-(2,2,2-trifluoroethyl)-1H-imidazol-5(4H)-one)] (19). Similar to Spinach2, Broccoli exhibits a high folding efficiency in vitro, but it shows markedly lower magnesium dependence for folding (19). In addition, Broccoli shows increased thermostability and is substantially shorter than Spinach2. The reduced magnesium dependence contributes to a nearly twofold increase in brightness in *E. coli* and allows robust imaging of tagged RNA in mammalian cells, without requiring magnesium supplementation in media (19). Broccoli may also be more resistant to cellular ribonucleases, allowing more Broccoli to be expressed in cells and ultimately leading to the increased fluorescence responsible for its selection. Thus, a combination of desirable features can be identified using selection in live cells (19).

Interestingly, unlike Spinach2, Broccoli does not require the use of a tRNA scaffold to promote its folding in vivo. This feature is highly advantageous because the tRNA scaffold can be recognized by cellular ribonucleases, possibly leading to aptamer cleavage and thereby limiting the overall fluorescence of an aptamer (49). These facts show that aptamer selection in living cells can produce aptamers that are so well folded that they do not require folding scaffolds.

Conceivably, directed evolution can lead to new photophysical properties, such as improved photostability or altered fluorescence emission spectra. For example, one could select the aptamers based on the presence of a red-shifted emission. Thus, the directed evolution approach described above could be used to identify distinct RNA aptamers that "tune" the fluorescence emission of a fluorophore.

Directed evolution: an approach to causing evolution of a nucleic acid or protein via selecting mutants that confer specific desirable properties

Expanding the Spectral Diversity of RNA–Fluorophore Complexes Using Plug-and-Play Fluorophores

The spectral properties of Spinach and Spinach2 are determined by their fluorophore, DFHBI, which exhibits an excitation maximum at 447 nm (55). However, filters commonly used for green fluorescence in fluorescence microscopes typically illuminate cells with ~480-nm radiation. As a result, Spinach–DFHBI complexes are inefficiently excited and exhibit suboptimal brightness in typical microscopy setups. This issue was addressed by designing novel DFHBI-like fluorophores that bind Spinach but exhibit altered excitation and emission maxima (55). A structure–activity relationship analysis of DFHBI showed that altering or adding halogen substituents on the benzylidene moiety did not markedly alter the fluorescence properties of altered compounds relative to those of DFHBI, although adding substituents on the imidazolinone moiety did result in Spinach–fluorophore complexes with altered spectral properties. For example, N-1 substitutions on the imidazolinone ring, including those involving trifluoroethyl and aminoethyl substituents, resulted in red-shifted excitation and emission spectra. Specifically, DFHBI-1T bound to Spinach and exhibited a 35-nm red shift in the excitation peak and a slight red shift in the emission peak. Similar spectral properties were also observed for Broccoli–DFHBI complexes (19). As a second example, substitution at the C-2 position of the imidazolinone ring also caused marked red shifts in the fluorescence emission spectra: DFHBI-2T [(Z)-4-(3,5-difluoro-4-hydroxybenzylidene)-1-methyl-2-(trifluoromethyl)-1H-imidazol-5(4H)-one)] bound to Spinach2 and exhibited a 53-nm red shift in the excitation maximum and a 22-nm red shift in the emission maximum, although the overall brightness was somewhat reduced owing to a decrease in the quantum yield (55). The increase in K_D to ~1.2 μM suggests that the bulky trifluoromethyl moiety in DFHBI-2T may exhibit steric hindrance with the Spinach2 aptamer.

Because the spectral properties of Spinach2–DFHBI-1T more closely match those needed for commonly used filter sets, Spinach2–DFHBI-1T is efficiently excited and exhibits increased fluorescence in cells (55). In addition to improved excitation, DFHBI-1T exhibits lower background fluorescence than does DFHBI, which already exhibited low background fluorescence in cells (55).

The modified fluorophores described above not only have improved brightness during fluorescence microscopic imaging but also provide the user with an opportunity to obtain fluorescence signals that are specific for different applications. These so-called plug-and-play fluorophores can alter the spectral properties of Spinach2 by simply adding different fluorophores to the culture media, allowing the spectral properties to be adjusted based on the specific spectral needs of the experiment.

Creation of additional fluorophores may also be possible; such fluorophores might include compounds that exhibit red fluorescence. The fluorophores in various red fluorescent proteins contain substitutions at the C-2 position that extend the π-bond delocalization (12). Fluorophores containing similar modifications may be capable of binding to Spinach and exhibiting red fluorescence.

Increasing the Sensitivity of RNA Imaging

An important research goal is imaging low-abundance RNAs in cells. The RNAs that have been imaged to date are expressed at high levels and form aggregates in either the cytosol or nucleus. In many cases, however, cellular RNAs are not present in aggregates, so imaging them would not benefit from a highly localized concentration of imaging tags. To increase the sensitivity, red fluorescent RNA–fluorophore complexes can be developed. Because there is less cellular autofluorescence in the red channel, imaging using a red RNA–fluorophore complex will likely have greater sensitivity than imaging using green tags. In addition, the use of fluorophores with higher extinction coefficients and higher quantum yields will result in higher brightness and sensitivity.

Another approach to increase the sensitivity of imaging is to tag RNA molecules with cassettes containing as many as 4, 8, 16, or even more aptamer tags. An important concern with regard to this approach is to ensure that the aptamers do not hybridize with each other in the same RNA. Such hybridization could potentially occur if the strands from one aptamer interact with the complementary strand in another aptamer. Thus, judicious insertion of mutations in each aptamer could help prevent interaptamer hybridization.

STRUCTURAL BASIS FOR SPINACH FLUORESCENCE

Structure of Spinach

The crystal structure of Spinach bound to DFHBI provides insights into the mechanism of RNA-induced fluorescence activation of DFHBI (34, 65). The 2.8-Å resolution structure shows that Spinach folds into a single coaxial helical stack. This stack contains an irregular junction that comprises three stacked tetrads: two potassium-stabilized G-quartets stacked above a mixed-sequence tetrad (**Figure 4**) (65). These tetrads constitute the Spinach G-quadruplex, which is unique among G-quadruplexes in that (*a*) the guanine residues are distant in sequence, and (*b*) it lacks the parallel folding topology seen for other RNA G-quadruplexes.

The DFHBI fluorophore is fully planar when bound to Spinach and is sandwiched between the top G-quartet and a planar U-A-U base triple (**Figure 4**) (65). In addition to these interactions, Spinach also makes contacts with DFHBI on the plane of its rings. The imidazolone oxygen and nitrogens exhibit hydrogen bonding with the RNA. Similarly, the phenolate oxygen of DFHBI hydrogen bonds with the RNA and with RNA-bound water, and each of the fluorine atoms coordinates two water molecules. The negative charges of the phenolate are surrounded by seven RNA phosphates that lie within an approximately 8-Å radius. This high concentration of negative charge appears to attract diffuse cations and to bridge RNA functional groups, waters, and DFHBI. These coordinated cations likely account for the selectivity of Spinach for the anionic form of DFHBI (65).

The structure of Spinach bound to DFHBI is similar to the GFP fluorophore (34, 65) in that both fluorophores have a planar configuration, which maximizes fluorescence by maintaining π-electron conjugation across the entire fluorophore. However, Spinach and GFP differ in how they achieve fluorophore planarity: Spinach stacks planar heterocyclic bases on each face of DFHBI, whereas GFP relies on van der Waals contacts with aliphatic moieties to conformationally restrain the chromophore, thereby inducing fluorescence (51, 59). In addition, GFP utilizes buried, ionizable amino acids to interact with the fluorophore (51), whereas Spinach binds DFHBI with formally neutral moieties and cations close to the fluorophore. This binding mechanism can allow the fluorescence of Spinach to be modulated by soluble cations. Another notable difference between Spinach and GFP is that the Spinach-bound DFHBI is partially accessible to bulk solvent, unlike the deeply buried HBI fluorophore in GFP (45, 66). This solvent accessibility enables DFHBI dissociation and association, but it may also permit fluorophore quenching by oxygen or other cytosolic constituents.

G-quadruplexes may be particularly well suited to inducing the fluorescence of HBI-like fluorophores because these quadruplexes provide a highly stable, flat, hydrophobic surface that is not readily obtained by other RNA structures. For example, structures such as conventional Watson–Crick base pairs or base triples often exhibit a degree of propeller twist (13). The G-quartet can also hydrogen bond to functional groups on the edges of the fluorophore (65), and its surface is

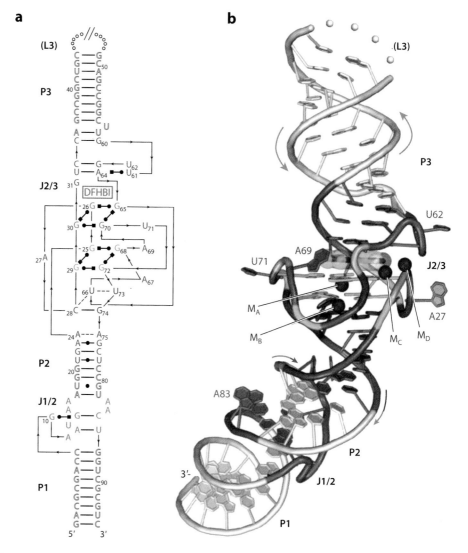

Figure 4

Structure of the Spinach–DFHBI complex. (*a*) Sequence and secondary structure of Spinach–DFHBI. The thin lines indicate chain connectivity; noncanonical base pairs are indicated with Leontis–Westhof symbols. Spinach folds into a single coaxial helical stack, which is ~110 Å long and contains three A-form duplexes (paired regions P1, P2, and P3). These duplexes are separated by two irregular junctions (J1/2 and J2/3). J2/3 forms the DFHBI binding domain, which contains a three-tetrad quadruplex comprising two G-quartets (*gold* and *cyan*) stacked above a mixed-sequence tetrad (*magenta*). The G-quartets are stabilized by two K+ ions (MA and MB in panel *b*). The DFHBI fluorophore is indicated in green. (*b*) Cartoon representation of the Spinach–DFHBI complex, color-coded as in panel *a*. The G-quartet that forms the base of the DFHBI binding pocket is indicated in gold. Purple spheres (labeled MA through MD) represent K+ ions. Figure adapted with permission from Warner et al. (2014). *Nature Structural & Molecular Biology* 21:658–63, copyright 2014 by Macmillan Publishers, Ltd. Abbreviation: DFHBI, (Z)-4-(3,5-difluoro-4-hydroxybenzylidene)-1,2-dimethyl-1H-imidazol-5(4H)-one.

large enough to accommodate both DFHBI and other RNA moieties on the same plane, allowing additional coplanar interactions with the fluorophore (65).

Possible Mechanisms of Improved DFHBI Quantum Yield after Spinach Binding

One important question in understanding the photophysics of the Spinach–DFHBI complex is as follows: How does Spinach bind to DFHBI and increase its quantum yield? At first glance, Spinach seems to enhance the behavior of DFHBI simply by binding to it and inhibiting isomerization around the methylene double bond. Indeed, the geometric restriction of DFHBI in a planar form between two planes composed of a G-quadruplex and a base triple can be an obvious explanation. It is also possible, however, that this simple packing constraint cannot account for the entire increase in quantum yield.

For example, the low quantum yield of DFHBI in the unbound state could result from relaxation from rotations around the bridging carbon bonds between two rings, but it could also result from nonradiative internal conversions from phenyl torsion or rotation around the imidazolinone bond or even excited-state intersystem crossing relaxation to the triplet state. In addition, when in the bound state, the charged RNA environment and hydrogen bonding interactions with the Spinach nucleic acids may alternately stabilize or destabilize the excited state of DFHBI and alternate the energy barrier during torsion or rotation around the bridging bond. Indeed, either a nearby negative charge around the electron acceptor or a nearby positive charge (e.g., Mg^{2+}) around the chromophore ring can decrease the electron transfer rate by destabilizing the charge transfer state, thus increasing the quantum yield. Excited-state decay measurements, including those generated by ultrafast fluorescence upconversion, polarization spectroscopy, and transient absorption spectroscopy, can be very useful for determining which mechanism dominates the suppression of nonradiative decay of the Spinach–DFHBI complex, as can calculations based on quantum chemical information, as evidenced in studies of GFP.

Understanding the Photobleaching Properties of Spinach

The Spinach–DFHBI complex displays relatively fast fluorescence decay under continuous large-dose light irradiation (27, 64), which partially limits its application for imaging low-abundance RNA. In contrast to the irreversible photobleaching mechanism of GFP, however, the decreased fluorescence intensity of the Spinach–DFHBI complex seems more likely to stem from a reversible photoconversion to a less-fluorescent state. Two different groups (27, 64) have proposed that the photoinduced *cis–trans* isomerization of DFHBI may account for this behavior.

The first of these groups, Wang et al. (64), reported that under blue light irradiation, DFHBI undergoes *cis–trans* photoisomerization, and compared with the more fluorescent Spinach–*cis*-DFHBI complex, the Spinach–*trans*-DFHBI complex is threefold less stable and one-third dimmer. To improve the signal-to-background contrast during long-term imaging, an optical lock-in detection (OLID) scheme was proposed for imaging Spinach-based probes (64). Han et al. (27) further argued that the fast *cis–trans* photoisomerization induces fast unbinding of the DFHBI from Spinach, and a new ground-state DFHBI can again bind with Spinach to recover the fluorescence. This argument was supported by the strong dependence of the fluorescence recovery rate on the DFHBI concentration. As a result, a pulsed illumination scheme, instead of a regular continuous-wave illumination scheme, was proposed to help retain the high fluorescence signal of the Spinach–DFHBI complex, and the time between pulses was chosen to allow fresh DFHBI to bind and recover the fluorescence (27).

Even though these schemes improve the performance of Spinach-based probes during imaging, the use of new RNA–fluorophore complexes that have higher photostability will simplify imaging.

Increased photostability may be achieved by RNA aptamers that more efficiently suppress light-induced fluorophore dissociation or fluorophore isomerization. Photostability will be especially important for applications that require high-intensity irradiation, such as in single-molecule or superresolution imaging.

USING SPINACH AND RELATED APTAMERS FOR IMAGING RNA IN LIVE CELLS

Spinach, Spinach2, and Broccoli can be used to tag RNAs for live-cell imaging in a manner analogous to the use of GFP-fusion proteins. In addition to expression in *E. coli* (46, 50, 54, 63), several RNAs have been expressed as fusion RNAs and imaged in mammalian cells, including 5S, a small ncRNA transcribed by RNA polymerase III that associates with the large ribosomal subunit (46); 7SK, an ncRNA that associates with transcription complexes; and CGG-repeat RNAs, which are linked to fragile X–associated tremor and ataxia syndrome (FXTAS) (57). In each case, fluorescence was not detectable in cells expressing a control RNA, whereas fluorescence was detected in cells expressing the imaging tag (57). In the case of 5S RNA, 5S–Spinach and 5S–Broccoli RNA fluorescence was detected throughout cells, with prominent fluorescence signals appearing as diffuse nuclear and cytosolic puncta (46). Fluorescence is particularly easy to detect after sucrose treatment, which leads to the formation of 5S RNA aggregates in the cytosol. These aggregates appear as distinctive puncta (46), and their distribution patterns are similar to those seen for endogenous 5S RNA in the same cell type (48). These data indicate that 5S–Spinach and 5S–Broccoli RNA fusions can be imaged in cells, including in the nucleus, and exhibit localizations consistent with endogenous RNA. Furthermore, the presence of the tag did not appear to affect the localization of the RNA for the RNAs tested (46, 57).

In contrast to eGFP, fluorescence is readily obtained after the Spinach RNA is synthesized, possibly ensuring that there are minimal temporal delays between RNA expression and RNA detection in living cells. Indeed, these tags can be used to image promoter activity using a FACS-based screen (19).

Several factors need to be considered when imaging RNA using Spinach in living cells. Imaging temperature could potentially influence fluorescence in living cells. Similarly, ion content in cells could affect imaging. Most RNAs are only able to achieve a folded structure at certain magnesium concentrations (10). Both Spinach and Spinach2 exhibit some magnesium dependence, and imaging is improved by adding exogenous magnesium to the culture media, which is expected to increase intracellular magnesium concentration. However, cells that exhibit low magnesium concentrations, or those that exhibit fluctuations in magnesium concentrations, could potentially influence the overall brightness or folding of Spinach. Broccoli exhibits reduced sensitivity to magnesium and is more thermostable than Spinach or Spinach 2, so this aptamer may be useful for overcoming the issues described above (19).

Another important consideration is aptamer folding. RNA aptamers are highly sensitive to adjacent sequences (39). Compared with Spinach, both Spinach2 and Broccoli show improved folding in diverse sequence contexts (19, 57). However, it is important to determine empirically whether the aptamer can fold properly when inserted into a target RNA. Therefore, an aptamer-tagged RNA should be synthesized in vitro before being expressed in living cells, and its molar fluorescence should be compared with that of a solution of the aptamer at the same concentration. These experiments should be performed in buffers that contain cytosolic ion concentrations. RNAs should only be expressed in living cells if the tagged RNA exhibits the expected fluorescence in solution. The development of so-called insulator sequences that provide a space between the target RNA and aptamers could also potentially reduce effects of the host RNA on aptamer folding.

Conceivably, aptamer insertion could also affect RNA stability; polyadenylation signals; or the function of microRNAs, which are typically located near the 3′ end of the transcript (24). Thus, it may be important to compare the properties of the tagged RNA with those of the endogenous RNA to ensure the physiologic properties and functions of the host RNA are retained.

FUTURE DIRECTIONS

Developing New Fluorescence Complexes Based On Non-HBI Fluorophores

Studies have demonstrated that HBI-like fluorophores are powerful imaging tools when complexed with RNA aptamers such as Spinach or Broccoli. The issue of whether fluorophore structures other than those in the HBI family can undergo similar conditional fluorescence and be useful for imaging RNA in cells remains an open one. Dolgosheina et al. (17) recently reported the selection of an RNA aptamer, called RNA Mango, that binds thiazole orange derivatives with low-nanomolar binding affinity. After binding, the fluorescence signal increased by 1,100-fold (17). The thiazole orange dye is well known to exhibit high cellular background fluorescence due to nonspecific binding with cellular DNA and RNA, and it exhibits rapid photobleaching (53). However, the high binding affinity of RNA Mango can partially enhance the signal-to-noise ratio when imaging, as only small amount of dye is needed. Future studies can address whether Mango can be used as a tag for genetically encoding fluorescent RNA in living cells.

The most promising compounds for RNA-dependent activation are a group of fluorophores that have been named molecular rotors. When in the excited state, these compounds undergo a twisting motion that leads to extremely low-fluorescence quantum yields (25). Interestingly, the twisted-state relaxation rates (and thus the fluorescence intensities) of these molecules have been known to depend strongly on qualities of the local environment, such as viscosity or polarity (25). Structurally, these molecular rotors consist of an electron donor and an acceptor linked by π conjugation. Example molecules include triphenylmethane (e.g., malachite green); p-N,N-(dimethylamino)benzonitrile (DMABN)-related structures (e.g., stilbenes); and [p-(dialkylamino)benzylidene]malononitrile (DBMN)-related structures (e.g., thioflavin T) (58). RNA aptamers could sterically inhibit the twisting motion or could tune the intramolecular charge transfer efficiency of the fluorophore between the twisted and local state. As a result, the excited twisted state would be unfavorable, leading to more radiative relaxation and thus enhanced quantum yield.

As mentioned above, unbound DFHBI displays very low cellular background fluorescence. However, low cellular background fluorescence is not seen with most other fluorophores, such as stilbene, triphenylmethane and cyanine dyes (23, 38). Indeed, even though aptamers that bind and activate the fluorescence of malachite green have been described (3), the high cellular background of this dye, as well as its ability to produce cytotoxic oxygen radicals, has limited the utility of these aptamers. The background fluorescence can be explained by partitioning into viscous membrane bilayers or nonspecific binding to cellular compounds. Background fluorescence due to nonspecific binding of thiazole orange to DNA was recently reduced by introducing a nitrile moiety that made the thiazole orange dye adopt a nonplanar configuration (53). Careful manipulation of fluorophore structures to minimize cellular interactions will be needed to ensure that new fluorophores used in RNA–fluorophore complexes have low background fluorescence.

Application of RNA–Fluorophore Complexes for Superresolution Imaging

Imaging RNA at high resolution in living cells is critical for obtaining insight into the functions of different RNA-based structures. Many of these RNA structures, such as PML bodies, polycomb bodies, Cajal bodies, and speckles, among others, are 1 μm or smaller in size (56), however, making it difficult to accurately resolve their shape and size using regular imaging techniques.

Superresolution imaging techniques to circumvent the classical diffraction-limited resolution barrier in light microscopy have been recently developed. These techniques can provide information on, for example, the localization and structural information of GFP-labeled proteins at a resolution of 10 nm, compared with a resolution of ~400 nm for epifluorescence microscopy (28). Fluorescent proteins have been applied in superresolution techniques such as stimulated emission depletion (STED) microscopy, and reversibly photoactivatable fluorescent proteins have been used to image protein structures with resolutions of less than 40 nm in photoactivated localization microscopy (PALM), stochastic optical reconstruction microscopy (STORM), and reversible saturable optically linear fluorescence transition (RESOLFT) microscopy (31, 33).

Superresolution imaging of RNA will require the RNA–fluorophore complexes to have several characteristics. Both high fluorescence brightness and high photostability during the on state are needed to generate enough photons to allow precise localization of single molecules. The reversible binding between RNAs and fluorophores can potentially provide the basis for the reversible transition between a fluorescent state and a dark state, thus breaking the diffraction barrier of imaging as used in STORM. RNAs bind and unbind fluorophores at specific k_{on} and k_{off} rates. The blinking rates of the photodeactivation (k_{off}) and the photoactivation (k_{on}) events should be balanced such that at a specific time, only a small portion of molecules are in the on state. In addition, the development of photoactivatable RNA–fluorophore complexes can be another important step in advancing RESOLFT-like superresolution RNA imaging. Considering the existence of several HBI fluorophore-based photoactivatable FPs, RNA–fluorophore complexes with similar photoactivation abilities can likely be developed. Indeed, as mentioned above, the observation of the fast, light-induced *cis–trans* isomerization of DFHBI indicates that the Spinach–DFHBI complex could potentially be evolved to be reversibly photoactivatable.

SUMMARY POINTS

1. RNAs have highly complex and dynamic cellular localization patterns. RNA imaging in living cells is important for determining the function and regulation of both noncoding and coding RNAs.

2. Genetic encoding markedly simplifies RNA imaging. Although useful, current GFP–MS2 or split GFP–based RNA imaging methods have potential challenges that could limit their applications.

3. RNA imaging can be realized by tagging with an RNA aptamer sequence that activates the fluorescence of a fluorophore. These fluorophores should be bioorthogonal and exhibit fluorescence only when specifically bound to the aptamer.

4. RNA aptamers can bind and switch on the fluorescence of small-molecule derivatives of the GFP fluorophore, HBI. An RNA aptamer that activates the fluorescence of a fluorophore similar to the one in eGFP, DFHBI, was named Spinach.

5. Newer RNA–fluorophore complexes, such as Spinach2 and Broccoli, have been generated and have improved folding and cell compatibility. So-called plug-and-play fluorophores allow the spectral properties of Spinach2 and Broccoli to be adjusted on the basis of experimental needs.

6. The crystal structure of Spinach bound to DFHBI reveals that fluorescence is achieved by forcing DFHBI planarity via sandwiching it between a G-quadruplex and a planar U-A-U base triple.

7. Spinach, Spinach2, and Broccoli can be used to tag RNAs for live-cell imaging. Several RNAs including 5S, 7SK, and CGG-repeat RNAs have been expressed and imaged in mammalian cells.

FUTURE ISSUES

1. Why does the Spinach-based complex display fast fluorescence decay under high-intensity light irradiation? How can its photostability be improved? How can new photostable RNA–fluorophore complexes be evolved?

2. Can new RNA–fluorophore complexes be generated to exhibit highly efficient red fluorescence, similar to what is seen with red fluorescent proteins?

3. How can the cellular behavior of RNA–fluorophore complexes be further improved to achieve high expression levels, efficient folding, and high stability?

4. Can the brightness and cellular performance of these aptamer tags be improved to image single RNA molecules in vivo?

5. Can fluorophores that are not based on HBI be developed, and what properties can these fluorophores confer to improve RNA imaging?

6. Can RNA–fluorophore complexes be developed that achieve the special requirements needed for superresolution imaging?

DISCLOSURE STATEMENT

Samie R. Jaffrey is a cofounder of Lucerna Technologies and is an author of patent applications related to Spinach and related aptamers. M.Y. is not aware of any affiliations, memberships, funding, or financial holdings that might be perceived as affecting the objectivity of this review.

ACKNOWLEDGMENTS

We thank members of the Jaffrey lab for helpful comments and suggestions. This work was supported by National Institutes of Health grants to S.R.J. (R01 NS064516 and R01 EB010249).

LITERATURE CITED

1. Anderson P, Kedersha N. 2002. Visibly stressed: the role of eIF2, TIA-1, and stress granules in protein translation. *Cell Stress Chaperones* 7:213–21
2. Aravin A, Gaidatzis D, Pfeffer S, Lagos-Quintana M, Landgraf P, et al. 2006. A novel class of small RNAs bind to MILI protein in mouse testes. *Nature* 442:203–7
3. Babendure JR, Adams SR, Tsien RY. 2003. Aptamers switch on fluorescence of triphenylmethane dyes. *J. Am. Chem. Soc.* 125:14716–17
4. Baffour-Awuah NA, Zimmer M. 2004. Hula-twisting in green fluorescent protein. *Chem. Phys.* 303:7–11

5. Bagni C, Greenough WT. 2005. From mRNP trafficking to spine dysmorphogenesis: the roots of fragile X syndrome. *Nat. Rev. Neurosci.* 6:376–87

6. Batista PJ, Chang HY. 2013. Long noncoding RNAs: cellular address codes in development and disease. *Cell* 152:1298–307

7. Beermann AE, Jay DG. 1994. Chromophore-assisted laser inactivation of cellular proteins. *Methods Cell Biol.* 44:715–32

8. Bertrand E, Chartrand P, Schaefer M, Shenoy SM, Singer RH, Long RM. 1998. Localization of ASH1 mRNA particles in living yeast. *Mol. Cell* 2:437–45

9. Bokman SH, Ward WW. 1981. Renaturation of *Aequorea* green-fluorescent protein. *Biochem. Biophys. Res. Commun.* 101:1372–80

10. Brion P, Westhof E. 1997. Hierarchy and dynamics of RNA folding. *Annu. Rev. Biophys. Biomol. Struct.* 26:113–37

11. Carlile TM, Rojas-Duran MF, Zinshteyn B, Shin H, Bartoli KM, Gilbert WV. 2014. Pseudouridine profiling reveals regulated mRNA pseudouridylation in yeast and human cells. *Nature* 515:143–46

12. Chudakov DM, Matz MV, Lukyanov S, Lukyanov KA. 2010. Fluorescent proteins and their applications in imaging living cells and tissues. *Physiol. Rev.* 90:1103–63

13. Clore GM, Gronenborn AM. 1985. Probing the three-dimensional structures of DNA and RNA oligonucleotides in solution by nuclear Overhauser enhancement measurements. *FEBS Lett.* 179:187–98

14. Cody CW, Prasher DC, Westler WM, Prendergast FG, Ward WW. 1993. Chemical structure of the hexapeptide chromophore of the *Aequorea* green-fluorescent protein. *Biochemistry* 32:1212–18

15. De S, Girigoswami A, Mandal S. 2002. Enhanced fluorescence of triphenylmethane dyes in aqueous surfactant solutions at supramicellar concentrations—effect of added electrolyte. *Spectrochim. Acta A* 58:2547–55

16. Derrien T, Johnson R, Bussotti G, Tanzer A, Djebali S, et al. 2012. The GENCODE v7 catalog of human long noncoding RNAs: analysis of their gene structure, evolution, and expression. *Genome Res.* 22:1775–89

17. Dolgosheina EV, Jeng SCY, Panchapakesan SSS, Cojocaru R, Chen PSK, et al. 2014. RNA Mango aptamer-fluorophore: a bright, high-affinity complex for RNA labeling and tracking. *ACS Chem. Biol.* 9:2412–20

18. Famulok M, Mayer G, Blind M. 2000. Nucleic acid aptamers—from selection in vitro to applications in vivo. *Acc. Chem. Res.* 33:591–99

19. Filonov GS, Moon JD, Svensen N, Jaffrey SR. 2014. Broccoli: rapid selection of an RNA mimic of green fluorescent protein by fluorescence-based selection and directed evolution. *J. Am. Chem. Soc.* 136:16299–308

20. Gold L, Polisky B, Uhlenbeck O, Yarus M. 1995. Diversity of oligonucleotide functions. *Annu. Rev. Biochem.* 64:763–97

21. Grate D, Wilson C. 1999. Laser-mediated, site-specific inactivation of RNA transcripts. *PNAS* 96:6131–36

22. Green R, Ellington AD, Szostak JW. 1990. In vitro genetic analysis of the *Tetrahymena* self-splicing intron. *Nature* 347:406–8

23. Guidry G. 1999. A method for counterstaining tissues in conjunction with the glyoxylic acid condensation reaction for detection of biogenic amines. *J. Histochem. Cytochem.* 47:261–64

24. Hafner M, Landthaler M, Burger L, Khorshid M, Hausser J, et al. 2010. Transcriptome-wide identification of RNA-binding protein and microRNA target sites by PAR-CLIP. *Cell* 141:129–41

25. Haidekker MA, Theodorakis EA. 2010. Environment-sensitive behavior of fluorescent molecular rotors. *J. Biol. Eng.* 4:11

26. Han J, Kim D, Morris KV. 2007. Promoter-associated RNA is required for RNA-directed transcriptional gene silencing in human cells. *PNAS* 104:12422–27

27. Han KY, Leslie BJ, Fei J, Zhang J, Ha T. 2013. Understanding the photophysics of the Spinach–DFHBI RNA aptamer–fluorogen complex to improve live-cell RNA imaging. *J. Am. Chem. Soc.* 135:19033–38

28. Hell SW. 2009. Microscopy and its focal switch. *Nat. Methods* 6:24–32

29. Hesselberth JR, Miller D, Robertus J, Ellington AD. 2000. In vitro selection of RNA molecules that inhibit the activity of ricin A-chain. *J. Biol. Chem.* 275:4937–42

19. Describes directed evolution of RNA–fluorophore complexes and the generation of Broccoli.

27. Describes a photophysical study of the photobleaching and photoconversion of the Spinach–DFHBI complex.

30. Hocine S, Raymond P, Zenklusen D, Chao JA, Singer RH. 2013. Single-molecule analysis of gene expression using two-color RNA labeling in live yeast. *Nat. Methods* 10:119–21

31. Hofmann M, Eggeling C, Jakobs S, Hell SW. 2005. Breaking the diffraction barrier in fluorescence microscopy at low light intensities by using reversibly photoswitchable proteins. *PNAS* 102:17565–69

32. Holeman LA, Robinson SL, Szostak JW, Wilson C. 1998. Isolation and characterization of fluorophore-binding RNA aptamers. *Fold. Des.* 3:423–31

33. Huang B, Bates M, Zhuang X. 2009. Super-resolution fluorescence microscopy. *Annu. Rev. Biochem.* 78:993–1016

34. Huang H, Suslov NB, Li NS, Shelke SA, Evans ME, et al. 2014. A G-quadruplex-containing RNA activates fluorescence in a GFP-like fluorophore. *Nat. Chem. Biol.* 10:686–91

35. Kiebler MA, Bassell GJ. 2006. Neuronal RNA granules: movers and makers. *Neuron* 51:685–90

36. Kojima S, Ohkawa H, Hirano T, Maki S, Niwa H, et al. 1998. Fluorescent properties of model chromophores of tyrosine-66 substituted mutants of *Aequorea* green fluorescent protein (GFP). *Tetrahedron Lett.* 39:5239–42

37. Kummer AD, Kompa C, Lossau H, Pollinger-Dammer F, Michel-Beyerle ME, et al. 1998. Dramatic reduction in fluorescence quantum yield in mutants of Green Fluorescent Protein due to fast internal conversion. *Chem. Phys.* 237:183–93

38. Likhtenshtein GI, Bishara R, Papper V, Uzan B, Fishov I, et al. 1996. Novel fluorescence-photochrome labeling method in the study of biomembrane dynamics. *J. Biochem. Biophys. Methods* 33:117–33

39. Martell RE, Nevins JR, Sullenger BA. 2002. Optimizing aptamer activity for gene therapy applications using expression cassette SELEX. *Mol. Ther.* 6:30–34

40. Meech SR. 2009. Excited state reactions in fluorescent proteins. *Chem. Soc. Rev.* 38:2922–34

41. Merzlyak EM, Goedhart J, Shcherbo D, Bulina ME, Shcheglov AS, et al. 2007. Bright monomeric red fluorescent protein with an extended fluorescence lifetime. *Nat. Methods* 4:555–57

42. Meyer KD, Saletore Y, Zumbo P, Elemento O, Mason CE, Jaffrey SR. 2012. Comprehensive analysis of mRNA methylation reveals enrichment in 3′ UTRs and near stop codons. *Cell* 149:1635–46

43. Mhlanga MM, Tyagi S. 2006. Using tRNA-linked molecular beacons to image cytoplasmic mRNAs in live cells. *Nat. Protoc.* 1:1392–98

44. Niwa H, Inouye S, Hirano T, Matsuno T, Kojima S, et al. 1996. Chemical nature of the light emitter of the *Aequorea* green fluorescent protein. *PNAS* 93:13617–22

45. Ormö M, Cubitt AB, Kallio K, Gross LA, Tsien RY, Remington SJ. 1996. Crystal structure of the *Aequorea victoria* green fluorescent protein. *Science* 273:1392–95

46. Paige JS, Wu KY, Jaffrey SR. 2011. RNA mimics of green fluorescent protein. *Science* 333:642–46

47. Parker R, Song H. 2004. The enzymes and control of eukaryotic mRNA turnover. *Nat. Struct. Mol. Biol.* 11:121–27

48. Paul CP, Good PD, Li SXL, Kleihauer A, Rossi JJ, Engelke DR. 2003. Localized expression of small RNA inhibitors in human cells. *Mol. Ther.* 7:237–47

49. Ponchon L, Dardel F. 2007. Recombinant RNA technology: the tRNA scaffold. *Nat. Methods* 4:571–76

50. Pothoulakis G, Ceroni F, Reeve B, Ellis T. 2013. The Spinach RNA aptamer as a characterization tool for synthetic biology. *ACS Synth. Biol.* 3:182–87

51. Remington SJ. 2011. Green fluorescent protein: a perspective. *Protein Sci.* 20:1509–19

52. Sando S, Narita A, Hayami M, Aoyama Y. 2008. Transcription monitoring using fused RNA with a dye-binding light-up aptamer as a tag: a blue fluorescent RNA. *Chem. Commun.* 33:3858–60

53. Shank NI, Pham HH, Waggoner AS, Armitage BA. 2013. Twisted cyanines: a non-planar fluorogenic dye with superior photostability and its use in a protein-based fluoromodule. *J. Am. Chem. Soc.* 135:242–51

54. Shu D, Khisamutdinov EF, Zhang L, Guo P. 2014. Programmable folding of fusion RNA in vivo and in vitro driven by pRNA 3WJ motif of phi29 DNA packaging motor. *Nucleic Acids Res.* 42:e10

55. Song W, Strack RL, Svensen N, Jaffrey SR. 2014. Plug-and-play fluorophores extend the spectral properties of Spinach. *J. Am. Chem. Soc.* 136:1198–201

56. Spector DL, Lamond AI. 2011. Nuclear speckles. *Cold Spring Harb. Perspect. Biol.* 3:a000646

34. Describes the crystal structure of the Spinach–DFHBI complex and provides insights into the mechanism of fluorescence activation (see also Reference 65).

46. Describes the initial generation of Spinach for RNA imaging.

57. Describes the
generation of Spinach2,
a Spinach variant with
improved folding and
imaging properties.

57. **Strack RL, Disney MD, Jaffrey SR. 2013. A superfolding Spinach2 reveals the dynamic nature of trinucleotide repeat RNA. *Nat. Methods* 10:1219–24**

58. Stsiapura VI, Maskevich AA, Kuzmitsky VA, Uversky VN, Kuznetsova IM, Turoverov KK. 2008. Thioflavin T as a molecular rotor: fluorescent properties of thioflavin T in solvents with different viscosity. *J. Phys. Chem. B* 112:15893–902

59. Tsien RY. 1998. The green fluorescent protein. *Annu. Rev. Biochem.* 67:509–44

60. Tyagi S. 2009. Imaging intracellular RNA distribution and dynamics in living cells. *Nat. Methods* 6:331–38

61. Tyagi S, Alsmadi O. 2004. Imaging native β-actin mRNA in motile fibroblasts. *Biophys. J.* 87:4153–62

62. Valencia-Burton M, McCullough RM, Cantor CR, Broude NE. 2007. RNA visualization in live bacterial cells using fluorescent protein complementation. *Nat. Methods* 4:421–27

63. van Nies P, Nourian Z, Kok M, van Wijk R, Moeskops J, et al. 2013. Unbiased tracking of the progression of mRNA and protein synthesis in bulk and in liposome-confined reactions. *ChemBioChem* 14:1963–66

64. Wang P, Querard J, Maurin S, Nath SS, Le Saux T, et al. 2013. Photochemical properties of Spinach and its use in selective imaging. *Chem. Sci.* 4:2865–73

65. Warner KD, Chen MC, Song W, Strack RL, Thorn A, et al. 2014. Structural basis for activity of highly efficient RNA mimics of green fluorescent protein. *Nat. Struct. Mol. Biol.* 21:658–63

66. Yang F, Moss LG, Phillips GN Jr. 1996. The molecular structure of green fluorescent protein. *Nat. Biotechnol.* 14:1246–51

67. Zhang X, Potty AS, Jackson GW, Stepanov V, Tang A, et al. 2009. Engineered 5S ribosomal RNAs displaying aptamers recognizing vascular endothelial growth factor and malachite green. *J. Mol. Recognit.* 22:154–61

Regulation of Rad6/Rad18 Activity During DNA Damage Tolerance

Mark Hedglin and Stephen J. Benkovic

Department of Chemistry, The Pennsylvania State University, University Park, Pennsylvania 16802; email: muh218@psu.edu, sjb1@psu.edu

Annu. Rev. Biophys. 2015. 44:207–28

The *Annual Review of Biophysics* is online at biophys.annualreviews.org

This article's doi: 10.1146/annurev-biophys-060414-033841

Keywords

DNA damage, PCNA, Rad6/Rad18, ubiquitin, DNA damage tolerance

Abstract

Replicative polymerases (pols) cannot accommodate damaged template bases, and these pols stall when such offenses are encountered during S phase. Rather than repairing the damaged base, replication past it may proceed via one of two DNA damage tolerance (DDT) pathways, allowing replicative DNA synthesis to resume. In translesion DNA synthesis (TLS), a specialized TLS pol is recruited to catalyze stable, yet often erroneous, nucleotide incorporation opposite damaged template bases. In template switching, the newly synthesized sister strand is used as a damage-free template to synthesize past the lesion. In eukaryotes, both pathways are regulated by the conjugation of ubiquitin to the PCNA sliding clamp by distinct E2/E3 pairs. Whereas monoubiquitination by Rad6/Rad18 mediates TLS, extension of this ubiquitin to a polyubiquitin chain by Ubc13–Mms2/Rad5 routes DDT to the template switching pathway. In this review, we focus on the monoubiquitination of PCNA by Rad6/Rad18 and summarize the current knowledge of how this process is regulated.

Contents

INTRODUCTION

Replicative polymerases (pols) have very stringent polymerase and proofreading domains and, thus, cannot accommodate damaged template bases. Consequently, progression of replication forks is stalled when such offenses are encountered during S phase. Failure to restart replication often results in double-strand breaks (DSBs) that may lead to gross chromosomal rearrangements, cell-cycle arrest, and cell death. Therefore, it is often more advantageous to circumvent such replicative arrests and to postpone repair of the offending damage in order to complete the cell cycle and maintain cell survival (1, 21, 34, 64–66, 100, 103, 128). Such a process, referred to as DNA damage tolerance (DDT), may be carried out either by translesion DNA synthesis (TLS) or by template switching. In TLS, the replicative pol is replaced with a specialized TLS pol that is able to catalyze stable, yet often erroneous, nucleotide incorporation opposite damaged templates, allowing replication to proceed (64, 100, 103, 128). In template switching, enzyme-catalyzed regression of the replication fork creates a chicken-foot structure in which the original template strands are reannealed, and the stalled primer terminus utilizes the newly synthesized sister strand as a damage-free template. Subsequent reversal of the chicken-foot structure reconstitutes the replication fork at a point beyond the damage, bypassing the block in an error-free manner. Both pathways have been observed in organisms ranging from bacteria, such as *Escherichia coli*, to humans, and many components of these pathways are well conserved (64, 100, 103, 122, 128). A major difference between DDT in eukaryotes and prokaryotes, however, is the use of the ubiquitin conjugation system as a regulatory mechanism (34, 122).

Ubiquitin is a small protein that is present exclusively in eukaryotes and that may be covalently attached to a target protein through an enzyme cascade. The E1 ubiquitin-activating enzyme activates ubiquitin and transfers it to an E2 ubiquitin-conjugating enzyme (Ubc), which catalyzes formation of an isopeptide bond between ubiquitin and a lysine residue on a target protein. An

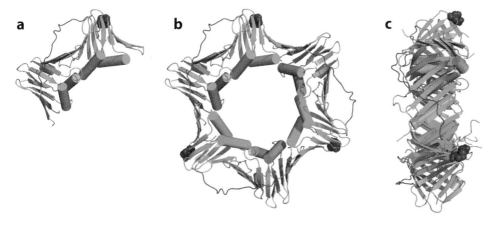

Figure 1

Structure of human proliferating cell nuclear antigen (PCNA). Model of PCNA generated using PyMOL (PDB ID: 1AXC) and shown in cartoon form. (*a*) The PCNA monomer consists of two independent domains, shown in gray (N-terminal) and green (C-terminal), joined by an interdomain connecting loop (IDCL), shown in magenta. Lysine residue 164 (K164) is shown as red spheres. Panels *b* and *c* show the front and side views of the PCNA trimer, respectively. The three PCNA monomers are arranged in a head-to-tail manner, resulting in structurally distinct faces. The face from which the C-termini protrude is referred to as the "C-terminal face" or "front side," and is highlighted in panel *b*. The side view of the PCNA trimer shown in panel *c* highlights the distinct differences between the two faces of PCNA. The "C-terminal face" or "front side" of PCNA shown on the left contains the IDCLs and interacts with replicative polymerases during normal DNA replication. K164, which is monoubiquitinated by Rad6/Rad18 in response to replication-blocking lesions, is on the opposite face; this face is referred to as the "back side" of PCNA.

E3 ubiquitin ligase can bind an E2 enzyme and a target protein simultaneously, mediating the specificity of this process (29). In response to sublethal doses of DNA-damaging agents that cause replication-blocking lesions, ubiquitin is conjugated to lysine residue 164 (K164) of a proliferating cell nuclear antigen (PCNA) monomer. No such modification occurs in untreated cells during S phase. Furthermore, the number of ubiquitins conjugated to PCNA by distinct E2/E3 pairs orchestrates DDT: Conjugation of a single ubiquitin by the Rad6/Rad18 pair mediates the TLS pathway, whereas extension of this ubiquitin to a polyubiquitin chain by Ubc13–Mms2/Rad5 diverts DDT to the template switching pathway (47). Over the past decade or so, researchers have invested much effort into delineating how the conjugation of ubiquitin to PCNA is regulated and how this posttranslational modification (PTM) orchestrates DDT. In this review, we focus on the monoubiquitination of PCNA by Rad6/Rad18 and the regulation of this process. We begin with a brief overview of the eukaryotic replisome.

THE EUKARYOTIC REPLISOME

Replicative DNA pols alone are distributive and achieve their characteristic high processivity by anchoring to ring-shaped sliding clamps that encircle double-stranded DNA (dsDNA) and slide freely along it. The eukaryotic sliding clamp, PCNA (**Figure 1**), has two structurally distinct faces and is a trimer of identical subunits. Each subunit consists of two independent domains joined by an interdomain connecting loop (IDCL). The C-terminal face of PCNA contains all C-termini and IDCLs and is a platform for interaction with the eukaryotic replicative pols, pol ε and pol δ (45). Specifically, the well-conserved PCNA-interacting peptide (PIP) box within replicative pols makes extensive contact with the IDCLs of PCNA (15). Orchestration of DNA

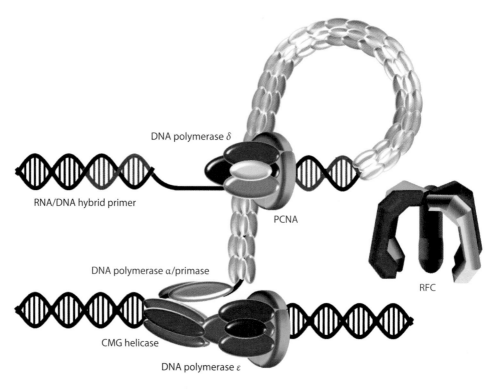

DNA polymerase δ

RNA/DNA hybrid primer

PCNA

DNA polymerase α/primase

RFC

CMG helicase

DNA polymerase ε

Figure 2

Model of the eukaryotic replisome shown in cartoon form. The leading and lagging strand replicative DNA polymerases (ε and δ, respectively), sliding clamp [proliferating cell nuclear antigen (PCNA)], clamp loader complex [replication factor C (RFC)], holo-helicase complex [Cdc45, Mcm2–7, GINS (CMG) helicase], primase complex (DNA polymerase α/primase), and single-stranded DNA–binding protein [replication protein A (RPA)] are involved in the formation of the eukaryotic replisome at each replication fork. The primase complex primes the lagging strand DNA generated via unwinding of the duplex DNA by CMG helicase. The RNA/DNA hybrid primers (*red*) are recognized by the RFC clamp loader, which subsequently loads PCNA onto the 3′ end of the primer. The replicative polymerases anchor to PCNA at the 3′ hydroxyl termini of the primer strands and extend them in the 5′ to 3′ direction. The single-stranded DNA generated during CMG helicase unwinding is coated with RPA.

replication also involves many accessory proteins, each of which has a unique role in enhancing the efficiency of this highly complex process. Together, PCNA, the replicative DNA pols, and these accessory proteins (discussed below) compose the replisome, which is responsible for the rapid and accurate replication of genomic DNA (**Figure 2**).

At each origin of replication, two replicative DNA helicases are loaded onto the DNA, one on each strand, and they utilize ATP to unwind dsDNA. In eukaryotes, the core of the replicative DNA helicase comprises the Mcm2–7 proteins, and it is loaded onto DNA in an inactive form. Subsequent activation occurs by the recruitment of the Cdc45 and GINS accessory proteins, forming the holo-helicase referred to as CMG (Cdc45, Mcm2–7, GINS). In contrast to most helicases, CMG translocates with a 3′–5′ polarity and, hence, tracks along the leading strand of the DNA (12, 80, 115). Upon unwinding of dsDNA by CMG, the single-stranded DNA (ssDNA) templates are bound by replication protein A (RPA), protecting them from cellular nucleases and preventing formation of alternative DNA structures (7, 131). The bifunctional DNA pol α/primase complex then synthesizes short, complementary RNA/DNA hybrid primers on the ssDNA templates for each Okazaki fragment and replication origin (33, 63, 97, 111, 142, 143). These hybrid primers are recognized by replication factor C (RFC), the clamp loader complex in eukaryotes. RFC utilizes ATP binding and hydrolysis to open PCNA rings and place them around the 3′ end of primer/template (P/T) junctions such that the C-terminal face of PCNA is oriented toward the terminal 3′ hydroxyl end of the hybrid primer, where DNA synthesis will initiate. Hence, the C-terminal face of PCNA is often referred to as its "front side" (45). For comparison, the highly conserved K164 residue is located on the opposite face, i.e., the "back side" of PCNA (**Figure 1**) (32). Replicative pols then bind to the front side of PCNA encircling DNA, completing formation of the replisome. Specifically, the CMG helicase selects and stabilizes DNA pol ε on the leading strand while DNA pol δ utilizes the hybrid primers synthesized every 100–250 nucleotides by the DNA pol α/primase complex on the lagging strand (38, 111) (**Figure 2**).

RAD6/RAD18 CONJUGATES UBIQUITIN TO PCNA ENCIRCLING A BLOCKED PRIMER/TEMPLATE JUNCTION

During normal DNA replication, the activities of the helicase and the replicative pols are tightly coupled, such that the amount of RPA-coated ssDNA is minimal. When a damaged template base is encountered, leading and lagging strand synthesis and/or helicase and polymerase activities become out of sync, leading to the buildup of RPA-coated ssDNA downstream of the offending damage (17, 19, 89). This structure recruits Rad6/Rad18 to the blocked P/T junction, where the Rad6/Rad18 complex catalyzes the conjugation of a single ubiquitin moiety (a process referred to herein as monoubiquitination) to K164 of the resident PCNA. This response can also be elicited by agents that block progression of replication forks without modifying (damaging) DNA at all, suggesting that RPA-coated ssDNA, rather than the actual DNA lesion, is the signal for Rad6/Rad18-mediated monoubiquitination of PCNA (11, 19, 23, 37, 44, 47, 73, 85, 86, 88, 90, 95, 105, 129). In vitro, Rad6/Rad18 can conjugate ubiquitin to all three monomers of a PCNA ring loaded onto DNA (44, 90). A single report (56) suggests that such conjugation may also occur in vivo, but further experiments are needed to confirm this and to ascertain whether such conjugation is required for DDT within the cell. Although there are roughly 10 E2 enzymes and more than 60 E3 ligases in eukaryotes, Rad6/Rad18 is the predominant E2/E3 pair responsible for the monoubiquitination of PCNA during DDT (29, 51, 118, 140). As the following section describes, the innate properties of Rad6 and Rad18 are uniquely attuned such that the Rad6/Rad18 complex is specifically targeted to PCNA present at stalled P/T junctions.

RAD6 AND RAD18 ARE A TAILOR-MADE MATCH FOR DNA DAMAGE TOLERANCE

Rad18 is a multidomain E3 ubiquitin ligase that functions as a homodimer. Dimerization occurs via an N-terminal RING domain. The Rad6-binding (R6B) domain is located at the C-terminus of Rad18 and interacts with the noncovalent ubiquitin interaction site on Rad6. This site is imperative for ubiquitin chain formation by Rad6, and its association with the R6B domain of Rad18 prevents this activity. The Rad18 RING domain also aids in Rad6 binding, independently of the R6B domain, and together these two domains form a stable interaction with Rad6. Dimerization of Rad18 is asymmetric, however, such that only one of the Rad6 binding sites is open. Thus, the Rad18 homodimer binds only a single Rad6. Whether the R6B and RING domains that bind to Rad6 are from the same or different Rad18 monomers remains unknown (4–6, 46, 50, 77, 90, 117).

Rad18 also contains distinct domains that bind DNA (the SAP domain), PCNA, and RPA (23, 54, 77, 90, 117). The PCNA-binding motif has been mapped to the N-terminal region of

Rad18 and acts independently of the other domains in this region. No sequence within this region shows any similarity to the classic PIP box (data not shown), however, and the amino acid residues involved in PCNA binding have yet to be identified (90). Furthermore, the location(s) on PCNA to which Rad18 binds remains unknown. Some reports suggest that Rad18 may not require access to the front side of PCNA for monoubiquitination, as overexpression of proteins that also bind to this side with high affinity, such as p15^{PAF} and p21, does not impair PCNA monoubiquitination (99, 113). Further experiments are needed to identify the Rad18-binding site(s) on PCNA. The SAP domain of Rad18 has a high preference for ssDNA, particularly that present at forked DNA substrates, and is required for assembly of Rad18 at stalled replication forks following DNA damage. Thus, the current model suggests that the SAP and RPA-binding domains together recruit Rad18 to RPA-coated ssDNA that builds up downstream of replication-blocking lesions. Once localized, the PCNA-binding domain of Rad18 directs it to the sliding clamp present at the blocked P/T junction (5, 23, 85, 90, 121). Note that Rad18 also contains ATPase and zinc finger (ZnF) domains. The function of the ATPase domain is unknown, but it has no effect on the DNA binding behavior of Rad18 or the Rad6/Rad18 complex and is dispensable for the interaction of Rad18 with Rad6 (5, 6, 54). The function of the ZnF domain is unclear; conflicting reports suggest that this domain has a role in DNA binding, Rad18 dimerization, ubiquitin binding, and controlling the cellular location of Rad18 (4, 54, 81, 117, 123).

Rad6 is an E2 Ubc that is highly conserved in eukaryotes and that can form independent complexes with alternative E3 ligases (6). Rad6 alone has an intrinsic ability to form polyubiquitin chains, and this activity is inhibited by its association with Rad18, permitting the conjugation of only single ubiquitin moieties to PCNA. Rad6 is also incapable of binding any nucleic acid, so by associating with Rad18, Rad6 is specifically targeted to RPA-coated ssDNA resulting from DNA damage (4). Once localized, the PCNA-binding domain of Rad18 is surmised to direct the ubiquitin-conjugating activity of Rad6 to PCNA encircling a blocked P/T junction. As discussed in the next section, the expression level, assembly, and cellular location of the Rad6/Rad18 complex are stringently controlled to ensure that the complex is poised for action when needed.

THE SPATIOTEMPORAL REGULATION OF THE RAD6/RAD18 COMPLEX PRIMES IT FOR DNA DAMAGE TOLERANCE

The expression levels of both Rad6 and Rad18 are cell cycle controlled. Interestingly, Rad18 expression decreases during S phase, whereas Rad6 expression gradually increases during S phase and peaks in late S/G$_2$ phase (72, 73, 75, 78). Upon exposure to agents that halt progression of replication forks, however, the expression levels of both proteins are upregulated (53, 73, 75, 78, 124). Such a response ensures that the supply of both proteins meets the demand for them, and this response may also both drive formation of the Rad6/Rad18 complex and control its cellular location.

During unperturbed DNA synthesis, Rad6 is present in both the cytoplasm and the nucleus, but very little of it is associated with DNA (72, 78). This is expected, as the DNA-binding activity of Rad6 depends entirely upon Rad18, which is downregulated in S phase. In response to DNA damage, Rad6 is redistributed exclusively to the nucleus, where it binds to chromatin and monoubiquitinates PCNA present at stalled replication forks (72, 73). Rad6 does not contain a nuclear localization signal, however (60), whereas Rad18 contains three (85), suggesting that the cellular location of Rad6 is dictated by Rad18 during DDT as follows. In the absence of DNA damage, low levels of Rad18 ensure that the nuclear concentration of the Rad6/Rad18 complex is low, allowing Rad6 to maintain its relationship with other E3 ligases; then, upon exposure to DNA-damaging agents, upregulation of Rad6 and Rad18 sequesters them into a complex that is directed to the nucleus, where the damaged chromatin resides. Future studies are needed to confirm this pathway.

PHOSPHORYLATION OF THE MAMMALIAN RAD6/RAD18 COMPLEX ENHANCES ITS ACTIVITY

Human Rad6 is phosphorylated at conserved serine residue 120 by cyclin-dependent kinase 9 (CDK9). This PTM increases the activity of Rad6 and is critical for its role in cell cycle progression, suggesting that this modification may also be vital for the role of Rad6/Rad18 in DDT. Indeed, knockdown of CDK9 reduces ubiquitination of PCNA (104, 108, 132). How regulation of this Rad6 PTM correlates with exposure to DNA damaging agents and DDT, however, is not known. Interestingly, the basal level of phosphorylated Rad18 present during unperturbed conditions is greatly enhanced in response to DNA damage by two kinases: Dbf4/Drf1-dependent Cdc7 kinase (DDK) and ATR/Chk1-dependent c-Jun N-terminal kinase (JNK) (9, 25). Identification of the latter kinase agrees with previous independent reports of a reduction in Rad18 foci at stalled replication forks (88) and of PCNA monoubiquitination (11) upon knockdown or inhibition of ATR (ataxia telangiectasia and Rad3-related), a DNA damage checkpoint kinase (14, 19, 23, 31, 86, 135).[1] Recent studies suggest that phosphorylation of Rad18 mediates its interaction with Polη.

In mammalian cells, Rad18 exists in complexes with Polη regardless of genotoxic stresses, owing to mutual binding domains within each protein. This interaction is modulated by DNA damage–dependent phosphorylation of the Polη-binding domain within Rad18. In the absence of DNA damage, a basal level of Rad18 is phosphorylated and associated with Polη. In response to UV irradiation, both DDK and JNK phosphorylate serine residues within the Polη-binding domain of Rad18. Each kinase is independent of the other, and both DDK and JNK promote the association of Rad18 with Polη. Interestingly, both kinases are essential for the cellular tolerance of UV-induced lesions and for the role of Rad18 in TLS (9, 25, 129, 139). Furthermore, Polη protein expression is induced upon exposure to UV irradiation (26, 69). Together, these distinct responses drive formation of the Rad18–Polη complex and the subsequent redistribution of cellular Polη to replication foci. Thus, by associating with Rad18, Polη may be chaperoned into the vicinity of stalled replication forks upstream of RPA-coated ssDNA. Once the complex is localized, however, Polη may actually direct Rad6/Rad18 to PCNA encircling stalled P/T junctions. This function is unique to Polη among TLS pols, distinct from the catalytic activity of Polη, and dependent upon the ability of Polη to bind PCNA (via its PIP box and flanking domains). Thus, by bridging Rad18 and PCNA, Polη stimulates PCNA monoubiquitination following UV irradiation (26). Combining both of these purported roles for the Rad18–Polη complex in TLS suggests a dynamic "horse-and-carriage" scenario in which (*a*) a basal level of Rad18 is phosphorylated and associated with Polη in the absence of DNA damage; (*b*) phosphorylation of Rad18 is greatly enhanced in response to UV irradiation, promoting its association with Polη and hitching the "carriage" to the "horse"; (*c*) functioning as the "horse," Rad18 pulls the Polη "carriage" to RPA-coated ssDNA; and (*d*) once it is localized to the damaged chromatin, Polη becomes the "horse" and directs the Rad18 "carriage" to PCNA residing at blocked P/T junctions, promoting monoubiquitination of PCNA.

---

[1]Numerous studies have observed that Rad6/Rad18-catalyzed monoubiquitination of PCNA did not depend on either ATM or ATR, suggesting that this process is independent of the DNA damage checkpoint. The reason for the discrepancy between these studies and those described above is currently unknown.

The aforementioned studies primarily utilized UV irradiation as the DNA-damaging agent, suggesting that the horse-and-carriage scenario described above is specific to UV-induced lesions. Indeed, Polη is responsible for the error-free bypass of cyclobutane pyrimidine dimers (CPDs), the major photoproduct of UV irradiation. Given the prominence of solar UV irradiation and the presence of at least three alternative TLS pols that can bypass CPDs erroneously, such a model may account for the highly efficient and error-free bypass of UV-induced CPDs within mammalian cells (136, 144). Rad6/Rad18, however, is responsible for the monoubiquitination of PCNA in response to all agents that elicit TLS, so this "horse-and-carriage" scenario may apply broadly to any circumstance in which progression of the replication fork is stalled. Several independent studies on benzo[a]pyrene diolepoxide (BPDE) suggest this may be the case. BPDE is a genotoxic metabolite of the chemical carcinogen benzo[a]pyrene that primarily forms guanine adducts that block the progression of replication forks. Similar to UV irradiation, these studies showed that exposure to BPDE induced JNK-dependent phosphorylation of Rad18 (9). In addition, treatment of DDK-depleted cells with BPDE specifically impaired the association of Polη with stalled replication forks (25), and in Polη-depleted cells, PCNA monoubiquitination by Rad6/Rad18 was decreased after BPDE treatment (26). One study also showed that (a) JNK activity depended upon the ATR kinase recruited to and activated by RPA-coated ssDNA and (b) replication fork arrest induced by either nucleotide depletion [via hydroxyurea (HU)] or UV irradiation promoted formation of Rad18–Polη complexes in vivo as well as their association to chromatin (9). Taken together, these findings suggest that the horse-and-carriage scenario is not genotoxin specific; rather, it describes a generic response solicited by RPA-coated ssDNA generated during S phase (139). Thus, of all available TLS pols within mammalian cells, Polη may be the default choice at any DNA lesion.

The apparent disparity in both accuracy and efficiency among various TLS events within mammalian cells raises many issues pertaining to how TLS pols are selected for bypass across a given DNA lesion. At one end of the spectrum are lesions induced by chemicals such as BPDE. Pol κ bypasses BPDE-induced lesions in an error-free manner in vitro and is responsible for their faithful replication in vivo (3, 70, 91, 116, 141). Polη, however, replicates past such lesions in an error-prone manner in vitro and, perhaps owing to the horse-and-carriage model, contributes to the mutagenic bypass of BPDE adducts in vivo (20, 59, 102, 141). At the other end of the spectrum are the two major UV-induced lesions that elicit TLS: the more-prominent CPD and the less-prominent pyrimidine (6–4) pyrimidone photoproducts [(6–4) photoproduct] (10). Polη accurately replicates across thymine–thymine (TT) CPDs in vitro and is responsible for the highly error-free (>90%) bypass of UV-induced CPDs in vivo (125, 136). In contrast, Polη has an eightfold preference for inserting an incorrect G residue opposite the 3′ T of a (6–4) TT photoproduct, yet TLS opposite these lesions is predominantly error-free (<2% mutation frequency), suggesting that another TLS pol must replicate past (6–4) photoproducts in vivo (52, 137). In the horse-and-carriage model, Polη binds to the front side of PCNA and is afforded ample opportunity for nucleotide incorporation. Does Polη simply insert a nucleotide across from a BPDE adduct, but not across from a (6–4) photoproduct? If so, how is this insertion (or lack thereof) ensured? How is the "correct" TLS pol selected for bypass of certain lesions but not others? The linked chaperoning activities of Rad18 and Polη during TLS raise these and many more intriguing questions.

THE ACTIVITY OF THE RAD6/RAD18 COMPLEX IS MEDIATED BY VARIOUS PROTEINS

Over the past 10 years or so, more and more seemingly unrelated proteins have been implicated in modulation of the activity of the Rad6/Rad18 complex in addition to their primary duties in other cellular pathways. For example, various proteins involved in DSB repair, such as BRCA1,

NBS1, PTIP, and Claspin-Timeless, have been shown to interact with Rad18 and/or PCNA and may mediate recruitment of the Rad6/Rad18 complex to blocked replication forks, enhancing monoubiquitination of PCNA during DDT. Similar behavior was also observed for two unrelated E3 proteins involved in initiation of DNA replication (CRL4^{CDT2}) and inhibition of p53-mediated apoptosis (SIVA1) (40, 42, 107, 119, 133, 135). Certain proteins have garnered considerable attention, each of which is summarized below.

ATP-Dependent Chromatin Remodelers

A plausible mechanism for enhancing monoubiquitination of chromatin-bound PCNA would be to provide Rad6/Rad18 with greater access to genomic DNA in response to DNA damage. In the cell, multisubunit ATP-dependent chromatin remodelers utilize the energy from ATP hydrolysis to remodel sections of chromatin, ultimately exposing or shielding the surrounding DNA. Expression of the highly conserved Ino80 complex is upregulated in S phase, during which it is recruited to and moves with active replication forks although the complex is dispensable for fork progression in unperturbed conditions (28, 83, 109, 110). A recent study observed that in *Saccharomyces cerevisiae*, Ino80 and its chromatin-remodeling activity were necessary for recruitment of Rad18 to MMS-stalled replication forks and for PCNA monoubiquitination. MMS is an alkylating agent that primarily forms methylated purine residues that cannot be accommodated by replicative pols, halting progression of replication forks. Ino80 was required for stabilization and efficient restart of MMS-stalled replication forks, a finding which is consistent with the ability of Ino80 to expose DNA neighboring a lesion and promote Rad6/Rad18-mediated ubiquitination of PCNA. It is unclear whether the exposed DNA facilitates recruitment of Rad18 directly or indirectly (through RPA). Interestingly, the role played by Ino80 may be specific to MMS-induced damage, as UV irradiation and HU treatment had marginal, if any, effects on PCNA ubiquitination in the absence of Ino80 (28). Others have observed, however, that Ino80 is required to stabilize HU-blocked replication forks, suggesting that Ino80 may be differentially involved in distinct pathways that deal with specific types of replicative stress (28, 87, 92, 110). What these alternative roles are and how such specificity is attained are unknown.

The RSC (remodels the structure of chromatin) complex is also purported to be associated with replication forks in *S. cerevisiae*, in which two isoforms are present and differ only in whether they contain the Rsc1 or Rsc2 subunit. Only the Rsc2 isoform is required for normal PCNA ubiquitination in response to either UV irradiation or HU treatment. In humans, Rsc1 and Rsc2 are fused together with Rsc4 to form BAF180. When BAF180 is depleted from human cells, ubiquitination of PCNA is reduced in untreated, control cells as well as in cells treated with either UV light, MMS, or HU. Furthermore, in BAF180-depleted cells, the amount of chromatin-bound PCNA, and Rad18, but not RPA, is substantially reduced following UV irradiation and fork progression is less efficient. Together, these observations suggest that the human RSC complex (referred to as PBAF) may enhance Rad6/Rad18-mediated ubiquitination of PCNA following DNA damage by stabilizing the amount of chromatin-bound PCNA as well as by promoting the binding of Rad6/Rad18 to chromatin in a manner independent of RPA deposition (87). How these feats are achieved, however, is unknown.

The nucleosome remodeling deacetylase (NuRD) complex couples ATPase and deacetylase activities to remodel chromatin. Recent evidence suggests that the mammalian NuRD complex may be targeted to UV-damaged chromatin by two transcriptional regulators, ZBTB1 and KAP-1. Upon UV exposure, ZBTB1 clusters into foci that colocalize with both CPDs and PCNA. Such behavior is mandatory for promoting Rad6/Rad18-mediated ubiquitination of PCNA, assembly of Polη foci, and cell survival following UV-related damage. Interestingly, recruitment of ZBTB1 to UV-damaged sites requires its ubiquitin-binding domain, suggesting that another unknown ubiquitinated protein recruits ZBTB1 to stalled replication forks. In addition, KAP-1 is strongly phosphorylated by an unknown kinase following UV irradiation and is targeted to chromatin by ZBTB1. Inhibition of either event diminishes both the association of Rad18 with chromatin and PCNA monoubiquitination. Interestingly, increasing chromatin relaxation in ZBTB1-knockdown cells appears to eliminate the need for ZBTB1 in Rad6/Rad18-mediated ubiquitination of PCNA following UV exposure (57). As phosphorylation of KAP-1 is known to initiate chromatin relaxation during DNA DSB repair (41), all of these observations suggest that ZBTB1 enhances PCNA monoubiquitination by targeting pKAP-1-dependent chromatin relaxation to UV-damaged sites. Further experiments, however, have suggested that the contribution of KAP-1 to chromatin remodeling following UV exposure differs from its role in chromatin remodeling during DNA DSB repair. Indeed, phosphorylation of KAP-1 in response to UV exposure is distinct from that observed in DNA DSB repair following treatment with ionizing radiation and is independent of the DNA damage checkpoint kinases ATM and ATR (57). In the realm of transcription, one role of KAP-1 is to recruit the NuRD complex to gene promoters, remodeling the surrounding chromatin (106). In undamaged human cells, a constitutive interaction of ZBTB1 with KAP-1 and a component of the NuRD complex was observed, suggesting that the role of pKAP-1 in chromatin relaxation following UV exposure may be recruitment of the NuRD complex to UV-induced lesions (57). Once localized, the NuRD complex can increase the accessibility of the surrounding DNA, directing Rad6/Rad18 to PCNA residing at a stalled P/T junction and enhancing PCNA monoubiquitination (57). Further experiments are needed to verify this model. As we have already pointed out, many unknowns remain for this pathway, and experiments are assuredly in progress to address each. Nonetheless, these and other studies on ATP-dependent chromatin remodelers clearly show that Rad6/Rad18 activity is modulated by chromatin accessibility.

p21

p21 is a cell-cycle regulator that exerts its control by inhibiting DNA synthesis via two independent domains. Its N-terminal cyclin/CDK-interaction domain binds to both cyclins and CDKs during G_1, particularly those involved in cell-cycle transitions, forming ternary complexes devoid of kinase activity. The activation of certain cyclin/CDK complexes in late G_1 is a key event in the commitment to S phase and is thought to allow the initiation of active replication forks. The C-terminal PIP motif of p21 binds tightly to PCNA, blocking its interaction with DNA pols and inhibiting DNA synthesis (101).

p21 is a target of p53 and is upregulated and transported to the nucleus upon exposure to agents that cause DNA strand breaks. When this occurs before S phase, p21 arrests the cell cycle, primarily via inhibition of CDKs. When DNA damage occurs after the cell has committed to S phase, p21 inhibits ongoing DNA synthesis by binding to PCNA (112). In contrast to the case for DNA strand breaks, modifications to the template bases of DNA may be accommodated during S phase via TLS, allowing DNA replication to resume without first correcting the damage. Under these circumstances, elevated p21 levels are detrimental, as TLS pols must gain access to PCNA. Even the low basal level of p21 that is maintained throughout S phase is sufficient to impair the interactions of TLS pols with chromatin-bound PCNA (71, 76, 114, 120). Furthermore, elevated p21 levels inhibit ubiquitination of PCNA (71, 113). Indeed, p21 levels decline, rather sharply, specifically in response to agents that halt progression of replication forks during S phase. Interestingly, exposure to these agents still elicits the p53 response, initiating transcription of the p21 promoter. For reasons unknown, however, RNA pol II is less efficient at traversing the p21 gene under these conditions. Thus, p21 mRNA does not accumulate, and no further p21 protein is synthesized. In addition, the basal level of p21 present at the time of damage is degraded by the proteasome (112). Other PCNA-binding proteins may aid in the degradation of p21 that is engaged with the sliding clamp by transiently promoting its detachment in response to DNA damage (71).

Owing to discrepancies in the literature, it is currently unclear how decreased p21 levels promote monoubiquitination of PCNA by Rad6/Rad18. One study observed that dissociation of p21 from PCNA, as well as its subsequent degradation, was necessary for PCNA monoubiquitination in cells, implying that access to the front side of PCNA is imperative for Rad6/Rad18 activity (71). In contrast, another study found that p21 lacking its PIP motif was almost as capable as full-length p21 in inhibiting PCNA ubiquitination, suggesting that the ability of p21 to modulate the ubiquitination of PCNA does not require these proteins to interact. Rather, the CDK-binding capacity of p21 must be negatively regulated to permit efficient PCNA ubiquitination (113). Indeed, p21 mutants lacking only functional CDK-binding domains did not alter monoubiquitination of PCNA in response to UV irradiation (76). Similarly, p15^{PAF}, a small protein much like p21, contains a highly conserved PIP box and interacts strongly with PCNA during S phase, but it has no effect on the ubiquitination of PCNA after UV irradiation (27, 48, 99, 138). Together, these findings suggest that Rad6/Rad18 does not interact with the front side of PCNA and/or that such interaction is not required for monoubiquitination of PCNA. Further experiments are needed to confirm or refute either of these models for the role of p21 in Rad6/Rad18-mediated DDT.

Spartan

Spartan (aka DVC1) is a multidomain protein that comprises an SHP box, a PIP box, and a UBZ4 ubiquitin-binding zinc finger. The SHP box is a known p97-binding motif and is required for association of Spartan with this protein. The latter two domains are highly conserved and mutually exclusive; binding of Spartan to unmodified PCNA is entirely dependent upon the PIP box, whereas only the UBZ domain is required for association with ubiquitin. Interestingly, Spartan also contains a SprT-like domain similar to that found in certain metalloproteases, but no such activity has been observed. It is unclear whether this domain is required for Spartan's function(s) in vivo (18, 24, 39, 55, 58, 74, 84).

Spartan expression is cell cycle regulated such that it peaks in S phase, persists through G$_2$ into early M phase, and is rapidly downregulated upon exiting mitosis. Spartan condenses into nuclear foci that colocalize with PCNA, and the proportion of cells with such foci peaks during S phase, suggesting that Spartan may have a role in unperturbed DNA replication (24, 74, 84). Upon exposure to agents such as UV irradiation, Spartan foci are dramatically enhanced. These foci are enriched in chromatin and colocalize with sites of DNA synthesis and DNA damage, ubiquitinated PCNA, Rad18, and RPA (18, 24, 39, 55, 74). Such behavior is entirely dependent upon both the PIP box and the UBZ domains of Spartan and is specific to agents that halt the progression of replication forks and induce monoubiquitination of PCNA (18, 24, 39, 55, 74, 84). Furthermore, Spartan levels gradually decline following UV-induced PCNA ubiquitination, suggesting that Spartan's function is transient and dependent on DNA damage (18). Although Spartan preferentially binds monoubiquitinated PCNA in vitro, one cannot assert that Spartan is directly recruited to monoubiquitinated PCNA in vivo, owing to conflicting reports in the literature (18, 24, 55, 74, 84). Interestingly, a fraction of cellular Spartan is ubiquitinated. This modification greatly reduces the ability of Spartan to bind ubiquitin and eliminates its recruitment to UV-induced nuclear foci, suggesting that ubiquitination of Spartan may mediate its role in DDT. However, the mechanism by which ubiquitination of Spartan is regulated in vivo is unknown (84).

Knockdown of Spartan sensitizes cells to killing by agents that cause replication forks to stall and increases the extent of UV-induced mutagenesis (18, 24, 39, 55, 74, 84). Furthermore, although relocalization of Spartan to sites of replication stress does not require its SHP domain (or p97 binding), only wild-type Spartan is able to rescue, suggesting that binding of Spartan to PCNA, ubiquitin, and p97 is required for its role(s) in DDT (18, 24, 39, 55, 84). Two opposing descriptions of Spartan's mode of action have emerged, and these descriptions are based on conflicting results. In one description, depletion of wild-type Spartan or mutation of its UBZ domain led to a pronounced persistence of UV-induced Polη foci, yet neither depletion nor mutation had any effect on either PCNA monoubiquitination or the association of Rad18 to chromatin following UV exposure (24, 84). However, overexpression of wild-type Spartan did suppress the interaction between Polη and monoubiquitinated PCNA, enhance recruitment of p97 into UV-induced foci, and lead to the removal of Polη from such foci and chromatin. Furthermore, an ATPase-deficient p97 targeted to UV-induced foci by Spartan failed to efficiently trigger removal of Polη. p97 [also known as valosin-containing protein (VCP)] remodels ubiquitinated proteins via its ATPase activity. Thus, once targeted to a stalled replication fork by its UBZ domain, Spartan may recruit p97 via its SHP domain to actively displace Polη from chromatin (24, 84).

In the second description, knockdown of Spartan decreased PCNA monoubiquitination and significantly reduced Polη recruitment to DNA damage sites following exposure to UV light, and only full-length Spartan rescued these behaviors (18, 39, 55). Similarly, transient overexpression of Spartan dramatically increased formation of Polη foci and eliminated the requirement for UV irradiation. This effect was impaired by mutation in either the UBZ domain or the PIP box of Spartan (55). Thus, this opposing description purports that Spartan binds to chromatin-bound PCNA through its PIP box and UBZ domain and suppresses the reduction of PCNA ubiquitination, perhaps via transient inhibition of USP1 (ubiquitin-specific protease 1), which is responsible for cleaving ubiquitin from PCNA following DDT (55, 127). Knockdown of Spartan in cells lacking USP1 still led to a reduction in PCNA ubiquitination, however, suggesting that Spartan may suppress the reduction of PCNA ubiquitination by other means (18, 55). Indeed, other studies observed that Spartan binds directly to Rad18 and to p97, inhibiting the activity of p97 and preventing extraction of Rad18 from chromatin in the latter case (18, 39, 55). Thus, Spartan may promote the formation of ubiquitinated PCNA in addition to inhibiting its destruction. Collectively, these activities serve to transiently enhance recruitment of TLS pols to stalled replication forks. Although there is no doubt that Spartan plays an imperative role in DDT, future experiments are needed to discern which, if either, of these models is correct.

RAD6/RAD18-MEDIATED DNA DAMAGE TOLERANCE IS SELECTED FOR WHEN A REPLICATION-BLOCKING LESION IS ENCOUNTERED

At least three distinct mechanisms may rescue a stalled replication fork during S phase. The two Rad6/Rad18-dependent pathways are primarily elicited when a small DNA adduct is encountered. The third possibility, homologous recombination (HR), is a very complex process that utilizes the undamaged sister chromatid as a homologous template to resume DNA synthesis. HR is functional throughout the S and G2 phases of the cell cycle and is primarily summoned for the repair of more drastic genomic offenses that cannot be replicated past, such as DNA strand breaks. HR can also rescue replication forks arrested at small DNA adducts, but it may be more harmful than good in such cases, as the process can trigger cell cycle arrest, and failed attempts can lead to gross chromosomal rearrangements. Indeed, eukaryotic cells have established a temporal hierarchy to avoid such disasters: The Rad6/Rad18-mediated pathways are elicited first at replication-blocking lesions, whereas HR serves as a so-called salvage pathway and is summoned only when the other pathways are malfunctioning (61, 79). In *S. cerevisiae*, conjugation of SUMO (small ubiquitin-like modifier) to PCNA proctors this hierarchy.

SUMO is a small posttranslational modifier in eukaryotes that is reversibly conjugated to a plethora of proteins involved in a broad range of cellular processes (30). During normal DNA replication within *S. cerevisiae*, SUMO is conjugated to K127 and/or K164 within PCNA, a process referred to herein as SUMOylation. K164 is highly conserved and is the predominant attachment site, whereas K127, which is less conserved, is a secondary site (47, 93). The interaction of DNA pols with PCNA is not affected by SUMOylation of either site (16). Similar to ubiquitination, only PCNA encircling DNA is SUMOylated in vivo (94). In complete contrast to ubiquitination, however, SUMOylation of PCNA (*a*) is upregulated in and limited to unperturbed S phase, (*b*) is not induced by sublethal levels of agents that elicit TLS, and (*c*) has a role in maintaining the integrity of the genome during normal DNA replication (47, 93, 94, 98, 130). This role is manifested through recruitment of the Srs2 helicase, which contains distinct domains that bind PCNA, SUMO, and Rad51 independently (2, 16, 93, 98). Rad51 is an imperative HR protein responsible for locating a homologous template within the sister chromatid and annealing it to the invading strand primer (61). Because of its tandem SUMO- and PCNA-binding domains, Srs2 preferentially interacts with SUMO–PCNA (2, 93). This behavior directs a portion of cellular Srs2 to SUMO–PCNA that is encircling genomic DNA (engaged in DNA replication), where Srs2 prohibits the initiation of HR during unperturbed S phase either by dissolving inappropriately placed Rad51 nucleoprotein filaments or by preventing their formation (16, 43, 62, 67, 93, 98, 126).

During normal DNA replication within *S. cerevisiae*, a significant portion of cellular PCNA is SUMOylated, predominantly at K164. Conjugation of SUMO to a given PCNA trimer is not refractory toward its subsequent ubiquitination, however, so removal of SUMO is not a prerequisite for ubiquitination (93, 94, 130). In fact, genetic studies in *S. cerevisiae* revealed that polyubiquitination-dependent template switching actually requires previous SUMOylation of PCNA (13), possibly to keep the HR machinery at bay in order to permit conjugation of ubiquitin to PCNA. Furthermore, the activity of Rad6/Rad18 toward a given PCNA trimer is directly enhanced by the presence of SUMO on the same clamp. The N-terminal half of Rad18 from *S. cerevisiae* contains both a PCNA-binding domain and a SUMO interaction motif (SIM) that mediates its noncovalent interaction with SUMO. This pairing accounts for preferential binding of SUMO–PCNA by Rad18 and dramatically improves the efficiency of ubiquitin conjugation to SUMO–PCNA compared to native PCNA. In vivo, this SIM–SUMO interaction enhances the recognition of PCNA engaged in DNA replication and contributes to the full activity of Rad6/Rad18 required for efficient ubiquitin-dependent DDT (96). Taken together, these findings suggest that SUMOylation of PCNA during normal DNA replication functions as a traffic cop in *S. cerevisiae*: SUMOylation of PCNA directs the recovery process toward Rad6/Rad18-mediated bypass in the event that a replication block is encountered by recruiting Srs2 to inhibit HR and/or by recruiting Rad6/Rad18 to promote ubiquitination of PCNA that is engaged in DNA replication (93, 96, 98).

SUMOylation of PCNA has only recently been observed in human cells and occurs at very low levels compared with those observed in *S. cerevisiae* (36, 82). Hence, studies analogous to those cited above are in their infancy. Nonetheless, some insight has been provided. The human Rad18 sequence lacks an obvious SIM, and the presence of SUMO on PCNA has no effect on the ability of the human Rad6/Rad18 complex to conjugate ubiquitin to PCNA in vitro (96). Thus, SUMO does not seem to promote ubiquitination of PCNA by recruiting the Rad6/Rad18 complex. However, a mechanism similar to that described above for Srs2 may exist in humans. The human protein PARI (PCNA-associated recombination inhibitor) contains a UvrD helicase–related domain, a PIP box, a SIM, and a Rad51-binding domain. In cells, PARI is found at very low levels, and a recent study suggests that SUMO–PCNA concentrates PARI to replication forks, where it suppresses HR by disrupting Rad51 filaments. Interestingly, PARI is not an active helicase and, in contrast to Srs2, which can move along DNA and remove multiple Rad51 molecules within a single binding encounter with DNA (82), PARI must be present in amounts stoichiometric to Rad51 in order to efficiently inhibit HR. As mentioned above, however, SUMO–PCNA levels are very low in human cells, so this method of HR suppression may not be the predominant one. Indeed, other human helicases may suppress HR by inhibiting various stages of initiation independently of SUMO–PCNA (8, 35, 49).

CONCLUDING REMARKS

It was first observed in 2002 that Rad6/Rad18 conjugated ubiquitin to eukaryotic PCNA in response to DNA-damaging agents that cause replication-blocking lesions. In the ensuing years, substantial efforts have begun to unveil the complexity and intricacies of this process. Because it involves multiple levels of regulation for a wide variety of circumstances, this process has been optimized to operate mostly during S phase and only on PCNA trimers encircling damaged DNA. In the pursuit of answers, however, more questions have been raised, particularly those pertaining to the spatiotemporal control of this process. For instance, where in relation to the replication fork does Rad6/Rad18-mediated DDT occur? There are currently two models that address this question (please see the excellent review, Reference 134). In one, replicative DNA synthesis on the afflicted strand and progression of the replication fork do not resume until the offending damage is bypassed. Hence, Rad6/Rad18 must conjugate ubiquitin to PCNA rings present at or near a replication fork, where the replisome may or may not remain intact. In the contrasting model, the replisome progresses ahead, and replicative DNA synthesis resumes downstream of the lesion, leaving behind a gap opposite the offending damage. In this case, Rad6/Rad18 and the ensuing DDT function behind the progressing replication fork (and the replisome) to fill in the gap. Given the ample experimental evidence for each, the two models may not be mutually exclusive. However, each model has many persisting questions. For instance, if DDT occurs at or near the replication fork, what is the composition of the blocked P/T junction? Do the replicative polymerases or other PCNA-binding proteins remain engaged? If so, how does Rad6/Rad18 gain access to the resident PCNA clamp? In contrast, if DDT occurs behind the replication fork, does the original PCNA ring stay behind with the gap? If so, how is it retained at the stalled P/T junction? Another pressing issue is the temporal correlation between the ubiquitination events (monoubiquitination versus polyubiquitination) and the DDT pathways (TLS versus template switching). The E2/E3 pairs involved in DDT act sequentially, suggesting that the DDT pathways also do so. Indeed, UV-induced lesions are bypassed predominantly by TLS in *S. cerevisiae*; template switching functions only as a backup (22, 95). Furthermore, a recent in vivo report suggests that the two Rad5-related proteins in human cells, HLTF and SHPRH, actually bind to Rad18 in a DNA damage–specific manner to enhance monoubiquitination of PCNA and recruitment of the appropriate TLS pol (68). Although instances in which template switching is solicited first cannot yet be ruled out, these reports suggest that the simpler yet potentially mutagenic TLS pathway is preferred over the faithful, more complex template switching pathway. But what dissuades Ubc13–Mms2/Rad5 from extending the single ubiquitin moieties on PCNA into polyubiquitin chains? Perhaps one of the many known ubiquitin-binding proteins involved in TLS? Is it a timing issue, that is, does TLS occur prior to the arrival of Ubc13–Mms2/Rad5 to the stalled P/T junction? Furthermore, what ultimately signals the extension of the monoubiquitin and solicitation of the template switching pathway, and when does this occur? A failed TLS attempt? These questions, in addition to those raised throughout the text, underscore the need for additional studies. Because the answers will require scrutiny of more quantitative data, in vitro biochemical experiments will play a vital role in answering these questions.

SUMMARY POINTS

1. Translesion DNA synthesis (TLS) is one of two DNA damage tolerance (DDT) pathways that can replicate past DNA lesions that halt the progression of replication forks. In TLS, the replicative polymerase is replaced with a specialized polymerase that is able to catalyze stable, yet often erroneous, nucleotide incorporation opposite damaged templates, allowing replicative DNA synthesis to resume.

2. DDT in eukaryotes is regulated by the E2/E3-catalyzed attachment of ubiquitin to K164 of the sliding clamp, PCNA. An E2 ubiquitin-conjugating enzyme catalyzes the attachment of ubiquitin to the target protein while an E3 ubiquitin ligase binds to an E2 enzyme and the target protein simultaneously, mediating the specificity of the conjugation.

3. Conjugation of a single ubiquitin by the E2/E3 pair Rad6/Rad18 mediates the TLS pathway of DDT, whereas extension of this ubiquitin to a polyubiquitin chain by the Ubc13–Mms2/Rad5 E2/E3 pair routes DDT to the other DDT pathway, template switching.

4. The buildup of RPA-coated ssDNA downstream of a replication-blocking lesion recruits Rad6/Rad18 to the blocked P/T junction, where the Ra6/Rad18 complex attaches a single ubiquitin to K164 of the resident PCNA. The innate properties of Rad6 and Rad18 are uniquely attuned such that the Rad6/Rad18 complex is specifically targeted to PCNA present at stalled P/T junctions.

5. Rad6 has an intrinsic ability to form polyubiquitin chains and contains neither a nuclear localization signal (NLS) nor any domain that interacts with PCNA, RPA, or DNA, whereas Rad18 contains multiple NLSs, as well as distinct domains that bind DNA, PCNA, and RPA. Thus, by pairing with Rad18, Rad6 is specifically recruited to PCNA residing at a blocked P/T junction within the nucleus, where Rad18 permits the conjugation of only single ubiquitin moieties by Rad6.

6. The expression level, assembly, and cellular location of the Rad6/Rad18 complex are stringently controlled by the cell cycle such that the nuclear concentration of the complex is low during unperturbed S phase. Upon exposure to agents that halt the progression of replication forks, upregulation of Rad6 and Rad18 sequesters them into a complex that is directed to the nucleus where the damaged chromatin resides.

7. The activity of the Rad6/Rad18 complex is regulated by PTMs to each protein, particularly phosphorylation, as well as by a multitude of accessory proteins that modulate the recruitment of Rad6/Rad18 to RPA-coated ssDNA by various mechanisms.

8. Eukaryotic cells have established a temporal hierarchy of DNA repair pathways when dealing with replication-blocking lesions; Rad6/Rad18-mediated TLS is elicited first, followed by Ubc13–Mms2/Rad5-mediated template switching, and homologous recombination serves as a salvage pathway that is summoned only when the other pathways are malfunctioning. In essence, this hierarchy is achieved by promoting the monoubiquitination of PCNA by Rad6/Rad18 while simultaneously inhibiting the initiation of homologous recombination.

DISCLOSURE STATEMENT

The authors are not aware of any affiliations, memberships, funding, or financial holdings that might be perceived as affecting the objectivity of this review.

ACKNOWLEDGMENTS

M.H. is supported by the National Cancer Institute of the National Institutes of Health under award number F32CA165471. The content is solely the responsibility of the authors and does not necessarily represent the official views of the National Institutes of Health.

LITERATURE CITED

1. Andersen PL, Xu F, Xiao W. 2008. Eukaryotic DNA damage tolerance and translesion synthesis through covalent modifications of PCNA. *Cell Res.* 18:162–73
2. Armstrong AA, Mohideen F, Lima CD. 2012. Recognition of SUMO-modified PCNA requires tandem receptor motifs in Srs2. *Nature* 483:59–63
3. Avkin S, Goldsmith M, Velasco-Miguel S, Geacintov N, Friedberg EC, Livneh Z. 2004. Quantitative analysis of translesion DNA synthesis across a benzo[*a*]pyrene-guanine adduct in mammalian cells: the role of DNA polymerase κ. *J. Biol. Chem.* 279:53298–305
4. Bailly V, Lamb J, Sung P, Prakash S, Prakash L. 1994. Specific complex formation between yeast RAD6 and RAD18 proteins: a potential mechanism for targeting RAD6 ubiquitin-conjugating activity to DNA damage sites. *Genes Dev.* 8:811–20
5. Bailly V, Lauder S, Prakash S, Prakash L. 1997. Yeast DNA repair proteins Rad6 and Rad18 form a heterodimer that has ubiquitin conjugating, DNA binding, and ATP hydrolytic activities. *J. Biol. Chem.* 272:23360–365
6. Bailly V, Prakash S, Prakash L. 1997. Domains required for dimerization of yeast Rad6 ubiquitin-conjugating enzyme and Rad18 DNA binding protein. *Mol. Cell. Biol.* 17:4536–43
7. Balakrishnan L, Bambara RA. 2011. Eukaryotic lagging strand DNA replication employs a multi-pathway mechanism that protects genome integrity. *J. Biol. Chem.* 286:6865–70
8. Barber LJ, Youds JL, Ward JD, McIlwraith MJ, O'Neil NJ, et al. 2008. RTEL1 maintains genomic stability by suppressing homologous recombination. *Cell* 135:261–71
9. Barkley LR, Palle K, Durando M, Day TA, Gurkar A, et al. 2012. c-Jun N-terminal kinase-mediated Rad18 phosphorylation facilitates Polη recruitment to stalled replication forks. *Mol. Biol. Cell* 23:1943–54
10. Beukers R, Eker APM, Lohman PHM. 2008. 50 years thymine dimer. *DNA Repair* 7:530–43
11. Bi X, Barkley LR, Slater DM, Tateishi S, Yamaizumi M, et al. 2006. Rad18 regulates DNA polymerase κ and is required for recovery from S-phase checkpoint-mediated arrest. *Mol. Cell. Biol.* 26:3527–40
12. Boos D, Frigola J, Diffley JFX. 2012. Activation of the replicative DNA helicase: Breaking up is hard to do. *Curr. Opin. Cell Biol.* 24:423–30
13. Branzei D, Vanoli F, Foiani M. 2008. SUMOylation regulates Rad18-mediated template switch. *Nature* 456:915–20
14. Brun J, Chiu RK, Wouters BG, Gray DA. 2010. Regulation of PCNA polyubiquitination in human cells. *BMC Res. Notes* 3:85
15. Bruning JB, Shamoo Y. 2004. Structural and thermodynamic analysis of human PCNA with peptides derived from DNA polymerase-δ p66 subunit and flap endonuclease-1. *Structure* 12:2209–19
16. Burkovics P, Sebesta M, Sisakova A, Plault N, Szukacsov V, et al. 2013. Srs2 mediates PCNA-SUMO-dependent inhibition of DNA repair synthesis. *EMBO J.* 32:742–55
17. Byun TS, Pacek M, Yee MC, Walter JC, Cimprich KA. 2005. Functional uncoupling of MCM helicase and DNA polymerase activities activates the ATR-dependent checkpoint. *Genes Dev.* 19:1040–52
18. Centore RC, Yazinski SA, Tse A, Zou L. 2012. Spartan/C1orf124, a reader of PCNA ubiquitylation and a regulator of UV-induced DNA damage response. *Mol. Cell* 46:625–35

19. Chang DJ, Lupardus PJ, Cimprich KA. 2006. Monoubiquitination of proliferating cell nuclear antigen induced by stalled replication requires uncoupling of DNA polymerase and mini-chromosome maintenance helicase activities. *J. Biol. Chem.* 281:32081–88

20. Chiapperino D, Kroth H, Kramarczuk IH, Sayer JM, Masutani C, et al. 2002. Preferential misincorporation of purine nucleotides by human DNA polymerase η opposite benzo[*a*]pyrene 7,8-diol 9,10-epoxide deoxyguanosine adducts. *J. Biol. Chem.* 277:11765–71

21. Chun ACS, Jin D-Y. 2010. Ubiquitin-dependent regulation of translesion polymerases. *Biochem. Soc. Trans.* 38:110–15

22. Daigaku Y, Davies AA, Ulrich HD. 2010. Ubiquitin-dependent DNA damage bypass is separable from genome replication. *Nature* 465:951–55

23. Davies AA, Huttner D, Daigaku Y, Chen S, Ulrich HD. 2008. Activation of ubiquitin-dependent DNA damage bypass is mediated by replication protein A. *Mol. Cell* 29:625–36

24. Davis EJ, Lachaud C, Appleton P, Macartney TJ, Nathke I, Rouse J. 2012. DVC1 (C1orf124) recruits the p97 protein segregase to sites of DNA damage. *Nat. Struct. Mol. Biol.* 19:1093–100

25. Day TA, Palle K, Barkley LR, Kakusho N, Zou Y, et al. 2010. Phosphorylated Rad18 directs DNA polymerase η to sites of stalled replication. *J. Cell Biol.* 191:953–66

26. Durando M, Tateishi S, Vaziri C. 2013. A non-catalytic role of DNA polymerase η in recruiting Rad18 and promoting PCNA monoubiquitination at stalled replication forks. *Nucleic Acids Res.* 41:3079–93

27. Emanuele MJ, Ciccia A, Elia AEH, Elledge SJ. 2011. Proliferating cell nuclear antigen (PCNA)-associated KIAA0101/PAF15 protein is a cell cycle-regulated anaphase-promoting complex/cyclosome substrate. *PNAS* 108:9845–50

28. Falbo KB, Alabert C, Katou Y, Wu S, Han J, et al. 2009. Involvement of a chromatin remodeling complex in damage tolerance during DNA replication. *Nat. Struct. Mol. Biol.* 16:1167–72

29. Finley D, Ulrich HD, Sommer T, Kaiser P. 2012. The ubiquitin-proteasome system of *Saccharomyces cerevisiae*. *Genetics* 192:319–60

30. Flotho A, Melchior F. 2013. Sumoylation: a regulatory protein modification in health and disease. *Annu. Rev. Biochem.* 82:357–85

31. Frampton J, Irmisch A, Green CM, Neiss A, Trickey M, et al. 2006. Postreplication repair and PCNA modification in *Schizosaccharomyces pombe*. *Mol. Biol. Cell* 17:2976–85

32. Freudenthal BD, Gakhar L, Ramaswamy S, Washington MT. 2010. Structure of monoubiquitinated PCNA and implications for translesion synthesis and DNA polymerase exchange. *Nat. Struct. Mol. Biol.* 17:479–84

33. Frick DN, Richardson CC. 2001. DNA primases. *Annu. Rev. Biochem.* 70:39–80

34. Friedberg EC. 2005. Suffering in silence: the tolerance of DNA damage. *Nat. Rev. Mol. Cell Biol.* 6:943–53

35. Fugger K, Mistrik M, Danielsen JR, Dinant C, Falck J, et al. 2009. Human Fbh1 helicase contributes to genome maintenance via pro- and anti-recombinase activities. *J. Cell Biol.* 186:655–63

36. Gali H, Juhasz S, Morocz M, Hajdu I, Fatyol K, et al. 2012. Role of SUMO modification of human PCNA at stalled replication fork. *Nucleic Acids Res.* 40:6049–59

37. Garg P, Burgers PM. 2005. Ubiquitinated proliferating cell nuclear antigen activates translesion DNA polymerases η and REV1. *PNAS* 102:18361–66

38. Georgescu RE, Langston L, Yao NY, Yurieva O, Zhang D, et al. 2014. Mechanism of asymmetric polymerase assembly at the eukaryotic replication fork. *Nat. Struct. Mol. Biol.* 21:664–70

39. Ghosal G, Leung JW-C, Nair BC, Fong K-W, Chen J. 2012. Proliferating cell nuclear antigen (PCNA)-binding protein C1orf124 is a regulator of translesion synthesis. *J. Biol. Chem.* 287:34225–33

40. Gohler T, Munoz IM, Rouse J, Blow JJ. 2008. PTIP/Swift is required for efficient PCNA ubiquitination in response to DNA damage. *DNA Repair* 7:775–87

41. Goodarzi AA, Kurka T, Jeggo PA. 2011. KAP-1 phosphorylation regulates CHD3 nucleosome remodeling during the DNA double-strand break response. *Nat. Struct. Mol. Biol.* 18:831–39

42. Han J, Liu T, Huen MSY, Hu L, Chen Z, Huang J. 2014. SIVA1 directs the E3 ubiquitin ligase RAD18 for PCNA monoubiquitination. *J. Cell Biol.* 205:811–27

43. Haracska L, Torres-Ramos CA, Johnson RE, Prakash S, Prakash L. 2004. Opposing effects of ubiquitin conjugation and SUMO modification of PCNA on replicational bypass of DNA lesions in *Saccharomyces cerevisiae*. *Mol. Cell. Biol.* 24:4267–74

44. Haracska L, Unk I, Prakash L, Prakash S. 2006. Ubiquitylation of yeast proliferating cell nuclear antigen and its implications for translesion DNA synthesis. *PNAS* 103:6477–82

45. Hedglin M, Kumar R, Benkovic SJ. 2013. Replication clamps and clamp loaders. *Cold Spring Harb. Perspect. Biol.* 5:a010165

46. Hibbert RG, Huang A, Boelens R, Sixma TK. 2011. E3 ligase Rad18 promotes monoubiquitination rather than ubiquitin chain formation by E2 enzyme Rad6. *PNAS* 108:5590–95

47. Hoege C, Pfander B, Moldovan GL, Pyrowolakis G, Jentsch S. 2002. *RAD6*-dependent DNA repair is linked to modification of PCNA by ubiquitin and SUMO. *Nature* 419:135–41

48. Hosokawa M, Takehara A, Matsuda K, Eguchi H, Ohigashi H, et al. 2007. Oncogenic role of KIAA0101 interacting with proliferating cell nuclear antigen in pancreatic cancer. *Cancer Res.* 67:2568–76

49. Hu Y, Raynard S, Sehorn MG, Lu X, Bussen W, et al. 2007. RECQL5/Recql5 helicase regulates homologous recombination and suppresses tumor formation via disruption of Rad51 presynaptic filaments. *Genes Dev.* 21:3073–84

50. Huang A, Hibbert RG, de Jong RN, Das D, Sixma TK, Boelens R. 2011. Symmetry and asymmetry of the RING–RING dimer of Rad18. *J. Mol. Biol.* 410:424–35

51. Huang J, Huen MSY, Kim H, Leung CCY, Glover JNM, et al. 2009. RAD18 transmits DNA damage signalling to elicit homologous recombination repair. *Nat. Cell Biol.* 11:592–603

52. Johnson RE, Haracska L, Prakash S, Prakash L. 2001. Role of DNA polymerase η in the bypass of a (6-4) TT photoproduct. *Mol. Cell. Biol.* 21:3558–63

53. Jones JS, Prakash L. 1991. Transcript levels of the *Saccharomyces cerevisiae* DNA repair gene RAD18 increase in UV irradiated cells and during meiosis but not during the mitotic cell cycle. *Nucleic Acids Res.* 19:893–98

54. Jones JS, Weber S, Prakash L. 1988. The *Saccharomyces cerevisiae RAD18* gene encodes a protein that contains potential zinc finger domains for nucleic acid binding and a putative nucleotide binding sequence. *Nucleic Acids Res.* 16:7119–31

55. Juhasz S, Balogh D, Hajdu I, Burkovics P, Villamil MA, et al. 2012. Characterization of human Spartan/C1orf124, an ubiquitin-PCNA interacting regulator of DNA damage tolerance. *Nucleic Acids Res.* 40:10795–808

56. Kannouche PL, Wing J, Lehmann AR. 2004. Interaction of human DNA polymerase η with monoubiquitinated PCNA: a possible mechanism for the polymerase switch in response to DNA damage. *Mol. Cell* 14:491–500

57. Kim H, Dejsuphong D, Adelmant G, Ceccaldi R, Yang K, et al. 2014. Transcriptional repressor ZBTB1 promotes chromatin remodeling and translesion DNA synthesis. *Mol. Cell* 54:107–18

58. Kim MS, Machida Y, Vashisht AA, Wohlschlegel JA, Pang Y-P, Machida YJ. 2013. Regulation of error-prone translesion synthesis by Spartan/C1orf124. *Nucleic Acids Res.* 41:1661–68

59. Klarer AC, Stallons LJ, Burke TJ, Skaggs RL, McGregor WG. 2012. DNA polymerase eta participates in the mutagenic bypass of adducts induced by benzo[a]pyrene diol epoxide in mammalian cells. *PLOS ONE* 7:e39596

60. Koken M, Reynolds P, Bootsma D, Hoeijmakers J, Prakash S, Prakash L. 1991. *Dhr6*, a *Drosophila* homolog of the yeast DNA-repair gene *RAD6*. *PNAS* 88:3832–36

61. Krejci L, Altmannova V, Spirek M, Zhao X. 2012. Homologous recombination and its regulation. *Nucleic Acids Res.* 40:5795–818

62. Krejci L, Van Komen S, Li Y, Villemain J, Reddy MS, et al. 2003. DNA helicase Srs2 disrupts the Rad51 presynaptic filament. *Nature* 423:305–09

63. Kuchta RD, Stengel G. 2010. Mechanism and evolution of DNA primases. *Biochim. Biophys. Acta* 1804:1180–89

64. Lange SS, Takata K, Wood RD. 2011. DNA polymerases and cancer. *Nat. Rev.* 11:96–110

65. Lehmann AR. 2005. Replication of damaged DNA by translesion synthesis in human cells. *FEBS Lett.* 579:873–76

66. Lehmann AR, Niimi A, Ogi T, Brown S, Sabbioneda S, et al. 2007. Translesion synthesis: Y-family polymerases and the polymerase switch. *DNA Repair* 6:891–99

67. Liberi G, Maffioletti G, Lucca C, Chiolo I, Baryshnikova A, et al. 2005. Rad51-dependent DNA structures accumulate at damaged replication forks in *sgs1* mutants defective in the yeast ortholog of BLM RecQ helicase. *Genes Dev.* 19:339–50

68. Lin JR, Zeman MK, Chen JY, Yee MC, Cimprich KA. 2011. SHPRH and HLTF act in a damage-specific manner to coordinate different forms of postreplication repair and prevent mutagenesis. *Mol. Cell* 42:237–49

69. Liu G, Chen X. 2006. DNA polymerase η, the product of the xeroderma pigmentosum variant gene and a target of p53, modulates the DNA damage checkpoint and p53 activation. *Mol. Cell. Biol.* 26:1398–413

70. Liu Y, Yang Y, Tang T-S, Zhang H, Wang Z, et al. 2014. Variants of mouse DNA polymerase κ reveal a mechanism of efficient and accurate translesion synthesis past a benzo[*a*]pyrene dG adduct. *PNAS* 111:1789–94

71. Logette E, Schuepbach-Mallepell S, Eckert MJ, Leo XH, Jaccard B, et al. 2011. PIDD orchestrates translesion DNA synthesis in response to UV irradiation. *Cell Death Differ.* 18:1036–45

72. Lyakhovich A, Shekhar MPV. 2003. Supramolecular complex formation between Rad6 and proteins of the p53 pathway during DNA damage-induced response. *Mol. Cell. Biol.* 23:2463–75

73. Lyakhovich A, Shekhar MPV. 2004. *RAD6B* overexpression confers chemoresistance: RAD6 expression during cell cycle and its redistribution to chromatin during DNA damage-induced response. *Oncogene* 23:3097–106

74. Machida Y, Kim MS, Machida YJ. 2012. Spartan/C1orf124 is important to prevent UV-induced mutagenesis. *Cell Cycle* 11:3395–402

75. Madura K, Prakash S, Prakash L. 1990. Expression of the *Saccharomyces cerevisiae* DNA repair gene *RAD6* that encodes a ubiquitin conjugating enzyme, increases in response to DNA damage and in meiosis but remains constant during the mitotic cell cycle. *Nucleic Acids Res.* 18:771–78

76. Mansilla SF, Soria G, Vallerga MB, Habif M, Martínez-López W, et al. 2013. UV-triggered p21 degradation facilitates damaged-DNA replication and preserves genomic stability. *Nucleic Acids Res.* 41:6942–51

77. Masuda Y, Suzuki M, Kawai H, Suzuki F, Kamiya K. 2012. Asymmetric nature of two subunits of RAD18, a RING-type ubiquitin ligase E3, in the human RAD6A-RAD18 ternary complex. *Nucleic Acids Res.* 40:1065–76

78. Masuyama S, Tateishi S, Yomogida K, Nishimune Y, Suzuki K, et al. 2005. Regulated expression and dynamic changes in subnuclear localization of mammalian Rad18 under normal and genotoxic conditions. *Genes Cells* 10:753–62

79. Mathiasen DP, Lisby M. 2014. Cell cycle regulation of homologous recombination in *Saccharomyces cerevisiae*. *FEMS Microbiol. Rev.* 38:172–84

80. McGlynn P. 2013. Helicases at the replication fork. *Adv. Exp. Med. Biol.* 767:97–121

81. Miyase S, Tateishi S, Watanabe K, Tomita K, Suzuki K, et al. 2005. Differential regulation of Rad18 through Rad6-dependent mono- and polyubiquitination. *J. Biol. Chem.* 280:515–24

82. Moldovan GL, Dejsuphong D, Petalcorin MI, Hofmann K, Takeda S, et al. 2012. Inhibition of homologous recombination by the PCNA-interacting protein PARI. *Mol. Cell* 45:75–86

83. Morrison AJ, Highland J, Krogan NJ, Arbel-Eden A, Greenblatt JF, et al. 2004. INO80 and γ-H2AX interaction links ATP-dependent chromatin remodeling to DNA damage repair. *Cell* 119:767–75

84. Mosbech A, Gibbs-Seymour I, Kagias K, Thorslund T, Beli P, et al. 2012. DVC1 (C1orf124) is a DNA damage–targeting p97 adaptor that promotes ubiquitin-dependent responses to replication blocks. *Nat. Struct. Mol. Biol.* 19:1084–92

85. Nakajima S, Lan L, Kanno S, Usami N, Kobayashi K, et al. 2006. Replication-dependent and -independent responses of RAD18 to DNA damage in human cells. *J. Biol. Chem.* 281:34687–95

86. Niimi A, Brown S, Sabbioneda S, Kannouche PL, Scott A, et al. 2008. Regulation of proliferating cell nuclear antigen ubiquitination in mammalian cells. *PNAS* 105:16125–30

87. Niimi A, Chambers AL, Downs JA, Lehmann AR. 2012. A role for chromatin remodellers in replication of damaged DNA. *Nucleic Acids Res.* 40:7393–403

88. Nikiforov A, Svetlova M, Solovjeva L, Sasina L, Siino J, et al. 2004. DNA damage-induced accumulation of Rad18 protein at stalled replication forks in mammalian cells involves upstream protein phosphorylation. *Biochem. Biophys. Res. Commun.* 323:831–37

89. Nitani N, Yadani C, Yabuuchi H, Masukata H, Nakagawa T. 2008. Mcm4 C-terminal domain of MCM helicase prevents excessive formation of single-stranded DNA at stalled replication forks. *PNAS* 105:12973–78

90. Notenboom V, Hibbert RG, van Rossum-Fikkert SE, Olsen JV, Mann M, Sixma TK. 2007. Functional characterization of Rad18 domains for Rad6, ubiquitin, DNA binding and PCNA modification. *Nucleic Acids Res.* 35:5819–30

91. Ogi T, Shinkai Y, Tanaka K, Ohmori H. 2002. Polκ protects mammalian cells against the lethal and mutagenic effects of benzo[a]pyrene. *PNAS* 99:15548–53

92. Papamichos-Chronakis M, Peterson CL. 2008. The Ino80 chromatin-remodeling enzyme regulates replisome function and stability. *Nat. Struct. Mol. Biol.* 15:338–45

93. Papouli E, Chen S, Davies AA, Huttner D, Krejci L, et al. 2005. Crosstalk between SUMO and ubiquitin on PCNA is mediated by recruitment of the helicase Srs2p. *Mol. Cell* 19:123–33

94. Parker JL, Bucceri A, Davies AA, Heidrich K, Windecker H, Ulrich HD. 2008. SUMO modification of PCNA is controlled by DNA. *EMBO J.* 27:2422–31

95. Parker JL, Ulrich HD. 2009. Mechanistic analysis of PCNA poly-ubiquitylation by the ubiquitin protein ligases Rad18 and Rad5. *EMBO J.* 28:3657–66

96. Parker JL, Ulrich HD. 2012. A SUMO-interacting motif activates budding yeast ubiquitin ligase Rad18 towards SUMO-modified PCNA. *Nucleic Acids Res.* 40:11380–88

97. Patel SS, Pandey M, Nandakumar D. 2011. Dynamic coupling between the motors of DNA replication: hexameric helicase, DNA polymerase, and primase. *Curr. Opin. Chem. Biol.* 15:595–605

98. Pfander B, Moldovan GL, Sacher M, Hoege C, Jentsch S. 2005. SUMO-modified PCNA recruits Srs2 to prevent recombination during S phase. *Nature* 436:428–33

99. Povlsen LK, Beli P, Wagner SA, Poulsen SL, Sylvestersen KB, et al. 2012. Systems-wide analysis of ubiquitylation dynamics reveals a key role for PAF15 ubiquitylation in DNA-damage bypass. *Nat. Cell Biol.* 14:1089–98

100. Prakash S, Johnson RE, Prakash L. 2005. Eukaryotic translesion synthesis DNA polymerases: specificity of structure and function. *Annu. Rev. Biochem.* 74:317–53

101. Prives C, Gottifredi V. 2008. The p21 and PCNA partnership: a new twist for an old plot. *Cell Cycle* 7:3840–46

102. Rechkoblit O, Zhang Y, Guo D, Wang Z, Amin S, et al. 2002. *trans*-Lesion synthesis past bulky benzo[a]pyrene diol epoxide N^2-dG and N^6-dA lesions catalyzed by DNA bypass polymerases. *J. Biol. Chem.* 277:30488–94

103. Sale JE, Lehmann AR, Woodgate R. 2012. Y-family DNA polymerases and their role in tolerance of cellular DNA damage. *Nat. Rev. Mol. Cell Biol.* 13:141–52

104. Sarcevic B, Mawson A, Baker RT, Sutherland RL. 2002. Regulation of the ubiquitin-conjugating enzyme hHR6A by CDK-mediated phosphorylation. *EMBO J.* 21:2009–18

105. Schmutz V, Wagner J, Janel-Bintz R, Fuchs RPP, Cordonnier AM. 2007. Requirements for PCNA monoubiquitination in human cell-free extracts. *DNA Repair* 6:1726–31

106. Schultz DC, Friedman JR, Rauscher FJ 3rd. 2001. Targeting histone deacetylase complexes via KRAB-zinc finger proteins: the PHD and bromodomains of KAP-1 form a cooperative unit that recruits a novel isoform of the Mi-2α subunit of NuRD. *Genes Dev.* 15:428–43

107. Sertic S, Evolvi C, Tumini E, Plevani P, Muzi-Falconi M, Rotondo G. 2013. Non-canonical CRL4A/4B^{CDT2} interacts with RAD18 to modulate post replication repair and cell survival. *PLOS ONE* 8:e60000

108. Shchebet A, Karpiuk O, Kremmer E, Eick D, Johnsen SA. 2012. Phosphorylation by cyclin-dependent kinase-9 controls ubiquitin-conjugating enzyme-2A function. *Cell Cycle* 11:2122–27

109. Shen X, Mizuguchi G, Hamiche A, Wu C. 2000. A chromatin remodelling complex involved in transcription and DNA processing. *Nature* 406:541–44

110. Shimada K, Oma Y, Schleker T, Kugou K, Ohta K, et al. 2008. Ino80 chromatin remodeling complex promotes recovery of stalled replication forks. *Curr. Biol.* 18:566–75

111. Simon AC, Zhou JC, Perera RL, van Deursen F, Evrin C, et al. 2014. A Ctf4 trimer couples the CMG helicase to DNA polymerase α in the eukaryotic replisome. *Nature* 510:293–97

112. Soria G, Gottifredi V. 2010. PCNA-coupled p21 degradation after DNA damage: the exception that confirms the rule? *DNA Repair* 9:358–64

113. Soria G, Podhajcer O, Prives C, Gottifredi V. 2006. P21$^{Cip1/WAF1}$ downregulation is required for efficient PCNA ubiquitination after UV irradiation. *Oncogene* 25:2829–38

114. Soria G, Speroni J, Podhajcer OL, Prives C, Gottifredi V. 2008. p21 differentially regulates DNA replication and DNA-repair-associated processes after UV irradiation. *J. Cell Sci.* 121:3271–82

115. Soultanas P. 2012. Loading mechanisms of ring helicases at replication origins. *Mol. Microbiol.* 84:6–16

116. Suzuki N, Ohashi E, Kolbanovskiy A, Geacintov NE, Grollman AP, et al. 2002. Translesion synthesis by human DNA polymerase κ on a DNA template containing a single stereoisomer of dG-(+)- or dG-(−)-*anti*-N^2-BPDE (7,8-dihydroxy-*anti*-9,10-epoxy-7,8,9,10-tetrahydrobenzo[*a*]pyrene). *Biochemistry* 41:6100–06

117. Tateishi S, Sakuraba Y, Masuyama S, Inoue H, Yamaizumi M. 2000. Dysfunction of human Rad18 results in defective postreplication repair and hypersensitivity to multiple mutagens. *PNAS* 97:7927–32

118. Terai K, Abbas T, Jazaeri AA, Dutta A. 2010. CRL4^{Cdt2} E3 ubiquitin ligase monoubiquitinates PCNA to promote translesion DNA synthesis. *Mol. Cell* 37:143–49

119. Tian F, Sharma S, Zou J, Lin S-Y, Wang B, et al. 2013. *BRCA1* promotes the ubiquitination of PCNA and recruitment of translesion polymerases in response to replication blockade. *PNAS* 110:13558–63

120. Tsanov N, Kermi C, Coulombe P, Van der Laan S, Hodroj D, Maiorano D. 2014. PIP degron proteins, substrates of CRL4^{Cdt2}, and not PIP boxes, interfere with DNA polymerase η and κ focus formation on UV damage. *Nucleic Acids Res.* 42:3692–706

121. Tsuji Y, Watanabe K, Araki K, Shinohara M, Yamagata Y, et al. 2008. Recognition of forked and single-stranded DNA structures by human RAD18 complexed with RAD6B protein triggers its recruitment to stalled replication forks. *Genes Cells* 13:343–54

122. Ulrich HD. 2011. Timing and spacing of ubiquitin-dependent DNA damage bypass. *FEBS Lett.* 585:2861–67

123. Ulrich HD, Jentsch S. 2000. Two RING finger proteins mediate cooperation between ubiquitin-conjugating enzymes in DNA repair. *EMBO J.* 19:3388–97

124. Varanasi L, Do PM, Goluszko E, Martinez LA. 2012. Rad18 is a transcriptional target of E2F3. *Cell Cycle* 11:1131–41

125. Varga A, Marcus AP, Himoto M, Iwai S, Szüts D. Analysis of CPD ultraviolet lesion bypass in chicken DT40 cells: polymerase η and PCNA ubiquitylation play identical roles. *PLOS ONE* 7:e52472

126. Veaute X, Jeusset J, Soustelle C, Kowalczykowski SC, Le Cam E, Fabre F. 2003. The Srs2 helicase prevents recombination by disrupting Rad51 nucleoprotein filaments. *Nature* 423:309–12

127. Villamil MA, Chen J, Liang Q, Zhuang Z. 2012. A noncanonical cysteine protease USP1 is activated through active site modulation by USP1-associated factor 1. *Biochemistry* 51:2829–39

128. Washington MT, Carlson KD, Freudenthal BD, Pryor JM. 2010. Variations on a theme: eukaryotic Y-family DNA polymerases. *Biochim. Biophys. Acta* 1804:1113–23

129. Watanabe K, Tateishi S, Kawasuji M, Tsurimoto T, Inoue H, Yamaizumi M. 2004. Rad18 guides polη to replication stalling sites through physical interaction and PCNA monoubiquitination. *EMBO J.* 23:3886–96

130. Windecker H, Ulrich HD. 2008. Architecture and assembly of poly-SUMO chains on PCNA in *Saccharomyces cerevisiae*. *J. Mol. Biol.* 376:221–31

131. Wold MS. 1997. Replication protein A: a heterotrimeric, single-stranded DNA-binding protein required for eukaryotic DNA metabolism. *Annu. Rev. Biochem.* 66:61–92

132. Wood A, Schneider J, Dover J, Johnston M, Shilatifard A. 2005. The Bur1/Bur2 complex is required for histone H2B monoubiquitination by Rad6/Bre1 and histone methylation by COMPASS. *Mol. Cell* 20:589–99

133. Yanagihara H, Kobayashi J, Tateishi S, Kato A, Matsuura S, et al. 2011. NBS1 recruits RAD18 via a RAD6-like domain and regulates Pol η-dependent translesion DNA synthesis. *Mol. Cell* 43:788–97

134. Yang K, Weinacht CP, Zhuang Z. 2013. Regulatory role of ubiquitin in eukaryotic DNA translesion synthesis. *Biochemistry* 52:3217–28

135. Yang XH, Shiotani B, Classon M, Zou L. 2008. Chk1 and Claspin potentiate PCNA ubiquitination. *Genes Dev.* 22:1147–52

136. Yoon J-H, Prakash L, Prakash S. 2009. Highly error-free role of DNA polymerase η in the replicative bypass of UV-induced pyrimidine dimers in mouse and human cells. *PNAS* 106:18219–24

137. Yoon J-H, Prakash L, Prakash S. 2010. Error-free replicative bypass of (6-4) photoproducts by DNA polymerase ζ in mouse and human cells. *Genes Dev.* 24:123–28

138. Yu P, Huang B, Shen M, Lau C, Chan E, et al. 2001. p15^PAF, a novel PCNA associated factor with increased expression in tumor tissues. *Oncogene* 20:484–89

139. Yuasa MS, Masutani C, Hirano A, Cohn MA, Yamaizumi M, et al. 2006. A human DNA polymerase η complex containing Rad18, Rad6 and Rev1; proteomic analysis and targeting of the complex to the chromatin-bound fraction of cells undergoing replication fork arrest. *Genes Cells* 11:731–44

140. Zhang S, Chea J, Meng X, Zhou Y, Lee EY, Lee MY. 2008. PCNA is ubiquitinated by RNF8. *Cell Cycle* 7:3399–404

141. Zhang Y, Wu X, Guo D, Rechkoblit O, Wang Z. 2002. Activities of human DNA polymerase κ in response to the major benzo[*a*]pyrene DNA adduct: error-free lesion bypass and extension synthesis from opposite the lesion. *DNA Repair* 1:559–69

142. Zheng L, Shen B. 2011. Okazaki fragment maturation: nucleases take centre stage. *J. Mol. Cell Biol.* 3:23–30

143. Zhou B, Arnett DR, Yu X, Brewster A, Sowd GA, et al. 2012. Structural basis for the interaction of a hexameric replicative helicase with the regulatory subunit of human DNA polymerase α-primase. *J. Biol. Chem.* 287:26854–66

144. Ziv O, Geacintov N, Nakajima S, Yasui A, Livneh Z. 2009. DNA polymerase ζ cooperates with polymerases κ and ι in translesion DNA synthesis across pyrimidine photodimers in cells from XPV patients. *PNAS* 106:11552–57

Structure Principles of CRISPR-Cas Surveillance and Effector Complexes

Tsz Kin Martin Tsui and Hong Li

Institute of Molecular Biophysics and Department of Chemistry and Biochemistry, Florida State University, Tallahassee, FL 32306; email: hong.li@fsu.edu

Annu. Rev. Biophys. 2015. 44:229–55

First published online as a Review in Advance on May 27, 2015

The *Annual Review of Biophysics* is online at biophys.annualreviews.org

This article's doi: 10.1146/annurev-biophys-060414-033939

Keywords

DNA interference, RNA silencing, ribonucleoprotein particles, prokaryote immunity

Abstract

The pathway of CRISPR-Cas immunity redefines the roles of RNA in the flow of genetic information and ignites excitement for next-generation gene therapy tools. CRISPR-Cas machineries offer a fascinating set of new enzyme assemblies from which one can learn principles of molecular interactions and chemical activities. The interference step of the CRISPR-Cas immunity pathway congregates proteins, RNA, and DNA into a single molecular entity that selectively destroys invading nucleic acids. Although much remains to be discovered, a picture of how the interference process takes place is emerging. This review focuses on the current structural data for the three known types of RNA-guided nucleic acid interference mechanisms. In it, we describe key features of individual complexes and we emphasize comparisons across types and along functional stages. We aim to provide readers with a set of core principles learned from the three types of interference complexes and a deep appreciation of the diversity among them.

Contents

INTRODUCTION

Clustered regularly interspaced short palindromic repeats (CRISPR): prokaryotic DNA loci that store invader genetic elements used for defending against invaders

Repeat: a short and repetitive DNA element within the CRISPR locus; often palindromic but can be nonpalindromic

Spacer: a unique short DNA element flanked by identical repeats within the CRISPR locus; often match genetic elements of invaders

The recent discovery of adaptive immunity in prokaryotes conferred by clustered regularly interspaced short palindromic repeats (CRISPR) and CRISPR-associated (Cas) proteins (3, 8, 18) has excited several scientific communities, including but not limited to those focused on microbiology, RNA biology, and biotechnology. The CRISPR-Cas loci are widespread in sequenced genomes of bacteria (~48%) and archaea (~84%). These loci provide microbes with defense against invading genetic elements in a sequence-specific manner; at a conceptual level, this defense mechanism is reminiscent of RNA interference in eukaryotes. The immunity mediated by CRISPR-Cas includes three functional processes: spacer acquisition, CRISPR RNA (crRNA) maturation, and target interference (**Figure 1**). The spacer acquisition step incorporates new spacers from the invading virus or plasmids into the CRISPR locus, the crRNA maturation step prepares functional crRNAs from the transcript of the repeat–spacer array, and the target interference step directs crRNA-guided cleavage of invading genetic elements. For extensive reviews on the CRISPR-Cas pathway, the reader is referred to References 5, 21, 35, 53, 77, 84, 86, 88, and 91.

All three functional processes are essential for CRISPR-Cas-mediated immunity and are of great interest to biotechnology and for industry applications. Both scholarly and practical interests in CRISPR-Cas biology demand a thorough understanding of its inner workings, especially the mechanisms that underlie molecular assembly, enzyme specificity, and regulatory interactions. Over the past several years, functional and structural data on CRISPR-Cas machineries have rapidly become available, providing unprecedented access to information about the mechanism(s) of multicomponent protein–nucleic acid assembly and nucleic acid interference. This

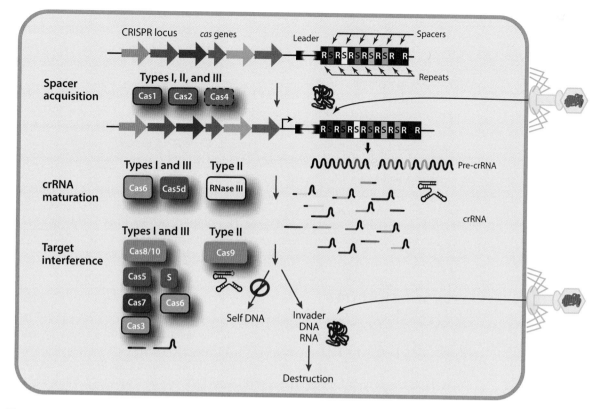

Figure 1

Overview of the CRISPR-Cas immunity pathways and their associated Cas proteins. In the spacer acquisition step, DNA segments are incorporated into the repeat–spacer array near the leader sequence. Cas1 and Cas2, and Cas4 in some organisms, are believed to be responsible for this process. Cas6, and in some cases Cas5d or endogenous RNase III, is the primary enzyme that processes precursor crRNA transcripts to generate mature crRNA. Additional maturation steps may take place in some systems, but these steps have not yet been characterized. During the target interference step, crRNA and the remaining Cas proteins assemble into three different types of ribonucleoprotein particles (crRNPs) that destroy invader nucleic acids and spare self nucleic acids. Abbreviations: Cas, CRISPR-associated; CRISPR, clustered regularly interspaced short palindromic repeats; crRNA, CRISPR RNA.

review summarizes the biochemical and structural discoveries related to the machineries responsible for nucleic acid interference mediated by CRISPR-Cas. Other excellent reviews of the similar and related processes can be found in References 2, 31, 32, 39, 45, 66, 86. In the following sections, we describe the nomenclature, function, organization, and nucleic acid interference models of all known interference complexes, and we aim to make mechanistic connections by comparing the available functional and structural data. We conclude with a discussion of the structural basis for genome editing applications.

CRISPR-Cas SYSTEMS

Functional CRISPR-Cas loci comprise a DNA repeat–spacer array, a set of *cas* genes, and a leader sequence. The locus-specific repeat sequences range from 23 to 48 nucleotides (nt) in length, and each bears the identity of a particular CRISPR-Cas system and dictates CRISPR-specific interactions (44). The repeats are interspersed with distinct spacer sequences that are roughly 24–70 nt long, and some of these sequences match regions of bacteriophage or plasmid DNA

(7, 34, 55, 62). The complementarity between the spacers and the invader genetic elements is the basis upon which the CRISPR-Cas systems target invaders for destruction. The leader sequence is believed to direct transcription of the repeat–spacer array and acquisition of new spacers (63, 94). With only one exception (12), Cas proteins are responsible for all three functional steps of the CRISPR-Cas immunity (21, 86).

Although the Cas proteins are overwhelmingly diverse (25, 48), bioinformatics and functional testing have helped to categorize most of them into ten broad superfamilies, Cas1–Cas10 (49, 50). Cas1 and Cas2 (11, 94), and possibly Cas4 (47), are involved in the spacer acquisition step, but their mechanism(s) of action remains uncharacterized. The crRNA maturation step is carried out by the Cas6 superfamily of endoribonucleases in most CRISPR-Cas systems (8, 10, 30, 46, 68), but, in systems that lack Cas6, this step is carried out either by a distinct Cas5 protein, Cas5d (58), or by the host RNase III in a *trans*-activating RNA-dependent manner (12) (**Figure 1**). During the interference stage, the crRNA is assembled with specific Cas proteins into CRISPR ribonucleoprotein (crRNP) complexes (**Figure 1**). crRNPs that search for but do not cleave target nucleic acids, termed surveillance crRNPs, recruit additional effector proteins to cleave target nucleic acids. Those that do cleave target nucleic acids are termed effector crRNPs.

TYPES AND SUBTYPES

CRISPR-Cas systems are categorized into three major types (I, II and III) primarily on the basis of the phylogeny of the best-conserved *cas1* gene and the combined presence of other *cas* genes, and each type is further divided into subtypes (49). All three types share the same functional paths (**Figure 1**), but they differ in the methods and machineries used to carry out these functions (**Figure 2**). Although types I and type III crRNPs are prevalent in both bacteria and archaea, type II crRNPs are found only in bacterial organisms. A given organism may possess one, two, or all of the CRISPR-Cas types; however, in organisms containing more than one CRISPR-Cas type, neither the interaction among different types nor the distribution of functional roles is known (9).

The three types of CRISPR-Cas systems produce functional crRNA using different methods. In the type I and type III systems, the crRNA is processed primarily by the Cas6 endoribonuclease. The mature crRNA bears a 7- or 8-nt 5′ tag derived from the 3′ portion of the repeat, the guide, and, in the cases where the 3′ region is not processed further, a stem loop derived from the 5′ portion of the repeat (10, 22, 30, 67, 68, 72, 74, 81) (**Figure 2**). In the type I-C system, in which Cas6 is absent, this process is carried out by the Cas5d endoribonuclease, and the crRNA bears a similar overall structure but has an 11-nt 5′ tag (58). Both the Cas6 and Cas5d associated with the type I system are typically single-turnover enzymes and are part of the interference complex (22, 30, 58, 72, 81). The Cas6 associated with the type III system often dissociates from the product after processing, however, and remains independent from the interference complexes (74, 76, 87) (**Figure 2**). The type II system employs the host RNase III endoribonuclease in a *trans*-activating crRNA (tracrRNA)-dependent manner and produces crRNAs bearing a 3′ tag that remains paired with the tracrRNA throughout the interference function (**Figure 2**) (12).

The three CRISPR-Cas types also differ in interference target and in the composition of their interference complexes. The type I CRISPR-Cas system targets DNA exclusively, whereas some subtypes of the type II and type III systems target DNA and others target RNA. Both type I and type III interference complexes are multi–Cas protein crRNPs that have a single RNA subunit (**Figure 2**). The genes encoding these crRNP proteins are typically arranged as a cassette or as an operon, but not all proteins encoded within the cassette are part of the interference complexes. Type II interference complexes comprise a single Cas9 protein and two different RNA subunits (**Figure 2**).

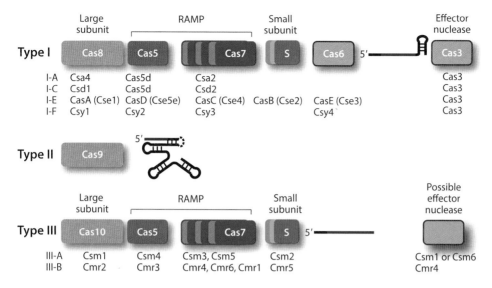

Figure 2

The principal components of the three types of interference complexes. Proteins are represented by colored bars, and crRNA are represented by lines. Type I and type III crRNPs share the same four fundamental protein classes (large subunit, small subunit, Cas5, and Cas7). The large subunit is Cas8 for type I crRNPs and Cas10 for type III crRNPs, and Cas5 and Cas7 are distinct classes of the repeat associated mysterious protein (RAMP) superfamily. Type I crRNPs recruit an effector protein, Cas3, for DNA cleavage. The effector protein for the DNA-targeting type III crRNPs is not yet known, although Csm1 and Csm6 are the speculated effector proteins for type III-A, and Cmr4 is believed to be the effector protein of the type III-B crRNP. The guide region of the crRNA is shown in red, and the region derived from the repeat sequences is shown in black. The type II crRNPs comprise Cas9, a crRNA, and a *trans*-activating RNA (tracrRNA). The crRNA and the tracrRNA maybe covalently linked by a stem loop (*dashed line*), resulting in a single guide RNA (sgRNA). The names of other individual Cas proteins used in specific crRNPs that have been identified so far are listed under the cartoon for each type. Abbreviations: Cmr, Cas module RAMP antiviral complex; Csm, Cas subtype *Mycobacterium tuberculosis* antiviral complex (Csm).

PRINCIPAL BUILDING BLOCKS

The need to define a common set of principal components of crRNPs arises from the multiple naming systems used for these complexes and the observed similarity in their three-dimensional organizations. The systematic naming system for the Cas proteins first proposed by Makarova & Koonin in 2011 (49), and refined in 2013 (50), best reflects the structural and functional similarities among the different types and subtypes of crRNPs. In their unified system, type II crRNPs comprise a single class of protein, Cas9, whereas both type I and type III crRNPs share four fundamental classes of proteins: the large subunit, the small subunit, Cas5, and Cas7 (**Figure 2**). The large subunit comprises the Cas8 class of proteins for type I crRNPs and the Cas10 class for the type III crRNPs. These two protein classes contain polymerase-like features, and proteins belonging to the Cas10 class are often fused with a histidine–aspartate (HD) nuclease domain. The small subunit in type I and type III crRNPs is a small α-helical protein that plays essential roles in complex assembly. Cas5 and Cas7 are distinct classes of the repeat associated mysterious protein (RAMP) superfamily that are characterized by the presence of the ferredoxin-like fold (47). The RAMP superfamily also includes other Cas protein classes such as Cas6 proteins, which process crRNA (47) and form part of the mature complexes for the subtype I-E, I-B, and I-F crRNPs because of their tight association with the processed crRNA.

Repeat associated mysterious proteins (RAMPs): proteins containing a ferredoxin-like fold and a glycine-rich loop; these proteins are the most abundant type of Cas protein

In addition to the stably bound protein factors, type I, and possibly type III-A, crRNPs recruit additional effector proteins to cleave their DNA targets. Type I crRNPs recruit the Cas3 nuclease-helicase for cleavage of target DNA after substrate binding, and this protein is thus a key component of the holo-complexes (**Figure 2**). Note that Cas3 also contains the same HD nuclease domain as that in the Cas10 protein, suggesting a frequent exchange of domains among Cas proteins. The identity of the effector protein for the type III-A crRNP remains elusive owing to limited biochemical data. A recent study showed that *Staphylococcus epidermidis* type III-A crRNP achieves DNA targeting in a transcription-dependent manner (23). In this case, the HD domain associated with the Cas10 subunit may be responsible for cleaving DNA (23, 65). Alternatively, type III-A crRNP recruits an unidentified effector protein to cleave DNA. The stable assemblies for both type III-B (RNA-cleaving) and type II-A (DNA-cleaving) crRNPs are associated with catalytic activities. Cas7 is believed to be the catalytic subunit of the III-B crRNPs, and Cas9 bears a RuvC domain and an HNH-like nuclease domains that are responsible for DNA cleavage.

DISCOVERY

Works from laboratories across the globe have resulted in isolation and biochemical characterization of representatives of type I, type II, and type III crRNPs. In all cases, bioinformatics analysis provided the initial guidance in the search for interference activities, and such analysis has made selective purification and reconstitution possible. In combination, traditional biochemical purification methods and modern sequencing and mass spectrometry techniques ultimately led to the isolation and characterization of nucleic acid–targeting crRNPs.

Among all types of crRNPs, the first to be isolated was a type I-E surveillance complex termed Cascade (CRISPR-associated complex for antiviral defense) isolated from *Escherichia coli* by Brouns et al. in 2008 (8). This complex was purified from cells overexpressing the CRISPR locus with a single affinity tag incorporated in various *cas* genes, and it was shown to contain five Cas proteins and a ∼57-nt crRNA (8). The five proteins, CasA (also called Cse1 or Cas8), CasB (also called Cse2 or small subunit), CasC (also called Cse4 or Cas7), CasD (also called Cas5e), and CasE (also called Cse3 or Cas6e) (**Figure 2**) are encoded by an operon containing *casA–casE*. CasE is the endoribonuclease responsible for processing crRNA by the Cascade (8). Specific gene knockout followed by phage resistance assay demonstrated the essential function of each protein against viral infection in vivo (8). The Cascades of type I-A (46), I-C (58), and I-F (92) were later isolated in a similar manner and found to contain analogous protein subunits, with two exceptions. The type I-C and type I-F Cascade contain only three (Csd1, Csd2, and Cas5d) and four (Csy1, Csy2, Csy3, and Csy4) subunits, respectively, although both complexes also contain a crRNA-processing endoribonuclease. The type I-C endoribonuclease Cas5d shares RNA recognition properties with both CasE and CasD of type I-E, and these shared properties led to a provocative model in which Cas5d plays the roles of both CasE and CasD (58). The type I-F Cascade lacks the CasB-equivalent subunit but its Csy1 subunit appears to contain a CasB-equivalent domain (92), suggesting a conserved Cascade organization.

The type II effector crRNPs were first demonstrated to have an in vivo DNA interference function in 2007 and 2010 (3, 18). In 2012, two different groups (19, 40) subsequently characterized the subunit composition and in vitro DNA cleavage activity of the *Streptococcus pyogenes* and *Streptococcus thermophilus* type II-A crRNPs. Type II-A crRNPs contain a single protein subunit, Cas9 (also Csn1), a crRNA of 39–42 nt in length, and a tracrRNA of ∼75 nt. The tracrRNA base pairs with the repeat region of the crRNA and is required for crRNA processing by the host RNase III in the presence of Cas9 (12, 24). Jinek et al. (40) further demonstrated that for the type II-A system, the crRNA and tracrRNA may be linked into a single guide RNA (sgRNA) by a

HD domain: a nuclease domain containing arrangements of histidine and aspartate residues, typically H—HD—D or HD—H—D

CRISPR-associated complex for antiviral defense (Cascade): the first reported CRISPR antiviral complex; belongs to the type I-E CRISPR-Cas system

tetraloop without affecting its DNA interference function, making this complex the simplest DNA interference complex known. A type II-B crRNP from *Francisella novicida* was reported around the same time, and this complex regulates endogenous gene expression in order to promote bacterial virulence without requiring catalytic centers for DNA cleavage (42, 70). The type II-B crRNP is believed to target mRNA and to contain Cas9, a tracrRNA of ~91 nt, and a small CRISPR/Cas-associated RNA (scaRNA) of ~48 nt (70), although the *F. novicida* Cas9 is also able to cleave DNA in vitro using its tracrRNA and crRNA (16). Several other type II systems similar to the *F. novicida* crRNP also contribute to pathogenesis of their host bacteria (70). The type II effector crRNPs are considered one of the most important discoveries in CRISPR-Cas studies, and these discoveries have resulted in an explosion of applications in many areas of biology.

The first antiplasmid immunity function by a type III crRNP was reported in 2008, when it was described for the type III-A Csm (Cas subtype *Mycobacterium tuberculosis* antiviral complex) from *S. epidermidis* (52). Affinity purification of the crRNA-containing Csm later resulted in identification of five associated Csm proteins (Csm1–Csm5) all encoded from the *cas10-csm* operon and a 31–67-nt crRNA (28, 29). The native Csm from *Sulfolobus solfataricus* (Sso) was also purified by a combination of affinity and ion exchange methods, but this complex was shown to contain eight Csm proteins and a crRNA (69). Surprisingly, one recent study showed that a type III-A Csm cleaves RNA rather than DNA in vitro (80). In 2009, Terns and colleagues (27) isolated another type III crRNP, the type III-B Cmr (Cas module RAMP antiviral complex), from the cell extract of the archaeon *Pyrococcus furiosus* (Pf). Interestingly, the Cmr was also shown to have RNA cleavage (27). The PfCmr contains six proteins, Cmr1–Cmr6, all of which are encoded from a tightly linked RAMP module (named after the predominant presence of RAMP proteins), and one of two distinct crRNAs, a 45-mer and a 39-mer species (27). Two other Cmrs were later isolated from *Thermus thermophilus* (Tt) (79) and *S. solfataricus* (95) and were found to have the same core composition, although the two complexes varied somewhat in the size of the crRNA and the number of Cmr proteins. The TtCmr has the same Cmr1–Cmr6 subunits as in the PfCmr, along with a 40- or 46-mer crRNA (79). In addition to containing Cmr1–Cmr6, the SsoCmr also has an Sso-specific Cmr7 protein (95). The precise size of the SsoCmr-associated crRNA has not been characterized, but it was estimated to be ~46 nucleotides (95). Similar to the PfCmr, both TtCmr and SsoCmr have RNA cleavage activities in vitro.

crRNA, tracrRNA, and sgRNA: type-specific small RNAs derived from CRISPR-related loci used by Cas proteins in guiding RNA processing or nucleic acid interference

Cas subtype *Mycobacterium tuberculosis* antiviral complex (Csm): type III-A under the unified system; first demonstrated DNA interference CRISPR-Cas system

Cas module RAMP antiviral complex (Cmr): type III-B under the unified system; first demonstrated RNA interference CRISPR-Cas system

FUNCTIONS

The process of RNA-guided nucleic acid destruction begins with assembly of functional crRNPs and ends with the capture and cleavage of the target nucleic acids. Similar to other ribonucleo-protein particles, this process involves intricate protein–protein, protein–nucleic acid, and nucleic acid–nucleic acid interactions, and it requires enzymatic activities that break the phosphodiester bond. In addition to these shared processes, the three types of crRNPs also exhibit type-specific functions, which we describe below.

Most crRNPs target DNA for destruction; type II-B and type III-B crRNPs are believed to also target RNA. The in vitro RNA cleavage activity of the type III-B complex has allowed us to learn its functional properties. Both a region of ~31–38 nt (depending on the size of crRNA) that is complementary to the guide region of the crRNA and a correctly assembled multisubunit Cmr were shown to be necessary and sufficient for RNA cleavage. Importantly, two of the three reported Cmrs exhibit the ability to make regularly spaced excisions, and this ability may be explained by two possible models of assembly (26, 64, 79). The first model is a single Cmr assembly bearing regularly spaced RNA cleavage centers. The second entails multiple Cmr assemblies of a regular size, each of which contains a single RNA cleavage center. Current structural data are consistent with the former model, but they do not exclude the latter. RNA cleavage by the Cmrs requires divalent ions, but the cleavage products are consistent with a metal-independent mechanism, suggesting that the metal ions play a structural rather than catalytic role.

In contrast to the type III-B crRNPs, the type I, type II-A, and type III-A crRNPs target DNA in vivo. Both type II-A and type III-A crRNPs were recently shown to also have RNA cleavage activity in vitro (60, 80), however, suggesting an RNA binding and cleavage mechanism that may be related to that for DNA. The DNA targeted by these crRNPs contains a sequence segment (protospacer) that is complementary to the guide region of the crRNA (spacer). During interference, the guide region of the crRNA pairs with the complementary strand of the protospacer to form a structure called an R-loop while a protein or proteins cleave both the complementary and the noncomplementary strands. Importantly, because the crRNA is also complementary to its encoding DNA, the crRNPs must be able to distinguish the self DNA from the invader DNA. The type III-A crRNP is believed to discriminate its own DNA on the basis of the repeat sequences flanking the complementary spacers (52). For type I and type II crRNPs, a 2–5-nt segment adjacent to the protospacer [protospacer-adjacent motif (PAM)], as well as the paired crRNA, is sufficient for crRNPs to control this specificity (13, 54). Protospacers lacking a PAM remain intact when challenged by crRNPs. Finally, the type I and type III-A DNA-targeting crRNPs must recruit effector proteins that perform the actual DNA cleavage.

Recent structural and biochemical data have provided important insights about each of the functions described above. Intricate molecular interaction networks and large molecular motions have been observed. Successful studies of distinct crRNPs have revealed unique mechanisms that are pertinent to individual complexes. However, comparisons of the overall and subunit structures have revealed surprising mechanistic links among remotely related crRNPs, including links between those that target DNA versus RNA.

ASSEMBLY

Studies of crRNPs by electron microscopy, X-ray crystallography, native mass spectroscopy, and biochemical techniques have revealed atomic or near atomic resolution models for several crRNPs belonging to each of the three main types. These structural models have provided important insights into crRNP assembly and function. Owing to the structural relatedness between type I and type III crRNPs, we discuss their assembly principles together, and we discuss those for the type II crRNP separately.

The preparation of homogeneous specimens in large quantities has been crucial to the success of the structural studies cited here. In all reported cases, recombinant proteins from bacterial expression systems and a combination of synthetic and in vitro transcribed RNA were used to assemble the complexes. However, assembling these complexes, including the crRNA, within the expression hosts using coexpression strategies has proven to be much more helpful and, in some cases, necessary. For the six-component type I-E Cascade complex, a plasmid bearing the gene encoding Cas8 and a tandem repeat–spacer array was cotransformed into expression *E. coli* cells with another plasmid bearing the operon encoding Cas5, Cas6, Cas7, and the small subunit (38, 57, 96). For the multicomponent type III complexes, either native purification (80) or subcomplex purification followed by assembly with synthetic RNA on gel filtration columns proved to be effective (6, 64, 78, 79). For the type II Cas9 protein, bacterial expression worked sufficiently well for protein production despite its large size, but the challenge of constructing the appropriate RNA and DNA molecules had to be overcome via nucleic acid engineering (41). A minimal chimera RNA between the crRNA and tracrRNA was found to be fully functional and was employed in structural studies (1, 59).

Protospacers:
exogenous nucleic acid elements with sequences that are complementary to those of CRISPR spacers

R-loop:
a three-stranded structure in which an RNA is hybridized to a complementary DNA strand, resulting in displacement of the noncomplementary strand

Protospacer-adjacent motif (PAM): a highly conserved and system-specific 2–5 nucleotide motif flanking one side of the protospacer that triggers DNA interference

Type I and Type III: Helical Assembly

Single-particle cryo-electron microscopy (cryoEM) and X-ray crystallographic studies have revealed detailed subunit arrangement and interaction information (33, 38, 43, 57, 90, 96). Combined EM, X-ray crystallographic, and mass spectrometry data for the type III-B Cmr (6, 64, 78, 79) are now available, as are negative-stained EM data for the type III-A Csm (69). In addition, crystal structures are available for many individual subunits of both type I and type III crRNPs (**Table 1**). These studies show that, despite having distant phylogeny, the type I and type III crRNPs share a surprisingly similar architecture. Analysis of the available crystal structures of individual subunits across type I and type III crRNPs suggests a propensity for a common helical assembly and for binding single-stranded crRNA. Type-specific differences have also been observed that may explain functional variations among crRNPs.

Type I and type III crRNPs are elongated in shape with a distinct head and a base flanking a helical body (**Figure 3**). The crRNA lies linearly along a central channel through the major groove of the helical assembly, and its $5'$ and $3'$ ends are anchored in the base and the head of this assembly, respectively. This architecture has been compared to the shapes of seahorses or sea worms (31). The four principal protein classes are arranged similarly in space in the crRNP structures regardless the type (**Figure 3**). Each crRNP contains a single copy of the large subunit, one or two Cas5 proteins, and varying numbers of copies of the small subunit and the Cas7 proteins. The most-conserved region of the crRNPs is the base, which comprises the large subunit and Cas5. The least-conserved region is the head, which comprises type-specific components. The head of the type I-E Cascade is formed by the crRNA-processing endonuclease Cas6 bound to the $3'$ hairpin of the crRNA, whereas those of the type III-A and type III-B complexes are formed by heterogeneous Cas7 proteins (**Figure 3**).

The most represented protein class in type I and type III crRNPs is the Cas7 class that forms the major helical backbone of the Cascade, the Csms, and the Cmrs (**Figures 3** and **4**, 7.1–7.6). Both the type I-E Cascade and the type III-B Cmrs contain six copies of Cas7, which may be either the same or different (**Figure 4**). Cascade contains six identical Cas7 proteins (CasC) (**Figures 3** and **4**, 7.1–7.6) (38, 57, 96), whereas the Cmr contains three different Cas7 proteins [Cmr4 (four subunits), Cmr1 (one subunit), and Cmr6 (one subunit)] (6, 64, 78, 79). The Sso type III-A Csm contains eight Cas7 proteins, which belong to five different subclasses (69), and the TtCsm contains seven Cas7 subunits, which belong to two different subclasses (80). However, the overall size and shape of the SsoCsm and the TtCsm are similar to those of the Cmr (**Figure 3**) (6, 69). The second multirepeat protein is the small subunit, which is represented either two or three times among the crRNPs (**Figures 3** and **4**, S.1–S.3). The small subunit forms the second backbone of the central body that complements the contour of the Cas7 backbone (**Figures 3** and **4**).

The similarity in assembly between the type I and type III crRNPs is further supported by structural similarities among the individual principal building blocks. The large subunits of both type I-E (Cas8) and type III-B (Cas10) crRNPs are multidomain and are dominated by helical secondary structures (**Figure 5**). Similarly, the small subunit is exclusively helical in both types (**Figure 5**). Both Cas7 and Cas5 belong to the RAMP superfamily, which includes proteins that are characterized by the ferredoxin-like fold and have structures that are comparable to that of a right hand (**Figures 4**, **6**, and **7**). The ferredoxin-like fold forms the core of the protein, or the palm. A long β-hairpin protruding between the second and the third core β-strands comprises the thumb, and a helical insertion between the first and the second core β-strands forms the fingers. Cas5 proteins seem to lack the fingers domain, suggesting that this domain is specific to Cas7 (**Figures 4** and **6**). The helical assembly of crRNPs arises from the filamentous characteristics of the Cas7 family of proteins. Cas7 can self-assemble in a head-to-tail (or thumb-to-palm) fashion and can thus extend

Table 1 List of crystal and electron microscopy (EM) structures of CRISPR ribonucleoproteins (crRNPs) and subunits*

crRNP or subunit name	Subtype and species	PDB ID (resolution)	Components	Notes
Crystal structures				
Cascade	I-E *Escherichia coli* K12 (*Ec*)	4U7U (3.0 Å)	Cas8, Cas5, Cas6, Cas7, small subunit, crRNA	First crystal structure of multisubunit CRISPR-Cas crRNP
Cascade	I-E *Escherichia coli* K12 (*Ec*)	1VY8 (3.2 Å)	Cas8, Cas5, Cas6, Cas7, small subunit, crRNA	First crystal structure of multisubunit CRISPR-Cas crRNP
Cascade	I-E *Escherichia coli* K12 (*Ec*)	4QYZ (3.0 Å)	Cas8, Cas5, Cas6, Cas7, small subunit, crRNA, ssDNA	First crystal structure of multisubunit CRISPR-Cas crRNP bound with an ssDNA substrate
Cas3	I-C *Thermobifida fusca* YX (*Tf*)	4QQW (2.7 Å)	Cas3, Fe^{3+} DNA,	First Cas3 structure
		4QQX (3.3 Å)	Cas3, Fe^{3+}, ATP	First Cas3 structure
		4QQY (3.1 Å)	Cas3, Fe^{3+} ADP	First Cas3 structure
		4QQZ (2.9 Å)	Cas3, Fe^{3+}, DNA, ANP	First Cas3 structure
Cas7 (Csa2)	I-A *Sulfolobus solfataricus* P2 (*Sso*)	3PS0 (2.0 Å)	Cas7	First type I-A Cas7 structure
Cas7 (Cmr4)	III-B *Pyrococcus furiosus* DSM 3638 (*Pf*)	4RDP (2.8 Å)	Cas7	First type III-B Cas7 structure
Cas7 (Csc2)	I-D *Thermofilum pendens* (*Tp*)	4TXD (1.8 Å)	Cas7	First type I-D Cas7 structure
Cas7 (Csm3)	III-A *Methanopyrus kandleri* (*Mk*)	4N0L (2.4 Å)	Cas7	First type III-A Cas7 structure
Cas5 (Cas5d)	I-C *Bacillus halodurans* (*Bh*)	4F3M (1.7 Å)	Cas5	First type I-C Cas5 structure; first Cas5 protein to show RNA processing activity
Cas5 (Cmr3)	III-B *Pyrococcus furiosus* DSM 3638 (*Pf*)	4H4K (2.8 Å)	Cas10, Cas5	Second type III-B Cas5 structure; α1 helix observed; thumb disordered
Cas5 (Cmr3)	II-B *Pyrococcus furiosus* DSM 3638 (*Pf*)	3W2W (2.5 Å)	Cas10, Cas5	Second type III-B Cas5 structure; thumb β-hairpin observed; α1 helix disordered
Cas8 (Cse1, CasA)	I-E *Acidimicrobium ferrooxidans* DSM 10331 (*Acf*)	4H3T (2.0 Å)	Cas8	
Cas10 (Cmr2)	III-B *Pyrococcus furiosus* DSM 3638 (*Pf*)	3UNG (2.3 Å)	Cas10	First type III-B Cas10 structure; ATP and metal binding observed
Small subunit (Cmr5)	III-B *Pyrococcus furiosus* DSM 3638 (*Pf*)	4GKF (2.1 Å)	Cmr5	
Small subunit (Cmr5)	III-B *Thermus thermophilus* HB8 (*Tt*)	2ZOP (2.1 Å)	Cmr5	
Small subunit (Cmr5)	III-B *Archaeoglobus fulgidus* (*Af*)	2OEB (1.6 Å)	Cmr5	
Small subunit (CasB)	I-E *Thermobifida fusca* (*Tf*)	4H79 (1.9 Å)	CasB	
Small subunit (CasB)	I-A *Thermus thermophilus* (*Tt*)	4H7A (2.6 Å)	CasB	

(Continued)

Table 1 (*Continued*)

crRNP or subunit name	Subtype and species	PDB ID (resolution)	Components	Notes
Cas9	II-A *Streptococcus pyogenes* SF370 (*Sp*)	4UN3 (2.6 Å)	Cas9, sgRNA, PAM-containing dsDNA	First Cas9 bound with a PAM-containing dsDNA
		4UN4 (2.4 Å)	Cas9, sgRNA, PAM-containing dsDNA with 2-nt mismatch	
		4UN5 (2.4 Å)	Cas9, sgRNA, PAM-containing dsDNA with 3-nt mismatch	
Cas9	II-A *Streptococcus pyogenes* (*Sp*)	4OO8 (2.5 Å)	Cas9, sgRNA, ssDNA	First Cas9 structure bound with sgRNA and ssDNA
Cas9	II-A *Streptococcus pyogenes* SF370 (*Sp*)	4CMP (2.6 Å)	Cas9	First apo Cas9 structures (II-A and II-C)
		4CMQ (3.1 Å)	Cas9, Mn^{2+}	
Cas9	II-C *Actinomyces naeslundii* (*An*)	4OGE (2.2 Å)	Cas9	
		4OGC (2.8 Å)	Cas9, Mn^{2+}	
EM structures				
Cmr	III-B *Thermus thermophilus* (*Tt*)	EMD-2418 (22 Å)	Cas10, Cas5, three different Cas7s (Cmr1, Cmr4, and Cmr6), small subunit, crRNA	First EM structure revealing a helical feature, six Cas7 repeats, and the base structure
Cmr	III-B *Pyrococcus furiosus* DSM 3638 (*Pf*)	EMD-6165 EMD-6166 (15 Å)	Cas10, Cas5, three different Cas7s (Cmr1, Cmr4, and Cmr6), small subunit, crRNA, ssRNA	First EM structure revealing the location of the HD domain and the α1 hooks
		EMD-6167 (12 Å)	Cas7 (Cmr4), small subunit	
Csm	III-A *Sulfolobus solfataricus* (*Sso*)	EMD-2420 (30 Å)	Cas10, Cas5, five different Cas7s, small subunit, crRNA	First EM structure of a type III-A complex
Csm	III-A *Thermus thermophilus* (*Tt*)	EMD-6122 (21 Å)	Cas10, Cas5, two different Cas7s (Csm3 and Csm5), small subunit, crRNA	Second EM structure of a type III-A complex
Cascade	I-E *Escherichia coli* K12 (*Ec*)	EMD-5314 (8.8 Å)	Cas8, Cas5, Cas6, Cas7, small subunit, crRNA	First high-resolution EM structure. Six Cas7 repeats observed
Cascade	I-E *Escherichia coli* K12 (*Ec*)	EMD-5315 (9.2 Å)	Cas8, Cas5, Cas6, Cas7, small subunit, crRNA, ssRNA	Discontinuous RNA duplex was observed
Cascade	I-E *Escherichia coli* K12 (*Ec*)	EMD-5929 (9 Å)	Cas8, Cas5, Cas6, Cas7, small subunit, crRNA, dsDNA	Conformational changes in the small and large subunits observed
Cascade	I-E *Escherichia coli* K12 (*Ec*)	EMD-5930 (20 Å)	Cas8, Cas5, Cas6, Cas7, small subunit, crRNA, dsDNA, Cas3	First structure reporting the locations of the dsDNA and the Cas3 binding site

*Abbreviations: Cas, CRISPR-associated; Cascade, CRISPR-associated complex for antiviral defense; Cmr, Cas module RAMP antiviral complex; Csm, Cas subtype Mycobacterium tuberculosis antiviral complex; crRNA, CRISPR RNA; ds, double-stranded; HD, histidine–aspartate; PAM, protospacer-adjacent motif; PDB, Protein Data Bank; RAMP, repeat associated mysterious protein; sgRNA, single guide RNA; ss, single-stranded.

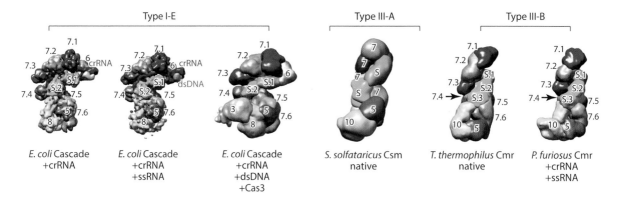

Figure 3

Architectural similarities between the type I and type III crRNPs. Electron microscopy densities are segmented for each complex and are colored according to the same scheme as that used for protein subunits in **Figures 1** and **2**. The crRNA is colored in red, and the target nucleic acids are colored in magenta. Various crRNPs belonging to different types are manually superimposed and displayed in the same orientation. The segment corresponding to a specific Cas protein is labeled by only the numerical component of the protein name (e.g., 10 indicates Cas10). Subunits that are repeated multiple times are labeled by the numerical name of the subunit followed by a number specifying the order of the repeat (e.g., 7.6 indicates the sixth Cas7). The small subunit is labeled S, S.1, S.2, or S.3. In the case of the type III-A crRNP, the exact number of repeats has not been determined for either Cas7 or the small subunit, so the corresponding densities are labeled "7" and "S," respectively. The reader is referred to **Table 1** for additional information. Abbreviations: Cas, CRISPR-associated; crRNA, CRISPR RNA; crRNP, CRISPR ribonucleoprotein; ds, double-stranded; *E. coli, Escherichia coli; P. furiosus, Pyrococcus furiosus*; ss, single-stranded; *S. solfataricus, Sulfolobus sofataricus; T. thermophilus, Thermus theromphilus*.

indefinitely in the absence of competing interactions (**Figures 4** and **7**). Structural studies of an isolated type III-B Cas7 and a Cas7–small subunit complex (Cmr4–Cmr5) support this structural property (6, 64, 78). The fact that crRNPs possess defined numbers of Cas7 subunits implies that the interactions between Cas7 and the base and head subunits must be stronger than its self-interactions.

Cas3 is the effector protein of the type I crRNPs and is associated with the crRNPs upon binding of cognate double-stranded DNA (dsDNA) (61). Cas3 belongs to the SF2 family of helicases and, not surprisingly, contains structural features of this family of enzymes (39) (**Figure 3**). Cas3 is placed near the base of the type I-E Cascade on the back surface of the large subunit (**Figure 3**).

RuvC-like domain: a nuclease domain with an RNase H fold that contains two metal ions and a combination of histidine, aspartate, and glutamate residues

HNH-like domain: a nuclease domain containing the hallmark ββα-metal active site formed by a metal ion and a combination of histidine, asparagine, and aspartate residues

Type II: Bilobe Architecture

Four crystal structures of the type II crRNP principal component, Cas9, from *S. pyogenes* (Sp) and *Actinomyces naeslundii* (An) have been obtained. These structures belong to Cas9 of type II-A and type II-C subtypes and include the apo structures of SpCas9 and AnCas9 (41), a structure of SpCas9 bound with an sgRNA and a 20-nt single-stranded DNA (ssDNA) (59), and the structure of SpCas9 bound with an sgRNA and a double-stranded DNA (dsDNA) substrate (1). Cas9 is a large protein (~100–190 kDa) with multiple juxtaposed domains belonging to two major lobes: a recognition (α-helical) lobe and a nuclease lobe. The nuclease lobe is further divided into three regions of interest: a RuvC-like domain, an HNH-like domain, and a PAM-interacting domain (PID) (**Figure 8**). The apo II-C Cas9 structures contain most of the nuclease lobe but only a partial recognition lobe (41). Upon binding nucleic acids, the recognition lobe reorganizes to engage them by undergoing a drastic conformational change (**Figure 8**).

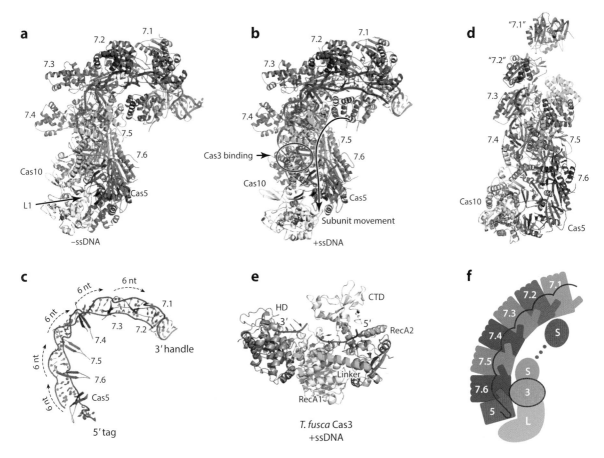

Figure 4

Crystal or combined electron microscopy (EM) and crystal structures of the type I-E Cascade (*a*,*b*,*c*), the type III-B Cmr (*d*), and the effector protein, Cas3 (*e*). Cas7 subunit repeats are colored in alternating dark blue and light blue. The large subunit and the small subunit are colored in yellow and green, respectively. Cas5 is colored in orange. The crRNA is colored in red and the target is colored in magenta. (*a*) The crystal structures of the *Escherichia coli* Cascade without a bound substrate DNA (PDB IDs: 4U7U and 1VY8); (*b*) The crystal structure of the *E. coli* Cascade with a single-stranded DNA (ssDNA) bound (PDB ID: 4QYZ). The direction of movement of the small subunit proteins upon binding of the ssDNA substrate is indicated by an arrow. The Cas3 binding site on the Cascade as determined by an EM method (see **Figure 3**) is indicated by an open circle. (*c*) The arrangement of the thumb β-hairpins of Cas5 and Cas7 repeats on the crRNA:ssDNA hybrid (PDB ID: 4QYZ). The Cas5 thumb interacts with the 5′ tag in a sequence-specific manner. The Cas7 thumbs insert into the crRNA:ssDNA heteroduplex, causing every sixth base pair to unwind. (*d*). The EM structure of the type III-B Cmr fitted with crystal structures of the Cas10–Cas5 heterodimer (PDB ID: 4K4K), the Cas7 filament (PDB ID: 4RDP), and the small subunit (PDB ID: 4GKF) with the EM density removed. A portion of the crRNA is modeled based on crRNA–Cascade interactions that have been adjusted for the different symmetry relationships among the Cas7 repeats of the Cmr. The locations of the Cmr1 ("7.2") and Cmr6 ("7.1") proteins are indicated by models from Cmr4 proteins (7.3–7.6) and are labeled with quotation marks. (*e*) The crystal structure of *Thermobifida fusca* Cas3 bound with an ssDNA (PDB ID: 4QQW). Colors are arbitrarily assigned to individual domains. Cas3 first binds and cleaves the noncomplementary strand using its histidine–aspartate (HD) domain and then processes the complementary strand using an uncharacterized mechanism. (*f*) Cartoon representation of the key features of type I and type III crRNP assemblies. Cas3 binding applies to only type I crRNPs. Abbreviations: Cas, CRISPR-associated; Cascade, CRISPR-associated complex for antiviral defense; Cmr, Cas module RAMP antiviral complex; crRNA, CRISPR RNA; crRNP, CRISPR ribonucleoprotein; CTD, C-terminal domain; PDB, Protein Data Bank; RAMP, repeat associated mysterious protein.

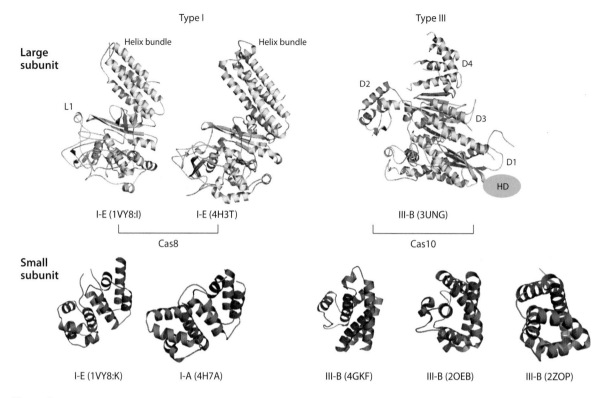

Figure 5

Similar structural classes of the large and small subunits between the type I and type III crRNPs. The large subunit proteins are shown in yellow, and the small subunit proteins are shown in green. The crRNP subtype and the PDB ID are indicated below the structure for each protein. **Table 1** contains additional information about these proteins. The L1 loop of the *Escherichia coli* Cas8 protein has been shown to interact with the protospacer-adjacent motif (PAM) sequence to prevent destruction of "self" DNA. The histidine–aspartate (HD) domain of Cas10 is not included in the crystal structure, and its position is indicated only on the basis of sequence connectivity. The bound ATP molecule in the Cas10 protein is shown in the stick model. The physiological importance of the ATP binding site on Cas10 remains unclear. D1–D4 refer to domains 1–4, respectively. Abbreviations: Cas, CRISPR-associated; crRNP, CRISPR ribonucleoprotein; PDB, Protein Data Bank.

crRNA RECOGNITION

Crystal structures of the *E. coli* type I-E crRNP in the presence and absence of ssDNA and an atomic model of the *P. furiosus* type III-B crRNP have provided insights into crRNA recognition, and, more importantly, how these two distantly related crRNPs share a similar crRNA recognition mechanism. In contrast, the crystal structures of the *S. pyogenes* type II-A crRNP reveal a drastically different crRNA recognition mechanism.

Type I and Type III crRNPs: Thumb Grips

So far, only one crystal structure among all type I and type III crRNPs allows detailed analysis of crRNA binding to crRNP proteins. The Wiedenheft and Wang laboratories independently obtained the crystal structure of the *E. coli* Cascade bound with a crRNA (38, 96), and the Bailey laboratory obtained the structure of the *E. coli* Cascade bound with a crRNA and the cognate ssDNA (57). These important structures have advanced our understanding of crRNA recognition by type I crRNPs.

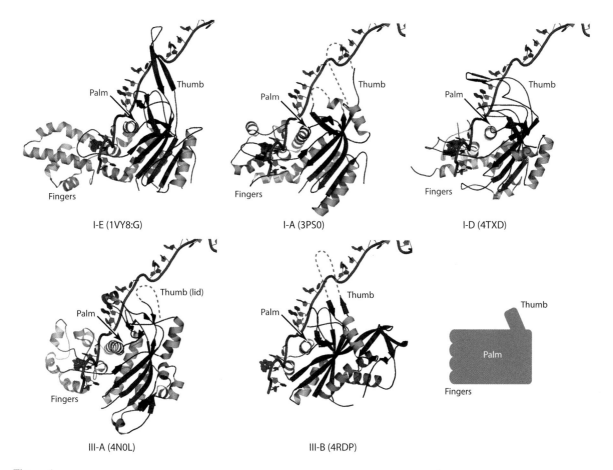

Figure 6

Similar Cas7 structures between type I type III CRISPR-Cas systems. Currently known Cas7 structures are superimposed with that of type I-E (PDB ID: IVY8, chain G) with bound crRNA. The type and the PDB ID for each Cas7 structure are indicated below it. **Table 1** contains additional information about these structures. Dashed lines indicate disordered regions in the crystal structures. The thumb hairpin loop is often disordered in RNA-free Cas7 structures, but this loop is expected to be stabilized in a manner similar to that depicted in the type I-E Cas7 structure (PDB ID: 1VY8, chain G). The right hand representation of the Cas7 structure is shown at the lower right, and key regions of this structure are labeled.

The 5′ tag of the crRNA (8 nt) is the key element of specificity. The backbone of the first eight nucleotides is bent into an S-shape; nucleotides 1–4 form the lower arc, and nucleotides 5–8 form the upper arc. The 5′ tag is completely engulfed by Cas5, Cas7.6 (the Cas7 subunit closest to Cas5), and to some degree, the L1 loop of the large subunit (**Figure 4**). The lower arc forms a tight loop that lies parallel to the first helix (α1) of the Cas5 palm domain. The upper arc bends less sharply and is pressed against the α1 helix of Cas7.6 by the β-hairpin thumb domain of Cas5 from below (**Figure 4**). The nucleobases of the first six nucleotides are engaged in close contact with the surrounding proteins. The first nucleotide interacts extensively with Cas7.6, the second and third interact with Cas5, and the fourth, fifth, and sixth interact with the L1 loop of the large subunit. These combined interactions likely impart the specificity required for crRNA association and explain the necessity of protein complex formation for specific binding of crRNA.

The guide (spacer) region of the crRNA extends along the helical contour formed by the six Cas7 repeats and is fixed on the protein surface by a set of spectacular thumb-to-palm interactions

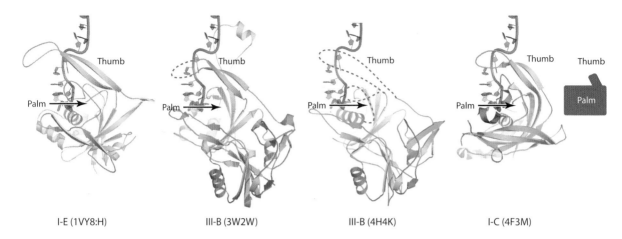

I-E (1VY8:H)   III-B (3W2W)   III-B (4H4K)   I-C (4F3M)

Figure 7

Similar Cas5 structures between the type I and type III CRISPR-Cas systems. Currently known Cas5 structures are superimposed with that of type I-E (PDB ID: IVY8, chain H) with bound crRNA. The type and the PDB ID for each protein are indicated below the appropriate structure. **Table 1** contains additional information about these structures. Dashed lines indicate the disordered regions in the crystal structures. The thumb hairpin loop is often disordered in RNA-free Cas5 structures, but this loop is expected to be stabilized in a manner similar to that depicted in the type I-E Cas5 structure (PDB ID: 1VY8, chain H). The right hand representation of the Cas5 structure is shown at the right, and key regions of the structure are labeled.

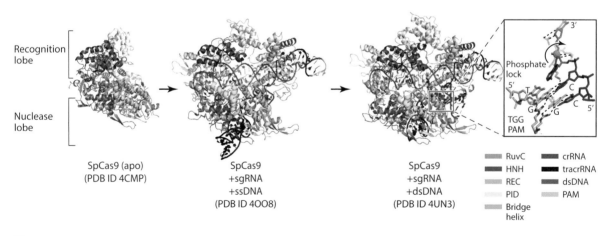

Figure 8

Structures of Cas9 and its complexes with RNA and DNA substrates. The domain color scheme is indicated at the lower right. Cas9 has a bilobe organization comprising the recognition lobe (*gray*) and the nuclease lobe (*dark blue, light blue,* and *yellow*) connected by an arginine-rich bridge helix (*green*). Large rearrangements of the recognition lobe are observed upon binding of the single guide RNA (sgRNA) and the complementary single-stranded DNA (ssDNA). More moderate arrangements are observed when double-stranded DNA (dsDNA) bearing the protospacer-adjacent motif (PAM) sequence associates. Additional information about the structures is found in **Table 1**. (*left*) Structure of the apo *Streptococcus pyogenes* (Sp) Cas9. (*middle*) Structure of SpCas9 bound with sgRNA and a complementary ssDNA. (*right*) Structure of SpCas9 bound with an sgRNA and a dsDNA substrate bearing the TGG PAM sequence. The PAM–Cas9 interactions are depicted in the inset. A pair of arginine residues forms nucleobase-specific hydrogen bonds with the PAM nucleotides GG. As a result, the +1 nucleotide of the complementary DNA strand splays out of the helical stack and pairs with the guide RNA. The phosphate backbone kink is stabilized by the phosphate lock loop.

among the Cas7 proteins (**Figure 4**). The thumbs are spaced evenly along the RNA with a 6-nt spacing (**Figure 4**). Each thumb inserts into the helical stack of the bases and presses the phosphate backbone against the α1 helix of the Cas7 above, thereby splaying every sixth base, and this splay is accompanied by a sharp kink of the phosphate backbone at this position (**Figure 4**). The contacts established between the RNA and proteins are nonspecific and thus can accommodate any sequences.

Comparison of the Cas5 and Cas7 protein structures between the type I and type III crRNPs suggests these proteins share a similar crRNA binding mechanism (**Figures 6** and **7**). Superimposition of RNA-free type III-B, I-A, I-D, and III-A Cas7 structures with the structure for RNA-loaded type I-E Cas7 of Cascade (7.6) reveals striking similarities among the thumb and palm domains of these proteins, and these similarities are likely to preserve the thumb-to-palm (or thumb grip) principle observed in *E. coli* Cascade (**Figure 6**). Similarly, superimposition of the RNA-free type III-B Cas5 structures with the RNA-bound type I-E Cas5 structure shows that although the thumb and palm elements of type III-B Cas5 are often disordered in isolation, these elements are likely engaged in similar interactions with the 5′ tag of the cognate crRNA (**Figure 7**). Interestingly, locations of the predicted thumbs of Cas5 and Cas7 in the assembled Cmr match those of regularly spaced α1 hook densities (64), supporting a preservation of the observed interactions between the thumb and the small subunit in the type III-B Cmr.

Type II: Bilobe Clamp

The principles of RNA interaction with the type II Cas9 protein are revealed by three significant SpCas9 structures (the apo structure, the ssDNA- and sgRNA-bound structure, and the dsDNA and sgRNA-bound structure) (1, 41, 59). The key elements recognized by the Cas9 of the type II crRNP include the repeat:antirepeat hybrid formed between the crRNA, the sgRNA, and the first stem loop of the tracrRNA, although the last two stem loops of the tracrRNA also play some roles in stabilizing the crRNP (40, 59). The repeat:antirepeat hybrid contains 10 bp interrupted by a 2,4-nucleotide internal loop (**Figure 8**). The duplex is buried at the interface between the two lobes of Cas9 and the first helical segment of the recognition lobe. The internal loop also contacts residues from the recognition lobe. The guide region (base paired with ssDNA) is engulfed in a sequence-independent manner by the arginine-rich bridge helix that connects the recognition lobe and the nuclease lobe, the recognition lobe, and the HNH-like domain (**Figure 8**). The 10–12 nt near the repeat interact most extensively with the bridge helix, which provides the structural basis for the so-called seed interaction for binding substrate DNA near the PAM sequence (82) in much the same way as the seed interaction observed at the guide–repeat junction for Cascade does (92). The second and third stem loops of the tracrRNA interact with residues from the PAM-interacting domain and the RuvC-like domain (**Figure 8**) (59). These two stem loops are not required for Cas9 function but can dramatically increase its catalytic efficiency (40, 59).

TARGET RECOGNITION

Type I and Type III: Base Pairs with a Stretch

Most known effector and surveillance complexes target dsDNA for interference, although the type I-E Cascade and the type III-A Csm can bind complementary ssRNA (80, 90). For the crRNA to gain access to the complementary strand of a dsDNA, the dsDNA must unwind. Furthermore, the crRNPs must also specifically recognize the PAM motif to distinguish self DNA from foreign DNA. The crystal structures of *E. coli* Cascade bound to ssDNA (57) and the combined EM and crystal structure models of the P*f*Cmr (6, 64) have provided insights into how the substrate DNA or RNA binds to the type I and type III crRNPs.

In the ssDNA-bound Cascade, the bound crRNA is partially exposed to solvent owing to the interdigitized thumb grips (**Figure 4**) and is thus unable to base pair with a target DNA. In addition, the phosphate backbone of crRNA closely follows the contour of the central filament, restricting the way in which the target can be paired with the crRNA. Interestingly, Cascade, and most likely the Cmr (with RNA substrate), overcomes these challenges via segmented base pairing. The bound crRNA–ssDNA heteroduplex deviates largely from the standard B- or A-form and does not hybridize continuously. The entire duplex is underwound and stretched longitudinally to match the entire assembly contour. Base pairing is interrupted every 6 bp by the inserted thumb β-hairpin, leading to an irregular and discontinuous RNA–DNA heteroduplex (**Figure 4**). The regularly disrupted base pairing is consistent with the fact that mutations occurring every 5 bp in target DNA are tolerated in vivo (73).

Each segment of 5 bp has a similar structure as a result of having similar interactions with the Cas7 repeats (**Figure 4**), suggesting that the protein assembly dictates the features of the target interactions. Strikingly, substrate binding is accompanied by a notable domain rotation of the large subunit and as much as 16 Å sliding of the two small subunits toward the base (**Figures 3 and 4**), demonstrating that DNA hybridization is a dynamic process.

In the combined EM and crystal structural models of the P*f*Cmr, a similar irregularity in the crRNA–RNA hybrid must occur, imposed by the helical contour and by the structural similarity between its Cas7 and that of Cascade (64) (**Figures 4 and 7**). Thus, the basic features observed in the Cascade crRNA–DNA hybrid are likely to be conserved between type I and type III crRNPs.

Given that the 5′ end of the Cascade-bound guide region has the strongest affinity for DNA (92), hybridization likely first takes place near the PAM sequence. This hybridization leads to small subunit sliding and large subunit rotation, then to hybridization of the next segment and perhaps to more small subunit sliding and large subunit rotation (**Figure 9a**). The cycle continues until the last segment is hybridized. Single-molecule experiments showed that base pairing is not stable until the last base pair at the distal end is formed (22), suggesting the importance of complete base pairing in DNA cleavage. It is believed that irregular and discontinuous base pairing allows for better mismatch detection and more accurate substrate capture than a single hybridization event does (57). This principle of heteroduplex formation has been compared to that facilitated by the DNA recombination protein RecA (57, 86).

Self Versus Foreign: The Protospacer-Adjacent Motif Meets the Phosphate Lock

DNA-targeting crRNPs must recognize and utilize the PAM sequence to prevent self-targeting. In vitro DNA binding studies of type I-E Cascade on dsDNA binding have shown that the R-loop forms only when PAM is present (75, 89). The use of a DNA substrate bearing the PAM sequence in both strands of the target DNA showed that the PAM sequence is preferentially recognized in the complementary strand (89). Similar studies with type II Cas9 complexes also demonstrated the importance of the PAM sequence in DNA interference (15, 16, 40). The type II crRNPs recognize the PAM sequence on the noncomplementary strand of the dsDNA rather than on the complementary strand (20, 40), however, suggesting a mechanistic difference between these systems at this step.

The nucleic acid structure captured by X-ray crystallography that most closely resembles an R-loop structure is that for the type II Cas9 bound with dsDNA, and this structure sheds light on how the PAM facilitates R-loop formation (1). To obtain the structure of a PAM-interacting

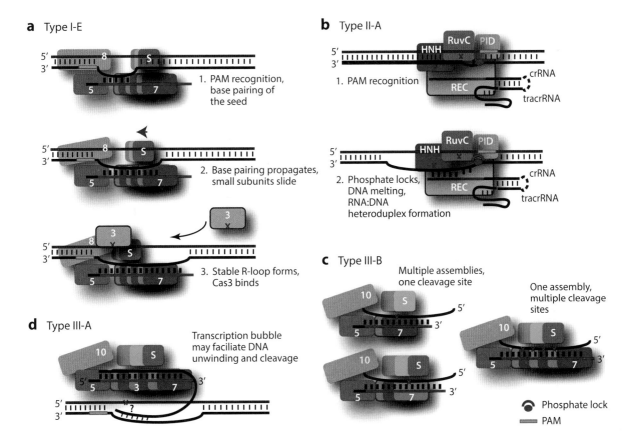

a Type I-E

5′
3′

8
S

5
7

1. PAM recognition, base pairing of the seed

5′
3′

8
S

5
7

2. Base pairing propagates, small subunits slide

3
X

5′
3′

3
Y
8
S

5
7

3. Stable R-loop forms, Cas3 binds

b Type II-A

5′
3′

HNH
RuvC
X
PID

REC

crRNA

tracrRNA

1. PAM recognition

5′
3′

HNH
RuvC
X
PID

REC

crRNA

tracrRNA

2. Phosphate locks, DNA melting, RNA:DNA heteroduplex formation

c Type III-B

Multiple assemblies, one cleavage site

10
S

5
7

5′
3′

10
S

5
7

5′
3′

One assembly, multiple cleavage sites

10
S

5
7

5′
3′

Phosphate lock
PAM

d Type III-A

Transcription bubble may faciliate DNA unwinding and cleavage

10
S

5
3
7

5′
3′

5′
3′

?

Figure 9

Nucleic acid target binding and cleavage models for type I, type II, and type III crRNPs. Red crosses indicate DNA or RNA cleavage sites. (*a*) Model of type I crRNP function. Upon recognition of the protospacer-adjacent motif (PAM) sequence on the complementary strand, the surveillance complex allows the so-called seed base pairing between the crRNA and the complementary DNA to occur. This pairing triggers sliding of the small subunit toward the base of the crRNP and domain rotation in the large subunit, freeing the downstream guide RNA for additional base pairing. This process continues until the ultimate formation of the R-loop. Cas3 is then recruited to the region in which the noncomplementary strand wraps around the helix bundle domain of the Cas8 protein, where itmakes the first excision. (*b*) Model of type II crRNP function. The DNA duplex is inspected by the Cas9 crRNP until the PAM sequence is recognized. A PAM sequence–interacting element such as the pair of arginine residues of the SpCas9 engages the PAM nucleotides, triggering unwinding of the adjacent base pairs and splaying of the first substrate nucleotide. The DNA–crRNA base pairing forms and is made possible by a stabilizing interaction between the severely kinked phosphate backbone and the phosphate lock loop of Cas9, and the pairing propagates while the DNA substrate unwinds. The HNH-like domain cleaves the complementary strand while the RuvC-like domain cleaves the noncomplementary strand. (*c*) Model of type III-B crRNP function. The crRNP has a stable assembly with multiple Cas7 repeats that may facilitate cleavage of the RNA base paired with the crRNA. The alternative model of multiple assemblies with varying Cas7 repeats is not depicted. Numbered subunits indicate respective proteins (e.g., 3 indicates Cas3, 8 indicates Cas8). Abbreviations: crRNA, CRISPR-RNA; crRNP, CRISPR ribonucleoprotein; PID, PAM-interacting domain; S, small subunit; Sp, *Streptococcus pyogenes*; tracrRNA, *trans*-activating RNA.

Cas9 complex, a partially active Cas9 containing a defective HNH-like domain and an active RuvC-like domain was incubated with an 83-nt sgRNA and a dsDNA substrate bearing the TGG PAM sequence on its noncomplementary strand. In the crystal structure, the RuvC-like domain cleaved the noncomplementary strand but left its 3′ cleavage product intact, allowing examination of PAM–Cas9 interactions. The duplex containing the PAM sequence lies at an ∼120° angle to the sgRNA–DNA heteroduplex, which is coaxial with the crRNA–tracrRNA duplex (**Figure 8**). Unlike the irregular crRNA–DNA heteroduplex observed in the type I and type III crRNPs, the sgRNA–DNA hybrid maintains a regular A-form helix, likely owing to its short length. The substrate strand is engaged in sequence-independent interactions mostly with the recognition lobe.

The PAM helix is nestled in a positively charged groove formed between the C-terminal domain (CTD) and the Topo-homology domain (collectively, the PID) (**Figure 8**). The PAM nucleotides TGG remain base paired (**Figure 8**). There is only slight tightening of the binding pocket on Cas9 compared with its PAM-free structure, suggesting a preformed PAM-binding channel. The structure identifies the DRKRY motif on a β-hairpin of the CTD in SpCas9 as the PAM-interaction unit, where the pair of arginine residues forms hydrogen bonds with the major groove edges of the two guanine nucleotides. The nucleotides on the target strand are not recognized by Cas9, providing the structural basis for the tolerance of mismatches in the PAM on this strand. The specific PAM–Cas9 interaction triggers local structural changes that destabilize the adjacent base pairing (**Figure 8**). In particular, a sharp kink in the target strand immediately downstream of the PAM motif is formed (**Figure 8**). The kink is necessary for the target strand to transition from pairing with the nontarget strand to pairing with the sgRNA. Nearby serine and lysine residues recognize the kinked phosphate group (called the phosphate lock) (**Figure 8**), which drives the conformational change of the target strand necessary for R-loop formation (**Figure 9**).

Although the protein elements interacting with the TGG PAM sequence are conserved in some type II-A Cas9 species, these elements can be different in or completely absent from others (1, 15, 16). Furthermore, the sequences and locations of the PAM vary widely (16). Thus, the principle learned from the SpCas9 studies may need to be revised once more Cas9–PAM interactions are observed.

TARGET CLEAVAGE

Various crRNPs employ different mechanisms to cleave target nucleic acids. The catalytic centers for the type I and type II crRNPs are readily identified and confirmed on the basis of both sequence homology to known nucleases and in vitro biochemical and structural studies. However, those associated with type III crRNPs are more difficult to discern because of the lack of clear homology and high-resolution structures. Thus, we summarize below the known mechanisms of how type I and type II crRNPs cleave target DNA and the predicted mechanisms of how type III-B crRNPs cleave RNA.

DNA Cleavage: Something Borrowed

The type I surveillance crRNPs do not display DNA cleavage activities; rather, they recruit Cas3-related effectors to cleave the target DNA. Many type I Cas3 proteins are large helicase–nuclease combinations, but some contain two separate interacting polypeptides [Cas3' being the helicase and Cas3'' being an HD nuclease]. A structure of a Cas3- and dsDNA-loaded Cascade was determined using cryoEM methods (33), and an atomic model of the complex was then constructed based on this structure using the ssDNA-loaded Cascade crystal structure (57). The modeled Cas3- and dsDNA-loaded Cascade shows that the PAM-proximal dsDNA is situated between the fingers domains of Cas7.6 and Cas7.5, and the complementary strand pairs with the bound crRNA while the noncomplementary strand traverses a positive path composed of the helix bundle of the large subunit and the two small subunits. This binding model places a region near the PAM sequence of the displaced noncomplementary strand on Cas3 and therefore predicts that the noncomplementary strand is nicked and further degraded by Cas3. Consistently, in vitro DNA cleavage experiments have shown that in the absence of ATP, only the noncomplementary strand is cleaved, whereas in the presence of ATP, both strands are cleaved processively (75).

The mechanism of how Cas3 interacts with and cleaves ssDNA was learned from recent crystal structures of *Thermobifida fusca* (type I-C) Cas3 bound with an ssDNA substrate and various nucleotides (37). The nuclease domain of Cas3 belongs to the family of metal-dependent HD nucleases, and its structure indeed resembles that of other HD proteins (37, 56). Cas3 has four domains: the HD domain, a RecA-like domain 1, a RecA-like domain 2, and a CTD. The two RecA-like domains form the helicase core, and the HD domain and the helicase core are arranged linearly with respect to the bound ssDNA, the 3′ and 5′ ends of which are anchored in the HD domain and the helicase core, respectively (**Figure 3**). The 3′ terminal phosphate group of the ssDNA is engaged in coordination interactions with two bound metal ions and is believed to be cleaved via a nucleophilic attack mediated by a metal-coordinated water molecule. The fact that ATP is required for Cas3 to cleave both DNA strands processively suggests that a large rearrangement in Cas3-bound Cascade is powered by ATP hydrolysis and is necessary for Cas3 to access the complementary strand. There is also some evidence indicating that negative supercoil in DNA can increase the efficiency of Cascade cleavage, perhaps via efficient conformational change and strand separation (89).

The type II Cas9 proteins also use well-characterized nuclease domains, the HNH-like and the RuvC-like domains, to cleave DNA. The HNH-like domain contains the hallmark ββα-metal active site, which typically comprises a coordinated metal; a water molecule; and aspartate, asparagine, and histidine residues. The coordinate metal ion is not observed in the currently known Cas9 structures owing to mutation of the catalytic histidine. Studies of other HNH nucleases suggest that the histidine acts as a general base to activate the water molecule, allowing it to attack the scissile phosphate in the in-line displacement reaction. The metal ion coordinated by the aspartate and asparagine residues and the oxygen atoms of the scissile phosphate stabilizes the phosphoanion transition state and the leaving group (83). The RuvC domain is also a well-characterized nuclease domain that contains two metal ions, two aspartate residues, a glutamate residue, and a histidine residue. In general, the two metals are simultaneously coordinated with a nonbridging oxygen of the scissile phosphate and a carboxylate group, enabling an activated hydroxyl group (typically water) to attack the scissile phosphate in the in-line displacement reaction (93). The current Cas9 structures still lack the detailed interactions between the DNA substrate and the nuclease domains at the active sites needed to confirm the proposed catalytic mechanisms.

RNA Cleavage: Shaping the Scissile Phosphate

Unlike the type I, type II, or type III-A effector/surveillance complexes that target DNA, the type III-B Cmr targets complementary RNA for destruction. Both the TtCmr and the PfCmr can make three, four, or five cuts, depending on the organism(s) and guide RNA used, although four cuts seem to be the most dominate product (6, 26, 64, 79). The last cleavage site (that closest to the 3′ end) on the target RNA is always 5 nt away from the last paired target nucleotide, and each of the remaining sites is located 6 nt upstream of the preceding site. The SsoCmr also cleaves RNA, but its cleavage pattern is somewhat different from that observed for the other two Cmrs. The SsoCmr does not cleave at regularly spaced sites; rather, it cleaves preferentially within AU-rich regions. The Sso complex also requires an unpaired flap at the 3′ end of the target nucleic acid, but the sequence of this flap is not important for cleavage. In addition, the SsoCmr cleaves both its guide RNA and its target RNA, and this activity depends on the presence of a 3′ overhang of the target RNA (95).

The fact that Cmrs cleave the target RNA at sites with a 6-nt spacing and the observation that the crRNA–DNA hybrid bound within Cascade has a 6-bp periodicity (38, 57, 96) may not be a coincidence. The four cleavage sites are reasonably attributed to the four Cas7 subunits that are separated by 6 bp of stretched RNA (64) (**Figure 9c**), a notion supported by modeling and mutagenesis studies. Furthermore, the observed set of striking $\alpha1$ hook structures is believed to act analogously to the Asp-Arg/Lys-Trp triad of the Cas7 that penetrates the cRNA–ssDNA duplex with regular 6-bp spacing (96). The distorted RNA bases at this 6-nt spacing have important implications for breakage of the phosphate backbone because the bases that are flipped outward facilitate formation of the necessary in-line conformation at the upstream scissile phosphate and can thus enhance the rate of bond breakage at these sites.

Despite the consistency between the structural data and the evenly spaced cleavage sites, the four Cmr4/four cleavage site model does not satisfactorily explain cleavage at three or five sites (26, 64, 79). Although the varying Cmr4 subunit model accounts for these cleavage sites better than the four Cmr4/four cleavage site model does (**Figure 9c**), the assemblies corresponding to varying Cmr4 subunits have not been captured by experiments, suggesting a high stability of the four-Cmr4 assembly. Alternatively, other Cas7 proteins may play a role in cleavage in some organisms, and the activity of a given Cmr4 may depend on its location within the helical assembly. Answers to these unresolved issues await high-resolution structures of the Cmr holo-complex.

The type III-A Csm was shown to cleave RNA in the same manner as the type III-B Cmr does (80). Furthermore, the Csm was recently shown to target DNA in a transcription-dependent manner (6). Given that these two complexes have a similar overall assembly, especially with respect to the arrangement of the Cas7 subunits (80), the Csm is believed to bind and cleave RNA according to the same principle as the Cmr. Thus, the Csm may use its ability to bind RNA in locating target DNA (**Figure 9d**), making it a dual-substrate cleavage crRNP.

APPLICATIONS

One of the most exciting prospects in the research on CRISPR-Cas immunity is development of new biotechnology that serves the needs of basic research and those of clinical applications. Both the CRISPR-Cas system as a whole and individual enzymes have been exploited for these purposes, which range from generating phage-resistant bacterial products (4) to altering specific genetic sequences in animal cells (85). The most powerful yet simple tool to have emerged from the CRISPR-Cas research to date is the Cas9-based genome editing system. Cloning customized sgRNA together with Cas9 in transfecting vector systems allows simultaneous delivery of the type II crRNP to cells that can then cleave almost any desired DNA target. The utility of the Cas9–sgRNA nuclease in eukaryotic cells is based on its ability to produce RNA-guided double-stranded breaks in genomes. These breaks can be repaired either by the error-prone process of nonhomologous end-joining or by the precise process of homology-directed repair. The superb adaptability and power of the programmable RNA-guided nuclease have been demonstrated in multiple organisms and cell types (for reviews on this topic, see References 36, 51, 71, 85).

Despite its promises and its rapid gain in popularity as a major genome editing tool, the Cas9–sgRNA system still has several limitations. A notable fraction of off-target nucleic acid degradation has been documented (17). A large sgRNA screening across multiple genes in different organisms suggests that the PAM sequence in use is not completely optimized (14). Although efforts using modified Cas9 resulted in fewer off-target effects, better systems with higher stringency are required for safe applications. Continued improvement in the Cas9 enzyme itself through either protein or tracrRNA engineering provides one solution to the problem. Alternatively, Cas9 enzymes from other species or multisubunit systems, such as the type I-E

Cascade and the type III-A crRNP, that have tighter requirements for the PAM sequence used could be developed to eliminate the off-target activities.

Targeting DNA alone may limit our ability to achieve full knockout owing to splice variants or inaccessible chromatin structures. In cases in which the cellular contexts do impact Cas9 accessibility, RNA interference (RNAi) or CRISPR-Cas RNA-targeting complexes such as the recently characterized PAM-dependent RNA-cleaving Cas9 system (60) may be used. Moreover, the type II-B Cas9 and the type III-B Cmr may be combined with the Cas9–sgRNA nuclease to achieve the best gene silencing result. As our basic knowledge on various CRISPR-Cas interference systems grows, newer and safer biotechnology tools are expected to emerge.

CONCLUDING REMARKS

The crRNPs carry out nucleic acid silencing function by a variety of methods that were initially thought to be unrelated. Although this observation remains true for type II crRNPs, structural and mechanistic connections between type I and type III crRNPs, as well as among type III subtypes, are now evident. Despite a distant phylogeny, the protein subunits that compose both type I type III crRNPs may be categorized into four principal classes that construct a similar architecture characterized by helical repeats. More importantly, the ways in which the crRNAs, and possibly the target nucleic acids (regardless of whether they are DNA or RNA), interact with the assembled crRNPs are strikingly similar. This mode of nucleic acid interaction is believed to result in both fidelity and silencing efficiency. The segmented target–guide base pairing cycle has a low tolerance for mismatches and allows multiple cleavage of the target.

Critical interactions that allow the crRNP to distinguish self from foreign DNA and that lead to a following testable model have been observed only in the case of the type II Cas9 crRNP. A pair of arginine residues stabilize the two guanine nucleotides of the PAM sequence, resulting in a kinked phosphate backbone of the complementary strand that is stabilized by the phosphate lock loop. The phosphate lock promotes unwinding of the DNA that in turn pairs with the guide RNA. Although innovative biologists are using sophisticated screening methods to quickly identify the most efficient and broadly applicable Cas9 technology, theoretical studies that may help validate and predict experimental results should also be undertaken, and, more importantly, such studies are needed to understand the fundamental basis for the observed cellular effects. Given the available crystal structures and the growing amount of experimental data on Cas9 specificity, these studies are now within reach.

Many questions surrounding the CRISPR-Cas pathway remain unanswered. Given the fact that both RNA and DNA may be cleaved by many crRNPs, what are the true interference targets of the CRISPR-Cas immunity process in cells? How do the multisubunit crRNPs recognize the correct PAM sequence? How do type III-A crRNPs achieve transcription-dependent DNA targeting? Do the energetics of PAM–Cas9 interactions support the formation of a DNA–RNA three-way junction of the R-loop? Do the energetics of segmented pairing support its hypothesized beneficial effect to fidelity? What defines the length of the helical assemblies of crRNPs? Would multicomponent systems also be a good choice for genome editing and RNA silencing? Do all crRNPs have roles in prokaryote development and in the virulence of pathogens? Continued mechanistic studies of crRNPs may reveal surprising answers to these questions.

DISCLOSURE STATEMENT

The authors are not aware of any affiliations, memberships, funding, or financial holdings that might be perceived as affecting the objectivity of this review.

ACKNOWLEDGMENTS

This work was supported by National Institutes of Health grant R01 GM099604 to H.L.

LITERATURE CITED

1. Anders C, Niewoehner O, Duerst A, Jinek M. 2014. Structural basis of PAM-dependent target DNA recognition by the Cas9 endonuclease. *Nature* 513:569–73
2. Bailey S. 2013. The Cmr complex: an RNA-guided endoribonuclease. *Biochem. Soc. Trans.* 41:1464–67
3. Barrangou R, Fremaux C, Deveau H, Richards M, Boyaval P, et al. 2007. CRISPR provides acquired resistance against viruses in prokaryotes. *Science* 315:1709–12
4. Barrangou R, Horvath P. 2012. CRISPR: new horizons in phage resistance and strain identification. *Annu. Rev. Food Sci. Technol.* 3:143–62
5. Barrangou R, Marraffini LA. 2014. CRISPR-Cas systems: Prokaryotes upgrade to adaptive immunity. *Mol. Cell* 54:234–44
6. Benda C, Ebert J, Scheltema RA, Schiller HB, Baumgärtner M, et al. 2014. Structural model of a CRISPR RNA-silencing complex reveals the RNA-target cleavage activity in Cmr4. *Mol. Cell* 56:43–54
7. Bolotin A, Quinquis B, Sorokin A, Ehrlich SD. 2005. Clustered regularly interspaced short palindrome repeats (CRISPRs) have spacers of extrachromosomal origin. *Microbiology* 151:2551–61
8. Brouns SJ, Jore MM, Lundgren M, Westra ER, Slijkhuis RJ, et al. 2008. Small CRISPR RNAs guide antiviral defense in prokaryotes. *Science* 321:960–64
9. Carte J, Christopher RT, Smith JT, Olson S, Barrangou R, et al. 2014. The three major types of CRISPR-Cas systems function independently in CRISPR RNA biogenesis in *Streptococcus thermophilus*. *Mol. Microbiol.* 93:98–112
10. Carte J, Wang R, Li H, Terns RM, Terns MP. 2008. Cas6 is an endoribonuclease that generates guide RNAs for invader defense in prokaryotes. *Genes Dev.* 22:3489–96
11. Datsenko KA, Pougach K, Tikhonov A, Wanner BL, Severinov K, Semenova E. 2012. Molecular memory of prior infections activates the CRISPR/Cas adaptive bacterial immunity system. *Nat. Commun.* 3:945
12. Deltcheva E, Chylinski K, Sharma CM, Gonzales K, Chao Y, et al. 2011. CRISPR RNA maturation by *trans*-encoded small RNA and host factor RNase III. *Nature* 471:602–7
13. Deveau H, Barrangou R, Garneau JE, Labonte J, Fremaux C, et al. 2008. Phage response to CRISPR-encoded resistance in *Streptococcus thermophilus*. *J. Bacteriol.* 190:1390–400
14. Doench JG, Hartenian E, Graham DB, Tothova Z, Hegde M, et al. 2014. Rational design of highly active sgRNAs for CRISPR-Cas9–mediated gene inactivation. *Nat. Biotechnol.* 32:1262–67
15. Esvelt KM, Mali P, Braff JL, Moosburner M, Yaung SJ, Church GM. 2013. Orthogonal Cas9 proteins for RNA-guided gene regulation and editing. *Nat. Methods* 10:1116–21
16. Fonfara I, Le Rhun A, Chylinski K, Makarova KS, Lecrivain AL, et al. 2014. Phylogeny of Cas9 determines functional exchangeability of dual-RNA and Cas9 among orthologous type II CRISPR-Cas systems. *Nucleic Acids Res.* 42:2577–90
17. Fu Y, Foden JA, Khayter C, Maeder ML, Reyon D, et al. 2013. High-frequency off-target mutagenesis induced by CRISPR-Cas nucleases in human cells. *Nat. Biotechnol.* 31:822–26
18. Garneau JE, Dupuis ME, Villion M, Romero DA, Barrangou R, et al. 2011. The CRISPR/Cas bacterial immune system cleaves bacteriophage and plasmid DNA. *Nature* 468:67–71
19. Gasiunas G, Barrangou R, Horvath P, Siksnys V. 2012. Cas9–crRNA ribonucleoprotein complex mediates specific DNA cleavage for adaptive immunity in bacteria. *PNAS* 109:E2579–86
20. Gasiunas G, Siksnys V. 2013. RNA-dependent DNA endonuclease Cas9 of the CRISPR system: Holy Grail of genome editing? *Trends Microbiol.* 21:562–67
21. Gasiunas G, Sinkunas T, Siksnys V. 2014. Molecular mechanisms of CRISPR-mediated microbial immunity. *Cell. Molec. Life Sci.* 71:449–65
22. Gesner EM, Schellenberg MJ, Garside EL, George MM, Macmillan AM. 2011. Recognition and maturation of effector RNAs in a CRISPR interference pathway. *Nat. Struct. Molec. Biol.* 18:688–92
23. Goldberg GW, Jiang W, Bikard D, Marraffini LA. 2014. Conditional tolerance of temperate phages via transcription-dependent CRISPR-Cas targeting. *Nature* 514:633–37

24. Gottesman S. 2011. Microbiology: dicing defence in bacteria. *Nature* 471:588–89

25. Haft DH, Selengut J, Mongodin EF, Nelson KE. 2005. A guild of 45 CRISPR-associated (Cas) protein families and multiple CRISPR/Cas subtypes exist in prokaryotic genomes. *PLOS Comput. Biol.* 1:e60

26. Hale CR, Cocozaki A, Li H, Terns RM, Terns MP. 2014. Target RNA capture and cleavage by the Cmr type III-B CRISPR–Cas effector complex. *Genes Dev.* 28:2432–43

27. Hale CR, Zhao P, Olson S, Duff MO, Graveley BR, et al. 2009. RNA-guided RNA cleavage by a CRISPR RNA-Cas protein complex. *Cell* 139:945–56

28. Hatoum-Aslan A, Maniv I, Marraffini LA. 2011. Mature clustered, regularly interspaced, short palindromic repeats RNA (crRNA) length is measured by a ruler mechanism anchored at the precursor processing site. *PNAS* 108:21218–22

29. Hatoum-Aslan A, Samai P, Maniv I, Jiang W, Marraffini LA. 2013. A ruler protein in a complex for antiviral defense determines the length of small interfering CRISPR RNAs. *J. Biol. Chem.* 288:27888–97

30. Haurwitz RE, Jinek M, Wiedenheft B, Zhou K, Doudna JA. 2010. Sequence- and structure-specific RNA processing by a CRISPR endonuclease. *Science* 329:1355–58

31. Heidrich N, Vogel J. 2013. Same same but different: new structural insight into CRISPR-Cas complexes. *Mol. Cell* 52:4–7

32. Hochstrasser ML, Doudna JA. 2015. Cutting it close: CRISPR-associated endoribonuclease structure and function. *Trends Biochem. Sci.* 40:58–66

33. Hochstrasser ML, Taylor DW, Bhat P, Guegler CK, Sternberg SH, et al. 2014. CasA mediates Cas3-catalyzed target degradation during CRISPR RNA-guided interference. *PNAS* 111:6618–23

34. Hols P, Hancy F, Fontaine L, Grossiord B, Prozzi D, et al. 2005. New insights in the molecular biology and physiology of *Streptococcus thermophilus* revealed by comparative genomics. *FEMS Microbiol. Rev.* 29:435–63

35. Horvath P, Barrangou R. 2010. CRISPR/Cas, the immune system of bacteria and archaea. *Science* 327:167–70

36. Hsu PD, Lander ES, Zhang F. 2014. Development and applications of CRISPR-Cas9 for genome engineering. *Cell* 157:1262–78

37. Huo Y, Nam KH, Ding F, Lee H, Wu L, et al. 2014. Structures of CRISPR Cas3 offer mechanistic insights into Cascade-activated DNA unwinding and degradation. *Nature Struct. Mol. Biol.* 21:771–77

38. Jackson RN, Golden SM, van Erp PB, Carter J, Westra ER, et al. 2014. Structural biology. Crystal structure of the CRISPR RNA-guided surveillance complex from *Escherichia coli*. *Science* 345:1473–79

39. Jackson RN, Lavin M, Carter J, Wiedenheft B. 2014. Fitting CRISPR-associated Cas3 into the helicase family tree. *Curr. Opin. Struct. Biol.* 24:106–14

40. Jinek M, Chylinski K, Fonfara I, Hauer M, Doudna JA, Charpentier E. 2012. A programmable dual-RNA–guided DNA endonuclease in adaptive bacterial immunity. *Science* 337:816–21

41. Jinek M, Jiang F, Taylor DW, Sternberg SH, Kaya E, et al. 2014. Structures of Cas9 endonucleases reveal RNA-mediated conformational activation. *Science* 343:1247997

42. Jones CL, Sampson TR, Nakaya HI, Pulendran B, Weiss DS. 2012. Repression of bacterial lipoprotein production by *Francisella novicida* facilitates evasion of innate immune recognition. *Cell. Microbiol.* 14:1531–43

43. Jore MM, Lundgren M, van Duijn E, Bultema JB, Westra ER, et al. 2011. Structural basis for CRISPR RNA-guided DNA recognition by Cascade. *Nat. Struct. Molec. Biol.* 18:529–36

44. Kunin V, Sorek R, Hugenholtz P. 2007. Evolutionary conservation of sequence and secondary structures in CRISPR repeats. *Genome Biol.* 8:R61

45. Li H. 2015. Structural principles of CRISPR RNA processing. *Structure* 23:13–20

46. Lintner NG, Kerou M, Brumfield SK, Graham S, Liu H, et al. 2011. Structural and functional characterization of an archaeal clustered regularly interspaced short palindromic repeat (CRISPR)-associated complex for antiviral defense (CASCADE). *J. Biol. Chem.* 286:21643–56

47. Makarova KS, Aravind L, Wolf YI, Koonin EV. 2011. Unification of Cas protein families and a simple scenario for the origin and evolution of CRISPR-Cas systems. *Biol. Direct* 6:38

48. Makarova KS, Grishin NV, Shabalina SA, Wolf YI, Koonin EV. 2006. A putative RNA-interference-based immune system in prokaryotes: computational analysis of the predicted enzymatic machinery, functional analogies with eukaryotic RNAi, and hypothetical mechanisms of action. *Biol. Direct* 1:7

49. Makarova KS, Haft DH, Barrangou R, Brouns SJ, Charpentier E, et al. 2011. Evolution and classification of the CRISPR-Cas systems. *Nat. Rev. Microbiol.* 9:467–77

50. Makarova KS, Wolf YI, Koonin EV. 2013. The basic building blocks and evolution of CRISPR–Cas systems. *Biochem. Soc. Trans.* 41:1392–400

51. Malina A, Mills JR, Cencic R, Yan Y, Fraser J, et al. 2013. Repurposing CRISPR/Cas9 for in situ functional assays. *Genes Dev.* 27:2602–14

52. Marraffini LA, Sontheimer EJ. 2008. CRISPR interference limits horizontal gene transfer in staphylococci by targeting DNA. *Science* 322:1843–45

53. Marraffini LA, Sontheimer EJ. 2010. CRISPR interference: RNA-directed adaptive immunity in bacteria and archaea. *Nat. Rev. Genet.* 11:181–90

54. Mojica FJM, Díez-Villaseñor C, García-Martínez J, Almendros C. 2009. Short motif sequences determine the targets of the prokaryotic CRISPR defence system. *Microbiology* 155:733–40

55. Mojica FJM, Díez-Villaseñor C, García-Martínez J, Soria E. 2005. Intervening sequences of regularly spaced prokaryotic repeats derive from foreign genetic elements. *J. Mol. Evol.* 60:174–82

56. Mulepati S, Bailey S. 2011. Structural and biochemical analysis of nuclease domain of clustered regularly interspaced short palindromic repeat (CRISPR)-associated protein 3 (Cas3). *J. Biol. Chem.* 286:31896–903

57. Mulepati S, Héroux A, Bailey S. 2014. Structural biology. Crystal structure of a CRISPR RNA–guided surveillance complex bound to a ssDNA target. *Science* 345:1479–84

58. Nam KH, Haitjema C, Liu X, Ding F, Wang H, et al. 2012. Cas5d protein processes pre-crRNA and assembles into a cascade-like interference complex in subtype I-C/Dvulg CRISPR-Cas system. *Structure* 20:1574–84

59. Nishimasu H, Ran FA, Hsu PD, Konermann S, Shehata SI, et al. 2014. Crystal structure of Cas9 in complex with guide RNA and target DNA. *Cell* 156:935–49

60. O'Connell MR, Oakes BL, Sternberg SH, East-Seletsky A, Kaplan M, Doudna JA. 2014. Programmable RNA recognition and cleavage by CRISPR/Cas9. *Nature* 516:263–66

61. Plagens A, Tjaden B, Hagemann A, Randau L, Hensel R. 2012. Characterization of the CRISPR/Cas subtype I-A system of the hyperthermophilic crenarchaeon *Thermoproteus tenax*. *J. Bacteriol.* 194:2491–500

62. Pourcel C, Salvignol G, Vergnaud G. 2005. CRISPR elements in *Yersinia pestis* acquire new repeats by preferential uptake of bacteriophage DNA, and provide additional tools for evolutionary studies. *Microbiology* 151:653–63

63. Pul U, Wurm R, Arslan Z, Geissen R, Hofmann N, Wagner R. 2010. Identification and characterization of *E. coli* CRISPR-*cas* promoters and their silencing by H-NS. *Molec. Microbiol.* 75:1495–512

64. Ramia NF, Spilman M, Tang L, Shao Y, Elmore J, et al. 2014. Essential structural and functional roles of the Cmr4 subunit in RNA cleavage by the Cmr CRISPR-Cas complex. *Cell Rep.* 9:1610–17

65. Ramia NF, Tang L, Cocozaki AI, Li H. 2014. *Staphylococcus epidermidis* Csm1 is a 3′–5′ exonuclease. *Nucleic Acids Res.* 42:1129–38

66. Reeks J, Naismith JH, White MF. 2013. CRISPR interference: a structural perspective. *Biochem. J.* 453:155–66

67. Reeks J, Sokolowski RD, Graham S, Liu H, Naismith JH, White MF. 2013. Structure of a dimeric crenarchaeal Cas6 enzyme with an atypical active site for CRISPR RNA processing. *Biochem. J.* 452:223–30

68. Richter H, Zoephel J, Schermuly J, Maticzka D, Backofen R, Randau L. 2012. Characterization of CRISPR RNA processing in *Clostridium thermocellum* and *Methanococcus maripaludis*. *Nucleic Acids Res.* 40:9887–96

69. Rouillon C, Zhou M, Zhang J, Politis A, Beilsten-Edmands V, et al. 2013. Structure of the CRISPR interference complex CSM reveals key similarities with Cascade. *Mol. Cell* 52:124–34

70. Sampson TR, Saroj SD, Llewellyn AC, Tzeng Y-L, Weiss DS. 2013. A CRISPR/Cas system mediates bacterial innate immune evasion and virulence. *Nature* 497:254–57

71. Sander JD, Joung JK. 2014. CRISPR-Cas systems for editing, regulating and targeting genomes. *Nat. Biotechnol.* 32:347–55

72. Sashital DG, Jinek M, Doudna JA. 2011. An RNA-induced conformational change required for CRISPR RNA cleavage by the endoribonuclease Cse3. *Nat. Struct. Molec. Biol.* 18:680–87

73. Semenova E, Jore MM, Datsenko KA, Semenova A, Westra ER, et al. 2011. Interference by clustered regularly interspaced short palindromic repeat (CRISPR) RNA is governed by a seed sequence. *PNAS* 108:10098–103

74. Shao Y, Li H. 2013. Recognition and cleavage of a nonstructured CRISPR RNA by its processing endoribonuclease Cas6. *Structure* 21:385–93

75. Sinkunas T, Gasiunas G, Waghmare SP, Dickman MJ, Barrangou R, et al. 2013. *In vitro* reconstitution of Cascade-mediated CRISPR immunity in *Streptococcus thermophilus*. *EMBO J.* 32:385–94

76. Sokolowski RD, Graham S, White MF. 2014. Cas6 specificity and CRISPR RNA loading in a complex CRISPR-Cas system. *Nucleic Acids Res.* 42:6532–41

77. Sorek R, Lawrence CM, Wiedenheft B. 2013. CRISPR-mediated adaptive immune systems in bacteria and archaea. *Annu. Rev. Biochem.* 82:237–66

78. Spilman M, Cocozaki A, Hale C, Shao Y, Ramia N, et al. 2013. Structure of an RNA silencing complex of the CRISPR-Cas immune system. *Mol. Cell* 52:146–52

79. Staals RHJ, Agari Y, Maki-Yonekura S, Zhu Y, Taylor DW, et al. 2013. Structure and activity of the RNA-targeting Type III-B CRISPR-Cas complex of *Thermus thermophilus*. *Mol. Cell* 52:135–45

80. Staals RHJ, Zhu Y, Taylor DW, Kornfeld JE, Sharma K, et al. 2014. RNA Targeting by the Type III-A CRISPR-Cas Csm Complex of *Thermus thermophilus*. *Mol. Cell* 56:518–30

81. Sternberg SH, Haurwitz RE, Doudna JA. 2012. Mechanism of substrate selection by a highly specific CRISPR endoribonuclease. *RNA* 18:661–72

82. Sternberg SH, Redding S, Jinek M, Greene EC, Doudna JA. 2014. DNA interrogation by the CRISPR RNA-guided endonuclease Cas9. *Nature* 507:62–67

83. Stoddard BL. 2005. Homing endonuclease structure and function. *Q. Rev. Biophys.* 38:49–95

84. Terns MP, Terns RM. 2011. CRISPR-based adaptive immune systems. *Curr. Opin. Microbiol.* 14:321–27

85. Terns RM, Terns MP. 2014. CRISPR-based technologies: prokaryotic defense weapons repurposed. *Trends Genet.* 30:111–18

86. van der Oost J, Westra ER, Jackson RN, Wiedenheft B. 2014. Unravelling the structural and mechanistic basis of CRISPR–Cas systems. *Nat. Rev. Microbiol.* 12:479–92

87. Wang R, Preamplume G, Terns MP, Terns RM, Li H. 2011. Interaction of the Cas6 riboendonuclease with CRISPR RNAs: recognition and cleavage. *Structure* 19:257–64

88. Westra ER, Swarts DC, Staals RHJ, Jore MM, Brouns SJJ, van der Oost J. 2012. The CRISPRs, they are a-changin': how prokaryotes generate adaptive immunity. *Annu. Rev. Genet.* 46:311–39

89. Westra ER, van Erp PBG, Künne T, Wong SP, Staals RHJ, et al. 2012. CRISPR immunity relies on the consecutive binding and degradation of negatively supercoiled invader DNA by Cascade and Cas3. *Mol. Cell* 46:595–605

90. Wiedenheft B, Lander GC, Zhou K, Jore MM, Brouns SJJ, et al. 2011. Structures of the RNA-guided surveillance complex from a bacterial immune system. *Nature* 477:486–89

91. Wiedenheft B, Sternberg SH, Doudna JA. 2012. RNA-guided genetic silencing systems in bacteria and archaea. *Nature* 482:331–38

92. Wiedenheft B, van Duijn E, Bultema JB, Waghmare SP, Zhou K, et al. 2011. RNA-guided complex from a bacterial immune system enhances target recognition through seed sequence interactions. *PNAS* 108:10092–97

93. Yang W. 2011. Nucleases: diversity of structure, function and mechanism. *Q. Rev. Biophys.* 44:1–93

94. Yosef I, Goren MG, Qimron U. 2012. Proteins and DNA elements essential for the CRISPR adaptation process in *Escherichia coli*. *Nucleic Acids Res.* 40:5569–76

95. Zhang J, Rouillon C, Kerou M, Reeks J, Brugger K, et al. 2012. Structure and mechanism of the CMR complex for CRISPR-mediated antiviral immunity. *Mol. Cell* 45:303–13

96. Zhao H, Sheng G, Wang J, Wang M, Bunkoczi G, et al. 2014. Crystal structure of the RNA-guided immune surveillance Cascade complex in *Escherichia coli*. *Nature* 515:147–50

Structural Biology of the Major Facilitator Superfamily Transporters

Nieng Yan

State Key Laboratory of Bio-membrane and Membrane Biotechnology, Center for Structural Biology, School of Medicine, Tsinghua-Peking Joint Center for Life Sciences, Tsinghua University, Beijing 100084, China; email: nyan@tsinghua.edu.cn

Annu. Rev. Biophys. 2015. 44:257–83

The *Annual Review of Biophysics* is online at biophys.annualreviews.org

This article's doi:
10.1146/annurev-biophys-060414-033901

Keywords

major facilitator superfamily, MFS, alternating access, membrane transport, GLUT1

Abstract

The ancient and ubiquitous major facilitator superfamily (MFS) represents the largest secondary transporter family and plays a crucial role in a multitude of physiological processes. MFS proteins transport a broad spectrum of ions and solutes across membranes via facilitated diffusion, symport, or antiport. In recent years, remarkable advances in understanding the structural biology of the MFS transporters have been made. This article reviews the history, classification, and general features of the MFS proteins; summarizes recent structural progress with a focus on the sugar porter family transporters exemplified by GLUT1; and discusses the molecular mechanisms of substrate binding, alternating access, and cotransport coupling.

Contents

INTRODUCTION

More than 800 genes in the human genome are thought to encode membrane transport proteins (37). These proteins have evolved to shepherd a wide variety of essential molecules, ranging from protons to folded proteins, as they move through the hydrophobic lipid bilayer. Transport proteins have been identified for even the small neutral molecules water and glycerol, which had been thought to traverse membrane merely via free diffusion (2). The presence of highly specific and diverse transport proteins provides the first layer of sophisticated regulation at the boundary between an organism and its environment. Transport proteins play a pivotal role in cellular growth, homeostasis, metabolism, and signal transduction.

Transport proteins comprise channels and transporters. Channel proteins are open to both sides of the membrane simultaneously when in a conducting state, and therefore they mediate only the diffusion of substrates down their electrochemical gradients. In contrast, transporters are capable of catalyzing the transmembrane movement of specific substrates uphill against their concentration gradients. To observe thermodynamic laws, a transporter must harness other forms of energy to drive the uphill translocation of specific substrates. Transporters can be classified into three types depending on their energy source: primary active transporters, secondary active transporters, and facilitators. Primary active transporters are powered by photons or by energy released from chemical reactions such as ATP hydrolysis. Secondary active transporters exploit the electrochemical potentials of a cotransporting ion or solute, such as a transmembrane proton or sodium gradient. To achieve energy coupling, a transporter must possess at least two gates that open alternately, never simultaneously (27, 93). Facilitators, also called uniporters, catalyze

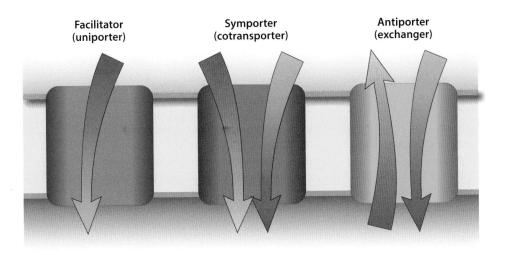

Figure 1

Schematic illustration of the three types of secondary active transporters. Facilitators catalyze substrate diffusion across the membrane down its concentration gradient. Symporters or antiporters use the energy released from the downhill translocation of one substrate to drive the uphill translocation of another substrate either in the same direction (symporters) or in the opposite direction (antiporters). The color gradients of the arrows indicate the transmembrane electrochemical gradients of the substrates.

diffusion of the substrates down their electrochemical gradients. These transporters are sometimes considered a subtype of secondary transporters that lacks cotransport coupling. In this article, the term "secondary transporters" refers to both secondary active transporters and facilitators.

The major facilitator superfamily (MFS) represents the largest among all groups of secondary transporters (20, 44, 90). This article reviews the research history, classification, and general structural features of these proteins, with a focus on recent advances in their structural biology.

THE MAJOR FACILITATOR SUPERFAMILY

The MFS is an ancient and ubiquitous transporter superfamily consisting of more than 15,000 sequenced members, and this number is growing rapidly with the continuing emergence of genome sequences (20, 44). Members of the MFS have an extraordinarily broad spectrum of substrates, including inorganic and organic ions, nucleosides, amino acids, short peptides, and lipids. MFS members comprise facilitators, symporters, and antiporters, which move substrates across membranes via facilitated diffusion, cotransport, or exchange, respectively (**Figure 1**). Owing to their fundamental significance in physiology, pathophysiology, and drug development, the MFS transporters, exemplified by the human glucose transporters GLUT1, GLUT2, GLUT3, and GLUT4 and by the *Escherichia coli* lactose permease LacY, have been the most rigorously investigated transporters with a long history.

The Early History of Major Facilitator Superfamily Protein Research

Studies of glucose permeation, the $Na^+:K^+$ pump (95), and action potentials (43) represent the early history of research into transporters, ion pumps, and ion channels, respectively. The earliest examination of glucose transport through biomembranes occurred nearly a century ago. In 1919, Edge reported in his thesis that the rate of glucose permeation through the human red blood cell membrane was affected by glucose concentration, an observation that was further confirmed by more systematic and quantitative examinations in 1930s and 1940s (4, 108). In 1948, LeFevre (64) provided experimental evidence supporting an active transport mechanism for glucose uptake into human red blood cells. He postulated a "carrier" concept without details as to molecular mechanism. In the early 1950s, Widdas (106, 107) elaborated on the carrier transfer hypothesis, extending it to account for the observed kinetics of placental glucose transfer. In the late 1970s, a liposome-based glucose uptake assay was reconstituted with partially purified proteins from erythrocytes (56, 57). The glucose transporter from red blood cells was then named GLUT1, and its amino acid sequence and 12–transmembrane segment (TM) topology were deduced by Lodish and colleagues in 1985 (73). Subsequently, three additional tissue-specific glucose transporters, GLUT2, GLUT3, and GLUT4, were cloned (5, 25, 26, 50, 102). The focus of GLUT research was then shifted toward identification and characterization of their disease-related variants and toward their mechanisms of regulation, structural characterization, and potential as drug targets (74).

LacY, one of three genes in the *Lac* operon (48, 49), was the first for which a gene product was shown to be associated with a specific transport activity (17, 23, 24). The transport function of LacY was extensively studied at a genetic level prior to 1980 (94). In 1980, Kaback, who had successfully prepared membrane vesicles derived from *E. coli* in the 1960s (55), demonstrated the proton gradient–dependent transport activities of LacY in isolated membrane vesicles (89). Since then, the Kaback group (30, 54) has conducted systematic investigations of LacY using a combination of biochemical, biophysical, and structural biology approaches.

In addition to GLUTs and LacY, dozens of MFS transporters have been identified that actively transport specific solutes, ions, and drugs in a wide variety of species, including bacteria, fungi, plants, and animals (36). The term "major facilitator superfamily" was coined in 1993 in an effort to phylogenetically classify these sequenced solute permeases and drug-resistance proteins (71). At that time, fewer than 60 proteins, comprising five clusters, were identified as belonging to the MFS. Since then, the number of sequenced and annotated MFS proteins has expanded rapidly (90).

Classification

Three major nomenclature and classification systems have been proposed for transporters. The Pfam protein families database is a comprehensive database of sequenced protein domains from all organisms (20), in which related protein families are grouped into clans. As of September 2014, the MFS clan (CL0015) consists of 25 families and 249,360 sequenced domains (**http://pfam. xfam.org/clan/MFS**) (**Table 1**).

The HUGO Gene Nomenclature Committee (HGNC) uses the solute carrier (SLC) system to classify human genes that encode membrane transport proteins, excluding channel proteins, ABC transporters, and ion pumps (37). In total, 395 genes in the human genome have been assigned to 52 SLC families (**http://slc.bioparadigms.org/**). Among these, 14 SLC families comprising 102 genes belong to the MFS (**Table 1**) (3).

A third classification system is presented by the Transport Classification Database (TCDB, **http://www.tcdb.org/**), which classifies representative transporters from all organisms on the basis of transport mechanism (two criteria), phylogenetic relations (two criteria), and substrates (one criterion), and which has a superfamily > family > subfamily hierarchy. In the TCDB, 8 of over 600 families, consisting of 864 annotated proteins, belong to the major facilitator superfamily (a superfamily that contains the MFS), and the MFS family (2.A.1) is further divided into 82 subfamilies (**Table 1**) (90).

Notably, structural biology has provided important insights into the understanding of the evolution and classification of membrane transporters. Proteins having no sequence similarity may

Table 1 Major facilitator superfamily (MFS) members and subfamilies in the Pfam, SLC, and TCDB databases

Members of the MFS clan (CL0015) in the Pfam database (249,360 domains)

Acatn

ATG22

BT1

CLN3

DUF1228

DUF791

Folate carrier

FPN1

FTR1

LacY Symp

MFS 1

MFS 1-like

MFS 2

MFS 3

MFS *Mycoplasma*

Nodulin-like

Nuc H symport

Nucleoside tran

OATP

PTR2

PUCC

Sugar tr

TLC

TRI12

UNC-93

Genomic Transport Database solute carrier series (SLC) families belonging to the MFS (102 proteins)

ID	Family description	Number of identified proteins
SLC2	Facilitative glucose transporters	14
SLC15	Proton oligopeptide cotransporter	4
SLC16	Monocarboxylate transporter	14
SLC17	Vesicular glutamate transporter	9
SLC18	Vesicular amine transporter	4
SLC19	Folate/thiamine transporter	3
SLC21/SLCO	Organic anion transporter	12
SLC22	Organic cation/anion/zwitterion transporter	23
SLC29	Facilitative nucleoside transporter	4
SLC33	Acetyl-CoA transporter	1
SLC37	Sugar-phosphate/phosphate exchanger	4
SLC43	Sodium-independent, system-L like amino acid transporter	3
SLC45	Putative sugar transporter	4
SLC46	Folate transporter	3

(Continued)

Table 1   (*Continued*)

Transport Classification Database (TCDB) families belonging to the MFS (864 proteins)

ID	Family description	Number of proteins
2.A.1	Major facilitator superfamily (MFS)	728
2.A.2	Glycoside-pentoside-hexuronide:cation symporter (GPH) family	37
2.A.12	ATP:ADP antiporter (AAA) family	20
2.A.17	Proton-dependent oligopeptide transporter (POT/PTR) family	40
2.A.48	Reduced folate carrier (RFC) family	6
2.A.60	Organo anion transporter (OAT) family	23
2.A.71	Folate-biopterin transporter (FBT) family	8
9.B.111	6TMS Lysyl tRNA synthetase (LysS) family	2

exhibit identical structural folds. For example, the structure of the formate channel FocA reveals an unexpected aquaporin fold (75, 105), and, consequently, the formate–nitrite transporter (FNT) family is now included in the major intrinsic protein (MIP) superfamily in the TCDB. Rapid progress in the structural identification of proteins with a leucine transporter (LeuT) fold has led to the reassignment of 11 families into the amino acid–polyamine-organocation (APC) superfamily (28, 111, 113). Thus, more families, for which structural information remains unknown at present, may eventually be included in the MFS.

These parallel classification and nomenclature systems have brought a certain degree of complexity and confusion. Each of the three systems has a distinct emphasis, however, so it cannot replace the others. The SLC system focuses on human transporters, whereas Pfam analyzes millions of sequences and classifies them based on domains. Effort has been made to correlate the Pfam and SLC systems (44). In this review, I rely on primarily the TCDB system when discussing representative proteins.

General Transport Mechanism

Our understanding of the general transport mechanism has been advanced as a result of decades of multidisciplinary studies. The solute carrier mechanism proposed by Widdas (107) has been gradually replaced by a more general alternating-access mechanism (51). The carrier mechanism suggests that transport of the solute requires a carrier (the transporter) that loads the substrate on one side of the lipid bilayer, swims across the membrane, and releases the cargo on the other side (107). The alternating-access mechanism, in contrast, predicts that to complete a transport cycle, the transporter must switch between at least two conformations, an outward-facing conformation and an inward-facing one, in order to allow alternating access to the substrate binding site from either side of the membrane (**Figure 2**).

A serious challenge to the carrier mechanism is the energy barrier involved in the trans-membrane displacement of a protein that presumably has an exposed hydrophilic surface. Although the alternating-access mechanism has become a prevailing one in the transporter field, however, recent structural studies have provided support for the "carrier" mechanism for several specific types of transporters, such as the bacterial aspartate transporter Glt_{Ph} (88), the Na^+:H^+ antiporters NhaA and NapA (63), the bile acid transporter ASBT (123), and the primary active energy-coupling factor (ECF) transporter (104, 112, 119). In these transporters, one domain, either the oligomerization domain, as in Glt_{Ph}, NhaA, NapA, and ASBT, or the transport subunit, as in the ECF transporters, provides the framework needed to support the movement of the substrate binding site across the membrane via a rigid-body rotation of the substrate binding

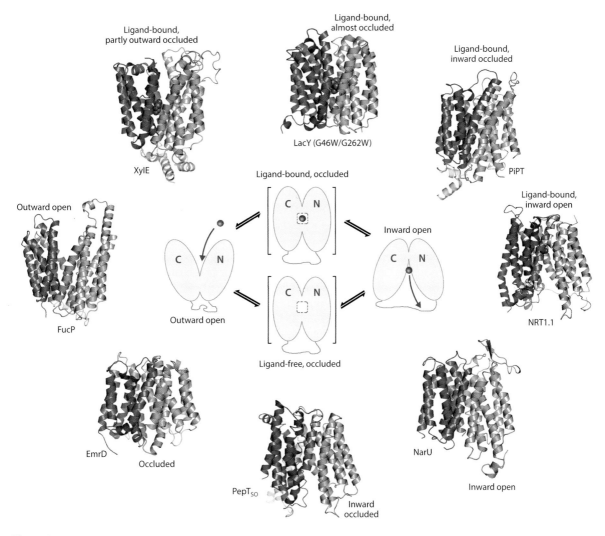

Figure 2

Distinct conformations of major facilitator superfamily (MFS) transporters. The representative structures for MFS transporters exhibit distinct conformations in a predicted alternating-access cycle. The N and C domains are colored in silver and blue, respectively. The bound ligands in XylE, LacY, PiPT, and NRT1.1 are shown as gray spheres. The PDB IDs for these structures are as follows: 3O7Q for FucP, 4GBY for XylE, 4OAA for LacY, 4J05 for PiPT, 4CL5 for NRT1.1, 4IU9 for NarU, 2XUT for PepT$_{So}$, and 2GFP for EmrD. An inventory for these structures can be found in **Table 2**. All structure figures were prepared with PyMol (13). In all side views in this article, the transporters are positioned with the cytoplasmic side at the bottom.

domain (93). This refined carrier mechanism, now referred to as the "elevator mechanism," can still be regarded as a specific form of alternating access. Thus, alternating access represents a general mechanism that can be applied to all known transporters (93, 115).

Physiology, Disease, and Pharmaceutical Perspectives

The MFS transporters have been a major focus of investigation not only because of their abundance, but also, and more importantly, because of their physiological and pathophysiological significance. As reflected in their names (**Table 1**), the MFS transporters are responsible for nutrient uptake, metabolite extrusion, and multidrug resistance. In essence, these proteins play a pivotal role in growth, metabolism, and homeostasis at cellular level in all organisms, and they are involved in a multitude of physiological processes such as development, neurotransmission, and signaling. Aberrant functions of MFS proteins have been associated with a plethora of debilitating diseases, such as cancer, gout, schizophrenia, epileptic seizure, amyotrophic lateral sclerosis (ALS), and Alzheimer's disease (18, 85, 87). In addition to being drug targets, the MFS transporters can also be employed for specific drug delivery (85).

A recent special issue of *Molecular Aspects of Medicine* was committed to providing a comprehensive review of the current understanding of SLC transporters from physiological, disease, and pharmaceutical perspectives (37). The following MFS families were covered in this issue: the SLC2 GLUT sugar porters (74); the SLC15 proton-coupled oligopeptide transporters (96); the SLC16 monocarboxylate transporters (34); the SLC17 organic anion transporters (87); the SLC18 vesicular neurotransmitter transporters (62); the SLC19 and SLC46 folate transporters (120); the SLC21/SLCO organic anion transporters (33); the SLC22 transporters of organic cations, anions, and zwitterions (58); the SLC29 facilitative nucleoside transporters (118); the SLC33 acetyl-CoA transporters (41); the SLC37 phosphate-linked sugar phosphate antiporters (9); the SLC43 facilitator system L–amino acid transporters (6); and the SLC45 putative sugar transporters (103). The relevance of the MFS transporters to cancer, exemplified by GLUT1, GLUT3, GLUT4, MCT1, MCT4, OCT1, OCT2, and OAT10, was also examined (18). As the expression levels of these transporters change in different types of cancer, activating or inhibiting them may serve as a principle for the development of anticancer drugs. Potential drug-targeting solute carriers, including the SLC2, SLC18, and SLC22 families, have also been studied (85).

The reviews listed above focus on SLC families, which are human transporters. The MFS transporters involved in the multidrug resistance in bacteria and fungi also have the potential for use in the development of new drugs against pathogenic microorganisms. Multidrug resistance and potential uses of MFS transporters from bacteria and fungi have been covered in recent reviews (10, 16).

STRUCTURAL BIOLOGY OF THE MAJOR FACILITATOR SUPERFAMILY TRANSPORTERS

Overview

Before the resolution of any crystal structure, comprehensive biochemical and biophysical approaches were combined to deduce structural information about MFS transporters (45, 53, 101). Electron crystallography was used to examine the structure of a bacterial oxalate:formate antiporter OxlT (40, 42). Despite the relatively low resolution (6.5 Å), the 12 TMs were correctly positioned in the projection. A breakthrough was finally achieved in 2003, when the first crystal structures of two MFS transporters, LacY (1) and the glycerol-3-phosphate transporter, GlpT (46), were reported simultaneously. Despite this inspiring start to the structural investigation of MFS transporters, the determination of new MFS structures proceeded more slowly, with the structure of the multidrug resistance protein EmrD in 2006 (117) and that of the L-fucose:proton symporter FucP in 2009 (11).

A structure boom for the MFS proteins finally arrived during the second decade of the 21st century. As many as 40 structures of 18 unique MFS proteins belonging to 9 MFS families have been deposited in the Protein Data Bank (PDB) as of September 15, 2014 (**Table 2**) (1, 11, 14, 15, 19, 31, 46, 47, 52, 77, 82–84, 97, 99, 100, 110, 114, 117, 121, 122). Although most of

Table 2 Structures, functions, and organisms for which structures of major facilitator superfamily (MFS) proteins have been resolved*

Protein	Function	MFS subfamily and TCDB ID	Organism	PDB ID(s)	Resolution limit (Å)	Year of the first structure	Conformation(s)
GLUT1	D-Glucose facilitator	Sugar porter (SP) 2.A.1.1.28	*Homo sapiens*	4PYP	3.1	2014	Inward open
XylE	D-Xylose:H$^+$ symporter	SP 2.A.1.1.3	*Escherichia coli*	4GBY, 4GBZ, 4GC0, 4JA3, 4JA4, 4QIQ	2.6	2012	1. Ligand-bound, partly occluded, outward-facing 2. Inward open 3. Partly occluded, inward-facing
GlcP	D-Gluose:H$^+$ symporter	SP 2.A.1.1.42	*Staphylococcus epidermidis*	4LDS	3.2	2013	Inward open
LacY	Lactose:H$^+$ symporter	Oligosaccaride:H$^+$ symporter (OHS) 2.A.1.5.1	*Escherichia coli*	1PV7, 2CFP, 2CFQ, 2V8N, 2Y5Y, 4OAA	2.95	**2003**	1. Inward open 2. Ligand-bound, occluded
FucP	L-Fucose:H$^+$ symporter	Fucose:H$^+$ symporter (FHS) 2.A.1.7.1	*Escherichia coli*	3O7Q, 3O7P	3.1	2009	Outward open
PiPT	Phosphate:H$^+$ symporter	Phosphate:H$^+$ symporter (PHS) 2.A.1.9.10	*Piriformospora indica*	4J05	2.9	2013	Ligand-bound, inward-facing, occluded
GlpT	Glycerol-3-phosphate:Pi antiporter	Organophosphate:Pi antiporter (OPA) 2.A.1.4.3	*Escherichia coli*	1P24	3.3	**2003**	Inward open
NarU	Nitrate:nitrite antiporter	Nitrate/Nitrite Porter (NNP) 2.A.1.8.10	*Escherichia coli*	4IU8, 4IU9	3	2013	1. Inward-facing, occluded 2. Partially inward open
NarK	Nitrate:nitrite antiporter	NNP: 2.A.1.8.1	*Escherichia coli*	4JR9, 4JRE	2.6	2013	1. Apo inward open; 2. Inward open with nitrite
EmrD	Drug:H$^+$ transproter	Drug:H$^+$ antiporter-1 (DHA1) 2.A.1.2.9	*Escherichia coli*	2GFP	3.5	2006	Occluded
YajR	Drug:H$^+$ symporter	DHA1: 2.A.1.2.60	*Escherichia coli*	3WDO	3.15	2013	Outward open

(Continued)

Table 2 *(Continued)*

Protein	Function	MFS subfamily and TCDB ID	Organism	PDB ID(s)	Resolution limit (Å)	Year of the first structure	Conformation(s)
MelB	Melibiose:sodium (or lithium or H^+) symporter	Glycoside-pentoside-hexuronide: cation symporter (GPH) 2.A.2.1.1	*Salmonella typhimurium*	4M64	3.4	2014	1. Outward partly occluded 2. Outward inactive
$PepT_{So}$	Peptide:H^+ symporter	Proton-dependent oligopeptide transporter (POT) 2.A.17.4.7	*Shewanella oneidensis*	2XUT	3.6	2011	Inward-facing, occluded
$PepT_{So2}$	Peptide:H^+ symporter	POT 2.A.17.4.7	*Shewanella oneidensis*	4LEP, 4TPH, 4TPG, 4TPJ	3.2	2013	Ligand-bound, inward open
$PepT_{St}$	Peptide:H^+ symporter	POT 2.A.17.1.6	*Streptococcus thermophilus*	4APS	3.3	2012	Inward open
GkPOT	Peptide:H^+ symporter	POT 2.A.17.1.7	*Geobacillus kaustophilus*	4IKV, 4IKW, 4IKX, 4IKY, 4IKZ	**1.9**	2013	Inward open
YbgH	Peptide:H^+ symporter	POT 2.A.17.1.4	*Escherichia coli*	4Q65	3.4	2014	Inward open
NRT1.1	Nitrate:H^+ symporter	POT 2.A.17.3.1	*Arabidopsis thaliana*	4OH3, 4CL4, 4CL5	3.25	2014	1. Apo inward open 2. Inward open with nitrate

*Bold text in cells indicates milestones in the study of MFS proteins. GLUT1 is the only human (*Homo sapiens*) MFS transporter for which a structure is available, 1.9 Å is the highest resolution among all MFS structures obtained to date, and 2003 is the year in which the first MFS structures were reported. Abbreviations: PDB, Protein Data Bank; TCDB, Transport Classification Database.

the structures were achieved using bacterial homologs, three came from eukaryotes: the human glucose transporter GLUT1 (14), the plant nitrate transporter NRT1.1 (82, 99), and a fungus phosphate transporter PiPT (83). GLUT1 represents the first and the only human SLC protein to have a known structure at an atomic resolution.

Another major breakthrough in the structural study of MFS transporters is the visualization of multiple conformations for one protein. Transporters undergo cycles of conformational shifts to achieve alternating access. Thus, obtaining structures of multiple conformations of a given protein has been an important goal for structural biologists seeking to understand its transport mechanism. The structures obtained for MFS transporters prior to 2013 did exhibit different conformations, but, unfortunately, the different conformations belonged to distinct transporters. Until 2013, none of the proteins had been captured in more than one conformational state (**Figure 2**) (115). Since then, however, structures for more than one conformational state of the D-xylose:proton symporter XylE (84, 110), LacY (60), the nitrate:nitrite antiporter NarU (114), and the melibiose:cation symporter MelB (19) have been obtained (**Table 2**).

This exciting progress has greatly advanced the mechanistic understanding of MFS proteins. In the next subsection, I review the common and distinct structural features of representative MFS transporters and the recent advancements in the structural elucidation of new MFS transporters. I then focus on GLUT1 and its bacterial homologs to discuss mechanistic insights.

General Structural Features of the Major Facilitator Superfamily

All of the MFS transporters share a common and characteristic core fold, known as the MFS fold (**Figure 3a**). To facilitate a structural description of it, I introduce a coordinate system whereby the two axes parallel to the membrane plane and corresponding to the major and minor axes of the oval-shaped cross-section of the protein are defined as axes a and b, respectively, and the axis perpendicular to the membrane plane is axis c (**Figure 3a**). A canonical MFS fold comprises two domains, each consisting of six consecutive TMs. The two domains, usually called the N and C domains, exhibit a twofold pseudosymmetry related by axis c. Within each domain, the six TMs are organized into a pair of inverted "3+3" repeats. In the N domain, TMs 1, 2, and 3 are related to TMs 4, 5, and 6 by an approximate 180° rotation around axis a; in the C domain, TMs 7, 8, and 9 have a similar relationship with TMs 10, 11, and 12 (**Figure 3a**).

The corresponding TMs in each repeat appear to play similar structural and functional roles (115). The first helix in each three-helix bundle (TMs 1, 4, 7, and 10) is positioned in the center of the transporter, and together, these helices directly constitute the transport path (**Figure 3a**). A large majority of the residues identified for substrate binding and cotransport coupling are located on these four helices. During a transport cycle, the interactions between TM1 and TM7 on the extracellular side occur in alternation with those between TM4 and TM10 on the cytoplasmic side to insulate the substrate binding site from the extramembrane milieu. Notably, although most of the TMs in MFS proteins are continuous helices, discontinuity occurs for TMs 1, 4, 7, and 10, possibly providing the structural adaptability needed for alternating access (14, 52, 100). TMs 2, 5, 8, and 11, which are positioned on the outside of the core helices along axis b, mediate the interface between the N and C domains. Residues in these segments that face the transport pathway may participate in substrate binding and cotransport coupling (100, 124). TMs 3, 6, 9, and 12 are placed on the outside of TMs 1, 4, 7, and 10 along axis a, supporting the structural integrity of the transporter (**Figure 3a**). Interestingly, in the context of the overall structure, corresponding TMs from two three-TM repeats always stand next to each other in opposite orientations (**Figure 3a**).

In addition to the core MFS fold, some members of the MFS may contain extra domains and motifs (**Figure 3b**). For example, all of the structures of proteins in the sugar porter (SP) family have

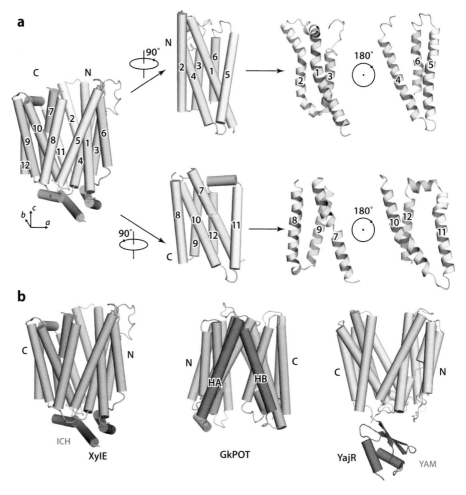

Figure 3

Structural features of the major facilitator superfamily (MFS) proteins. (*a*) A canonical MFS fold. The 12-TM structure in an MFS fold contains two discretely folded domains, the N and C domains, which are related by an approximate 180° rotation around axis *c* (defined at the bottom of the panel). Each domain consists of two inverted 3-TM repeats. The corresponding helices in each of these units have the same color. (*b*) Unique structural elements from distinct MFS subfamilies. Abbreviations: ICH, intracellular helical; MBD, methyl-CpG-binding domain protein 2; TM, transmembrane segment; YAM, YajR/AraEP/MBD.

an intracellular helical (ICH) domain, which comprises three or four helices between the N and C domains and one short helix at the C terminus. The ICH domain is essential for intracellular gating in XylE and GLUT1 (14, 79, 100). The structures of the bacterial peptide transporters from the proton-dependent oligopeptide transporter (POT) family all contain two extra TMs, designated HA and HB, which are inserted between the N and C domains. The inserted helical hairpin is missing in the POT protein NRT1.1 from *Arabidopsis thaliana*, supporting the conclusion that these extra TMs are not ubiquitous to proteins in the POT subfamily (12). Nevertheless, a recent study of the POT protein YbgH demonstrated that the internal rigidity of the helical hairpin is important for their transport activity (121). In the multidrug resistance transporter YajR, an independently folded YAM [YajR/AraEP/ methyl-CpG-binding domain protein 2 (MBD)] domain follows the C-terminus of the TM domain, although the function of this soluble domain remains unclear (52).

Recent Progress in the Structural Study of the Major Facilitator Superfamily

A summary of the structural advances of MFS transporters prior to 2013 can be found in a minireview by Yan (115). Below is a brief review of the major achievements in structural biology of the MFS over the past two years. An inventory of all of the resolved MFS protein structures can be found in **Table 2**.

The sugar porter family: GLUT1 and its bacterial homologs XylE and GlcP. The glucose transporters GLUT1–GLUT4 represent some of the physiologically most important and most rigorously characterized transporters. Their significance in physiology and disease has been reviewed recently (74, 115) and is not discussed here. GLUTs have been the targets of active structural research for decades. However, the daunting challenges involved in working with eukaryotic membrane proteins have prevented any major progress on the structural determination of GLUTs (35). Before the crystal structure of human GLUT1 was elucidated in early 2014 (14), homology models of GLUTs were generated based on the crystal structures of their bacterial homolog, XylE.

GLUTs belong to the SP subfamily (**Table 2**), the members of which are responsible for the cellular uptake of glucose and other monosaccharides or disaccharides in all kingdoms of life (7, 39, 66, 81, 109). Among the bacterial homologs, XylE from *E. coli* shares ~30% sequence identity and ~50% similarity with human GLUT1–GLUT4. The crystal structure of XylE was first obtained in an outward-facing and partly occluded conformation, bound to its substrate, D-xylose; its inhibitor, D-glucose; and a glucose derivative, 6-bromo-6-deoxy-D-glucose, at resolutions of 2.8, 2.9, and 2.6 Å, respectively (100). Subsequently, two more conformations of XylE, the inward open and partly inward occluded conformations, were captured (84). Despite the relatively low resolution and severe anisotropy in X-ray diffraction, the backbones of these structures were clearly resolved. Thus, for the first time, the structures of both outward-facing and inward-facing conformations of the same MFS transporter were obtained, and XylE therefore became another prototypal MFS protein for structural and mechanistic examinations.

The structure of the inward open conformation of the D-glucose:proton symporter GlcP from *Staphylococcus epidermidis* was determined at a resolution of 3.2 Å (47). The structures of XylE and GlcP provide an important framework for mechanistic understanding of the SP transporters and for homology modeling of the physiologically more relevant GLUTs.

Finally, the crystal structure of the human GLUT1, which exhibits an inward open conformation, was determined at a resolution of 3.2 Å (**Figure 4***a*). Four key factors contributed to the success of GLUT1 structure determination (14). First, the previously identified glycosylation site N45 was substituted with threonine to prevent potential heterogeneity caused by glycosylation. Second, a single point mutation, E329Q, which was suggested to lock the transporter in an inward-facing state (92), was introduced to improve conformational homogeneity. Third, the crystallization trials were carried out at 4°C to stabilize the protein. Finally, the detergent nonyl-β-D-glucopyranoside (β-NG) was used in the last step of GLUT1 purification and crystallization. The electron density of a β-NG molecule could be unambiguously resolved in the structure. Interestingly, the glucoside of β-NG, which is reminiscent of D-glucose, is bound to the structure in a manner similar to the binding of D-glucose to XylE (**Figure 4***b*). Because of the chirality of glucoside and the presence of the aliphatic tail, the β-NG molecule can bind only to the inward-facing conformation of GLUT1. Therefore, the specific detergent molecule also contributes to the stabilization of the inward open conformation.

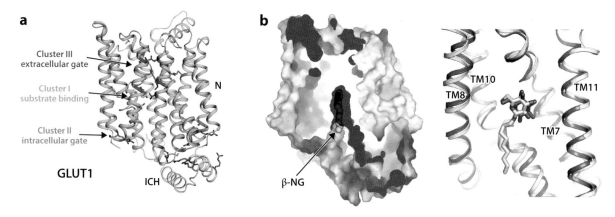

Figure 4

The structure of the human glucose transporter GLUT1 in an inward open conformation. (*a*) Mapping of disease-related mutations on the GLUT1 structure identified three clusters, which are important for substrate binding or for the extracellular or intracellular gating of GLUT1. (*b*) A molecule of the detergent β-NG is bound in the central cavity. The coordination of the sugar moiety of β-NG by GLUT1 is similar to the binding of D-glucose by XylE. The structures of GLUT1 (*blue*) and XylE (*pale cyan*) are superimposed relative to their respective C domains. The ligands are shown using stick diagrams. Abbreviations: β-NG, nonyl-β-D-glucopyranoside; ICH, intracellular helical domain.

The GLUT1 structure allows mapping of over 40 mutations associated with GLUT1 deficiency syndrome (also known as De Vivo syndrome) (14). These mutations are predominantly clustered in three regions. Cluster I overlaps with the substrate binding site; cluster II mediates the interactions between the TM domain and the ICH domain, contributing to the closure of the intracellular gate; and cluster III is involved in the contacts between the N and C domains on the extracellular side, representing the extracellular gate. Structure-guided analysis of disease-related mutations thus facilitates mechanistic understanding of both GLUT1 and the SP proteins in general (14) (**Figure 4***a*).

The aforementioned ICH domain is observed in all SP structures, indicating that this domain is a general feature of the SP subfamily. The SP transporters share several conserved signature motifs (38, 70, 84, 100), which are exclusively positioned on the cytoplasmic side of the structure, lining up the interface between the TM and ICH domains and supporting an essential functional role of the ICH domain. Structural comparison suggests that the ICH domain may serve as a latch to stabilize the outward-facing conformation of the transporter (14, 100).

The proton-dependent oligopeptide transporter family: GkPOT and NRT1.1. The POT or PTR family comprises proton symporters that catalyze the cellular uptake of short peptides. A subfamily in plants, exemplified by NRT1.1, permeates nitrogenous ligands (65). Importantly, the human SLC15 POT proteins PepT1 and PepT2 have direct pharmaceutical relevance through uptake of a variety of drugs (96). Thus, proteins belonging to the POT family have been actively pursued for structural characterizations. With the exception of the nitrate transporter from *Arabidopsis thaliana*, NRT1.1, the POT structures obtained to date are for a number of bacterial homologs, including PepT$_{So}$ (77), PepT$_{St}$ (97), PepT$_{So2}$ (31, 32), GkPOT (15), and YbgH (121) (**Table 2**).

A comprehensive review on the structural biology of the POT/PTR family was published recently (76). Here, I would like to bring particular attention to the structure of GkPOT, a peptide:proton symporter in *Geobacillus kaustophilus*. The crystals were obtained in the lipidic cubic phase (LCP), and the diffraction reached 1.9 Å (15). The structure can be superimposed well with other bacterial POT homologs for which crystals were obtained in detergent micelles, partially alleviating the concern that the structures of a membrane transporter may be distorted by detergents.

NRT1.1 is the only plant MFS protein for which detailed structural information is available (82, 99). This protein exhibits dual affinities for nitrate. The phosphorylation of T101 serves as the signal to switch from a low-affinity to a high-affinity state. Interestingly, the structure of NRT1.1 revealed a dimeric assembly in the crystal. Zheng and coworkers (122) examined the oligomerization status of NRT1.1 in a detergent solution by cross-linking and in oocyte membranes by Förster resonance energy transfer (FRET) spectroscopy analysis. The dimerization of wild-type NRT1.1 was confirmed in both experiments. Furthermore, a phosphomimetic mutant of NRT1.1, T101D, which exhibits high-affinity nitrate transport activity, was shown to be a monomer in the lipid bilayer. These studies established the correlations between the phosphorylation and oligomerization states of NRT1.1 (99). Whether disruption of the dimer interface without phosphorylation of T101 is sufficient to convert NRT1.1 from the low-affinity to the high-affinity state remains to be studied.

Other families: the PHS, NNP, and GPH subfamilies. The structural gallery of MFS proteins has been expanded to contain more subfamilies, including the phosphate:H$^+$ symporter family (PHS), the nitrate:nitrite porter family (NNP), and the glycoside-pentoside-hexuronide:cation symporter (GPH) family (**Table 2**).

The phosphate:H$^+$ symporter PiPT, from the fungus *Piriformospora indica*, represents the first eukaryotic MFS protein for which an atomic structure was obtained. The structure was captured in a ligand-bound, inward occluded state at a resolution of 2.9 Å and serves as a framework for the elucidation of the substrate binding and proton coupling mechanism (83).

The structures of the nitrate:nitrite antiporters NarU and NarK from *E. coli* were determined at resolutions of 3.0 and 2.6 Å, respectively (114, 122). Both proteins were captured in inward-facing conformations. Each asymmetric unit of the NarU crystal contains two molecules, one in the occluded conformation and the other in a partially inward open state (114). The structures of NarK were also obtained in two inward open states: ligand-free and phosphate-bound (122). The NNP structures in three distinct conformational states provide insights into their functional mechanisms.

A crystal structure of the melibiose permease MelB in *Salmonella typhimurium* was obtained at a resolution of 3.4 Å (19). The four molecules in each asymmetric unit exhibit two conformations, the partly outward occluded conformation and the outward inactive conformation. Notably, MelB can catalyze the symport of melibiose with Na$^+$, Li$^+$, or H$^+$. Structural analysis identified a trigonal bipyramid geometry, composed of the D55/59/124 and Y120/T121/T373 side chains, as a potential cation binding site. Replacing any of the residues at positions 55/59/121/124 with cysteine led to altered cation selectivity, supporting the notion of the geometry described above as a cation binding site. The structures of MelB provide a framework for understanding the coupling and alternating-access mechanism of the MFS Na$^+$ symporters.

LacY. LacY has been a prototype for the study of secondary transporters. After its first structure (an inward open conformation) was determined, a decade of rigorous effort failed to capture another conformation. The breakthrough was finally made in early 2014. Through rational design, two conserved residues, G46 and G262, located on the extracellular segments of TM2 and TM8, respectively, were replaced by tryptophan residues. These two residues are positioned on the interface between the N and C domains. Substitution of glycine with a bulky residue is

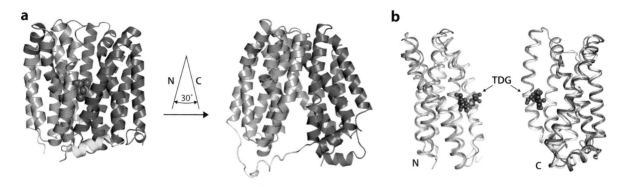

Figure 5

State transition of LacY is achieved via rigid-body rotation of the two domains. (*a*) Structural comparison of LacY between the TDG-bound, nearly occluded, outward-facing conformation (*left*) and the inward open conformation (*right*). A 30° concentric rotation around axis *b* (see **Figure 3a**) results in the transition from the outward occluded to inward open state. (*b*) Domain superimposition of the two structures of LacY. The N and C domains in the two structures exhibit almost identical conformations, supporting the notion of a rigid-body rotation of the two domains. Abbreviation: TDG, D-galactopyranosyl-1-thio-β, D-galactopyranoside.

predicted either to open the interface of the two domains on the extracellular side or to destabilize the inward open conformation. Indeed, the structure of the tryptophan-modified LacY variant (G46W/G262W) exhibits a ligand-bound and almost occluded outward-facing conformation (**Figure 5a**) (60). The conformational shift from the outward occluded state to an inward open one involves a 30° concentric rotation of the two domains around axis *b* (**Figures 3a and 5a**). Pairwise superimposition of the respective N and C domains suggests a rigid-body rotation of the two domains during the conformational shift (**Figure 5b**).

STRUCTURE-GUIDED MECHANISTIC ELUCIDATION

Structural information lays out the foundation for mechanistic investigations. Three fundamental mechanisms need to be addressed for all of the MFS transporters: the molecular basis underlying substrate selectivity; the conformational changes that take place during an alternating-access cycle; and, most importantly, the coupling mechanisms for antiporters and symporters. The exciting progress in the structural elucidation of MFS proteins in the past couple of years has further advanced our understanding of these fundamental mechanisms.

Substrate Binding

The structurally elucidated MFS transporters all contain a single substrate binding cavity located in the center of the membrane and enclosed by the N and C domains. Before their ligand-bound structures were determined, many MFS transporters were subjected to mutagenesis to identify residues that recognize substrate; examples of some of the transporters studied are LacY, GalP, FucP, and PepT$_{St}$ (115). Structures of XylE in complex with three different ligands revealed the first picture of substrate coordination by an MFS transporter (100), and structures of substrate-bound transporters were subsequently resolved for PiPT, NarK, LacY, and PepT$_{So2}$. These structures reveal two common features: Multiple aromatic residues are positioned surrounding the trapped substrate, insulating it from the extramembrane environment, and the ligands are usually asymmetrically coordinated by the two domains.

In all MFS symporters and facilitators with known ligand-bound structures, it appears that one domain provides the primary binding site, whereas the other contributes few coordinating residues. For example, in the partly outward occluded conformation of XylE, the bound ligand is predominantly coordinated by the C domain, and the N domain contributes only three binding residues (100). In the inward open GLUT1 structure, the glucoside of β-NG is exclusively coordinated by residues from the C domain in a manner almost identical to the coordination of D-glucose by XylE (**Figure 4b**) (14). In the inward occluded PiPT structure, the bound phosphate is closer to the C domain and is coordinated by six residues from the C domain and by only two from the N domain (83). In the outward occluded LacY structure, the bound ligand is closer to the N domain, which provides more coordinating residues than the C domain does. Therefore, the N domain appears to serve as the primary substrate binding site in LacY (60). In the recently reported peptide-bound inward open PepT$_{So2}$ structure, the tripeptide is also coordinated mainly by residues in the N domain (31).

The only exception to date is seen in the structure of nitrite-bound NarK, in which the two domains appear to contribute equally to substrate binding. Note that NarK is an antiporter, whereas the others mentioned above are all symporters. It remains to be further investigated whether the observed patterns of substrate binding, which are asymmetric for symporters and symmetric for antiporters, can be generalized to other MFS proteins, and if so, whether such patterns are associated with the transport mechanisms of antiporters and symporters.

Alternating Access

Multiple conformations for each MFS transporter, which have been observed for several distinct proteins, provide the framework for a mechanistic understanding of alternating access. Mounting evidence has demonstrated that the state transitions for an MFS protein involve both domain rotation and local structural rearrangements. For LacY, the transition from the outward occluded to the inward open state requires a 30° rigid-body rotation of the two domains. In XylE, NarU (114), and MelB (19), however, local structural rearrangements of specific TMs are observed between distinct states. I discuss XylE as a representative example because it has been captured in three distinct conformations (**Figure 6**)

For XylE, the transition from the ligand-bound, partly outward occluded state to the inward open state requires an approximately 16° concentric domain rotation around axis *b* (**Figure 6a**). Meanwhile, structural rearrangements occur in the extracellular segment of TM7, the cytoplasmic fragment of TM10, and in the cytoplasmic fragment and extracellular tip of TM11 (**Figure 6b**). Interestingly, the N domain remains unaltered during the state transition. Because the C domain provides the primary substrate binding site for XylE, the local conformational changes of the C domain involving TM7 and TM10 may be associated with substrate binding and release. The rigid-body rotation of the N domain results in the alternative exposure of the substrate binding site to one side of the membrane or the other (14).

A partly inward occluded state was captured in the absence of ligand for XylE (84). Comparison with the inward open structure reveals a local bending of TM10 on the cytoplasmic side toward the central cavity, resulting in the partly occluded state (**Figure 6c**). Similar conformational changes were observed between the inward open PepT$_{St}$ (77) and the inward occluded PepT$_{So}$ (77). These structural observations suggest that the conformational rearrangements underlying an alternating-access cycle are more complex than a simple rigid-body rotation, or the so-called rocker-switch model (46). XylE has become a prototypal protein for the study of alternating access. A complete picture of the alternating-access cycle for XylE relies on successful determination of the structure of XylE in its outward open state.

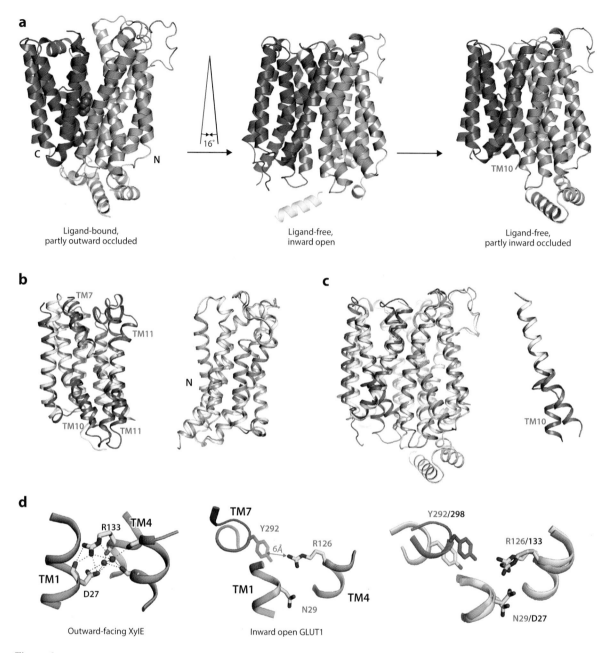

Figure 6

Alternating-access and proton coupling mechanisms of XylE. (*a*) Structures of XylE in three conformations. PDB IDs for the three structures are as follows: 4GBY (*left*), 4QIQ (*middle*), and 4JA3 (*right*). (*b*) Superimpositions of the individual domains between the outward-facing and inward open states. The inward open XylE is colored in pale cyan in panels *b* and *c*. The regions with local conformational shifts are highlighted in orange. (*c*) Structural comparison of the inward open and partly inward occluded states of XylE. The only difference occurs in the cytoplasmic segment of TM10, which is highlighted on the right. (*d*) Structural comparison of the outward-facing conformation of XylE with the inward open conformation of GLUT1. The hydrogen bonds are represented by red dashed lines. The rightmost illustration depicts the superimposed structures of GLUT1 and XylE relative to their respective N domains. Abbreviation: TM, transmembrane segment.

The Coupling Mechanism of Major Facilitator Superfamily Proton Symporters

The coupling mechanism through which an active transporter utilizes the energy released from the downhill translocation of one substrate to drive the uphill movement of the other remains mostly enigmatic. Among the secondary active transporters, the proton symporters have been relatively well characterized (116). The understanding of the coupling mechanism for MFS proton symporters prior to 2012 has already been summarized in several reviews (22, 54, 115). Here, I focus on some recent discoveries that may facilitate mechanistic interpretation of proton coupling in SP proton symporters.

An aspartic acid residue at position 27 of XylE (69), which corresponds to D32 in the galactose:proton symporter GalP (91) and D22 in GlcP (47), plays a critical role in proton coupling. The mutation D27N in XylE, or D22N in GlcP, led to elimination of proton-dependent active symport, but not counterflow activity (47, 69). The mechanism by which D27 of XylE and the corresponding aspartic acid residues in the other SP proteins affect the coupling remained largely unknown until the structural determination of GLUT1, which revealed a tantalizing clue.

In the outward-facing XylE structure (100), D27 on TM1 forms a network of hydrogen bonds with the invariant R133 on TM4 (**Figure 6d**). This structure was obtained at pH 9.5, suggesting that D27 may be deprotonated. In the inward open GLUT1 structure, N29, which corresponds to D27 of XylE, mimics a permanently protonated state of aspartic acid. It is of particular note that R126 of GLUT1, which corresponds to R133 of XylE, does not interact with N29 (**Figure 6d**). Thus, one can reasonably speculate that in XylE, upon protonation of D27, the side chain of R133 would be released, possibly triggering the outward-to-inward transition. Note that the guanidinium group of R126 in GLUT1 is approximately 6 Å away from the benzene ring of Y292, so these groups likely form cation–π interactions in the inward open GLUT1 (**Figure 6d**). In the outward-facing XylE, the aromatic ring of Y298, which corresponds to Y292 of GLUT1, is approximately 9 Å away from the guanidinium group of R133, placing these residues too far apart for cation–π interactions (**Figure 6d**). Therefore, a comparison of the facilitator GLUT1 and the proton symporter XylE provides an important clue to understanding the proton coupling mechanism.

Uniporters catalyze only the translocation of a substrate down its concentration gradient (**Figure 1**). The conformational switches of the transporters are the key to completing a transport cycle. In GLUT1, the ligand-free protein may prefer an outward open conformation because of the extensive interactions between the TM and ICH domains (**Figure 4a**). Substrate binding at the central site on the C domain may induce closure of the N and C domains on the extracellular side, leading to a rearrangement of interactions on both sides of the bound substrate. When the binding affinity between the N and C domains on the extracellular side of the membrane exceeds that on the intracellular side, the protein may switch to the inward open conformation. Once GLUT1 adopts the inward open conformation, the substrate is exposed to a low-concentration milieu, and the equilibrium shifts toward substrate dissociation. The empty uniporter then returns to the outward-facing conformation (**Figure 7**).

For proton-driven symporters, the translocation of proton and substrate are obligatorily coupled. The general transport mechanism of a proton-coupled symporter such as XylE may be similar to that of the uniporter if the substrate (xylose) and the obligatory ligand (proton) are considered as a single entity (**Figure 7**). Because there are two types of substrates, however, the key difference between a symporter and a facilitator is that the translocation of one substrate (sugar or H$^+$) cannot be completed without that of the other. The detailed mechanism of the complete transport cycle awaits further characterization, but this analysis provides a tentative answer to one step of the cycle for XylE. In the absence of H$^+$, arrival of the sugar induces the closure of the N and C domains, but the protein cannot complete the outward-to-inward transition because the

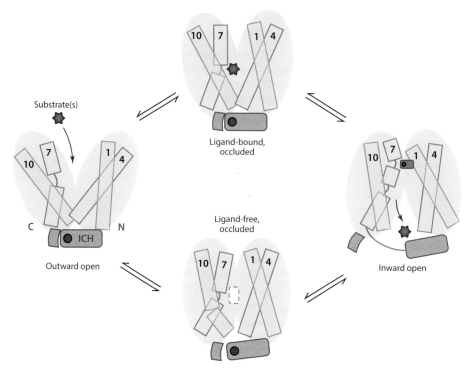

Figure 7

A working model for the sugar porter (SP) family, showing a revised version of the alternating-access model in **Figure 2**. The outward open structure remains to be determined, but the other conformations are derived from the appropriate XylE and GLUT1 structures. The intracellular helical domain (ICH) is illustrated as a latch that strengthens the intracellular gate in the outward open conformation. The extracellular gate comprises a few residues from TM1, TM4, and TM7, which are illustrated by the red zone in the inward open cartoon. Substrate(s) refers to one solute in facilitators and to two cotransported chemicals in symporters. Abbreviation: TM, transmembrane segment.

switch, namely residue R133, is sequestered by deprotonated D27 (**Figure 6d**). Protonation of D27 releases R133, which may subsequently reach out to interact with the C domain and thereby trigger the outward-to-inward transition. In the inward-facing conformation, the equilibrium may be shifted toward deprotonation because the environment has a low proton concentration. Deprotonation may be an essential step for the release of the substrate into a high-concentration environment. The deprotonated and substrate-released transporter then returns to the outward open conformation.

Many detailed mechanisms, such as the translocation route and the alternating-access mechanism for H⁺, remain to be investigated. In addition, one key element that distinguishes symporters from uniporters remains unclear—the inward open, substrate-released symporter cannot return to the outward-facing conformation without deprotonation, whereas a uniporter can achieve this switch despite its permanently protonated state. Further experimental characterizations, as well as molecular dynamics (MD) simulations, are likely required to address these remaining issues.

PERSPECTIVE

The exciting progress in the structural elucidation of MFS transporters in recent years has provided significant insights into our understanding of their mechanisms of activity. Despite these advances, however, several important issues remain to be addressed. Four examples of these issues are discussed in the following subsections.

Structural Determination of Additional Major Facilitator Superfamily Subfamilies

As summarized in **Table 2**, the 18 MFS proteins whose structures have been reported so far belong to nine families. However, the structures of most MFS families, especially those of families with significant physiological and pharmaceutical relevance such as the vesicular glutamate or amine transporters, are yet to be resolved (**Table 1**). Although all MFS proteins share a common structural fold, the unique features of specific families may support their specific biological functions. Obtaining the atomic structure for MFS members that have been identified as drug targets is of particular importance. The information provided by the homologous models, especially those of distantly related proteins, may not be sufficient for structure-guided drug design. Therefore, structural determination of the MFS members that are of direct physiological and pharmaceutical relevance represents one major direction for the study of the structural biology of MFS proteins in the future.

Elucidation of the Major Facilitator Superfamily Transport Mechanism

Although structures of multiple conformations are available for XylE and a few other MFS proteins, there is inadequate information on any MFS transporter to propose a complete alternating-access cycle. The outward open conformational state is still missing for XylE. A multitude of techniques, including the introduction of specific point mutations (14, 29, 60), chemical cross-linking (21, 80, 88), and cocrystallization with binders such as antibodies or nanobodies (86, 98), have been developed and have proven useful for facilitating the generation and structural determination of a desired conformation.

The revolutionary advances in cryo electron microscopy (cryoEM) are reshaping structural biology. The structures of extremely challenging targets for crystallography (59), exemplified by the ion channel TRPV1 (8, 67) and the membrane complex γ-secretase, were resolved by cryoEM at reasonable resolutions (68). CryoEM also has the advantage of revealing multiple conformations of the target macromolecules through classification (72). Whether high-resolution structural determination of the MFS proteins, for which monomers have an average molecular weight of approximately 50 kDa, can be reliably performed by single-particle cryoEM analysis remains to be seen.

In addition to capturing a complete alternating-access cycle, the coupling mechanism remains the most intriguing and challenging unresolved issue in the study of MFS symporters and antiporters. Elucidation of the coupling mechanism may require combination of multiple approaches. Finally, kinetic investigations of the transport process represent another challenging aspect for the mechanistic understanding of MFS proteins.

Modulation of Major Facilitator Superfamily Proteins by Lipids

During protein purification and crystallization, the native environment for membrane proteins—the lipid bilayer—is destroyed. This presents a challenge for researchers seeking to better understand the behavior of MFS proteins, as the surrounding lipids are an integral component for the structure and function of a membrane transporter. However, the study of the modulation of membrane proteins by lipids has been a grave challenge, owing to the difficulty of dealing with lipid molecules. Because an MFS transporter undergoes a large degree of conformational change during the alternating-access cycle, the surrounding lipids in their native environment are likely to affect the function, kinetics, or even thermodynamics of the transporter. The modulation of MFS transporters by specific lipids has yet to be systematically explored. Development and application of new technologies are required to advance our understanding of the interactions between integral membrane proteins and their surrounding lipids (61).

Deorphanization of Major Facilitator Superfamily Members

Despite rapid progress in the structural and mechanistic understanding of MFS transporters, an important aspect of their study remains, namely, characterization of the functions of many MFS proteins. Even for the rigorously characterized human proteins (**Table 1**), the physiological function, localization, and substrates for the majority of the SLC transporters, including GLUT6–GLUT14, remain largely enigmatic. Consequently, most of the MFS members are still orphan transporters. For example, an MFS member in mice, Mfsd2a, was only recently identified as an essential transporter for the omega-3 fatty acid decosahexaeoic acid (78). Together, the deorphanization and annotation of MFS members, especially those in humans and mammals, represent a major challenge for the future study of the MFS.

DISCLOSURE STATEMENT

The author is not aware of any affiliations, memberships, funding, or financial holdings that might be perceived as affecting the objectivity of this review.

ACKNOWLEDGMENTS

I thank Dr. Liang Feng, Dr. Brendan Lehnert, Dr. Yigong Shi, and Dr. Ting Zhu for critical reading of the article. This work was supported by funds from the Ministry of Science and Technology of China (2015CB910101) and from the National Natural Science Foundation of China (31125009). The research of N.Y. was supported in part by an International Early Career Scientist grant from the Howard Hughes Medical Institute and by an endowed professorship from Bayer Healthcare.

LITERATURE CITED

1. Abramson J, Smirnova I, Kasho V, Verner G, Kaback HR, Iwata S. 2003. Structure and mechanism of the lactose permease of *Escherichia coli*. *Science* 301:610–15
2. Agre P. 2004. Aquaporin water channels. *Biosci. Rep.* 24:127–63
3. Almén MS, Nordström KJ, Fredriksson R, Schiöth HB. 2009. Mapping the human membrane proteome: a majority of the human membrane proteins can be classified according to function and evolutionary origin. *BMC Biol.* 7:50
4. Bang O, Orskov SL. 1937. Variations in the permeability of the red blood cells in man, with particular reference to the conditions obtaining in pernicious anemia. *J. Clin. Investig.* 16:279–88
5. Birnbaum MJ, Haspel HC, Rosen OM. 1986. Cloning and characterization of a cDNA encoding the rat brain glucose-transporter protein. *PNAS* 83:5784–88
6. Bodoy S, Fotiadis D, Stoeger C, Kanai Y, Palacín M. 2013. The small SLC43 family: facilitator system l amino acid transporters and the orphan EEG1. *Mol. Asp. Med.* 34:638–45
7. Büttner M. 2007. The monosaccharide transporter(-like) gene family in *Arabidopsis*. *FEBS Lett.* 581:2318–24

8. Cao E, Liao M, Cheng Y, Julius D. 2013. TRPV1 structures in distinct conformations reveal activation mechanisms. *Nature* 504:113–18

9. Chou JY, Jun HS, Mansfield BC. 2013. The SLC37 family of phosphate-linked sugar phosphate antiporters. *Mol. Asp. Med.* 34:601–11

10. Costa C, Dias PJ, Sá-Correia I, Teixeira MC. 2014. MFS multidrug transporters in pathogenic fungi: Do they have real clinical impact? *Front. Physiol.* 5:197

11. Dang S, Sun L, Huang Y, Lu F, Liu Y, et al. 2010. Structure of a fucose transporter in an outward-open conformation. *Nature* 467:734–38

12. Daniel H, Spanier B, Kottra G, Weitz D. 2006. From bacteria to man: archaic proton-dependent peptide transporters at work. *Physiology* 21:93–102

13. DeLano WL. 2002. The PyMOL Molecular Graphics System. **http://www.pymol.org**

14. Deng D, Xu C, Sun P, Wu J, Yan C, et al. 2014. Crystal structure of the human glucose transporter GLUT1. *Nature* 510:121–25

15. Doki S, Kato HE, Solcan N, Iwaki M, Koyama M, et al. 2013. Structural basis for dynamic mechanism of proton-coupled symport by the peptide transporter POT. *PNAS* 110:11343–48

16. Dos Santos SC, Teixeira MC, Dias PJ, Sá-Correia I. 2014. MFS transporters required for multidrug/multixenobiotic (MD/MX) resistance in the model yeast: understanding their physiological function through post-genomic approaches. *Front. Physiol.* 5:180

17. Ehring R, Beyreuther K, Wright JK, Overath P. 1980. In vitro and in vivo products of *E. coli* lactose permease gene are identical. *Nature* 283:537–40

18. El-Gebali S, Bentz S, Hediger MA, Anderle P. 2013. Solute carriers (SLCs) in cancer. *Mol. Asp. Med.* 34:719–34

19. Ethayathulla AS, Yousef MS, Amin A, Leblanc G, Kaback HR, Guan L. 2014. Structure-based mechanism for Na$^+$/melibiose symport by MelB. *Nat. Commun.* 5:3009

20. Finn RD, Bateman A, Clements J, Coggill P, Eberhardt RY, et al. 2014. Pfam: the protein families database. *Nucleic Acids Res.* 42:D222–30

21. Fluman N, Ryan CM, Whitelegge JP, Bibi E. 2012. Dissection of mechanistic principles of a secondary multidrug efflux protein. *Mol. Cell* 47:777–87

22. Forrest LR, Krämer R, Ziegler C. 2011. The structural basis of secondary active transport mechanisms. *Biochim. Biophys. Acta* 1807:167–88

23. Fox CF, Carter JR, Kennedy EP. 1967. Genetic control of the membrane protein component of the lactose transport system of *Escherichia coli*. *PNAS* 57:698–705

24. Fox CF, Kennedy EP. 1965. Specific labeling and partial purification of the M protein, a component of the β-galactoside transport system of *Escherichia coli*. *PNAS* 54:891–99

25. Fukumoto H, Kayano T, Buse JB, Edwards Y, Pilch PF, et al. 1989. Cloning and characterization of the major insulin-responsive glucose transporter expressed in human skeletal muscle and other insulin-responsive tissues. *J. Biol. Chem.* 264:7776–79

26. Fukumoto H, Seino S, Imura H, Seino Y, Eddy RL, et al. 1988. Sequence, tissue distribution, and chromosomal localization of mRNA encoding a human glucose transporter-like protein. *PNAS* 85:5434–38

27. Gadsby DC. 2009. Ion channels versus ion pumps: the principal difference, in principle. *Nat. Rev. Mol. Cell Biol.* 10:344–52

28. Gao X, Lu F, Zhou L, Dang S, Sun L, et al. 2009. Structure and mechanism of an amino acid antiporter. *Science* 324:1565–68

29. Gao X, Zhou L, Jiao X, Lu F, Yan C, et al. 2010. Mechanism of substrate recognition and transport by an amino acid antiporter. *Nature* 463:828–32

30. Guan L, Kaback HR. 2006. Lessons from lactose permease. *Annu. Rev. Biophys. Biomol. Struct.* 35:67–91

31. Guettou F, Quistgaard EM, Raba M, Moberg P, Low C, Nordlund P. 2014. Selectivity mechanism of a bacterial homolog of the human drug-peptide transporters PepT1 and PepT2. *Nat. Struct. Mol. Biol.* 21:728–31

32. Guettou F, Quistgaard EM, Tresaugues L, Moberg P, Jegerschold C, et al. 2013. Structural insights into substrate recognition in proton-dependent oligopeptide transporters. *EMBO Rep.* 14:804–10

33. Hagenbuch B, Stieger B. 2013. The *SLCO* (former *SLC21*) superfamily of transporters. *Mol. Asp. Med.* 34:396–412

34. Halestrap AP. 2013. The *SLC16* gene family—structure, role and regulation in health and disease. *Mol. Asp. Med.* 34:337–49

35. He Y, Wang K, Yan N. 2014. The recombinant expression systems for structure determination of eukaryotic membrane proteins. *Protein Cell* 5:658–72

36. Hediger MA. 1994. Structure, function and evolution of solute transporters in prokaryotes and eukaryotes. *J. Exp. Biol.* 196:15–49

37. Hediger MA, Clémençon B, Burrier RE, Bruford EA. 2013. The ABCs of membrane transporters in health and disease (SLC series): introduction. *Mol. Asp. Med.* 34:95–107

38. Henderson PJ, Maiden MC. 1990. Homologous sugar transport proteins in *Escherichia coli* and their relatives in both prokaryotes and eukaryotes. *Philos. Trans. R. Soc. Lond. B* 326:391–410

39. Henderson PJF, Baldwin SA. 2012. Structural biology: bundles of insights into sugar transporters. *Nature* 490:348–50

40. Heymann JAW, Sarker R, Hirai T, Shi D, Milne JLS, et al. 2001. Projection structure and molecular architecture of OxlT, a bacterial membrane transporter. *EMBO J.* 20:4408–13

41. Hirabayashi Y, Nomura KH, Nomura K. 2013. The acetyl-CoA transporter family SLC33. *Mol. Asp. Med.* 34:586–89

42. Hirai T, Heymann JAW, Shi D, Sarker R, Maloney PC, Subramaniam S. 2002. Three-dimensional structure of a bacterial oxalate transporter. *Nat. Struct. Biol.* 9:597–600

43. Hodgkin AL, Huxley AF. 1945. Resting and action potentials in single nerve fibres. *J. Physiol.* 104:176–95

44. Höglund PJ, Nordström KJV, Schiöth HB, Fredriksson R. 2011. The solute carrier families have a remarkably long evolutionary history with the majority of the human families present before divergence of Bilaterian species. *Mol. Biol. Evol.* 28:1531–41

45. Hruz PW, Mueckler MM. 2001. Structural analysis of the GLUT1 facilitative glucose transporter. *Mol. Membr. Biol.* 18:183–93

46. Huang Y, Lemieux MJ, Song J, Auer M, Wang DN. 2003. Structure and mechanism of the glycerol-3-phosphate transporter from *Escherichia coli*. *Science* 301:616–20

47. Iancu CV, Zamoon J, Woo SB, Aleshin A, Choe JY. 2013. Crystal structure of a glucose/H$^+$ symporter and its mechanism of action. *PNAS* 110:17862–67

48. Jacob F, Monod J. 1961. Genetic regulatory mechanisms in the synthesis of proteins. *J. Mol. Biol.* 3:318–56

49. Jacob F, Perrin D, Sanchez C, Monod J. 1960. Operon: a group of genes with the expression coordinated by an operator. *C. R. Hebd. Seances Acad. Sci.* 250:1727–29

50. James DE, Brown R, Navarro J, Pilch PF. 1988. Insulin-regulatable tissues express a unique insulin-sensitive glucose transport protein. *Nature* 333:183–85

51. Jardetzky O. 1966. Simple allosteric model for membrane pumps. *Nature* 211:969–70

52. Jiang D, Zhao Y, Wang X, Fan J, Heng J, et al. 2013. Structure of the YajR transporter suggests a transport mechanism based on the conserved motif A. *PNAS* 110:14664–69

53. Kaback HR, Sahin-Tóth M, Weinglass AB. 2001. The kamikaze approach to membrane transport. *Nat. Rev. Mol. Cell Biol.* 2:610–20

54. Kaback HR, Smirnova I, Kasho V, Nie Y, Zhou Y. 2011. The alternating access transport mechanism in LacY. *J. Membr. Biol.* 239:85–93

55. Kaback HR, Stadtman ER. 1966. Proline uptake by an isolated cytoplasmic membrane preparation of *Escherichia coli*. *PNAS* 55:920–27

56. Kasahara M, Hinkle PC. 1976. Reconstitution of D-glucose transport catalyzed by a protein fraction from human erythrocytes in sonicated liposomes. *PNAS* 73:396–400

57. Kasahara M, Hinkle PC. 1977. Reconstitution and purification of the D-glucose transporter from human erythrocytes. *J. Biol. Chem.* 252:7384–90

58. Koepsell H. 2013. The SLC22 family with transporters of organic cations, anions and zwitterions. *Mol. Asp. Med.* 34:413–35

59. Kühlbrandt W. 2014. Microscopy: Cryo-EM enters a new era. *eLIFE* 3:e03678

60. Kumar H, Kasho V, Smirnova I, Finer-Moore JS, Kaback HR, Stroud RM. 2014. Structure of sugar-bound LacY. *PNAS* 111:1784–88

61. Laganowsky A, Reading E, Allison TM, Ulmschneider MB, Degiacomi MT, et al. 2014. Membrane proteins bind lipids selectively to modulate their structure and function. *Nature* 510:172–75

62. Lawal HO, Krantz DE. 2013. SLC18: vesicular neurotransmitter transporters for monoamines and acetylcholine. *Mol. Asp. Med.* 34:360–72

63. Lee C, Kang HJ, von Ballmoos C, Newstead S, Uzdavinys P, et al. 2013. A two-domain elevator mechanism for sodium/proton antiport. *Nature* 501:573–77

64. LeFevre PG. 1948. Evidence of active transfer of certain non-electrolytes across the human red cell membrane. *J. Gen. Physiol.* 31:505–27

65. Léran S, Varala K, Boyer J-C, Chiurazzi M, Crawford N, et al. 2014. A unified nomenclature of NITRATE TRANSPORTER 1/PEPTIDE TRANSPORTER family members in plants. *Trends Plant Sci.* 19:5–9

66. Li F, Ma C, Wang X, Gao C, Zhang J, et al. 2011. Characterization of *Sucrose transporter* alleles and their association with seed yield-related traits in *Brassica napus* L. *BMC Plant Biol.* 11:168

67. Liao M, Cao E, Julius D, Cheng Y. 2013. Structure of the TRPV1 ion channel determined by electron cryo-microscopy. *Nature* 504:107–12

68. Lu P, Bai XC, Ma D, Xie T, Yan C, et al. 2014. Three-dimensional structure of human γ-secretase. *Nature* 512:166–70

69. Madej MG, Sun L, Yan N, Kaback HR. 2014. Functional architecture of MFS D-glucose transporters. *PNAS* 111:E719–27

70. Maiden MC, Davis EO, Baldwin SA, Moore DC, Henderson PJ. 1987. Mammalian and bacterial sugar transport proteins are homologous. *Nature* 325:641–43

71. Marger MD, Saier MH Jr. 1993. A major superfamily of transmembrane facilitators that catalyse uniport, symport and antiport. *Trends Biochem. Sci.* 18:13–20

72. Meyerson JR, Kumar J, Chittori S, Rao P, Pierson J, et al. 2014. Structural mechanism of glutamate receptor activation and desensitization. *Nature* 514:328–34

73. Mueckler M, Caruso C, Baldwin SA, Panico M, Blench I, et al. 1985. Sequence and structure of a human glucose transporter. *Science* 229:941–45

74. Mueckler M, Thorens B. 2013. The SLC2 (GLUT) family of membrane transporters. *Mol. Asp. Med.* 34:121–38

75. Murata K, Mitsuoka K, Hirai T, Walz T, Agre P, et al. 2000. Structural determinants of water permeation through aquaporin-1. *Nature* 407:599–605

76. Newstead S. 2014. Molecular insights into proton coupled peptide transport in the PTR family of oligopeptide transporters. *Biochim. Biophys. Acta* 1850:488–99

77. Newstead S, Drew D, Cameron AD, Postis VL, Xia X, et al. 2011. Crystal structure of a prokaryotic homologue of the mammalian oligopeptide–proton symporters, PepT1 and PepT2. *EMBO J.* 30:417–26

78. Nguyen LN, Ma D, Shui G, Wong P, Cazenave-Gassiot A, et al. 2014. Mfsd2a is a transporter for the essential omega-3 fatty acid docosahexaenoic acid. *Nature* 509:503–6

79. Oka Y, Asano T, Shibasaki Y, Lin J-L, Tsukuda K, et al. 1990. C-terminal truncated glucose transporter is locked into an inward-facing form without transport activity. *Nature* 345:550–53

80. Oldham ML, Chen J. 2011. Crystal structure of the maltose transporter in a pretranslocation intermediate state. *Science* 332:1202–5

81. Özcan S, Johnston M. 1999. Function and regulation of yeast hexose transporters. *Microbiol. Mol. Biol. Rev.* 63:554–69

82. Parker JL, Newstead S. 2014. Molecular basis of nitrate uptake by the plant nitrate transporter NRT1.1. *Nature* 507:68–72

83. Pedersen BP, Kumar H, Waight AB, Risenmay AJ, Roe-Zurz Z, et al. 2013. Crystal structure of a eukaryotic phosphate transporter. *Nature* 496:533–36

84. Quistgaard EM, Löw C, Moberg P, Trésaugues L, Nordlund P. 2013. Structural basis for substrate transport in the GLUT-homology family of monosaccharide transporters. *Nat. Struct. Mol. Biol.* 20:766–68

85. Rask-Andersen M, Masuram S, Fredriksson R, Schiöth HB. 2013. Solute carriers as drug targets: current use, clinical trials and prospective. *Mol. Asp. Med.* 34:702–10

86. Rasmussen SGF, Choi H-J, Fung JJ, Pardon E, Casarosa P, et al. 2011. Structure of a nanobody-stabilized active state of the β2 adrenoceptor. *Nature* 469:175–80

87. Reimer RJ. 2013. SLC17: a functionally diverse family of organic anion transporters. *Mol. Asp. Med.* 34:350–59

88. Reyes N, Ginter C, Boudker O. 2009. Transport mechanism of a bacterial homologue of glutamate transporters. *Nature* 462:880–85

89. Robertson DE, Kaczorowski GJ, Garcia ML, Kaback HR. 1980. Active transport in membrane vesicles from *Escherichia coli*: The electrochemical proton gradient alters the distribution of the *lac* carrier between two different kinetic states. *Biochemistry* 19:5692–702

90. Saier MH Jr, Reddy VS, Tamang DG, Västermark Å. 2014. The transporter classification database. *Nucleic Acids Res.* 42:D251–58

91. Sanderson NM, Qi D, Steel A, Henderson PJF. 1998. Effect of the $D^{32}N$ and $N^{300}F$ mutations on the activity of the bacterial sugar transport protein, GalP. *Biochem. Soc. Trans.* 26:S306

92. Schürmann A, Doege H, Ohnimus H, Monser V, Buchs A, Joost H-G. 1997. Role of conserved arginine and glutamate residues on the cytosolic surface of glucose transporters for transporter function. *Biochemistry* 36:12897–902

93. Shi Y. 2013. Common folds and transport mechanisms of secondary active transporters. *Annu. Rev. Biophys.* 42:51–72

94. Shuman HA. 1981. The use of gene fusions of study bacterial transport proteins. *J. Membr. Biol.* 61:1–11

95. Skou JC. 1957. The influence of some cations on an adenosine triphosphatase from peripheral nerves. *Biochim. Biophys. Acta* 23:394–401

96. Smith DE, Clémençon B, Hediger MA. 2013. Proton-coupled oligopeptide transporter family SLC15: physiological, pharmacological and pathological implications. *Mol. Asp. Med.* 34:323–36

97. Solcan N, Kwok J, Fowler PW, Cameron AD, Drew D, et al. 2012. Alternating access mechanism in the POT family of oligopeptide transporters. *EMBO J.* 31:3411–21

98. Steyaert J, Kobilka BK. 2011. Nanobody stabilization of G protein-coupled receptor conformational states. *Curr. Opin. Struct. Biol.* 21:567–72

99. Sun J, Bankston JR, Payandeh J, Hinds TR, Zagotta WN, Zheng N. 2014. Crystal structure of the plant dual-affinity nitrate transporter NRT1.1. *Nature* 507:73–77

100. Sun L, Zeng X, Yan C, Sun X, Gong X, et al. 2012. Crystal structure of a bacterial homologue of glucose transporters GLUT1–4. *Nature* 490:361–66

101. Thorens B, Mueckler M. 2010. Glucose transporters in the 21st century. *Am. J. Physiol. Endocrinol. Metab.* 298:E141–45

102. Thorens B, Sarkar HK, Kaback HR, Lodish HF. 1988. Cloning and functional expression in bacteria of a novel glucose transporter present in liver, intestine, kidney, and β-pancreatic islet cells. *Cell* 55:281–90

103. Vitavska O, Wieczorek H. 2013. The SLC45 gene family of putative sugar transporters. *Mol. Asp. Med.* 34:655–60

104. Wang T, Fu G, Pan X, Wu J, Gong X, et al. 2013. Structure of a bacterial energy-coupling factor transporter. *Nature* 497:272–76

105. Wang Y, Huang Y, Wang J, Cheng C, Huang W, et al. 2009. Structure of the formate transporter FocA reveals a pentameric aquaporin-like channel. *Nature* 462:467–72

106. Widdas WF. 1951. Inability of diffusion to account for placental glucose transfer in the sheep. *J. Physiol.* 115:36–37

107. Widdas WF. 1952. Inability of diffusion to account for placental glucose transfer in the sheep and consideration of the kinetics of a possible carrier transfer. *J. Physiol.* 118:23–39

108. Wilbrandt W, Guensberg E, Lauener H. 1947. Admission of glucose by erythrocyte membrane. *Helv. Physiol. Pharmacol. Acta* 5:C20–22

109. Wilson-O'Brien AL, Patron N, Rogers S. 2010. Evolutionary ancestry and novel functions of the mammalian glucose transporter (GLUT) family. *BMC Evol. Biol.* 10:152

110. Wisedchaisri G, Park M-S, Iadanza MG, Zheng H, Gonen T. 2014. Proton-coupled sugar transport in the prototypical major facilitator superfamily protein XylE. *Nat. Commun.* 5:4521

111. Wong FH, Chen JS, Reddy V, Day JL, Shlykov MA, et al. 2012. The amino acid-polyamine-organocation superfamily. *J. Mol. Microbiol. Biotechnol.* 22:105–13

112. Xu K, Zhang M, Zhao Q, Yu F, Guo H, et al. 2013. Crystal structure of a folate energy-coupling factor transporter from *Lactobacillus brevis*. *Nature* 497:268–71

113. Yamashita A, Singh SK, Kawate T, Jin Y, Gouaux E. 2005. Crystal structure of a bacterial homologue of Na^+/Cl^--dependent neurotransmitter transporters. *Nature* 437:215–23

114. Yan H, Huang W, Yan C, Gong X, Jiang S, et al. 2013. Structure and mechanism of a nitrate transporter. *Cell Rep.* 3:716–23

115. Yan N. 2013. Structural advances for the major facilitator superfamily (MFS) transporters. *Trends Biochem. Sci.* 38:151–59

116. Yan N. 2013. Structural investigation of the proton-coupled secondary transporters. *Curr. Opin. Struct. Biol.* 23:483–91

117. Yin Y, He X, Szewczyk P, Nguyen T, Chang G. 2006. Structure of the multidrug transporter EmrD from *Escherichia coli*. *Science* 312:741–44

118. Young JD, Yao SYM, Baldwin JM, Cass CE, Baldwin SA. 2013. The human concentrative and equilibrative nucleoside transporter families, SLC28 and SLC29. *Mol. Asp. Med.* 34:529–47

119. Zhang P, Wang J, Shi Y. 2010. Structure and mechanism of the S component of a bacterial ECF transporter. *Nature* 468:717–20

120. Zhao R, Goldman ID. 2013. Folate and thiamine transporters mediated by facilitative carriers (SLC19A1-3 and SLC46A1) and folate receptors. *Mol. Asp. Med.* 34:373–85

121. Zhao Y, Mao G, Liu M, Zhang L, Wang X, Zhang XC. 2014. Crystal structure of the *E. coli* peptide transporter YbgH. *Structure* 22:1152–60

122. Zheng H, Wisedchaisri G, Gonen T. 2013. Crystal structure of a nitrate/nitrite exchanger. *Nature* 497:647–51

123. Zhou X, Levin EJ, Pan Y, McCoy JG, Sharma R, et al. 2014. Structural basis of the alternating-access mechanism in a bile acid transporter. *Nature* 505:569–73

124. Zhou Y, Jiang X, Kaback HR. 2012 . Role of the irreplaceable residues in the LacY alternating access mechanism. *PNAS* 109:12438–42

RELATED RESOURCES

Genomic Transporter Database, SLC series (the SLC Tables): **http://slc.bioparadigms.org/**
Membrane proteins of known structures: **http://blanco.biomol.uci.edu/mpstruc/**
The MFS Clan (CL0015) in the Pfam protein families database: **http://pfam.xfam.org/clan/MFS**
Transporter Classification Database: **http://www.tcdb.org/**

Specification of Architecture and Function of Actin Structures by Actin Nucleation Factors*

Colleen T. Skau and Clare M. Waterman†

Cell Biology and Physiology Center, National Heart, Lung, and Blood Institute, National Institutes of Health, Bethesda, Maryland 20892; email: colleen.skau@nih.gov, watermancm@nhlbi.nih.gov

Annu. Rev. Biophys. 2015. 44:285–310

The *Annual Review of Biophysics* is online at biophys.annualreviews.org

This article's doi:
10.1146/annurev-biophys-060414-034308

*This is a work of the US Government and is not subject to copyright protection in the United States.

†Corresponding author

Keywords

formin, Arp2/3, contractile ring, stress fiber, lamellipodium

Abstract

The actin cytoskeleton is essential for diverse processes in mammalian cells; these processes range from establishing cell polarity to powering cell migration to driving cytokinesis to positioning intracellular organelles. How these many functions are carried out in a spatiotemporally regulated manner in a single cytoplasm has been the subject of much study in the cytoskeleton field. Recent work has identified a host of actin nucleation factors that can build architecturally diverse actin structures. The biochemical properties of these factors, coupled with their cellular location, likely define the functional properties of actin structures. In this article, we describe how recent advances in cell biology and biochemistry have begun to elucidate the role of individual actin nucleation factors in generating distinct cellular structures. We also consider how the localization and orientation of actin nucleation factors, in addition to their kinetic properties, are critical to their ability to build a functional actin cytoskeleton.

Contents

INTRODUCTION

Actin assembly in motile cells is critical for several processes, from protruding the leading edge of a cell to regulating transcription to controlling organelle shape and size. To accomplish these functions, a cell builds several distinct actin structures, and coordination of actin polymerization among these structures presents a significant challenge for the cell. Although some regulation may be accomplished via compartmentalization or differential localization of actin-binding proteins, it is unlikely that these mechanisms alone are able to specify the variety of actin structures. Therefore, cells use a diverse group of actin nucleation factors to spatially and temporally construct different actin structures, and the organization and dynamics of these structures are defined by the nucleation factor. Many actin nucleation factors have been identified and biochemically characterized, although much about their in vivo localization, roles, and regulation remains unknown. In this review, we explore the role of actin nucleation factors in constructing three different geometries of actin structures: dendritic networks, actin bundles, and isotropic networks (**Figure 1**). We first describe why cells require actin nucleation factors, along with the molecular mechanisms of the three main classes of actin nucleators. We then discuss the organization of actin structures in the cell and how the properties and orientation of each nucleator contribute to the different classes of structures.

THE BIOCHEMISTRY OF ACTIN IN CELLS

Why Are Actin Nucleation Factors Essential?

Actin nucleation is tightly controlled because (*a*) the critical concentration for assembly of actin monomers into filaments (F-actin) is low, and (*b*) actin filament assembly is energetically costly:

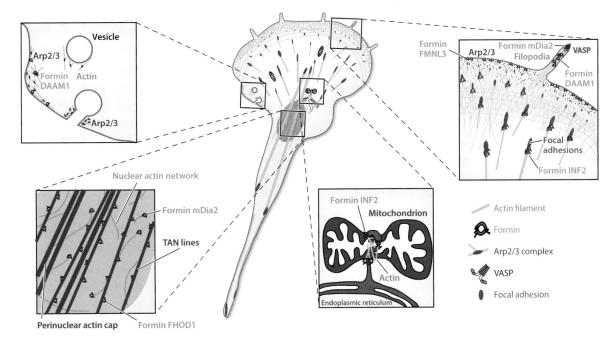

Figure 1

Different actin nucleators specify architecturally and functionally distinct actin structures. (*Center*) Diagram showing actin organization in a motile cell. Actin is shown in green, the Arp2/3 complex at the branch point of two filaments is shown in purple, and the FH2 homodimers of formins are shown in orange. Insets highlight organelles with associated actin structures, including vesicles, focal adhesions, mitochondria, and the nucleus, and show these structures in greater detail. Note the different geometries of actin associated with different organelles. For clarity, only the best-characterized actin nucleator is shown for each actin structure, and only some of the described actin structures are shown. Some actin structures are not depicted; these include cell–cell junctions, the contractile ring, ventral stress fibers, and blebs. Abbreviations: Arp2/3, actin-related proteins 2 and 3; DAAM1, disheveled-associated activator of morphogenesis 1; FHOD1, FH1/FH2 domain-containing protein 1; FMNL3, formin-like protein 3; INF2, inverted formin-2; mDia2, mouse diaphanous-related formin 2; TAN lines, transmembrane actin-associated nuclear lines; VASP, vasodilator-stimulated phosphoprotein.

the rate-limiting step for spontaneous actin assembly is the formation of the trimer. However, the vast majority of monomeric globular actin (G-actin) in the cell is bound by G-actin-sequestering proteins, such as profilin, that prohibit spontaneous nucleation (92, 132). To regulate the assembly of sequestered actin monomers, cells use actin nucleation factors, three main classes of which are found in most mammalian cells. These different classes form distinct actin structures that perform different functions in cells. They are the actin-related proteins 2 and 3 (Arp2/3) complex and its activating factors, tandem monomer binding proteins (TMBPs), and formins.

What Are the Mechanistic Differences Between the Three Main Classes of Actin Nucleation Factors?

The first actin nucleation factor to be discovered was the Arp2/3 complex (70, 124), which nucleates a new actin filament as a branch off of the side of an existing filament at an approximately 70° angle (81, 108). The core of this seven-member complex comprises Arp2 and Arp3, which are structurally similar to actin monomers (77, 94, 124), and the complex cannot function without a

TMBP: tandem monomer binding protein

Table 1 Proteins associated with the actin-related protein 2 and 3 (Arp2/3) complex

Abbreviation	Description
NPF	Nucleation-promoting factor
WASP/N-WASP	Wiskott–Aldrich syndrome protein/neural-WASP
WAVE	WASP family verprolin-homologous protein
WASH	WASP and Scar homology protein
WHAMM	WASP homolog associated with actin, membranes, and microtubules
JMY	Junction-mediating and -regulatory protein
GMF	Glia maturation factor
WIP	WASP-interacting protein
CARMIL	Capping protein, Arp2/3, and myosin I linker

nucleation promoting factor (NPF) (for review, see Reference 96). The NPFs are grouped into related families described in **Table 1**: WASP/N-WASP, WAVE, WASH, and WHAMM (28, 33). After nucleation, the Arp2/3 complex does not affect the rate of assembly at the fast-growing barbed end of the actin filament; rather the complex remains associated with the pointed end (3, 81). Thus the Arp2/3 complex, activated by an NPF, nucleates the development of a branch from an existing actin filament.

The two other families of actin nucleation factors create unbranched filaments. The first family, TMBPs, includes Spire, Cordon-bleu, leiomodin, VopL/F, and JMY, and members of this family bind at least three actin monomers via WH2 domains, mimicking the stable actin trimer (91, 139). Similar to the Arp2/3 complex, TMBPs bind the pointed end of the filament and leave the barbed end free (91). Vasodilator-stimulated phosphoprotein (VASP) is related to this group, and this protein has been reported to have nucleation properties in vitro (43), although it likely functions as an elongation factor in vivo and, unlike other TMBPs, regulates assembly at the barbed end of filaments (13, 109, 126). Thus, diverse TMBPs utilize different mechanisms of monomer clustering to stabilize the formation of linear actin filaments with free barbed ends.

The second family of linear filament nucleation factors, formins, stabilizes the spontaneously formed actin trimer and remains processively associated with the fast-growing barbed end of a filament, regulating its elongation (61). Formins have a conserved actin polymerization core consisting of the FH1 (formin homology 1) and FH2 (formin homology 2) domains. The proline-rich coils of the FH1 domain bind profilin–actin complexes and promote addition of actin monomers to the barbed end of the filament, which is bound by the FH2 domain. The FH2 domain is a homodimer that binds like a ring around the outside of three interacting actin monomers, stabilizing the actin seed and regulating monomer addition at the barbed end (86, 131). Flexibility between the halves of the homodimer allows the formin to remain processively bound to the growing barbed end of the actin filament (62, 131). Formins are therefore unique as actin nucleators, which remain bound to the growing barbed end of linear actin filaments. The next sections describe how these diverse actin nucleators define distinct actin structures.

VASP:
vasodilator-stimulated phosphoprotein

DENDRITIC NETWORKS

The following subsections discuss the structure, composition, and function of dendritic actin networks, along with how the Arp2/3 complex defines and controls them.

How Do the Properties of the Arp2/3 Complex Define the Functional Properties of Dendritic Networks?

Dendritic networks are used to generate pushing force against a membrane wherever they are found in the cell, and the properties of the Arp2/3 complex make it ideal for formation of structures that participate in this pushing process. Many NPFs are associated with the membrane and thus locally activate the Arp2/3 complex there (96). Filaments near the membrane push against it via a Brownian ratchet mechanism upon incorporation of new monomers at their barbed ends (138). Stochastic, rapid incorporation of capping protein onto the free barbed ends of these filaments distributes force along the entire edge of the membrane, allowing the dendritic network to act as an expanding gel (72). At the leading edge of a cell, compression from the membrane curves the actin filaments away from it, and as the Arp2/3 complex branches off of the convex side of a curved actin filament more frequently than off of the concave side (93), the Arp2/3 complex is biased toward generating productive branches that are oriented toward the leading edge of the cell (93). The dendritic network is therefore equipped to handle compressive forces from the membrane and to provide force over a large two-dimensional area (93). Thus, specific properties of the Arp2/3 complex tailor it to generate a force-producing dendritic network at the leading-edge membrane.

AJ: adherens junction

The leading edge of a cell is not the only structure that employs a network polymerized by Arp2/3, however. Endocytosis, bacterial pathogens, and cell–cell junctions also use Arp2/3-created actin networks to push against membranes. The organization and role of this actin network are less well established for the case of endocytosis than for the other two examples. Endocytic actin may be arranged similarly to the lamellipodial network. Alternatively, growth at the inner surface of an object such as a vesicle may exert squeezing forces as the Arp2/3 gel expands around it (93). The bacterium *Listeria* takes advantage of squeezing forces generated by Arp2/3-mediated actin polymerization to rocket around inside cells and spread to neighboring cells (66), and endocytic vesicles may use a similar structure. The Arp2/3 complex is also critical in formation of adherens junctions (AJs) at cell–cell contacts (1, 47). Initial contacts may be formed using Arp2/3-mediated lamellipodia similar to those seen at the protruding edge of a cell, although cells forming AJs are not motile. As it does for lamellipodia, the Arp2/3 complex produces a force-generating network used for pushing a membrane in both endocytic vesicles and AJs. We now discuss the organization of Arp2/3-generated structures in greater detail.

Lamellipodia. Nucleation of the branched actin network that makes up the lamellipodium depends on the Arp2/3 complex and, in fact, this structure was the first for which the importance of the Arp2/3 complex was characterized. The following sections describe current knowledge regarding the organization and dynamics of the lamellipodium as generated by the Arp2/3 complex and other actin nucleation factors.

What is the architecture of the lamellipodium? The lamellipodium is a thin, veil-like region of cytoplasm that dynamically protrudes and retracts along the front edge of migrating cells based on the directed polymerization of actin filaments (46). Lamellipodia in migrating cells contain a dendritic meshwork of actin filaments and extend laterally up to tens of micrometers along the cell edge, although they are typically less than two micrometers wide (105). When membrane tension is low, actin polymerization drives the membrane forward to protrude the leading edge. When tension is high, however, polymerization drives retrograde flow, which, coupled to extracellular matrix adhesion, generates traction to drive cell movement (121, 123). Thus, polymerization of the actin network at the lamellipodium is the motor that drives the cell forward.

ADF: actin
depolymerizing factor

CME:
clathrin-mediated
endocytosis

What proteins are necessary and sufficient for generation of a lamellipodium? The proteins essential for generating a functional Arp2/3 network are actin; Arp2/3 with an NPF; cofilin; capping protein; and an actin monomer–binding protein, profilin (66). Because the Arp2/3 complex is intrinsically inactive, the NPF localization is critical for determining where Arp2/3 polymerizes actin (28, 70, 125). Thus, association of NPFs with the membrane at the leading edge of the cell is essential for the Arp2/3 complex to generate a lamellipodium. The actin-severing protein actin depolymerizing factor (ADF)/cofilin is also important for generating a lamellipodium via actin turnover (14, 83). In motile cells, ADF/cofilin is localized behind the lamellipodial network, where it severs older actin filaments (7, 71, 108). This severing promotes monomer recycling and thereby supplies the Arp2/3 at the leading edge of the cell with enough G-actin to drive rapid membrane protrusion (90). Capping protein also increases branching by blocking the assembly of filaments and thus directs monomers toward new nucleation by the Arp2/3 complex (2). Additional proteins that regulate the Arp2/3 complex, including cortactin and coronin, are also found at the edge, and new Arp2/3-regulatory proteins such as WASP-interacting protein (WIP), capping protein, Arp2/3 and myosin I linker (CARMIL), and glial maturation factor (GMF) are under active study (for review, see Reference 22). Together, Arp2/3 and its NPFs directly drive the polymerization of a dendritic actin mesh, and this process critically depends on actin monomers being released by ADF/cofilin-based severing and funneled to the Arp2/3 complex by capping protein.

How do other actin nucleation factors contribute to formation of the lamellipodium? Recent work indicates that other actin nucleation factors besides Arp2/3 play a role in generating lamellipodia. The formin FMNL2 (also called FRL3) accumulates in filopodia and at the lamellipodium (15), where it works with the Arp2/3 complex to regulate the rate of protrusion (15). Other formins have also been proposed to contribute to the formation of lamellipodia, including the Diaphanous formin mDia2 (134) and inverted formin-2 (INF2) (103a), although details about their roles in that process remain unclear (**Table 2**) (for review, see Reference 63). The dendritic network generated by Arp2/3 is critical for lamellipodial protrusion; other actin nucleation factors at the leading edge of the cell likely make a secondary contribution (66).

Endocytosis and vesicles. Extensive biochemical and cell biological work in yeast has clearly delineated an essential role for actin polymerization by the Arp2/3 complex in endocytosis. In fact, the steps of the endocytic pathway in yeast are spatially and temporally well characterized. However, the role of actin polymerization in mammalian cell endocytosis is much less well studied, and the geometries of the actin structures in endocytosis remain poorly understood.

Is actin essential for mammalian endocytosis? Although actin is essential for endocytosis in yeast, the role of actin assembly in clathrin-mediated endocytosis (CME) in mammalian cells is debated (for review, see Reference 79). Initial studies indicated that the role of actin varied depending on the cell type and on whether the cells were adherent or in suspension (36). Thus, actin was thought to play an accessory role in endocytosis. Several studies also indicated that the importance of actin depended on local membrane tension and on the ability of clathrin to assemble on a membrane under tension (9, 17, 65). Taken together, these studies suggest that actin has a supporting role in mammalian endocytosis.

What is the source of actin for endocytosis? Other studies have identified an essential role for actin in CME (73, 75, 136), suggesting that it likely generates force at the membrane. Both the Arp2/3 complex and N-WASP localize to sites of endocytosis (74). Electron microscopy has shown short,

Table 2 Formins described in the text, grouped by family

Protein name	Structural affiliation(s)
FH1/FH2	Formin homology domains 1/2
mDia1	Adherens junctions Dorsal stress fibers Cortex and/or blebs
mDia2	Lamellipodia Filopodia Contractile ring Nucleus
FHOD1	TAN lines Transverse arcs
DAAM1	Filopodia Ventral stress fibers (?) Cortical nodes
FMNL1	Cortex/blebs
FMNL2/FRL3	Filopodia Lamellipodial protrusion
FMNL3/FRL2	Filopodia
FMN1	Adherens junctions
INF2	Mitochondrial fission Stress fiber assembly

branched filaments and the Arp2/3 complex at sites of clathrin-coated pit invagination, where the barbed ends of actin filaments were directed toward internalizing clathrin structures (29). We therefore propose that actin generated by Arp2/3 is critical for the later stages of endocytosis and plays a role in pushing the plasma membrane around a forming vesicle, similar to its role in pushing the plasma membrane forward at the leading edge of a cell. However, how actin generated by Arp2/3 is organizationally related to lamellipodial actin is unknown.

Adherens junctions. AJs are dynamic complexes of proteins that connect neighboring cells to each other. Extracellular cadherin molecules connect to each other and span the plasma membrane, where they interact with catenin molecules inside the cell. Catenins can bind directly to the actin cytoskeleton, and they can also interact with other actin-binding proteins (for review, see Reference 76). However, the organization of actin at AJs remains somewhat unknown.

What is the role of the Arp2/3 complex in adherens junctions? Arp2/3-mediated dendritic actin networks are also critical for structures that connect cells. Adherens junctions rely on the homotypic interaction between cadherins in adjacent cells and catenins that link cadherins to the cortical actin cytoskeleton (for review, see Reference 76). The Arp2/3 complex can bind to E-cadherin directly and localize to AJs, where it can regulate actin polymerization (60). The Arp2/3 complex, in conjunction with its activators (60, 76), is required to establish and maintain AJs (1, 47, 118). Similar to a lamellipodium, a dendritic actin network at the cell edge can push the membrane outward, allowing extensive contact with neighboring cells and the formation of junctions.

Are other actin assembly factors associated with adherens junctions? Some evidence also suggests that the formins Diaphanous 1 (Dia1) and Formin 1 (FMN1) may be important at AJs (23, 57), but inhibition of formins in general does not disrupt cell–cell junctions (110). Interestingly, however, in some cell types, the cortical actin cytoskeleton underlying the plasma membrane at the site of AJs is composed of linear actin bundles rather than a dendritic meshwork (47). Thus actin at AJs may comprise either two distinct networks, one made by a formin and the other by the Arp2/3 complex, or a single network resulting from the cooperation between formins and Arp2/3. We postulate that the network created by the Arp2/3 complex is more important for the initial generation of AJs by pushing the membrane forward (and thus promoting contact with neighboring cells) using a mechanism common to all dendritic networks.

ACTIN BUNDLES

What Are the Functional Differences Between Dendritic Networks and Linear Bundles?

In contrast to the relatively uniform dendritic networks that generate pushing force over a large area, linear actin bundles are heterogeneous: some of these structures are composed of filaments of uniform polarity, whereas others are bundles of filaments with mixed polarity. The roles of linear actin bundles are also heterogeneous. Bundles with uniform polarity can push a membrane forward at a very local site or can act as a noncontractile tether that connects one organelle in the cell to a contractile actin network. Once they are connected to the contractile networks, uniform polarity bundles can be used to pull on targets. Conversely, mixed polarity bundles are intrinsically contractile and can therefore provide constriction forces to deform substrates or generate force by shortening. Thus, owing to organizational differences generated by actin nucleators, linear bundles of actin filaments play roles that are distinct from those played by dendritic networks and by each other.

How Do the Molecular Properties of Formins Contribute to Generation of Diverse Linear Bundle Structures?

Formins generate linear actin structures with specific properties. Different formins have different biochemical properties, and these properties define organizational and functional differences among linear structures (52). Formins can define an actin structure both directly and indirectly. The variation among kinetic properties of formins allows them to act directly on actin structure formation by nucleating and assembling actin at different rates and by modifying actin filaments by bundling or severing them. Additionally, recent evidence shows that application of force to formins can modulate the rate of actin polymerization (51). These parameters define how a structure grows and disassembles. Formins can also act indirectly by modifying the flexibility and twist of actin filaments (88), and these changes can alter which actin-binding proteins associate with which actin bundles (103, 112). Thus, the biochemical properties of formins make them well-suited to generating both uniform and mixed polarity bundles that have a variety of kinetic properties (**Table 2**).

The orientation of formins within a structure is critical to defining its geometry (**Figure 2**). Formins can polymerize actin structures with either uniform or mixed polarity because in contrast to the Arp2/3 complex, formins do not have an intrinsic nucleation bias. Therefore, the polarity of a bundle must be defined by physical tethering. To create a bundle of uniform polarity, for example, formins localized to a defined spot in the cell would all be oriented in the same direction,

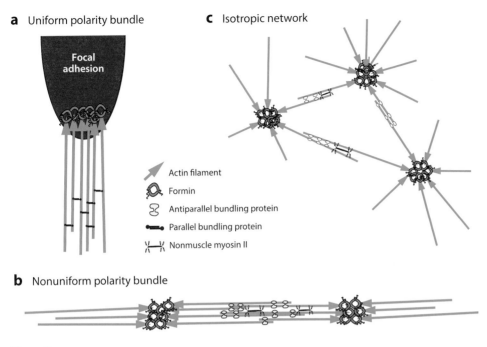

a Uniform polarity bundle   **c** Isotropic network

Focal adhesion

➤ Actin filament

Formin

Antiparallel bundling protein

Parallel bundling protein

Nonmuscle myosin II

b Nonuniform polarity bundle

Figure 2

Orientation of formin actin nucleators may define the geometry of linear actin structures. Formin molecules are shown in orange, and actin filaments are shown in green; the fast-growing barbed end of each filament is marked by an arrowhead. (*a*) Formins oriented in the same direction generate a uniform polarity bundle, for example, at the focal adhesion. A cross-linking protein specific for filaments oriented in the same direction is also shown. (*b*). Formins oriented back to back in linear arrays generate bundles with mixed polarity. A cross-linking protein specific for filaments oriented in the antiparallel direction is also shown, as are myosin II minifilaments. (*c*) Formins oriented back to back in discrete location, called pom-poms, generate isotropic networks. A cross-linking protein specific for filaments oriented in the antiparallel direction is also shown, as are myosin II minifilaments.

and the barbed ends of the actin filaments would be retained at a single location (**Figure 2*a***). To create a bundle of mixed polarity, however, formins would have to be spaced along the bundle track and oriented away from each other. This orientation would result in polymerization of filaments with barbed ends grouped at the location of the tethered formin but with pointed ends moving in opposite directions (**Figure 2*b***). Interestingly, some formins associate with microtubules, and this association may provide an actin-independent mechanism for localization (37). Thus, formin orientation is critical to the ability of formins to generate bundles of both uniform and mixed polarity, although the mechanisms of orienting and tethering these proteins are unknown. We now describe each type of bundle, providing specific examples of distinct bundle structures and what is known about how nucleators define these structures.

UNIFORM POLARITY ACTIN BUNDLES

What Are the Roles of Uniform Polarity Actin Bundles?

Actin bundles with uniform polarity have two main roles. They can push the membrane forward, as filopodia do, or they can act as noncontractile tethers. Bundles of uniform polarity are not effective substrates for myosin II; however, they can be connected to contractile actin networks, from which the tethered bundles can transmit force to other structures. Bundles with uniform polarity can be generated in multiple ways. Formins localized at a single site could orient in the same direction relative to each other and thus polymerize filaments in the same direction. Alternatively, bundling proteins, such as fascin, or motor proteins, such as myosin, could align filaments into a bundle. At least two structures in the cell are made up of actin filaments with uniform polarity: filopodia and dorsal stress fibers (SF). We also postulate that, given their function and organization, transmembrane actin-associated nuclear (TAN) lines may be composed of bundles of uniform polarity. We now discuss the architecture and role of each structure, along with what is known about how each is polymerized.

Filopodia. One of the most obvious structures on many motile cells is a series of thin spikes extending from the plasma membrane at intervals around the cell. Although these structures were originally identified as microvilli, they have since been recognized as being a separate kind of dynamic protrusion with their own actin organization and function: the filopodia. Furthermore, recent work has begun to delineate different roles for different types of filopodia in a single cell.

What are filopodia? Filopodia are slender, finger-like projections that protrude from the edge of a cell and are made up of a plasma membrane–enclosed array of actin filaments bundled together by fascin (for review, see Reference 16). Individual actin filaments within a bundle span the entire length of the filopodium and are oriented such that their fast-growing barbed ends are at the distal tip (82). Similar to the dendritic network, actin polymerization at the tip of a filopodium pushes the membrane forward; in contrast to the dendritic network, however, the main role of most filopodia is not to drive cell motility. Filopodia are critical for early cell spreading by functioning as local sensors, termed "sticky fingers," that allow integrins to detect properties of the extracellular matrix and find permissive attachment sites (38). The ability of filopodia to protrude dynamically is critical for their ability to explore space, and the mechanism underlying this dynamic protrusion is in contrast to that of the dendritic actin network, which provides more force but cannot be fully remodeled as rapidly.

How are filopodial bundles generated by actin nucleation factors? Filopodia are embedded in the dendritic actin mesh at the leading edge of the cell (90, 98), although it is still unclear whether initiation of filopodia formation depends on an actin nucleation factor. Original models propose that long filaments form spontaneously within the dendritic network, whereupon VASP prevents capping and promotes elongation at the filopodial tip (109, 135). Subsequent work, however, has shown that the formin mDia2 plays an important role in filopodia formation (100, 134). VASP and Dia2 interact at filopodia (32, 99). mDia2 may therefore protect filaments in the lamellipodium from capping, promoting their elongation, and may also promote the association of lamellipodial filaments with VASP through its interaction with mDia2 (134, 135). The details of this interaction are still under study (8, 13, 126), but it now seems clear that the formin Dia2 cooperates with VASP to promote the assembly of filopodia.

mDia2 is not the only formin thought to play a role in filopodia assembly. Recent work has shown that the formin DAAM1 (disheveled-associated activator of morphogenesis 1) localizes along the length of the filopodium in a manner dependent on its physical interaction with fascin (50). Depletion of DAAM1 leads to losses of filopodial integrity and number (50). DAAM1 appears to function primarily as a bundling protein, rather than as a polymerase (50). Along the length of filopodia, DAAM1 may work with mDia2 as part of a hand-off mechanism to help elongate filaments, but this has not been demonstrated. Additionally, the formin FRL2 (also called FMNL3) localizes to the tips of filopodia and can induce filopodia formation, although the mechanisms underlying these behaviors are not entirely clear (44). Thus, multiple actin nucleation factors may function together to generate a filopodial bundle. Critically, filopodial actin nucleators must be gathered at the tip of the filopodium and must all be oriented in the same direction to ensure that actin polymerization drives membrane protrusion, rather than filament polymerization back into the cell.

Interestingly, some cell types can produce multiple kinds of filopodia, depending on biochemical differences among the actin nucleation factors that create the protrusions (13, 126). In Schneider 2 (S2) cells from *Drosophila*, filopodia formed by Ena, a member of the VASP family, are more dynamic but shorter than those produced by Dia (13). Similarly, mammalian fibroblasts expressing either VASP or mDia2 generate filopodia that have different dynamics, morphology, and number but similar molecular compositions (8). Thus, a single cell type can express multiple types of filopodial protrusions that may have different in vivo roles.

Dorsal stress fibers. Both electron microscopy and fluorescence microscopy allow visualization of an intricate network of apparently parallel actin bundles that span the length of many cell types. Even before any molecular mechanism for generating these fibers was proposed, two distinct networks could be identified in cells spread on a solid substrate: one near the dorsal side of the cell, and one at the ventral side near the substrate. These fibers were coincident with the long-identified stress fibers or tension striae, and further examination revealed that actin was providing this tension. The following sections describe different types of actin stress fibers.

What are the organization and function of dorsal stress fibers? Actin SF can be divided into three categories on the basis of their cellular location and assembly mechanisms: dorsal SF, ventral SF, and transverse arcs (48). Of these, only dorsal SF bundles have uniform polarity; transverse arcs and ventral stress fibers have nonuniform polarity. Therefore, we discuss only dorsal SF in this subsection; transverse arcs and ventral SF are considered with other nonuniform bundles.

In culture, dorsal SF run roughly perpendicular to the leading edge of migrating cells and terminate with their barbed ends at a focal adhesion on the ventral side of adherent cells (48). Because the filaments in the dorsal SF have a uniform orientation, they largely lack myosin II (48, 111). However, the ends of the bundles not associated with focal adhesions connect either to the contractile actin mesh on the dorsal side of the cell or to rearward-flowing transverse arcs (48). Force transmitted to focal adhesions from the dorsal cortex through dorsal SF is critical for the elongation and maturation of these structures (27). We further postulate that the uniform orientation of filaments in dorsal SF is critical for their ability to direct this elongation; pulling on noncontractile dorsal SF by the cortical actin mesh generates a unidirectional force for focal adhesion elongation. If dorsal SF were mixed polarity bundles, this pulling could result in bundle stretching and less transmission of force to the focal adhesions. Recent work (84, 103a) has indicated that dorsal SF play a critical role in generating the elongated fibrillar adhesions used by fibroblasts to remodel and build the ECM. Thus, despite being localized near the leading edge of cells, dorsal SF are not used for pushing the membrane forward; rather, these structures appear to be involved in rearrangement of proteins at focal adhesions via their connection to a contractile actin network.

How are uniformly oriented dorsal stress fibers generated? The formation of dorsal SF relies on the uniform orientation of formins at focal adhesions; the uniformity of formin orientation tethers the barbed ends of all actin filaments at these adhesions. Hotulainen & Lappalainen (48) proposed that the formin mDia1 contributes to elongation of stress fibers from the distal side of

MTOC: microtubule
organizing center

LINC: linker of
nucleus and
cytoskeleton

focal adhesions; however, neither mDia1 nor mDia2, which may also play a role in SF formation (41), has been localized to dorsal SF. We have now shown (103a) that the formin INF2 localizes to the proximal end of dorsal SF at the junction with focal adhesions, and INF2 nucleates and polymerizes actin at that location. In fact, polymerization of actin at the proximal end of dorsal SF is critical for the transition of focal adhesions into fibrillar adhesions. Thus dorsal SF are generated by actin filament polymerization in a uniform direction from a discrete spot, the focal adhesion, and these fibers function as a tether to transmit force from the contractile actin network to focal adhesions in a defined direction.

TAN lines and the nucleus. The term dorsal SF has largely been applied to the actin bundles terminating in a focal adhesion near the edge of the cell and reaching toward the dorsal side of the cell to connect to the actin cortex there. However, some stress fibers terminate in focal adhesions and run all the way across the dorsal side of the nucleus. The following section considers these fibers to be distinct from dorsal SF despite their somewhat similar locations.

Why does a cell need actin around the nucleus? Positioning the nucleus in migrating cells is a significant challenge given the size and relative inflexibility of the nucleus compared with those of the cytoplasm. Cells migrating into a scratch wound use an actin-based system to position their nuclei toward the rear of the cell and behind the microtubule organizing center (MTOC), which is oriented toward the leading edge (39, 40). As cell migration into the wound is impaired in the absence of active nuclear positioning systems (69), actin-based positioning of the large, rigid nucleus is a key to efficient cell migration.

How are actin structures that control nuclear position organized, and how are they formed? The major structures shown to control nuclear position are TAN lines, which are composed of aligned actin bundles that run along the dorsal side of the nucleus parallel to the axis of migration, and linear arrays of the LINC (linker of nucleus and cytoskeleton) complex that connects the nucleus to these actin cables (69). Linear organization of LINC proteins on the dorsal side of the nucleus depends on the actin cables (64, 69). The organization of these actin cables has not been conclusively shown, although we hypothesize that they are uniformly oriented actin bundles, given their orientation along the nucleus and their ability to align other protein complexes. In fact, we suggest that TAN lines could function similarly to dorsal SF; that is, they transmit force generated by the contractile actin mesh to proteins integral to the nuclear envelope, and the nuclear envelope proteins in turn reorganize in the direction of applied force. However, it is unclear whether these cables contain myosin II; they may in fact be contractile bundles of nonuniform orientation.

What does this mechanism suggest about the orientation of formins that might nucleate actin cables for TAN lines? Similar to creation of dorsal SF by formins at focal adhesions, formins for TAN lines must all have the same fixed orientation. In contrast to the case of dorsal SF, however, there is no evidence to suggest that the barbed ends of TAN lines are localized to a single location. Instead, we suggest that rearward contraction of stress fibers from the edges of cells could form cables of actin with formins scattered throughout them. Bundling by a protein specific for filaments oriented in the same direction could orient the formins. Alternatively, recent work shows that the formin FHOD1 is critical for TAN line function, although this protein does not nucleate the dorsal actin cables directly (64). Thus, this formin could possibly direct actin cable orientation. The mechanism by which actin cables with oriented polarity on the dorsal side of the nucleus are generated remains to be elucidated.

NONUNIFORM POLARITY ACTIN BUNDLES

What Are the Roles of Nonuniform Actin Bundles?

Many linear actin structures in the cell are composed of mixed polarity filaments. We propose that generation of bundles with nonuniform polarity relies on nucleating factors having a fixed orientation such that the barbed ends of filaments are clustered at a particular location while the pointed ends protrude away; many such locations oriented in a linear fashion would generate a mixed polarity bundle (**Figure 2b**). Alternatively, mixed polarity bundles could be generated by rearrangement of uniform polarity filaments in the dendritic network, as the network contraction model for contractile arcs suggests (117).

Nonuniform polarity bundles are a substrate for myosin II, and the action of myosin II on these bundles results in one of two actions: constriction if the filaments are in a ring and bundle shortening if the filaments are in a linear bundle. For instance, the contractile ring constricts as filaments of alternating polarity slide past each other owing to myosin II activity (78). A similar mechanism may drive mitochondrial fission: actin assembles around the mitochondrion and aids in constricting it via a myosin II-dependent mechanism (45). Additionally, as transverse arcs move from the cell edge to the cell center, they shorten as a result of the action of myosin and control the shape of the cell by doing so (20, 21, 48). Thus, nonuniform polarity bundles are critical for constriction or shortening mechanisms that exert the forces needed to control shape.

Cytokinesis and the contractile ring. A ring of filamentous structures has been seen at the ingressing furrows of cells, particularly those of invertebrate eggs, for almost 50 years (1). Whether this ring pulls the plasma membrane in as the cell divides or merely guides membrane deposition has been a subject of much debate, as has the mechanism of filament constriction. However, studies on a variety of organisms have begun to reach a consensus regarding the mechanism of contractile ring assembly. The following subsections describe current knowledge regarding the role of actin in mammalian cell division.

What structures are responsible for dividing a cell? Assembly of the contractile ring in mammalian cells begins at anaphase onset. MgcRacGAP activity results in localization of RhoA to the midzone of the cell (for review, see Reference 78), where local stimulation of RhoA activity promotes actin polymerization and myosin II activity (89). Myosin II activity causes membrane-linked actin filaments to slide past each other, providing the force needed for ingression of the cleavage furrow (19), so it is critical that actin filaments in the ring are mixed in polarity. The scaffold protein anillin also localizes to the cleavage furrow, where it links the actomyosin ring to the septins that deform the membrane (85). In comparison with the detailed genetic and biochemical work describing the actions of cytokinesis in yeast, however, assembly and organization of the contractile ring in mammalian cells are not well understood.

How is the contractile ring formed in mammalian cells? RhoA promotes actin polymerization through formin activation (for review, see Reference 140). Whether there is a specific formin at contractile rings remains unclear, although evidence has shown that Arp2/3 has only a minor role at best. Recent work has suggested that mDia2 may be involved in contractile ring assembly, as loss of mDia2 results in contractile ring defects (122). However, data regarding the role of the closely related formin mDia1 present conflicting accounts. Examination of formins belonging to the Dia family found increased binucleate cells when mDia2 was lost, but not when mDia1 was lost (122). In contrast, recent work on cortical actin polymerization identified mDia1 as a critical component of cell division (18). The orientation of formins that generate the contractile ring is another open issue. To create bundles with mixed polarity, formins would have to be fixed relative to each other in a back to back configuration. This could be accomplished by two formin spots on both sides of the contractile ring, each of which polymerizes filaments in both directions around it. However, studies in fission yeast have shown that formin in the contractile ring localizes to a series of spots around the cell and polymerizes filaments radially in all directions from each spot (128). Only filaments that are in the correct orientation to be captured by myosin and that are in nearby spots are incorporated into the contractile ring; off-target filaments are destroyed by cofilin (116, 128). It is unknown whether similar mechanisms are utilized by the Dia formins in vertebrate cells.

Mitochondrial fission. Although cell division by a constricting ring of actin has been studied for decades, the idea that rings of actin could be used for constriction elsewhere in the cell has been shown only recently. Specifically, mechanisms similar to those involved in cell division may also be at play in mitochondrial division.

How are specific actin structures involved in mitochondrial fission? Cell division requires assembly of an actin ring that is tens of microns in diameter. However, smaller actin rings can be used to divide organelles within the cell. Depletion of F-actin leads to a loss of mitochondrial fission and to reduced accumulation of the dynamin-related protein Drp1, which is also critical for mitochondrial fission (11, 31). Recent evidence has also suggested that myosin II plays an important role at sites of mitochondrial fission (58). As with the contractile ring, this myosin-mediated constriction mechanism strongly indicates that the actin filaments at the site of mitochondrial division are oriented in an antiparallel arrangement.

How does actin polymerize at sites of mitochondrial fission? INF2 is essential for the actin polymerization necessary for recruitment of Drp1 (59). INF2-generated actin filaments appear at sites of close contact between the endoplasmic reticulum (ER) and mitochondria (59). A model of mitochondrial fission, termed mitokinesis, has been proposed, in which INF2-generated actin filaments localize to the mitochondria via the ER and "preconstrict" the mitochondria using a mechanism similar to the constriction of a contractile ring (45). Drp1 is then able to localize and complete fission via ring formation of a ring, similar to the behavior of dynamin (45). It is interesting to consider how the ER would be able to position INF2 molecules to generate filaments with mixed polarity if mitokinesis is in fact similar to cytokinesis.

Transverse arcs. In addition to dorsal SF that run along the length of the cell, motile cells contain other types of linear actin bundles. The following subsections discuss dynamic transverse arcs, which assemble and flow rearward from the leading edge of the cell. Transverse arcs from different cell types vary in thickness; some cell types, such as osteosarcoma cells, show prominent transverse arcs, whereas others, such as fibroblasts, have thinner arcs. We focus specifically on the common assembly mechanism and roles of transverse arcs that are likely the same in many cell types (48).

What are the characteristics of transverse arcs? In contrast to dorsal SF, transverse arcs run parallel to the leading edge of the cell and do not terminate in focal adhesions (48). Transverse arcs flow toward the center of the cell at the same speed as retrograde flow from the leading edge and disappear in front of the nucleus (104). Both α-actinin and myosin are found in sarcomeric patterns along transverse arcs, indicating that they are mixed polarity bundles (48). In fact, transverse arcs can be seen condensing from short actin bundles in live cells (48).

How are transverse arcs formed and what is their role? Multiple mechanisms for formation of transverse arcs have been proposed. These arcs may assemble from short pieces of the lamellipodium that are annealed end-to-end (48, 104). This mechanism does not require a specific arc-associated actin nucleator, as the actin in the annealed pieces is from the Arp2/3-generated lamellipodial network. The formin FHOD1 (FH1/FH2 domain-containing protein 1) has been shown to be necessary for arc-driven cell spreading (49), however, and in the absence of FHOD1, both dorsal SF and transverse arcs are lost (102). Interestingly, FHOD1 does not appear to polymerize actin; rather, FHOD1 appears to bundle it (101). Therefore, FHOD1 may play a critical role in knitting arcs together through its ability to specifically localize to areas of antiparallel actin organization (101, 102). The contribution of bundling by FHOD1 versus that by α-actinin or myosin II remains unclear, however. If actin nucleation by a formin is required for assembly of transverse arcs, the formin in question would have to be distributed throughout the bundle in spots in which molecules were oriented back to back, as described for the contractile ring. This fixed orientation of formins would then ensure the presence of overlapping stretches of filaments with opposite polarity needed to form a mixed polarity bundle.

Myosin II acts on transverse arcs in two directions: shortening them from side to side as the sarcomeres contract, and thereby limiting the width of the cell (20), and contracting them rearward, which exerts force on the dorsal SF to flatten the lamella and to drive elongation of focal adhesions (see the subsection titled "Dorsal stress fibers") (12, 84). Thus, in addition to promoting cell spreading (49), arcs may help maintain the shape of cells (21), and may help slow retrograde flow to promote focal adhesion assembly in some cell types (20). Because these actions rely on the shortening of arcs, the nonuniform polarity of filaments in the arcs is essential for their activity. However, the mechanism by which these functions are regulated is unknown.

Ventral stress fibers and graded polarity bundles. In addition to the dorsal SF, which rise from the leading edge of a motile cell toward the dorsal cell cortex, cells contain actin bundles along their ventral surfaces that often display a sarcomere-like pattern of organization. Initial observations largely differentiated these stress fibers from dorsal SF solely on the basis of their location; recent work, however, has begun to show that dorsal and ventral SF have different mechanisms of assembly and likely play different roles in the cell.

What are ventral stress fibers? Ventral SF are the third major type of stress fiber in motile cells (48, 104). In contrast to dorsal SF, ventral SF are essentially parallel to the bottom of the cell and are found underneath the cell body, often terminating in a focal adhesion at each end (48, 104). One type of ventral SF is the graded polarity bundle (30). These long, overlapping bundles of actin span the ventral side of the cell and exhibit unusual filament orientation; as their name suggests, the polarity of the filaments changes depending on their position in the cell (30). Filaments within a graded polarity bundle that are located near the leading edge of the cell are uniform in orientation, whereas those in the center of the cell have mixed polarities (30). It is unclear whether all SF on the ventral side of the cell have a graded polarity organization. Studies have shown that ventral SF in some cells are limited to the area under the cell body and do not extend all the way to the cell edge as graded polarity bundles do (105). Therefore, graded polarity bundles are likely a specific type of ventral SF.

How are ventral stress fibers formed and what is their role? The formation of graded polarity bundles is a challenging problem, as their dynamics appear to vary along the length of the bundle (30). One mechanism suggests that these bundles are formed from filopodia that become disconnected from the lamellipodium (4), but additional filament growth would be necessary for the new graded polarity bundle to span the length of the cell. No specific actin nucleation factor has been shown to be essential for or localized to graded polarity bundles or to any kind of ventral SF. Interestingly, however, the myosin IIB isoform concentrates toward the rear of migrating cells, and recent work (5) has shown that the formin DAAM1 colocalizes with myosin IIB and specifically regulates the myosin IIB-containing actin network. This finding raises the following question: How might DAAM1 polymerize actin for graded polarity bundles and/or ventral SF? As with other types of mixed polarity bundles, generation of the filament arrangement needed for formation of graded polarity bundles would rely on spots of DAAM1 being oriented back to back along the track of the ventral SF. Perhaps myosin IIB, which acts more as a tensile cross-linker than as a stepping motor, serves to localize DAAM1 to spots along the rear of the cell.

The role played by ventral SF is also unknown; they may help regulate contraction in the rear of a migrating cell (113) or movement of the cell body. As it is difficult to specifically eliminate ventral stress fibers, however, their contribution to motility is as yet undefined. Ventral SF also associate with adhesions under the center of the cell where fibrillogenesis of fibronectin occurs in fibroblasts, so they may also regulate this process. Further work that allows independent inhibition of ventral SF is necessary to conclusively establish their role.

The perinuclear actin cap. Although a great deal of work in the field of actin in cell biology has focused on its role at the leading edge of the cell, specifically concentrating on SF and the lamellipodium, cells also contain many other actin structures. In recent years, particular interest has developed in understanding how the actin cytoskeleton can mechanically influence the nucleus. In addition to playing a role in nuclear positioning (see the subsection titled "TAN lines and the nucleus"), new evidence suggests that actin can also control other aspects of the nucleus.

What is the perinuclear actin cap? The shape of nuclei in most cells correlates with the overall shape of the cell, thus suggesting that the two are connected (10). In fact, a dense cap of actin bundles on the dorsal side of the nucleus orients along the long axis of the cell and coordinates cell and nuclear shape in a manner dependent on interaction with lamins (54). The actin cap appears to differ from TAN lines, as loss of it leads specifically to the misregulation of nuclear shape that has been implicated in laminopathies, rather than to nuclear positioning defects (55, 56). Therefore, the perinuclear cap is a distinct actin structure found particularly in cells under shear stress that regulates the shape of the nucleus (54, 56).

How is the actin cap generated? Actin cap fibers terminate in a specific subset of focal adhesions that are located near the periphery of the cell and that are critical for mechanotransduction to the nucleus (54, 56). As with ventral SF, termination at both ends in focal adhesions indicates that these bundles are likely composed of mixed polarity filaments and may be generated by similar mechanisms. The actin at the actin cap is significantly more dynamic than that in the dorsal and ventral SF, suggesting specific nucleation by a formin, although the formin involved has not yet been identified (55). Perhaps a formin could interact with proteins in the outer nuclear membrane to polymerize actin there, or some factor at the nuclear membrane could locally activate a nearby formin. Alternatively, the actin cap–associated adhesions could have their own formin, which gathers barbed ends and polymerizes actin out of the adhesions, promoting generation of mixed polarity bundles when the two populations meet over the nucleus. How the actin cap is polymerized remains an open issue.

ERM: ezrin, radixin, moesin

ISOTROPIC NETWORKS

How Are Isotropic Networks Formed in Cells, and How Are They Used?

Although the most apparent structures in motile cells are linear actin bundles and the dendritic network at the lamellipodium, other actin networks exist, some of which are essentially isotropic in nature. Isotropic networks can be used to stabilize structures in cell; for instance, the cell cortex helps control cell shape and integrity and regulates pressure release in the form of blebs. The isotropic nature of the network provides stability without concentrating force generation at any single point. The actin polymerized inside the nucleus appears to be an isotropic network that plays a role in helping to regulate transcription, rather than to control shape, although nuclear actin may also have an unappreciated structural role. Therefore isotropic networks serve a variety of incompletely understood functions in the cell.

How isotropic networks are generated is also somewhat unclear. We postulate that they result from the interaction between two classes of nucleators, Arp 2/3 and formins, both of which have been implicated in nuclear actin and play a role in the functioning of the cortex. How would a cell generate filaments with uniform polarity, but arranged in a network rather than linearly? The orientation of the filaments is likely controlled by the orientation of the formins. As described above, (see the section titled "Nonuniform Polarity Actin Bundles") orienting formins back to back generates filaments with pointed ends projecting in opposite directions. In the case of isotropic networks, formins are radially organized with uniform polarity with respect to each other, as in the center of a pom-pom (**Figure 2c**), rather than simply aligning back to back along a linear track. The filaments these formins generate will therefore have barbed ends gathered at the center of the pom-pom and pointed ends extending away from it. How Arp2/3 plays into this network is unknown. As a dendritic network is ideal for generating force at a membrane, perhaps these radiating formin-nucleated filaments act as a scaffold for the dendritic network that in turn supports the membrane. How interaction between classes of nucleators generates isotropic networks remains a fascinating area of research.

The mesenchymal cell cortex. In contrast to the highly organized cortex of erythrocytes, the cortex of mesenchymal cells is poorly understood and likely lacks the rigid structure of red blood cells. However, recent work has begun to show the importance of the actin cortex in providing structure for the cell and in regulating migration.

What is the organization of the actin cortex? The surface of the cell proximal to the plasma membrane is lined with an actin mesh known as the actin cortex (80, 130). This contractile actin network is critical for maintaining cell shape and cytoplasmic coherence (95), but the organization and dynamics of this actin mesh are only beginning to be elucidated. Several actin-binding proteins are localized to the actin cortex (for review, see Reference 97), but the roles of only a few of these proteins have been defined. For example, the ERM (ezrin, radixin, moesin) proteins link the cortex to the membrane (35). Additionally, the cross-linking protein filamin is known to localize to the cortex and link it to the membrane (107, 120). The precise organization of this mesh has not been elucidated.

How is actin at the cortex polymerized? Recent studies have highlighted the complex dynamics of the actin cortex. Loss of the Arp2/3 complex reduces the expression of actin under the membrane and impairs cell motility (127). However, a recent study also shows that the cortex is organized into dense motile actin nodes from which pom-poms of actin filaments emanate, dependent on myosin IIA, the cross-linking protein filamin A, and the formin DAAM1 (68). Interestingly, this organization resembles the well-characterized assembly of a contractile ring in fission yeast; in fission yeast, the ring comprises a series of cross-linked formin-containing nodes that contract toward each other (116, 128). How DAAM1 and Arp2/3 work together or with other actin nucleation factors to generate the submembranous actin cortex remains unclear.

Blebbing cells. The role of blebs in cell migration is a developing frontier in motility research. Fascinatingly, in vivo imaging has revealed cell migration via bleb-based motility in live mice. Although this migration mechanism is by no means as thoroughly studied as lamellipodium-based migration, ongoing work from multiple labs not only has shown that cells can migrate by blebbing but also has begun to describe the physical properties behind this motility.

What is the role of actin in the dynamics of membrane blebs? Dynamic blebs are pressure-driven, non-actin-dependent membrane protrusions that are generated spontaneously at the edges of cells. Recent work has begun to elucidate the role of blebbing as a novel mode of migration for cells in vivo (for review, see Reference 24). Blebs are formed by disruption of the membrane–cortex connection and by bulging of the membrane (26, 87). In their earliest stages, protruding blebs are devoid of actin (87), and as expansion halts, ERM proteins are recruited to the bleb membrane prior to actin recruitment (25). The actin cortex is then rebuilt within the bleb, and myosin localizes to the bleb neck, where it acts on the newly built cortex to retract the bleb (25). In contrast to lamellipodia, blebs do not rely on actin polymerization for protrusion and do not have specific attachment points to the substrate; thus, the role of actin in bleb-driven cell migration is less clear. The cortical actin network may be responsible for generating force perpendicular to the surface to allow cells to "chimney" forward via a bleb (106), but the molecular details of this mechanism are not yet known.

How is actin rebuilt on the membrane of a bleb? The molecular mechanisms involved in rebuilding the actin cortex in a bleb are a topic of much research. One spliceoform of the formin FMNL1, which is restricted to hematopoietic-derived cells and certain cancers, is involved in the formation of dynamic blebs in blood cells, and other formins and the Arp2/3 complex do not appear to be involved (42). In migrating melanoma cells, however, the situation appears quite different. Proteomics analyses of blebs have indicated roles for several formins and for the Arp2/3 complex at the actin cortex (18). Subsequent work identified distinct, critical contributions of mDia1 and the Arp2/3 complex to the formation of a blebbing cell cortex (18). Furthermore, Arp2/3 can potentiate the effects of mDia1 at the cortex (18). Perhaps rapid branching by the Arp2/3 complex provides the barbed ends needed for mDia1 to bind and assemble. This behavior suggests a different mechanism of isotropic network formation than the pom-pom model described above. Here, the Arp2/3 complex establishes the geometry of a dendritic network, and a formin acts on that network to rapidly expand it. A major difference between these two models is the localization of the formins; in the pom-pom model, multiple formins cluster at discrete spots, whereas in the Arp2/3-potentiation model, individual formins assemble actin filaments away from Arp2/3 nodes. Careful examination of actin and actin nucleation factors at the cortex will reveal the assembly mechanisms. Together these data reveal novel roles for formins working with the Arp2/3 complex in polymerizing the cortical actin mesh underlying the membrane.

Actin in the nucleus. Among controversial topics in actin research, the presence of actin in the nucleus has been second only to perhaps the presence of actin in bacteria. Although earlier studies suggested that actin was absent from the nucleus, recent careful biochemical and microscopy studies have shown that actin does exist in the nucleus, either as short filaments or as monomers.

MAL: megakaryocytic acute leukemia protein

Why does a cell need actin in the nucleus? In addition to cytoplasmic actin, which helps control the shape and position of the nucleus, actin assembles within the nucleus itself to control transcription through the megakaryocytic acute leukemia protein (MAL) (115). In the absence of nuclear actin polymerization, MAL shuttles rapidly between the nucleus and the cytoplasm (115). Polymerized nuclear actin binds to MAL and retains it in the nucleus, where low levels of G-actin also inhibit actin-dependent nuclear export (115). Thus, although the presence of F-actin in the nucleus has been controversial, nuclear actin may play a role in regulating transcription in somatic cells.

How does actin polymerize in the nucleus? How nuclear actin polymerizes is not fully understood. Transcriptional studies indicate that WASP is expressed inside the nucleus and that Arp2/3 specifically may have a role in regulating transcription (137). Furthermore, blocking nuclear export leads to actin polymerization via mDia2 accumulation in the nucleus (6). Activation of mDia2 in the nucleus increases F-actin, nuclear accumulation of MAL, and transcription (6). As both Arp2/3 and a formin have been found in the nucleus, multiple nuclear actin networks may exist, or the actin nucleation factors may cooperate.

CONCLUSIONS AND FUTURE DIRECTIONS

In this article, we have described many of the known actin structures in migratory cells, along with their mechanisms of assembly. The problem of how so many different actin structures can assemble in a temporally and spatially regulated way within one cytoplasm remains a fascinating one in cell biology, and its answer no doubt relies on the actin nucleating proteins, namely, the Arp2/3 complex, formins, and the TMBPs. Although it is tempting to speculate that a distinct nucleator is associated with each structure, there are now several examples of actin assembly factors working together, such as the cell cortex and filopodia, and many nucleators that localize to more than one structure. Of particular interest in this latter group is the formin mDia1, which appears to be required by many cellular structures, but the localization of which remains undefined. mDia1 may represent a transient nucleator presence at these structures, perhaps nucleating the first filaments then handing off further assembly to other factors. As new actin structures are frequently being described, however, assigning a single nucleation factor to each structure becomes ever more complicated, and understanding how nucleation factors synergize becomes ever more important. Furthermore, many actin nucleators, particularly those in the TMBP family and some divergent formins, do not yet have any known role in cells. Therefore much remains to be understood about the construction of a spatially organized, dynamically coordinated actin cytoskeleton in motile cells.

One tantalizing prospect for the future of understanding how the actin cytoskeleton is connected involves the use of cutting-edge superresolution microscopy techniques. Because the diameter of an actin filament is far below the resolution limit of a light microscope, visualizing the fine details of actin structures has been difficult and has generally been confined to complicated electron microscopy studies with limited molecular specificity (69, 128). New superresolution microscopy techniques, such as structured illumination (SIM), photoactivated localization microscopy (PALM), and stochastic optical reconstruction microscopy (STORM), and variations of these techniques allow for accurate description of actin structures with high molecular detail (34, 53, 114, 129). So far, these techniques have produced stunningly detailed characterization of several actin structures in cells, including focal adhesions, junctions, axons, and TAN lines (53, 67, 119, 129), but the characterizations have remained more descriptive than predictive. Other localization techniques such as single-molecule tracking of individual formins offer further promise for understanding the role of actin nucleators in living cells (133). A challenge for the field going forward is how to apply the power of superresolution microscopy to gain mechanistic insight into the mechanical integration and dynamic organization of the actin cytoskeleton in living cells.

SUMMARY POINTS

1. Different actin nucleation factors generate different geometries among actin structures: Arp2/3 creates branched structures, whereas formins and TMBPs create linear filaments.

2. Several actin structures rely prominently on branched actin filaments: lamellipodia, endocytic vesicles, and AJs.

3. Other actin structures are composed primarily of linear actin filaments created by formins: actin bundles found in filopodia, TAN lines, and various types of stress fibers.

4. Contractile actin structures such as the contractile ring are also linear filaments generated by formins, as are structures involved in mitochondrial division.

5. Isotropic networks such as those found at the cell cortex or in the nucleus may involve cooperation between formins and the Arp2/3 complex.

6. Both the localization and the specific orientation of formin molecules are critical for determining the molecular properties of organizationally and functionally diverse actin bundles.

DISCLOSURE STATEMENT

The authors are not aware of any affiliations, memberships, funding, or financial holdings that might be perceived as affecting the objectivity of this review.

ACKNOWLEDGMENTS

This work was supported by the National Heart, Lung, and Blood Institute Division of Intramural Research.

LITERATURE CITED

1. Abu Taha A, Taha M, Seebach J, Schnittler H-J. 2014. ARP2/3-mediated junction-associated lamellipodia control VE-cadherin–based cell junction dynamics and maintain monolayer integrity. *Mol. Biol. Cell* 25:245–56

2. Akin O, Mullins RD. 2008. Capping protein increases the rate of actin-based motility by promoting filament nucleation by the Arp2/3 complex. *Cell* 133:841–51

3. Amann KJ, Pollard TD. 2001. The Arp2/3 complex nucleates actin filament branches from the sides of pre-existing filaments. *Nat. Cell Biol.* 3:306–10

4. Anderson TW, Vaughan AN, Cramer LP. 2008. Retrograde flow and myosin II activity within the leading cell edge deliver F-actin to the lamella to seed the formation of graded polarity actomyosin II filament bundles in migrating fibroblasts. *Mol. Biol. Cell* 19:5006–18

5. Ang S-F, Zhao Z, Lim L, Manser E. 2010. DAAM1 is a formin required for centrosome re-orientation during cell migration. *PLOS ONE* 5:e13064

6. Baarlink C, Wang H, Grosse R. 2013. Nuclear actin network assembly by formins regulates the SRF coactivator MAL. *Science* 340:864–67

7. Bamburg JR. 1987. Distribution and cellular localization of actin depolymerizing factor. *J. Cell Biol.* 105:2817–25

8. Barzik M, McClain LM, Gupton SL, Gertler FB. 2014. Ena/VASP regulates mDia2-initiated filopodial length, dynamics, and function. *Mol. Biol. Cell* 25:2604–19

9. Batchelder EM, Yarar D. 2010. Differential requirements for clathrin-dependent endocytosis at sites of cell–substrate adhesion. *Mol. Biol. Cell* 21:3070–79

10. Belin BJ, Mullins RD. 2013. What we talk about when we talk about nuclear actin. *Nucleus* 4:291–97

11. Bereiter-Hahn J, Vöth M, Mai S, Jendrach M. 2008. Structural implications of mitochondrial dynamics. *Biotechnol. J.* 3:765–80

12. Bershadsky AD, Ballestrem C, Carramusa L, Zilberman Y, Gilquin B, et al. 2006. Assembly and mechanosensory function of focal adhesions: experiments and models. *Eur. J. Cell Biol.* 85:165–73

13. Bilancia CG, Winkelman JD, Tsygankov D, Nowotarski SH, Sees JA, et al. 2014. Enabled negatively regulates Diaphanous-driven actin dynamics in vitro and in vivo. *Dev. Cell* 28:394–408

14. Blanchoin L, Pollard TD, Hitchcock-DeGregori SE. 2001. Inhibition of the Arp2/3 complex-nucleated actin polymerization and branch formation by tropomyosin. *Curr. Biol.* 11:1300–304

15. Block J, Breitsprecher D, Kühn S, Winterhoff M, Kage F, et al. 2012. FMNL2 drives actin-based protrusion and migration downstream of Cdc42. *Curr. Biol.* 22:1005–12

16. Bornschlögl T. 2013. How filopodia pull: what we know about the mechanics and dynamics of filopodia. *Cytoskeleton* 70:590–603

17. Boulant S, Kural C, Zeeh J-C, Ubelmann F, Kirchhausen T. 2011. Actin dynamics counteract membrane tension during clathrin-mediated endocytosis. *Nat. Cell Biol.* 13:1124–31

18. Bovellan M, Romeo Y, Biro M, Boden A, Chugh P, et al. 2014. Cellular control of cortical actin nucleation. *Curr. Biol.* 24:1628–35

19. Bresnick AR. 1999. Molecular mechanisms of nonmuscle myosin-II regulation. *Curr. Opin. Cell Biol.* 11:26–33

20. Burnette DT, Manley S, Sengupta P, Sougrat R, Davidson MW, et al. 2011. A role for actin arcs in the leading-edge advance of migrating cells. *Nat. Cell Biol.* 13:371–81

21. Burnette DT, Shao L, Ott C, Pasapera AM, Fischer RS, et al. 2014. A contractile and counterbalancing adhesion system controls the 3D shape of crawling cells. *J. Cell Biol.* 205:83–96

22. Campellone KG, Welch MD. 2010. A nucleator arms race: cellular control of actin assembly. *Nat. Rev. Mol. Cell Biol.* 11:237–51

23. Carramusa L, Ballestrem C, Zilberman Y, Bershadsky AD. 2007. Mammalian diaphanous-related formin Dia1 controls the organization of E-cadherin-mediated cell-cell junctions. *J. Cell Sci.* 120:3870–82

24. Charras G, Paluch E. 2008. Blebs lead the way: how to migrate without lamellipodia. *Nat. Rev. Mol. Cell Biol.* 9:730–36

25. Charras GT, Hu C-K, Coughlin M, Mitchison TJ. 2006. Reassembly of contractile actin cortex in cell blebs. *J. Cell Biol.* 175:477–90

26. Charras GT, Yarrow JC, Horton MA, Mahadevan L, Mitchison TJ. 2005. Non-equilibration of hydrostatic pressure in blebbing cells. *Nature* 435:365–69

27. Choi CK, Vicente-Manzanares M, Zareno J, Whitmore LA, Mogilner A, Horwitz AR. 2008. Actin and α-actinin orchestrate the assembly and maturation of nascent adhesions in a myosin II motor-independent manner. *Nat. Cell Biol.* 10:1039–50

28. Co C, Wong DT, Gierke S, Chang V, Taunton J. 2007. Mechanism of actin network attachment to moving membranes: barbed end capture by N-WASP WH2 domains. *Cell* 128:901–13

29. Collins A, Warrington A, Taylor KA, Svitkina T. 2011. Structural organization of the actin cytoskeleton at sites of clathrin-mediated endocytosis. *Curr. Biol.* 21:1167–75

30. Cramer LP. Siebert M, Mitchison TJ. 1997. Identification of novel graded polarity actin filament bundles in locomoting heart fibroblasts: implications for the generation of motile force. *J. Cell Biol.* 136:1287–305

31. De Vos KJ, Allan VJ, Grierson AJ, Sheetz MP. 2005. Mitochondrial function and actin regulate dynamin-related protein 1-dependent mitochondrial fission. *Curr. Biol.* 15:678–83

32. Dent EW, Kwiatkowski AV, Mebane LM, Philippar U, Barzik M, et al. 2007. Filopodia are required for cortical neurite initiation. *Nat. Cell Biol.* 9:1347–59

33. Derivery E, Gautreau A. 2010. Generation of branched actin networks: assembly and regulation of the N-WASP and WAVE molecular machines. *Bioessays* 32:119–31

34. Engel U. 2014. Structured illumination superresolution imaging of the cytoskeleton. *Methods Cell Biol.* 123:315–33

35. Fehon RG, McClatchey AI, Bretscher A. 2010. Organizing the cell cortex: the role of ERM proteins. *Nat. Rev. Mol. Cell Biol.* 11:276–87

36. Fujimoto LM, Roth R, Heuser JE, Schmid SL. 2000. Actin assembly plays a variable, but not obligatory role in receptor-mediated endocytosis. *Traffic* 1:161–71

37. Gaillard J, Ramabhadran V, Neumanne E, Gurel P, Blanchoin L, et al. 2011. Differential interactions of the formins INF2, mDia1, and mDia2 with microtubules. *Mol. Biol. Cell* 22:4575–87

38. Galbraith CG, Yamada KM, Galbraith JA. 2007. Polymerizing actin fibers position integrins primed to probe for adhesion sites. *Science* 315:992–95

39. Gomes ER, Jani S, Gundersen GG. 2005. Nuclear movement regulated by Cdc42, MRCK, myosin, and actin flow establishes MTOC polarization in migrating cells. *Cell* 121:451–63

40. Gundersen GG, Worman HJ. 2013. Nuclear positioning. *Cell* 152:1376–89

41. Gupton SL, Eisenmann K, Alberts AS, Waterman-Storer CM. 2007. mDia2 regulates actin and focal adhesion dynamics and organization in the lamella for efficient epithelial cell migration. *J. Cell Sci.* 120:3475–87

42. Han Y, Eppinger E, Schuster IG, Weigand LU, Liang X, et al. 2009. Formin-like 1 (FMNL1) is regulated by N-terminal myristoylation and induces polarized membrane blebbing. *J. Biol. Chem.* 284:33409–17

43. Hansen SD, Mullins RD. 2010. VASP is a processive actin polymerase that requires monomeric actin for barbed end association. *J. Cell Biol.* 191:571–84

44. Harris ES, Gauvin TJ, Heimsath EG, Higgs HN. 2010. Assembly of filopodia by the formin FRL2 (FMNL3). *Cytoskeleton* 67:755–72

45. Hatch AL, Gurel PS, Higgs HN. 2014. Novel roles for actin in mitochondrial fission. *J. Cell Sci.* 127:4549–60

46. Heath JP, Holifield BF. 1993. On the mechanisms of cortical actin flow and its role in cytoskeletal organisation of fibroblasts. *Symp. Soc. Exp. Biol.* 47:35–56

47. Hoelzle MK, Svitkina T. 2012. The cytoskeletal mechanisms of cell–cell junction formation in endothelial cells. *Mol. Biol. Cell* 23:310–23

48. Hotulainen P, Lappalainen P. 2006. Stress fibers are generated by two distinct actin assembly mechanisms in motile cells. *J. Cell Biol.* 173:383–94

49. Iskratsch T, Yu C-H, Mathur A, Liu S, Stévenin V, et al. 2013. FHOD1 is needed for directed forces and adhesion maturation during cell spreading and migration. *Dev. Cell* 27:545–59

50. Jaiswal R, Breitsprecher D, Collins A, Corrêa IR Jr, Xu M-Q, Goode BL. 2013. The formin Daam1 and fascin directly collaborate to promote filopodia formation. *Curr. Biol.* 23:1373–79

51. Jégou A, Carlier M-F, Romet-Lemonne G. 2013. Formin mDia1 senses and generates mechanical forces on actin filaments. *Nat. Commun.* 4:1883

52. Johnson M, East DA, Mulvihill DP. 2014. Formins determine the functional properties of actin filaments in yeast. *Curr. Biol.* 24:1525–30

53. Kanchanawong P, Shtengel G, Pasapera AM, Ramko EB, Davidson MW, et al. 2010. Nanoscale architecture of integrin-based cell adhesions. *Nature* 468:580–84

54. Khatau SB, Hale CM, Stewart-Hutchinson PJ, Patel MS, Stewart CL, et al. 2009. A perinuclear actin cap regulates nuclear shape. *PNAS* 106:19017–22

55. Khatau SB, Kim D-H, Hale CM, Bloom RJ, Wirtz D. 2010. The perinuclear actin cap in health and disease. *Nucleus* 1:337–42

56. Kim D-H, Khatau SB, Feng Y, Walcott S, Sun SX, et al. 2012. Actin cap associated focal adhesions and their distinct role in cellular mechanosensing. *Sci. Rep.* 2:555

57. Kobielak A, Pasolli HA, Fuchs E. 2004. Mammalian formin-1 participates in adherens junctions and polymerization of linear actin cables. *Nat. Cell Biol.* 6:21–30

58. Korobova F, Gauvin TJ, Higgs HN. 2014. A role for myosin II in mammalian mitochondrial fission. *Curr. Biol.* 24:409–14

59. Korobova F, Ramabhadran V, Higgs HN. 2013. An actin-dependent step in mitochondrial fission mediated by the ER-associated formin INF2. *Science* 339:464–67

60. Kovacs EM, Goodwin M, Ali RG, Paterson AD, Yap AS. 2002. Cadherin-directed actin assembly. *Curr. Biol.* 12:379–82

61. Kovar DR, Pollard TD. 2004. Insertional assembly of actin filament barbed ends in association with formins produces piconewton forces. *PNAS* 101:14725–30

62. Kozlov MM, Bershadsky AD. 2004. Processive capping by formin suggests a force-driven mechanism of actin polymerization. *J. Cell Biol.* 167:1011–17

63. Kühn S, Geyer M. 2014. Formins as effector proteins of Rho GTPases. *Small GTPases* 5:e29513

64. Kutscheidt S, Zhu R, Antoku S, Luxton GWG, Stagljar I, et al. 2014. FHOD1 interaction with nesprin-2G mediates TAN line formation and nuclear movement. *Nat. Cell Biol.* 16:708–15

65. Liu AP, Loerke D, Schmid SL, Danuser G. 2009. Global and local regulation of clathrin-coated pit dynamics detected on patterned substrates. *Biophys. J.* 97:1038–47

66. Loisel TP, Boujemaa R, Pantaloni D, Carlier M-F. 1999. Reconstitution of actin-based motility of *Listeria* and *Shigella* using pure proteins. *Nature* 401:613–16

67. Lorenzo DN, Badea A, Davis J, Hostettler J, He J, et al. 2014. A PIK3C3–Ankyrin-B–Dynactin pathway promotes axonal growth and multiorganelle transport. *J. Cell Biol.* 207:735–52

68. Luo W, Yu C, Lieu ZZ, Allard J, Mogilner A, et al. 2013. Analysis of the local organization and dynamics of cellular actin networks. *J. Cell Biol.* 202:1057–73

69. Luxton GWG, Gomes ER, Folker ES, Vintinner E, Gundersen GG. 2010. Linear arrays of nuclear envelope proteins harness retrograde actin flow for nuclear movement. *Science* 329:956–59

70. Machesky LM, Reeves E, Wientjes F, Mattheyse FJ, Grogan A, et al. 1997. Mammalian actin-related protein 2/3 complex localizes to regions of lamellipodial protrusion and is composed of evolutionarily conserved proteins. *Biochem. J.* 328:105–12

71. Maciver SK, Weeds AG. 1994. Actophorin preferentially binds monomeric ADP-actin over ATP-bound actin: consequences for cell locomotion. *FEBS Lett.* 347:251–56

72. Mejillano MR, Kojima S, Applewhite DA, Gertler FB, Svitkina TM, Borisy GG. 2004. Lamellipodial versus filopodial mode of the actin nanomachinery: pivotal role of the filament barbed end. *Cell* 118:363–73

73. Merrifield CJ. 2004. Seeing is believing: imaging actin dynamics at single sites of endocytosis. *Trends Cell Biol.* 14:352–58

74. Merrifield CJ, Qualmann B, Kessels MM, Almers W. 2004. Neural Wiskott Aldrich Syndrome Protein (N-WASP) and the Arp2/3 complex are recruited to sites of clathrin-mediated endocytosis in cultured fibroblasts. *Eur. J. Cell Biol.* 83:13–18

75. Messa M, Fernández-Busnadiego R, Sun EW, Chen H, Czapla H, et al. 2014. Epsin deficiency impairs endocytosis by stalling the actin-dependent invagination of endocytic clathrin-coated pits. *eLife* 3:e03311

76. Michael M, Yap AS. 2013. The regulation and functional impact of actin assembly at cadherin cell–cell adhesions. *Semin. Cell Dev. Biol.* 24:298–307

77. Michaille JJ, Gouy M, Blanchet S, Duret L. 1995. Isolation and characterization of a cDNA encoding a chicken actin-like protein. *Gene* 154:205–9

78. Miller AL. 2011. The contractile ring. *Curr. Biol.* 21:R976–78

79. Mooren OL, Galletta BJ, Cooper JA. 2012. Roles for actin assembly in endocytosis. *Annu. Rev. Biochem.* 81:661–86

80. Morone N, Fujiwara T, Murase K, Kasai RS, Ike H, et al. 2006. Three-dimensional reconstruction of the membrane skeleton at the plasma membrane interface by electron tomography. *J. Cell Biol.* 174:851–62

81. Mullins RD, Heuser JA, Pollard TD. 1998. The interaction of Arp2/3 complex with actin: nucleation, high affinity pointed end capping, and formation of branching networks of filaments. *PNAS* 95:6181–86

82. Narita A, Mueller J, Urban E, Vinzenz M, Small JV, Maéda Y. 2012. Direct determination of actin polarity in the cell. *J. Mol. Biol.* 419:359–68

83. Nishida E, Maekawa S, Muneyuki E, Sakai H. 1984. Action of a 19K protein from porcine brain on actin polymerization: a new functional class of actin-binding proteins. *J. Biochem.* 95:387–98

84. Oakes PW, Beckham Y, Stricker J, Gardel ML. 2012. Tension is required but not sufficient for focal adhesion maturation without a stress fiber template. *J. Cell Biol.* 196:363–74

85. Oegema K, Savoian MS, Mitchison TJ, Field CM. 2000. Functional analysis of a human homologue of the *Drosophila* actin binding protein anillin suggests a role in cytokinesis. *J. Cell Biol.* 150:539–52

86. Otomo T, Tomchick DR, Otomo C, Panchal SC, Machius M, Rosen MK. 2005. Structural basis of actin filament nucleation and processive capping by a formin homology 2 domain. *Nature* 433:488–94

87. Paluch E, Piel M, Prost J, Bornens M, Sykes C. 2005. Cortical actomyosin breakage triggers shape oscillations in cells and cell fragments. *Biophys. J.* 89:724–33

88. Papp G, Bugyi B, Ujfalusi Z, Barkó S, Hild G, et al. 2006. Conformational changes in actin filaments induced by formin binding to the barbed end. *Biophys. J.* 91:2564–72

89. Piekny AJ, Glotzer M. 2008. Anillin is a scaffold protein that links RhoA, actin, and myosin during cytokinesis. *Curr. Biol.* 18:30–36

90. Pollard TD, Borisy GG. 2003. Cellular motility driven by assembly and disassembly of actin filaments. *Cell* 112:453–65

91. Rebowski G, Boczkowska M, Hayes DB, Guo L, Irving TC, Dominguez R. 2008. X-ray scattering study of actin polymerization nuclei assembled by tandem W domains. *PNAS* 105:10785–90

92. Reichstein E, Korn ED. 1979. *Acanthamoeba* profilin. a protein of low molecular weight from *Acanthamoeba castellanii* that inhibits actin nucleation. *J. Biol. Chem.* 254:6174–79

93. Risca VI, Wang EB, Chaudhuri O, Chia JJ, Geissler PL, Fletcher DA. 2012. Actin filament curvature biases branching direction. *PNAS* 109:2913–18

94. Robinson RC, Turbedsky K, Kaiser DA, Marchand JB, Higgs HN, et al. 2001. Crystal structure of Arp2/3 complex. *Science* 294:1679–84

95. Rossier OM, Gauthier N, Biais N, Vonnegut W, Fardin M-A, et al. 2010. Force generated by actomyosin contraction builds bridges between adhesive contacts. *EMBO J.* 29:1055–68

96. Rottner K, Hänisch J, Campellone KG. 2010. WASH, WHAMM and JMY: regulation of Arp2/3 complex and beyond. *Trends Cell Biol.* 20:650–61

97. Salbreux G, Charras G, Paluch E. 2012. Actin cortex mechanics and cellular morphogenesis. *Trends Cell Biol.* 22:536–45

98. Schafer DA, Mooseker MS, Cooper JA. 1992. Localization of capping protein in chicken epithelial cells by immunofluorescence and biochemical fractionation. *J. Cell Biol.* 118:335–46

99. Schirenbeck A, Arasada R, Bretschneider T, Stradal TEB, Schleicher M, Faix J. 2006. The bundling activity of vasodilator-stimulated phosphoprotein is required for filopodium formation. *PNAS* 103:7694–99

100. Schirenbeck A, Bretschneider T, Arasada R, Schleicher M, Faix J. 2005. The Diaphanous-related formin dDia2 is required for the formation and maintenance of filopodia. *Nat. Cell Biol.* 7:619–25

101. Schönichen A, Mannherz HG, Behrmann E, Mazur AJ, Kühn S, et al. 2013. FHOD1 is a combined actin filament capping and bundling factor that selectively associates with actin arcs and stress fibers. *J. Cell Sci.* 126:1891–1901

102. Schulze N, Graessl M, Blancke Soares A, Geyer M, Dehmelt L, Nalbant P. 2014. FHOD1 regulates stress fiber organization by controlling the dynamics of transverse arcs and dorsal fibers. *J. Cell Sci.* 127:1379–93

103. Skau CT, Neidt EM, Kovar DR. 2009. Role of tropomyosin in formin-mediated contractile ring assembly in fission yeast. *Mol. Biol. Cell* 20:2160–73

103a. Skau CT, Plotnikov SV, Doyle AD, Waterman CM. 2015. Inverted formin 2 in focal adhesions promotes dorsal stress fiber and fibrillar adhesion formation to drive extracellular matrix assembly. *PNAS* 112:E2447–56

104. Small JV, Rottner K, Kaverina I, Anderson KI. 1998. Assembling an actin cytoskeleton for cell attachment and movement. *Biochim. Biophys. Acta* 1404:271–81

105. Small JV, Stradal T, Vignal E, Rottner K. 2002. The lamellipodium: where motility begins. *Trends Cell Biol.* 12:112–20

106. Sroka J, von Gunten M, Dunn GA, Keller HU. 2002. Phenotype modulation in non-adherent and adherent sublines of Walker carcinosarcoma cells: the role of cell-substratum contacts and microtubules in controlling cell shape, locomotion and cytoskeletal structure. *Int. J. Biochem. Cell Biol.* 34:882–99

107. Stossel TP, Condeelis J, Cooley L, Hartwig JH, Noegel A, et al. 2001. Filamins as integrators of cell mechanics and signalling. *Nat. Rev. Mol. Cell Biol.* 2:138–45

108. Svitkina TM, Borisy GG. 1999. Arp2/3 complex and actin depolymerizing factor/cofilin in dendritic organization and treadmilling of actin filament array in lamellipodia. *J. Cell Biol.* 145:1009–26

109. Svitkina TM, Bulanova EA, Chaga OY, Vignjevic DM, Kojima S, et al. 2003. Mechanism of filopodia initiation by reorganization of a dendritic network. *J. Cell Biol.* 160:409–21

110. Tang VW, Brieher WM. 2012. α-Actinin-4/FSGS1 is required for Arp2/3-dependent actin assembly at the adherens junction. *J. Cell Biol.* 196:115–30

111. Tojkander S, Gateva G, Schevzov G, Hotulainen P, Naumanen P, et al. 2011. A molecular pathway for myosin II recruitment to stress fibers. *Curr. Biol.* 21:539–50

112. Ujfalusi Z, Kovács M, Nagy NT, Barkó S, Hild G, et al. 2012. Myosin and tropomyosin stabilize the conformation of formin-nucleated actin filaments. *J. Biol. Chem.* 287:31894–904

113. Vallenius T. 2013. Actin stress fibre subtypes in mesenchymal-migrating cells. *Open Biol.* 3:130001

114. Van den Dries K, Schwartz SL, Byars J, Meddens MBM, Bolomini-Vittori M, et al. 2013. Dual-color superresolution microscopy reveals nanoscale organization of mechanosensory podosomes. *Mol. Biol. Cell* 24:2112–23

115. Vartiainen MK, Guettler S, Larijani B, Treisman R. 2007. Nuclear actin regulates dynamic subcellular localization and activity of the SRF cofactor MAL. *Science* 316:1749–52

116. Vavylonis D, Wu J-Q, Hao S, O'Shaughnessy B, Pollard TD. 2008. Assembly mechanism of the contractile ring for cytokinesis by fission yeast. *Science* 319:97–100

117. Verkhovsky AB, Svitkina TM, Borisy GG. 1999. Network contraction model for cell translocation and retrograde flow. *Biochem. Soc. Symp.* 65:207–22

118. Verma S, Shewan AM, Scott JA, Helwani FM, den Elzen NR, et al. 2004. Arp2/3 activity is necessary for efficient formation of E-cadherin adhesive contacts. *J. Biol. Chem.* 279:34062–70

119. Versaevel M, Braquenier J-B, Riaz M, Grevesse T, Lantoine J, Gabriele S. 2014. Super-resolution microscopy reveals LINC complex recruitment at nuclear indentation sites. *Sci. Rep.* 4:7362

120. Wang K, Ash JF, Singer SJ. 1975. Filamin, a new high-molecular-weight protein found in smooth muscle and non-muscle cells. *PNAS* 72:4483–86

121. Wang YL. 1985. Exchange of actin subunits at the leading edge of living fibroblasts: possible role of treadmilling. *J. Cell Biol.* 101:597–602

122. Watanabe S, Ando Y, Yasuda S, Hosoya H, Watanabe N, et al. 2008. mDia2 induces the actin scaffold for the contractile ring and stabilizes its position during cytokinesis in NIH 3T3 cells. *Mol. Biol. Cell* 19:2328–38

123. Waterman-Storer CM, Desai A, Bulinski JC, Salmon ED. 1998. Fluorescent speckle microscopy, a method to visualize the dynamics of protein assemblies in living cells. *Curr. Biol.* 8:1227–30

124. Welch MD, DePace AH, Verma S, Iwamatsu A, Mitchison TJ. 1997. The human Arp2/3 complex is composed of evolutionarily conserved subunits and is localized to cellular regions of dynamic actin filament assembly. *J. Cell Biol.* 138:375–84

125. Welch MD, Iwamatsu A, Mitchison TJ. 1997. Actin polymerization is induced by Arp2/3 protein complex at the surface of *Listeria monocytogenes*. *Nature* 385:265–69

126. Winkelman JD, Bilancia CG, Peifer M, Kovar DR. 2014. Ena/VASP enabled is a highly processive actin polymerase tailored to self-assemble parallel-bundled F-actin networks with Fascin. *PNAS* 11:4121–26

127. Wu C, Haynes EM, Asokan SB, Simon JM, Sharpless NE, et al. 2013. Loss of Arp2/3 induces an NF-κB–dependent, nonautonomous effect on chemotactic signaling. *J. Cell Biol.* 203:907–16

128. Wu J-Q, Sirotkin V, Kovar DR, Lord M, Beltzner CC, et al. 2006. Assembly of the cytokinetic contractile ring from a broad band of nodes in fission yeast. *J. Cell Biol.* 174:391–402

129. Wu Y, Kanchanawong P, Zaidel-Bar R. 2015. Actin-delimited adhesion-independent clustering of E-cadherin forms the nanoscale building blocks of adherens junctions. *Dev. Cell* 32:139–54

130. Xu K, Babcock HP, Zhuang X. 2012. Dual-objective storm reveals three-dimensional filament organization in the actin cytoskeleton. *Nat. Methods* 9:185–88

131. Xu Y, Moseley JB, Sagot I, Poy F, Pellman D, et al. 2004. Crystal structures of a formin homology-2 domain reveal a tethered dimer architecture. *Cell* 116:711–23

132. Xue B, Robinson RC. 2013. Guardians of the actin monomer. *Eur. J. Cell Biol.* 92:316–32

133. Yamashiro S, Mizuno H, Watanabe N. 2015. An easy-to-use single-molecule speckle microscopy enabling nanometer-scale flow and wide-range lifetime measurement of cellular actin filaments. *Methods Cell Biol.* 125:43–59

134. Yang C, Czech L, Gerboth S, Kojima S, Scita G, Svitkina T. 2007. Novel roles of formin mDia2 in lamellipodia and filopodia formation in motile cells. *PLOS Biol.* 5:e317

135. Yang C, Svitkina T. 2011. Filopodia initiation: focus on the Arp2/3 complex and formins. *Cell Adhes. Migr.* 5:402–8

136. Yarar D, Waterman-Storer CM, Schmid SL. 2005. A dynamic actin cytoskeleton functions at multiple stages of clathrin-mediated endocytosis. *Mol. Biol. Cell* 16:964–75

137. Yoo Y, Wu X, Guan J-L. 2007. A novel role of the actin-nucleating Arp2/3 complex in the regulation of RNA polymerase II-dependent transcription. *J. Biol. Chem.* 282:7616–23

138. Zhu J, Mogilner A. 2012. Mesoscopic model of actin-based propulsion. *PLOS Comput. Biol.* 8:e1002764

139. Zuchero JB, Coutts AS, Quinlan ME, La Thangue NB, Mullins RD. 2009. p53-cofactor JMY is a multifunctional actin nucleation factor. *Nat. Cell Biol.* 11:451–59

140. Zuo Y, Oh W, Frost JA. 2014. Controlling the switches: Rho GTPase regulation during animal cell mitosis. *Cell. Signal.* 26:2998–3006

Structural Symmetry in Membrane Proteins*

Lucy R. Forrest

Computational Structural Biology Group, Porter Neuroscience Center, National Institute of Neurological Disorders and Stroke, National Institutes of Health, Bethesda, Maryland 20852; email: lucy.forrest@nih.gov

Annu. Rev. Biophys. 2015. 44:311–37

The *Annual Review of Biophysics* is online at biophys.annualreviews.org

This article's doi:
10.1146/annurev-biophys-051013-023008

Keywords

oligomer, internal repeats, inverted-topology repeats, asymmetry, alternating access

Abstract

Symmetry is a common feature among natural systems, including protein structures. A strong propensity toward symmetric architectures has long been recognized for water-soluble proteins, and this propensity has been rationalized from an evolutionary standpoint. Proteins residing in cellular membranes, however, have traditionally been less amenable to structural studies, and thus the prevalence and significance of symmetry in this important class of molecules is not as well understood. In the past two decades, researchers have made great strides in this area, and these advances have provided exciting insights into the range of architectures adopted by membrane proteins. These structural studies have revealed a similarly strong bias toward symmetric arrangements, which were often unexpected and which occurred despite the restrictions imposed by the membrane environment on the possible symmetry groups. Moreover, membrane proteins disproportionately contain internal structural repeats resulting from duplication and fusion of smaller segments. This article discusses the types and origins of symmetry in membrane proteins and the implications of symmetry for protein function.

Contents

INTRODUCTION

Symmetry, defined as the property of having the same appearance from two or more vantage points, is an aesthetically appealing and common feature of natural systems (52). In the structure of macromolecules and, in that of proteins in particular, researchers have identified a multitude of symmetries and pseudosymmetries, which appear to have a range of functional advantages (50, 70). As we reach the milestone of identifying 500 unique structures of membrane proteins (112, 155, 161), reviewing the prevalence and mechanistic significance of symmetry in this special class of proteins seems timely.

After briefly introducing the major functional classes of integral membrane proteins, I discuss the emergence of symmetry in their structures as a result of gene duplication or oligomerization. I then describe the specific types of symmetry observed thus far, as well as their mechanistic implications. This discussion focuses on membrane proteins with chains spanning the entire lipid bilayer one or more times [in contrast to monotopic, membrane-associated proteins (13, 155)]. I conclude with open questions and exciting future directions for the field.

FUNCTIONS OF MEMBRANE PROTEINS

Approximately 25–35% of the genes in a genome encode for integral membrane proteins (3, 81, 123). These proteins perform a wide variety of functions that can be grouped into four types: receptors, channels and transporters, enzymes, and cofactor scaffolds.

Receptors

Lipid bilayers serve as hydrophobic barriers that protect the interior of cells and organelles, but they also impede numerous essential processes. So-called receptor proteins facilitate the transmission of information across membranes. In response either to light or to chemical signals from the exterior of the cell, these proteins adopt different states or conformations and thereby modulate their ability to interact with other proteins in the interior of the cell. The family of seven-transmembrane (TM)-helix G protein–coupled receptors (GPCRs) is the most prominent example, and it constitutes the largest functional class in eukarya (3). Receptor tyrosine kinases (RTKs) comprise another large and important family of membrane proteins in this class (83).

Domain: a functional and structural unit of protein, typically between 100 and 250 amino acids in length

Channels and Transporters

The second-most abundant membrane proteins, accounting for between 2 and 15% of the genes in a given genome (3, 5), are those that facilitate selective passage of chemicals across the lipid membrane. In the simplest case, proteins called channels create pores through which ions and other molecules diffuse passively, that is, down their concentration gradients. To regulate this process, many channels incorporate so-called gating mechanisms that respond to environmental stimuli such as voltage or ligand binding.

Cells also need to expel toxic compounds and to take up rare nutrients, and doing so typically requires movement against a concentration gradient, also known as active transport. So-called primary active transporters derive the energy for such processes from ATP hydrolysis or from light conversion. ATP hydrolysis is catalyzed by protein domains residing outside the membrane that are tightly coupled to the membrane-spanning domain through which the substrate passes.

Many primary transporters also serve as ion pumps; that is, they accumulate, for example, H^+ or Na^+ ions on one side of the membrane and thereby generate an electrochemical gradient. Such concentration gradients are used as an energy source by membrane proteins known as secondary active transporters. Specifically, these proteins power the movement of one substrate against its gradient by harnessing the energy released from the dissipation of the gradient of a different substrate. The transport process may involve the substrates moving either in the same (symport) direction or the opposite (antiport) direction. In all cases, these transporters function according to so-called alternating-access mechanisms (67), whereby the binding sites for the substrates are alternately exposed to one side of the membrane or the other, but not to both at the same time (reviewed in, for example, Reference 43).

Membrane Enzymes

Many enzymatic reactions carried out by water-soluble proteins are also conducted by enzymes that are integrally embedded in the membrane. The membrane setting facilitates access to hydrophobic substrates such as TM helices destined for proteolysis, but it must also allow access to reactive water molecules. Recent structural studies have shown that membrane enzymes achieve this feat by means of different strategies. For example, the TM helices of UbiA prenyltransferases surround a central hydrophilic active site cavity that is accessible to hydrophobic substrates from the membrane via a hydrophobic tunnel (62). In contrast, the trimeric enzyme diacylglycerol kinase A (DgkA), which phosphorylates lipid headgroups, forms three distinct active sites at the height of the lipid–water interface on the outer surface of the enzyme (86). Perhaps the most unexpected strategy is the aqueous microenvironment within the hydrophobic region of the lipid bilayer created by an exposed hydrophilic patch on the outer surface of membrane proteases. This patch is thought to be the active site for proteolysis (reviewed in References 35, 160).

Cofactor Scaffolding Proteins

The orientational confinement imposed by the lipid bilayer can also hold a functional advantage. During photosynthesis, for example, light is absorbed by cofactors in so-called light-harvesting complexes (LHCs) and, by way of resonance energy transfer, activates neighboring photosynthetic reaction centers (PRCs). By fixing the relative positions of their cofactors at a specific distance apart, LHCs and PRCs create optimal conditions for light absorption and transfer. Similarly, electron-transfer reactions in the membranes of mitochondria and respiratory bacteria are facilitated by a series of scaffolding proteins known as complexes I to IV, which serve to fix the positions of various iron-containing redox centers. Ultimately, both photosynthesis and respiration result in an H^+ or Na^+ electrochemical gradient across the membrane, which is harnessed by a significantly more dynamic membrane motor protein called ATP synthase (also known as complex V) to energize the production of ATP. See, for example, Reference 155 for a review of these processes.

FUNCTIONAL DIVERSITY, PROTEIN SIZE, AND SYMMETRY

The assortment of functions described above appears to require a very diverse array of protein architectures. A possible evolutionary strategy to achieve this diversity is to create larger proteins and complexes from smaller structural units (50, 85). This strategy likely has a number of advantages: creation of new protein surfaces capable of binding to different molecules; enhanced stability, for example, by shielding of hydrophobic surfaces that are narrower than the membrane width (10, 116); conformational stability of multimeric complexes; and the potential to support cooperative or other regulatory mechanisms, for example, by tethering distinct functions within heterooligomers. As I explain below, larger proteins are created either by the assembly of multiple subunits, or by the fusion of duplicated or dissimilar genes; symmetry appears to be an intrinsic consequence of both of these processes (50, 85).

Oligomerization

The simplest mechanism by which larger proteins are formed is through assembly into homooligomers or heterooligomers. Oligomerization is remarkably common; Levy et al. (85) showed that between one-half and two-thirds of all proteins form obligate complexes. Unfortunately, the equivalent numbers for membrane protein structures have not been well documented, although a cursory analysis of the Protein Data Bank of Transmembrane Proteins (PDBTM) (151) suggests that a similarly large fraction of membrane proteins (~65%) are obligate oligomers; that is, they have more than one membrane-spanning subunit (85) (see **Figure 1**).

Symmetry is found in ~85% of protein complexes and is therefore the norm (85). It has been proposed that symmetry arises naturally from the fact that symmetric protein–protein interfaces contain duplications of all pairwise contacts. Thus, the most favorable interactions are also duplicated, leading to more stable interfaces than those achievable by nonsymmetric complexes (4, 100). A simple survey of available structures (as in the section titled "Symmetry in Membrane Protein Structures"; see **Tables 1–3** and **Figure 2**) suggests that membrane protein oligomers are also predominantly symmetric, although a systematic statistical analysis would be desirable. It will also be important to assess whether the above arguments regarding interface energies also apply within the context of the hydrophobic membrane environment, as well as whether the reduced degrees of freedom in the membrane either enhance or diminish this inherent predisposition toward symmetry.

Gene Fusion

A second solution to the need for larger and/or more complex proteins is to combine preexisting domains by gene fusion (50). Indeed, the majority of all proteins (55–67%) contain multiple detectable subdomains (107). When considering only membrane proteins, however, the tendency

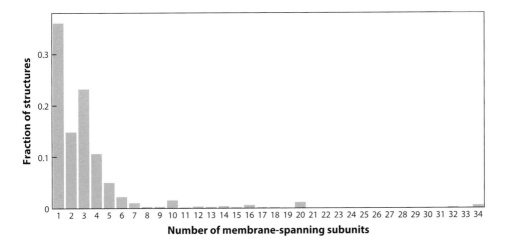

Figure 1

Degree of oligomer formation in membrane protein structures, shown as the fraction of structures that contain one or more membrane-spanning subunits. Data were taken from the Protein Data Bank of Transmembrane Proteins (PDBTM) database (151) dated August 1, 2014, which contains 2,241 proteins. No filtering to remove low-resolution or redundant models was applied. Thus, each data point may contain several representatives from the same structural family. This analysis is necessarily biased toward proteins that crystallize and that are well studied (108). The oligomers are formed via interactions between membrane domains and/or between fused water-soluble domains.

is reversed: only approximately 30% of these proteins contain multiple, independently functioning TM domains (93). Notably, this lack of fusion between membrane protein domains is not due to an inherent inability of their genes to fuse: Indeed, as many as 90% of membrane proteins contain water-soluble domains (93). Thus, it may be that the reduced dimensionality of the membrane enhances the stability of protein–protein interactions, reducing the need for gene fusion of the membrane domains (93).

If fusion of membrane-spanning segments is indeed less common than fusion of water-soluble domains, then one must assume that more complicated membrane protein functions, such as co-operativity, occur preferentially via oligomerization. However, the fraction of membrane protein oligomers in PDBTM (**Figure 1**) is similar to that found for all proteins (85). A more systematic analysis of available membrane protein structures may help to resolve this apparent discrepancy.

Internal Repeats

The discussion above pertains to the fusion of domains with independent functionality. However, larger proteins can also be constructed by fusion of genes encoding small protein segments; for example, fusion may occur after duplication of secondary structure elements (102), which results in internal structural repeats. Of the proteins containing detectable internal repeats, roughly half are symmetric, suggesting that these proteins originated from concurrent duplication and fusion of genes that encoded homooligomeric complexes (1). In other cases, duplication and subsequent fusion of segments that did not previously form oligomers may have resulted in nonsymmetric internal repeats (1). In either case, after fusion, internal repeat sequences are independently exposed to selective point mutations. Thus, in the absence of a specific functional reason to maintain perfect internal symmetry, the primary sequences of the repeats are very likely to diverge, resulting in structures that are internally pseudosymmetric rather than symmetric (108).

Internal repeats: duplications of a structural element or sequence motif within a single polypeptide chain

Table 1 Membrane proteins of known structure with nonsymmetrical or twofold symmetrical architectures

Order	None	Perpendicular C₂	Perpendicular pC₂	Planar C₂	Planar pC₂	Planar 2₂	Dihedral pD₂
Receptor, enzyme	OST (95), Proteases (88), TatC (135), YidC (82)	AMPAR (142), **Class C GPCR (79)**, **Complex III (163)**, **Complex IV (64)**, **Glycophorin A (103)**, **PS-II (155)**, Rhodanese (34), RTK (83)	Complex II (147), DsbB (63), NMDAR (73), PRC (27), Rhodopsin (21), UbiA (62),				
Primary transporter	P-type ATPase (149)	ABC export (25), ABC import I (60), ABC import II (97), **SR-II (51)**	ABC export (2), ABC import I (124), BR (21)		*ABC import II* (97)*		
Secondary transporter		CDF (99), SemiSWEET (164), **APC (36)**, **CLC (31)**, **DASS (106)**, **EIIC (17)**	MATE (54), SWEET (65), RND* (33)	SMR (41, 152)	*CLC* (31), APC* (45), CaCA (89), CNT* (69), DASS* (106), EAAT* (22), NCS2 (98), NPA1* (140)*	*Mrp* (32)*	*MFS (58)*
Channel	BcsA (117)	MgtE (53), **SKT (16)**, **CLC (31)**		Gramicidin A (6)	Amt (76), FNT* (157), MIP* (114), SecY (153), TMBIM (18), UT (84)		

Protein families (or one subunit of a larger complex) are organized by symmetry order, axis orientation (perpendicular or parallel to the membrane), and symmetry group. Citations are for structures, analyses thereof, or reviews describing each family. pC_2 indicates a pseudo-C_2 symmetry axis. Bold text indicates a possible regulatory role (e.g., stability, cooperativity). Blue text indicates asymmetry. Italic text indicates that the corresponding symmetry axis runs through the helices of the two repeats (interdigitating repeats). Asterisks indicate listed symmetry is found within a protomer in an oligomeric complex. pD_n indicates n-fold dihedral pseudosymmetry. Protein names, abbreviations, and, in some cases, functions are as follows: ABC, ATP binding cassette; AMPAR, α-amino-3-hydroxy-5-methyl-4-isoxazolepropionic acid receptor; Amt, ammonia channels; APC, amino acid/polyamine/organocation superfamily, which includes the Na^+-coupled amino acid transporter LeuT, and the betaine/carnitine/choline transporter (BCCT) families; BcsA, subunit A of the cellulose synthesis and translocation system; BR, bacteriorhodopsin, a light-driven H^+ pump; CaCA, Ca^{2+}:cation antiporter family; CDF, cation diffusion facilitator; CLC, Cl^- channel family, which includes Cl^-/H^+ antiporters; CNT, concentrative nucleoside transporter; complex II, succinate:ubiquinone reductase; complex III, cytochrome bc_1; complex IV, cytochrome c oxidase aa_3; DASS, divalent anion:Na^+ symporter; DsbB, disulfide bond formation protein B, a thiol oxidase responsible for disulfide bond formation in *Escherichia coli*; EAAT, excitatory amino acid transporter; EIIC, subunit C of the phosphoenolpyruvate–carbohydrate phosphotransferase transport system; FNT, formate/nitrite transporter; GPCR, G protein–coupled receptor; MATE, multidrug and toxin extrusion transporter; MFS, major facilitator superfamily, which exhibits a hitherto unappreciated twofold dihedral symmetry; MgtE, Mg^{2+} channels; MIP, major intrinsic proteins; Mrp, Na^+/H^+ antiporter related to the transport domains in complex I of the respiratory chain; NCS2, nucleobase:cation symporter-2; NMDAR, N-methyl-D-aspartate receptor; NPA1, Na^+/H^+ antiporter 1; OST, oligosaccharyl transferase; PRC, photosynthetic reaction center; rhodanese is a thiosulfate-cyanide sulfurtransferase; RND, resistance-nodulation-division transporter; RTK, receptor tyrosine kinase; SecY, protein-conducting channel; SKT, superfamily of K^+ transporters; SMR, small multidrug resistance; SR-II, sensory rhodopsin II, a light-driven ion pump that forms a dimer through its transducer protein (HtrII); SWEET, sugar transporters of the SWEET (monomer), SemiSWEET (heterodimer), and Pnu (monomer) families; TatC, twin-arginine protein transport component; TMBIM, transmembrane Bax inhibitor motif family; UbiA, prenyl-transferase family; UT, urea transporter; YidC, Sec-independent membrane protein insertion chaperone.

Table 2 Membrane proteins of known structure with threefold or fourfold symmetrical architectures

Order	Threefold		Fourfold		
Group	C_3	pC_3	C_4	pC_4	D_4
Receptor, enzyme	DgkA (86), MAPEG (40), plant LHC2 (94), pMMO (90)	Complex IV (64), NOR (57), pMMO* (90)			
Primary transporter		M-PPase (75)			
Secondary transporter	**BCCT** (133), **RND** (120), **CNT** (69), **EAAT** (167)	MCP (128)			
Channel	CTR (26), DEG-eNaC (68), Dermcidin (143), P2XR (74), RND (30), **Amt** (76), **OMP** (139), **SLAC** (19), **UT** (84)	DEG-eNaC (68), UreI* (146)	AMPAR[†] (142), KcsA (29), M2 (61), Nav (127), **MIP** (114)	NMDAR[†] (73), SKT (16),	AQP-0 (49)

Protein families (or one subunit of a larger complex) are organized by symmetry order and symmetry group. Citations are for structures, analyses thereof, or reviews describing each family. D_n indicates n-fold dihedral symmetry; pC_n indicates a pseudo-C_n symmetry axis. Bold text indicates a possible regulatory role (e.g., stability, cooperativity). Blue text indicates asymmetry. Asterisks indicate listed symmetry is found within a protomer in an oligomeric complex. Daggers indicate mixed symmetry: C_4 symmetry applies only in the channel region, whereas the entire complex has an overall twofold symmetry or pseudosymmetry. Protein names, abbreviations, and, in some cases, functions are as follows: Amt, ammonia channels; AMPAR, α-amino-3-hydroxy-5-methyl-4-isoxazolepropionic acid-subtype glutamate receptor; AQP-0, aquaporin-0, an MIP-family member; BCCT, betaine/choline/carnitine transporters, which belong to the amino acid/polyamine/organocation (APC) superfamily, and therefore also exhibit pC_2 symmetry (see **Table 1**); BR, bacterial rhodopsin family of light-driven H⁺ pumps; Complex IV, cytochrome c oxidase; CNT, concentrative nucleoside transporters; CTR, copper uptake proteins; DEG-eNaC, degenerin epithelial sodium channel family, including acid-sensing ion channels (ASICs), which can form both homomeric and heteromeric channels; DgkA, diacylglycerol kinase A; EAAT, excitatory amino acid transporter; KcsA, K⁺ channel from *Streptomyces lividans*; M2, influenza virus M2 proton-selective ion channel; MAPEG, membrane-associated proteins in eicosanoid and glutathione mechanism; MCP, mitochondrial carrier protein; MIP, major intrinsic protein superfamily, which includes the aquaporin family of proteins; M-PPase, membrane pyrophosphatase; Nav, voltage-gated sodium channel; NMDAR, N-methyl-D-aspartate subtype glutamate receptor; NOR, nitric oxide reductase; P2XR, P2X receptor channel; plant LHC2, plant light-harvesting complex II; pMMO, particulate methane monooxygenase; OMP, outer-membrane β-barrel protein; RND, resistance-nodulation-division transporter, with a channel component in the outer membrane; SKT, superfamily of K⁺ transporters; SLAC, slow anion channel; UreI, proton-gated inner-membrane urea channel; UT, urea transporter.

The first studies of internal structural pseudosymmetry in membrane proteins suggested that the proportion of available membrane protein structures containing pseudosymmetry is as high as one-half (21, 55), although a recent study using a more conservative repeat-detection strategy identified pseudosymmetry in only ~24% of membrane protein structures (121). The discrepancy between these studies suggests that a quarter of membrane proteins may contain highly divergent internal repeats that are difficult to detect, although the possibility that recently reported structures are less pseudosymmetric remains. Regardless of the exact frequency, given that the proportion of all folds found to be internally pseudosymmetric was ~18%, available membrane protein structures are clearly enriched in internal pseudosymmetry compared with water-soluble proteins (121).

For a few membrane protein families, hints of these internal structural duplications were identified based on sequence analyses, long before structures were available (see, for example, References 125, 137). However, many other duplications were too distantly related (<10% identity) to be detected by such methods (21, 55, 77, 121).

Pseudosymmetric proteins: two or more protein segments with differing sequences but shared topological arrangements (folds) of their backbones

Table 3   Membrane proteins of known structure with fivefold or higher symmetrical architectures

Order	Fivefold		Sixfold		Sevenfold	Eightfold or higher
Group	C_5	pC_5	C_6	D_6	C_7	C_{8+} or pC_{8+}
Receptor, enzyme						Bacterial LH2 [C_{8-9}] (112), LH1 [C_{16}] (122)
Primary transporter						F/V/A-ATPase c-rings* [C_8, C_{10}–C_{15}, and pC_{11}] (110)
Secondary transporter						
Channel	pLGICs (56), CorA (101), **FNT** (157)	Bestrophin (166), pLGIC (115), SLAC* (19)	MARVEL (7), **UreI** (146)	Cx (104)	MscS (9), CDC (130)	Cytolysin [C_{12}] (119), OMA [C_8] (28), OMP [pC_8–pC_{24}] (37)

Protein families (or one subunit of a larger complex) are organized by symmetry order and symmetry group. Citations are for structures, analyses thereof, or reviews describing each family. pC_n indicates a pseudo-C_n symmetry axis; D_n indicates n-fold dihedral symmetry. Higher-order symmetry groups are given in brackets. Bold text indicates a proposed regulatory role (e.g., stability, cooperativity). Asterisks indicate listed symmetry is found within a larger oligomeric complex. Protein names, abbreviations, and, in some cases, functions, are as follows: CDC, cholesterol-dependent cytolysin pore-forming toxin; CorA, Mg^{2+} channel family; Cx, connexin; Cytolysin, α-helical pore-forming toxin; FNT, formate/nitrite transporter; LH1, light-harvesting complex (LHC)-1; bacterial LH2, bacterial LHC-2; MARVEL, myelin and lymphocyte (MAL) and related proteins for vesicle trafficking and membrane link family; MscS, small mechanosensitive channel; OMA, outer-membrane auxiliary proteins, including the Wza polysaccharide translocon; OMP, outer-membrane β-barrel protein; pLGIC, pentameric ligand-gated ion channels, or Cys-loop receptors, which include homomeric receptors, as in the bacterial ELIC channel, and heteromeric complexes such as the nicotinic acetylcholine receptor; SLAC, slow anion channel; UreI, proton-gated inner membrane urea channel.

Figure 2

Types of point symmetry in membrane protein structures. Structures are shown as cartoon helices, viewed down onto the membrane. Colored segments indicate symmetric elements, such as independent chains or internal repeats (indicated by asterisks); nonsymmetric elements are shown in gray. Labels in the lower left corner of each box indicate the symmetry or pseudosymmetry type for that structure. $ModB_2$ (PDB ID: 2ONK), from the homodimeric molybdate type I ATP binding cassette (ABC) importer has twofold symmetry (60), and rhodopsin has twofold pseudosymmetry (21); in both cases, the symmetry axis runs perpendicular to the membrane. Pseudosymmetry about a twofold (2_2) screw axis parallel to the membrane plane is seen only in the Mrp antiporter-like subunits of complex I (Nqo14; see **Figure 4**). EmrE (PDB ID: 3B5D) is an asymmetric homodimer in its antiparallel form (20). BsYetJ (PDB ID: 4PGW) is a pH-dependent Ca^{2+} channel from the transmembrane (TM) Bax inhibitor motif (TMBIM) family and contains a pseudosymmetric inverted repeat; the closed form is shown (18). NCX cation antiporters (PDB ID: 3V5U) contain asymmetric inverted repeats and are therefore both asymmetric and pseudosymmetric (89). The symmetry axis in EmrE, NCX, BsYetJ, and Nqo14 lies parallel to the membrane. Fucose permease (PDB ID: 3O7Q) is a major facilitator superfamily (MFS) member (23). The MFS fold contains twofold C_2 pseudosymmetry axes, one perpendicular to and another parallel to the membrane plane, and it therefore exhibits dihedral D_2 pseudosymmetry; the approximately coincident axes of the six–TM helix N- and C-terminal domains are shown independently. The outward open form of fucose permease shown is also asymmetric (131). Human five-lipooxygenase activating protein (FLAP) (PDB ID: 2Q7M) is an enzyme belonging to the family of membrane-associated proteins involved in eicosanoid and glutathione metabolism (MAPEG), and has threefold C_3 symmetry (40). M-PPase (PDB ID: 4AV3) is a Na^+-pumping membrane pyrophosphatase from *Thermatoga maritima* with threefold pseudosymmetry (75). Nav is a tetrameric voltage-gated Na^+ channel from *Arcobacter butzleri* (PDB ID: 3RVZ) with fourfold rotational symmetry (127). TrkH (PDB ID: 3PJZ) is a K^+ channel from the superfamily of K^+ transporters (SKT) with fourfold pseudosymmetry (16). In both Nav and TrkH, the cation pore follows the symmetry axis. TehA (PDB ID: 3M73, chain A) is a pentameric slow anion channel (SLAC) homolog with fivefold rotational symmetry (19). Connexin26 (PDB ID: 2ZW3) is a gap junction; each hexameric hemichannel exhibits C_6 symmetry, and each hemichannel spans one membrane, leading to an overall dihedral symmetry (104). α-Hemolysin (PDB ID: 7AHL) is a toxin that assembles to form a C_7-symmetric pore (144). The F-type ATP synthase membrane rotor c-ring (PDB ID: 2XND) shows C_8 (or higher) symmetry (159). Symmetry axes were defined using SymD v1.3 (78), and figures were made with PyMOL v1.7 (Schrödinger LLC; **http://www.pymol.org**).

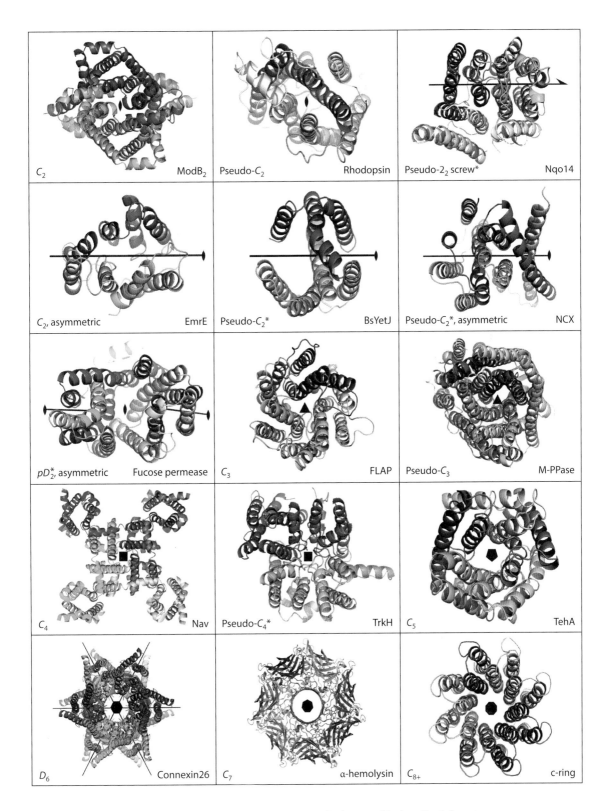

C_2 ModB$_2$	Pseudo-C_2 Rhodopsin	Pseudo-2_2 screw* Nqo14
C_2, asymmetric EmrE	Pseudo-C_2* BsYetJ	Pseudo-C_2*, asymmetric NCX
pD_2^*, asymmetric Fucose permease	C_3 FLAP	Pseudo-C_3 M-PPase
C_4 Nav	Pseudo-C_4* TrkH	C_5 TehA
D_6 Connexin26	C_7 α-hemolysin	C_{8+} c-ring

SYMMETRY IN MEMBRANE PROTEIN STRUCTURES

Lipid bilayers contain a planar symmetry that divides the hydrophobic core in half and reflects the two leaflets. One might therefore expect that some membrane proteins contain a similar structural symmetry, namely, one about an axis running along the midplane of the membrane. Nevertheless, one should keep in mind that the chemical environments on the two sides of the membrane typically are not equivalent.

Nonsymmetric Membrane Proteins

By definition, the ~35% of soluble and membrane proteins that are monomeric (50, 85) (**Figure 1**) cannot adopt oligomeric symmetry. Moreover, 57–82% of individual domains also contain no internal repeats (21, 121) and therefore also lack any detectable symmetry. Such nonsymmetric proteins ought to be well suited to detecting differences between the environments on each side of the membrane (50). Indeed, no class of receptor with known structures, namely GPCRs, ligand-gated ion channels, and enzyme-linked receptors such as RTKs, exhibits any apparent symmetry with respect to the membrane plane. Nevertheless, proteins belonging to all these families feature structural symmetry around an axis perpendicular to the membrane (see the subsection titled "Symmetry with the axis perpendicular to the membrane plane").

Enzymatic reactions in the membrane appear to be accomplished readily by nonsymmetric architectures. These include oligosaccharide transferase (OST) (95), aspartate proteases (88), site-2-proteases (38), and rhomboid proteases (158, 162) (**Table 1**). Nonsymmetric folds are also found in the protein translocation systems YidC (82) and TatC (135), as well as in a cellulose synthesis and translocation system, the BcsA/BcsB complex (117). In the latter case, the eight TM helices of BcsA are organized into pairs, but they are not related by symmetry. Finally, the P-type ATPases, which constitute one of the largest families of primary transporters (149), are clearly nonsymmetric (**Table 1**). Such a lack of symmetry is unusual among transport proteins.

Given that ~35% of membrane proteins are monomeric (**Figure 1**), one might expect the list of nonsymmetric proteins given in **Table 1** to be significantly longer. Perhaps the monomeric proteins instead contain internal symmetry. It has been estimated that as many as ~25–50% of domains contain no internal pseudosymmetry and therefore should be listed as nonsymmetric in **Table 1** (21, 121); it is possible that the automated approaches used in those studies underestimate the occurrence of internal repeats because the evolutionary divergence of these repeats makes their relationships difficult to detect (1, 121). As a telling example, most GPCRs have been classified as nonsymmetric (121), even though rhodopsin (a GPCR) contains a clear structural duplication of three transmembrane (TM) helices (21). Thus, the repeats in GPCRs seem to have diverged significantly. An effective strategy for identifying symmetry in these structures might therefore be to assign pseudosymmetry to a given structural class based on an analysis of all known structures in that class, rather than using representative folds.

Cyclic Symmetry

When surveying the most common symmetry groups in oligomeric structures, Levy et al. (85) found that 80% of oligomers contained dihedral symmetry, whereas only 20% were cyclic. In contrast, internally duplicated segments are >90% rotationally symmetric (121). A survey of available symmetries in membrane proteins (both internal and oligomeric; see **Tables 1–3** and **Figure 2**) corroborates previous observations that membrane proteins differ from water-soluble proteins in that the vast majority of membrane protein symmetries are cyclic (21, 121), even for oligomers. Indeed, only a few cases with dihedral symmetry were found (see the subsection titled

"Dihedral and Plane Symmetries"). In contrast, almost all imaginable cyclic symmetry groups are found in the available membrane protein structures (**Figure 2**).

Symmetry with the axis perpendicular to the membrane plane. The majority of symmetric membrane proteins contain a rotational symmetry about an axis that runs perpendicular to the membrane plane (**Figure 2**). This type of symmetry axis implies that the N-terminal and C-terminal ends of all involved chains are located on the same side of the membrane, presumably simplifying the insertion process.

Protomer:
a single subunit of a homooligomeric subunit, as distinct from a monomer, which is a nonoligomeric entity

Asymmetric proteins: protein segments with similar folds that adopt distinct conformations of their backbones within the context of the same fold

Take your partner by the hand: cyclic twofold (C_2) symmetry and pseudosymmetry with a perpendicular axis. The simplest symmetric arrangement, and among the most common in membrane proteins, involves a 180° rotation around an axis perpendicular to the membrane (C_2, **Table 1**). As described below, ideal C_2 symmetry is found in homooligomeric complexes, whereas C_2 pseudosymmetry is observed both within heterooligomeric complexes and between internal repeats (**Figure 2**). In cases in which this association is known to be required for function, the symmetric elements almost always create a binding site or pathway at their interface (**Table 1**).

Signaling receptors such as RTKs, for example, create a ligand binding site at the dimer interface (83, 87). Each protomer contains extracellular and intracellular domains that are connected by a single TM helix. Binding of the ligand to the extracellular domains causes dimerization or triggers a conformational change within a preexisting dimer (83). Recent structures obtained by NMR of isolated TM helix homodimers, for example, ErbB2 (11), and heterodimers, for example, ErbB1/ErbB2 (113), are consistent with C_2 symmetry or pseudosymmetry extending into the membrane.

Primary transporters of the ATP binding cassette (ABC) transporter family assemble using C_2 perpendicular symmetry, creating both a substrate pathway and ATP binding sites at the dimer interface (132). All ABC transporters contain two TM domains (TMDs) and two ABCs (also known as nucleotide binding domains, NBDs), which are assembled either from separate chains or from fused domains. Notably, the NBDs create two off-axis binding sites for ATP using a head-to-tail arrangement, whereas the substrate pathway typically follows the symmetry axis.

Four different classes of ABC transporters have been identified (96): ABC exporters and three types of ABC importers, called type I, type II, and energy coupling factor (ECF) importers. Simple homodimers are found in three of these classes, for example, forming local C_2 symmetry in the TM domains of the type I importer ModB$_2$ (60) (**Figure 2**) and in those of the type II importer BtuC$_2$ (97). Heterodimeric ABC transporters, in contrast, come together in pseudo-C_2-symmetric complexes, as exemplified by MalF and MalG, which form the TM segments of the ABC importer MalFGK (124). In some cases, one NBD has lost the ability to hydrolyze ATP. A structure of an ABC exporter with one of these so-called degenerate NBDs contains a nucleotide bound to only one site, creating an asymmetry in these soluble domains (59); such asymmetry has intriguing functional implications (as reviewed in, for example, Reference 147).

Perpendicular pseudo-C_2-symmetry is also seen in some secondary transporters (**Table 1**; **Figures 2** and **3**), notably in the largest class, the major facilitator superfamily (MFS) (126). Structural studies confirmed that the MFS fold contains two lobes of six TM helices, each lining a central pathway (58). Interestingly, the multidrug and toxin extrusion (MATE) transporters, such as NorM (54), and the resistance-nodulation-division (RND) transporters, exemplified by AcrB (33), also contain two domains of six TM helices lining a central pathway. Nevertheless, the topological arrangements of the helices differ between these three folds.

Beyond the aforementioned functional roles, dimerization of membrane proteins also appears to be a common strategy for regulation (**Table 1**), for example, by enhancing stability or

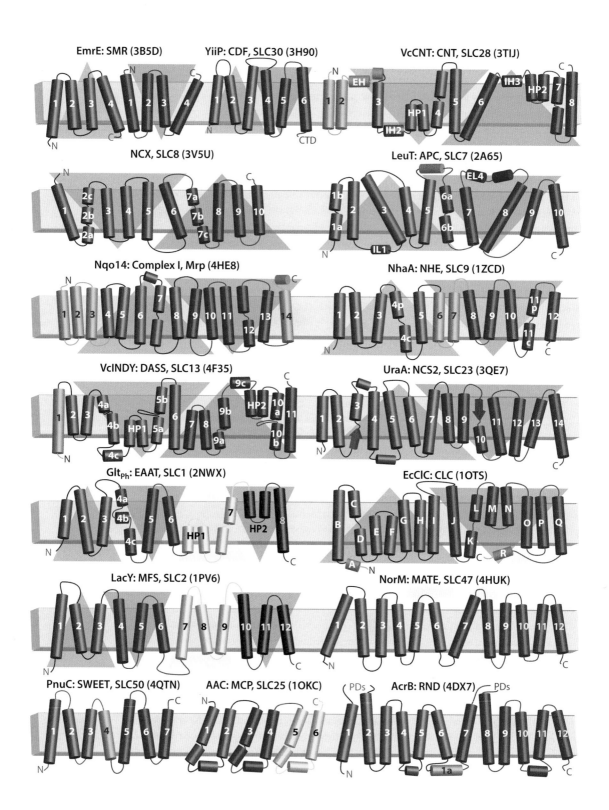

introducing allostery. Dimerization of class C GPCRs allows them unique modes of activation (79). By extension, the occurrence and functional relevance of homooligomerization and heterooligomerization by class A GPCRs is the focus of intense study (39).

Threefold symmetry is often found in regulatory roles. As mentioned in the subsection titled "Membrane Enzymes," the trimeric enzyme DgkA is proposed to form active sites at the interface between adjacent protomers in a threefold symmetric arrangement (**Table 2**). The positioning of these sites on the exterior of the protein at the level of the lipid headgroups provides access for both hydrophobic (diacylglycerol) and hydrophilic (ATP) substrates (86). Homotrimeric assemblies also create channels and pathways. Examples include the P2X ATP-gated ion channels (74) and the outer membrane protein component of the RND efflux systems called TolC (30). Membrane proteins with diverse functions are assembled from triplicated internal repeats with pseudo-C_3 symmetry (**Table 2**). In the ion-pumping pyrophosphatases (M-PPases) (**Figure 2**) (75, 91) and mitochondrial carrier proteins (MCPs) (**Figure 3**) (128), for example, these repeats surround the central substrate binding sites and/or pathways.

Strikingly, no perfectly threefold-symmetric structures have been reported for transporters, at least not for their core transport units (**Table 2**). Homotrimeric assemblies of secondary transporters and channels are common, however, apparently for regulatory reasons. For example, trimerization of the Na^+-coupled aspartate transporter Glt_{Ph}, a homolog of the excitatory amino acid transporters (EAATs), may help stabilize the protein within the membrane during its large, elevator-like conformational change (22, 134).

Interestingly, asymmetry between protomers is also seen in trimeric transporter assemblies such as the RND transporter AcrB (120) (**Table 2**). Furthermore, within each protomer of AcrB, two parallel repeats (**Table 1**; **Figure 3**) cycle through three distinct conformational states, resulting in H^+ uptake (33). These changes in the membrane domains are mechanically transduced to a periplasmic domain; this domain also cycles through three distinct states, resulting in drug extrusion. The asymmetry in the trimer results from coupling of the transport cycles of the three protomers, owing to an extensive interface between the periplasmic domains. This asymmetric coupling mechanism may minimize the extent of drug backflow (33). Interactions involving the cytoplasmic tails of neighboring protomers (133) also lead to an asymmetry in the trimeric Na^+-coupled betaine transporter, BetP (150), possibly providing a mechanism for the increase in its transport rate in response to osmotic stress (138).

←

Figure 3

Transmembrane topologies of secondary transporters with known structure. The outside of the cell or organelle is oriented to the top. Protein name, family name, and human solute carrier (SLC) nomenclature, if applicable, are given for each protein, and representative PDB IDs are given in parentheses. Helices are represented as cylinders, and strands are represented as arrows. Each inverted-topology repeat is highlighted using a triangle; the bases of these triangles indicate the side of the N terminus for each segment. The cation diffusion facilitator (CDF) dimerizes through contacts between C-terminal domains (CTDs). The PnuC protein includes an additional N-terminal TM helix (not shown) that is not conserved among SWEET transporters; semiSWEET transporters (e.g. 164) resemble a dimer of TM1–3 and TM4–6 of the vitamin B_3 transporter, PnuC, but with a domain swap (66). Nqo14 is a subunit of the NADH:oxidoreductase complex I, related to the Mrp family cation exchangers; see **Figure 4** for more details. Abbreviations: AAC, ADP–ATP carrier; APC, amino acid/polyamine/organocation superfamily; CLC, Cl^- channels/antiporters; CNT, concentrative nucleoside transporter; DASS, divalent anion:Na^+ symporter; EAAT, excitatory amino acid transporter; MATE, multidrug and toxin extruder protein; MCP, mitochondrial carrier protein; MFS, major facilitator superfamily; NCS2, nucleobase cation symporter-2; NCX, Na^+/Ca^{2+} cation exchanger; NHE, Na^+/H^+ exchanger; RND, resistance-nodulation-division transporter; PDs, periplasmic domains; SMR, small multidrug resistance; SWEET, sugar transporter; Vc, *Vibrio cholera*; YiiP, H^+-coupled Zn^{2+} transporter from *Escherichia coli*.

Higher cyclic symmetries in channels and other systems. The creation of a central pathway is a common feature of parallel membrane protein oligomers (**Figure 2**), resulting in hollow rings with between 3-fold and 12-fold symmetry (**Tables 2** and **3**). Tetramers include K^+ and Na^+ channels such as the voltage-gated Na^+ channel NavAb (127) (**Figure 2**), the M2 H^+ channel from influenza A virus (61), and the channel regions of ionotropic glutamate receptors (iGluRs) such as the AMPA-subtype receptor (142). Many channels are pentameric, e.g., the anion channel TehA from the plant slow anion channel (SLAC) family (19) (**Figure 2**), although hexamers, such as a MARVEL [myelin and lymphocyte (MAL) and related proteins for vesicle trafficking and membrane link family]-domain channel called synaptophysin (7); heptamers, such as the small mechanosensitive channel, MscS (9); and octamers, as in the outer membrane polysaccharide translocon Wza (28), have all been observed. The largest pore-forming oligomers are constructed from toxins such as the cytolysins (130) (**Table 3**), using both α-helical and β-barrel TM segments (155). Indeed, a toxin called perfringolysin O may create a pore-forming complex with 40–50 protomers; such a complex would undoubtedly represent the highest cyclic symmetry order in a membrane protein (130, 141).

Rings of membrane proteins perform roles other than pore formation (**Table 3**). For example, LHCs form ovals or rings to transfer the light energy harnessed during photosynthesis to PRCs located in the center of the complex (**Table 3**) (112, 122). Another example is the rotor ring of the F-type ATP synthases. The rotor rings are likely to be plugged by lipids (129) and facilitate H^+ or Na^+ permeation at their outer surface as they rotate against an adjacent static subunit (71, 129). Because three ATP molecules are synthesized for every revolution of the ring, the number of subunits in the rotor ring (which in most cases equals the number of transported ions) determines the thermodynamic capacity of the enzyme to synthesize ATP (109).

Pseudosymmetry is less common in α-helical complexes of higher order (**Tables 2** and **3**, **Figure 2**), although some channels are composed of repeated elements (e.g. TrkH; see Reference 16), and other channels and receptors are known to form heteromers (e.g., heterotetrameric NMDA-subtype iGluRs, which are formed of dimers of heterodimers; see Reference 73), as do some of the membrane rings of rotary ATPase enzymes (109). In contrast, in outer-membrane β-barrel proteins (OMPs), the β-strands typically belong to a continuous polypeptide chain and are related by an 8-fold to 24-fold rotational pseudosymmetry (37) (**Table 3**).

Mixed symmetries. In some heteromeric membrane protein complexes it is possible to identify subdomains whose symmetries vary. In these cases, the membrane domain often exhibits a higher symmetry order than that of the extramembrane domains. Examples include the ATP synthases and ATPases, which have membrane rotor rings that adopt C_8 or higher symmetry or pseudosymmetry (see the subsection titled "Higher cyclic symmetries in channels and other systems") and which are connected by so-called stalk segments to a large catalytic domain that comprises a trimer of heterodimers related by C_6 pseudosymmetry (as reviewed in, for example, Reference 71).

As mentioned in the subsection titled "Higher cyclic symmetries in channels and other systems," the channel regions of iGluRs have fourfold rotational symmetry (in AMPA-subtype receptors; see Reference 142) or pseudosymmetry (in NMDA-subtype receptors; see Reference 73). Remarkably, however, the same protein chains that form the channel extend into extracellular domains that have only twofold symmetry (or pseudosymmetry) because the domains are arranged as pairs of local dimers (73, 111, 142). Thus, iGluRs exhibit mixed symmetries within the same protein chain.

The membrane-bisecting axis of rotation. The discovery in recent years of multiple examples of rotational symmetries about axes that run along a plane bisecting the membrane has been a surprising one (**Figure 2**). Prior to these findings, the only example of such a protein was a unique bacterial channel-forming antibiotic called gramicidin A, which is composed of D-amino-acids that cause it to form a β-helix (14). Gramicidin A is too short to span the entire lipid bilayer and so forms head-to-head dimers related by a planar C_2 symmetry axis, thereby satisfying its hydrogen-bonding potential within the hydrophobic membrane core (6). For typical α-helical transmembrane helices, however, the membrane-bisecting axis of rotation raises energetic conundrums because the protein must either (*a*) insert nonhelical segments deep into the bilayer and risk exposing polar groups to the hydrophobic core or (*b*) insert the entire protein with dual TM topologies, seemingly a challenge for the insertion machinery. Such issues of membrane protein folding are reviewed in Reference 12.

Most of the membrane-bisecting C_2 symmetries relate internal repeats with an odd number of TM helices (**Figure 2**). As a result, the topologies of these repeats are inverted with respect to one another, placing their N termini on opposite sides of the membrane (**Figure 3**, **Table 1**) and resulting in C_2 pseudosymmetry. The only characterized dimers whose protomers are related by a symmetry axis oriented in this way are the small multidrug resistance (SMR) transporters (**Figures 2** and **3**) and the FluC fluoride channel (145).

An underappreciated distinction emerges when comparing inverted-topology folds, namely the orientation of the membrane-bisecting symmetry axis relative to the repeats. The symmetry axis may lie in between the two repeats of a protein, in which case each repeat has an independent fold (see the EmrE structure in **Figure 2**), or the axis may pass through the center of both repeats, in which case the helices of the two repeats must interdigitate (see the NCX and fucose permease structures in **Figure 2**).

Adjacent inverted-topology repeats. Interestingly, inverted-repeat folds in which the repeats are adjacent to the axis of symmetry are found mostly in channels (**Table 1**). Many of these channels are specific for small polar molecules such as water (aquaporin 1, Aqp1; Reference 114), urea (*Desulfovibrio vulgaris* urea transporter, dvUT; Reference 84), or ammonia (AmtB; Reference 76). In addition, adjacent inverted-topology repeats are found in channels and transporters for small anions (e.g., CLC family transporters and channels) (31) and for cations, as in the Bax inhibitor homolog, BsYetJ (**Figure 2**) (18). Unusually, the two three–TM helix repeats in BsYetJ surround the seventh TM helix, through which the pseudosymmetry axis also passes (**Figure 2**).

With the exception of BsYetJ, the interface between adjacent repeats typically defines two symmetry-equivalent pathways that lead from either side of the membrane to the center of the protein (44). This strategy for channel formation seems to be evolutionarily parsimonious because a single duplication leads to a narrow pathway that is well suited to conducting small molecules (145).

Interdigitating inverted-topology repeats. Proteins that contain interdigitating inverted-topology structural repeats have arguably the most complex of the known membrane protein folds (**Figure 3**), and these proteins are mainly involved in secondary transport (italicized elements in **Table 1**). However, interlocking repeat elements also contribute to subdomains in larger transporters; for example, in type II ABC importers, four TM helices within each lobe contribute to a pseudosymmetric inverted repeat (21, 97). Similarly, each twofold symmetric lobe in the MFS fold is itself composed of interdigitating three–TM helix inverted-topology repeats (58), leading to an overall twofold dihedral pseudosymmetry (**Figures 2** and **3**). As a result, the MFS fold can be considered to contain interlocking inverted-topology repeats of six TM helices (131). As described in the subsection titled "Asymmetry in membrane proteins," a functional advantage of such interlocking inverted-topology repeats may be an ability to adopt asymmetric states that fulfill the requirements for alternating access.

Topology: the direction of threading of protein segments back and forth across the membrane

Dual-topology: the ability of a protein to insert into the membrane in both orientations with equal probability; also known as undecided or frustrated topology

Inverted-topology repeats: membrane protein segments in a single chain inserted in opposite orientations, and related by a twofold axis running parallel to the membrane

Domain swapping: the positional exchange of one or more secondary structure elements from neighboring protomers in an oligomeric complex

Interdigitation leads to wide spacing between contiguous helices (in sequence), implying that the isolated repeats are unlikely to be well folded. The resulting interfaces between interlocked helices are indistinguishable in nature from those in the interior of proteins (50), namely, they have minimal hydration and extensive hydrophobic cores, in stark contrast to the interfaces of typical oligomers. The folding of interdigitated proteins must therefore be a complex process, particularly in the context of the membrane, and it would be interesting to examine whether individual inverted-topology repeats can exist as independently folded units.

The possible evolutionary origins of such a complex fold are also enigmatic. However, their interfaces are reminiscent of those in domain-swapping water-soluble proteins (92), and this similarity may provide a useful starting point for further inquiry.

Asymmetry in membrane proteins. Although symmetric and pseudosymmetric arrangements predominate, many membrane proteins exhibit a structural asymmetry that is essential for function (blue elements in **Tables 1** and **2**). Asymmetry in a homooligomer has the evolutionary handicap that the asymmetric interface must evolve to optimize interactions with two different environments simultaneously (50). This disadvantage may explain the rarity of such interfaces, but functional advantages appear in some cases to compensate that energetic cost.

The first example of functional asymmetry in membrane proteins was provided by the homodimeric SMR transporter EmrE (20, 41, 152). In structures of EmrE, the two identical protein chains adopt an antiparallel orientation with different conformations and, as a result, create a pathway to one side of the membrane only (**Figure 2**). This fold is an example of classical asymmetry. Around the same time, a distinctive asymmetry was also found to underlie the formation of the outward-facing state of an amino acid transporter, LeuT (44, 45). The asymmetry in LeuT was obscured by the pseudosymmetry of the repeats (165), which contain <10% identical residues and therefore also exhibit some level of inherent structural divergence. Once detected, however, the asymmetry could be taken advantage of, and used to model an alternate state. Specifically, each repeat was used as a template for homology modeling of the other repeat, so that each repeat adopts the other conformation. In this way, by threading the sequence of the first repeat onto the structure of the second repeat, and vice versa, the two halves of the protein swap conformations. This conformation swapping strategy applied to LeuT resulted in a model of an inward-facing state (45), the general features of which are remarkably consistent with a structure determined subsequently (80).

These findings imply that, by creating an asymmetry between the two repeats, proteins such as EmrE and LeuT can adopt two states, consistent with an alternating-access cycle (i.e., with pathways leading to one side of the membrane or the other). Thus, to transition to the other major conformation in the transport cycle, the protein undergoes asymmetry exchange, wherein the first repeat (or protomer) adopts the conformation of the second repeat (or protomer), and vice versa (41, 45), resulting in a new asymmetric structure that is open to the other side of the membrane. Given that substrate accumulation in physiological contexts is driven only by the balance of substrate concentrations and the associated membrane potentials, all conformations of the transporter must be similarly accessible from an energetic standpoint, without any additional input (unlike primary transporters, for which a direct energy input is required). The degeneracy of structural states implied by the asymmetry-exchange mechanism described above is an elegant solution to this requirement.

The repeat-swapping strategy for modeling the structures of alternate states of asymmetric transporters has since been applied to proteins with diverse structural folds (**Figure 3**), including the aspartate transporter Glt_{Ph} (22), the Na^+/Ca^{2+} exchanger (NCX) from the Ca^{2+}:cation exchanger family (CaCA) (89), lactose permease from the MFS (131), and NhaA from the Na^+:H^+

antiporter (NPA) family (140). Notably, all of these folds comprise inverted repeats with inter-digitating helices (italicized elements in **Table 1**, **Figure 2**). A model of an alternate state was generated for each of these cases, and the predicted global conformational changes were later validated by structures (42, 43, 134, 156) or other biophysical and biochemical evidence (131, 140). Importantly, NMR spectroscopy data support the proposal that antiparallel EmrE functions by exchanging between degenerate states (118). Thus, the asymmetry-exchange mechanism underlies alternating access by both homodimers and pseudosymmetric interdigitating inverted repeats.

How do asymmetric transporters optimize their substrate pathways to interact equally favorably with two different environments (50), that is, to both achieve protein–protein packing and interact with substrate and/or aqueous solution? In Glt_{Ph}, these interfaces comprise smooth surfaces with both polar and hydrophobic character (134), which is likely to reduce the probability of the protein becoming trapped in one state.

A notable conundrum posed by the asymmetry-exchange mechanism is the role of symmetric states. Let us consider two subunits, A and B, both of which can adopt two conformations, i and j. The asymmetric states of the transporter can thus be defined as A_iB_j or A_jB_i. What prevents the formation of A_iB_i or A_jB_j? Might one of these arrangements correspond to an occluded state or, possibly, to a leaky state (105)?

Intriguingly, asymmetry has recently been detected in the antiparallel homodimeric F^- channel, FluC (C. Miller, personal communication), although the reason why a channel requires asymmetry is unclear. Still, pure asymmetry such as that found in EmrE and FluC is rare, and the inverted repeats of asymmetry-exchanging transporters typically have divergent sequences. Pseudosymmetry may therefore play an important role in adapting secondary transporters to diverse substrates and conditions. In some cases, the breakdown in symmetry may also reduce the free energy of one state over the other just enough to provide preferential conformations of the transporter, for example, while awaiting substrate binding. Analysis of putative common ancestors of asymmetry-exchanging transporters may therefore provide useful insights into the minimal requirements for secondary transport.

Note that in principle, it is possible to achieve such diversity and conformational bias using heterodimeric proteins rather than fused internal repeats. As heterodimers are relatively rare among secondary transporters, fusing two domains into a single larger protein may have additional advantages, for example, in terms of stability or folding within the membrane.

Face-to-back inverted-topology repeats. Remarkably, a pseudosymmetry involving a screw axis with a membrane-bisecting axis was recently identified within a membrane protein subunit related to Na^+/H^+ antiporters of the Mrp family (32) (**Table 1**, **Figure 2**). Specifically, the multimeric NADH:ubiquinone oxidoreductase, or complex I of the respiratory chain, was demonstrated to contain a five–TM helix internal repeat within each of three subunits (Nqo12, Nqo13, and Nqo14) responsible for H^+ pumping (**Figure 4**). Because they are related by a pseudotwofold screw axis (2_2) rather than a rotational axis (C_2), however, the repeats are oriented face-to-back, rather than adjacent or interdigitating (32). An additional domain (Nqo8), which also contains one of these repeat units, is located close to the NADH:ubiquinone electron transfer site (8). This structure shows how the screw axis is well suited to creating a linear (in effect, helical) array of subunits with repeated interactions. The repeated arrangement presumably facilitates multiple simultaneous pathway openings and closures in response to electron transfer at one end of the complex. The interfaces between repeats in Nqo14 and Nqo13, for example, are similar to those between repeats within each subunit (**Figure 4**). Molecular dynamics simulation studies indicate that the formation of aqueous proton channels that open alternately to either side of the membrane may require

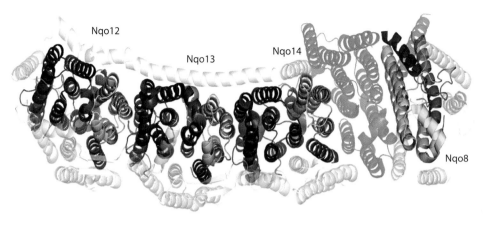

Nqo12

Nqo13

Nqo14

Nqo8

Figure 4

The membrane domain of complex I from *Thermus thermophilus* (8) (PDB ID: 4HE8) viewed from the periplasm. Inverted-topology repeats related by a twofold (2_2) screw axis are colored blue to red for the first repeat unit or dark gray for the second repeat unit. The single repeat unit in the Nqo8 subunit has the same transmembrane topology as the first repeat units in the other three domains, but this domain is more tilted than Nqo12, Nqo13, and Nqo14 are, and it is rotated by 180° around an axis perpendicular to the membrane plane (cf. *dark blue helices*). Nqo8 is separated from Nqo14 by several additional subunits (*purple*). Other nonsymmetric segments and subunits are shown in white.

exchange between symmetry-related states (72), similar to the asymmetry-exchange mechanism described above in the subsection titled "Asymmetry in membrane proteins."

Dihedral and Plane Symmetries

Dihedral and planar symmetries contain within them a twofold symmetry axis and are therefore in principle compatible with membranes. In dihedral symmetry, however, there must be rotational twofold axes both perpendicular to and parallel to the membrane plane (154). Thus, dihedral symmetry within a protein spanning a single membrane potentially exposes polar groups to the hydrophobic membrane core. One possible solution is found in protein complexes that span two membranes. For example, in gap junctions, two hemichannels, one per membrane, are stacked up to create a pore across the two membranes. Each hemichannel is formed by a hexamer of connexin proteins with C_6 symmetry, and the entire gap junction exhibits a dihedral (D_6) symmetry (104) (**Table 3**, **Figure 2**). Similarly, in the lens of the eye, aquaporin-0 (AQP-0) tetramers pack head-to-head into octamers that span the membranes of the lens fiber cells, creating a D_4 dihedral symmetry (**Table 2**) (49).

Dihedral symmetry can also be achieved by interchelating the repeated elements. MFS transporters, which have a dimer of inverted repeats, satisfy this requirement. As mentioned in the subsection titled "Interdigitating inverted-topology repeats," these proteins have a twofold pseudosymmetry axis perpendicular to the membrane that relates the six–TM helix halves, combined with a twofold pseudosymmetry axis parallel to the membrane that relates two interchelated three–TM helix repeats in each half (**Figures 2** and **3**). Thus, MFS transporters contain D_2 dihedral pseudosymmetry (**Table 2**) while maintaining the unsatisfied hydrogen bond potential in the aqueous solution away from the hydrophobic membrane core.

Although they are rare, plane symmetries, which are created by translations in two directions, are found in arrays of membrane proteins at specific cellular structures. These include ribbons of claudin proteins at epithelial tight junctions (46, 148) and arrays of AQP-0 octamers (15). Both specific and nonspecific properties of the lipids may be critical for the formation of such arrays (24, 48).

Higher-Order Cubic and Space-Group Symmetries

The planar nature of lipid membranes renders the three-dimensional arrangements associated with higher-order cubic or space-group symmetries unavailable to membrane proteins. However, attachments to scaffolding or anchoring proteins may result in the formation of spatially ordered complexes by assemblies of membrane proteins.

Dynamic Transitions Between Symmetry Types

Many membrane proteins function via dynamic conformational changes. The example of secondary transporters described in the subsection titled "The membrane-bisecting axis of rotation" illustrates how such a functional conformational cycle can involve a transition between two low-energy asymmetric states. Other proteins may require transitions from symmetric to asymmetric states or transitions from one type of symmetry to another. Channel gating and/or activation can involve asymmetric intermediates or progressive, stepwise conformational changes of independent subunits. For example, the closed channel form of the Bax inhibitor homolog BsYetJ is pseudosymmetric (**Figure 2**), but the open form is asymmetric, owing to a movement of a single TM helix (18). In voltage-gated cation channels, each pore-lining subunit is connected to a voltage-sensing domain (see the Nav structure in **Figure 2**) for which voltage-induced movements are transmitted to the channel-lining helices to increase the probability that the helices adopt an open conformation. For example, it has been shown that during activation of the tetrameric *Shaker* K^+ channel, the gating in each subunit is independent, and therefore the complex must visit asymmetric intermediate conformations (168). However, the combined activation of all four subunits is required to form a new, symmetric, open state of the channel.

The subunits in iGluRs can also be activated independently by ligand binding, leading to intermediate conductance states (136). Nevertheless, the complete activation event appears to involve a transition in the extracellular domains from one twofold pseudosymmetric arrangement to a distinct arrangement that is also twofold pseudosymmetric (111). Conformational changes associated with the channel becoming desensitized to its ligand, in contrast, involve a transition to a fourfold-symmetric state in those same extracellular domains. Remarkably, throughout all of these changes in the extracellular domains, the TM channel in iGluRs apparently retains an overall fourfold pseudosymmetry (111).

SUMMARY POINTS

1. Membrane protein structures to date exhibit a wide range of symmetries and pseudosymmetries from twofold to planar arrays, including mixtures of symmetries within a larger complex, but most conform to cyclic point-group symmetry.

2. The fraction of oligomers in available membrane protein structures is apparently similar to that of water-soluble proteins, but membrane protein structures contain a higher proportion of internal repeats. Overall, membrane proteins may exhibit symmetry more frequently than water-soluble proteins do.

3. Inverted-topology (pseudo)symmetries create channels and pathways through the membrane.

4. Asymmetry has been observed in secondary transporters and in one channel; the majority of these proteins have folds comprising inverted-topology repeats or protomers, both interdigitated and adjacent.

5. Both identical (homooligomeric) and divergent (pseudosymmetric internal repeat) protein sequences use asymmetry-exchange mechanisms to create degenerate alternate states consistent with alternating-access transport mechanisms.

6. Conformational changes in membrane proteins can involve transitions between different symmetry types.

FUTURE ISSUES

1. Systematic analysis of the growing number of membrane protein structures will be needed to further classify symmetries, pseudosymmetries, oligomerization, and internal repeats in membrane proteins. Continued efforts in structural biology, particularly in noncrystallographic methods such as cryo-electron microscopy will be needed to fill in gaps in fold space.

2. Which factors govern asymmetry in secondary transporters, and how is the balance of asymmetric states affected by substrate binding? How do these factors change for different transporter architectures, and how are they affected by individual point mutations? What is the advantage of fused repeats over small dimeric proteins?

3. Do symmetric (or pseudosymmetric) states play a role in secondary transport by asymmetry-exchange mechanisms, for example, as occluded/closed or leak states?

4. What factors define the boundary between channel and transporter functions (with symmetric and asymmetric functional states, respectively), especially in folds such as the CLCs?

5. What was the evolutionary pathway of inverted-topology interlocking repeats? Are the individual repeats stable as separate entities? Bioinformatic and folding studies of the simplest cases, such as NCX, may help identify contributions from, for example, circular permutation or domain swapping.

6. Did all inverted-topology folds arise from divergent evolution of a single ancestor, or did they arise as a result of convergent evolution from many dual-topology proteins?

DISCLOSURE STATEMENT

The author is not aware of any affiliations, memberships, funding, or financial holdings that might be perceived as affecting the objectivity of this review.

ACKNOWLEDGMENTS

Thanks to José Faraldo-Gómez for helpful discussions, suggestions and comments on the manuscript. This work was supported by the Intramural Research Program of the National Institutes of Health, National Institute of Neurological Disorders and Stroke.

LITERATURE CITED

1. Abraham A-L, Pothier J, Rocha EPC. 2009. Alternative to homo-oligomerisation: the creation of local symmetry in proteins by internal amplification. *J. Mol. Biol.* 394(3):522–34

2. Aller SG, Yu J, Ward A, Weng Y, Chittaboina S, et al. 2009. Structure of P-glycoprotein reveals a molecular basis for poly-specific drug binding. *Science* 323(5922):1718–22

3. Almén MS, Nordström KJV, Fredriksson R, Schiöth HB. 2009. Mapping the human membrane proteome: a majority of the human membrane proteins can be classified according to function and evolutionary origin. *BMC Biol.* 7(1):50

4. André I, Strauss CEM, Kaplan DB, Bradley P, Baker D. 2008. Emergence of symmetry in homooligomeric biological assemblies. *PNAS* 105(42):16148–52

5. Arabidopsis Genome Initiative. 2000. Analysis of the genome sequence of the flowering plant *Arabidopsis thaliana*. *Nature* 408(6814):796–815

6. Arseniev AS, Lomize AL, Barsukov IL, Bystrov VF. 1986. Gramicidin A transmembrane ion-channel. Three-dimensional structure reconstruction based on NMR spectroscopy and energy refinement. *Biol. Membr.* 3(11):1077–104 (from Russian)

7. Arthur CP, Stowell MHB. 2007. Structure of synaptophysin: a hexameric MARVEL-domain channel protein. *Structure* 15(6):707–14

8. **Baradaran R, Berrisford JM, Minhas GS, Sazanov LA. 2013. Crystal structure of the entire respiratory complex I. *Nature* 494:443–48**

9. Bass RB, Strop P, Barclay M, Rees DC. 2002. Crystal structure of *Escherichia coli* MscS, a voltage-modulated and mechanosensitive channel. *Science* 298(5598):1582–87

10. Benjamini A, Smit B. 2012. Robust driving forces for transmembrane helix packing. *Biophys. J.* 103(6):1227–35

11. Bocharov EV, Mineev KS, Volynsky PE, Ermolyuk YS, Tkach EN, et al. 2008. Spatial structure of the dimeric transmembrane domain of the growth factor receptor ErbB2 presumably corresponding to the receptor active state. *J. Biol. Chem.* 283(11):6950–56

12. **Bowie JU. 2013. Structural biology. Membrane protein twists and turns. *Science* 339(6118):398–99**

13. Bracey MH, Cravatt BF, Stevens RC. 2004. Structural commonalities among integral membrane enzymes. *FEBS Lett.* 567(2–3):159–65

14. Busath DD. 1993. The use of physical methods in determining gramicidin channel structure and function. *Annu. Rev. Physiol.* 55:473–501

15. Buzhynskyy N, Sens P, Behar-Cohen F, Scheuring S. 2011. Eye lens membrane junctional microdomains: a comparison between healthy and pathological cases. *New J. Phys.* 13(8):085016

16. Cao Y, Jin X, Huang H, Derebe MG, Levin EJ, et al. 2011. Crystal structure of a potassium ion transporter, TrkH. *Nature* 471(7338):336–40

17. Cao Y, Jin X, Levin EJ, Huang H, Zong Y, et al. 2011. Crystal structure of a phosphorylation-coupled saccharide transporter. *Nature* 473(7345):50–54

18. Chang Y, Bruni R, Kloss B, Assur Z, Kloppmann E, et al. 2014. Structural basis for a pH-sensitive calcium leak across membranes. *Science* 344(6188):1131–35

19. Chen Y-H, Hu L, Punta M, Bruni R, Hillerich B, et al. 2010. Homologue structure of the SLAC1 anion channel for closing stomata in leaves. *Nature* 467(7319):1074–80

20. Chen Y-J, Pornillos O, Lieu S, Ma C, Chen AP, Chang G. 2007. X-ray structure of EmrE supports dual topology model. *PNAS* 104(48):18999–19004

21. Choi S, Jeon J, Yang J-S, Kim S. 2008. Common occurrence of internal repeat symmetry in membrane proteins. *Proteins* 71(1):68–80

22. Crisman TJ, Qu S, Kanner BI, Forrest LR. 2009. Inward-facing conformation of glutamate transporters as revealed by their inverted-topology structural repeats. *PNAS* 106(49):20752–7

23. Dang S, Sun L, Huang Y, Lu F, Liu Y, et al. 2010. Structure of a fucose transporter in an outward-open conformation. *Nature* 467(7316):734–38

24. Davies KM, Anselmi C, Wittig I, Faraldo-Gómez JD, Kühlbrandt W. 2012. Structure of the yeast F_1F_O-ATP synthase dimer and its role in shaping the mitochondrial cristae. *PNAS* 109:13602–7

8. The first structure of a face-to-back inverted-topology repeat.

12. Insightful overview of membrane protein insertion and folding, particularly important for dual-topology proteins.

25. Dawson RJP, Locher KP. 2006. Structure of a bacterial multidrug ABC transporter. *Nature* 443(7108):180–85

26. De Feo CJ, Aller SG, Siluvai GS, Blackburn NJ, Unger VM. 2009. Three-dimensional structure of the human copper transporter hCTR1. *PNAS* 106(11):4237–42

27. Deisenhofer J, Epp O, Miki K, Huber R, Michel H. 1985. Structure of the protein subunits in the photosynthetic reaction centre of *Rhodopseudomonas viridis* at 3 Å resolution. *Nature* 318(6047):618–24

28. Dong C, Beis K, Nesper J, Brunkan-LaMontagne AL, Clarke BR, et al. 2006. Wza the translocon for *E. coli* capsular polysaccharides defines a new class of membrane protein. *Nature* 444(7116):226–29

29. Doyle DA, Morais Cabral J, Pfuetzner RA, Kuo A, Gulbis JM, et al. 1998. The structure of the potassium channel: molecular basis of K$^+$ conduction and selectivity. *Science* 280(5360):69–77

30. Du D, Wang Z, James NR, Voss JE, Klimont E, et al. 2014. Structure of the AcrAB–TolC multidrug efflux pump. *Nature* 509(7501):512–15

31. Dutzler R, Campbell EB, Cadene M, Chait BT, MacKinnon R. 2002. X-ray structure of a ClC chloride channel at 3.0 Å reveals the molecular basis of anion selectivity. *Nature* 415(6869):287–94

32. Efremov RG, Sazanov LA. 2011. Structure of the membrane domain of respiratory complex I. *Nature* 476(7361):414–20

33. Eicher T, Seeger MA, Anselmi C, Zhou W, Brandstätter L, et al. 2014. Coupling of remote alternating-access transport mechanisms for protons and substrates in the multidrug efflux pump AcrB. *eLIFE* 3:e03145

34. Eichmann C, Tzitzilonis C, Bordignon E, Maslennikov I, Choe S, et al. 2014. Solution NMR structure and functional analysis of the integral membrane protein YgaP from *Escherichia coli*. *J. Biol. Chem.* 289(34):23482–503

35. Erez E, Fass D, Bibi E. 2009. How intramembrane proteases bury hydrolytic reactions in the membrane. *Nature* 459(7245):371–78

36. Fang Y, Jayaram H, Shane T, Kolmakova-Partensky L, Wu F, et al. 2009. Structure of a prokaryotic virtual proton pump at 3.2 Å resolution. *Nature* 460(7258):1040–43

37. Fairman JW, Noinaj N, Buchanan SK. 2011. The structural biology of β-barrel membrane proteins: a summary of recent reports. *Curr. Opin. Struct. Biol.* 21(4):523–31

38. Feng L, Yan H, Wu Z, Yan N, Wang Z, et al. 2007. Structure of a site-2 protease family intramembrane metalloprotease. *Science* 318(5856):1608–12

39. Ferre S, Casado V, Devi LA, Filizola M, Jockers R, et al. 2014. G protein–coupled receptor oligomerization revisited: functional and pharmacological perspectives. *Pharmacol. Rev.* 66(2):413–34

40. Ferguson AD, McKeever BM, Xu S, Wisniewski D, Miller DK, et al. 2007. Crystal structure of inhibitor-bound human 5-lipoxygenase-activating protein. *Science* 317(5837):510–12

41. Fleishman SJ, Harrington SE, Enosh A, Halperin D, Tate CG, Ben-Tal N. 2006. Quasi-symmetry in the cryo-EM structure of EmrE provides the key to modeling its transmembrane domain. *J. Mol. Biol.* 364(1):54–67

42. Forrest LR. 2013. Structural biology. (Pseudo-)symmetrical transport. *Science* 339(6118):399–401

43. Forrest LR, Krämer R, Ziegler C. 2011. The structural basis of secondary active transport mechanisms. *Biochim. Biophys. Acta* 1807(2):167–88

44. Forrest LR, Rudnick G. 2009. The rocking bundle: a mechanism for ion-coupled solute flux by symmetrical transporters. *Physiology* 24:377–86

45. Forrest LR, Zhang Y-W, Jacobs MT, Gesmonde J, Xie L, et al. 2008. Mechanism for alternating access in neurotransmitter transporters. *PNAS* 105(30):10338–43

46. Furuse M, Sasaki H, Fujimoto K, Tsukita S. 1998. A single gene product, claudin-1 or -2, reconstitutes tight junction strands and recruits occludin in fibroblasts. *J. Cell Biol.* 143(2):391–401

47. George AM, Jones PM. 2012. Perspectives on the structure–function of ABC transporters: the Switch and Constant Contact Models. *Prog. Biophys. Mol. Biol.* 109(3):95–107

48. Gonen T, Cheng Y, Sliz P, Hiroaki Y, Fujiyoshi Y, et al. 2005. Lipid–protein interactions in double-layered two-dimensional AQP0 crystals. *Nature* 438(7068):633–38

49. Gonen T, Sliz P, Kistler J, Cheng Y, Walz T. 2004. Aquaporin-0 membrane junctions reveal the structure of a closed water pore. *Nature* 429(6988):193–97

31. The only known structure of a membrane protein containing inverted-topology repeats.

41. Structural modeling using electron microscopy data for antiparallel EmrE; the authors propose an asymmetry-exchange mechanism.

45. Authors propose asymmetry exchange for pseudosymmetric repeats in LeuT and demonstrate accessibility of proposed pathway.

50. **Goodsell DS, Olson AJ. 2000. Structural symmetry and protein function.** *Annu. Rev. Biophys. Biomol. Struct.* 29:105–53

51. Gordeliy VI, Labahn J, Moukhametzianov R, Efremov R, Granzin J, et al. 2002. Molecular basis of transmembrane signalling by sensory rhodopsin II-transducer complex. *Nature* 419(6906):484–87

52. Gross DJ. 1996. The role of symmetry in fundamental physics. *PNAS* 93(25):14256–59

53. Hattori M, Tanaka Y, Fukai S, Ishitani R, Nureki O. 2007. Crystal structure of the MgtE Mg^{2+} transporter. *Nature* 448(7157):1072–75

54. He X, Szewczyk P, Karyakin A, Evin M, Hong W-X, et al. 2010. Structure of a cation-bound multidrug and toxic compound extrusion transporter. *Nature* 467(7318):991–94

55. Hennerdal A, Falk J, Lindahl E, Elofsson A. 2010. Internal duplications in α-helical membrane protein topologies are common but the nonduplicated forms are rare. *Protein Sci.* 19(12):2305–18

56. Hilf RJC, Dutzler R. 2008. X-ray structure of a prokaryotic pentameric ligand-gated ion channel. *Nature* 452(7185):375–79

57. Hino T, Matsumoto Y, Nagano S, Sugimoto H, Fukumori Y, et al. 2010. Structural basis of biological N_2O generation by bacterial nitric oxide reductase. *Science* 330(6011):1666–70

58. Hirai T, Heymann JAW, Shi D, Sarker R, Maloney PC, Subramaniam S. 2002. Three-dimensional structure of a bacterial oxalate transporter. *Nat. Struct. Biol.* 9(8):597–600

59. Hohl M, Briand C, Grütter MG, Seeger MA. 2012. Crystal structure of a heterodimeric ABC transporter in its inward-facing conformation. *Nat. Struct. Mol. Biol.* 19(4):395–402

60. Hollenstein K, Frei DC, Locher KP. 2007. Structure of an ABC transporter in complex with its binding protein. *Nature* 446(7132):213–16

61. Hong M, DeGrado WF. 2012. Structural basis for proton conduction and inhibition by the influenza M2 protein. *Protein Sci.* 21(11):1620–33

62. Huang H, Levin EJ, Liu S, Bai Y, Lockless SW, Zhou M. 2014. Structure of a membrane-embedded prenyltransferase homologous to UBIAD1. *PLOS Biol.* 12(7):e1001911

63. Inaba K, Murakami S, Suzuki M, Nakagawa A, Yamashita E, et al. 2006. Crystal structure of the DsbB-DsbA complex reveals a mechanism of disulfide bond generation. *Cell* 127(4):789–801

64. Iwata S, Ostermeier C, Ludwig B, Michel H. 1995. Structure at 2.8 Å resolution of cytochrome *c* oxidase from *Paracoccus denitrificans*. *Nature* 376(6542):660–69

65. Jaehme M, Guskov A, Slotboom DG. 2014. Crystal structure of the vitamin B_3 transporter PnuC, a full-length SWEET homolog. *Nat. Struct. Mol. Biol.* 21:1013–15

66. Jaehme M, Guskov A, Slotboom DG. 2015. The twisted relation between Pnu and SWEET transporters. *Trends Biochem. Sci.* 40(4):183–88

67. Jardetzky O. 1966. Simple allosteric model for membrane pumps. *Nature* 211(5052):969–70

68. Jasti J, Furukawa H, Gonzales EB, Gouaux E. 2007. Structure of acid-sensing ion channel 1 at 1.9 Å resolution and low pH. *Nature* 449(7160):316–23

69. Johnson ZL, Cheong C-G, Lee S-Y. 2012. Crystal structure of a concentrative nucleoside transporter from *Vibrio cholerae* at 2.4 Å. *Nature* 483(7390):489–83

70. Jones CP, Ferré-D'Amaré AR. 2015. RNA quaternary structure and global symmetry. *Trends Biochem. Sci.* 40(4):211–20

71. Junge W, Lill H, Engelbrecht S. 1997. ATP synthase: an electrochemical transducer with rotatory mechanics. *Trends Biochem. Sci.* 22(11):420–23

72. Kaila VRI, Wikström M, Hummer G. 2014. Electrostatics, hydration, and proton transfer dynamics in the membrane domain of respiratory complex I. *PNAS* 111(19):6988–93

73. Karakas E, Furukawa H. 2014. Crystal structure of a heterotetrameric NMDA receptor ion channel. *Science* 344(6187):992–97

74. Kawate T, Michel JC, Birdsong WT, Gouaux E. 2009. Crystal structure of the ATP-gated $P2X_4$ ion channel in the closed state. *Nature* 460(7255):592–98

75. Kellosalo J, Kajander T, Kogan K, Pokharel K, Goldman A. 2012. The structure and catalytic cycle of a sodium-pumping pyrophosphatase. *Science* 337(6093):473–76

76. Khademi S, O'Connell J III, Remis J, Robles-Colmenares Y, Miercke LJW, Stroud RM. 2004. Mechanism of ammonia transport by Amt/MEP/Rh: structure of AmtB at 1.35 Å. *Science* 305(5690):1587–94

50. An excellent and comprehensive discussion of symmetry in all classes of proteins.

77. Khafizov K, Staritzbichler R, Stamm M, Forrest LR. 2010. A study of the evolution of inverted-topology repeats from LeuT-fold transporters using AlignMe. *Biochemistry* 49(50):10702–13

78. Kim C, Basner J, Lee B. 2010. Detecting internally symmetric protein structures. *BMC Bioinform.* 11(1):303

79. Kniazeff J, Prézeau L, Rondard P, Pin J-P, Goudet C. 2011. Dimers and beyond: the functional puzzles of class C GPCRs. *Pharmacol. Ther.* 130(1):9–25

80. Krishnamurthy H, Gouaux E. 2012. X-ray structures of LeuT in substrate-free outward-open and apo inward-open states. *Nature* 481(7382):469–74

81. Krogh A, Larsson B, von Heijne G, Sonnhammer ELL. 2001. Predicting transmembrane protein topology with a hidden Markov model: application to complete genomes. *J. Mol. Biol.* 305(3):567–80

82. Kumazaki K, Chiba S, Takemoto M, Furukawa A, Nishiyama K, et al. 2014. Structural basis of Sec-independent membrane protein insertion by YidC. *Nature* 509(7501):516–20

83. Lemmon MA, Schlessinger J. 2010. Cell signaling by receptor tyrosine kinases. *Cell* 141(7):1117–34

84. Levin EJ, Quick M, Zhou M. 2009. Crystal structure of a bacterial homologue of the kidney urea transporter. *Nature* 462(7274):757–61

85. Levy ED, Pereira-Leal JB, Chothia C, Teichmann SA. 2006. 3D complex: a structural classification of protein complexes. *PLOS Comput. Biol.* 2(11):e155

86. Li D, Lyons JA, Pye VE, Vogeley L, Aragão D, et al. 2013. Crystal structure of the integral membrane diacylglycerol kinase. *Nature* 497(7450):521–24

87. Li E, Hristova K. 2010. Receptor tyrosine kinase transmembrane domains: function, dimer structure and dimerization energetics. *Cell Adhes. Migr.* 4(2):249–54

88. Li X, Dang S, Yan C, Gong X, Wang J, Shi Y. 2014. Structure of a presenilin family intramembrane aspartate protease. *Nature* 493(7430):56–61

89. Liao J, Li H, Zeng W, Sauer DB, Belmares R, Jiang Y. 2012. Structural insight into the ion-exchange mechanism of the sodium/calcium exchanger. *Science* 335(6069):686–90

90. Lieberman RL, Rosenzweig AC. 2005. Crystal structure of a membrane-bound metalloenzyme that catalyses the biological oxidation of methane. *Nature* 434(7030):177–82

91. Lin S-M, Tsai J-Y, Hsiao C-D, Huang Y-T, Chiu C-L, et al. 2012. Crystal structure of a membrane-embedded H$^+$-translocating pyrophosphatase. *Nature* 484(7394):399–403

92. Liu Y, Eisenberg D. 2002. 3D domain swapping: as domains continue to swap. *Protein Sci.* 11(6):1285–99

93. Liu Y, Gerstein M, Engelman DM. 2004. Transmembrane protein domains rarely use covalent domain recombination as an evolutionary mechanism. *PNAS* 101(10):3495–97

94. Liu Z, Yan H, Wang K, Kuang T, Zhang J, et al. 2004. Crystal structure of spinach major light-harvesting complex at 2.72 Å resolution. *Nature* 428(6980):287–92

95. Lizak C, Gerber S, Numao S, Aebi M, Locher KP. 2011. X-ray structure of a bacterial oligosaccharyltransferase. *Nature* 474(7351):350–55

96. Locher KP. 2009. Structure and mechanism of ATP-binding cassette transporters. *Phil. Trans. R. Soc. B.* 364(1514):239–45

97. Locher KP, Lee AT, Rees DC. 2002. The *E. coli* BtuCD structure: a framework for ABC transporter architecture and mechanism. *Science* 296(5570):1091–98

98. Lu F, Li S, Jiang Y, Jiang J, Fan H, et al. 2011. Structure and mechanism of the uracil transporter UraA. *Nature* 472(7342):243–46

99. Lu M, Fu D. 2007. Structure of the zinc transporter YiiP. *Science* 317(5845):1746–48

100. Lukatsky DB, Zeldovich KB, Shakhnovich EI. 2006. Statistically enhanced self-attraction of random patterns. *Phys. Rev. Lett.* 97(17):178101

101. Lunin VV, Dobrovetsky E, Khutoreskaya G, Zhang R, Joachimiak A, et al. 2006. Crystal structure of the CorA Mg^{2+} transporter. *Nature* 440(7085):833–37

102. Lynch M, Conery JS. 2000. The evolutionary fate and consequences of duplicate genes. *Science* 290(5494):1151–55

103. MacKenzie KR, Prestegard JH, Engelman DM. 1997. A transmembrane helix dimer: structure and implications. *Science* 276(5309):131–33

104. Maeda S, Nakagawa S, Suga M, Yamashita E, Oshima A, et al. 2009. Structure of the connexin 26 gap junction channel at 3.5 Å resolution. *Nature* 458:597–602

105. Mager S, Min C, Henry DJ, Chavkin C, Hoffman BJ, et al. 1994. Conducting states of a mammalian serotonin transporter. *Neuron* 12(4):845–59

106. Mancusso R, Gregorio GG, Liu Q, Wang DN. 2012. Structure and mechanism of a bacterial sodium-dependent dicarboxylate transporter. *Nature* 491(7425):622–26

107. Marsden RL, Lee D, Maibaum M, Yeats C, Orengo CA. 2006. Comprehensive genome analysis of 203 genomes provides structural genomics with new insights into protein family space. *Nucleic Acids Res.* 34(3):1066–80

108. Marsh JA, Teichmann SA. 2015. Structure, dynamics, assembly, and evolution of protein complexes. *Annu. Rev. Biochem.* In press. doi: 10.1146/annurev-biochem-060614-034142

109. Matthies D, Zhou W, Klyszejko AL, Anselmi C, Yildiz Ö, et al. 2014. High-resolution structure and mechanism of an F/V-hybrid rotor ring in a Na^+-coupled ATP synthase. *Nat. Commun.* 5:5286

110. Meier T, Faraldo-Gómez JD, Börsch M. 2011. ATP synthase: a paradigmatic molecular machine. In *Molecular Machines in Biology*, ed. J Frank, pp. 208–38. New York: Cambridge Univ. Press

111. Meyerson JR, Kumar J, Chittori S, Rao P, Pierson J, et al. 2014. Structural mechanism of glutamate receptor activation and desensitization. *Nature* 514(7522):328–34

112. McLuskey K, Roszak AW, Zhu Y, Isaacs NW. 2009. Crystal structures of all-alpha type membrane proteins. *Eur. Biophys. J.* 39(5):723–55

113. Mineev KS, Bocharov EV, Pustovalova YE, Bocharova OV, Chupin VV, Arseniev AS. 2010. Spatial structure of the transmembrane domain heterodimer of ErbB1 and ErbB2 receptor tyrosine kinases. *J. Mol. Biol.* 400(2):231–43

114. Mitsuoka K, Murata K, Walz T, Hirai T, Agre P, et al. 1999. The structure of aquaporin-1 at 4.5-Å resolution reveals short α-helices in the center of the monomer. *J. Struct. Biol.* 128(1):34–43

115. Miyazawa A, Fujiyoshi Y, Unwin N. 2003. Structure and gating mechanism of the acetylcholine receptor pore. *Nature* 423(6943):949–55

116. Mondal S, Johnston JM, Wang H, Khelashvili G, Filizola M, Weinstein H. 2013. Membrane driven spatial organization of GPCRs. *Sci. Rep.* 3:2909

117. Morgan JLW, Strumillo J, Zimmer J. 2013. Crystallographic snapshot of cellulose synthesis and membrane translocation. *Nature* 493(7431):181–86

118. Morrison EA, DeKoster GT, Dutta S, Vafabakhsh R, Clarkson MW, et al. 2012. Antiparallel EmrE exports drugs by exchanging between asymmetric structures. *Nature* 481(7379):45–50

119. Mueller M, Grauschopf U, Maier T, Glockshuber R, Ban N. 2009. The structure of a cytolytic α-helical toxin pore reveals its assembly mechanism. *Nature* 459(7247):726–30

120. Murakami S, Nakashima R, Yamashita E, Matsumoto T, Yamaguchi A. 2006. Crystal structures of a multidrug transporter reveal a functionally rotating mechanism. *Nature* 443(7108):173–79

121. **Myers-Turnbull D, Bliven SE, Rose PW, Aziz ZK, Youkharibache P, et al. 2014. Systematic detection of internal symmetry in proteins using CE-Symm. *J. Mol. Biol.* 426(11):2255–68**

122. Niwa S, Yu L-J, Takeda K, Hirano Y, Kawakami T, et al. 2014. Structure of the LH1–RC complex from *Thermochromatium tepidum* at 3.0 Å. *Nature* 508(7495):228–32

123. Nugent T, Jones DT. 2009. Transmembrane protein topology prediction using support vector machines. *BMC Bioinform.* 10(1):159

124. Oldham ML, Khare D, Quiocho FA, Davidson AL, Chen J. 2007. Crystal structure of a catalytic intermediate of the maltose transporter. *Nature* 450(7169):515–21

125. Pao GM, Wu L-F, Johnson KD, Höfte H, Chrispeels MJ, et al. 1991. Evolution of the MIP family of integral membrane transport proteins. *Mol. Microbiol.* 5(1):33–37

126. Pao SS, Paulsen IT, Saier MH. 1998. Major facilitator superfamily. *Microbiol. Mol. Biol. Rev.* 62(1):1–34

127. Payandeh J, Scheuer T, Zheng N, Catterall, WA. 2011. The crystal structure of a voltage-gated sodium channel. *Nature* 475(7356):353–58

128. Pebay-Peyroula E, Dahout-Gonzalez C, Kahn R, Trézéguet V, Lauquin GJ-M, Brandolin G. 2003. Structure of mitochondrial ADP/ATP carrier in complex with carboxyatractyloside. *Nature* 426(6962):39–44

129. Pogoryelov D, Krah A, Langer JD, Yildiz Ö, Faraldo-Gómez JD, Meier T. 2010. Microscopic rotary mechanism of ion translocation in the F(o) complex of ATP synthases. *Nat. Chem. Biol.* 6(12):891–99

121. Recent assessment of internal pseudosymmetry indicating that membrane proteins are enriched in symmetric structural repeats.

130. Popoff MR. 2014. Clostridial pore-forming toxins: powerful virulence factors. *Anaerobe* 30:220–38

131. Radestock S, Forrest LR. 2011. The alternating-access mechanism of MFS transporters arises from inverted-topology repeats. *J. Mol. Biol.* 407(5):698–715

132. Rees DC, Johnson E, Lewinson O. 2009. ABC transporters: the power to change. *Nat. Rev. Mol. Cell Biol.* 10(3):218–27

133. Ressl S, van Scheltinga ACT, Vonrhein C, Ott V, Ziegler C. 2009. Molecular basis of transport and regulation in the Na^+/betaine symporter BetP. *Nature* 457(7234):47–52

134. Reyes N, Ginter C, Boudker O. 2009. Transport mechanism of a bacterial homologue of glutamate transporters. *Nature* 462(7275):880–85

135. Rollauer SE, Tarry MJ, Graham JE, Jääskeläinen M, Jäger F, et al. 2012. Structure of the TatC core of the twin-arginine protein transport system. *Nature* 492(7428):210–14

136. Rosenmund C, Stern-Bach Y, Stevens CF. 1998. The tetrameric structure of a glutamate receptor channel. *Science* 280(5369):1596–99

137. Saraste M, Walker JE. 1982. Internal sequence repeats and the path of polypeptide in mitochondrial ADP/ATP translocase. *FEBS Lett.* 144(2):250–54

138. Schiller D, Rübenhagen R, Krämer R, Morbach S. 2004. The C-terminal domain of the betaine carrier BetP of *Corynebacterium glutamicum* is directly involved in sensing K^+ as an osmotic stimulus. *Biochemistry* 43(19):5583–91

139. Schirmer T, Keller TA, Wang YF, Rosenbusch JP. 1995. Structural basis for sugar translocation through maltoporin channels at 3.1 Å resolution. *Science* 267(5197):512–14

140. Schushan M, Rimon A, Haliloglu T, Forrest LR, Padan E, Ben-Tal N. 2012. A model-structure of a periplasm-facing state of the NhaA antiporter suggests the molecular underpinnings of pH-induced conformational changes. *J. Biol. Chem.* 287(22):18249–61

141. Shepard LA, Shatursky O, Johnson AE, Tweten RK. 2000. The mechanism of pore assembly for a cholesterol-dependent cytolysin: Formation of a large prepore complex precedes the insertion of the transmembrane β-hairpins. *Biochemistry* 39(33):10284–93

142. Sobolevsky AI, Rosconi MP, Gouaux E. 2009. X-ray structure, symmetry and mechanism of an AMPA-subtype glutamate receptor. *Nature* 462(7274):745–56

143. Song C, Weichbrodt C, Salnikov ES, Dynowski M, Forsberg BO, et al. 2013. Crystal structure and functional mechanism of a human antimicrobial membrane channel. *PNAS* 110(12):4586–91

144. Song L, Hobaugh MR, Shustak C, Cheley S, Bayley H, Gouaux JE. 1996. Structure of staphylococcal α-hemolysin, a heptameric transmembrane pore. *Science* 274(5294):1859–65

145. Stockbridge RB, Robertson JL, Kolmakova-Partensky L, Miller C. 2013. A family of fluoride-specific ion channels with dual-topology architecture. *eLIFE* 2:e01084

146. Strugatsky D, McNulty R, Munson K, Chen C-K, Soltis SM, et al. 2013. Structure of the proton-gated urea channel from the gastric pathogen *Helicobacter pylori*. *Nature* 493(7431):255–58

147. Sun F, Huo X, Zhai Y, Wang A, Xu J, et al. 2005. Crystal structure of mitochondrial respiratory membrane protein complex II. *Cell* 121(7):1043–57

148. Suzuki H, Nishizawa T, Tani K, Yamazaki Y, Tamura A, et al. 2014. Crystal structure of a claudin provides insight into the architecture of tight junctions. *Science* 344:304–7

149. Toyoshima C, Nakasako M, Nomura H, Ogawa H. 2000. Crystal structure of the calcium pump of sarcoplasmic reticulum at 2.6 Å resolution. *Nature* 405:647–55

150. Tsai C-J, Khafizov K, Hakulinen J, Forrest LR, Krämer R, et al. 2011. Structural asymmetry in a trimeric Na^+/betaine symporter, BetP, from *Corynebacterium glutamicum*. *J. Mol. Biol.* 407:368–81

151. Tusnády GE, Dosztányi Z, Simon I. 2005. PDB_TM: selection and membrane localization of trans-membrane proteins in the protein data bank. *Nucleic Acids Res.* 33:D275–78

152. Ubarretxena-Belandia I, Baldwin JM, Schuldiner S, Tate CG. 2003. Three-dimensional structure of the bacterial multidrug transporter EmrE shows it is an asymmetric homodimer. *EMBO J.* 22:6175–81

153. van den Berg B, Clemons WM, Collinson I, Modis Y, Hartmann E, et al. 2004. X-ray structure of a protein-conducting channel. *Nature* 427(6969):36–44

154. Venkatakrishnan AJ, Levy ED, Teichmann SA. 2010. Homomeric protein complexes: evolution and assembly. *Biochem. Soc. Trans.* 38:879–82

155. Vinothkumar KR, Henderson R. 2010. Structures of membrane proteins. *Q. Rev. Biophys.* 43(1):65–158

156. Waight AB, Pedersen BP, Schlessinger A, Bonomi M, Chau BH, et al. 2013. Structural basis for alternating access of a eukaryotic calcium/proton exchanger. *Nature* 499(7456):107–10

157. Wang Y, Huang Y, Wang J, Cheng C, Huang W, et al. 2009. Structure of the formate transporter FocA reveals a pentameric aquaporin-like channel. *Nature* 462(7272):467–72

158. Wang Y, Zhang Y, Ha Y. 2006. Crystal structure of a rhomboid family intramembrane protease. *Nature* 444:179–80

159. Watt IN, Montgomery MG, Runswick MJ, Leslie AG, Walker JE. 2010. Bioenergetic cost of making an adenosine triphosphate molecule in animal mitochondria. *PNAS* 107(39):16823–27

160. White SH. 2006. Rhomboid intramembrane protease structures galore! *Nat. Struct. Mol. Biol.* 13:1049–51

161. White SH, ed. 2015. *Membrane Proteins of Known 3D Structure*, updated Feb. 19. Stephen White Lab. UC Irvine, Irvine, CA. **http://blanco.biomol.uci.edu/mpstruc/**

162. Wu Z, Yan N, Feng L, Oberstein A, Yan H, et al. 2006. Structural analysis of a rhomboid family intramembrane protease reveals a gating mechanism for substrate entry. *Nat. Struct. Mol. Biol.* 13:1084–91

163. Xia D, Yu C-A, Kim H, Xia J-Z, Kachurin AM, et al. 1997. Crystal structure of the cytochrome bc_1 complex from bovine heart mitochondria. *Science* 277(5322):60–66

164. Xu Y, Tao Y, Cheung LS, Fan C, Chen LQ, et al. 2014. Structures of bacterial homologues of SWEET transporters in two distinct conformations. *Nature* 515(7527):448–52

165. Yamashita A, Singh SK, Kawate T, Jin Y, Gouaux E. 2005. Crystal structure of a bacterial homologue of Na^+/Cl^--dependent neurotransmitter transporters. *Nature* 437:215–23

166. Yang T, Liu Q, Kloss B, Bruni R, Kalathur RC, et al. 2014. Structure and selectivity in bestrophin ion channels. *Science* 346(6207):355–59

167. Yernool D, Boudker O, Jin Y, Gouaux E. 2004. Structure of a glutamate transporter homologue from *Pyrococcus horikoshii*. *Nature* 431(7010):811–18

168. Zagotta WN, Hoshi T, Aldrich RW. 1994. Shaker potassium channel gating. III: evaluation of kinetic models for activation. *J. Gen. Physiol.* 103(2):321–62

155. A systematic and thorough review of structures and functions of membrane proteins up to 2009.

The Synaptic Vesicle Release Machinery

Josep Rizo* and Junjie Xu

Departments of Biophysics, Biochemistry, and Pharmacology, University of Texas Southwestern Medical Center, Dallas, Texas 75390; email: jose@arnie.swmed.edu

Annu. Rev. Biophys. 2015. 44:339–67

The *Annual Review of Biophysics* is online at biophys.annualreviews.org

This article's doi:
10.1146/annurev-biophys-060414-034057

*Corresponding author.

Keywords

membrane fusion, SNAREs, Synaptotagmin, Complexin, Munc18, Munc13

Abstract

Extensive research has yielded crucial insights into the mechanism of neurotransmitter release, and working models for the functions of key proteins involved in release. The SNAREs Syntaxin-1, Synaptobrevin, and SNAP-25 play a central role in membrane fusion, forming SNARE complexes that bridge the vesicle and plasma membranes and that are disassembled by NSF–SNAPs. Exocytosis likely starts with Syntaxin-1 folded into a self-inhibited closed conformation that binds to Munc18-1. Munc13s open Syntaxin-1, orchestrating SNARE complex assembly in an NSF–SNAP–resistant manner together with Munc18-1. In the resulting primed state, with partially assembled SNARE complexes, fusion is inhibited by Synaptotagmin-1 and Complexins, which also perform active functions in release. Upon influx of Ca^{2+}, Synaptotagmin-1 activates fast release, likely by relieving the inhibition caused by Complexins and cooperating with the SNAREs in bringing the membranes together. Although alternative models exist and fundamental questions remain unanswered, a definitive description of the basic release mechanism may be available soon.

Contents

INTRODUCTION

Brain function depends critically on the ability of neurons to communicate with one another via neurotransmitters that are released from presynaptic terminals by Ca^{2+}-triggered synaptic vesicle exocytosis. Release requires the docking of synaptic vesicles at specialized areas of the plasma membrane called active zones, a priming reaction or reactions that leave the vesicles ready for release, and fast fusion of the vesicle and plasma membranes upon Ca^{2+} influx caused by an action potential (147). Each step can be modulated, allowing an exquisite regulation of the release probability in varied presynaptic plasticity processes that underlie diverse forms of information processing in the brain (117). Correspondingly, the sophisticated machinery that controls neurotransmitter release is formed by core proteins that have homologs in most types of intracellular membrane traffic and that underlie a conserved mechanism of membrane fusion, as well as by many specialized components that confer the tight regulation of release. Even the core proteins have unique properties that likely emerged in response to the regulatory requirements of synaptic vesicle fusion. Thus, elucidating the mechanism of membrane fusion is of the utmost interest to cell biology in general, but from the point of view of neuroscience it is also fundamental to understanding how the ancient process of membrane fusion, which evolved billions of years ago in eukaryotic cells, became adapted to provide the primary means by which neurons send signals to one another, ensuring that synaptic vesicle fusion does not occur prematurely but rather at the right place, at the right time, and with the right probability.

Research on neurotransmitter release is in an exciting moment because the wealth of information that has been accumulated for more than two decades has provided crucial insights into the mechanism of release and, although fundamental questions remain unanswered, a clear understanding of this mechanism may be reached in the next few years. Factors that govern release and belong to the core protein families involved in intracellular membrane traffic include N-ethylmaleimide sensitive factor (NSF), soluble NSF adaptor proteins (SNAPs), the SNAP receptors (SNAREs), Munc18-1, Munc13s, and Rab3s. Among them, the SNAREs clearly play a central role in membrane fusion, and other proteins are often considered to be SNARE regulators. However, Munc18-1 and Munc13s are essential for release and may play direct parts in fusion rather than merely have regulatory functions. Moreover, even proteins with specialized roles in release, such as Synaptotagmin-1 (Syt1) and Complexins, may also act directly in fusion. Defining how all of these proteins function together is necessary to gain a true understanding of the mechanism of release. Because of the vast amount of literature, it is impractical to provide a comprehensive account of this field, and several reviews covering different aspects of synaptic exocytosis have appeared recently (13, 70, 96, 126, 143, 148). In this review we discuss primarily the mechanistic aspects, summarizing the most central concepts and emphasizing recent key advances. We first describe the core of the release machinery—focusing mainly on the SNAREs, Munc18-1, and Munc13s—and later we discuss the mechanisms of action of Syt1 and Complexins as crucial regulators of release. We also mention some key results from studies of other membrane traffic systems that have helped in understanding the mechanism of membrane fusion.

MECHANICS OF MEMBRANE FUSION

Theoretical and experimental studies indicate that physiological membrane fusion requires the approach of the two membranes, the bending of the bilayers to destabilize them, the formation of a stalk intermediate where the proximal bilayer leaflets have fused, the merger of the distal leaflets to yield a fusion pore, and expansion of the fusion pore (25) (**Figure 1a**). This view has been strongly supported by recent X-ray diffraction data showing that the stalk intermediate, the central element in this model, can be formed by a variety of lipid systems (2). Thus, although alternative mechanisms of fusion cannot be ruled out, the stalk model constitutes a guide to envisioning how proteins might induce membrane fusion. The theoretical work has suggested that the total energy required for fusion ranges from 40 to 100 $k_B T$ (29, 91). This estimate is uncertain and depends on the lipid composition, but these calculations give an idea of how much energy needs to be provided by proteins to induce fusion. It is also important to consider how energy is applied to the membranes. For instance, a combination of forces that bend the membranes (e.g., **Figure 1a**, *red arrows*) is expected to induce fusion more efficiently than the application of only pulling forces, which would bring membranes into close proximity but would not fuse them (**Figure 1b**).

THE CORE RELEASE MACHINERY

The SNARE Complex

SNARE proteins are critical for most types of intracellular membrane traffic and are character-ized by ~65-residue sequences called SNARE motifs that have high propensities to form coiled coils (71, 96, 148). The neuronal SNAREs that mediate synaptic exocytosis are the synaptic vesi-cle protein Synaptobrevin/VAMP (vesicle-associated membrane protein) and the plasma mem-brane proteins SNAP-25 (synaptosomal-associated protein of 25 kDa; no relation to SNAPs) and Syntaxin-1. SNAP-25 has two SNARE motifs, and Synaptobrevin and Syntaxin-1 each contain one SNARE motif that precedes a C-terminal transmembrane (TM) region (**Figure 1c**). The three SNAREs assemble into a tight SNARE complex (142) that consists of a four-helix bundle formed by the SNARE motifs (115, 150) (**Figure 1d**) and that brings the membranes into close proximity; this realization arose from electron microscopy images of the SNARE complex and led to the fundamental notion that the energy released upon SNARE complex assembly is used to in-duce membrane fusion (60). These and other results led to the textbook model whereby a vesicle SNARE (v-SNARE; Synaptobrevin here) binds to the target membrane SNAREs (t-SNAREs; Syntaxin-1 and SNAP-25 here) to draw the membranes together and induce fusion (**Figure 2a**).

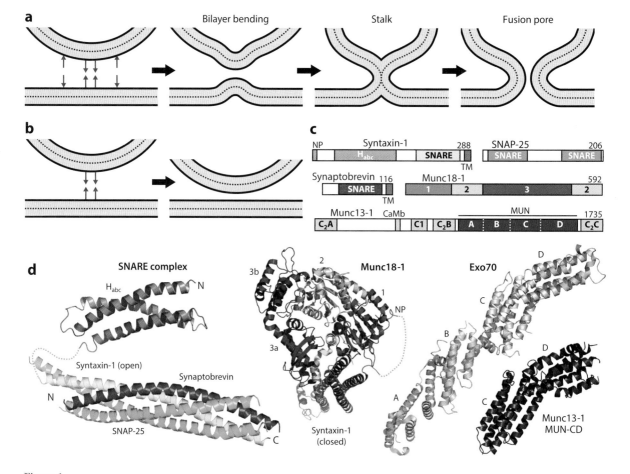

Figure 1

The stalk model and the core of the neurotransmitter release machinery. (*a*) Diagrams depicting key steps of the stalk model of membrane fusion. After the two membranes are brought into close proximity, forces that bend the membranes destabilize the bilayers, leading to a stalk intermediate where the proximal leaflets have merged; the fusion pore is formed after fusion of the distal leaflets. The last step, expansion of the fusion pore, is not shown. The red arrows illustrate the concept that a combination of pulling and pushing forces could be critical to bending the membranes. (*b*) Diagram illustrating the notion that pulling forces alone could bring the membranes closer but would not bend them. (*c*) Domain diagrams of Synaptobrevin, Syntaxin-1, SNAP-25, Munc18-1, and Munc13-1. Numbers on the right above the diagrams indicate the length of the proteins. The four subdomains of the Munc13-1 MUN domain are labeled A–D. The same color coding is used throughout the figures except that Munc18-1 has a single color in **Figure 2c**. (*d*) Three-dimensional structures of the Syntaxin-1 H_{abc} domain, the SNARE complex, the Munc18-1–closed Syntaxin-1 complex, the Munc13-1 MUN-CD region, and Exo70; the latter shows the structural similarity between the MUN domain and a tethering factor (Protein Data Bank accession codes 1BR0, 1SFC, 3C98, 2B1E, and 3SWH, respectively). N and C indicate the N terminus of the Syntaxin-1 H_{abc} domain and the C terminus of the SNARE complex. Dotted curves represent the sequences linking the N-peptide with the H_{abc} domain and the H_{abc} domain with the SNARE complex, which were not present or observed in the structures. Abbreviations: CaMb, calmodulin-binding region; NP, Syntaxin-1 N-peptide; SNARE, SNAP receptor (SNARE) motif.

After fusion, the SNARE complex is disassembled by NSF, an ATPase from the AAA protein family, with the assistance of SNAPs (142) to recycle the SNAREs for another round of fusion (7, 101). NSF and SNAPs are also universal components of intracellular fusion machineries, which are believed to function using the same basic mechanism outlined here. Note, however, that in some systems the two SNARE motifs of SNAP-25 are in two distinct SNAREs, and that the concept of v- and t-SNAREs becomes confusing for homotypic fusion, where both membranes contain the four SNARE motifs. The finding that the SNARE complex contains a conserved polar layer formed by an arginine from Synaptobrevin and three glutamines from Syntaxin-1 and SNAP-25 led to a more general classification into R- and Q_a-, Q_b-, and Q_c-SNAREs, depending on their predicted location in the SNARE complex (45).

Do the SNAREs Constitute a Minimal Membrane Fusion Machinery?

Reconstitution experiments that revealed lipid mixing between liposomes containing Synaptobrevin and liposomes containing Syntaxin-1–SNAP-25 led to the proposal that the SNAREs constitute a minimal membrane fusion machinery (162). However, observation of content mixing is essential to demonstrate membrane fusion, as extensive lipid mixing can occur with very little content mixing (20, 186). A multitude of subsequent reconstitution studies have yielded a wide variety of results (reviewed in 126). For instance, some data indicated that a single SNARE complex is sufficient for lipid and content mixing (156), but another study revealed that Synaptobrevin liposomes can dock to Syntaxin-1–SNAP-25 liposomes for 30 minutes without lipid mixing (80), suggesting that the formation of SNARE complexes is not sufficient for fusion. A recent study using nanodiscs, which are model disk-like bilayers surrounded by a scaffolding protein, indicated that one neuronal SNARE complex is sufficient to fuse two nanodiscs (136); however, no fusion was observed in another study even when a neuronal SNARE complex bridging the two nanodiscs was fully assembled (137). The variability in results from different studies likely arises from multiple factors, such as the method of reconstitution and the protein-to-lipid ratios in the liposome assays (126), or the size of the nanodiscs in the latter experiments. Hence, all of these results need to be interpreted with caution and, ultimately, their relevance needs to be evaluated through correlations with physiological data.

When evaluating the minimal model from an energetic point of view, it is important to keep in mind the potential contributions from different sections of the SNARE complex. Thus, most models assume that for both Syntaxin-1 and Synaptobrevin, the SNARE motif, the TM region, and the linker domain (LD) between them can form a continuous helix (**Figure 2a**, state ❸). Such helix continuity has been observed in the crystal structure of a SNARE complex including the TM regions (145), which revealed interactions between the LD and TM regions of Syntaxin-1 and Synaptobrevin in addition to those involving the SNARE motifs (**Figure 2b**). Moreover, different regions of the SNARE motifs within the four-helix bundle can make distinct energetic contributions, as the SNARE complex can assemble in steps, zippering from the N terminus to the membrane-proximal C terminus (**Figure 2a**). Indeed, there is evidence for formation of partially assembled SNARE complexes in neurons (144); and intermediates where only the N-terminal half (NTH) of the SNARE complex is assembled have been detected in vitro (24, 79, 87, 137, 153). In these partially assembled states, the C-terminal half (CTH) of the Synaptobrevin SNARE motif is believed to be unstructured, while the CTHs of the Syntaxin-1 and SNAP-25 SNARE motifs may become unstructured too (153) or may remain helical, forming a three-helix bundle (79) (**Figure 2a**, state ❶).

Stepwise SNARE complex assembly has been clearly observed with magnetic (105) and optical tweezers (51). The use of optical tweezers yielded estimates for the free energies associated with the assembly of different sections of the SNARE complex: 35 $k_B T$ for the NTH, 28 $k_B T$ for the CTH, and 8 $k_B T$ for the LDs. The overall free energy of SNARE-complex formation was estimated to be 68 $k_B T$ (51), which is extremely high for protein–protein interactions. Although estimates obtained with atomic-force microscopy or the surface-force apparatus are lower, in the 30 $k_B T$ range (88, 90), these data indicate that the free energy of assembly of a few SNARE complexes (or perhaps only one) could be sufficient to induce membrane fusion. In this context, functional studies in synapses and chromaffin cells have suggested that two or three SNARE complexes are required for Ca^{2+}-triggered exocytosis (107, 140); these findings correlate with an analysis of the dependence of the synaptic vesicle release probability on Syntaxin-1 levels, which yielded a Hill coefficient of 2.5 (4). Note, however, that in vivo other proteins, such as Syt1, likely provide additional energy for membrane fusion (see subsection titled Synaptotagmin-1).

A fundamental question is how the energy of SNARE-complex formation is applied to the membranes. Assembly of the two halves (NTH and CTH) of the SNARE four-helix bundle consumes most of this energy and is expected to produce pulling forces that bring the two membranes

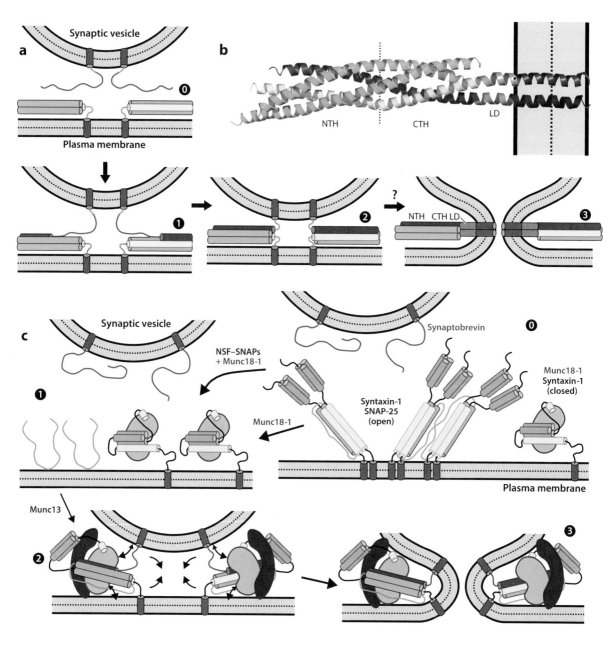

within approximately 4 nm of each other (**Figure 2a**, state ❷). However, without other forces (e.g., **Figure 1a**, *left*), it is unclear how the pulling forces can bend the membranes to induce fusion (**Figure 1b**). Indeed, the observation of stable docking between membranes containing Synaptobrevin and membranes containing Syntaxin-1–SNAP-25 (80, 137) provides strong evidence that states with partially or fully assembled SNARE complexes (e.g., **Figure 2a**, states ❶ and ❷) can be formed without inducing fusion. As mentioned above, the Syntaxin-1 and Synaptobrevin LDs can form α-helices that could bind to each other and bring the membranes closer, but the energy associated with such binding (8 k_BT) is likely to be insufficient to induce fusion. Moreover, flexibility in the LDs, which has been observed by electron paramagnetic resonance (77), would help to uncouple the energy of SNARE-complex formation from the membranes. Interactions of the highly basic LDs with the membranes could also help to bring the membranes into closer proximity, but it is uncertain to what extent. Note, also, that the insertion of flexible sequences in the LD of Synaptobrevin strongly impairs Ca^{2+}-triggered exocytosis, but spontaneous neurotransmitter release and slower forms of exocytosis in chromaffin cells are much less affected (33, 75), indicating that the nature of the LDs may be crucial for the coupling of Ca^{2+} sensing to fast fusion but not for membrane fusion per se. These findings also argue against the functional importance of the formation of continuous helices involving the SNARE motifs, LDs, and TM regions. Importantly, neurotransmitter release can still occur when the TM regions of Syntaxin-1 and Synaptobrevin are replaced by lipid anchors (184), in correlation with results from reconstitution experiments with yeast vacuolar SNAREs (169). Thus, the SNARE TM regions are not essential for membrane fusion.

In summary, SNARE complexes are critical for membrane fusion and produce strong pulling forces to bring two membranes together, but it is not clear how these forces can induce membrane fusion in the absence of other proteins. Although SNARE complexes can induce fusion under some conditions (e.g., 156), it should be noted that images from cryo-electron microscopy of fusion reactions mediated by the SNAREs alone revealed the formation of wide bilayer–bilayer interfaces that presumably proceed to fusion through extended hemifusion diaphragms (63). These results suggest that either the mechanism of physiological membrane fusion is considerably different from that predicted by the stalk model (**Figure 1a**) or that the SNAREs alone cannot induce fusion by a physiologically relevant mechanism.

←

Figure 2

Models of how the core neurotransmitter release machinery may induce membrane fusion. (*a*) Model of membrane fusion induced by the SNAREs alone. Only the SNARE motifs, linker domains (LDs), and the transmembrane (TM) regions are shown. NTH and CTH indicate the N- and C-terminal halves of the SNARE complex. The model postulates that the SNARE complex assembles from the N to the C terminus in distinct stages that lead to membrane fusion, and predicts that, for both Syntaxin-1 and Synaptobrevin, the SNARE motifs, LDs, and TM regions form continuous helices. The distinct states are numbered ❶ to ❸, but note that there could be additional intermediates in the assembly pathway (88). (*b*) Crystal structure of the neuronal SNARE complex including the LDs and TM regions in different shades of gray (Protein Data Bank accession code 3IPD). (*c*) Model of synaptic vesicle fusion mediated by the SNAREs, Munc18-1, and the Munc13-1 MUN domain, with the assistance of NSF–SNAPs. The model predicts that the starting point for exocytosis is not the Syntaxin-1–SNAP-25 complex, which is highly heterogeneous, but the Munc18-1-closed Syntaxin-1 complex, which may be formed directly or after disassembly of the Syntaxin-1–SNAP-25 complex by NSF–SNAPs (states ❶ and ❶). The Munc13-1 MUN domain opens Syntaxin-1 and, together with Munc18-1, orchestrates assembly of the SNARE complex; this initially leads to a primed state with partially assembled SNARE complexes (state ❷) that is ready for membrane fusion (state ❸) upon Ca^{2+} influx, but it may also be able to fuse spontaneously. For simplicity, other key components of the release machinery such as Synaptotagmin-1 and Complexins are not shown. The black arrows in state ❷ illustrate the notion that a combination of forces helps to bend the membranes to induce fusion (as in **Figure 1a**) and results when the SNAREs pull the membranes together at the same time that Munc18-1 or the Munc13-1 MUN domain, or both, hinder the approach of the membranes because of the steric hindrance caused by their bulk. Abbreviations: NSF, N-ethylmaleimide sensitive factor; SNAP, soluble NSF adaptor proteins; SNAREs, SNAP receptors.

An additional concern regarding the minimal model is that the t-SNARE complex formed by Syntaxin-1 and SNAP-25, which presumably serves as the acceptor for Synaptobrevin, is commonly assumed to consist of a three-helix bundle (**Figure 2a**, state ❶), but SNARE motifs have a strong tendency to form four-helix bundles rather than three-helix bundles. Indeed, Syntaxin-1 and SNAP-25 normally form complexes with a 2:1 stoichiometry where the missing Synaptobrevin SNARE motif is replaced by a second Syntaxin-1 SNARE motif (167) (**Figure 2c**, state ❶), and can form other four-helix bundles due to the promiscuity of these SNARE motifs, thus yielding diverse kinetic traps that hinder the formation of SNARE complexes (126). In addition, Syntaxin-1–SNAP-25 complexes have a tendency to aggregate (94), likely because the two SNAP-25 SNARE motifs can be incorporated into separate four-helix bundles (**Figure 2c**, state ❶). These findings raise the question as to whether these heterogeneous Syntaxin-1 SNARE complexes constitute an appropriate starting point for an exquisitely regulated biological process, such as neurotransmitter release (94). Moreover, an aspect that is often overlooked is that NSF and SNAPs disrupt not only ternary SNARE complexes but also Syntaxin-1 SNARE complexes (94, 161). Correspondingly, in reconstitution experiments, lipid mixing caused by the SNAREs alone is inhibited by NSF–SNAPs (161), but these factors were not included in most reconstitution studies with the neuronal SNAREs.

SNARE Regulatory Sequences

Below, we discuss how some of the issues raised above are clarified by the interplay between the SNAREs and other key components of the release machinery. This interplay is mediated in part by sequences that precede the SNARE motif in some SNAREs, particularly those of the Syntaxin family. Syntaxin-1 contains a short sequence at the N terminus, which is called N-peptide, and an N-terminal three-helix bundle known as the H_{abc} domain (47) that in isolated Syntaxin-1 binds back to the SNARE motif, forming a closed conformation and thus inhibiting SNARE-complex formation (41) (**Figures 1c,d** and **2c**, states ❶ and ❶). The roles of the N-peptide and the closed conformation are intimately related to Munc18-1 and will be discussed in more detail below, but here we note that the N-peptide plays a crucial role in release (185), and the closed conformation provides a key point for the regulation of release as shown by the finding that a so-called LE mutation—which helps open Syntaxin-1 and facilitates SNARE-complex formation (41)—increases the release probability and the speed of release (1, 52). These findings led to the proposal that the number of SNARE complexes in primed vesicles dictates the efficiency and kinetics of evoked release. Ongoing research is unraveling to what extent the properties of Syntaxin-1 are specialized for the particular regulatory requirements of neurotransmitter release or are conserved in other membrane traffic systems. For instance, the N-peptide is shared by some SNAREs of the Syntaxin family but not by others (42, 43, 177); and although the H_{abc} domain is present in all Syntaxins, the closed conformation is adopted by some Syntaxins but not others (43, 44, 49, 108, 177).

Munc18-1

Munc18-1 is a member of the Sec1/Munc18 (SM) protein family that, like the SNAREs, has critical roles in most types of intracellular membrane traffic (19, 148, 152). The importance of SM protein function is well illustrated by the total abrogation of neurotransmitter release observed in Munc18-1 knockout mice (160), and multiple studies have suggested that Munc18-1 is involved in synaptic vesicle docking, priming, and fusion (19, 148, 152). These diverse functions are mediated, at least in part, by multiple types of interactions between Munc18-1 and the neuronal SNAREs, particularly Syntaxin-1. Thus, Munc18-1 binds tightly to Syntaxin-1 (62) folded in the closed conformation (41, 106), to the Syntaxin-1 N-terminal region through both the N-peptide and the H_{abc} domain (34, 39, 76, 135), and to the four-helix bundle of the SNARE complex (39, 135, 171).

The crystal structure of Munc18-1 bound to closed Syntaxin-1 showed that Munc18-1 has an arch-shaped architecture with three domains (**Figure 1c**) that form a cavity where closed Syntaxin-1 binds (106) (**Figures 1d** and **2c**, states ❶ and ❷). Domain 3 of Munc18-1 can be divided in two subdomains (3a and 3b). Domain 1 and subdomain 3a form the cavity of Munc18-1, which makes extensive contacts with the H_{abc} domain and the SNARE motif of Syntaxin-1; in addition, the Syntaxin-1 N-peptide binds to domain 1 of Munc18-1 on the side opposite to the cavity (**Figures 1d** and **2c**, states ❶ and ❷). The site of Munc18-1 that binds to the SNARE four-helix bundle is unclear because there is evidence that binding is mediated by the Munc18-1 cavity (134, 171) or by subdomain 3a at the other side of the cavity (66, 111), while the Munc18-1 homolog from the yeast plasma membrane, Sec1p, appears to bind to the SNARE complex via a groove between domains 1 and 2 (61).

Ongoing research is unraveling the distinct roles of the different types of interactions between Munc18-1 and the SNAREs, which can be inhibitory, activating, or perhaps fundamental for membrane fusion. Correspondingly, reconstitutions studies with the neuronal SNAREs and Munc18-1 have revealed that Munc18-1 has both stimulatory and inhibitory activities (129, 135). These results did not explain the essential nature of Munc18-1 in release because the stimulatory effects of Munc18-1 were rather modest compared with those caused by Syt1 without Munc18-1 (26, 174). Nevertheless, reconstitution experiments with Munc18-1 and the SNAREs have provided key insights and established clear correlations with functional data (see below), suggesting that these experiments recapitulate some key aspects of Munc18-1 function.

After it was found that Sec1p does not bind to Sso1p, its cognate Syntaxin-1 (18), the tight interaction between Munc18-1 and closed Syntaxin-1 appeared to be a specialized feature of neuronal exocytosis, and other types of SM protein–Syntaxin-1 interactions have been identified (12, 43, 44, 177). However, this picture is changing as additional complexes between SM proteins and closed Syntaxins are being identified (15, 49). In the synapse, the binary interaction of Munc18-1 with Syntaxin-1 stabilizes the closed conformation (23) and hinders formation of the SNARE complex (14, 93), thus gating the entry of Syntaxin-1 into SNARE complexes (52) and likely providing a key point for the regulation of neurotransmitter release during the presynaptic plasticity processes involving Munc13s, which have a central role in opening Syntaxin-1 (93) (see subsection titled Munc13s). However, the binary interaction between Syntaxin-1 and Munc18-1 also plays a positive part by stabilizing both proteins (52, 160). Moreover, the Syntaxin-1–Munc18-1 complex is probably crucial for vesicle docking (50, 52), and its physiological importance is further supported by clear correlations between Syntaxin-1 binding and Munc18-1 function (58).

The functional importance of the interaction between the Syntaxin-1 N-peptide and Munc18-1 has been supported by diverse physiological data (e.g., 72, 76, 185, but see 59, 103). The binding of the isolated N-peptide to Munc18-1 is weak, but it can cooperate with interactions of Munc18-1 with closed Syntaxin-1 in the binary complex or with the H_{abc} domain in open Syntaxin-1 (14, 39, 66, 76). Based on reconstitution data (116, 134), the interaction between the Syntaxin-1 N-peptide and Munc18-1 likely cooperates also with Munc18-1 binding to the SNARE four-helix bundle. These results suggest that the binding of the Syntaxin-1 N-peptide to Munc18-1 plays a critical role in keeping Munc18-1 associated with the SNARE machinery throughout the steps that lead to release, thus linking the binary interaction between Munc18-1 and closed Syntaxin-1 with other downstream interactions between Munc18-1 and the SNAREs that have key active roles in release and involve open Syntaxin-1 within the SNARE complex (**Figure 2c**). Interestingly, removing the N-peptide abrogates the function of Syntaxin-1 in spontaneous release, in vesicle priming, and in evoked release, whereas removal of the H_{abc} domain strongly affects spontaneous release and vesicle priming but not evoked release (185). These results correlate with reconstitution assays whereby the N-peptide but not the H_{abc} domain has been found to be crucial for the stimulation of SNARE-dependent lipid mixing caused by Munc18-1 (134). Moreover, these assays also have shown that the N-peptide still supports the Munc18-1 stimulation of lipid mixing when removed from Syntaxin-1 and attached to SNAP-25, in correlation with the finding that Syntaxin-1 function in *Caenorhabditis elegans* can be rescued by two separate N- and C-terminal fragments (116). These observations suggest that, although the N-peptide is present in some Syntaxins but not in others (42, 43, 177), other SNAREs may contain the N-peptide in some systems and, hence, the N-peptide may be a universal feature in intracellular membrane traffic.

Altogether, the available data lead to a model whereby the binary Syntaxin-1–Munc18-1 complex is critical for the docking and priming of synaptic vesicles; however, after Syntaxin-1 is opened and the SNARE complex forms, the H_{abc} domain is dispensable, and Munc18-1 binding to the Syntaxin-1 N-peptide and to the SNARE four-helix bundle are critical for membrane fusion (**Figure 2c**, states ❷ and ❸). In this model, the lack of a strong perturbation in evoked release upon deletion of the H_{abc} domain (185) may result from compensation between decreased priming and increased release probability. Note, also, that the interaction of Munc18-1 with the four-helix bundle might be directly involved in fusion (39, 124) (see the subsection titled Synergy Among Munc18-1, Munc13s, NSF, and SNAPs) but, unfortunately, the binding mode has not been characterized in detail. Reconstitution data have suggested that the stimulatory effect of Munc18-1 on lipid mixing requires interactions with Synaptobrevin within the four-helix bundle (135), but this notion has not been tested in vivo. Clearly, a key event in the model of **Figure 2c** is the opening of Syntaxin-1, which is mediated by Munc13s.

Munc13s

Munc13s and invertebrate Unc13 are large proteins (approximately 200 kDa) from presynaptic active zones that also have a crucial function in neurotransmitter release, as shown by the total abrogation of release observed in *unc13* nulls and in mice bearing a double knockout of Munc13-1 and -2 (5, 121, 158). These proteins contain a large module called the MUN domain that is responsible for this crucial function (8), and several additional domains (illustrated in **Figure 1c** for Munc13-1). These domains control diverse forms of regulation of release during presynaptic plasticity, likely by modulating the key function of the MUN domain; additionally, the C_2A domain provides a link to Rab3-interacting molecules (RIMs), large Rab3 effectors that have multiple roles in additional forms of presynaptic plasticity (reviewed recently in 126). Here we focus on the central function of the MUN domain in release.

The finding that Syntaxin-1 bearing the LE mutation that helps open its closed conformation (41) can partially rescue release in *C. elegans unc13* nulls (122) suggested that Munc13s play a role in opening Syntaxin-1. The Munc13-1 MUN domain has been found to interact with membrane-anchored SNARE complexes and Syntaxin-1–SNAP-25 heterodimers (56, 164), and also to bind weakly to Munc18-1 and to the Syntaxin-1 SNARE motif (93). Moreover, the MUN domain has been shown to dramatically accelerate the transition from the closed Syntaxin-1–Munc18-1 complex to the SNARE complex, likely by extracting the Syntaxin-1 SNARE motif from the closed conformation and providing a template for SNARE complex assembly (93). These results leave little doubt that Munc13s mediate the opening of Syntaxin-1, thus orchestrating SNARE-complex formation together with Munc18-1 (**Figure 2c**); the results also illustrate how weak interactions can play key parts in promoting conformational transitions in proteins. However, it is worth noting that the partial rescue of release in *unc13* nulls by the Syntaxin-1 LE mutant in *C. elegans* (122) may have been favored by strong overexpression, and that the LE mutant does not appear to rescue release in Munc13-1/2 double knockout mice (52). These findings suggest that the MUN domain has another critical function in neurotransmitter release in addition to opening Syntaxin-1.

Sequence analyses have shown that the MUN domain has a low but significant homology to subunits from diverse tethering complexes—such as the exocyst, the Golgi-associated retrograde protein (GARP), the conserved oligomeric Golgi (COG), and Dsl1p (113)—which function in distinct membrane compartments (reviewed in 180). The structures of these subunits are elongated and include four subdomains consisting of helix bundles (A to D), as illustrated for the exocyst subunit Exo70 (38) in **Figure 1d**. As predicted, the structure of a Munc13-1 fragment spanning the C and D subdomains (MUN-CD) revealed a striking similarity with the tethering complex subunits (89) (**Figure 1d**). These findings suggest that tethering factors, Munc13s, and the related neuronal proteins called calcium-dependent activator protein for secretion (CAPS) form a family that has been named complex associated with tethering containing helical rods (CATCHR) (180) and that has a general function (or functions) in membrane traffic (126). This general function may be to provide a physical link between vesicles and target membranes (sometimes called docking and sometimes called tethering), a function that is well established for tethering complexes (180), and is supported for Munc13s/Unc13 by electron microscopy analyses of synapses (57, 139, 163) as well as by reconstitution data (11). Moreover, as described above for Munc13-1, tethering factors bind to SNARE proteins and can accelerate SNARE complex assembly (e.g., 119), which may thus be an additional general function of this protein family. Note, however, that the docking or tethering function can be performed by other unrelated protein complexes—such as the transport protein particle (TRAPP) or homotypic fusion and vacuole protein sorting (HOPS) complexes—in some membrane traffic systems (165, 180), and that tethering factors can interact with the SNAREs that are not from the Syntaxin family (e.g., 119, 141). These findings suggest that the docking and assembly of the SNARE complex may be mediated by similar but not identical mechanisms in different systems. Finally, we also note that the Munc13-1 MUN domain bound to the SNARE complex (56, 93) may also perform a direct role in membrane fusion (**Figure 2c**; see also next subsection).

Synergy Among Munc18-1, Munc13s, NSF, and SNAPs

The data summarized above suggest a model whereby the starting point for the pathway that leads to neurotransmitter release is the closed Syntaxin-1–Munc18-1 complex and where assembly of the SNARE complex is orchestrated by Munc13s in cooperation with Munc18-1, leading to a primed state with partially assembled SNARE complexes (**Figure 2c**, state ❷). This model has been supported by reconstitution experiments showing that liposomes containing the Syntaxin-1–Munc18-1 complex fuse with Synaptobrevin liposomes in a manner that strictly requires Munc13-1 and SNAP-25, and that is enhanced by Syt1 (94). This mechanism contrasts with the textbook model whereby the Syntaxin-1–SNAP-25 t-SNARE complex constitutes the starting point that binds to the v-SNARE Synaptobrevin (**Figure 2a**), which underlies the fact that most reconstitution studies of synaptic vesicle fusion used liposomes containing Syntaxin-1–SNAP-25. In principle, the observation of fusion between these liposomes and Synaptobrevin liposomes supports the textbook model, but these studies could not account for the essential roles of Munc18-1 and Munc13s for neurotransmitter release, and did not include NSF–SNAPs, which disassemble Syntaxin-1–SNAP-25 complexes (94, 161). Importantly, the highly efficient fusion between Syntaxin-1–SNAP-25 proteoliposomes and Synaptobrevin liposomes stimulated by Syt1 is abolished by the addition of NSF and α-SNAP, and in the presence of these factors, Munc18-1 and Munc13-1 are then required for fusion (94). These results are reminiscent of seminal findings that were made earlier in reconstitutions of yeast vacuolar fusion; these findings showed that the HOPS tethering complex, which includes the SM protein Vps33p, plays a critical role in membrane fusion by enabling assembly of *trans*-SNARE complexes in the presence of Sec17p and Sec18p (168), the yeast homologs of SNAPs and NSF. This convergence of data from two distant forms of membrane traffic provides compelling evidence that a fundamental function of SM proteins and tethering factors, including Munc13s, is the orchestration of SNARE complex assembly in a cellular environment that has abundant NSF–SNAPs and, hence, favors SNARE complex disassembly.

The notion that the closed Syntaxin-1–Munc18-1 complex, rather than the Syntaxin-1–SNAP-25 complex, constitutes the starting point for synaptic vesicle exocytosis is supported by the observation that Munc18-1 displaces SNAP-25 from its complex with Syntaxin-1 (94). However, high-resolution imaging has revealed colocalization of Munc18-1 with both Syntaxin-1 and SNAP-25 at the neuronal plasma membrane, and the colocalization of Munc18-1 and SNAP-25 required the Syntaxin-1 N-peptide (114). A plausible interpretation of these data that also integrates what is known about interactions between Munc18-1 and the SNAREs is that, because Syntaxin-1 and SNAP-25 are abundant, it is practically unavoidable to have a dynamic equilibrium at the plasma membrane between closed Syntaxin-1–Munc18-1 complexes and Syntaxin-1–SNAP-25 complexes, and some of the Syntaxin-1-SNAP-25 complexes may have Munc18-1 bound to the Syntaxin-1 N-terminal region. As discussed above, the Syntaxin-1–SNAP-25 complexes are heterogeneous, have a tendency to aggregate, and normally have a 2:1 stoichiometry, thus providing a poor starting point for synaptic vesicle fusion. The model in **Figure 2c** proposes that at the sites of exocytosis, the productive pathway that leads to fusion selects for Syntaxin-1–Munc18-1 complexes, perhaps through the docking mechanisms discussed below. The Syntaxin-1–SNAP-25 complexes existing in the plasma membrane could serve as reservoirs that can be converted to the Syntaxin-1–Munc18-1 complex by direct replacement of SNAP-25 with Munc18-1 or with the assistance of NSF and SNAPs, which facilitate such replacement on membranes, likely by disassembling oligomeric Syntaxin-1–SNAP-25 complexes (94). In this context, Sec17p and Sec18p have been found to act in a synergistic way with HOPS to promote SNARE activity in reconstitutions of yeast vacuolar fusion (104), suggesting that formation of off-pathway complexes by the t-SNAREs can constitute a strong hindrance that is eliminated through their disassembly by Sec17p and Sec18p.

A key question is whether SM proteins and associated tethering factors normally remain bound to *trans*-SNARE complexes after orchestrating their assembly. In studies of yeast vacuolar fusion, HOPS prevented disassembly of *trans*-SNARE complexes by Sec17p and Sec18p (168), which must involve an association of HOPS with the SNAREs. Conversely, neuronal trans-SNARE complexes have been reported to be resistant to NSF–SNAPs (161), raising the possibility that Munc18-1 and Munc13s are dispensable after SNARE complex assembly has been orchestrated. However, the following findings suggest that Munc18-1 or the Munc13 MUN domain, or both, remains associated with *trans*-SNARE complexes after their assembly: (*a*) the ability of Munc18-1 and Munc13-1 to suppress the inhibition caused by NSF–α-SNAP in the reconstitutions of synaptic vesicle fusion (94), (*b*) the crucial importance of Munc18-1, Munc13s, and the Syntaxin-1 N-peptide for release (5, 121, 158, 160, 185), and (*c*) the observation that interactions of Munc18-1 and the Munc13-1 MUN domain with the SNARE four-helix bundle are enhanced by the membrane-anchoring of the SNAREs (56, 135) (**Figure 2c**, state ❷). In addition to potentially protecting from interference by NSF–SNAPs, the bound Munc18-1 or Munc13 MUN domain (or both) may play a direct role in membrane fusion because of its bulk, which would hinder the approach of the two membranes. Thus, the combination of these hindrance forces with the pulling forces caused by the SNAREs could help bend the membranes to initiate fusion (39, 124) (**Figure 2c**), a mechanism that might be much more efficient than that supported by the SNAREs alone and might be less sensitive to flexibility in the SNARE LDs. Structural studies of SNARE complexes bound to SM proteins or tethering factors, or both, ideally between two membranes, will be critical to assess the validity of this model or other models that have been proposed to explain the essential nature of SM proteins for membrane fusion (e.g., 19, 148).

The mechanism of docking is another central aspect that remains to be elucidated. At the synapse, this mechanism likely involves Rab3s, which are members of the Rab family of small GTPases that normally have docking roles in intracellular membrane traffic (16). Although it is unclear how the function of Rab3 relates to the SNARE–Munc18-1–Munc13 machinery, the report of a direct interaction between Rab3A and Munc18-1 (55) suggests a mechanism whereby the binding of Rab3A to the closed Syntaxin-1–Munc18-1 complex mediates docking and selects for this complex to favor the mechanism (**Figure 2c**) over pathways involving Syntaxin-1–SNAP-25 complexes. This proposal is consistent with the importance of Munc18-1 and Syntaxin-1 for docking (52) and is supported by imaging data showing that the formation of new docking sites for secretory granules coincides with the accumulation of Rab3A, Syntaxin-1, and Munc18-1 at these sites, and that Munc13 and SNAP-25 are recruited later (50). Note, however, that Munc13s have also been implicated in docking (57, 139, 163) and that an alternative docking mechanism that could also select for closed Syntaxin-1–Munc18-1 complexes involves the binding of Rab3s to effectors in the plasma membrane, such as RIMs, which in turn can recruit Munc13s by forming a tripartite Rab3—RIM—Munc13 complex (40). In addition, Munc13s may also mediate docking via SNARE and membrane interactions independently of Rab3s (11), and some data have suggested that docking is mediated by a SNAP-25–Syt1 interaction (32), although this mechanism cannot underlie docking in general since Syt1 is not conserved in other membrane traffic systems.

In summary, the model in **Figure 2c** integrates much of the experimental evidence, but it would be premature to rule out the textbook model (**Figure 2a**) or other alternative models because multiple fundamental questions remain unanswered. Moreover, elucidating the mechanism of release requires an understanding of how the functions of the core machinery are coupled to those of crucial proteins with specialized roles, such as Syt1 and Complexins.

REGULATION OF NEUROTRANSMITTER RELEASE BY SYNAPTOTAGMIN-1 AND COMPLEXINS

Synaptotagmin-1

Ca^{2+}-triggered neurotransmitter release exhibits two components: a fast, synchronous phase that occurs within less than 0.5 ms after Ca^{2+} influx, and a slower, asynchronous phase (147). It is now well established that members of the Synaptotagmin family act as Ca^{2+} sensors in synaptic exocytosis and other types of Ca^{2+}-evoked secretion, and that there is an interplay between the two phases of release, as well as with spontaneous release. Thus, Syt1 (and the closely related Syt2 and Syt9) acts as the Ca^{2+} sensor for synchronous release, and both asynchronous and spontaneous release are enhanced in its absence, whereas Syt7 acts as the Ca^{2+} sensor for asynchronous release (reviewed in 147). Hence, some of the interplay may arise because of competition between distinct Ca^{2+} sensors for common targets (e.g., SNARE complexes) at release sites. Here we focus on the mechanism of action of Syt1 in fast release, and only mention some results from other forms of release that have provided important insights into this mechanism. Recent reviews have covered diverse aspects of Syt1 function (13, 21, 70, 125, 147).

Syt1 is a synaptic vesicle protein, but this localization does not appear to be essential for its function because Syt1 targeted to the plasma membrane can support fast release (68). Two C_2

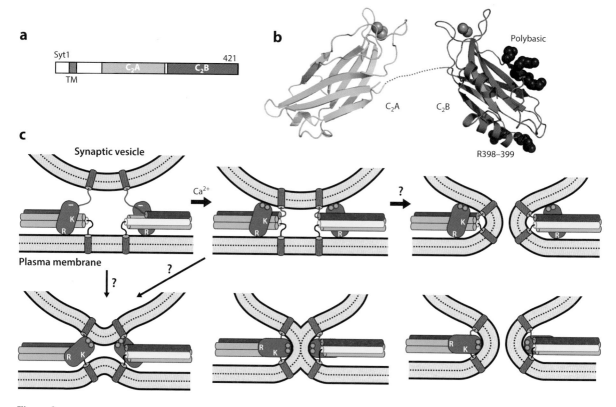

Figure 3

Structure and function of Synaptotagmin-1 (Syt1). (*a*) Domain diagram of Syt1. (*b*) Structures of the Ca^{2+}-bound Syt1 C$_2$A and C$_2$B domains (Protein Data Bank accession codes 1BYN and 1K5W, respectively). Ca^{2+} ions are shown as orange spheres. The side chains of the polybasic region and the arginines R398 and R399 at the bottom of C$_2$B are shown as dark blue spheres. (*c*) Models of Syt1 function. In the top subpanels, the Syt1 C$_2$B domain is shown initially bound to partially assembled SNARE complexes through the polybasic region (indicated by K) and to the plasma membrane through R398 and R399 (indicated by R), while repelling the vesicle membrane because of the negative charge of the Ca^{2+}-binding loops (indicated by minus sign). Upon Ca^{2+} influx, Ca^{2+} binding to the C$_2$B domain induces binding to the vesicle membrane, thus helping to bring the membranes together and inducing membrane fusion in cooperation with C-terminal zippering of the SNARE complex. In the bottom subpanels, the C$_2$B Ca^{2+}-binding loops help to bend the membranes and to form the stalk intermediate by binding to the membranes and stabilizing structures with high positive curvature. R398 and R399 are proposed to bind to the SNARE complex to hold the C$_2$B domain in the correct position to allow it to exert its action on the membranes. In both models, the C$_2$B Ca^{2+}-binding loops could also bind to the plasma membrane, but the interplay with Complexins is more readily explained if these loops bind to the vesicle membrane. For simplicity, the C$_2$A domain is not shown, but it is expected that it cooperates with the C$_2$B domain in phospholipid binding and, perhaps, membrane bridging or membrane bending. Abbreviations: SNARE, SNAP receptor.

domains (the C$_2$A and C$_2$B domains) form most of the Syt1 cytoplasmic region (**Figure 3*a***). The C$_2$A and C$_2$B domains bind three and two Ca^{2+} ions, respectively, via five aspartate residues located in loops at the top of β-sandwich structures (46, 132, 149, 155) (**Figure 3*b***). These loops also mediate Ca^{2+}-dependent binding of the C$_2$ domains to negatively charged phospholipids through hydrophobic residues that insert into the acyl layer and interactions of the phospholipid head groups with basic residues and the bound Ca^{2+} ions (22, 46, 182), which induce an electrostatic switch in the C$_2$ domains (133). Mutations that increase or decrease the apparent Ca^{2+} affinity of Syt1 in Ca^{2+}-dependent phospholipid binding lead to parallel decreases in the Ca^{2+} dependence of neurotransmitter release (48, 120); these findings showed the functional importance of this activity and demonstrated the Ca^{2+}-sensing role of Syt1 in release. Such functional importance was also shown by the strong impairment in release caused by disrupting Ca^{2+} binding to the C_2B domain or even by replacing a single, hydrophobic residue in the C_2B domain top loops with glutamate (95, 110); at the same time these findings revealed the crucial nature of the C_2B domain for release. The effects of similar mutations in the C_2A domain are less drastic, but this domain does play an important role in release (86, 110, 138, 146). Interestingly, replacing one of the aspartate Ca^{2+} ligands from the C_2A domain with glutamate, which disrupts Ca^{2+} binding but does not neutralize the charge, impairs release more strongly than aspartate-to-asparagine mutations, showing the importance of neutralizing the aspartate residues for release (146). Note, also, that Ca^{2+} binding to the Syt7 C_2A domain is more important than Ca^{2+} binding to the C_2B domain for asynchronous release (6).

The functional importance of Syt1–membrane interactions and the discovery that Syt1 dramatically enhances the activity of the neuronal SNAREs in reconstitution experiments in a Ca^{2+}-dependent manner (26, 154) suggested that Syt1 cooperates with the SNAREs in inducing membrane fusion. Intriguingly, Syt1 clusters chromaffin granules and liposomes (31), and data from cryo-electron microscopy showed that a Syt1 fragment spanning its two C_2 domains (C_2AB) binds simultaneously to two membranes in a Ca^{2+}-dependent manner, bringing them into close proximity (approximately 4 nm) (3, 131). Both the C_2A and the C_2B domains contribute to this membrane-bridging activity, but the C_2B domain has a preponderant role due to the abundance of positive charges around its surface, which could explain its key importance for release. These findings led to a model whereby Syt1 cooperates with the SNAREs in membrane fusion by helping to bring the membranes together in a Ca^{2+}-dependent manner that underlies the dependence of neurotransmitter release on Ca^{2+} (3) (**Figure 3c**, top subpanels). In this model, repulsion between the membranes and the negatively charged Ca^{2+}-binding regions of the C_2 domains hinders fusion before Ca^{2+} influx, and simultaneous binding to the two membranes upon Ca^{2+} influx provides energy to induce fusion that adds to the energy arising from final SNARE complex zippering. In support of this model, mutation of two arginines (R398 and R399) that are located at the bottom of the C_2B domain, opposite to the Ca^{2+}-binding region (**Figure 3b**), and that are critical for the membrane-bridging activity of C_2AB strongly impairs the stimulatory effect of C_2AB in lipid-mixing assays in vitro as well as Syt1 function in neurons (174). Subsequent studies have provided abundant data supporting the notion that the membrane-bridging activity is key for the stimulatory effect of Syt1 in reconstitution experiments (e.g., 67, 112, 157). This activity may be performed by parallel or antiparallel orientations, or both, of the two C_2 domains (64, 131) and depends on a delicate balance between interactions in *cis* with the Synaptobrevin membrane and in *trans* with the Syntaxin-1–SNAP-25 membrane (84, 159).

An additional mechanism that could underlie a role for Syt1 in fusion is the induction of positive membrane curvature due to the insertion of the Ca^{2+}-binding loops into the membranes (98), which could facilitate membrane bending, stalk formation, or opening of the fusion pore, or a combination of these (**Figure 3c**, bottom subpanels). This model does not explain the crucial function of R398 and R399 at the bottom of the C_2B domain, and the data from negative-stain electron microscopy that supported the model by showing liposome tubulation induced by Syt1 C_2AB need to be interpreted with caution because the negative stain strongly perturbs membranes and practically no tubulation was observed by cryo-electron microscopy (3, 125, 131). Nevertheless, some correlations have been established between the effects of Syt1 mutations on the tubulation-inducing tendency and their effects on Syt1 function (68, 92, 98), and this is an attractive mechanism that may be compatible with the notion that Syt1 bridges membranes. Thus, after helping to bring the membranes together, the Syt1 C_2 domains may reorient to facilitate membrane bending and the subsequent steps leading to fusion (**Figure 3c**). A key to distinguishing between these and other proposed models of Syt1 function is to understand the role (or roles) of interactions between Syt1 and the SNAREs, which we discuss in the subsection titled Interplay Among Synaptotagmin-1, the SNAREs, and Complexins.

Complexins

Complexins are small, soluble proteins that bind tightly to the SNARE complex (102) and have both active and inhibitory roles in neurotransmitter release. The active roles are manifested by the marked decreases in evoked release observed upon knockout or knockdown of Complexins-1 and -2 (Cpx1 and Cpx2), the two major mammalian isoforms, or in *Complexin* nulls in invertebrates (65, 69, 99, 100, 118). There is also a decrease in vesicle priming upon knockout or knockdown of Cpx1 and Cpx2 (172, 178), although this effect is milder than the total abrogation of priming observed in the absence of Munc18-1 or Munc13s (158, 160). Because Cpx1 binding stabilizes the SNARE complex, it was proposed that there may be more than one priming step, and in the second step Complexins stabilize partially assembled SNARE complexes (24). The inhibitory role of Complexins emerged initially from functional, biophysical, and reconstitution studies that led to a model whereby Cpx1 inhibits release and Syt1 releases this inhibition (53, 127, 128, 151). Later, increases in spontaneous release that varied over a wide range were observed in the absence of Complexins in several systems (65, 69, 99, 100), but in Cpx1–3 triple knockout mice spontaneous release actually decreases (176). These different results likely arise because of a delicate balance between the active and inhibitory functions of Complexins (173). Diverse functional evidence showed that Complexins function together with Syt1 to trigger and synchronize the release of neurotransmitters, but they can also act independently of Syt1, likely in conjunction with other Ca^{2+} sensors (17, 35, 172, 178), and the dramatic increase in spontaneous release observed in *Complexin* nulls requires Syt1 (73).

Cpx1 is highly flexible in isolation, with some α-helical structure that is stabilized upon binding to the SNARE complex (109). Binding is mediated by a central helix that packs in an antiparallel orientation against the Synaptobrevin and Syntaxin-1 SNARE motifs, and is preceded by an accessory helix (**Figure 4a,b**). Each of these two domains, as well as the N- and C-terminal regions of Cpx1, has specific functions in release, although the underlying mechanisms are still being unraveled. The central helix is crucial for all Cpx1 functions (100, 175), likely because it stabilizes the SNARE complex and places the remaining Cpx1 sequences in the right positions to perform different functions. The accessory helix has an inhibitory role (100, 175) that we discuss in more detail below. The N-terminal region is critical for the active role of Complexins, which may arise because it helps to release the inhibition caused by the accessory helix and/or because it binds to the C terminus of the SNARE complex, perhaps providing additional stabilization energy to induce fusion (100, 172, 175). The C-terminal region contributes to both the active and inhibitory roles of Complexins (74) and binds phospholipids, an activity that has been attributed a positive function, based on reconstitution experiments (36, 130), and an inhibitory function, based on functional studies in *C. elegans* (166).

The inhibitory function of the Cpx1 accessory helix was proposed to arise from partial (175) or full (54) insertion of this helix into partially assembled SNARE complexes, thus preventing C-terminal zippering of the complexes (**Figure 4c**). Full insertion is highly unlikely because the accessory helix contains only one hydrophobic residue, but the model was supported by the finding that superclamp mutations, involving substitutions of charged residues with hydrophobic ones, enhance the inhibition of cell–cell fusion by Cpx1; it was also supported by a poorclamp mutation that reduced the inhibition caused by Cpx1 (54). The crystal structure

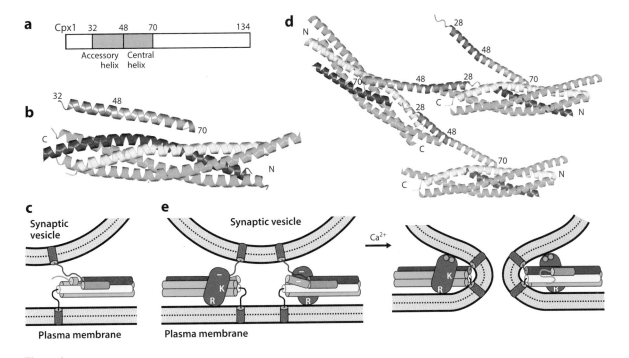

Figure 4

Structure and function of Complexins. (*a*) Domain structure of Complexin-1 (Cpx1). Numbers indicate the domain boundaries. (*b*) Structure of the Cpx1 (residues 26–83)–SNARE complex (Protein Data Bank accession code 1KIL). (*c*) Model of how part of the accessory helix of Cpx1 could insert into a partially assembled SNARE complex to hinder C-terminal zippering and thus inhibit membrane fusion. (*d*) Structure of the complex between Cpx1 (residues 26–83) and a SNARE complex with C-terminally truncated Synaptobrevin (Protein Data Bank accession code 3RK3). Three copies of the complex are shown to illustrate the zigzag array that underlies crystallization. In panels *b* and *d*, N and C indicate the N and C termini of the SNARE complex; residue numbers show the boundaries of the Cpx1 accessory and central helices. (*e*) Model whereby the negatively charged accessory helix of Cpx1 hinders membrane fusion through electrostatic and steric repulsion with the vesicle membrane. The Syt1 C_2B Ca^{2+}-binding loops could add to this repulsion before Ca^{2+} influx (*left*), but Ca^{2+}-triggered binding of the C_2B domain to the vesicle membrane forces melting of the Cpx1 accessory helix and brings the membranes together to induce fusion (as in **Figure 3c**). For simplicity, the N- and C-terminal regions of Cpx1 are not shown. Abbreviation: SNARE, SNAP receptor.

of a Synaptobrevin-truncated SNARE complex bound to a Cpx1 superclamp mutant containing three charge-to-hydrophobic substitutions revealed insertion of the accessory helix in *trans* to another SNARE complex, leading to a zigzag array (**Figure 4d**) that was proposed to help set the stage for fusion (79). However, this binding mode is very unlikely for wild-type Cpx1 because it would place three charged residues in hydrophobic environments; correspondingly, extensive NMR analyses have shown that the wild-type Cpx1 accessory helix does not insert into truncated SNARE complexes in solution and found no evidence for insertion in solution even for the triple superclamp mutant (153). Moreover, the triple superclamp mutation was found to have slightly stimulatory or no effects on release in mice, whereas the poorclamp mutation impaired release (153), findings that were in sharp contrast to the results from cell–cell fusion assays. Conversely, a superclamp mutation did increase the inhibition of release by Complexin in *Drosophila*, while a poorclamp mutation had no effect (27). Hence, functional data have not provided clear correlations in support of the insertion or zigzag models, and biophysical data argue strongly against these models for wild-type Cpx1, but it may be premature to rule them out. Intriguingly, the finding that increasing or decreasing the negative charge of the Cpx1 accessory helix respectively inhibits or stimulates release led to a natural model whereby the negatively charged accessory helix inhibits release through electrostatic and steric repulsion with the membranes (153) (**Figure 4e**). This model needs further testing, but is attractive because it makes sense from a biophysical point of view and readily explains the interplay between Cpx1 and Syt1 that we discuss next.

Interplay Among Synaptotagmin-1, the SNAREs, and Complexins

The notion that Syt1 releases the inhibition caused by Complexins arose in part from the finding that Syt1 C_2AB displaces a Cpx1 fragment spanning the accessory and central helices (Cpx1 residues 26–83) from membrane-anchored SNARE complexes, which involves simultaneous interactions of C_2AB with the SNAREs and the membranes (30, 151). Such displacement was not observed for full-length Cpx1, and Syt1 C_2AB and Cpx1 residues 26–83 can bind simultaneously to the SNARE complex in solution (170). Rationalizing these data and, more generally, understanding the role (or roles) in release of interactions between Syt1 and the SNAREs has been hindered because many types of such interactions have been described, some of which were Ca^{2+} dependent or Ca^{2+} independent, and involved different SNAREs or distinct Syt1 sites, or both (reviewed in 21, 124). Hence, it is unclear which of these interactions are physiologically relevant or arise merely from the promiscuous nature of these highly charged proteins. Syt1–t-SNARE binding has been proposed to mediate SNARE complex assembly upon Ca^{2+} influx (9), but this model is difficult to reconcile with the roles of Munc18-1, Munc13s, and Complexin in priming. Nevertheless, interactions of Syt1 with Syntaxin-1 or SNAP-25, or both, could be important because they most likely mediate the binding of Syt1 and the SNARE complex, and, hence, may be critical in facilitating cooperation between Syt1 and the SNAREs in membrane fusion. Attempts to determine the binding sites for the Syt1–SNARE complex have yielded some contradictory results, but insights into which sites are more likely to be relevant were brought by the biochemical interplay between Syt1 and Cpx1 in SNARE-complex binding.

A majority of results, including data from electron paramagnetic resonance and fluorescence spectroscopy studies, indicated that a polybasic region at the side of the C_2B domain β-sandwich (**Figure 3b**) constitutes the binding site for the SNARE complex (e.g., 30, 78, 81, 123), and multiple results mapped the Syt1 binding site to an acidic patch of SNAP-25 in the middle of the SNARE complex (e.g., 78, 123), which is distinct from the Cpx1 binding site. These results agree with the finding that C_2AB and Cpx1 bind simultaneously to the SNARE complex (170), and place the Syt1 C_2B domain in an ideal position to bridge the membranes, as proposed in **Figure 3c**. Moreover, this location of the C_2B domain may also explain the fact that C_2AB competes with Cpx1 residues 26–83 for binding to membrane-anchored SNARE complexes because binding of the C_2B Ca^{2+} binding loops to the membrane while C_2B remains bound to the SNAREs could cause strong steric clashes between the Cpx1 accessory helix and the membrane (**Figure 4e**). Hence, these observations lead naturally to a model whereby, before Ca^{2+} influx, both Syt1 and Cpx1 are bound to a partially assembled SNARE complex, hindering membrane fusion because of the electrostatic repulsion of the Cpx1 accessory helix and the Syt1 C_2B domain Ca^{2+} binding loops with the phospholipids; upon Ca^{2+} binding to Syt1, the binding of the C_2B Ca^{2+} binding loops to the membrane forces melting of the Cpx1 accessory helix, which is quite flexible (24, 153), and brings the two membranes together in cooperation with full C-terminal zippering of the SNARE complex (**Figure 4e**). Since C_2AB does not displace full-length Cpx1 from membrane-anchored SNARE complexes (170), this model predicts that Cpx1 remains bound through its central helix and additional interactions of the N terminus with the SNAREs (172) and of the C terminus with the lipids (130, 166). The model also postulates that the Syt1 C_2A domain cooperates in fusion by binding to one membrane, thus increasing the overall energy of Syt1–membrane interactions, or perhaps also by bridging both membranes or helping to stabilize positive membrane curvature.

This model is attractive because it is consistent with a large amount of data, but other results suggest other distinct possibilities. Thus, some data have indicated that the Syt1 binding site on the SNARE complex is located at another acidic patch toward the C terminus of SNAP-25 (181). The binding of Syt1 to this site would clash with Cpx1 and, hence, it is unlikely to dominate in solution, but it is plausible that a rearrangement occurs upon Ca^{2+}-dependent membrane binding to favor binding to this C-terminal SNAP-25 site, which could underlie the observed displacement of Cpx1 residues 26–83 by C_2AB (30). Note also that the Ca^{2+} binding region of the C_2A domain has also been implicated in SNARE-complex binding (92), and the C_2B domain polybasic region also has been shown to mediate binding to phospholipids, particularly to phosphatidylinositol 4,5-bisphosphate (PIP_2) (21, 78). Moreover, data from single-particle fluorescence resonance energy transfer (FRET) have suggested that the binding site for the SNARE complex is in the bottom of the Syt1 C_2B domain (28). Some light may have been brought into this confusing picture by NMR data showing that the C_2B domain polybasic region constitutes the primary binding site for the SNARE complex in C_2AB in solution, whereas the Ca^{2+} binding region of the C_2A domain and R398 and R399 at the bottom of the C_2B domain mediate additional, weaker binding modes that promote C_2AB–SNARE complex aggregation (183). These results support the models in **Figures 3c** and **4e**, and suggest that these weaker binding sites are observed because both the C_2A domain Ca^{2+} binding region and the bottom of the C_2B domain are positively charged regions that, in the absence of their native targets (the membranes), have a tendency to bind to negatively charged species, such as the SNARE complex. However, the relevance of these weaker binding sites cannot be ruled out. For instance, the binding of the bottom of the C_2B domain to a negative patch in the SNARE complex might be key to positioning the domain in an ideal orientation to help bend the membranes (**Figure 3c**, bottom subpanels).

Reconstitution experiments have provided important insights into how the SNAREs, Syt1, and Complexins cooperate in release, but have also raised some questions. Syt1 C_2AB dramatically simulates the activity of the neuronal SNAREs in reconstitution assays (26, 154), as described above, and single-vesicle assays revealed that full-length Syt1 and the neuronal SNAREs induce efficient content mixing, although expansion of the fusion pore is slow (80, 83), and the dependence on Ca^{2+} varied drastically among studies. Thus, one study found optimal fusion at 10 μM Ca^{2+}, which is similar to the Ca^{2+} concentrations required for release (147), and a decrease in fusion at higher Ca^{2+} concentrations (85); another study observed a cooperative Ca^{2+} dependence with an apparent affinity of 3 mM (80). Efficient fusion at lower Ca^{2+} concentrations was observed later by the same group (37). Cell–cell fusion assays and reconstitutions with the neuronal SNAREs often have revealed only inhibitory (53, 128) or only stimulatory (80, 130, 179) activities for Complexins; intriguingly, Ca^{2+} dramatically increased the stimulatory activity in one case (179), but the biochemical basis for this effect is unclear. Some reconstitutions incorporating Syt1 did reveal inhibitory activities of Complexins in the absence of Ca^{2+} and stimulatory activities upon the addition of Ca^{2+} (82, 97). Moreover, single-vesicle fusion assays used in combination with cryo-electron microscopy have suggested that Syt1 promotes fast fusion starting from point contacts between liposomes, and that Syt1 and Cpx1 together synchronize fast fusion with Ca^{2+} influx (37, 82). Hence, these assays have established some clear correlations with biological data, despite lacking Munc18-1 and Munc13s. Overall, the results obtained agree with the model in **Figure 4e**, but they may also be compatible with other models.

OUTLOOK

The results summarized above, and many others that we could not cover, show that astounding progress has been made toward understanding the mechanism of neurotransmitter release, but fundamental questions remain to be answered, and it is still unclear whether the different models shown in **Figures 2–4** can be integrated into a single, coherent model of release. The reconstitution of synaptic vesicle fusion with the eight most central components of the release machinery—namely the three SNAREs, Munc18-1, Munc13-1, Syt1, NSF, and α-SNAP (94)—suggests that the underlying ideas on how these proteins function are likely to be correct. However, although it is clear that Munc18-1 and Munc13s orchestrate SNARE complex assembly, a crucial question is whether additionally Munc18-1 or Munc13s, or both, remain bound to the SNARE complex, thus playing a direct role in membrane fusion (**Figure 2c**). It is also unclear whether a physiologically relevant docking mechanism occurred in these reconstitutions because Rab3s were not included. In this context, the strong enhancement of fusion caused by the Syt1 C_2 domains (94) may arise from both a docking-like activity—due to their ability to bridge two membranes, which may not be relevant in vivo—and a direct role in fusion that arises from the same ability and is physiologically relevant. Similarly, the reconstitutions incorporating the SNAREs together with Syt1 or Complexins, or both (e.g., 82, 85, 97, 154, 157), clearly appear to be capturing some key aspects of the functions of these proteins, but it is unclear whether the docking effects observed in these experiments (e.g., 36, 78) reflect biologically relevant mechanisms or they arise from protein–membrane interactions that do not mediate docking in vivo although they may be important downstream from docking. Moreover, the crucial nature of Munc18-1 and Munc13s for neurotransmitter release and the observation of extended liposome–liposome interfaces in cryo-electron microscopy images of reconstitutions that do not incorporate both of these proteins (10, 37, 63) raise the question of to what extent reconstitutions lacking Munc18-1 and Munc13s can reproduce the true mechanism of synaptic vesicle fusion. Note, also, that although current models provide some ideas about how the release machinery brings membranes together and bends them, we are far from understanding how fusion pores form and expand. Clearly, images of fusion intermediates occurring in reconstitutions incorporating all of the key proteins and structures of *trans*-SNARE complexes with bound Munc18-1, Munc13-1, or Syt1, or a combination of these, will be extremely helpful in addressing these questions. Although these studies will be challenging, we believe that a clear description of the mechanism of neurotransmitter release may be within reach in the next few years.

SUMMARY POINTS

1. The SNAREs Syntaxin-1, Synaptobrevin, and SNAP-25 play a central role in membrane fusion, forming SNARE complexes that bridge the vesicle and plasma membranes and that are disassembled by NSF–SNAPs.

2. Exocytosis likely starts with Syntaxin-1 folded into a self-inhibited closed conformation that binds to Munc18-1, providing a key point for regulation of neurotransmitter release.

3. Munc13s open Syntaxin-1, orchestrating SNARE complex assembly in an NSF–SNAP-resistant manner together with Munc18-1.

4. Additionally, Munc18-1 or Munc13s, or both, may have a direct role in membrane fusion in cooperation with the SNAREs.

5. Synaptotagmin-1 acts as the Ca^{2+} sensor that triggers fast neurotransmitter release. Ca^{2+}-dependent binding of the Synaptotagmin-1 C_2 domains to phospholipids is critical for this function.

6. Complexins play active and inhibitory functions in neurotransmitter release, in a tight interplay with Synaptotagmin-1 and the SNAREs.

7. Synaptotagmin-1 may activate release by releasing the inhibition caused by Complexins, by cooperating with the SNAREs in bringing the two membranes together, by facilitating the bending of the membranes, or by a combination of these three activities.

8. Alternative models exist and fundamental questions remain unanswered.

FUTURE ISSUES

1. Do Munc18-1 and Munc13s play a direct role in membrane fusion, in addition to orchestrating SNARE complex assembly?

2. What is the physiological mechanism of synaptic vesicle docking? Are there multiple mechanisms of docking that may be partially redundant?

3. Can current models of neurotransmitter release be integrated into a coherent model that explains a majority of the available data?

4. Structural studies of protein complexes mediating membrane docking and fusion will be key to addressing these questions.

DISCLOSURE STATEMENT

The authors are not aware of any affiliations, memberships, funding, or financial holdings that might be perceived as affecting the objectivity of this review.

ACKNOWLEDGMENTS

We apologize to the many authors whose work could not be cited because of space limitations. Our work in this area is supported by grants from the Welch Foundation (I-1304) and the National Institutes of Health (NS037200 and NS040944) to J.R.

LITERATURE CITED

1. Acuna C, Guo Q, Burre J, Sharma M, Sun J, Sudhof TC. 2014. Microsecond dissection of neurotransmitter release: SNARE-complex assembly dictates speed and Ca^{2+} sensitivity. *Neuron* 82:1088–100

2. Aeffner S, Reusch T, Weinhausen B, Salditt T. 2012. Energetics of stalk intermediates in membrane fusion are controlled by lipid composition. *PNAS* 109:E1609–18

3. Arac D, Chen X, Khant HA, Ubach J, Ludtke SJ, et al. 2006. Close membrane–membrane proximity induced by Ca^{2+}-dependent multivalent binding of synaptotagmin-1 to phospholipids. *Nat. Struct. Mol. Biol.* 13:209–17

4. Arancillo M, Min SW, Gerber S, Munster-Wandowski A, Wu YJ, et al. 2013. Titration of Syntaxin1 in mammalian synapses reveals multiple roles in vesicle docking, priming, and release probability. *J. Neurosci.* 33:16698–714

5. Aravamudan B, Fergestad T, Davis WS, Rodesch CK, Broadie K. 1999. Drosophila UNC-13 is essential for synaptic transmission. *Nat. Neurosci.* 2:965–71

6. Bacaj T, Wu D, Yang X, Morishita W, Zhou P, et al. 2013. Synaptotagmin-1 and synaptotagmin-7 trigger synchronous and asynchronous phases of neurotransmitter release. *Neuron* 80:947–59

7. Banerjee A, Barry VA, DasGupta BR, Martin TF. 1996. N-Ethylmaleimide-sensitive factor acts at a prefusion ATP-dependent step in Ca^{2+}-activated exocytosis. *J. Biol. Chem.* 271:20223–26

8. Basu J, Shen N, Dulubova I, Lu J, Guan R, et al. 2005. A minimal domain responsible for Munc13 activity. *Nat. Struct. Mol. Biol.* 12:1017–18

9. Bhalla A, Chicka MC, Tucker WC, Chapman ER. 2006. Ca^{2+}-synaptotagmin directly regulates t-SNARE function during reconstituted membrane fusion. *Nat. Struct. Mol. Biol.* 13:323–30

10. Bharat TA, Malsam J, Hagen WJ, Scheutzow A, Sollner TH, Briggs JA. 2014. SNARE and regulatory proteins induce local membrane protrusions to prime docked vesicles for fast calcium-triggered fusion. *EMBO Rep.* 15:308–14

11. Boswell KL, James DJ, Esquibel JM, Bruinsma S, Shirakawa R, et al. 2012. Munc13-4 reconstitutes calcium-dependent SNARE-mediated membrane fusion. *J. Cell Biol.* 197:301–12

12. Bracher A, Weissenhorn W. 2002. Structural basis for the Golgi membrane recruitment of Sly1p by Sed5p. *EMBO J.* 21:6114–24

13. Brunger AT, Weninger K, Bowen M, Chu S. 2009. Single-molecule studies of the neuronal SNARE fusion machinery. *Annu. Rev. Biochem.* 78:903–28

14. Burkhardt P, Hattendorf DA, Weis WI, Fasshauer D. 2008. Munc18a controls SNARE assembly through its interaction with the Syntaxin N-peptide. *EMBO J.* 27:923–33

15. Burkhardt P, Stegmann CM, Cooper B, Kloepper TH, Imig C, et al. 2011. Primordial neurosecretory apparatus identified in the choanoflagellate. *Monosiga brevicollis. PNAS* 108:15264–69

16. Cai H, Reinisch K, Ferro-Novick S. 2007. Coats, tethers, Rabs, and SNAREs work together to mediate the intracellular destination of a transport vesicle. *Dev. Cell* 12:671–82

17. Cao P, Yang X, Sudhof TC. 2013. Complexin activates exocytosis of distinct secretory vesicles controlled by different synaptotagmins. *J. Neurosci.* 33:1714–27

18. Carr CM, Grote E, Munson M, Hughson FM, Novick PJ. 1999. Sec1p binds to SNARE complexes and concentrates at sites of secretion. *J. Cell Biol.* 146:333–44

19. Carr CM, Rizo J. 2010. At the junction of SNARE and SM protein function. *Curr. Opin. Cell Biol.* 22:488–95

20. Chan YH, van LB, Boxer SG. 2009. Effects of linker sequences on vesicle fusion mediated by lipid-anchored DNA oligonucleotides. *PNAS* 106:979–84

21. Chapman ER. 2008. How Does synaptotagmin trigger neurotransmitter release? *Annu. Rev. Biochem.* 77:615–41

22. Chapman ER, Davis AF. 1998. Direct interaction of a Ca^{2+}-binding loop of synaptotagmin with lipid bilayers. *J. Biol. Chem.* 273:13995–4001

23. Chen X, Lu J, Dulubova I, Rizo J. 2008. NMR analysis of the closed conformation of Syntaxin-1. *J. Biomol. NMR* 41:43–54

24. Chen X, Tomchick DR, Kovrigin E, Arac D, Machius M, et al. 2002. Three-dimensional structure of the complexin/SNARE complex. *Neuron* 33:397–409

25. Chernomordik LV, Kozlov MM. 2008. Mechanics of membrane fusion. *Nat. Struct. Mol. Biol.* 15:675–83

26. Chicka MC, Hui E, Liu H, Chapman ER. 2008. Synaptotagmin arrests the SNARE complex before triggering fast, efficient membrane fusion in response to Ca^{2+}. *Nat. Struct. Mol. Biol.* 15:827–35

27. Cho RW, Kummel D, Li F, Baguley SW, Coleman J, et al. 2014. Genetic analysis of the Complexin trans-clamping model for cross-linking SNARE complexes in vivo. *PNAS* 111:10317–22

28. Choi UB, Strop P, Vrljic M, Chu S, Brunger AT, Weninger KR. 2010. Single-molecule FRET-derived model of the synaptotagmin 1-SNARE fusion complex. *Nat. Struct. Mol. Biol.* 17:318–24

29. Cohen FS, Melikyan GB. 2004. The energetics of membrane fusion from binding, through hemifusion, pore formation, and pore enlargement. *J. Membr. Biol.* 199:1–14

30. Dai H, Shen N, Arac D, Rizo J. 2007. A quaternary SNARE-synaptotagmin-Ca^{2+}-phospholipid complex in neurotransmitter release. *J. Mol. Biol.* 367:848–63

31. Damer CK, Creutz CE. 1994. Synergistic membrane interactions of the two C2 domains of synaptotagmin. *J. Biol. Chem.* 269:31115–23

32. de Wit H, Walter AM, Milosevic I, Gulyas-Kovacs A, Riedel D, et al. 2009. Synaptotagmin-1 docks secretory vesicles to Syntaxin-1/SNAP-25 acceptor complexes. *Cell* 138:935–46

33. Deak F, Shin OH, Kavalali ET, Sudhof TC. 2006. Structural determinants of Synaptobrevin 2 function in synaptic vesicle fusion. *J. Neurosci.* 26:6668–76

34. Deak F, Xu Y, Chang WP, Dulubova I, Khvotchev M, et al. 2009. Munc18-1 binding to the neuronal SNARE complex controls synaptic vesicle priming. *J. Cell Biol.* 184:751–64

35. Dhara M, Yarzagaray A, Schwarz Y, Dutta S, Grabner C, et al. 2014. Complexin synchronizes primed vesicle exocytosis and regulates fusion pore dynamics. *J. Cell Biol.* 204:1123–40

36. Diao J, Cipriano DJ, Zhao M, Zhang Y, Shah S, et al. 2013. Complexin-1 enhances the on-rate of vesicle docking via simultaneous SNARE and membrane interactions. *J. Am. Chem. Soc.* 135:15274–77

37. Diao J, Grob P, Cipriano DJ, Kyoung M, Zhang Y, et al. 2012. Synaptic proteins promote calcium-triggered fast transition from point contact to full fusion. *eLife* 1:e00109

38. Dong G, Hutagalung AH, Fu C, Novick P, Reinisch KM. 2005. The structures of exocyst subunit Exo70p and the Exo84p C-terminal domains reveal a common motif. *Nat. Struct. Mol. Biol.* 12:1094–100

39. Dulubova I, Khvotchev M, Liu S, Huryeva I, Sudhof TC, Rizo J. 2007. Munc18-1 binds directly to the neuronal SNARE complex. *PNAS* 104:2697–702

40. Dulubova I, Lou X, Lu J, Huryeva I, Alam A, et al. 2005. A Munc13/RIM/Rab3 tripartite complex: from priming to plasticity? *EMBO J.* 24:2839–50

41. Dulubova I, Sugita S, Hill S, Hosaka M, Fernandez I, et al. 1999. A conformational switch in Syntaxin during exocytosis: role of munc18. *EMBO J.* 18:4372–82

42. Dulubova I, Yamaguchi T, Arac D, Li H, Huryeva I, et al. 2003. Convergence and divergence in the mechanism of SNARE binding by Sec1/Munc18-like proteins. *PNAS* 100:32–37

43. Dulubova I, Yamaguchi T, Gao Y, Min SW, Huryeva I, et al. 2002. How Tlg2p/Syntaxin 16 'snares' Vps45. *EMBO J.* 21:3620–31

44. Dulubova I, Yamaguchi T, Wang Y, Sudhof TC, Rizo J. 2001. Vam3p structure reveals conserved and divergent properties of Syntaxins. *Nat. Struct. Biol.* 8:258–64

45. Fasshauer D, Sutton RB, Brunger AT, Jahn R. 1998. Conserved structural features of the synaptic fusion complex: SNARE proteins reclassified as Q- and R-SNAREs. *PNAS* 95:15781–86

46. Fernandez I, Arac D, Ubach J, Gerber SH, Shin O, et al. 2001. Three-dimensional structure of the synaptotagmin 1 C_2B-domain: synaptotagmin 1 as a phospholipid binding machine. *Neuron* 32:1057–69

47. Fernandez I, Ubach J, Dulubova I, Zhang X, Sudhof TC, Rizo J. 1998. Three-dimensional structure of an evolutionarily conserved N-terminal domain of Syntaxin 1A. *Cell* 94:841–49

48. Fernandez-Chacon R, Konigstorfer A, Gerber SH, Garcia J, Matos MF, et al. 2001. Synaptotagmin I functions as a calcium regulator of release probability. *Nature* 410:41–49

49. Furgason ML, MacDonald C, Shanks SG, Ryder SP, Bryant NJ, Munson M. 2009. The N-terminal peptide of the Syntaxin Tlg2p modulates binding of its closed conformation to Vps45p. *PNAS* 106:14303–8

50. Gandasi NR, Barg S. 2014. Contact-induced clustering of Syntaxin and munc18 docks secretory granules at the exocytosis site. *Nat. Commun.* 5:3914

51. Gao Y, Zorman S, Gundersen G, Xi Z, Ma L, et al. 2012. Single reconstituted neuronal SNARE complexes zipper in three distinct stages. *Science* 337:1340–43

52. Gerber SH, Rah JC, Min SW, Liu X, de Wit H, et al. 2008. Conformational switch of Syntaxin-1 controls synaptic vesicle fusion. *Science* 321:1507–10

53. Giraudo CG, Eng WS, Melia TJ, Rothman JE. 2006. A clamping mechanism involved in SNARE-dependent exocytosis. *Science* 313:676–80

54. Giraudo CG, Garcia-Diaz A, Eng WS, Chen Y, Hendrickson WA, et al. 2009. Alternative zippering as an on-off switch for SNARE-mediated fusion. *Science* 323:512–16

55. Graham ME, Handley MT, Barclay JW, Ciufo LF, Barrow SL, et al. 2008. A gain-of-function mutant of Munc18-1 stimulates secretory granule recruitment and exocytosis and reveals a direct interaction of Munc18-1 with Rab3. *Biochem. J.* 409:407–16

56. Guan R, Dai H, Rizo J. 2008. Binding of the Munc13-1 MUN domain to membrane-anchored SNARE complexes. *Biochemistry* 47:1474–81

57. Hammarlund M, Palfreyman MT, Watanabe S, Olsen S, Jorgensen EM. 2007. Open Syntaxin docks synaptic vesicles. *PLOS Biol.* 5:e198

58. Han GA, Malintan NT, Saw NM, Li L, Han L, et al. 2011. Munc18-1 domain-1 controls vesicle docking and secretion by interacting with Syntaxin-1 and chaperoning it to the plasma membrane. *Mol. Biol. Cell* 22:4134–49

59. Han L, Jiang T, Han GA, Malintan NT, Xie L, et al. 2009. Rescue of Munc18-1 and -2 double knockdown reveals the essential functions of interaction between Munc18 and closed Syntaxin in PC12 cells. *Mol. Biol. Cell* 20:4962–75

60. Hanson PI, Roth R, Morisaki H, Jahn R, Heuser JE. 1997. Structure and conformational changes in NSF and its membrane receptor complexes visualized by quick-freeze/deep-etch electron microscopy. *Cell* 90:523–35

61. Hashizume K, Cheng YS, Hutton JL, Chiu CH, Carr CM. 2009. Yeast Sec1p functions before and after vesicle docking. *Mol. Biol. Cell* 20:4673–85

62. Hata Y, Slaughter CA, Sudhof TC. 1993. Synaptic vesicle fusion complex contains unc-18 homologue bound to Syntaxin. *Nature* 366:347–51

63. Hernandez JM, Stein A, Behrmann E, Riedel D, Cypionka A, et al. 2012. Membrane fusion intermediates via directional and full assembly of the SNARE complex. *Science* 336:1581–84

64. Herrick DZ, Kuo W, Huang H, Schwieters CD, Ellena JF, Cafiso DS. 2009. Solution and membrane-bound conformations of the tandem C2A and C2B domains of synaptotagmin 1: evidence for bilayer bridging. *J. Mol. Biol.* 390:913–23

65. Hobson RJ, Liu Q, Watanabe S, Jorgensen EM. 2011. Complexin maintains vesicles in the primed state in *C. elegans*. *Curr. Biol.* 21:106–13

66. Hu SH, Christie MP, Saez NJ, Latham CF, Jarrott R, et al. 2011. Possible roles for Munc18-1 domain 3a and Syntaxin1 N-peptide and C-terminal anchor in SNARE complex formation. *PNAS* 108:1040–45

67. Hui E, Gaffaney JD, Wang Z, Johnson CP, Evans CS, Chapman ER. 2011. Mechanism and function of synaptotagmin-mediated membrane apposition. *Nat. Struct. Mol. Biol.* 18:813–21

68. Hui E, Johnson CP, Yao J, Dunning FM, Chapman ER. 2009. Synaptotagmin-mediated bending of the target membrane is a critical step in Ca^{2+}-regulated fusion. *Cell* 138:709–21

69. Huntwork S, Littleton JT. 2007. A complexin fusion clamp regulates spontaneous neurotransmitter release and synaptic growth. *Nat. Neurosci.* 10:1235–37

70. Jahn R, Fasshauer D. 2012. Molecular machines governing exocytosis of synaptic vesicles. *Nature* 490:201–7

71. Jahn R, Scheller RH. 2006. SNAREs—engines for membrane fusion. *Nat. Rev. Mol. Cell Biol.* 7:631–43

72. Johnson JR, Ferdek P, Lian LY, Barclay JW, Burgoyne RD, Morgan A. 2009. Binding of UNC-18 to the N-terminus of Syntaxin is essential for neurotransmission in *Caenorhabditis elegans*. *Biochem. J.* 418:73–80

73. Jorquera RA, Huntwork-Rodriguez S, Akbergenova Y, Cho RW, Littleton JT. 2012. Complexin controls spontaneous and evoked neurotransmitter release by regulating the timing and properties of synaptotagmin activity. *J. Neurosci.* 32:18234–45

74. Kaeser-Woo YJ, Yang X, Sudhof TC. 2012. C-terminal complexin sequence is selectively required for clamping and priming but not for Ca^{2+} triggering of synaptic exocytosis. *J. Neurosci.* 32:2877–85

75. Kesavan J, Borisovska M, Bruns D. 2007. v-SNARE actions during Ca^{2+}-triggered exocytosis. *Cell* 131:351–63

76. Khvotchev M, Dulubova I, Sun J, Dai H, Rizo J, Sudhof TC. 2007. Dual modes of Munc18-1/SNARE interactions are coupled by functionally critical binding to Syntaxin-1 N terminus. *J. Neurosci.* 27:12147–55

77. Kim CS, Kweon DH, Shin YK. 2002. Membrane topologies of neuronal SNARE folding intermediates. *Biochemistry* 41:10928–33

78. Kim JY, Choi BK, Choi MG, Kim SA, Lai Y, et al. 2012. Solution single-vesicle assay reveals PIP2-mediated sequential actions of synaptotagmin-1 on SNAREs. *EMBO J.* 31:2144–55

79. Kummel D, Krishnakumar SS, Radoff DT, Li F, Giraudo CG, et al. 2011. Complexin cross-links pre-fusion SNAREs into a zigzag array. *Nat. Struct. Mol. Biol.* 18:927–33

80. Kyoung M, Srivastava A, Zhang Y, Diao J, Vrljic M, et al. 2011. In vitro system capable of differentiating fast Ca^{2+}-triggered content mixing from lipid exchange for mechanistic studies of neurotransmitter release. *PNAS* 108:E304–13

81. Lai AL, Huang H, Herrick DZ, Epp N, Cafiso DS. 2011. Synaptotagmin 1 and SNAREs form a complex that is structurally heterogeneous. *J. Mol. Biol.* 405:696–706

82. Lai Y, Diao J, Cipriano DJ, Zhang Y, Pfuetzner RA, et al. 2014. Complexin inhibits spontaneous release and synchronizes Ca²⁺-triggered synaptic vesicle fusion by distinct mechanisms. *eLife* 3:e03756

83. Lai Y, Diao J, Liu Y, Ishitsuka Y, Su Z, et al. 2013. Fusion pore formation and expansion induced by Ca²⁺ and synaptotagmin 1. *PNAS* 110:1333–38

84. Lai Y, Shin YK. 2012. The importance of an asymmetric distribution of acidic lipids for synaptotagmin 1 function as a Ca²⁺ sensor. *Biochem. J.* 443:223–29

85. Lee HK, Yang Y, Su Z, Hyeon C, Lee TS, et al. 2010. Dynamic Ca²⁺-dependent stimulation of vesicle fusion by membrane-anchored synaptotagmin 1. *Science* 328:760–63

86. Lee J, Guan Z, Akbergenova Y, Littleton JT. 2013. Genetic analysis of synaptotagmin C2 domain specificity in regulating spontaneous and evoked neurotransmitter release. *J. Neurosci.* 33:187–200

87. Li F, Kummel D, Coleman J, Reinisch KM, Rothman JE, Pincet F. 2014. A half-zippered SNARE complex represents a functional intermediate in membrane fusion. *J. Am. Chem. Soc.* 136:3456–64

88. Li F, Pincet F, Perez E, Eng WS, Melia TJ, et al. 2007. Energetics and dynamics of SNAREpin folding across lipid bilayers. *Nat. Struct. Mol. Biol.* 14:890–96

89. Li W, Ma C, Guan R, Xu Y, Tomchick DR, Rizo J. 2011. The crystal structure of a Munc13 C-terminal module exhibits a remarkable similarity to vesicle tethering factors. *Structure* 19:1443–55

90. Liu W, Montana V, Parpura V, Mohideen U. 2009. Single molecule measurements of interaction free energies between the proteins within binary and ternary SNARE complexes. *J. Nanoneurosci.* 1:120–29

91. Liu W, Parpura V. 2010. SNAREs: could they be the answer to an energy landscape riddle in exocytosis? *Sci. World J.* 10:1258–68

92. Lynch KL, Gerona RR, Kielar DM, Martens S, McMahon HT, Martin TF. 2008. Synaptotagmin-1 utilizes membrane bending and SNARE binding to drive fusion pore expansion. *Mol. Biol. Cell* 19:5093–103

93. Ma C, Li W, Xu Y, Rizo J. 2011. Munc13 mediates the transition from the closed Syntaxin-Munc18 complex to the SNARE complex. *Nat. Struct. Mol. Biol.* 18:542–49

94. Ma C, Su L, Seven AB, Xu Y, Rizo J. 2013. Reconstitution of the vital functions of Munc18 and Munc13 in neurotransmitter release. *Science* 339:421–25

95. Mackler JM, Drummond JA, Loewen CA, Robinson IM, Reist NE. 2002. The C₂B Ca²⁺-binding motif of synaptotagmin is required for synaptic transmission in vivo. *Nature* 418:340–44

96. Malsam J, Kreye S, Sollner TH. 2008. Membrane fusion: SNAREs and regulation. *Cell. Mol. Life Sci.* 65:2814–32

97. Malsam J, Parisotto D, Bharat TA, Scheutzow A, Krause JM, et al. 2012. Complexin arrests a pool of docked vesicles for fast Ca²⁺-dependent release. *EMBO J.* 31:3270–81

98. Martens S, Kozlov MM, McMahon HT. 2007. How synaptotagmin promotes membrane fusion. *Science* 316:1205–8

99. Martin JA, Hu Z, Fenz KM, Fernandez J, Dittman JS. 2011. Complexin has opposite effects on two modes of synaptic vesicle fusion. *Curr. Biol.* 21:97–105

100. Maximov A, Tang J, Yang X, Pang ZP, Sudhof TC. 2009. Complexin controls the force transfer from SNARE complexes to membranes in fusion. *Science* 323:516–21

101. Mayer A, Wickner W, Haas A. 1996. Sec18p (NSF)-driven release of Sec17p (α-SNAP) can precede docking and fusion of yeast vacuoles. *Cell* 85:83–94

102. McMahon HT, Missler M, Li C, Sudhof TC. 1995. Complexins: cytosolic proteins that regulate SNAP receptor function. *Cell* 83:111–19

103. Meijer M, Burkhardt P, de Wit H, Toonen RF, Fasshauer D, Verhage M. 2012. Munc18-1 mutations that strongly impair SNARE-complex binding support normal synaptic transmission. *EMBO J.* 31:2156–68

104. Mima J, Hickey CM, Xu H, Jun Y, Wickner W. 2008. Reconstituted membrane fusion requires regulatory lipids, SNAREs and synergistic SNARE chaperones. *EMBO J.* 27:2031–42

105. Min D, Kim K, Hyeon C, Cho YH, Shin YK, Yoon TY. 2013. Mechanical unzipping and rezipping of a single SNARE complex reveals hysteresis as a force-generating mechanism. *Nat. Commun.* 4:1705

106. Misura KM, Scheller RH, Weis WI. 2000. Three-dimensional structure of the neuronal-Sec1-Syntaxin 1a complex. *Nature* 404:355–62

107. Mohrmann R, de Wit H, Verhage M, Neher E, Sorensen JB. 2010. Fast vesicle fusion in living cells requires at least three SNARE complexes. *Science* 330:502–5

108. Nicholson KL, Munson M, Miller RB, Filip TJ, Fairman R, Hughson FM. 1998. Regulation of SNARE complex assembly by an N-terminal domain of the t-SNARE Sso1p. *Nat. Struct. Biol.* 5:793–802

109. Pabst S, Hazzard JW, Antonin W, Sudhof TC, Jahn R, et al. 2000. Selective interaction of complexin with the neuronal SNARE complex: determination of the binding regions. *J. Biol. Chem.* 275:19808–18

110. Paddock BE, Wang Z, Biela LM, Chen K, Getzy MD, et al. 2011. Membrane penetration by synaptotagmin is required for coupling calcium binding to vesicle fusion in vivo. *J. Neurosci.* 31:2248–57

111. Parisotto D, Pfau M, Scheutzow A, Wild K, Mayer MP, et al. 2014. An extended helical conformation in domain 3a of Munc18-1 provides a template for SNARE (soluble N-ethylmaleimide-sensitive factor attachment protein receptor) complex assembly. *J. Biol. Chem.* 289:9639–50

112. Park Y, Hernandez JM, van den BG, Ahmed S, Holt M, et al. 2012. Controlling synaptotagmin activity by electrostatic screening. *Nat. Struct. Mol. Biol.* 19:991–97

113. Pei J, Ma C, Rizo J, Grishin NV. 2009. Remote homology between Munc13 MUN domain and vesicle tethering complexes. *J. Mol. Biol.* 391:509–17

114. Pertsinidis A, Mukherjee K, Sharma M, Pang ZP, Park SR, et al. 2013. Ultrahigh-resolution imaging reveals formation of neuronal SNARE/Munc18 complexes in situ. *PNAS* 110:E2812–20

115. Poirier MA, Xiao W, Macosko JC, Chan C, Shin YK, Bennett MK. 1998. The synaptic SNARE complex is a parallel four-stranded helical bundle. *Nat. Struct. Biol.* 5:765–69

116. Rathore SS, Bend EG, Yu H, Hammarlund M, Jorgensen EM, Shen J. 2010. Syntaxin N-terminal peptide motif is an initiation factor for the assembly of the SNARE-Sec1/Munc18 membrane fusion complex. *PNAS* 107:22399–406

117. Regehr WG. 2012. Short-term presynaptic plasticity. *Cold Spring Harb. Perspect. Biol.* 4:a005702

118. Reim K, Mansour M, Varoqueaux F, McMahon HT, Sudhof TC, et al. 2001. Complexins regulate a late step in Ca^{2+}-dependent neurotransmitter release. *Cell* 104:71–81

119. Ren Y, Yip CK, Tripathi A, Huie D, Jeffrey PD, et al. 2009. A structure-based mechanism for vesicle capture by the multisubunit tethering complex Dsl1. *Cell* 139:1119–29

120. Rhee JS, Li LY, Shin OH, Rah JC, Rizo J, et al. 2005. Augmenting neurotransmitter release by enhancing the apparent Ca^{2+} affinity of synaptotagmin 1. *PNAS* 102:18664–69

121. Richmond JE, Davis WS, Jorgensen EM. 1999. UNC-13 is required for synaptic vesicle fusion in *C. elegans*. *Nat. Neurosci.* 2:959–64

122. Richmond JE, Weimer RM, Jorgensen EM. 2001. An open form of Syntaxin bypasses the requirement for UNC-13 in vesicle priming. *Nature* 412:338–41

123. Rickman C, Jimenez JL, Graham ME, Archer DA, Soloviev M, et al. 2006. Conserved prefusion protein assembly in regulated exocytosis. *Mol. Biol. Cell* 17:283–94

124. Rizo J, Chen X, Arac D. 2006. Unraveling the mechanisms of synaptotagmin and SNARE function in neurotransmitter release. *Trends Cell Biol.* 16:339–50

125. Rizo J, Rosenmund C. 2008. Synaptic vesicle fusion. *Nat. Struct. Mol. Biol.* 15:665–74

126. Rizo J, Sudhof TC. 2012. The membrane fusion enigma: SNAREs, Sec1/Munc18 proteins, and their accomplices—guilty as charged? *Annu. Rev. Cell Dev. Biol.* 28:279–308

127. Roggero CM, De Blas GA, Dai H, Tomes CN, Rizo J, Mayorga LS. 2007. Complexin/synaptotagmin interplay controls acrosomal exocytosis. *J. Biol. Chem.* 282:26335–43

128. Schaub JR, Lu X, Doneske B, Shin YK, McNew JA. 2006. Hemifusion arrest by complexin is relieved by Ca^{2+}-synaptotagmin I. *Nat. Struct. Mol. Biol.* 13:748–50

129. Schollmeier Y, Krause JM, Kreye S, Malsam J, Sollner TH. 2011. Resolving the function of distinct Munc18-1/SNARE protein interaction modes in a reconstituted membrane fusion assay. *J. Biol. Chem.* 286:30582–90

130. Seiler F, Malsam J, Krause JM, Sollner TH. 2009. A role of complexin–lipid interactions in membrane fusion. *FEBS Lett.* 583:2343–8

131. Seven AB, Brewer KD, Shi L, Jiang QX, Rizo J. 2013. Prevalent mechanism of membrane bridging by synaptotagmin-1. *PNAS* 110:E3243–52

132. Shao X, Fernandez I, Sudhof TC, Rizo J. 1998. Solution structures of the Ca^{2+}-free and Ca^{2+}-bound C_2A domain of synaptotagmin I: does Ca^{2+} induce a conformational change? *Biochemistry* 37:16106–15

133. Shao X, Li C, Fernandez I, Zhang X, Sudhof TC, Rizo J. 1997. Synaptotagmin-Syntaxin interaction: the C2 domain as a Ca^{2+}-dependent electrostatic switch. *Neuron* 18:133–42

134. Shen J, Rathore SS, Khandan L, Rothman JE. 2010. SNARE bundle and Syntaxin N-peptide constitute a minimal complement for Munc18-1 activation of membrane fusion. *J. Cell Biol.* 190:55–63

135. Shen J, Tareste DC, Paumet F, Rothman JE, Melia TJ. 2007. Selective activation of cognate SNAREpins by Sec1/Munc18 proteins. *Cell* 128:183–95

136. Shi L, Shen QT, Kiel A, Wang J, Wang HW, et al. 2012. SNARE proteins: one to fuse and three to keep the nascent fusion pore open. *Science* 335:1355–59

137. Shin J, Lou X, Kweon DH, Shin YK. 2014. Multiple conformations of a single SNAREpin between two nanodisc membranes reveal diverse pre-fusion states. *Biochem. J.* 459:95–102

138. Shin OH, Xu J, Rizo J, Sudhof TC. 2009. Differential but convergent functions of Ca^{2+} binding to synaptotagmin-1 C_2 domains mediate neurotransmitter release. *PNAS* 106:16469–74

139. Siksou L, Varoqueaux F, Pascual O, Triller A, Brose N, Marty S. 2009. A common molecular basis for membrane docking and functional priming of synaptic vesicles. *Eur. J. Neurosci.* 30:49–56

140. Sinha R, Ahmed S, Jahn R, Klingauf J. 2011. Two Synaptobrevin molecules are sufficient for vesicle fusion in central nervous system synapses. *PNAS* 108:14318–23

141. Sivaram MV, Saporita JA, Furgason ML, Boettcher AJ, Munson M. 2005. Dimerization of the exocyst protein Sec6p and its interaction with the t-SNARE Sec9p. *Biochemistry* 44:6302–11

142. Sollner T, Bennett MK, Whiteheart SW, Scheller RH, Rothman JE. 1993. A protein assembly–disassembly pathway in vitro that may correspond to sequential steps of synaptic vesicle docking, activation, and fusion. *Cell* 75:409–18

143. Sorensen JB. 2009. Conflicting views on the membrane fusion machinery and the fusion pore. *Annu. Rev. Cell Dev. Biol.* 25:513–37

144. Sorensen JB, Wiederhold K, Muller EM, Milosevic I, Nagy G, et al. 2006. Sequential N- to C-terminal SNARE complex assembly drives priming and fusion of secretory vesicles. *EMBO J.* 25:955–66

145. Stein A, Weber G, Wahl MC, Jahn R. 2009. Helical extension of the neuronal SNARE complex into the membrane. *Nature* 460:525–28

146. Striegel AR, Biela LM, Evans CS, Wang Z, Delehoy JB, et al. 2012. Calcium binding by synaptotagmin's C_2A domain is an essential element of the electrostatic switch that triggers synchronous synaptic transmission. *J. Neurosci.* 32:1253–60

147. Sudhof TC. 2013. Neurotransmitter release: the last millisecond in the life of a synaptic vesicle. *Neuron* 80:675–90

148. Sudhof TC, Rothman JE. 2009. Membrane fusion: grappling with SNARE and SM proteins. *Science* 323:474–77

149. Sutton RB, Davletov BA, Berghuis AM, Sudhof TC, Sprang SR. 1995. Structure of the first C_2 domain of synaptotagmin I: a novel Ca^{2+}/phospholipid-binding fold. *Cell* 80:929–38

150. Sutton RB, Fasshauer D, Jahn R, Brunger AT. 1998. Crystal structure of a SNARE complex involved in synaptic exocytosis at 2.4 A resolution. *Nature* 395:347–53

151. Tang J, Maximov A, Shin OH, Dai H, Rizo J, Sudhof TC. 2006. A complexin/synaptotagmin 1 switch controls fast synaptic vesicle exocytosis. *Cell* 126:1175–87

152. Toonen RF, Verhage M. 2007. Munc18-1 in secretion: lonely Munc joins SNARE team and takes control. *Trends Neurosci.* 30:564–72

153. Trimbuch T, Xu J, Flaherty D, Tomchick DR, Rizo J, Rosenmund C. 2014. Re-examining how complexin inhibits neurotransmitter release. *eLife* 3:e02391

154. Tucker WC, Weber T, Chapman ER. 2004. Reconstitution of Ca^{2+}-regulated membrane fusion by synaptotagmin and SNAREs. *Science* 304:435–38

155. Ubach J, Zhang X, Shao X, Sudhof TC, Rizo J. 1998. Ca^{2+} binding to synaptotagmin: how many Ca^{2+} ions bind to the tip of a C_2-domain? *EMBO J.* 17:3921–30

156. van den Bogaart G, Holt MG, Bunt G, Riedel D, Wouters FS, Jahn R. 2010. One SNARE complex is sufficient for membrane fusion. *Nat. Struct. Mol. Biol.* 17:358–64

157. van den Bogaart G, Thutupalli S, Risselada JH, Meyenberg K, Holt M, et al. 2011. Synaptotagmin-1 may be a distance regulator acting upstream of SNARE nucleation. *Nat. Struct. Mol. Biol.* 18:805–12

158. Varoqueaux F, Sigler A, Rhee JS, Brose N, Enk C, et al. 2002. Total arrest of spontaneous and evoked synaptic transmission but normal synaptogenesis in the absence of Munc13-mediated vesicle priming. *PNAS* 99:9037–42

159. Vennekate W, Schroder S, Lin CC, van den Bogaart G, Grunwald M, et al. 2012. *Cis-* and *trans-*membrane interactions of synaptotagmin-1. *PNAS* 109:11037–42

160. Verhage M, Maia AS, Plomp JJ, Brussaard AB, Heeroma JH, et al. 2000. Synaptic assembly of the brain in the absence of neurotransmitter secretion. *Science* 287:864–69

161. Weber T, Parlati F, McNew JA, Johnston RJ, Westermann B, et al. 2000. SNAREpins are functionally resistant to disruption by NSF and αSNAP. *J. Cell Biol.* 149:1063–72

162. Weber T, Zemelman BV, McNew JA, Westermann B, Gmachl M, et al. 1998. SNAREpins: minimal machinery for membrane fusion. *Cell* 92:759–72

163. Weimer RM, Gracheva EO, Meyrignac O, Miller KG, Richmond JE, Bessereau JL. 2006. UNC-13 and UNC-10/rim localize synaptic vesicles to specific membrane domains. *J. Neurosci.* 26:8040–47

164. Weninger K, Bowen ME, Choi UB, Chu S, Brunger AT. 2008. Accessory proteins stabilize the acceptor complex for Synaptobrevin, the 1:1 Syntaxin/SNAP-25 complex. *Structure* 16:308–20

165. Wickner W. 2010. Membrane fusion: five lipids, four SNAREs, three chaperones, two nucleotides, and a Rab, all dancing in a ring on yeast vacuoles. *Annu. Rev. Cell Dev. Biol.* 26:115–36

166. Wragg RT, Snead D, Dong Y, Ramlall TF, Menon I, et al. 2013. Synaptic vesicles position complexin to block spontaneous fusion. *Neuron* 77:323–34

167. Xiao W, Poirier MA, Bennett MK, Shin YK. 2001. The neuronal t-SNARE complex is a parallel four-helix bundle. *Nat. Struct. Biol.* 8:308–11

168. Xu H, Jun Y, Thompson J, Yates J, Wickner W. 2010. HOPS prevents the disassembly of trans-SNARE complexes by Sec17p/Sec18p during membrane fusion. *EMBO J.* 29:1948–60

169. Xu H, Zick M, Wickner WT, Jun Y. 2011. A lipid-anchored SNARE supports membrane fusion. *PNAS* 108:17325–30

170. Xu J, Brewer KD, Perez-Castillejos R, Rizo J. 2013. Subtle interplay between synaptotagmin and complexin binding to the SNARE complex. *J. Mol. Biol.* 425:3461–75

171. Xu Y, Su L, Rizo J. 2010. Binding of Munc18-1 to Synaptobrevin and to the SNARE four-helix bundle. *Biochemistry* 49:1568–76

172. Xue M, Craig TK, Xu J, Chao HT, Rizo J, Rosenmund C. 2010. Binding of the complexin N terminus to the SNARE complex potentiates synaptic-vesicle fusogenicity. *Nat. Struct. Mol. Biol.* 17:568–75

173. Xue M, Lin YQ, Pan H, Reim K, Deng H, et al. 2009. Tilting the balance between facilitatory and inhibitory functions of mammalian and *Drosophila* complexins orchestrates synaptic vesicle exocytosis. *Neuron* 64:367–80

174. Xue M, Ma C, Craig TK, Rosenmund C, Rizo J. 2008. The Janus-faced nature of the C_2B domain is fundamental for synaptotagmin-1 function. *Nat. Struct. Mol. Biol.* 15:1160–68

175. Xue M, Reim K, Chen X, Chao HT, Deng H, et al. 2007. Distinct domains of complexin I differentially regulate neurotransmitter release. *Nat. Struct. Mol. Biol.* 14:949–58

176. Xue M, Stradomska A, Chen H, Brose N, Zhang W, et al. 2008. Complexins facilitate neurotransmitter release at excitatory and inhibitory synapses in mammalian central nervous system. *PNAS* 105:7875–80

177. Yamaguchi T, Dulubova I, Min SW, Chen X, Rizo J, Sudhof TC. 2002. Sly1 binds to Golgi and ER Syntaxins via a conserved N-terminal peptide motif. *Dev. Cell* 2:295–305

178. Yang X, Kaeser-Woo YJ, Pang ZP, Xu W, Sudhof TC. 2010. Complexin clamps asynchronous release by blocking a secondary Ca^{2+} sensor via its accessory α helix. *Neuron* 68:907–20

179. Yoon TY, Lu X, Diao J, Lee SM, Ha T, Shin YK. 2008. Complexin and Ca^{2+} stimulate SNARE-mediated membrane fusion. *Nat. Struct. Mol. Biol.* 15:707–13

180. Yu IM, Hughson FM. 2010. Tethering factors as organizers of intracellular vesicular traffic. *Annu. Rev. Cell Dev. Biol.* 26:137–56

181. Zhang X, Kim-Miller MJ, Fukuda M, Kowalchyk JA, Martin TF. 2002. Ca^{2+}-dependent synaptotagmin binding to SNAP-25 is essential for Ca^{2+}-triggered exocytosis. *Neuron* 34:599–611

182. Zhang X, Rizo J, Sudhof TC. 1998. Mechanism of phospholipid binding by the C_2A-domain of synaptotagmin I. *Biochemistry* 37:12395–403

183. Zhou A, Brewer KD, Rizo J. 2013. Analysis of SNARE complex/synaptotagmin-1 interactions by one-dimensional NMR spectroscopy. *Biochemistry* 52:3446–56

184. Zhou P, Bacaj T, Yang X, Pang ZP, Sudhof TC. 2013. Lipid-anchored SNAREs lacking transmembrane regions fully support membrane fusion during neurotransmitter release. *Neuron* 80:470–83

185. Zhou P, Pang ZP, Yang X, Zhang Y, Rosenmund C, et al. 2013. Syntaxin-1 N-peptide and Habc-domain perform distinct essential functions in synaptic vesicle fusion. *EMBO J.* 32:159–71

186. Zick M, Wickner WT. 2014. A distinct tethering step is vital for vacuole membrane fusion. *eLife* 3:e03251

Cumulative Index of Contributing Authors, Volumes 40–44

Garcia-Ojalvo J, 42:605–27
Garren M, 43:65–91
Gaub HE, 41:497–518
Giesa T, 42:651–73
Giusti F, 40:379–408
Gohon Y, 40:379–408
Golding I, 40:63–80
Goormaghtigh E, 40:379–408
Goldman DH, 43:119–40
Goldstein LSB, 43:141–69
Greene EC, 42:241–63
Grewer C, 42:95–120
Grimm C, 44:167–86
Grossman E, 41:557–84
Grossman JP, 41:429–52
Groves JT, 41:543–56
Gruner SM, 40:81–98; 44:33–51
Guittet E, 40:379–408

H

Ha T, 41:295–319
Han L, 43:331–55
Hass MAS, 44:53–75
Hedglin M, 44:207–28
Hegemann P, 44:167–86
Henn A, 41:247–67
Hill CP, 42:29–49
Hilser VJ, 41:585–609
Holmes KC, 40:169–86
Honig B, 43:193–210
Hsin J, 40:187–203
Hughes AL, 43:41–63
Hurley JH, 40:119–42

I

Inman J, 42:583–604
Inagaki F, 44:101–22

J

Jacobson MP, 42:289–314
Jaffrey SR, 44:187–206
Ji B, 44:1–32
Johnson CH, 40:143–67
Johnson JE, 41:473–96
Jun S, 44:123–42

K

Kaiser CM, 43:119–40
Kaul N, 40:267–88

Kent SBH, 41:41–61
Kim CU, 40:81–98
Kish-Trier E, 42:29–49
Kleinschmidt JH, 40:379–408
Kodera N, 42:393–414
Kolodny R, 42:559–82
Kondev J, 42:469–91
Kozlov AG, 41:295–319
Kruse K, 40:315–36
Kühlbrandt W, 40:379–408
Kussell E, 42:493–514

L

Lattman EE, 44:33–51
Le Bon C, 40:379–408
Lee EH, 40:187–203
Levitt M, 42:559–82
Lew MD, 41:321–42
Li H, 44:229–55
Li Z, 42:315–35
Lima CD, 43:357–79
Lippincott-Schwartz J, 43:303–29
Lohman TM, 41:295–319
Loose M, 40:315–36
Luger K, 40:99–117
Luo M, 42:191–215

M

Ma B, 42:169–89
McIntosh DB, 44:123–42
Mager T, 42:95–120
Maillard RA, 43:119–40
Mäkelä T, 41:227–46
Mariuzza RA, 42:191–215
Martinez KL, 40:379–408
Matysik J, 42:675–99
Medalia O, 41:557–84
Mobley DL, 42:121–42
Moerner WE, 41:321–42
Mondragón A, 42:537–57
Moore PB, 41:1–19
Morlot S, 42:629–49
Motlagh HN, 41:585–609
Mulder FAA, 44:53–75
Muramoto K, 40:205–23

N

Naismith JH, 41:157–77
Napetschnig J, 42:443–68

Nelson DR, 41:371–402
Nissen P, 40:243–66
Noda NN, 44:101–22
Nussinov R, 42:169–89

O

Okan OB, 41:205–25

P

Palmgren MG, 40:243–66
Park E, 41:21–40
Patel DJ, 41:343–70
Pereyaslavets L, 42:559–82
Perkins TT, 43:279–302
Petrey D, 43:193–210
Picard M, 40:379–408
Pollack L, 40:225–42
Popot J-L, 40:379–408
Pucci B, 40:379–408
Puchner EM, 41:497–518

Q

Qian H, 41:179–204

R

Rambo R, 42:415–41
Rando OJ, 43:41–63
Rapoport TA, 41:21–40
Rath A, 41:135–55
Razinia Z, 41:227–46
Read RJ, 42:265–87
Richardson DC, 42:1–28, 265–87
Richardson JS, 42:1–28, 265–87
Rienstra CM, 42:515–36
Rizo J, 44:339–67
Roux A, 42:629–49
Rué P, 42:605–27
Rusconi R, 43:65–91

S

Sachs JN, 40:379–408
Samson AO, 42:559–82
Sanchez A, 42:469–91
Sanders CR, 41:81–101
Sauls JT, 44:123–42
Scheraga HA, 40:1–39
Schneider F, 44:167–86

Schönichen A, 42:289–314
Schulten K, 40:187–203
Schwille P, 40:315–36
Selenko P, 43:171–92
Sen A, 44:77–100
Sengupta P, 43:303–29
Serganov A, 41:343–70
Shan S-o, 43:381–408
Shaw DE, 41:429–52
Shcherbakova DM, 43:303–29
Sheinin MY, 42:583–604
Shi Y, 42:51–72
Shinzawa-Itoh K, 40:205–23
Shivashankar GV, 40:361–78
Skau CT, 44:285–310
Song WJ, 43:409–32
Sonner JM, 42:143–67
Sontz PA, 43:409–32
Soppina V, 40:267–88
Stenmark H, 40:119–42
Stewart PL, 40:143–67
Stocker R, 43:65–91
Streich FC Jr, 43:357–79
Strümpfer J, 40:187–203
Su C-C, 43:93–117
Sun Y, 41:519–42

T

Taheri-Araghi S, 44:123–42
Tainer JA, 42:415–41

Terwilliger TC, 42:265–87
Tezcan F, 43:409–32
Thompson MA, 41:321–42
Tinoco I Jr, 43:1–17
Tribet C, 40:379–408
Tsai C-J, 42:169–89
Tsui TKM, 44:229–55
Tu Y, 42:337–59

U

Uchiashi T, 42:393–414

V

van Heijenoort C, 40:379–408
van Horn WD, 41:61–81
Veesler D, 41:473–96
Velikovsky A, 42:191–215
Venkatachalam V, 43:211–32
Verhey KJ, 40:267–88
Verkhusha VV, 43:303–29
Voth GA, 42:73–93

W

Walden H, 43:257–78
Wang MD, 42:583–604
Waterman CM, 44:285–310
Webb BA, 42:289–314
Wien F, 40:379–408
Wilson CAM, 43:119–40

Wilson RC, 42:217–39
Woodside MT, 43:19–39
Wrabl JO, 41:585–609
Wu H, 42:443–68

X

Xu H, 41:429–52
Xu J, 44:339–67

Y

Yadav V, 44:77–100
Yan N, 44:257–83
Yang Y, 42:315–35
Yeates TO, 41:41–61
Ylänne J, 41:227–46
Yoshikawa S, 40:205–23
You M, 44:187–206
Yu EW, 43:93–117

Z

Zhan J, 42:315–35
Zhang X, 43:381–408
Zhou H-X, 42:361–92
Zhou Y, 42:315–35
Zhu P, 41:269–93
Zito F, 40:379–408
Zoonens M, 40:379–408
Zuckerman DM, 40:41–62
Zwerger M, 41:557–84